Data Structures, Algorithms, and Performance

Derick Wood
University of Waterloo

ADDISON-WESLEY PUBLISHING COMPANY
Reading, Massachusetts • Menlo Park, California • New York
Don Mills, Ontario • Wokingham, England • Amsterdam • Bonn
Sydney • Singapore • Tokyo • Madrid • San Juan • Milan • Paris

Library of Congress Cataloging-in-Publication Data

Wood, Derick, 1940–
    Data structures and their performance / Derick Wood.
       p.   cm.
    Includes bibliographical references and index.
    ISBN 0-201-52148-2
    1. Data structures (Computer science)   2. Abstract data types
   (Computer science)   I. Title.
   QA76.9.D35W66   1993
   005.7'3—dc20   91-31025
                                       CIP

The programs and applications presented in this book have been included for their instructional value. They have been tested with care, but are not guaranteed for any particular purpose. The publisher does not offer any warranties or representations, nor does it accept any liabilities with respect to the programs or applications.

1 2 3 4 5 6 7 8 9 10-HA-95949392

Dedication: To C.C. and M.

P R E F A C E

Data structures, which are used to represent data, are one side of the programming coin; algorithms are the other side. Just as a coin has two sides, and we cannot remove either one, programming has the two sides of data structures and algorithms, and we cannot ignore either one. The choice of representation of a program's data is as central to program design as is the choice of algorithm. Having said this, we focus primarily on data structures and their performance, and secondarily on algorithms. We have to make wise choices of representations; therefore, we must have a basic knowledge of data representations and their properties. We aim to provide you with the strengths and weaknesses of data strucutres within the context of programming and algorithms, so that you can make wise choices.

The study of data structures is exciting and rewarding. The basic ideas are simple, yet many problems raised by these simple ideas are challenging and often unsolved. When we have to decide what should be taught in a data-structures course, the only agreement seems to be on the course title.

This text has been written for a junior- or senior-level course in data structures. Our goals are to introduce you to the world of data structures, to show you how to evaluate data structures, to help you obtain insight into data strucures, and to give you the basis for making wise choices of data structures. We introduce the overarching framework of abstract data types (ADTs) in Chapter 1 and present the three approaches to performance evaluation (empirical, simulational, and analytical) in Chapter 2. We also discuss the three approaches to analytical evaluation, namely, worst case, expected case, and amortized case. Amortized analysis, which can be thought of as worst-case batch analysis, is a recently introduced and powerful tool for evaluating algorithms and data structures. In Chapters 3 and 4 we provide a medium-paced, detailed review of lists and maps. The core of the text is Chapters 5 through 14 in which we present the more advanced topics of trees, strings, sets, tables, dictionaries, partitions, sorting, and graphs. The pace is brisker and less detailed. Finally, in Chapter 15, we preview six advanced data structures (skip lists, quad trees, k-d trees, segment trees, range trees, and hierarchical trees) and two advanced data-structuring techniques (dynamization and persistence).

This text has a different emphasis to that of other currently available data-structure texts. Specifically, it

- is down to earth, yet does not mire the reader in details;
- uses an ADT framework in a consistent manner;

- emphasizes the choice of efficient data structures for specific groups of operations or ADTs;

- shuns the encyclopedic study of data structures by focusing on those structures that are efficient, easy to implement, or have some inherent interest;

- covers data structures that are used to solve real-world problems;

- presents material on main-memory and disk data structures in an integrated manner;

- introduces a number of recently developed data structures (in the core are red–black trees, splay trees, linear-hash tables, Fibonacci queues, priority-search trees, and union-deunion-find structures; in the preview are skip lists, quad trees, k-d trees, segment trees, range trees, and hierarchical trees);

- introduces two new data-structuring techniques: dynamization and persistence;

- discusses three algotirhms that are the basis of utilities (string edit distance [diff], Boyer-Moore-Horspool pattern matching [grep], Ziv-Lempel-Welch compression [compress]);

- uses worst-case, expected-case, and amortized case analyses throughout;

- encourages the simulational and empirical evaluation of data structures.

We use Pascal to provide detailed, example implementations of ADT operations and pseudo-Pascal when we give partial implementations. Each chapter ends not only with a set of exercises, but also with a history section that provides references to the data-structuring literature. We use "*" to indicate a difficult section or exercise; the *-ed sections can be omitted on a first reading. An instructor's manual will be available for instructors who adopt the text.

ACKNOWLEDGMENTS

My interest in data structures was kindled in 1968, when Colin J. Bell, my tentative PhD supervisor, managed to complete the expected-case analysis of binary search trees under updates that performed fringe rebalancing. It was only in 1975, however, that I began to carry out research in the area of data structures and algorithms as a result of a long-term collaboration in formal-language theory with Hermann Maurer and Arto Salomaa. In parallel with that research, Hermann and I investigated a new class of balanced binary trees that we called *neighbor trees*. My interest in tree-like data structures took fire, and the flame continues to burn today.

Over the years my interest in data structures was fanned by collaborators, colleagues, and students. Without them this book would never have been written. In alphabetical order they are: Jon Bentley, Ricardo Baeza-Yates, Anne

Brüggemann-Klein, Helen Cameron, Bernard Chazelle, Herbert Edelsbrunner, Vladimir Estivill-Castro, Gaston Gonnet, Ralf-Hartmut Güting, Yoshihide Igarashi, Rolf Klein, Hans-Peter Kriegel, Tony Lai, Paul Larson, Ted Leslie, Michael Li, Ming Li, Heikki Mannila, David Matthews, Kurt Mehlhorn, Ian Munro, Naomi Nishimura, Otto Nurmi, Thomas Ottmann, Mark Overmars, Stott Parker, Darrell Raymond, Gregory Rawlins, Arny Rosenberg, Michael Schrapp, Bernhard Seeger, Raimund Seidel, Murray Sherk, Hannes Siz, Eljas Soisalon-Soininen, Frank Tompa, Esko Ukkonen, Vijay Vaishnavi, Jan van Leeuwen, Emo Welzl, Peter Widmayer, and Chee Yap.

Six of these individuals deserve a special mention. Vladimir Estivill-Castro corrected and tested my Pascal subprograms and also obtained the simulation results; Paul Larson was a fount of wisdom about hashing methods; David Matthews provided the statistical approach to the length of text sequences discussed in Chapter 2; Bernhard Seeger tutored me about external data structures for multidimensional data, most of which was omitted; Murray Sherk gave valuable feedback about the amortized analysis of sequential search and splay trees; and Frank Tompa counseled me on the topic of abstract data types.

This text was a family project; without the continual encouragement, organization, and support of my wife Mary, and without the typesetting of Calvin and Charlton, it would never have seen the light of day. Anne Brüggemann-Klein gave selflessly of her TEXnical knowledge. (The original manuscript was prepared using Leslie Lamport's LATEX and Donald Knuth's TEX.) The text was written while I was a fulltime faculty member in the Data Structuring Group, Department of Computer Science, The University of Waterloo, which provided an exciting environment that I will miss. Draft versions of the text were used on unsuspecting undergraduates at the Univeristy of Waterloo, many of whom provided constructive feedback.

Good reviewers are hard to find. I am grateful to Dan Hirschberg, Stan Kwasny, Tony Marsland, Chartel Martel, Jon Mauney, Bernard Moret, Gary Newell, Andrew Olson, Michael Quinn, Dana Richards, Hanan Samet, Maarten van Swaay, and Ralph Wilkerson, who gave unsparingly of their time in their critical evaluation of drafts of this book. A book is never finished, it is only published; therefore, I am solely responsible for all errors and omissions. Please send me your comments and corrections either in writing to: Department of Computer Science, University of Western Ontario, London Ontario N6A 5B7 Canada, or by e-mail to dwood@csd.uwo.ca or dwood@watdragon.waterloo.edu.

Keith Wollman was the CS editor at A-W who decided to undertake this project, and when he was promoted, Peter Gordon more than ably took over at short notice. Helen Goldstein, Assistant Editor, was a delight to work with. I am grateful to the three of them for their help and understanding. Lyn Dupre, the developmental editor, cut my manuscript into English prose with her sharp, yet gracious, pen. Finally Helen Wythe and Denise Descoteaux nursed the book through the perils of production and marketing.

C O N T E N T S

Review

1

Data Structures and Data Types

Algorithms and data structures are the warp and woof of programming. We construct a program from an algorithm by choosing representations for its data. Each data representation defines a data structure, and each program accesses and manipulates its data structures with a small number of different operations, such as insert a new value, remove a value, or return the most recently added value. The values that a data structure takes, together with the operations on it, specify an **abstract data type (ADT).** Conversely, given an ADT, there are many data structures that support its operations. The fundamental question addressed by this text is this: How do we choose data structures wisely? We should choose a data structure that not only supports the operations of the given ADT, but also—and more important—supports the operations *efficiently.* In other words, although we require correctness, we are concerned primarily with the time and memory (or space) used by a data structure.

We put these ideas into practice by exploring, in this text, the ADTs that are fundamental to the study of data structures and programming. At the same time, these ADTs serve to introduce the data structures that support them efficiently. We begin, in Section 1.1, with an introduction to data-structure design and to the fundamental notion of an ADT. We continue, in Section 1.2, by studying the reversal problem and two different solutions for it. This problem is used as a vehicle to explore the idea of an ADT in more detail. We describe, in Section 1.4, a functional method of specifying the operations of ADTs, and discuss the representation and implementation of ADTs. The reversal problem also serves to introduce two basic ADTs: the QUEUE and the STACK. Both ADTs maintain the chronological order of arrival of elements, but they differ in the operations that they allow. In Sections 1.5 and 1.6, we examine the representation and implementation of QUEUE and STACK, respectively. In both cases, we provide performance reports that summarize our evaluation of the alternative implementations; we also provide ratings of the implementations. One representation of QUEUE— the cursor representation—leads us directly into the issue of memory management, which we discuss in more detail in Section 13.5.

ADTs have become an accepted part of the programming process. Newer programming languages, such as Ada, provide ADTs in their full generality; older languages, such as Pascal, provide only a reasonable starting point. Furthermore, ADTs are treated as objects in programming languages such as C++ and Smalltalk, in which they are the primary programming concept. We use Pascal in this text, not because it is the most appropriate language, but rather because it is the language most widely used and understood by students.

1.1   DATA-STRUCTURE DESIGN

The goals of data-structure design are the same as those of program design—primarily, correctness and efficiency, and secondarily, modularity, robustness, portability, and maintainability. In addition, and as important, good data-structure design supports the goals of good program design.

1.1.1   The Top-Down, Bottom-Up Approach

Data-structure design is best viewed within a framework that combines both the top-down and bottom-up design techniques. Given a program specification, we normally use **top-down design** to develop the program; during this development, we isolate data-structure specifications, treating the data structures as **black boxes** around which we continue to design the program. We then use these specifications to design the data structures. Based on the cumulative experience of the programming community, we already know many frequently occurring data-structure specifications. Thus, we can explore the design of data structures with known specifications, without knowing the programming problems they are to solve. This exploration is, inherently, the **bottom-up design** of programs; we produce modules that can be combined to give programs. Within this framework, we can concentrate, without distraction, on the efficiency of data structures in terms of time and space. Conversely, if a previously designed data structure can be used to solve a given programming problem, the associated program does not need to know how the data structure works; it needs to know only how to access the data structure.

1.1.2   Levels of Refinement

When we refine data-structure specifications, we encounter five levels of refinement:

1. **Data reality:** We have the data themselves, with no interpretation and no omissions.

2. **Data abstraction:** We focus on or abstract those aspects of the data that are relevant to our problem.

3. **Data relatedness:** We identify the relationships among the data that are relevant to our problem.

4. **Data representation:** We design a representation of those aspects of the data captured in the abstraction, and create an implementation of the data's explicit relationships.

5. **Data encoding:** We design a representation of the data and of their relationships in terms of predefined data abstractions.

To ensure that you understand these ideas, we consider an example of route finding. In Section 1.2, we consider a second example in much more detail. We are given the task of designing a computer-based city road system that answers queries of the form, "How do you drive to *X* from *Y*?" The route-finding problem can be stated as follows: *Find a route, by road, from point A to point B within the city.* The *data reality* comprises the data themselves, with no interpretation and no omissions. Here, the data reality comprises the roads and the locations of *A* and *B*. At the next level, we focus on, or abstract, those aspects of the data that are relevant to our problem; this step gives us a *data abstraction,* or model. What do we abstract from the road system? There are several possibilities: the intersections of the roads, the distances between access points, the types of road (highway, four lane, two lane, one way, two way), and so on. If we create the wrong abstraction, we will solve the wrong problem. For simplicity, we assume that the roads are two way; hence, we need to know only the roads and their intersections.

We next identify the *data relationships* that are relevant to the problem. In addition, we decide which of these relationships should be made explicit, and which should remain implicit. The distinction is that the **implicit relationships** should be derivable from the **explicit relationships.** We treat the explicit relationships as the basis of all other relationships of interest. For route finding, we need to know which roads meet at each intersection; we make this relationship explicit. We may also need to know all intersections on a given road, or all roads that occur two intersections from this one. These relationships we leave implicit. At this stage, the relationships can be captured as an **edge-labeled graph;** see Fig. 1.1. The nodes are the intersections; the edges are the road segments between intersections; and the edge labels identify the roads.

At the fourth level, we design a *data representation* for those aspects of the data captured in the abstraction; moreover, we design an implementation of the explicit relationships. Here, for example, we may use a Boolean matrix or array, indexed by pairs of roads. Entries are **true** if there is an intersection at which both roads meet, and are **false** otherwise; see Chapter 13 for other representations. We have used a two-dimensional array, a data type that is available in programming

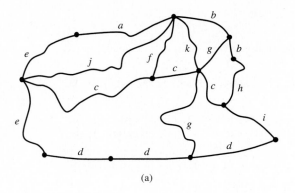

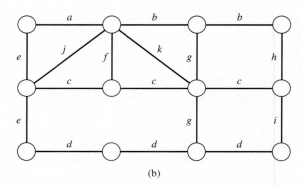

Figure 1.1 Route-finding problem. (a) A simple road system, and (b) its associated abstraction as an edge-labeled graph.

languages such as Pascal; we call it a **language data type.** Observe that representation and efficiency concerns surface at this level for the first time. It is important to realize that there are many possible data representations, even when efficiency is a primary goal.

Note that a representation and implementation may be cast in terms of some other data abstraction, in which case we continue by refining the design of the new abstraction. Eventually, however, we must reach the level of the predefined, basic data abstractions. At this level, data representation is called *data encoding.* The difference in terminology stems from our inability to change the bottom level of representation. At the intermediate representational levels, we can explore many different alternatives; at the data-encoding level, however, our choices are restricted. We have to represent the data using the structures available at the bottom level.

The refinement of a data-structure design is like the peeling of an onion; see Fig. 1.2. Since the first and last levels of data-structure design are beyond our

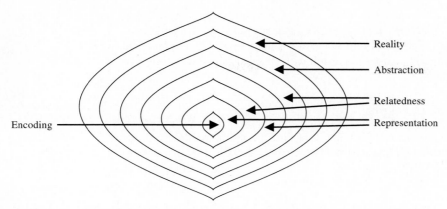

Figure 1.2 Onion skins and data-structure refinement. The two outermost skins of the onion correspond to the levels of data reality and abstraction. The successive pairs of skins correspond to the levels of data relatedness and representation, and the core corresponds to data encoding.

control, we focus on the remaining three. The three levels of data abstraction, data relatedness, and data representation are captured by the notion of ADTs and their representation and implementation.

1.1.3 Abstract Data Types

Assume that we are given

- A set of elements or values
- A finite set of operations on these elements

We consider this combination to define an ADT. An ADT is abstract not because it is theoretical, but rather because it is an abstraction of the data and their operations; the data's representation and the operations' implementation are of no interest at this level. Programming languages such as Pascal have a number of built-in data types that we call *language data types*. The Pascal language data types are **array, boolean, char, integer, pointer, real,** and **record.** Of these types, **array, pointer,** and **record** are used to construct more complex user-defined types in Pascal. We cannot change the representation and implementation of language data types; both have already been determined for us by the compiler writer.

In a Pascal program, the ADTs are represented and implemented in terms of language data types and of other ADTs. Thus, the data-encoding level is the representation of ADTs in terms of language data types. Reversing the whole picture, language data types are the foundation and the ADTs are the upper stories.

Throughout the text, we specify ADTs by defining their values and the operations on them. Given an ADT specification, we implement it by choosing a representation of the ADT values in terms of other ADTs and language data types, and by coding Pascal functions or procedures that carry out the ADT operations.

We face the issue of efficiency, in space and time, whenever we implement an ADT. The aim of this text is to provide you with efficient implementations and an evaluation of them.

1.1.4 The Benefits of ADTs

During program design, we discover the data and the operations they allow; together, they define an ADT. In mathematical terms, an ADT is a set of elements and a finite number of well-defined operations on these elements—an algebra. In programming terms, an ADT is a black box that supports the required functionality.

ADTs have taken a central place in program design for two reasons. First, ADTs enable us to split a program into separate modules that can be implemented independently. Such a separation helps us to write clear, correct, maintainable, and portable programs by hiding the representation and implementation of the data, in each module, from all other modules. Second, ADTs are the foundation stone of what have come to be known as **objects,** which have given rise to object-oriented programming and object-oriented programming languages such as C++.

During the design of a program, we can postpone the implementation of the ADTs; we can write the program using the ADT operations to access the corresponding data. Thus, ADTs

- Provide natural modules that aid in the development of correct programs
- Separate concerns—we can design programs and data structures separately and independently
- Hide information—we do not need to know how the programs' ADTs are implemented
- Are portable—they can be used in other programs
- Enable us to develop prototypes rapidly
- Allow and encourage us to delay decisions about their final implementation until late in the development cycle

1.2 THE REVERSAL PROBLEM

Having defined ADTs and discussed their benefits, we treat in more detail a second problem: the reversal problem. We use the reversal problem to emphasize the differences between an ADT and a non-ADT approach by giving two solutions to the problem. The ADT solution also introduces two basic ADTs—the QUEUE and the STACK ADTs—which we then explore in detail. The **reversal problem** can be stated as follows: *Given two character sequences A and B, is A the same as B read backward or, equivalently, is B the same as A read backward?* For example, if $A = (b,a,d)$ and $B = (d,a,b)$, then A is the reversal of B. If, however, $B = (d,a,b,b,l,e)$, this relation no longer holds. Although we state the problem for only character sequences, it can be extended to sequences of any type of element. Our goal is to write a program that inputs two sequences and checks whether one is the other's reversal. The problem is not difficult to solve, but it is interesting because of the data-abstraction and data-representation issues that it introduces.

We first observe that we should scan A and B from opposite ends and compare corresponding elements to check whether A is the reversal of B. If we scan A from the first element to the last element, then we should scan B from the last to first element, and vice versa. Alternatively, we may compare the first element in A and the last element in B, and if they match, we remove them and repeat this process. If they do not match, A is not the reversal of B. With either approach, we need to treat A and B similarly, but in opposite orders. An attempt at a solution might result in Program 1.1; it leaves much to be desired. The first and, perhaps, obvious comment is that we have restricted the number of characters to be at most 100, but we have not tested for this restriction when the characters are input. Second, we have integrated into the program the chosen representation of the data—a one-dimensional array or **block** of characters. It is nontrivial for us, even for this simple program segment, to change the representation without redesigning the program. Of course, this redesign is neither arduous nor intellectually challenging; for more complex problems, however, we prefer to avoid redesign. We cannot afford the time, effort, and cost to start afresh each time we change the data representation. We should separate the data and their access from the rest of the program; we should use ADTs.

1.3 DATA ABSTRACTION REVISITED

In Program 1.1, the representation of the data and their access is integrated into the program. To separate these aspects from the program, we stand back and ask: What kind of data do we have and how do we access them? *Taking this stance is the process of abstraction*—it combines the two levels of data abstraction and data relatedness introduced in Section 1.1.2.

The data for the reversal problem are described as two character sequences. They do not constitute character sets; rather, they define character sequences. We access both sequences as follows:

1. Create the initially empty sequence: The assignments $Apt := 0$ and $Bpt := 0$ result in the creation of two empty sequences.

2. Append a single character to the end of a sequence: The statements $Apt := Apt + 1$; $read(instreamA, A[Apt])$ result in the addition of a character at the end of A.

3. Scan a sequence one element at a time: We can scan from first to last, or last to first.

```
program Reversal(instreamA,instreamB);
{ The identifiers instreamA and instreamB denote the two streams
    of input for the program. The sequence A is input from instreamA,
    and the sequence B is input from instreamB.
    The program inputs the two sequences A and B and tests whether A
    is equal to the reverse of B, outputting an appropriate message
    in either case.}

var A,B: array[1..100] of char;
    i,Apt,Bpt: integer;
    equal: boolean;
begin
    {We input the two sequences.}
    Apt:= 0;
    while not eof(instreamA) do
    begin Apt:= Apt + 1;
        read(instreamA,A[Apt])
    end;

    Bpt:= 0;
    while not eof(instreamB) do
    begin Bpt:= Bpt + 1;
        read(instreamB,B[Bpt])
    end;

    {Now we compare the two sequences.}
    if Apt = Bpt
    then begin
        i:= 0; equal:= true;
        while (i < Apt) and equal do
        begin
            i:= i + 1;
            equal:= A[i] = B[Bpt - i + 1];
        end;
        if equal
        then {A equals B reversed-output appropriate message.}
        else {A does not equal B reversed-output appropriate message.}
    end
    else {A does not equal B reversed-output appropriate message.}
end.
```

used too much space to answer

Program 1.1   The non-ADT solution to the reversal problem for character sequences.

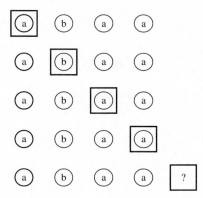

Figure 1.3 The five successive window positions for the sequence *A*.

The two operations described in step 3 are **traversals**—they visit all the elements of the sequence once and only once in a predefined order. A sequence has two natural traversal orders—first to last and last to first; we use both of them here.

Now, we consider *A* and *B* separately and in more detail. We append elements to the end of *A* during the input phase and, during the comparison phase, we traverse these elements from first to last. Schematically, we have provided a **window** that we move from the first element to the last element; see Fig. 1.3. We can see only a single element in the window; a window can contain neither two or more elements simultaneously nor only a part of an element. A window may, however, be over none of the elements; in this case, it is over the **after-last** position. Initially, we place the window over the first element. We then move it over the second element, then over the third element, and so on, until it is over the after-last position. We never move the window back, so we do not need to save the elements that have already been in the window. This interpretation suggests that we view the traversal as the combined operation "examine the earliest element" followed by "delete the earliest element"; see Fig. 1.4. Since we can examine and delete elements independently of inserting them, conceptually, we have a second window that is always over the latest element. The second window is used only when we insert an element; we insert an element beyond the window, and then we move the window over the new latest element. The specification of an ADT that we have given is similar to a well-known, fundamental ADT, the QUEUE ADT. The QUEUE ADT accesses data in a **first-in, first-out (FIFO)** order. The important relationship that is captured by QUEUE is a chronological one; QUEUE maintains the arrival order of elements. The QUEUE ADT is specified by the following five operations:

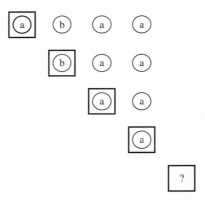

Figure 1.4   The deletion view of the five window positions for sequence
             A, given in Fig. 1.3.

1. Create an empty queue.
2. Test whether a queue is empty.
3. Add a new latest element to a queue.
4. Examine the earliest element of a queue.
5. Delete the earliest element of a queue.

When we reinterpret the sequence *A* as a chronologically ordered sequence, where the earliest element is the first element and the latest element is the last element, we see that the QUEUE ADT is an appropriate abstraction for *A*.

A similar examination of *B* shows that not only do we append elements, but also we traverse the sequence from last to first. Introducing a window provides the window positions shown in Fig. 1.5. Observe that we now have a **before-first** position for the window. We never reexamine elements that have appeared in the window; therefore, we may remove them after we have examined them (see Fig. 1.6). Since we insert, delete, and examine from the same window position in *B,* we need only one window. We have specified an ADT that is similar to another fundamental ADT, the STACK ADT. The STACK ADT accesses data in a **last-in, first-out (LIFO)** order; it maintains the arrival order of the elements, a chronological relationship. STACK is specified by the following five operations:

1. Create an empty stack.
2. Test whether a stack is empty.
3. Add a new latest element to a stack.
4. Examine the latest element of a stack.
5. Delete the latest element of a stack.

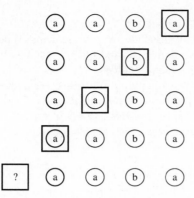

Figure 1.5 The five successive window positions for the sequence *B*.

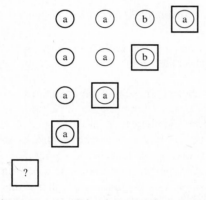

Figure 1.6 The deletion view of the five window positions for sequence *B*, given in Fig. 1.5.

1.4 ADT SPECIFICATION

We specify an ADT, in this text, with partial functions and English. The advantage of this approach is that functional notation is easily transcribed into Pascal and other programming languages, yet it cannot be confused with programming-language notation. In addition, programming notation denotes a computational process, whereas functional notation denotes a relationship.

In Section 1.3, we specified the QUEUE and STACK ADTs informally. We now demonstrate the level of formalism we use throughout this text by specifying their operations once more.

1.4.1 The QUEUE ADT

A queue maintains the chronological order of insertion of new elements. When we insert an element, it becomes the latest element in the queue, whereas we examine and delete the earliest element in the queue.

We formalize the five QUEUE operations using partial functions. We assume that each queue is a sequence of elements from some type *elementtype*. The set E denotes the values of type *elementtype*, B the values {**true**, **false**} of type *Boolean*, and Q the values of type QUEUE of *elementtype*. We specify the five operations as follows:

1. *Empty*: $\rightarrow Q$: The function value *Empty* is an empty queue.

2. *IsEmpty*: $Q \rightarrow B$: The function value *IsEmpty*(*Q*) is **true** if *Q* is an empty queue; otherwise, it is **false**.

3. *Insert*: $E \times Q \rightarrow Q$: The function value *Insert*(*e*,*Q*) is *Q* with *e* as its new latest element.

4. *Examine*: $Q \rightarrow E$: The function value *Examine*(*Q*) is undefined if *Q* is empty; otherwise, it is the earliest element in *Q*.

5. *Delete*: $Q \rightarrow Q$: The function value *Delete*(*Q*) is undefined if *Q* is empty; otherwise, it is *Q* without its earliest element.

We use the function names, which we have chosen for the QUEUE operations, for all similar ADT operations in this text. This generic nomenclature is helpful; we can recognize the similarity of ADT operations more easily.

Whenever a function value is undefined, we expect it to correspond, in an implementation, to an error report. For convenience, we introduce the notion of a value **undef** that is returned by a function in these circumstances. In an implementation, however, there is no such single value—"undefined" means that the value cannot be predicted from the definition of the function. Observe that, for any function *f*, *f* (...,**undef**,...) is undefined.

The method of specification that we have introduced is a mixture of the formal and the informal. It provides a formal syntax for writing specifications (functional notation), but it uses an informal approach to defining the semantics or meaning of the operations (English). The approach serves us well, since we do not want to reason about the formal properties of ADTs in this text.

The operation *Empty* gives an empty queue, and the operation *Insert* gives a new, larger queue from a given queue; we therefore call these operations **constructors.** Analogously, we call *Delete* a **destructor,** because repeated applications destroy a queue. We call *IsEmpty* a **checker.** The remaining operation, *Examine*, manipulates queues, so we call it a **manipulator.** This four-way classification of ADT operations is helpful—we can grow data structures only with constructors, can destroy them only with destructors, can check conditions that they satisfy only with checkers, and can examine and modify them only with manipulators.

1. **procedure** *Empty* (**var** *Q* : QUEUE);
2. **function** *IsEmpty* (*Q* : QUEUE) : **boolean**;
3. **procedure** *Insert* (*e* : *elementtype*; **var** *Q* : QUEUE);
4. **procedure** *Examine* (**var** *e* : *elementtype*; *Q* : QUEUE);
5. **procedure** *Delete* (**var** *Q* : QUEUE);

Figure 1.7   The Pascal subprogram headings for QUEUE.

An important issue raised by the specification of QUEUE is that we have defined operations as functions. Mathematically, this definition means that *Insert*(*e*,*Q*) always produces a new queue (when *e* and *Q* are defined). In a program, however, we normally want to modify *Q* so that it becomes the new queue. The main reasons for modification are to save time (it takes time for a program to produce a new copy of a queue) and space (the many copies that are produced during a program's execution do not necessarily disappear). In Pascal, we accomplish such a modification by writing *Insert* as a procedure rather than as a function, with its queue argument as a **var** parameter. Because the implementation and the formal specification should correspond, this transformation is unfortunate—the correspondence is lost. We resolve this problem by introducing the auxiliary notion of version. We say that *Insert*(*e*,*Q*) produces a new **version** of the queue *Q,* rather than a new queue. It may appear that we are splitting hairs, but versions enable us to relate *Q* to *Insert*(*e*,*Q*). In an implementation, we do not produce a new copy of *Q* with *e* as its latest element; rather, we modify the current version of *Q* and, hence, change it forever. Versions correspond, in a natural way, to the notion of a variable parameter in Pascal and in other programming languages. (Another reason that we use procedures rather than functions in Pascal is because Pascal functions can return only the scalar values **boolean**, **char**, **integer**, **pointer**, and **real**.) From the specification of QUEUE given previously, we derive the Pascal subprogram headings for QUEUE in Fig. 1.7.

1.4.2 The STACK ADT

Like a queue, a stack also maintains the chronological order of arrival of elements. The difference is that, although a newly inserted element becomes the latest element, we examine and delete the latest element. The STACK ADT has been implemented in a number of computer architectures and it is used as an automata-theoretical model in the form of the pushdown automaton. It is used to implement procedure calls, to evaluate expressions, to compile Pascal programs, and to allocate memory.

Letting S denote the set of all values of STACK of *elementtype*, the five STACK operations are specified as follows:

1. *Empty*: $\rightarrow S$: The function value *Empty* is an empty stack.

2. *IsEmpty*: $S \rightarrow B$: The function value *IsEmpty(S)* is **true** if S is empty; otherwise, it is **false**.

3. *Insert*: $E \times S \rightarrow S$: The function value *Insert(e,S)* is S with e as its new latest element.

4. *Examine*: $S \rightarrow E$: The function value *Examine(S)* is undefined if S is empty; otherwise, it is the latest element in S.

5. *Delete*: $S \rightarrow S$: The function value *Delete(S)* is undefined if S is empty; otherwise, it is S without its latest element.

1.4.3   The Reversal Problem: An ADT Solution

We are now in a position to give a solution to the reversal problem based on queues and stacks. To avoid naming conflicts, we add the prefix Q to the names of all QUEUE operations, and add S to the names of the STACK operations. We assume that the appropriate declarations for QUEUE and STACK have been precompiled and are available via a library of such ADT implementations. The new version of the program is Program 1.2.

1.4.4   Partial Functions in Practice

In practice, partial functions raise an obvious difficulty: They are not total! We must face and deal with the possibility that a function may be undefined for some arguments. Of course, such undefined function values correspond to an error condition, but how should we deal with them in a program? We have provided ADT operations that enable us to check for some undefined results *before* an operation is used. For example, *Examine(Q)* is undefined for the queue Q if Q is empty. Because we have already an operation that tests whether a queue is empty, we can ensure that *Examine(Q)* is well defined by embedding it in a test for emptiness. In other words, we should always write

```
{Examine(Q)}
if IsEmpty(Q)
then error('Attempting to examine an empty queue')
else Examine(Q);
```

rather than

```
Examine(Q);
```

To ensure that the users of an ADT are aware of the dangers of using an operation, we state what conditions should hold before that operation is used. This statement is called a **precondition.** In addition, assuming that the operation is used when the precondition holds, we also state what conditions hold after its use. This statement is the corresponding **postcondition.** For example, we annotate a call of *Examine* with

```
program Reversal(instreamA,instreamB);
{This version of Reversal uses the ADTs QUEUE and STACK.}

library myADT(QUEUE,STACK);
{We obtain the ADT implementations from the library myADT.}

var A: QUEUE; B: STACK;
    a,b,e: elementtype; test: boolean;
begin
    QEmpty(A); {We initialize queue A to be the first sequence.}
    while not eof(instreamA) do
    begin read(e);
        QInsert(e,A)
    end;

    SEmpty(B); {We initialize stack B to be the second sequence.}
    while not eof(instreamB) do
    begin read(e);
        SPush(e,B)
    end;

    {We test A and B for equality by repeatedly examining an element
    from both, deleting them, and comparing them.}
    test:= true;
    while not QIsEmpty(A) and not SIsEmpty(B) and test do
    begin QExamine(a,A); QDelete(A);
        STop(b,B); SPop(B);
        test:= a = b
    end;

    {We determine if A = B and take the appropriate action.}
    if test and QIsEmpty(A) and SIsEmpty(B)
    then {A equals B reversed}
    else {A doesn't equal B reversed}
end.
```

Program 1.2   An ADT solution to the reversal problem.

```
{pre: Q is not empty.}
Examine(Q);
{post: Q is not empty and Examine(Q)
    is the earliest element in }
```

and a call of *Insert* with

```
{pre: true is the vacuous precondition.}
Insert(e,Q);
{post: Insert(e,Q) is not empty, and
     e is the latest element in Insert(e,Q).}
```

We can annotate similarly the calls of the other QUEUE operations.

1.4.5 ADT Specification in Pascal

The preconditions and postconditions that we espoused in Section 1.4.4 have a
wider use than our discussion suggests. They can be used to specify the meaning
of an operation, since a postcondition tells us what conditions hold after the operation. We can use this approach when specifying ADT operations in Pascal.
Although we still use English to describe the preconditions and postconditions, it
is possible to convert them into a more rigorous formalism. We illustrate the
approach with the Pascal headings for QUEUE taken from Fig. 1.7. The new version of these headings is given in Fig. 1.8.

```
1. procedure Empty(var Q: QUEUE);
   {pre: vacuous.
   post: Q is an empty queue.}
2. function IsEmpty(Q: QUEUE): boolean;
   {pre: vacuous.
   post: IsEmpty(Q) is true if Q is an empty queue,
   and is false otherwise.}
3. procedure Insert(e: elementtype; var Q: QUEUE);
   {pre: vacuous.
   post: Q after is the same as Q before, except that
   it has e as its new latest element.}
4. procedure Examine(var e: elementtype; Q: QUEUE);
   {pre: Q is nonempty.
   post: e is the value of the earliest element of Q.}
5. procedure Delete(var Q: QUEUE);
   {pre: Q is nonempty.
   post: Q after is the same as Q before, without
   its earliest element.}
```

Figure 1.8   The Pascal specification of the QUEUE operations
                 with preconditions and postconditions.

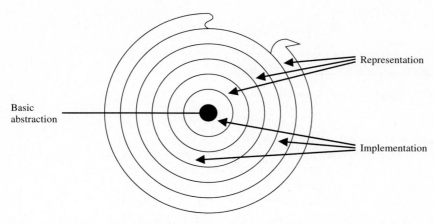

Figure 1.9 Onion skins and layers of representation and implementation. From the outside of the onion, pairs of skins correspond to the choices of representation and implementation. The core of the onion corresponds to the uncovered basic abstraction.

1.4.6 Layers of Representation and Implementation

Program 1.2 solves the reversal problem when we provide implementations of QUEUE and STACK. We must code the operations in the chosen programming language—Pascal, in our case. Our code is dependent, however, on other ADTs. For example, we might code the QUEUE operations directly using a block representation of a queue, as we do in the next section. Immediately, we are using the ADT ARRAY. If we are dealing with a queue of characters, then our code uses the ADT CHARACTER. In other words, beneath each abstraction, there is another abstraction, unless it is a basic abstraction. In terms of the simile of Section 1.1.2, we peel the skins of an onion to reveal the different layers of refinement; see Fig. 1.9. The difference here is that these layers are layers of representation and implementation, rather than layers of refinement.

1.5 QUEUE REPRESENTATIONS

Because a queue must maintain the chronological order of arrival of elements, the simplest representations are **linear structures** based on real-world examples of a queue—for example, a queue in a post office or a bank. In the real world, a queue is not the only method that is used to ensure fair treatment. An alternative approach, seen in bakeries, uses numbering. A new customer takes the next available number, whereas the staff maintain a counter of the last number served. This method is called **time stamping.** We could implement QUEUE in a similar man-

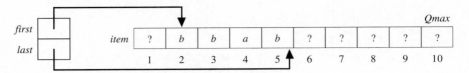

Figure 1.10   A block representation of a queue.

ner, assigning the current time to each arrival and representing the elements in either a nonlinear or a non–chronologically ordered structure. We delay presenting such an approach until Chapter 11, when we introduce priority queues that allow even more flexibility.

Here, we consider two basic linear representations of QUEUE: the block and pointer representations, which use the language data types **array** and **pointer**, respectively. In both cases, we use two windows that are hidden from the user of the ADT and are thus called **implicit windows.**

1.5.1   Block Representations

In Program 1.1, we represented A as a block of characters; hence, we first examine representations of queues based on blocks. Slightly abstracting the representation of A in Program 1.1, we represent the two windows and their positions with two indices *first* and *last* that index the earliest and latest elements, respectively. This choice suggests the structure displayed in Fig. 1.10. The maximum size of a queue is defined by the constant *Qmax*. In Pascal, the data structure can be captured by the following declarations:

```
const Qmax = 10; {say}
type QUEUE = record
                first,last: integer;
                item: array [1..Qmax] of elementtype;
             end;
```

We begin by discussing the implementation of *Insert*, *Examine*, and *Delete*. One method of coding them is shown in Program 1.3. Observe that *Q.first* and *Q.last* are playing a game of tag; each deletion increments *Q.first*, and each insertion increments *Q.last*. Repeated deletions without insertions cause the value of *Q.first* to catch up with the value of *Q.last*. At this stage, there is one element left in *Q*; see Fig. 1.11(a). A subsequent deletion causes *Q.first* to be equal to *Q.last* + 1, and *Q* is now empty; see Fig. 1.11(b). This effect indicates how we should code *Empty* and *IsEmpty*; see Program 1.3.

One problem with the preceding representation is that whenever we delete an element, that element's location is never used again. Therefore, after *Qmax* deletions, we cannot insert any more elements in *Q*, even though the block *Q.item* is completely free. The solution to this recycling problem is simple. We use **wrap-around;** that is, we consider the block be circular, as shown in Fig. 1.12. In this

```
procedure Empty(var Q: QUEUE);
{pre: vacuous.
    post: Q is an empty queue.}
begin Q.first:= 1; Q.last:= 0; end;


function IsEmpty(Q: QUEUE): boolean;
{pre: vacuous.
    post: IsEmpty(Q) is true if Q is an empty queue;
        otherwise, it is false.}
begin IsEmpty:= (Q.last + 1) = Q.first end;
procedure Insert(e: elementtype; var Q: QUEUE);
{pre: vacuous.
    post: Q after is the same as Q before, except that
        it has a new latest element e.}
begin
    if Q.last < Qmax
    then begin Q.last:= Q.last + 1;
        Q.item[Q.last]:= e
    end
    else error('Queue is full')
end;
procedure Examine(var e: elementtype; Q: QUEUE);
{pre: Q is nonempty.
    post: e is the value of Q's earliest element.}
begin
    if IsEmpty(Q)
    then error('Queue is empty')
    else e:= Q.item[Q.first]
end;
procedure Delete(var Q: QUEUE);
{pre: Q is nonempty.
    post: Q after is the same as Q before, without its earliest
        element.}
begin
    if IsEmpty(Q)
    then error('Queue is empty')
    else Q.first:= Q.first + 1
end;
```

Program 1.3 The block implementation of the QUEUE operations.

setting, index 1 is the next index after index 10. To ensure that the index values remain within the index range, we use the modulus operation. Hence, it is more convenient to index the block from $0..Qmax - 1$, rather than from $1..Qmax$; see Fig. 1.13. To increment *last,* we write

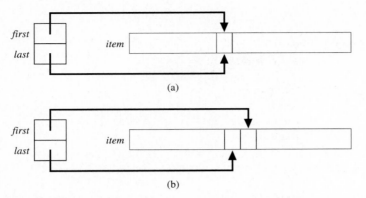

Figure 1.11   Examples of the block representation of queues. Queues with (a) one element and (b) no elements.

```
Q.last:= (Q.last + 1) mod Qmax,
```

rather than

```
Q.last:= Q.last + 1.
```

We treat *first* similarly. A queue is empty if $Q.first = (Q.last + 1)$ **mod** $Qmax$, so, initially, we let $Q.first = 0$ and $Q.last = Qmax - 1$. But what happens when a queue is full? A queue is full when the last element of the queue is followed immediately by the first element; see Fig. 1.13. In other words, $Q.first = (Q.last + 1)$ **mod** $Qmax$. Unfortunately, this condition is the same as the one that we specified for an empty queue; therefore, we cannot use this condition to differentiate between an empty queue and a full queue. We resolve this problem by defining a queue to be full when it contains $Qmax - 1$ elements; that is, it is full when

```
Q.first = (Q.last + 2) mod Qmax.
```

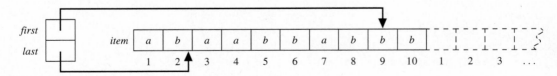

Figure 1.12   The wraparound representation of a queue.

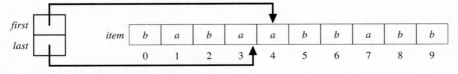

Figure 1.13   The wraparound representation of a full queue.

An alternative approach, explored in Exercise 1.16, is to maintain the number of elements in the queue. The wraparound implementation of the five operations is given in Program 1.4.

```
procedure Empty(var Q: QUEUE);
{pre: vacuous.
     post: Q is an empty queue.}
begin Q.first:= 0; Q.last:= Qmax - 1 end;

function IsEmpty(Q: QUEUE): boolean;
{pre: vacuous.
     post: IsEmpty(Q) is true if Q is an empty queue};
          otherwise, it is false.}
begin IsEmpty:= Q.first = (Q.last + 1) mod Qmax end;

procedure Insert(e: elementtype; var Q: QUEUE);
{pre: vacuous.
     post: Q after is the same as Q before, except
          that it has a new latest element e.}
begin
    if Q.first = (Q.last + 2) mod Qmax
    then error('The queue is full')
    else begin Q.last:= (Q.last + 1) mod Qmax;
         Q.item[Q.last]:= e
    end
end;

procedure Examine(var e: elementtype: Q: QUEUE);
{pre: Q is nonempty.
     post: e is the value of Q's earliest element.}
begin
    if IsEmpty(Q)
    then error('The queue is empty')
    else e:= Q.item[Q.first]
end;

procedure Delete(var Q: QUEUE);
{pre: Q is nonempty.
   post: Q after is the same as Q before, without
          its earliest element.}
begin
    if IsEmpty(Q)
    then error('The queue is empty')
    else Q.first:= (Q.first + 1) mod Qmax
end;
```

Program 1.4 The block implementation of the QUEUE operations with wraparound.

Figure 1.14   The drawing of a singly linked list.

1.5.2   Pointer Representations

One problem with block representations is that they restrict queues to have a pre-defined maximum length. One natural way to avoid this restriction, in Pascal and in many other programming languages, is to use a pointer representation. Recall that a **singly linked list** is a structure in which each cell or node is linked by a pointer to its unique successor. We usually draw such structures as shown in Fig. 1.14. In the simplest form, a header points to the first cell in the list, and the last node has a null-successor pointer. (A null pointer is represented by the constant **nil** in Pascal.) Since a queue should have two windows, we represent them with a header that has two pointers, one to the earliest cell and one to the latest cell. This discussion leads to a representation of QUEUE in Pascal that is captured with the following declarations:

```
type linktype = ↑ celltype;
     celltype = record
                     item: elementtype;
                     successor: linktype
                end;


QUEUE = record
            first, last: linktype;
        end;
```

Observe that, in principle, it is sufficient to have the header point to the earliest cell of the list, since we can move the window pointer to the end of the list when we need the corresponding window to be there. For reasons of efficiency, we have defined the header to point to both the earliest and latest cells; see Fig. 1.15. We represent an empty queue as shown in Fig. 1.16. We insert an element into a queue by creating a new cell for it, making the last cell point to the new cell, and changing $Q.last$ to point to the new cell, which has now become the last cell. This operation is shown in Fig. 1.15, with the modified links drawn as dashed lines. Similarly, we delete an element from a queue by returning its cell and modifying $Q.first$ to point to the new first cell, if there is one. We show these changes in Fig. 1.15. If a queue has only one element, then, when we delete an element, we change the values of both $Q.first$ and $Q.last$ to **nil**. The singly linked list implementation of the QUEUE operations is given in Program 1.5.

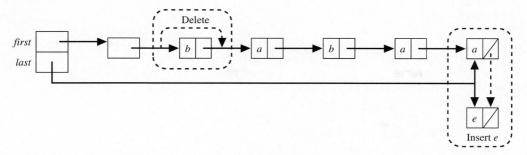

Figure 1.15   The singly linked list representation of a queue with insertion and deletion.

Figure 1.16   The singly linked list representation of an empty queue.

1.5.3   Cursor Representations

Languages such as BASIC and FORTRAN do not support pointer types; therefore, we cannot have pointer representations in such languages. We can, however, use block indices to represent pointer values, and use a global block of cells to hold the queues that we need. When indices are used in this way, they are called **cursors.** We present the singly linked list representation of QUEUE with cursors instead of pointers, creating a noncontiguous block representation of QUEUE. The example in Fig. 1.17 is a cursor version of the singly linked list of Fig. 1.15, where we have declarations similar to the following Pascal declarations:

```
const Qmax = ?;

type cursortype = 0..Qmax;
     celltype = record
                    item: elementtype;
                    successor: cursortype
                end;
     QUEUE = record
                 first,last: cursortype
             end;

var cells: array[1..Qmax] of celltype;
```

```
procedure Empty(var Q: QUEUE);
{pre: vacuous.
    post: Q is an empty queue.}
begin Q.first:= nil; Q.last:= nil end;

function IsEmpty(Q: QUEUE): boolean;
{pre: vacuous.
    post: IsEmpty(Q) is true if Q is an empty queue},
        otherwise, it is false.}
begin IsEmpty:= Q.first = nil end;

procedure Insert(e: elementtype;  var  Q: QUEUE);
{pre: vacuous.
    post: Q after is the same as Q before, except that
        it has a new latest element e.}
var p: linktype;
begin new(p); p ↑.item:= e; p ↑.successor:= nil;
    if Q.first = nil
    then Q.first:= p
    else Q.last ↑.successor:=  p;
    Q.last:= p;
end;

procedure Examine(var e: elementtype; Q: QUEUE);
{pre: Q is nonempty.
    post: e is the value of Q's earliest element.}
var p: linktype;
begin
    if IsEmpty(Q)
    then error('Queue is empty')
    else begin p:= Q.first; e:= p ↑.item end
end;

procedure Delete(var Q: QUEUE);
{pre: Q is nonempty.
    post: Q after is the same as Q before, without its
        earliest element.}
var p: linktype;
begin
    if IsEmpty(Q)
    then error('Queue is empty')
    else begin p:= Q.first; Q.first := p ↑.successor;
        dispose(p);
        if Q.first = nil then Q.last:= nil
    end
end;
```

Program 1.5   The singly linked list implementation of the QUEUE operations.

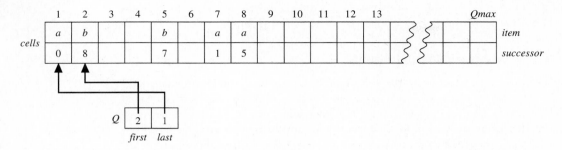

Figure 1.17 The first cursor representation of a queue.

In this representation, the cursor value 0 corresponds to the pointer value **nil**. Alternatively, since some languages do not even have the record structure, we can use, in this case, declarations similar to the following Pascal declarations:

```
const Qmax = ?;
      first = 1;
      last = 2;

type cursortype = 0..Qmax;
     QUEUE = array[first..last] of cursortype;

var items: array[1..Qmax] of elementtype;
    successors: array [1..Qmax] of cursortype;
```

The example of the first cursor representation given in Fig. 1.17 now appears as shown in Fig. 1.18.

The replacement of pointers by cursors introduces an additional problem: Whenever we do an insertion into a queue in a cursor representation, how do we

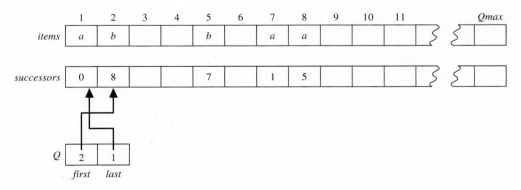

Figure 1.18 The second cursor representation of a queue.

find a free cell? We address this issue in Section 1.5.4; we discuss it in more detail in Section 13.5.

1.5.4 Memory Management

When we add cells or nodes to a linked-list data structure, we need to obtain additional memory locations; when we delete nodes, we can release their associated memory locations. In the pointer implementation of QUEUE, we have been shielded from the details of this process by the Pascal run-time environment, which provides the two procedures *new* and *dispose* to request and release memory locations. We now take the wraps off these two procedures and discuss how we can handle a request for or a release of memory locations.

Memory is a recyclable commodity, as are the videotapes in a video rental store. Just as a videotape is either rented or available, so memory either is **allocated** and in use by a process, or is available and **free** to be given to a process. Memory cannot evaporate. Just as a video-store manager has to keep track of the store's stocks—what is on loan and to whom, and what is in the store—a **memory manager** has to keep track of what memory locations are allocated and to which process, and what memory locations are free. We have a consumer–supplier relationship in which a consumer both **requests** memory from the supplier and **releases** or **returns** memory to the supplier, and the supplier grants requests for memory and accepts returned memory. Observe the duality in this model: The supplier releases (returns) memory when a consumer requests some, and takes (requests) memory when a consumer returns some.

In Ada, Pascal, and many other programming languages, memory is requested and returned in two different ways; by the **system** and by the **user.** Whenever a subprogram is called, its parameters and local variables are allocated memory and, correspondingly, when the call terminates, that memory is released. The request for and return of memory are initiated by the system, in this case. On the other hand, when we require memory for a pointer variable—say, p—in a Pascal program, we must request the memory with the call *new(p)*; it is user initiated. Similarly, in Pascal, we return the memory with the call *dispose(p)*. For example, given the Pascal type declarations

```
type linktype = ↑celltype;
     celltype = record
                    item: integer;
                    successor: linktype
                end;
```

for singly linked lists of integers, and variables p and q of type *linktype*, the sequence of statements

```
new(p); p ↑.item:= 3; p ↑.successor:= nil;
new(q); q ↑.item:= 5; q ↑.successor:= nil;
```

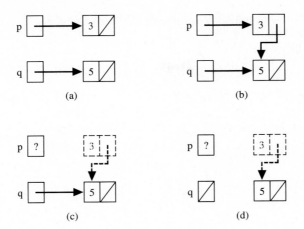

Figure 1.19 Creation of orphans in singly linked lists by *dispose* in Pascal.

gives the result depicted in Fig. 1.19(a). If we now execute

```
p ↑.successor:= q
```

we obtain the singly linked lists shown in Fig. 1.19(b). Note that p and q share a cell. From the definition of Pascal, we expect

```
dispose(p)
```

to release the first cell in p's list and p itself to become undefined, as shown in Fig. 1.19(c). In other words, *dispose* releases only the cell pointed to by its argument. We can still access the second cell in p's list because q points to it. If, however, we had executed

```
q:= nil; dispose(p)
```

the picture would be somewhat different; see Fig. 1.19(d). We have returned the first cell in p's list, but not the second cell; more important, the second cell is in limbo—it has been **orphaned.** The main difficulty with a user releasing allocated memory is that, if the user is not careful, orphans can be left lying around—the program is unable to access them, so they can never be released. Contrast this situation with the system request for and release of memory that occurs with subprogram calls. In this case, memory allocated on entry to a subprogram is released automatically on exit.

After this explanation of what happens, from the user's viewpoint, when *new(p)* and *dispose(p)* are executed, we consider what happens from the viewpoint of the Pascal run-time environment. Here, we explore the simpler memory-management problem that occurs with the first cursor representation of QUEUE;

see Section 1.5.3. We postpone, until Section 13.5, a discussion of more general and complex memory-management issues.

Recall that we have a global block

```
var cells: array[1..Qmax] of celltype;
```

with the supporting type declarations

```
const Qmax = ?;

type cursortype = 0..Qmax;
     celltype = record
                      item: elementtype;
                      successor: cursortype
                  end;
     QUEUE = record
                   first,last: cursortype
               end;
```

Each call of *IsEmpty* creates an empty queue that is represented with a record that has both fields set to 0; it does not change *cells*. *Insert* and *Delete*, however, should request and return cells, so we need a mechanism to keep track of the free cells. The mechanism should prevent two different queues from using the same cells in the global block. We use a **free list,** represented as a singly linked list, for this purpose. Initially, the free list contains all the cells in the array *cells*; see Fig. 1.20. On each call *Insert(e,Q)*, we mimic the singly linked list implementation of QUEUE by requesting a new cell and linking it to the current cell; see Program 1.6. Conversely, *Delete(Q)* removes the first cell from *Q,* if there is one, and returns it for further use; see Program 1.6. The implementation of the other operations is left to Exercise 1.2.

The request for a new cell and the return of a cell are, in this environment, easy to code. We have a global variable *freelist* that is the header of the free list, and we initialize the free list using the procedure *Initialize*; see Program 1.7. The three operations—*Request, Return,* and *Initialize*—are the operations of an ADT for memory management; this view is explored in more detail in Section 13.5. The use of a free list is an important technique for managing memory in many different situations, as we shall see in Section 13.5.

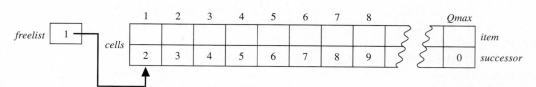

Figure 1.20   The initial free list.

```
procedure Insert(e: elementtype; var Q: QUEUE);
{pre: vacuous.
    post: Q after is the same as Q before, except that
    it has a new latest element e.}
var p: cursortype;
begin Request(p);
    cells[p].item:= e;
    cells[p].successor:= 0;
    if Q.first = 0
    then Q.first:= p
    else cells[Q.last].successor:= p;
    Q.last:= p;
end;

procedure Delete(var Q: QUEUE);
{pre: Q is nonempty.
    post: Q after is the same as Q before, without its
    earliest element.}
var p: cursortype;
begin
    if Q.first = 0
    then error('Queue is empty')
    else begin p:= Q.first;
        Q.first:= cells[p].successor;
        Return(p);
        if Q.first = 0 then Q.last:= 0
    end
end;
```

Program 1.6   The cursor version of the singly linked list implementation
                of the QUEUE operations *Insert* and *Delete*.

Because Pascal is a strongly typed language, we must incorporate separate
Initialize, *Request*, and *Return* procedures for each ADT that we implement with
cursors, in addition to the global block of cells for each ADT. For this reason,
when we discuss memory management more fully, in Section 13.5, we do not
give Pascal implementations of the algorithms. Normally, memory-management
algorithms are implemented in weakly typed programming languages, such as C.

1.5.5 Performance Reports

Throughout this text, we evaluate the efficiency of the data structures that we use
to implement ADTs. We present our underlying assumptions more rigorously in
Chapter 2; here, we introduce the ideas at a more intuitive level.

```
procedure Request(var p: cursortype);
{This procedure returns the index of a free cell, if there
    is one, by deleting one from the free list.}
begin
    if freelist = 0
    then error('There are no free cells')
    else begin
        p:= freelist;
        freelist:= cells[freelist].successor
    end
end;


procedure Return(var p: cursortype);
{This procedure releases the cell indexed by p by
    inserting it into the free list.}
begin
    cells[p].successor:= freelist;
    freelist:= p
end;


procedure Initialize;
{This procedure initializes the free list.}
var i: cursortype;
begin
    for i:= 1 to Qmax - 1 do
        cells[i].successor:= i + 1;

    freelist:= 1;
    cells{qmax].successor:= 0
end;
```

Program 1.7   The memory-management procedures for the cursor representation of QUEUE.

First, we evaluate the wraparound implementation of QUEUE given in Program 1.4. For simplicity, we assume that each high-level operation in Pascal takes 1 unit of time. In particular, an arithmetic operation, a Boolean operation, a subscripting operation, a record-selection operation, and an assignment operation each take 1 time unit. Based on this assumption, the procedure *Empty* takes 5 time units, because it has two assignment operations, one arithmetic operation, and two record-selection operations. Analogously, *IsEmpty* takes 6 time units. Note that we have ignored the time taken to make the corresponding procedure calls. The remaining three operations contain one conditional statement each and, also, *Insert* and *Examine* assign an *elementtype* value. We assume that a conditional statement takes 1 time unit plus the time units taken by its Boolean expression and the time units taken by its more time-consuming alternative. This scenario is a worst-case assumption that we shall usually make when evaluating data structures. Also, we assume that an *elementtype* assignment takes T_e time units. These additional assumptions enable us to compute the time units taken by *Delete*, *Insert*, and *Examine* as, at most, 11, $13 + T_e$, and $9 + T_e$ time units, respectively.

The simplistic assumptions we have made demonstrate that all five operations take time that is independent of the queue size. Moreover, *Empty*, *IsEmpty*, and *Delete* take time that is also independent of *elementtype*. Only *Insert* and *Examine* take time that depends on *elementtype*. We say that *Empty*, *IsEmpty*, and *Delete* are **constant-time operations,** whereas *Insert* and *Examine* are constant time only when we can predetermine the value of T_e. Because we are dealing with ADTs and data structures that have the type *elementtype* as a parameter, we must realize that the time taken by the ADT operations can depend on *elementtype*. We make this point in only this first chapter; we ignore the issue in subsequent chapters.

We now evaluate, in a similar fashion, the singly linked list implementation of a queue given in Program 1.5. Two new parameters enter the field: the time units T_{new} needed to obtain a new cell, and the time units $T_{dispose}$ needed to return an unneeded cell. Also, we let the operator $\uparrow$ take 1 time unit. Based on these additional assumptions, *Empty* and *IsEmpty* take 4 and 3 time units, respectively, whereas *Delete*, *Insert*, and *Examine* take, at most, $15 + T_{dispose}$, $16 + T_{new} + T_e$, and $8 + T_e$ time units, respectively. Thus, both *Insert* and *Delete* depend on the vagaries of the Pascal run-time environment—in particular, they depend on its method of managing main memory. We emphasize the importance of this observation, because, as programmers, we have no control over the Pascal run-time environment. The times T_{new} and $T_{dispose}$ are independent of the queue size and *elementtype*. As we shall see, in Section 13.5, the operations *new* and *dispose* may not be constant-time operations, although, for the simple memory-management scheme that we have described in Section 1.5.4 for cursor representations, *new* and *dispose* are constant-time operations. Having pointed out these facts of programming life, we ignore them from now on, and assume that T_{new} and $T_{dispose}$ are each 1 time unit. In Table 1.1, we summarize the performance results, for the two implementations of QUEUE, where "1" denotes constant time.

In Table 1.2, we provide performance ratings for the wraparound and singly linked list representations of QUEUE, and list some of their advantages and disadvantages. These subjective ratings are based on the performances of the representations. When we rate a representation "excellent," we imply that it should almost always be chosen. Our first choice of representation is the wraparound block representation, closely followed by the singly linked list representation. The wraparound representation uses block indexing, which is often faster than pointer chasing, and it avoids the space overhead of pointers. All block representations have a predefined maximum size, whereas pointer representations do not have this limitation. Hence, the wraparound representation is preferred whenever we know the maximum possible size of a queue; in all other situations, the pointer representation is preferred.

Table 1.1   A comparison of the worst-case times taken by the two
QUEUE implementations.

	QUEUE implementation	
Operation	Wraparound block	Singly linked
Empty	1^a	1
IsEmpty	1	1
Insert	$1 + T_e$	$1 + T_e$
Examine	$1 + T_e$	$1 + T_e$
Delete	1	1

[a] 1 denotes constant time.

Table 1.2   Performance ratings of the wraparound and singly linked list
implementations of QUEUE.

QUEUE implementation	Rating	Comments
Wraparound block	Excellent	No extra space; predefined maximum size
Singly linked	Very good	Extra linkage space; no predefined size

1.6   STACK REPRESENTATIONS

The natural way to implement STACK is as a linear structure that mirrors real-world stacks—for example, the push–pop stack of plates in a cafeteria. A linear structure maintains the arrival order of elements directly. Although we may introduce time stamping to avoid having to use a linear structure, we choose linear structures for their efficiency. Because the implementations of STACK are similar to those of QUEUE, we emphasize only the differences. The major difference is that all STACK operations take place in one window, which makes the implementations somewhat simpler to code.

1.6.1   A Block Representation

The simplest block representation is depicted in Fig. 1.21; the elements are assigned contiguous locations in a block of size *Smax*. The window and the window position are represented by the index *top* of the latest element. The representation can be captured by the following Pascal declarations:

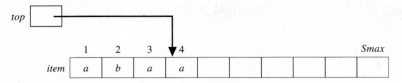

Figure 1.21   A block representation of a stack.

```
const Smax = 10; {say}
type STACK = record
                 top: 0..Smax;
                 item: array[1..Smax] of elementtype
             end;
```

Initially, *top* is 0; it is incremented by 1 whenever an element is added, and is decremented by 1 whenever an element is deleted. The five STACK operations are easy to code, so we leave their coding to Exercise 1.6.

1.6.2   A Pointer Representation

Since we access a stack through only one window, we represent the window of a stack as a pointer to a singly linked list; see Fig. 1.22. Note that an empty stack is represented by a **nil** pointer value. This discussion suggests the following Pascal type definitions:

```
type linktype = ↑celltype;
     celltype = record
                    item: elementtype;
                    successor: linktype
                end;
     STACK = linktype;
```

We leave the implementation of the five STACK operations to Exercise 1.7.

1.6.3   Performance Reports

Although we have not given implementations of the stack operations for the two representations that we have considered, we can intuit their behavior from their similarity to the queue implementations given in Section 1.5. We anticipate that

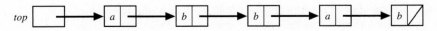

Figure 1.22   A singly linked list representation of a stack.

Table 1.3   A comparison of the worst-case times taken by the two
                 STACK implementations.

	STACK implementation	
Operation	Block	Singly linked
Empty	1^{a}	1
IsEmpty	1	1
Insert	$1 + T_e$	$1 + T_e$
Examine	$1 + T_e$	$1 + T_e$
Delete	1	1

[a] 1 denotes constant time.

Table 1.4   Performance ratings of the two implementations of STACK.

STACK implementation	Rating	Comments
Block	Excellent	Simple implementation; no extra space; predefined maximum size
Singly linked	Very good	Extra linkage space; no predefined size

Empty and *IsEmpty* take constant time in both representations, whereas *Delete* takes constant time in the block representation and takes at least $1 + T_{\text{dispose}}$ time units in the pointer representation. In addition, *Insert* takes at least $1 + T_e$ time units in the block representation and at least $1 + T_e + T_{\text{new}}$ time units in the pointer representation; *Examine* takes at least $1 + T_e$ time units in both representations. We leave the details of the evaluation to Exercise 1.8. In Table 1.3, we summarize the times of the STACK operations; in Table 1.4, we rate the two representations. We prefer to use the block representation when the predefined maximum size is acceptable, because it is easy to code, and because it uses indexing rather than pointer chasing, which is usually more efficient.

1.7   SUMMARY

We introduced data-structure design as the companion of algorithm design; they are the two principal ingredients of successful program construction. We identified five levels of refinement in the design of data structures: data reality, data abstraction, data relatedness, data representation, and data encoding. Of these levels, the levels of data abstraction, relatedness, and representation are treated as the specification, representation, and implementation of an ADT, where an ADT is a set of domain values and a finite set of operations on them. Each ADT must, at some level, be represented in a programming language in terms of its language data types. We believe that multilayered representations provide much of the power of ADTs; other contributors are information hiding, representation independence, implementation independence, and modularity.

We focused attention on the notion of ADTs using the reversal problem to introduce them. We introduced two fundamental ADTs: the QUEUE and STACK. Both ADTs maintain the arrival, or chronological, order of elements. They differ in only their *Insert* operations. We examine and delete the earliest element in a queue; we examine and delete the latest element in a stack. A queue displays first-in, first-out (FIFO) behavior; a stack displays last-in, first-out (LIFO) behavior.

We provided representations and partial implementations of both QUEUE and STACK. There are only two efficient possibilities for a representation: the block and pointer representations. Both approaches have their merits, but the block representations have an edge because they are simple to implement.

When a programming language does not support pointers, pointer representations are implemented as cursor representations. These representations, in turn, lead to the issues of memory management. We introduced the concept of a free list, which we can use to keep track of free cells. Further discussion of memory management is postponed to Section 13.5.

1.8 HISTORY

The separation of data from their representation took longer to gain a foothold in the programming community than did the separation of subprograms from programs. The debut of modern programming can be seen in the books of Dijkstra (1976), Gries (1981), and Linger, Mills, and Witt (1979). More specifically, top-down design is discussed in detail in Yourdon (1975). The first published treatment of stepwise refinement is in Wirth (1971), who used this approach in his text (Wirth, 1973). Myers (Myers et al., 1975) provides a treatment of modular programming.

Our introduction to data-structure design follows that of Tompa (1980; 1990). Morris (1973) was the first person to point out that ADTs are not just sets of values—they also include the legal operations on the values and, hence, constitute an algebra. The texts of Martin (1986) and Thomas, Robinson, and Emms (1988) are the most accessible texts that deal with the correctness of ADT representations and implementations. A useful and readable collection of articles on ADTs is to be found in the book edited by Yeh (1978). Cleaveland (1986) and Bishop (1986) discuss ADTs within programming languages. The text of Welsh, Elder, and Bustard (1984) demonstrates the ADT approach in a Pascal-like environment. ADTs are central to the concept of object-oriented programming; Meyer (1988) provides one of the best introductions to this approach.

The distinctions between a purely functional approach to ADTs, in which new values are always created (value semantics), and an approach that includes assignment, in which values can be modified (object semantics), are covered in detail in Martin (1986). The idea of using a functional approach that allows new values to be versions of old values (version semantics), rather than completely new values, was suggested by Frank Tompa (1990). As an approach to specifying ADTs, it falls between value and object semantics, because it provides a restricted inheritance of values.

The issue of efficient memory management is crucial to the implementation of operating systems, see Silberschatz, Peterson, and Galvin (1991), and of programming languages, see Aho, Sethi, and Ullman (1988) and Knuth (1968).

EXERCISES

1.1: We say that a string is a *palindrome* if it is the same as its reversal. Develop a program *Palindrome* that reads in a string and checks whether the string is a palindrome. Specify an appropriate ADT for this problem.

1.2: Implement and test one of the cursor representations of a queue.

1.3: The ADT RQUEUE abstracts the notion of a **readable queue,** which is a queue that allows us to read its elements from the earliest to the latest without deleting them. To support this extension, we introduce a third implicit window. We have four additional operations to support this activity: *Start, ReadElement, Next,* and *IsAfterLast. Start* initializes the third window to be over the earliest element, if there is one; *ReadElement* reads the element in the third window; *Next* advances the third window unless it is at the after last position; and *IsAfterLast* checks whether the third window is beyond the latest element. How would you represent RQUEUE using either a block or a pointer representation? Choose one representation and implement the nine RQUEUE operations.

1.4: In the definition of RQUEUE in Exercise 1.3, we have avoided the issue of what happens when the original QUEUE operations and the additional RQUEUE operations are interleaved. For example, consider what happens when we move the third window over the second element and there are three deletions! Discuss the interleaving problem. Suggest at least two techniques to deal with it.

1.5: The DEQUE ADT is more general than either the QUEUE or STACK ADTs in that it allows reading, insertion, and deletion of both earliest and latest elements. We replace *Delete, Insert,* and *Examine* by six operations: *DeleteFirst, DeleteLast, InsertFirst, InsertLast, ExamineFirst,* and *ExamineLast.* How would you represent a DEQUE using either a block or a pointer representation? Choose one representation and implement the eight DEQUE operations.

1.6: Code the five STACK operations in Pascal, using the block implementation.

1.7: Code the five STACK operations in Pascal, using the singly linked list implementation.

1.8: Carry out an analysis of the five stack operations for one of the STACK implementations.

1.9: Rather than using two different ADTs to solve the reversal problem, we can use a single ADT, which we call TWOSEQ to denote a two-ended sequence. The TWOSEQ ADT is an abstraction of a sequence that allows insertions at both ends. It has two insertion operations: *InsertFirst* and *InsertLast*. For clarity, we rename the examination and deletion operations *ExamineFirst* and *DeleteLast*. Provide a detailed specification of the six operations for TWOSEQ, and suggest an efficient representation and implementation. Moreover, rewrite Program 1.1 in terms TWOSEQ.

1.10: Specify the STACK and QUEUE ADTs using the TWOSEQ ADT of Exercise 1.9. Then demonstrate how you can implement one of these ADTs using the two-ended sequence operations.

1.11: An RSTACK ADT is similar to the RQUEUE ADT of Exercise 1.3. Specify the necessary additional operations, choose a representation of RSTACK, and code an implementation based on the chosen representation.

1.12: The usual form of arithmetic expressions is known as **infix;** however, we can define two other forms—**prefix** and **postfix** expressions—that avoid the use of parentheses. The definition of prefix expressions is left to Exercise 1.13; we consider postfix expressions here. For simplicity, we allow only the binary operators +, −, *, and /. A single value or variable is always a postfix expression, and, if E_1 and E_2 are postfix expressions, then $E_1 E_2 +$, $E_1 E_2 −$, $E_1 E_{2*}$, and $E_1 E_2 /$ are postfix expressions. As can be deduced from this recursive definition, operands precede their operators in postfix expressions.

    a. Design an algorithm to evaluate postfix expressions of real values.

    b. Design an algorithm that converts fully parenthesized infix expressions into postfix expressions. Can you modify your algorithm to treat infix expressions that are not fully parenthesized?

1.13: Recursively define prefix expressions—that is, expressions in which operators precede their operands.

Design and implement an algorithm to produce a prefix expression from an infix expression.

1.14: In a post office, if a clerk closes a window, the people in the line for that window have to join other lines. This observation motivates the introduction of two new operations for queues: *Catenate*: $Q \times Q \to Q$ and *Shuffle*: $Q \times Q \to Q$. The function value *Catenate* (Q_1, Q_2) is the result of appending Q_2 to Q_1; and the function value *Shuffle* (Q_1, Q_2) is the result of interleaving the elements of Q_2 with those of Q_1 so that the odd-numbered elements are from Q_1 and the even-numbered elements are from Q_2.

Implement these two new queue operations for the singly linked list representation of QUEUE.

1.15: Another operation that we might want in an ADT QUEUE is *Size*: $Q \to \mathcal{N}$; the function value $Size(Q)$ is the number of elements in Q.

Implement this operation for QUEUE using a block or pointer representation.

1.16:   Consider a block representation of QUEUE that uses wraparound and maintains the values *first* and *size*—the position of the earliest element and the size of the queue, respectively. Provide an implementation of QUEUE using this representation. Compare and contrast this representation with the one discussed in Section 1.5.1.

2

Performance Measurement

We address efficiency in data-structure design by providing methods to measure and compare the performance of data structures. We measure the performance of a data structure that supports a given ADT by measuring the performance of its implementation. This observation implies that we need to treat only the performance measurement of programs, since the methods apply equally well to data structures. In Sections 2.1, 2.2, and 2.3, we discuss the three methods of measuring performance: empirical, simulational, and analytical. Then, in Section 2.4, we introduce the asymptotic method of comparing the performance of programs and, hence, of data structures. In particular, the big-oh and big-Ω notations are defined. We are led to the existence of performance barriers or lower bounds that, in turn, lead to the definition of two basic computational models: the main-memory or random-access–machine model, and the external-memory or direct-access–memory model. Finally, in Section 2.5, we demonstrate the basic methods of analyzing the worst-case performance of recursive procedures.

With the **empirical approach,** we run a system with real-world input to estimate the system's performance. Here, the estimates are only as good as the input; the closer the chosen input to the expected input, the more accurate the estimates. For example, a computer-center manager develops a **benchmark** of programs that reflect the center's usage characteristics. The benchmark is used to evaluate new computer systems or changes in the current one.

With the **simulational approach,** we construct a computer model of a system, and then estimate the system's performance by evaluating the model's performance with simulated data. In this case, the estimates are only as good as the model and the input; the more accurate the model and simulated input, the more accurate the estimates.

Finally, with the **analytical approach,** we begin by constructing a mathematical or theoretical model of the system whose performance we are measuring;

we then use theoretical techniques to derive estimates of the system's performance. We must remember that the estimates are only as good as our model; the more accurate the model, the more accurate the estimates. In Section 1.5.5, we exercised this method with the model that we shall continue to use, in a slightly modified form.

In the automobile industry, for example, there are well-developed mathematical models that predict an automobile's drag when given its speed and acceleration. Using such a model, engineers can predict the performance of a new automobile. Similarly, based on the same mathematical model, a computer model can be implemented that takes into account features that are not incorporated into the mathematical model—it simulates the automobile. Using known automobiles and their observed performance, an engineer can test and calibrate the computer model. The performance of the new automobile can then be computed, in a variety of circumstances, based on the new auto's speed and acceleration. Simulational models are easier, less expensive, and faster to modify than is a scale model in a wind tunnel, which is the older method of simulation. In addition, it is easier, with a computer simulation, to run thousands of tests and to concentrate on specific aspects of the design during test runs. Finally, no automobile manufacturer would be persuaded to build a new car without seeing that car in action—she would demand an empirical test of performance. No prospective owner would buy a car without taking it for a test drive.

2.1   EMPIRICAL MEASUREMENT

The most realistic evaluation strategy is to run a system with real data. Just as automobile-magazine publishers test drive new cars, so we have to test run new programs, and even new implementations. The difference between the empirical and analytical or simulational evaluations is that, with the former, we execute real programs with real data. The predictions of a model, either analytical or simulational, are only as accurate as the model; eventually, we have to face the real world and to dirty our hands. Once we have analyzed the performance of a data structure, we usually want to decide how efficient that data structure is. We can compare it with other data structures for the same problem, or with the best results possible for the problem. For example, if we are doing an empirical comparison of two programs, we normally compare timings on the same machine with the same compiler and, if possible, with the same data. Since we use ADTs in the solution of programming problems, we prefer to measure the performance of an ADT implementation in the program that uses it. We call this technique **evaluation in context.** We may be tempted to evaluate a data structure by itself, outside of the user program, but we obtain a more realistic assessment when we evaluate it in its context. The contextual approach is applicable not only to empirical measurement, but also to simulational and analytical measurement.

In the real world, we evaluate a system by monitoring that system's behavior over time. To evaluate programs, we embed them, conceptually, in a **monitor** that

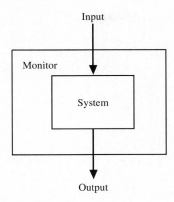

Figure 2.1 An empirical monitor scheme.

gathers and maintains statistics about the execution-time performance of the program; see Fig. 2.1. In practice, we often implement monitors by embedding the monitoring actions in a program. The function of such a monitor can be as simple as checking the time at the beginning and end of a run and computing the input data size, or as complex as overseeing the times taken by the execution of groups of statements and the number of times each group is executed. In the latter mode, the monitor functions as a **profiler.** Profilers are useful for fine tuning programs; fortunately, they are normally available as standalone tools.

2.2 SIMULATIONAL MEASUREMENT

The simulational approach to evaluating a program (and any system) is to construct a computer model of the program and then to monitor the model's performance with simulated data. Because a program is, trivially, its own model, running a simulation normally means, in this context, running a program with simulated data. On the other hand, when carrying out a simulational evaluation of a data structure, we should attempt to obtain the evaluation within the data structure's context, as we should for an empirical simulation. Occasionally, a program may be replaced by a simplified computer model, but that is the exception rather than the rule. In Section 2.2.1, we describe the approach using *ESearch* and *MSearch* as example programs whose behavior we want to simulate. In Section 2.2.2, we describe how to construct a good pseudorandom-number generator, and we provide a Pascal implementation of an efficient and robust one. Finally, in Section 2.2.3, we argue, on statistical grounds, what the length of a test sequence should be when we perform a simulational evaluation of programs such as *ESearch* and *MSearch*.

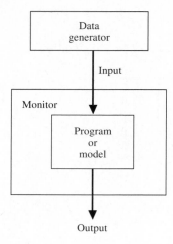

Figure 2.2   The general simulation scheme.

2.2.1   A Simulation

The general setup for a simulation is shown in Fig. 2.2. The program or model is encapsulated in a monitor that gathers and maintains statistics about the execution-time performance of the program. The **data generator** provides input data according to some probability distribution, which usually is prespecified and is based on a **pseudorandom-number generator.** Occasionally, we might wish to consider "all" possible input data of a given size—for example, all permutations of $1..n$, when evaluating a sorting program. In this case, the data generator has to enumerate the input data of the given size without repetitions. To illustrate the simulational approach, we introduce a search problem and two solutions for it that we use throughout this section to illustrate the ideas: *Given an integer $n \geq 1$ and an array D containing n distinct elements in the first n cells, determine for a sequence of query elements (queries) which of them are in D.*

The first solution uses **exhaustive sequential searching.** We compare each query element with the element in position 1, the element in position 2, and so on, until either the query element is matched or the list is exhausted; this approach is depicted in Fig. 2.3(a). Alternatively, we can use **move-to-front sequential searching**. We take the same actions as before, except that, whenever the query element is matched, we move it to the first position and move each of the intermediate elements one position to the right; Fig. 2.3(a) shows the first phase, and Fig. 2.3(b) shows the second phase.

We provide Pascal implementations of the algorithms for the two solutions in Programs 2.1 and 2.2. The functions are called *ESearch*, for exhaustive search, and *MSearch*, for move-to-front search. In both cases, we assume that the following global declarations have been made:

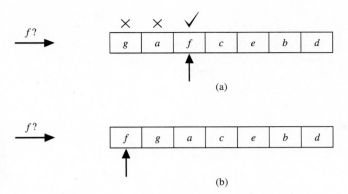

Figure 2.3 Sequential searching for the element *f* in list. (a) Exhaustive
searching. The position of the element *f* is unchanged.
(b) Move-to-front searching. The element *f* is moved to the
front of the list.

```
function ESearch(q: elementtype; D: ourarray): integer;
{D contains n distinct elements in positions 1..n, and q
    is the query element. If q appears in positions 1..n of D,
    then ESearch returns the unique position of q;
    otherwise, ESearch returns 0.
    This approach is called (exhaustive) sequential search.}

var i: integer;

begin D[nplusone]:= q;
    {We add q as the last element to ensure loop termination.}

    i:= 1;
    while D[i] <> q do i:= i + 1;
    {On termination, i is the position of the
        earliest appearance of q in D.}

    if i = nplusone
    then ESearch:= 0 {The search was unsuccessful.}
    else ESearch:= i {The search was successful.}
end ESearch;
```

Program 2.1 A Pascal implementation of exhaustive sequential search.

```
const n = ?; {n ≥ 1 is the number of elements in the given array.}
    nplusone = ?; {nplusone = n + 1}
type ourarray = array[1..nplusone] of elementtype;
```

```
function MSearch(q: elementtype; var D: ourarray): integer;
{D contains n distinct elements in positions 1..n, and q is the
    query element. If q appears in positions 1..n of D, then
    MSearch returns 1, moves q to position 1, and moves the
    elements in positions 1.. (i - 1) to positions 2..i, respectively.
    Otherwise, MSearch returns 0.
    This approach is called move-to-front sequential search.}

var i,j: integer;

begin D[nplusone]:= q;
    {We add q as the last element to ensure loop termination.}

    i:= 1;
    while D[i] <> q do i:= i + 1;
    {On termination, i is the position of the
        earliest appearance of q in D.}

    if i = nplusone
    then MSearch:= 0 {The search was successful.}
    else begin {The search was unsuccessful.}
        {Move the elements one position to the right.}
        for j:= i - 1 downto 1 do D[j + 1]:= D[j];
        D[1]:= q; MSearch:= 1
    end
end MSearch;
```

Program 2.2   A Pascal implementation of move-to-front sequential search.

We also assume that the first n positions of D contain n distinct elements and that *elementtype* allows equality tests to be performed. The functions *ESearch* and *MSearch* return 0 if the given query element is not in D; otherwise, they return the query element's position in D. Note that, normally, we would write *MSearch* as a Boolean procedure; we have written it to return the values 0 and 1 so that *ESearch* and *MSearch* are interchangeable. In addition, we use the **sentinel technique** to ensure that the search always terminates within the array bounds; that is, we always add the query as the $(n + 1)$th element before starting the search.

We use the same input data for each function so that we can compare the functions. Simulation provides **averaged results;** therefore, using the same data is not strictly necessary.

We take a simple-minded approach to the simulation. Assume that the n elements in the array are the n integers $1..n$, in random order, and that the integers have probabilities $p_1,...,p_{n+1}$, where p_{n+1} is the probability of unsuccessful search and p_i, $1 \leq i \leq n$, is the probability that integer i is accessed. We produce

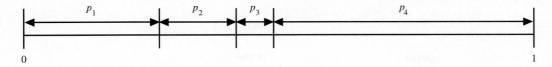

Figure 2.4   Interpreting probabilities as lengths of intervals.

query sequences with elements from $1..n + 1$ such that the probability of occurrence of each i, $1 \leq i \leq n + 1$, approximates p_i. The $n + 1$ probabilities can either be provided or be generated pseudorandomly.

How do we generate such a sequence? Since the probabilities sum to 1, we can think of them as lengths of intervals in the real interval $(0,1]$ that excludes 0, but includes 1. For example, if $n = 3$, then we have four intervals, the first ending at p_1, the second ending at $p_1 + p_2$, and so on; see Fig. 2.4. Thus, if we generate a pseudorandom number x in the interval $(0,1]$, then x corresponds to an access of element i if it is in the interval

$$\left(\sum_{j=1}^{i-1} p_j, \ \sum_{j=1}^{i} p_j \right],$$

and x corresponds to an unsuccessful access if it is in the interval $(1 - p_{n+1}, 1]$.

Having solved the data-generation problem, we must decide what statistics to collect. The simplest statistic is the number of elements the search function examines for each query—**the average number of probes** over the query sequence. We leave to Exercises 2.3 and 2.4 the exploration of other possibilities. But what should the monitor report? Again, we take the simplest approach; the monitor reports the average number of probes at intervals of 100 queries. Should we base our results on one query sequence or on many? We consider 100 sequences to minimize the effects of anomalies that might be produced by individual sequences. Finally, how long should the query sequence be? We would like each element to be examined at least once, so there should be at least n queries; we prefer to use at least n^2. We make this choice to minimize the occurrence of anomalies.

The monitor must keep track of the cumulative numbers of probes during each query sequence and over all query sequences. The monitor's final report, in its simplest form, is a table, as shown in Table 2.1. It is usually better, however, to display the results as a plot, as shown in Fig. 2.5. Plots are a valuable visual tool because they can be superimposed to provide a visual comparison of the results.

For the results of the simulation to be acceptable, we must ensure that the pseudorandom-number generator does, indeed, generate numbers that satisfy randomness tests, and that our decisions on the length of a query sequence are based soundly. We discuss these two issues in Sections 2.2.2 and 2.2.3.

Table 2.1   The monitor's final report of the cumulative number of probes for *ESearch* and *MSearch*.

Operation	No. of queries	No. of probes	Average no. of probes	Time (secs)	Average time ($\mu secs$)
ESearch	50	26566.0	531.3200	0.05	1000
	100	53302.0	533.0200	0.12	1200
	200	105439.0	527.1950	0.24	1200
	500	266364.0	532.7280	0.52	1040
	1000	529699.0	529.6990	0.96	960
	2000	1031442.0	515.7210	2.11	1055
	5000	2585498.0	517.0996	4.95	990
	10000	5190314.0	519.0314	10.10	1010
MSearch	50	34286.0	685.7200	0.10	2000
	100	53940.0	539.4000	0.09	900
	200	84654.0	423.2700	0.18	900
	500	150926.0	301.8520	0.38	760
	1000	219862.0	219.8620	0.45	450
	2000	321294.0	160.6470	0.68	340
	5000	647248.0	129.4496	1.52	304
	10000	1138614.0	113.8614	2.74	274

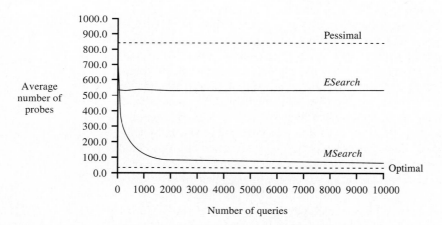

Figure 2.5   The superimposed plots of the cumulative numbers of probes for *ESearch* and *MSearch*, as obtained by simulational analysis.

2.2.2   Pseudorandom Numbers

Every simulation needs a pseudorandom-number generator. We can design and implement a good generator; alternatively, if we use someone else's, then we should ensure that it is a good one. The simplest pseudorandom-number generators are based on modulo arithmetic, using the **linear congruential method.** This method uses the current pseudorandom number to generate the next one, through a computation that has the general form

$$(ab + 1) \bmod m,$$

where a is the current pseudorandom number, b is some integer constant, and m is some large positive integer. This computation gives integers in the range $0..m - 1$; they are not really random, but we expect that they will appear to be if we choose $b,m,$ and the initial or **seed** value of a appropriately. Usually, m is a power of 2 or 10 close to the word size. The value chosen for b should not be too small or too large with respect to $m,$ it should end with the digits 21, and there should be no particular "pattern" among its other digits. Choosing b to be a number that has one fewer digit than m does is a good choice. For example, if $m = 1$ million, then choosing $b = 472,321$ is reasonable, as is choosing $b = 734,921$; choosing $b = 555,521$ is, however, not reasonable. Finally, the seed value of a should not produce small cycles; we should avoid 0.

Because b is chosen close to the word size and a also may be close to the word size, the product ab may cause overflow. This product is, however, only an intermediate result; in reality, we need to compute $(ab + 1) \bmod m$. Fortunately, the properties of modular arithmetic allow us to rewrite this computation as

$$(ab + 1) \bmod m = ((ab \bmod m) + 1) \bmod m;$$

that is, we need to compute only the product of a and b modulo m. Based on this observation, we split both a and b into two parts as follows. With the previous example ($m = 1$ million), we split a into

$$a = a_1 10^3 + a_0,$$

where $0 \le a_0, a_1 < 1000$; and, similarly,

$$b = b_1 10^3 + b_0.$$

Now, ab can be rewritten as

$$(a_1 10^3 + a_0)(b_1 10^3 + b_0) = a_1 b_1 10^6 + (a_1 b_0 + a_0 b_1) 10^3 + a_0 b_0,$$

and, because $m = 1$ million, immediately $a_1 b_1 10^6 \bmod m = 0$, we discard the leading term. This simplification leaves

$$ab \bmod m = ((a_1 b_0 + a_0 b_1) 10^3 + a_0 b_0) \bmod m.$$

Again, using the properties of modular arithmetic, we can rewrite the right-hand side of this equation as

$$(((a_1b_0 + a_0b_1) \bmod m^{1/2})m^{1/2} + a_0b_0) \bmod m,$$

and we can discard the most significant three digits of the first term, because the first term's value is at least m and at most $m^{3/2}$.

We can program the final pseudorandom-number generator in Pascal, as shown in Program 2.3. We have left open two issues. First, we often want pseudorandom numbers that are in a range that is much smaller than $0..(m - 1)$. How do we obtain them? Second, if we want pseudorandom real numbers between 0 and 1, how do we obtain them?

In answer to the first question, if we want a pseudorandom integer in a smaller range $1..r$, say, then we compute $\lfloor r \times (a/m) \rfloor$. In this way, we use the most

```
function Multiply(p,q: integer): integer;
{This function performs multiplication modulo modulus, a global integer
    constant, using the technique described in Section 2.2.2. It
    requires that the global constant modulus be an even power of 10
    less than the word size, and that the global integer constant
    sqrtmod be the square root of modulus.}
var plower,pupper,qlower,qupper: integer;

begin
    plower:= p mod sqrtmod;
    pupper:= p div sqrtmod;
    qlower:= q mod sqrtmod;
    qupper:= q div sqrtmod;
    Multiply:= (((plower*qupper + pupper*qlower) mod sqrtmod) * sqrtmod
                + plower*qlower) mod modulus;
end;


function Random: integer;
{This function computes a pseudorandom integer using the linear
    congruential method. It uses Multiply to do modulo multiplication
    to avoid overflow. It requires the global integer constants modulus,
    sqrtmod, and multiplier, and the global integer variable seed.
    The value of Random is an integer in the range 0..modulus - 1.
    The constant multiplier and the variable seed should be given values
    as suggested in Section 2.2.2.}

begin
    seed:= (Multiply (seed, multiplier) + 1) mod modulus;
    Random:= seed;
end;
```

Program 2.3 A Pascal implementation of a pseudorandom number generator.

significant digits of a; in Pascal, we compute $(a*r)$ **div** m, but, to avoid overflow, we split the computation again. The obvious way to obtain a pseudorandom integer is to use the least significant digits of a with a **mod** r. Unfortunately, the integers obtained in this way are not at all random; see Exercise 2.6. In answer to the second question, if we want a pseudorandom real number between 0 and 1, we simply return the real value a/m.

The linear congruential method is simple to implement, but its use requires care. The choices of the seed value of a, the multiplier b, and the modulus m are critical. Therefore, we would like to have a method of checking that each sequence of pseudorandom numbers is, for our purposes, random. Unfortunately, no such guarantee can be given. Nonetheless, we can apply various statistical tests of randomness to a sequence. If a sequence passes the tests, we are prepared to accept that it is random.

The simplest such test is the **chi-squared test.** Its aim is to test whether the distribution of the numbers in the sequence has a reasonable spread. Assume that we generate n integers in the range $[0,r)$; then, we would expect, for values of n large with respect to r, that there are n/r occurrences of each integer. The frequencies should not, however, be exactly the same; otherwise, the sequence would not be random. Letting f_i denote the number of occurrences of i in the sequence, we compute

$$\chi^2 = \frac{r}{n} \sum_{i=0}^{r-1} (f_i - n/r)^2.$$

Observe that this value is 0 if the frequencies are exactly n/r. If $n > 10r$, we expect χ^2 to be within $2\sqrt{r}$ of r. The implementation of this method is left to Exercise 2.7. There are other statistical tests that can be applied; one of them is discussed in Exercise 2.8.

2.2.3 The Length of a Test Sequence[*]

How long should a test sequence be to ensure that the results of a simulation are sufficiently accurate? This question requires a statistical answer. We do not attempt to answer it in general; rather, we answer it for the simulational evaluation of *ESearch*, described in Section 2.2.2, that estimates the expected number of probes in a successful search. The ideas are applicable, however, to any simulational evaluation.

Given n elements $e_1,...,e_n$ in positions $1,...,n$ of an array with access probabilities $p = p_1,...,p_n$, the expected number of probes μ_p is

$$\sum_{i=1}^{n} ip_i$$

and the variance σ_p^2 of the number of probes is

$$\sum_{i=1}^{n} i^2 p_i - \mu_p^2 \; .$$

Assume, however, that *we do not know the probability distribution,* yet we still want to obtain a good approximation to μ_p and, perhaps, to σ_p^2. Or, alternatively, assume that we want to confirm the analytic results by simulation.

The basic idea is to carry out an initial simulational experiment. For *ESearch,* we apply k queries, for some $k \geq n$, that we have chosen. Having finished this experiment, we estimate the value of μ_p, and we determine whether this estimate is sufficiently reliable by examining the precision of a confidence interval based on the estimated value of μ_p. (The confidence interval is a range of values for μ_p that is consistent with the estimated value of μ_p, the observed variability in the various numbers of probes used during the simulational experiment, and the statistical behavior of such experiments.) If it is, we have a long enough query sequence; otherwise, we derive a new value for k and iterate the process. We now flesh out the details.

If the query sequence is $q = q_1,...,q_k$, where q_i takes X_i probes, then the sequence $X = X_1,...,X_k$, has mean

$$\overline{X} = \frac{1}{k} \sum_{i=1}^{k} X_i \; .$$

Now $\overline{X}$ is an estimate of μ_p, and we want to determine how accurate an estimate it is. We begin by deciding how precise the estimate should be. Let us use a 95-percent confidence interval for μ_p with a width of ±10 percent of the value of μ_p —a reasonable choice for the precision of the estimate. A width of ±5 percent would be a still more stringent choice, but we want to emphasize that there is no simplistic connection between the confidence level associated with an interval estimate of μ_p and the absolute width of that interval. We now compute the sample size needed to achieve this precision based on the estimated mean and variance. If the computed sample size is smaller than k, then k is an acceptable sample size for the required precision; otherwise, we repeat the experiment with the computed sample size.

The approximate 95-percent confidence interval for μ_p based on a query sequence of length m is

$$\overline{X} \pm 1.96 \sigma_p / \sqrt{m} \; .$$

Although we do not know σ_p, we can estimate it using the standard deviation s of the sequence X, where

$$s = \sqrt{\frac{\sum_{i=1}^{k} X_i^2 - k\overline{X}^2}{k - 1}} \; .$$

The required confidence-interval estimate for μ_p is specified to be

$$[\overline{X} - \overline{X}/10, \overline{X} + \overline{X}/10];$$

it has width $\overline{X}/5$. But the estimated 95-percent confidence interval based on the values $\overline{X}$, s, and m is

$$[\overline{X} - 1.96s/\sqrt{m}, \overline{X} + 1.96s/\sqrt{m}],$$

with width $3.92s/\sqrt{m}$. This confidence interval implies that

$$\overline{X}/5 \geq 3.92s/\sqrt{m},$$

since the confidence interval computed from the estimate must be no larger than 20 percent of $\overline{X}$. In other words,

$$m \geq (19.6s/\overline{X})^2.$$

If k is smaller than the minimal value of m that satisfies this inequality, then we repeat the experiment with k equal to this minimal value; otherwise, the chosen query length is sufficient.

2.3   ANALYTICAL MEASUREMENT

Analyzing the performance of a data structure (or program) is not always easy; fortunately, many analyses have been done already. In this text, we not only provide the results of such analyses when they exist, but also introduce the methods of analysis.

In this section, we introduce the analytical method; in Sections 2.4 and 2.5, we discuss the comparison of analytical measures and the analysis of recursive subprograms, respectively.

2.3.1   An Analytical Primer

Do you remember solving problems of this form in high school? *In construction company A, it takes three workers 8 hours to dig a trench 6 feet deep, 12 feet long, and 3 feet wide. How long does it take 12 workers to dig a trench of the same depth and width, but 36 feet long?*

Well, analyzing the (abstract) time taken by any program is a similar task. We usually are not as interested in the precise answers, however, as we are in the relationships among the variables. In the sample problem, worker-hours (wh) are linearly proportional to the length (l) of the trench; that is,

$$wh = a_1 l + b_1,$$

for some nonnegative constants a_1 and b_1. The equation for wh implies that, when we double the length of the trench, we almost double the worker-hours required, because

$$2a_1l + b_1 = 2wh - b_1.$$

The relationship is best visualized as shown in the plot in Fig. 2.6.

We have abstracted the real world of trench digging by ignoring such factors as ability, speed, strength, organization, and coffee breaks, to produce a **mathematical model** of trench digging for the given construction company.

If a second construction company, company B, claims that its workers can dig trenches much faster than can company A's, we shall want to test its claim. We formulate the company B's equation, after observing the workers, as

$$wh = a_2l + b_2.$$

Assuming that $-b_2/a_2 \leftarrow b_1/a_1$ and $b_2 > b_1$, we obtain the additional plot shown in Fig. 2.6. We can see that for trenches of length at most $\bar{l}$, we complete the job faster with company A; for trenches of greater than this length, we complete the job faster with company B. The second group of workers, however, still exhibits a linear relationship between the worker-hours and trench length. In both cases, doubling the trench length takes almost twice the worker-hours. The **rate of change** or **growth** of worker-hours is the key to our understanding of trench digging by these two companies.

For example, if a third construction company, company C, advertised trench digging for which doubling the trench length quadrupled the required worker-hours, we would probably dismiss it from further consideration. We should do so because

$$wh = a_3l^2 + b_3l + c_3$$

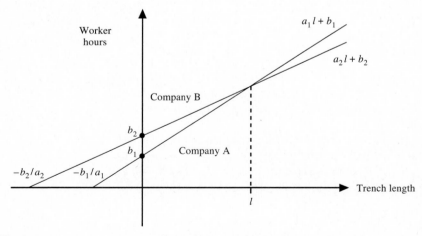

Figure 2.6   A plot of worker-hours versus trench length for two
trench-digging companies, A and B.

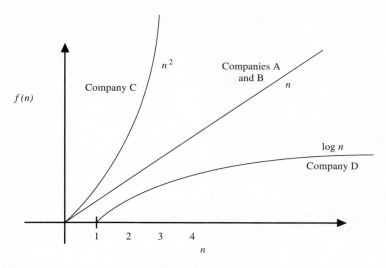

Figure 2.7 The growth rates of log n, n, and n^2.

is the corresponding quadratic equation, which grows much faster than a linear equation. On the other hand, if a fourth company, company D, claimed that doubling the trench length added only a constant number of worker-hours, we would almost certainly want to examine its claim more thoroughly. In this case, we have the logarithmic relationship

$$wh = a_4 \log l + b_4,$$

and it grows much more slowly than does the linear relationship. The growth rates of the three functions are compared in Fig. 2.7.

The trench-digging model has abstracted trench length and worker-hours, and their relationship, as the foci of our concerns. What should we abstract in our models of programs and their execution?

First, we ignore the specific values in the input data and consider only the "size" of, or the number of items in, the input data. For example, with a sorting program, we consider only the number of items to be sorted, rather than the items themselves. Second, our main concerns are how long a program takes to execute and how much space it uses during execution. The **abstract measure of time** that we use is the number of specified operations in a computation. For example, with a sorting program, we might count the key comparisons, the data movements, the elements examined, or the disk accesses. With a matrix program, we might count the arithmetic operations. With a program based on graphs, we might count the edges or nodes that are accessed. With a recursive subprogram, we might count the number of recursive calls.

Similarly, the **abstract measure of space** that we use is the number of input data elements and the number of units of extra space (an element takes 1 unit of space) introduced in the computation; the real space taken by each element is ignored at this level of detail. With a recursive subprogram, we might count the maximum depth of recursion, since each call uses extra space.

In all cases, we discard the inessential operations and preserve the essential ones. This selection is the essence and function of abstraction—to simplify, yet to retain sufficient detail to satisfy the requirements. Selection is also the reason that the analytic approach is so powerful; its results are independent of specific machines of the same type.

2.3.2   The Choice of Measures

Our goal is to relate the abstract size of the input data to the abstract time and abstract space used by a given program. In practice, we will be satisfied if we can provide an upper bound on the abstract time and space used by a program, rather than the exact time and space used. Even abstract time and space, however, depend on the specific input data, rather than just on the data's size. For a given input-data size, the time and space used by a program can vary widely. For example, with a sorting program, when the input data are almost sorted, the program often terminates much sooner than it would otherwise. We take this variation into account by considering three types of measure: **worst case, expected case,** and **amortized case.** Before defining the three types of measure more precisely, we investigate the functions *ESearch* and *MSearch*, given in Programs 2.1 and 2.2, respectively.

In *ESearch*, the time taken by the **while** loop dominates *ESearch*'s execution time, if we assume that all Pascal operations take the same time. The time taken by the **while** loop depends on the position of the query element. For example, in Fig. 2.8, *f* is in position 3, so the **while**-loop header is executed three times in this case. Thus, the simplest model for *ESearch* is that it takes

$$i \text{ time units}$$

for a query *q,* when *q* is in the *i*th position, $1 \le i \le n + 1$.

A similar argument for *MSearch* leads to either

$$2i \text{ time units}$$

for a query *q,* when *q* is in the *i*th position, $1 \le i \le n$, or to

$$n + 1 \text{ time units}$$

when *q* is in the $(n + 1)$th position. The times taken by *MSearch* are different, because of the second loop.

We can abstract time for *ESearch* and *MSearch* in four alternative ways as the number of **loop repetitions,** the number of **probes** or positions examined dur-

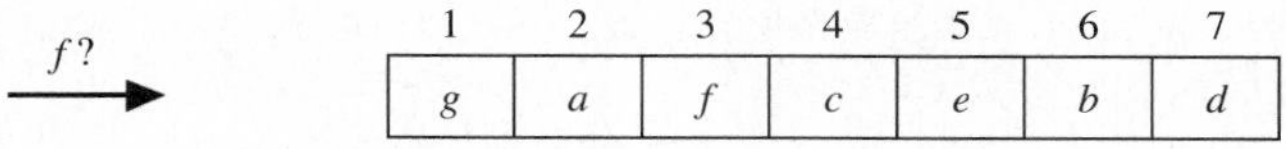

$f?$

1	2	3	4	5	6	7
g	a	f	c	e	b	d

Figure 2.8 Exhaustive sequential searching.

ing a search, the number of **locations visited,** or the number of **element comparisons.** If we consider comparisons or probes, then *MSearch* takes exactly i time units when q is in the ith position, $1 \leq i \leq n + 1$.

Is abstract time a good approximation to real time? In Table 2.2, we tabulate the real time taken by *ESearch* and *MSearch* using the Berkeley Pascal compiler on a VAX 8650 running under UNIX 4.3BSD. In the same table, we provide the four abstract times. The plots of the four abstract times are shown in Fig. 2.9. Observe that each of the abstract times provides a reasonable approximation to the real times taken by the algorithms; each of them is linearly proportional to the real time. For example, we can express the time taken by *ESearch* as

$$ap + b,$$

where p is the number of probes. With the values given in Table 2.2, we can conclude that

$$a = 1.88 \text{ and } b = 5.87.$$

Table 2.2 The abstract and real times for *ESearch* and *MSearch*.

Operation	Position	Time (μs)	No. of comps.	No. of loop reps.	No. of probes	No. of locations
ESearch	5	24.37	5	4	5	5
	10	26.99	10	9	10	10
	20	41.38	20	19	20	20
	50	100.02	50	49	50	50
	100	188.63	100	99	100	100
	200	369.49	200	199	200	200
	500	1007.18	500	499	500	500
	1000	1888.10	1000	999	1000	1000
MSearch	5	24.20	5	4	5	9
	10	47.02	10	9	10	19
	20	88.36	20	19	20	39
	50	215.08	50	49	50	99
	100	428.97	100	99	100	199
	200	862.53	200	199	200	399
	500	2149.02	500	499	500	999
	1000	4353.93	1000	999	1000	1999

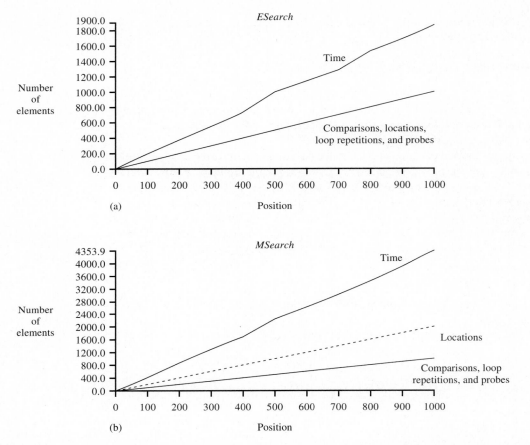

Figure 2.9 Plots of abstract and real times. (a) The plot for *ESearch*. (b) The plot for *MSearch*.

Although we want only to relate the size of the input data to the time and space requirements of a given program, we have to decide which time and which space requirements to use. For example, with *ESearch*, the size of the input data is the number n of elements in the array D. But it takes one probe or comparison to search for the element in the first position, and n probes to search for the element in the last position. Which time—1, n, or somewhere in between—should be associated with input size n? Similarly, in a sorting program with input-data size n, there are $n!$ different permutations of the input values, and each one may have a different sorting time.

As we mentioned, the usual approach is to consider three different measures. The first and simplest is the pessimistic measure—for each input-data size, we choose those data that have the largest possible time and space requirements. This measure is the **worst-case measure.** (Its optimistic companion, **the best-case**

measure, is rarely used.) It provides an upper bound on the time and space requirements for any input data of the same size. For both *ESearch* and *MSearch*, the worst-case time can be expressed by a time function, $T_\omega : \mathcal{N} \to \mathcal{N}$, from input-data size to abstract time units, defined by

$$T_\omega(n) = n + 1,$$

if we choose the number of probes (or comparisons) as our abstraction of time. Since units of time (and space) are nonnegative integers, the codomain of all time functions is $\mathcal{N} = \{0,1,2,...\}$. Moreover, the size of the input data is assumed to be a nonnegative integer; hence, the domain of a time (and space) function is also N .

For searching problems, we often distinguish between successful and unsuccessful search performance. Letting $s_\omega(n)$ and $u_\omega(n)$ be the corresponding worst-case time functions, we have

$$s_\omega(n) = n$$

and

$$u_\omega(n) = n + 1,$$

for the numbers of probes or comparisons in successful and unsuccessful searches, respectively, for both *ESearch* and *MSearch*.

The second measure takes the pragmatic or what-we-expect-to-happen view. For each input-data size, we compute the expected time and space requirements. This measure is thus the **expected-case measure.** For the measure to be well defined, we must know the probability distribution over all input data of the same size. Usually, we assume that all input data of the same size are equally likely to occur; we make the *assumption of a uniform probability distribution.* For example, with *ESearch*, we may assume that, for each n, all elements in D are equally likely to be accessed; moreover, we assume that unsuccessful search does not occur. Let p_i be the probability of accessing the element in position i. Since there are n elements, $p_i = 1/n$. Because finding the element at position i takes i probes, that element contributes

$$ip_i = i/n$$

probes to the expected number of probes. The sum of these contributions is the **expected number of probes;** it is

$$\sum_{i=1}^{n} i/n = n(n+1)/2n$$

$$= (n+1)/2 .$$

Informally, we expect any search to take us halfway down the array.

If unsuccessful search can occur with probability p_{n+1} and the elements in the array are equally likely to be accessed, then $p_i = (1 - p_{n+1})/n$, $1 \leq i \leq n$. Since $0 \leq p_{n+1} \leq 1$, we obtain a similar result for the expected number of probes; namely, we expect to probe at least the first half of the array. The derivation of this result is left to Exercise 2.1. We can generalize these results for any probability distribution as follows. If p_i is the access probability of the element at position i in the array, and p_{n+1} is the probability of unsuccessful search, then the expected number of probes is

$$\sum_{i=1}^{n+1} i p_i .$$

In Section 8.3, we reconsider sequential search in this general setting, and present an expected-case analysis of *MSearch*.

Finally, we turn to an increasingly important measure, the **amortized-case measure,** which measures the average time taken by a *worst-case sequence* of queries. Sometimes, the worst-case measure is too pessimistic, in the sense that, in a sequence of similar operations, the individual operations cannot all simultaneously attain their worst-case performance. Hence, considering the performance of a worst-case sequence of operations can give us more insight into the behavior of a data structure. For example, this approach is extremely successful for *MSearch*, as we shall prove in Section 8.3. *ESearch* and *MSearch* have the same amortized performance for unsuccessful search, but they differ for successful search. With *ESearch*, we obtain a worst-case sequence of size $s \geq 1$ by letting each query in the sequence be the element in the nth position. The total number of probes for such a sequence is

$$sn;$$

thus, the amortized-case and the worst-case behavior of *ESearch* are the same, but, as we shall prove in Section 8.3.3, this assertion does not hold for *MSearch*. In the next subsection, we demonstrate that, for a variant of STACK, an amortized analysis gives a view of reality more representative than that afforded by a worst-case analysis.

2.3.3 Stacks and Amortization

We demonstrate amortization's usefulness with a variant of STACK that we call MSTACK, for **multidelete stack**. MSTACK has the same operations as STACK, except that we replace the operation *Delete* with *MDelete*, which is allowed to remove more than one element at a time. More formally, $MDelete : \mathcal{N} \times S \to S$: The function value $MDelete(i,S)$ is undefined if S has fewer than i elements; otherwise, $MDelete(i,S)$ is S without its latest i elements. Observe that $MDelete(0,S)$ is S itself, $MDelete(n,S)$ is equivalent to *Empty* if S contains exactly n elements, and $MDelete(1,S)$ simulates the STACK *Delete* operation.

What effect does *MDelete* have on the performance of a representation and implementation of MSTACK? With a block representation, it has no effect at all. However, with a singly linked list representation in which we dispose of deleted cells, *Delete*(i,S) takes $O(i)$ time, 1 time unit for each disposal, when we ignore the time to dispose of a deleted cell. In other words, for a multidelete stack S that contains n elements, the worst-case time of *MDelete* is $O(n)$, which is linear in the number of elements in the multidelete stack. For the ADT STACK, on the other hand, *Delete* is a constant-time operation in the worst case.

Although the worst-case analysis of *MDelete* is correct, it does not tell the whole story. When we apply *MDelete* m times, to a multidelete stack, then, this coarse analysis leads us to believe, the m multideletions should take $\Omega(mn)$ time in total. But this bound is too high, because we cannot delete more elements than we have inserted. Thus, m calls of *MDelete* cannot take more time than the time taken to insert n elements in the first place.

We resolve this difficulty by using amortization. In an amortized analysis, we look at the total time taken by a sequence of operations, averaged over the length of the sequence, rather than at the time taken by one operation. In addition, we consider worst-case sequences of operations. Amortized analysis takes us beyond single-operation worst-case analysis. In the situations where it provides insight, such as in the singly linked list implementation of MSTACK, it tells us that, although a single operation can be time consuming, there cannot be too many time-consuming operations.

We prove the following fact for MSTACK.

Fact 2.1   *Any sequence of $n > 0$ insertion and multideletion operations on an empty multidelete stack takes $O(n)$ time when the stack is implemented with a singly linked list. Thus, multideletions take constant time, when the time taken by a sequence of insertions and multideletions is averaged over the length of the sequence; that is, the each MSTACK operation takes constant time, in the amortized case.*

Proof: Assume that a given sequence of operations contains m *Inserts* and $n - m$ *MDeletes*, in some specified order, where $0 \le m \le n$; further assume that the result of the sequence is not **undef**. Now, *Insert*, in the singly linked list representation of MSTACK, can be implemented to take constant times; therefore, m insertions take $O(m)$ time. Moreover, the largest stack that can be produced with m insertions is one that has exactly m elements; therefore, the $n - m$ *MDeletes* cannot delete more than m elements. This observation implies that $0 \le n - m \le m$. Because the deletion of a single element can be implemented to take constant time, the total time taken by the $n - m$ multideletions is also $O(m)$. Finally, since $m \le n$, the time taken by the n operations is $O(n)$.

Note that the argument is also valid when the n operations give the result **undef**.

The second statement of the fact follows immediately from the first one. $\square$

2.4 PERFORMANCE COMPARISON
AND EVALUATION

We have presented three methods for measuring the performance of data structures and programs. As we shall see, however, we often have different data structures that solve the same problem. It is natural to ask, therefore, which we should choose. In other words, we want to be able to evaluate a new data structure or program by comparing its performance with that of previous approaches. Such a comparison is applicable to the three methods of measuring performance. Normally, any comparison we make should compare apples with apples, not with oranges. For example, in an empirical comparison, we should time solutions on the same machine under the same operating system and compiler. (Often, empirical evaluation compares apples and oranges; for example, we run benchmarks on different machines to compare the machines' performances. We assume that, in our more restricted setting, we do not perform this type of comparison.) Analytically, if we count probes in one solution, we should count probes in the others.

There is, however, a second and deeper level of comparison that we use. We evaluate a new program or data structure by comparing its performance with the **performance barrier** inherent in the problem, rather than with different programs and data structures. Performance barriers make sense only within the framework of analytical measurement, where they are usually called **lower bounds.**

Lower-bound results are, essentially, negative results. They make claims such as this: Searching for a given query element in a block of n distinct elements using only equality testing cannot be done in fewer than n comparisons in the worst case. If the number of comparisons is our abstraction of time, then we are saying that the number of comparisons taken by exhaustive sequential searching, which we discussed in Section 2.3.2, cannot be reduced, *in the worst case.*

Proving lower bounds is more difficult than is comparing data structures and programs, because what a lower bound tells us is this: Whatever data structure or program we propose for this problem, it cannot beat the lower bound. Such wide-ranging performance-barrier claims are unusual; normally, we have to restrict our attention to specific classes of programs and data structures. In the example lower bound of the last paragraph, we included only programs that use equality comparisons to find a query element. We assumed that the data are in a block and the elements are distinct. The assumptions about what operations we allow and at what cost specify a **model of computation.**

We use a simple operation-based model of computation that is sufficient for our purposes. Together with the model of main memory that we present in Section 2.5.3, it gives the model for a **random-access machine** that enables us to express lower bounds for a number of the ADTs studied in the text. Complementing this model, we also consider an abstraction of external memory, a model of a **disk** or **direct-access memory,** in Section 2.5.4. The abstraction allows us to compare the performance of ADTs represented externally without getting lost in detail.

Before presenting these two models, we begin by discussing the asymptotic comparison of functions, since we need to be able to see how two different time (or space) functions grow with respect to each other. Then, we summarize how we can combine time and space functions algebraically.

2.4.1 Asymptopia

If we measure the performance of an algorithm analytically, then we obtain a time or space function $f(n)$ of the input size n. We then want to answer questions of the following form:

- What is the value of $f(1000)$?
- How do $f(1000)$ and $f(2000)$ compare?
- How do $f(n)$ and $g(n)$, for some other function $g(n)$, compare?

The second question is a special case of

- What happens when we double the input size?

No matter how $f(n)$ is defined, we can almost always evaluate it for specific values of n; however, if we want to compare $f(n)$ and $f(2n)$ (or $f(4n)$), for example, evaluation is not an option. If $f(n)$ is given in **closed form**[1]—for example, $f(n) = 2^n$ —we see that $f(2n)/f(n) = 2^{2n}/2^n = 2^n = f(n)$; in other words, doubling the input size results in squaring the time or space taken. This fact tells us a great deal about the **growth rate** of f. In general, we cannot obtain such simple characterizations of growth rate, so we have two goals. First, we need to be able to estimate the growth rate of a given time or space function. Second, we need to be able to compare the growth rates of two such functions. We need the first ability to evaluate one algorithm for a given problem; we need the second ability to compare two algorithms for a given problem or to compare an algorithm and a lower bound for a given problem.

Our approach for both goals is to compare the **asymptotic growth rates** of functions; we investigate what happens, in the limit, when the argument approaches infinity. We use this approach to provide simpler functions (which are easier to understand) that approximate asymptotically a given function. This technique is valuable, since a time function may not have a closed form (or we may not be able to find one) or, even if it has one, the closed form may be too complex for us to handle and understand. We determine the goodness of an approximation by comparing the growth rates of the original function and that function's approximation. The two basic comparison methods are the following. If

---

[1] A function is in **closed form** if the function's definition is given in terms of the function's arguments, and of no other variables.

$$\frac{f(n)}{g(n)} = 1 \text{ as } n \to \infty,$$

then we say that $f(n)$ is asymptotic to $g(n)$, and we denote this fact by writing

$$f(n) \sim g(n).$$

If

$$\frac{f(n)}{g(n)} = 0 \text{ as } n \to \infty,$$

then we say that $f(n)$ grows more slowly than $g(n)$, and we denote this fact by writing

$$f(n) \wr g(n).$$

For almost all pairs $f(n)$ and $g(n)$ of functions that we shall see, we have $f(n) \wr g(n)$, $g(n) \wr f(n)$, or $f(n) \sim cg(n)$, for some positive constant c determined by the functions.

Rather than using $\wr$ and $\sim$, we prefer to use the coarser **big-oh notation,** since it suppresses unimportant detail and is more uniformly applicable. Recall, from the trench-digging problem discussed in Section 2.3.1, that we compared the **rate of change** or **rate of growth** of worker-hours required by four construction companies. We compared the companies by plotting the corresponding functions. In general, this approach is inconvenient, so we define the big-oh notation that we use for comparing growth rates.

Given two functions $f,g:\mathcal{N} \to \mathcal{N}$ we say that f **is big oh of** g if there are a constant $c > 0$ and an integer $n_0 \geq 1$ such that, for all $n \geq n_0$,

$$f(n) \leq cg(n).$$

We write this inequality as $f(n)$ is $O(g(n))$. Informally, whenever we say that $f(n)$ is $O(g(n))$, we imply that f **grows no faster than does** g, for sufficiently large n— the rate of growth of f is bounded from above. Thus, whenever $f(n) \sim g(n)$ or $f(n) \wr g(n)$, we know that $f(n)$ is $O(g(n))$. It is not difficult to show that n^2 is $O(n^3)$; n^k is $O(n^l)$, $0 \leq k \leq l$; and n^k is $O(2^n)$, $k \geq 0$. Moreover, n^3 is not $O(n^2)$; n^l is not $O(n^k)$, $0 \leq k < l$; and 2^n is not $O(n^k)$, $k \geq 0$. We leave these demonstrations to Exercise 2.X; here, we consider the case $f(n) = 6n^2 - 2n + 7$ and $g(n) = n^3 + n$.

We show that $f(n)$ is $O(g(n))$, by letting $n_0 = 1$ and $c = 15$. Now, $f(n)$ is $O(g(n))$ if

$$6n^2 - 2n + 7 \leq 15n^3 + 15n,$$

for all $n \geq 1$, and this inequality holds if

$$0 \leq 15n^3 - 6n^2 + 17n - 7,$$

for all $n \geq 1$. Now, because $n \geq 1$, $17n - 7 \geq 10$ and $(15n - 6)n^2 \geq 9$, for all $n \geq 1$; hence, $f(n)$ is $O(g(n))$.

The converse does not hold, however. Assume that $g(n)$ is $O(f(n))$, and argue by contradiction. In this case, there are an $n_0 \geq 1$ and a constant $c > 0$ such that

$$n^3 + n \leq c(6n^2 - 2n + 7),$$

for all $n \geq n_0$. Again, this inequality holds if

$$n^3 - 6cn^2 + (2c + 1)n - 7c \leq 0,$$

for all $n \geq n_0$. For all $n > \max(n_0, 4, 6c)$, however, we have $n^3 > 6cn^2$ and $(2c + 1)n > 7c$. This conclusion yields a contradiction; hence, $g(n)$ is not $O(f(n))$.

By similar arguments, we can show that $f(n)$ is $O(n^2)$ and $g(n)$ is $O(n^3)$. For example, letting $n_0 = 2$ and $c = 7$, we have $6n^2 - 2n + 7 \leq 7n^2$, for all $n \geq 2$. Similarly, letting $n_0 = 1$ and $c = 2$, we find that $n^3 + n \leq 2n^3$, for all $n \geq 1$. These simplifications of $f(n)$ and $g(n)$ focus our attention on their **dominating terms.** The dominating term of a polynomial is particularly simple to find—it is the highest-degree term. For functions that are not polynomials, however, the dominating terms are not so obvious. Given $h(n) = \log\sqrt{n} + 2^{\sqrt{\log n}}$, what is the dominating term? Fortunately, the functions we consider in this text are not so complex. We have low-degree polynomials (1, n, n^2, n^3), logarithmic functions ($\log^* n$, $\log \log n$, $\log n$, $\log^2 n$), and combinations of functions ($n \log \log n$, $n \log n$, $n \log^2 n$, $n^2 \log n$).

Big-oh notation does not completely capture the rate of growth—it only bounds that rate from above. When we analyze the time, $T(n)$, taken by a program, in the worst case, say, and we have two bounds $f(n)$ and $g(n)$ for $T(n)$, then we choose the tighter bound. (If $f(n) \nmid g(n)$, then $T(n)$ is $O(f(n))$ is the tighter bound.) Whenever we have both $f(n)$ is $O(g(n))$ and $g(n)$ is $O(f(n))$, however, we are assured that f and g grow at the same rate, for sufficiently large n. If we know only that $f(n)$ is $O(g(n))$, for some unknown function f and known function g, then f may, in fact, grow much more slowly than does g. We find ourselves in this situation whenever we attempt to analyze the time and space requirements of a program. The time and space functions are unknown, and we try to find functions that not only bound them from above, but also exhibit the same rate of growth.

We need a notation to express that a function is **bounded from below** by a second function. We use **big-Ω notation.** Given two functions f and g, we say that $f(n)$ is $\Omega(g(n))$, if there are a constant $c > 0$ and an integer $n_0 \geq 1$ such that, for all $n \geq n_0$,

$$f(n) \geq cg(n).$$

Observe immediately that

$$f(n) \text{ is } \Omega(g(n)) \text{ iff } g(n) \text{ is } O(f(n)).$$

This definition of big Ω is neither the only possible one, nor necessarily the most useful one; however, it is sufficient for our purposes. An alternative definition is explored in Exercise 2.10.

When $f(n)$ is $\Omega(g(n))$, we infer that f **grows no more slowly than does** g—it bounds the rate of growth of f from below.

2.4.2 Big-Oh Algebra[*]

We have deliberately written

$$f(n) \text{ is } O(g(n)),$$

rather than

$$f(n) = O(g(n)),$$

to emphasize that the relationship is not symmetric; we cannot write

$$O(g(n)) \text{ is } f(n).$$

Despite this asymmetry, there are several algebraic laws for big-oh notation that can be proved. We give two of them here; others are explored in Exercise 2.11.

We often want to combine big-oh terms using summation and product. In these cases, there are several simple identities available, as we now demonstrate. Given two big-oh relationships, $f_1(n)$ is $O(g_1(n))$ and $f_2(n)$ is $O(g_2(n))$, then

$$a(n) = f_1(n) + f_2(n) \text{ is } O(g_1(n) + g_2(n))$$

and

$$p(n) = f_1(n) f_2(n) \text{ is } O(g_1(n)g_2(n)).$$

We prove the big-oh relationship for $a(n)$, leaving that for $p(n)$ to Exercise 2.12. By definition, there exist integers n_1 and n_2 and constants c_1 and c_2 such that

$$f_i(n) \le c_i g_i(n),$$

for all $n \ge n_i$, $i = 1, 2$. Hence,

$$a(n) = f_1(n) + f_2(n)$$
$$\le c_1 g_1(n) + c_2 g_2(n),$$

for all $n \ge n_0 = \max(n_1, n_2)$. But, letting $c = \max(c_1, c_2)$,

$$a(n) \le c(g_1(n) + g_2(n)),$$

for all $n \ge n_0$; that is,

$$a(n) \text{ is } O(g_1(n) + g_2(n)).$$

Special cases of the sum and product relationships occur when $g_1(n)$ is $O(g_2(n))$. Observe that, in this case, we have

$$a(n) \text{ is } O(g_2(n))$$

and

$$p(n) \text{ is } O(g_2^2(n)).$$

Another special case of these results occurs when $g_1(n)$ is $O(1)$. We obtain

$$a(n) \text{ is } O(1 + g_2(n)),$$

and, since $1 + g_2(n)$ is $O(g_2(n))$, we have

$$a(n) \text{ is } O(g_2(n))$$

and

$$p(n) \text{ is } O(1 \cdot g_2(n));$$

because $1 \cdot g_2(n)$ is $O(g_2(n))$, we have

$$p(n) \text{ is } O(g_2(n)).$$

In both cases, the constant function is absorbed, as we would expect. We have to be careful, however, of summations of the form

$$\sum_{i=1}^{n} a_i ,$$

where the a_i are nonnegative constants, since they are not $O(1)$, but rather are $O(n)$.

2.4.3 The Random-Access–Machine Model

In the **random-access–machine model (RAM model),** we assume that main memory is a one-dimensional array or block of cells; see Fig. 2.10. It is indexed by addresses in the range $0..M - 1$, where M is some power of 2. The time required to access a cell is assumed to be independent of that cell's location—we say that main memory has **random access.** Current access times are of the order of 1 microsecond per byte, since most current machines perform at least 1 million instructions per second (MIPS). This model, which is close to reality, implies that

Figure 2.10   Main memory viewed as a block of cells.

all structures we discuss in this text are, at some level, mapped into a block. When stating and proving lower bounds, we enhance this basic model with the basic operations that are allowed—for example, element comparisons.

2.4.4   The Direct-Access–Memory Model

In the **direct-access–memory model (DAM model),** we assume that the only kind of external memory available is a hard-disk unit. A hard-disk unit consists of one or more **disks** and one or more **arms;** see Fig. 2.11. The disks rotate at a constant speed and both sides of each disk are used. Reading and writing are accomplished by **read–write heads** on the arms. Each set of arms moves as one unit; individual arms cannot move alone. Typical disk units have two heads on each arm. When the arms are fixed, each head can access the data on one **track**—a track is a circular path on the surface of each disk. Thus, each arm in a unit accesses the same track on each side of each disk; such a set of tracks is called a **cylinder.** When there are two heads on each arm, the cylinder is, in reality, two cylinders—one for each head.

    A disk address is also in the range of $0..(M - 1)$, for some large M. It is more meaningful, however, to think of the address as comprising a cylinder number, a track number, and, finally, a block number within the track; see Fig. 2.4. The cylinder number causes the arm unit to move to the position of the given cylinder; the track number activates the corresponding head; and the block number determines the position on the track at which the head begins to read or write. Access is certainly neither random nor sequential; it is somewhere in between. Moving the arms to the correct cylinder is called **seeking;** the time this operation takes is called **seek time.** Current units have an **average seek time** (ast) of approximately 20 milliseconds. Activation of the appropriate head is essentially instantaneous, but the waiting time for the required block to come under the head, called **rotational latency,** is usually significant. Current units have an **average rotational**

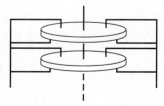

Figure 2.11   The disk or direct-access–memory model of external memory.

latency time (arlt) of approximately 10 milliseconds. Finally, the block is identified and the unit begins to read from or write to it. There is a small start-up delay before reading or writing begins; after this delay, the rate of transfer is constant. In current units, the **data-transfer rate** is approximately 2500 bytes per millisecond. We normally assume a block size of 2400 bytes, so the time taken to transfer one block, ignoring seeks, is approximately 1 millisecond. This time is called the **block transfer time** (btt). If we are accessing n blocks on a disk in a random fashion, then the time taken is expected to be

$$n \times (ast + arlt + btt) \text{ milliseconds.}$$

If the blocks are read sequentially, however, then the time taken is expected to be

$$(ast + arlt + n \times btt) \text{ milliseconds,}$$

which is shorter by approximately $n \times (ast + arlt) \approx 30n$ milliseconds. In most situations we encounter, however, blocks are accessed randomly. So, when we refer to **disk access time,** we mean the expected time to access one block; that is,

$$(ast + arlt + btt) \text{ milliseconds.}$$

We can **directly access** any location on a disk, but the time required depends on the position of the arms and on the position of the disk with respect to the arms. For this reason, we compare external structures by the number of disk accesses they use, rather than by the time taken to perform them. When we want to provide a ballpark estimate of the time taken by an external structure, we base it on the disk access time.

2.5 THE ANALYSIS OF RECURSIVE SUBPROGRAMS

Analyzing the time and space requirements of recursive subprograms is, conceptually, more difficult than is analyzing them for nonrecursive subprograms. We consider only the worst-case analysis of recursive subprograms; the expected-case analysis is beyond the scope of this text. As we shall see, we often design recursive subprograms when we implement operations on recursively defined data structures. Moreover, we obtain recursive subprograms in many other situations too; for example, when we use divide and conquer to design a subprogram, the latter normally will be recursive. It is natural, therefore, to ask how we can analyze the time and space requirements of such subprograms. The standard answer to this question is that we express the time or space requirements recursively. This approach yields a **recurrence equation,** which we then have to solve. We present, in Sections 2.5.1, 2.5.2, and 2.5.3, three techniques that enable us to solve many of the analysis problems we shall meet. In addition, in Section 2.5.4, we provide solutions to three general recurrence equations that are sufficient for the needs of this text.

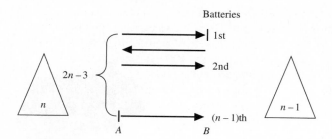

Figure 2.12   A general strategy that can be used to solve the problem of the battery-powered car.

2.5.1 The Battery-Powered–Car Problem

Assume that we have a battery-powered car that we can drive k kilometers with one new battery. We are able to carry at most one battery in addition to the one in use. Given a dump of n batteries at some point A on a highway, how far away from A, using the n batteries, can we drive the car? We assume that we use batteries from only the specified dump, and measure the distance to the farthest point from A that we can reach. Given the kilometerage of the car, we can drive a total of nk kilometers, the maximum possible distance, by carrying one additional battery at a time, driving k kilometers away from A, changing the battery, and driving k kilometers back to A. Unfortunately, we will have driven only k kilometers from A, if there are an odd number of batteries in the original dump. If there are an even number of batteries in the original dump, we will end up at A and, therefore, will be 0 kilometers from A.

If the dump contains only one battery, then we can drive exactly k kilometers from A. Otherwise, by using one battery to move the remaining batteries to a new location, and by doing this dump relocation repeatedly, we can drive the car farther than k kilometers from A. We carry $n - 1$ batteries, one at a time, to a new location x kilometers from the dump, using exactly one battery. We have to make a round trip of $2x$ kilometers for the first $n - 2$ batteries and a one-way trip of x kilometers for the last, or $(n - 1)$th, battery. Since we can drive the car k kilometers with one battery and we want to get as far from A as possible, we deduce that

$$2(n - 2)x + x = k;$$

that is, $x = k/(2n - 3)$ kilometers.

A general strategy has emerged; see Fig. 2.12: *Move the dump x kilometers down the road using one battery for this purpose. If n > 1, then the moving the dump takes 2n − 3 trips and the dump is moved x = k/(2n − 3) kilometers.* In Program 2.4, we give a Pascal implementation of this strategy. It is impossible to improve the three-battery solution given by this strategy. We can, however,

```
function Distance(n: integer): real;
{The value k is a global constant, the number of kilometers that we
    can drive the battery-powered car with one battery;
    n is the initial number of batteries; and  Distance(n)
    returns the distance that we can drive the battery-powered car
    when we drive it according to the rules given in Section 2.5.1,
    and use the recursive strategy also given in Section 2.5.1.}

begin
    if n = 1
    then Distance:= k
        {We use one battery to drive the car as far from A as possible.}
    else Distance:= k/(2*n - 3) + Distance(n - 1)
        {We use one battery to move the remaining n - 1 batteries
            a distance of k/(2n - 3) kilometers from A.}
end {Distance};
```

Program 2.4   The Pascal function *Distance* that provides a good solution
to the problem of the battery-powered car.

improve the four-battery solution by using more batteries to move the dump; see
Exercises 2.14 and 2.15.

We introduced the problem of the battery-powered car and the recursive
strategy to give us a recursive subprogram to analyze. Let $T(n)$ denote the time
units taken by *Distance*(n), $n \geq 1$. (Since there is only one computation for each n,
the worst-case and expected-case times are the same.) Mirroring the recursive
formulation of *Distance*, we express $T(n)$ recursively as follows:

$$T(1) = a,$$
$$T(n) = b + T(n - 1), n > 1,$$

for some constants $a,b > 0$. How do we obtain this **recurrence equation?** We
begin by executing the call *Distance*(1). It leads to the **then** alternative of the conditional statement in Program 2.4, and this alternative, clearly, takes a constant
time of, say, a time units. On the other hand, *Distance*(n), for $n > 1$, leads to the
else alternative, which is an assignment that includes a recursive call of *Distance*.
By definition, the evaluation of *Distance*$(n - 1)$ takes $T(n - 1)$ time units. Thus,
we are left with evaluating $k/(2*n - 3)$ and the $+$ operation, which take, in total,
constant time—say, $b > 0$.

We have expressed $T(n)$ recursively, but we prefer a closed-form solution
that gives $T(n)$ in terms of only n. Therefore, we must try to solve the recurrence
equation. This one is particularly simple. We use **unrolling**; that is, we first evaluate $T(n - 1)$ on the right-hand side of the recurrence equation, then evaluate the
resulting expression that contains $T(n - 2)$, and so on. Unrolling gives

```
procedure Generic(n: integer;...);

begin
    if n = 1
    then Action A {This step is the termination step.}
    else begin {This step is the recursive step.}
        Action B;
        Generic(n div 2,...);
        Action C
    end
end{Generic};
```

Program 2.5   The procedure *Generic*.

$$
\begin{aligned}
T(n) &= b + T(n-1) \\
&= b + b + T(n-2) \\
&= b + b + \cdots + b + T(1) \\
&= \underbrace{b + b + \cdots + b}_{n-1} + a
\end{aligned}
$$

after *n* evaluations of *T*. Thus,

$$
T(n) = b(n-1) + a,
$$

or, letting $c = \max(a,b)$, we can rewrite this equation as $T(n) \le cn$; in which case, $T(n)$ is $O(n)$. Using mathematical induction, it is not difficult to prove that this solution is correct; see Exercise 2.24.

2.5.2   Tabulation and Restriction[*]

We extend our range of techniques for solving recurrence equations with tabulation and domain restriction. We **tabulate** the values of a recursively defined function to discover a pattern among them, and thereby intuit a solution. We then modify this method by solving the recurrence equation for a **restricted domain** and attempting to prove that this solution holds in general. As a second example, consider the procedure *Generic* in Program 2.5. When $n > 1$, *Generic(n)* carries out action B, calls *Generic* recursively on one-half of the data, and then performs action C. Its termination step carries out only action A. The structure of *Generic* occurs so frequently that we should understand it thoroughly; we shall use it repeatedly in Chapter 8, for example.

Letting $T(n)$ be the time units taken by *Generic(n)*, in the worst case, we can express $T(n)$ recursively as

$$T(1) = a$$
$$T(n) = b + c + T(\lfloor n/2 \rfloor), n > 1,$$

where a, b, and c are the time units taken by actions A, B, and C, respectively, in the worst case.

Assuming that a, b, and c are constants, we try to express $T(n)$, in closed form, in terms of n. The recurrence equation appears more difficult than the one we solved in Section 2.5.1 because it includes the floor function. Once we tabulate the values of $T(n)$, for small values of n, however, we see a pattern emerge that enables us to intuit the solution. Let $d = b + c$, for convenience. Tabulating T for the first 15 values of n gives us

$$T(1) = a,$$
$$T(2) = a + d,$$
$$T(3) = a + d,$$
$$T(4) = a + 2d,$$
$$T(5) = a + 2d,$$
$$T(6) = a + 2d,$$
$$T(7) = a + 2d,$$
$$T(8) = a + 3d,$$

$$\cdot \quad \cdot$$

$$\cdot \quad \cdot$$

$$\cdot \quad \cdot$$

$$T(15) = a + 3d.$$

From these values, we intuit that, if we express n as

$$n = 2^k + l,$$

where $k = \lfloor \log n \rfloor$ and $0 \le l < 2^k$, then

$$T(n) = a + kd$$
$$= a + \lfloor \log n \rfloor d.$$

The formal proof of this formula is left to Exercise 2.25. We have argued that $T(n)$ is $O(\log n)$, but what if actions B and C take time linear in the input size? That is, what if there is some constant $d > 0$ such that $T(B \,\&\, C) \le dn$. (Action A again takes a time units, where a is a constant.) This assumption gives us a different recurrence equation for $T(n)$; namely,

$$T(1) = a,$$
$$T(n) = dn + T(\lfloor n/2 \rfloor), n > 1.$$

We take the same approach as before; we tabulate the values of $T(n)$, for small values of n:

$$T(1) = a,$$
$$T(2) = a + 2d,$$
$$T(3) = a + 3d,$$
$$T(4) = a + 6d,$$
$$T(5) = a + 7d,$$
$$T(6) = a + 9d,$$
$$T(7) = a + 10d,$$
$$T(8) = a + 14d,$$
$$T(9) = a + 15d.$$

Although there is a pattern in the values of $T(n)$, it is not so easy to identify. Rather than solving the recurrence equation directly, we first consider its solution for restricted values of n. The recurrence for $T(n)$ divides n by 2; thus, if we choose n to be a power of 2, then we can ignore the floor function. Letting $n = 2^k$, for some $k \geq 1$, we determine, by unrolling, that

$$T(2^k) = d(2^k + 2^{k-1} + \cdots + 2^1) + a.$$

If we replace the constants a and d by $e = \max(a,d)$, then we can simplify the equation for $T(2^k)$ to

$$T(2^k) \leq e(2^{k+1} - 1),$$

which in turn can be rewritten as

$$T(n) \leq 2en,$$

for $n = 2^k$, $k \geq 1$.

We have learned that $T(n)$ is $O(n)$, for n a power of 2. We now conjecture that this relationship holds also for arbitrary values of n, and attempt to prove this conjecture by induction; see Exercise 2.26.

2.5.3 The Difference Operator[*]

We now add **differencing** to our arsenal of techniques for solving recurrence equations. To introduce it, we consider a third generically structured recursive procedure, *BrandX* in Program 2.6. *BrandX* also appears frequently; we use it whenever we split the input data into two halves and treat each half separately and recursively in the same way. We shall see examples of its use in Chapters 5 and 12.

```
procedure BrandX(n: integer;...);

begin
    if n = 1
    then Action A {This step is the termination step.}
    else begin {This step is the recursion step.}
        Action B;
        BrandX(n div 2,...);
        Action C
        BrandX(n - (n div 2),...);
        Action D
    end
end{BrandX};
```

Program 2.6   The procedure *BrandX*.

Assuming that action A takes a time units, in the worst case, and that actions B, C, and D together take b time units, in the worst case, we can express the time $T(n)$ taken by *BrandX(n,...)*, in the worst case, as

$$T(1) = a,$$
$$T(n) = b + T(\lceil n/2 \rceil) + T(\lfloor n/2 \rfloor), n > 1.$$

Using tabulation once more, we find that $T(n) = an + b(n-1)$, $n \geq 1$, and, hence, $T(n)$ is $O(n)$. The proof that this solution is correct is left to Exercise 2.27.

We are more interested, however, in solving the recurrence equation when b is a linear function of the input size—namely, when $b \leq dn$. The recurrence equation can be rewritten as

$$T(1) = a,$$
$$T(n) = dn + T(\lceil n/2 \rceil) + T(\lfloor n/2 \rfloor), n > 1.$$

If we tabulate the values of $T(n)$, we obtain

$$T(1) = a,$$
$$T(2) = 2a + 2d,$$
$$T(3) = 3a + 5d,$$
$$T(4) = 4a + 8d,$$
$$T(5) = 5a + 12d,$$
$$T(6) = 6a + 16d,$$
$$T(7) = 7a + 20d,$$
$$T(8) = 8a + 24d.$$

In this case, we can see a pattern emerging if we examine the differences between adjacent values of $T(n)$. Define the **difference operator** Δ, for a function $f(n)$, by

$$\Delta f(n) = f(n + 1) - f(n).$$

The difference operator bears a number of similarities to the differential operator D, where

$$Df(x) = \lim_{h \to \infty} \frac{f(x + h) - f(x)}{h}.$$

The similarities and differences are the subjects of Exercise 2.28. The important aspect of differences is that we can express $f(n)$ in terms of a sum of differences; that is,

$$f(n) = f(1) + \sum_{i=1}^{n-1} \Delta f(i) \ .$$

We evaluate $\Delta T(n)$ for small values of n to find

$$\Delta T(1) = a + 2d,$$
$$\Delta T(2) = a + 3d,$$
$$\Delta T(3) = a + 3d,$$
$$\Delta T(4) = a + 4d,$$
$$\Delta T(5) = a + 4d,$$
$$\Delta T(6) = a + 4d,$$
$$\Delta T(7) = a + 4d,$$
$$\Delta T(8) = a + 5d.$$

The beginnings of a pattern emerge! Because $T(n)$ can be expressed as a sum of differences, if we can find a closed form for $\Delta T(n)$, then we may be able to find a closed form for $T(n)$. Now,

$$\begin{aligned}
\Delta T(n) &= T(n + 1) - T(n) \\
&= d + T(\lceil (n + 1)/2 \rceil) - T(\lfloor (n + 1)/2 \rfloor) \\
&\quad + T(\lceil n/2 \rceil) - T(\lfloor n/2 \rfloor) \\
&= d + T(\lfloor (n + 2)/2 \rfloor) - T(\lfloor n/2 \rfloor) \\
&= d + \Delta T(\lfloor n/2 \rfloor),
\end{aligned}$$

where we have used the identity $\lfloor (m + 1)/2 \rfloor = \lceil m/2 \rceil$ twice. We have expressed $\Delta T(n)$ as the following recurrence equation:

$$f(1) = a + 2d,$$
$$f(n) = d + f(\lfloor n/2 \rfloor), n > 1.$$

Apart from the constants, this recurrence equation is reminiscent of the first recurrence equation that we obtained for *Generic*; hence, we know that the solution for $f(n)$ is

$$f(n) = a + (2 + k)d, n \geq 1,$$

where $n = 2^k + l$ with $k = \lfloor \log n \rfloor$ and $0 \leq l < 2^k$. Thus,

$$T(n) = a + \sum_{i=1}^{n-1} \Delta T(i)$$

$$= a + \sum_{i=1}^{n-1} [a + (2 + k_i)d],$$

where $i = 2^{k_i} + l_i$ with $k_i = \lfloor \log i \rfloor$ and $0 \leq l_i < 2^{k_i}$. Therefore,

$$T(n) = an + 2(n - 1)d + d \sum_{i=1}^{n-1} k_i,$$

and, as we shall see in Chapter 8, the term

$$\sum_{i=1}^{m} k_i$$

is the internal path length of a minimal-height binary tree with m internal nodes. The sum

$$\sum_{i=1}^{m} k_i$$

is $O(m \log m)$; hence, $T(n)$ is $O(n \log n)$.

2.5.4 Recurrence Equations with Standard Solutions

Some recurrences occur so frequently that we state their general solutions as the following facts.

Fact 2.2 Let

$$T(n) \leq \begin{cases} a, & n = 1; \\ bT(n/c) + an, & n \geq 2; \end{cases}$$

for integer constants $a,b,c \geq 1$. Then,

$$T(n) \text{ is } \begin{cases} O(n), & b < c; \\ O(n \log n), & b = c; \\ O(n^{\log_c a}), & b > c. \end{cases}$$

Fact 2.3 Let

$$T(n) = \begin{cases} a, & n = 1; \\ bT(n-1) + a, & n \geq 2; \end{cases}$$

for integer constants $a,b \geq 1$. Then,

$$T(n) \text{ is } \begin{cases} O(n), & b = 1; \\ O(2^n), & b > 1. \end{cases}$$

Fact 2.4 Let

$$T(n) = \begin{cases} a, & n = 1; \\ bT(n/c) + a, & n \geq 2; \end{cases}$$

for integer constants $a,b,c \geq 1$. Then,

$$T(n) \text{ is } \begin{cases} O(\log n), & b = 1; \\ O(n), & b = c. \end{cases}$$

None of these results are difficult to establish, so we leave their derivation to Exercise 2.29.

2.6 SUMMARY

The performance evaluation of data structures is one of the two main themes of this text. We evaluate performance in three different and complementary ways:

1. Empirical: We monitor an implementation of a data structure with real data obtained from an application.

2. Simulational: We monitor an implementation of a data structure with simulated data generated pseudorandomly, according to some probability distribution.

3. Analytical: We analyze an abstract model of a data structure to provide an evaluation in terms of abstract time or space. There are three kinds of evaluation that we use:

   a. Worst case: We calculate the maximum attainable time or space a data structure uses for one operation; this measure is pessimistic.

b. Expected case: We calculate the time or space that a data structure expects to use for one operation. We normally assume that all data of a given size are equally likely to occur.

c. Amortized case: We calculate the time or space that a data structure uses for a worst-possible sequence of operations possibly averaged over the length of the sequence.

We showed how to analyze a number of recursive procedures using recurrence equations that we have solved by the methods of unrolling (repeatedly evaluate the right-hand sides), tabulation (evaluate the function for small values of the argument, attempt to discover a pattern, and intuit a solution), and differencing (form the differences between consecutive function values, and attempt to solve this new function). In all cases, we used mathematical induction to establish the correctness of the solution.

When comparing analytic performance, we need to ensure that we count the same operations in each case. We normally restrict our attention to the same basic set of operations when discussing the same problem. The assumptions we make provide a model of computation. We described two related models: the RAM model and the DAM model. In the RAM model, we have random access to main memory, in constant time, together with some appropriate operations—for example, comparisons and addition. In the DAM model, we have direct access to disk, in constant time, but, in this case, we are more interested in the number of disk accesses than in the time each one takes. We ignore all other operations in this model, because disk accesses take about 30,000 times as long as do random accesses in main memory.

We provided big-oh and big-Ω notation as the basic tools for the asymptotic comparison of abstract times and space needed by two or more data structures. Furthermore, we introduced the notion of a performance barrier, or a lower bound, for each problem relative to a given model of computation.

2.7 HISTORY

The analytical, systematic approach to performance measurement was introduced by Knuth, and is the major theme of Knuth's *Art of Computer Programming* (1968; 1973). Aho and colleagues (1974) subsequently established the current terminology and analyzed many algorithms. Sequential search and the move-to-front heuristic are discussed in more detail in Section 8.3. The move-to-front heuristic was analyzed by McCabe (1965) and independently by Hendricks (1976) and Rivest (1976). The treatment of pseudorandom numbers is based on Knuth (1969) and Sedgewick (1988). The checking for a long-enough query sequence in a simulation is based on the suggestions of Matthews (1990); the ideas are covered in basic statistical texts—see Moore (1979), for example.

The problem of the battery-powered car is an adaptation of the Jeep problem of Fine (Fine, 1947; Gale, 1970; Phipps, 1947; Wood, 1984). The approach to finding the solution to a recurrence equation that we have given is based on the ideas in Graham and associates (1989).

The main-memory model or RAM model is standard; see Aho and associates (1974), for example. The disk or DAM model is based on the models given by Folk and Zoellick (1987), and Salzberg (1988); the specific timings are based on those given by Salzberg.

EXERCISES

2.1: Derive the expected number of probes for sequential search in a block containing n distinct elements in positions $1..n$ when the probability of unsuccessful search is not 0, and the elements in the block are equally likely to be accessed.

2.2: Carry out the simulation of *ESearch* and *MSearch*, as discussed in Section 2.2, to compute the expected number of probes, for three probability distributions that you choose.

2.3: Repeat Exercise 2.2, but compute the expected number of comparisons.

2.4: Repeat Exercise 2.2, but also compute the variance of the number of probes.

2.5: Invent a new heuristic for sequential search. Compare its performance with that of *MSearch* using simulation.

2.6: There are two methods of generating pseudorandom integers in the range $1..r$, $r < m$, where m is the modulus of the pseudorandom-number generator. The first extracts the most significant digits of the pseudorandom integer; the second extracts the least significant digits.

Design an experiment to compare the randomness of pseudorandom integers obtained by these two methods.

2.7: Implement the chi-squared test. Use it to test one of the pseudorandom-number generators that is available to you.

2.8: Given a sequence of integers $i_0, i_1, ..., i_k$, generated by a pseudorandom-number generator that uses the linear congruential method with modulus m, examine all pairs (i_{2j}, i_{2j+1}), $j \geq 0$, and count the number of times each pair (u, v) of integers occurs, where $0 \leq u, v < m$. Apply the chi-squared test to these m^2 categories, with probability $1/m^2$ in each category.

2.9: Prove that n^3 is not $O(n^2)$; n^l is not $O(n^k)$, $0 \leq k < l$; and 2^n is not $O(n^k)$, $k \geq 0$.

2.10: An alternative asymmetric definition of big Ω is this one: We say that $f(n)$ is $\Omega'(g(n))$ if there is a constant $c > 0$ and there are infinitely many values of n, for which $f(n) \geq cg(n)$. Compare Ω and Ω'; in particular, if $f(n)$ is $\Omega(g(n))$, is $f(n)$ $\Omega'(g(n))$? Does the converse hold?

2.11: Prove the following results about big-oh notation:
    a. $f(n)$ is $O(g(n))$ and $g(n)$ is $O(h(n))$ imply that $f(n)$ is $O(h(n))$.
    b. $f(n)$ is $O(g(n))$ implies that for any constant $c > 0$, $cf(n)$ is $O(g(n))$.

    c. $f(n)$ is $O(h(n))$ and $g(n)$ is $O(h(n))$ imply that $f(n) + g(n)$ is $O(h(n))$.

    d. $f(n)$ is $O(g(n))$ implies that for all $k \geq 1$, $f^k(n)$ is $O(g^k(n))$.

2.12: Given that $p(n) = f_1(n)f_2(n)$ and $f_i(n)$ is $O(g_i(n))$, $i = 1,2$, prove that $p(n)$ is $O(g_1(n)g_2(n))$.

2.13: Based on the Pascal function *Distance* in Program 2.4, set up a recurrence equation for the distance the car can travel with n batteries in the dump. Solve the recurrence equation in terms of the **harmonic numbers**,

$$H_n = 1 + 1/2 + 1/3 + \cdots + 1/n.$$

2.14: Prove that the distance we can drive the battery-powered car with three batteries, using the strategy given in Section 2.5.1, cannot be increased.

2.15: Suggest a solution to the four-battery instance of the problem of the battery-powered car that enables us to drive the car farther than does the solution in Section 2.5.1. Generalize your solution to obtain an improved solution for the case of n batteries, when $n > 4$. Code your solution as a Pascal function $D(n)$, and derive a closed-form solution of the recurrence equation for the time taken by $D(n)$.

2.16: Assuming that the only addition operations in Pascal are *addone* and *subtractone*, which add 1 to and subtract 1 from a given value, respectively, define recursive functions to add and subtract two arbitrary integers. Express the time taken by these functions with two recurrence equations. Then solve the recurrence equations.

2.17: Write a recursive function to compute the value of $\binom{m}{n}$, for $m,n \geq 0$. Analyze the time taken by the function.

2.18: Write a recursive function to compute the determinant of a square integer matrix. Analyze the time taken by the function.

2.19: The Towers of Hanoi problem is as follows. You are given a board that has three pegs. On one peg, the origin, n disks, $n \geq 1$, are stacked. No two disks have the same diameter, and the disks are stacked in sorted order, with the largest on the bottom and smallest on the top. The only permissible move is to remove the topmost disk from one peg and to place that disk on another peg such that it either rests on the board or sits on top of a larger disk. You want to move the tower of disks on the origin peg to another peg.

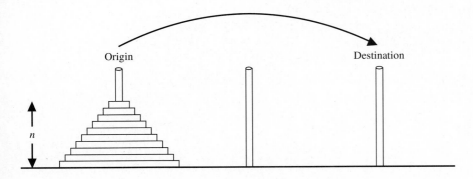

Write a recursive procedure to output the sequence of moves necessary to transfer all n disks from the specified starting peg to a second specified target peg. Ensure that the minimum possible number of moves is used. Establish and solve a recurrence equation for the number of disk moves. Can you prove that this number is the minimum?

2.20: The $f91$ function is defined for $n \geq 0$ as follows:

$$f91(n) = \begin{cases} n - 10 & \text{if } n > 100; \\ f91(f91(n + 11)), & \text{otherwise.} \end{cases}$$

Evaluate $f91(121)$ and $f91(90)$. Analyze the number of recursive calls made by the $f91$ function.

2.21: A cubic box with x-centimeter sides encloses another cubic box if x is at least 2 centimeters; otherwise, it contains a valuable secret. The enclosed box has sides that are 5 millimeters shorter than those of the outer box. Write a recursive function that, given the size of the outer box, returns the number of boxes that need to be opened to reveal the secret. Establish a closed-form expression for the number of boxes in terms of x, the size of the outer box.

2.22: Generalize to four pegs the recursive solution for the Towers of Hanoi problem that you gave in Exercise 2.19. Use the following strategy. Given at least three disks on a starting peg, move the topmost disk to the extra peg, move the remaining disks to the target peg using your three-peg solution, and then move the disk from the extra peg to the largest peg. When there are only one or two disks on the starting peg, move them as you did in the three-peg case. It is well known that the number of moves given by this strategy is not minimal. Illustrate this fact with an example. Derive a recurrence equation for the number of moves taken by this strategy. Solve the equation.

2.23: Modify *BrandX*, in Program 2.6, to give *BrandY* that, for $n \geq 3$, divides the data into three equal parts and calls itself recursively on each part. Derive and solve a recurrence equation for the time taken by *BrandY*, in the worst case, assuming that the various actions take constant time. Does *BrandY* perform more efficiently than does *BrandX*? Explain your answer.

2.24: Given the recurrence equation

$$T(1) = a,$$
$$T(n) = b + T(n - 1), n > 1,$$

for some constants $a,b > 0$, prove by induction that $T(n)$ is $O(n)$.

2.25: Given the recurrence equation

$$T(1) = a,$$
$$T(n) = b + T(\lfloor n/2 \rfloor), n > 1,$$

for some constants $a,b > 0$, obtained from *Generic*, given in Program 2.5, prove that $T(n) = a + \lfloor \log n \rfloor b$.

2.26: Given the recurrence equation

$$T(1) = a,$$
$$T(n) = dn + T(\lfloor n/2 \rfloor), n > 1,$$

for some constants $a,d > 0$, prove that $T(n) \leq 2en$, where $e = \max(a,d)$.

2.27: Given the recurrence equation

$$T(1) = a,$$
$$T(n) = b + T(\lceil n/2 \rceil) + T(\lfloor n/2 \rfloor), \ n > 1,$$

for some constants $a, b > 0$, prove that $T(n) = an + b(n - 1)$.

2.28: There are a number of parallels between the difference operator and the differential operator; this exercise explores a few of them. For $m \geq 0$, define $x^{\underline{m}} = x(x - 1) \cdots (x - m + 1)$ and $x^{\overline{m}} = x(x + 1) \cdots (x + m - 1)$. By definition, $x^{\underline{0}} = x^{\overline{0}} = 1$.

   a. Prove that $\Delta(x^{\underline{m}}) = mx^{\underline{m-1}}$. (Compare with $D(x^m) = mx^{m-1}$.)
   b. Prove that $g(x) = \Delta f(x)$ if and only if

   $$\sum g(x)\delta x = f(x) + C,$$

   where

   $$\sum g(x)\delta x$$

   is the class of functions whose difference is $g(x)$, and C is any function $p(x)$ such that $p(x + 1) = p(x)$. (Compare with $g(x) = Df(x)$ if and only if $\int g(x)dx = f(x) + C$.)
   c. Given $g(x) = \Delta f(x)$, prove that

   $$\sum_{a}^{b} g(x)\delta x = f(b) - f(a).$$

   (Compare with $g(x) = Df(x)$ implies that $\int_{a}^{b} g(x)dx = f(b) - f(a)$.)
   d. Prove that

   $$\sum_{a}^{b} g(x)\delta x = \sum_{a \leq k < b} g(k).$$

   e. Prove that

   $$\sum_{a}^{b} g(x)\delta x + \sum_{b}^{c} g(x)\delta x = \sum_{a}^{c} g(x)\delta x.$$

   (Compare with $\int_{a}^{b} g(x)dx + \int_{b}^{c} g(x)dx = \int_{a}^{c} g(x)dx$.)
   f. Prove that

   $$\sum_{0 \leq k < n} k^{\underline{m}} = n^{\underline{m+1}}/(m + 1).$$

   (Compare with $\int_{0}^{n} x^m \, dx = n^{m+1}/(m + 1)$.)
   g. Prove that $(x + y)^{\underline{2}} = x^{\underline{2}} + 2x^{\underline{1}}y^{\underline{1}} + y^{\underline{2}}$. (Compare with $(x + y)^2 = x^2 + 2xy + y^2$.)
   h. Prove that, for functions $u(x)$ and $v(x)$, $\Delta(uv) = u\Delta v + Ev\Delta u$, where $Ef(x) = f(x + 1)$ is the **shift operator.** (Compare with $D(uv) = uDv + vDu$.)
   i. Prove that, for functions $u(x)$ and $v(x)$,

   $$\sum u\Delta v = uv - \sum Ev\Delta u,$$

   where $Ef(x) = f(x + 1)$ is the shift operator. (Compare with $\int uDv = uv - \int vDu$.)

2.29: Sketch the proofs of Facts 2.2, 2.3, and 2.4, given in Section 2.5.4.

2.30: Consider the following recursive algorithm that, given a block $D[1..n]$ of distinct integers, finds the minimum and maximum values in D. If $n = 1$, then $Min = Max = D[1]$, otherwise we find, recursively, *MinL* and *MaxL* in $D[1..\lfloor n/2 \rfloor]$, find, recursively, *MinR* and *MaxR* in $D[\lfloor n/2 \rfloor + 1..n]$, and combine these results by letting *Min* = min(*MinL,MinR*) and *Max* = max(*MaxL,MaxR*). Set up a recurrence equation for the number of integer comparisons performed by the algorithm. Solve the equation.

2.31:   A polynomial $p(x)$ in x of degree $n \geq 0$ has the form

$$a_n x^n + a_{n-1}^{n-1} + \cdots + a_0,$$

where the a_i are the coefficients.

    a.   Design a recursive algorithm that, given the values of n and x and the values of $a_n,...,a_0$, will return the value of $p(x)$. For simplicity, assume that $a_n,...,a_0$ and x take only integer values.

    b.   Derive a recurrence equation for the number of scalar multiplications taken by your algorithm in terms of the degree of the given polynomial and solve it to give a closed-form expression for the number of scalar multiplications.

    c.   It is possible to construct an algorithm that uses exactly n multiplications. Does yours? If it does not, try again.

2.32:   **a.**   Prove that n^m is $O(n^p)$, when $m \leq p$.

       b.   Prove that, for any two functions $f(n)$ and $g(n)$, $f(n) + g(n)$ is $O(f(n) + g(n))$.

2.33:   Strictly speaking, $O(g(n))$ does not stand for one function $f(n)$; rather, it denotes the set of all functions $f(n)$ such that $f(n) \leq cg(n)$, for some constant $c > 0$. Thus, "$f(n)$ is $O(g(n))$" means that $f(n)$ is a member of the set of functions $O(g(n))$. This clarification enables us to use big-oh notation unambiguously on the left- and right-hand sides of statements, such as

$$n^2 + O(n) \text{ is } O(n^2).$$

In other words, for all $c > 0$, there is a constant $d > 0$ such that $n^2 + cn \leq dn^2$, for all $n \geq 0$.

    a.   Prove that $O(f(n)) + O(g(n))$ is $O(f(n) + g(n))$.

    b.   Prove, for any polynomial $p(n) = a_m n^m + \cdots + a_0$, that $p(n)$ is $O(n^m)$. This simplification corresponds to the rule that the highest-degree term dominates the behavior of a polynomial.

    c.   Prove that $O(f(n))O(g(n))$ is $O(f(n)g(n))$.

    d.   Prove that $O(f(n)g(n))$ is $f(n)O(g(n))$.

    e.   Prove that $O(f^2(n))$ is $O(f(n))^2$.

2.34:   Prove the following identities for floor and ceiling, for all $n \geq 0$.

    a. $n = \lfloor n/2 \rfloor + \lceil n/2 \rceil$.

    b. $\lfloor x \rfloor = n$ if and only if $n \leq \lfloor x \rfloor < n + 1$.

    c. $\lfloor x + n \rfloor = \lfloor x \rfloor + n$ and $\lceil x + n \rceil = \lceil x \rceil + n$.

    d. $\lfloor -x \rfloor = -\lceil x \rceil$ and $\lceil -x \rceil = -\lfloor x \rfloor$.

    e. $\lfloor \sqrt{\lfloor x \rfloor} \rfloor = \lfloor \sqrt{x} \rfloor$, for $x \geq 0$.

    f. $\lfloor (n+1)/2 \rfloor = \lceil n/2 \rceil$.

    g. $\lfloor (n + m - 1)/m \rfloor = \lceil n/m \rceil$, which is a generalization of the identity in part (f).

2.35:   Solve the recurrence equation

$$\begin{aligned} T(1) &= a, \\ T(n) &= b + T(n-1)/2, \, n > 1, \end{aligned}$$

using the techniques described in this chapter. Express $T(n)$ in both closed and big-oh forms.

2.36: Solve the recurrence equation

$$T(1) = a,$$
$$T(n) = b + 3/2T(\lfloor n/2 \rfloor), n > 1.$$

Express the solution in closed form.

2.37: You are given the generic recurrence equation

$$T(1) = a,$$
$$T(n) = bn\log^k n + T(\lfloor n/2 \rfloor) + T(\lceil n/2 \rceil), n > 1;$$

for some $k > 0$.

    a. By considering only values of n that are powers of 2, deduce the asymptotic value of $T(n)$.

    b. Derive a general closed-form solution for $T(n)$.

CHAPTER 3

Lists

In the previous chapter, we introduced the chronologically ordered ADTs QUEUE and STACK as the basic examples of ADTs with restricted access. We now present the LIST and SIMPLIST ADTs, which are generalizations of the previous two ADTs. Although we can consider them to be chronologically ordered, we are no longer restricted to inserting latest elements—we can insert elements from any time. For this reason, we prefer to think of these ADTs as lists in the everyday sense. Mathematically, we define a list L of $n \geq 0$ elements inductively as follows: If $n = 0$, then L is the empty list that contains no elements; otherwise, L consists of an element followed by a list of $n - 1$ elements. This definition reflects our intuition that we can write about the first element, the ith element, and the last element of a list. We allow insertion, deletion, and reading at *any* position in a list. To support this generality of access, we introduce explicit window-manipulation operations, and we consider two different ADTs: LIST and SIMPLIST. The LIST ADT has explicit windows and explicit window-manipulation operations; a user can define as many windows as she likes. The SIMPLIST ADT has one implicit window; a user can manipulate the window only by using the window-manipulation operations. We find it useful to have two window positions that are both outside a list, one before the first element, the *before-first* position, and one after the last element, the *after-last* position; see Fig. 3.1. An empty list has these two window positions and no others. We investigate how we can implement LIST and SIMPLIST efficiently, and demonstrate, as an example of their use, how we can use LIST to represent single-variable polynomials.

Why do we need the generality afforded by LIST and SIMPLIST? The immediate answer is that we do not always want it, but, at the same time, we often need more generality than we are given by QUEUE and STACK. An important example is the editing of a text file. Many text editors treat a text file as a list of lines of text. They need to be able to move through the lines, to add to them, to

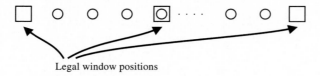

Legal window positions

Figure 3.1   Legal window positions.

delete them, to modify them, and so on. A queue or stack of lines of text is insufficient for this purpose, because we cannot access an element in the middle of a queue or stack without deleting elements. Clearly, the queue and stack representations are not viable choices for a text file. Furthermore, when editing a text file, we often refer to more than one line at a time. Both queues and stacks allow only one element at a time to be accessed. Finally, we need to be able to insert a new line and to delete a line at *any* position in a text file, not just at one end. (At a lower level, we want to insert and delete characters anywhere in a line too.)

A second example is the maintenance of a bibliography. Bibliographies are normally kept in sorted order (for example, sorted by author). A new entry can be added anywhere in the sorted order, and any entry can be deleted. This is one reason that index-card files used to be used to maintain bibliographies. It is as easy to add a new card as it is to remove an old one.

A third example is the manipulation of polynomials. As we shall see in Section 3.3, we can represent single-variable polynomials with the LIST ADT, and can use the LIST operations to implement polynomial operations such as addition and multiplication.

Before exploring polynomials, we specify the LIST ADT, in Section 3.1, and we discuss copying and equality testing in Section 3.2. Immediately after we present the polynomial manipulation example, in Section 3.3, we present various representations for LIST, in Section 3.4, and compare their performances. Finally, in Section 3.5, we specify SIMPLIST and prove that, when the singly linked list representation is used, we can obtain better performance than we can with the same representation of LIST. In particular, we establish that any sequence of SIMPLIST operations takes time linear in the number of operations—a second example of an amortized time bound.

3.1   LIST SPECIFICATION

The windows that we introduce are tied or bound to LIST; we cannot use the windows of some other ADT with LIST. Because we have made window manipulation explicit, we have an additional ADT—the *windowtype* ADT—that we need to specify hand in hand with the specification of LIST. We cannot define either LIST or *windowtype* in isolation; each needs the other. We discuss *windowtype*, in somewhat more detail, in Section 3.7. A *windowtype* variable denotes a window, and its value determines the associated window position. A window and a window position are abstract concepts, so a window variable's value may not be the position of the window itself; it may tell us only where to find that position. Despite these ambiguities, for simplicity, we normally refer to a *windowtype* variable as a window, and refer to its value as a window position.

Let B be the set of *Boolean* values, E be the set of *elementtype* values, L be the set of LIST values, and W be the set of *windowtype* values or positions (strictly speaking, positions of legal slots for windows) with respect to LIST. Note that *windowtype* and LIST are mutually dependent ADTs.

1. *Empty*: $\rightarrow L$: The function value *Empty* is an empty list that has two associated window positions, before first and after last.

2. *IsEmpty*: $L \rightarrow B$: The function value *IsEmpty(L)* is **true** if L is an empty list; otherwise, it is **false**.

3. *BeforeFirst*: $L \rightarrow W$: The function value *BeforeFirst(L)* is the before-first position.

4. *AfterLast*: $L \rightarrow W$: The function value *AfterLast(L)* is the after-last position.

5. *IsBeforeFirst*: $W \times L \rightarrow B$: The function value *IsBeforeFirst(w,L)* is **true** if the window w is over the before-first position of L; otherwise, it is **false**.

6. *IsAfterLast*: $W \times L \rightarrow B$: The function value *IsAfterLast(w,L)* is **true** if the window w is over the after-last position of L; otherwise, it is **false**.

7. *Next*: $W \times L \rightarrow W$: The function value *Next(w,L)* is undefined if the window w is over the after-last position of L; otherwise, it is the window position of the next element in L (if there is one; otherwise, it is over the after-last position).

8. *Previous*: $W \times L \rightarrow W$: The function value *Previous(w,L)* is undefined if the window w is over the before-first position of L; otherwise, it is the window position of the previous element in L (if there is one; otherwise, it is over the before-first position).

9. *Examine*: $W \times L \rightarrow E$: The function value *Examine(w,L)* is the value of the element in the window w, if w is over an element; otherwise, it is undefined.

10. *Replace*: $E \times W \times L \rightarrow L$: The function value *Replace(e,w,L)* is L with the element in the window w replaced by e, if w is over an element; otherwise, it is undefined.

11. *InsertAfter*: $E \times W \times L \rightarrow W \times L$: The function value *InsertAfter(e,w,L)* is undefined if w is the after-last position in L; otherwise, it is (w,L'), where L' is the same as L, except that an extra element e occurs after the window position w in L.

12. *InsertBefore*: $\mathcal{E} \times W \times L \to W \times L$: The function value *InsertBefore* (*e*,*w*,*L*) is undefined if *w* is the before-first position in *L*; otherwise, it is (*w*,*L'*), where *L'* is the same as *L*, except that an extra element *e* occurs before the window position *w* in *L*.

13. *Delete*: $W \times L \to W \times L$: The function value *Delete*(*w*,*L*) is undefined if *w* is the before-first or after-last window position in *L*; otherwise, it is (*w'*,*L'*), where *L'* is the same as *L*, except that the element of *L* in *w* is absent and *w'* is equal to *Next*(*w*,*L*).

The operations we have introduced fall into the four groups we introduced in Chapter 1. First, we have the *constructors Empty*, *InsertAfter*, and *InsertBefore*. Second, we have the *destructor Delete*. Third, we have the *checkers IsEmpty*, *IsBeforeFirst*, and *IsAfterLast*. Finally, we have the *manipulators BeforeFirst*, *AfterLast*, *Next*, and *Previous*, and the examination and replacement operations, *Examine* and *Replace*.

The specification of the LIST and *windowtype* operations is not as as simple as we suggest. For example, assume that we have a list *L* with exactly one element *a* and that we have two windows *w* and *x* in *L*. Then, the following sequence of operations places *w* and *x* over *a*:

```
BeforeFirst(w,L); Next(w,L);
BeforeFirst(x,L); Next(x,L);
```

Now, if we execute the operation

```
Delete(w,L);
```

then, by the specification of *Delete*, *w* is over the after-last position in *L*. The specification of *Delete* considers only one window; thus, the window *x* is undefined, because *a* is no longer in *L*.

We can refine the specification of the LIST operations in various ways to resolve such multiple-window problems. For example, if there is more than one window over an element *e* in a list and we modify the list through one of the windows, then we can specify that the other windows over *e* become undefined. Alternatively, we can specify that the other windows be treated in the same way that the modifying window is treated. In practice, the major difficulty with these solutions is that we should be able to identify the windows over an element in any chosen representation of LIST. The treatment of these issues is beyond the scope of this text; we shall continue to specify ADTs with explicit windows without solving the issues.

3.2 COPYING AND EQUALITY TESTING

When dealing with standard types in Pascal and other languages, we assume, without comment, the existence of two basic operations—assignment and equality testing. For example, for the types *elementtype* and *windowtype*, we assume that assignment is available and that we can test two *windowtype* values for

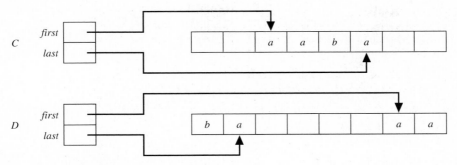

Figure 3.2 Two equal queues.

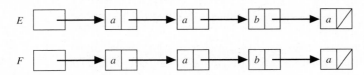

Figure 3.3 Two equal singly linked lists.

equality. With more complex types and with user-defined types such as QUEUE, STACK, and LIST, such operations may not be given. Therefore, we may need to add assignment and equality testing to the basic operations and to code them in terms of the basic operations. What does it mean to assign the value of one variable to another variable? What does it mean for two variables to be equal? These interrelated questions need to be answered.

To make our discussion more concrete, we consider blocks and singly linked lists. Given two blocks A and B of type **array**$[1..10]$ **of char**, we agree that A is equal to B if $A[1] = B[1],...,A[10] = B[10]$. Similarly, if we are using the block representation of QUEUE with wraparound that we defined in Section 1.5.1, two queues C and D of elements should be equal if their corresponding elements are equal and if they have the same number of elements; see Fig. 3.2. In other words,

$$C.e[C.first] = D.e[D.first],...,C.e[C.last] = D.e[D.last].$$

Again, given two singly linked lists E and F of elements, we say that they are equal if their corresponding elements are equal; see Fig. 3.3.

The common thread running through these examples is that equality depends on only the elements and their relative positions. It does not depend, at all, on the cells that hold the elements. Mathematically, this notion of equality is called **isomorphism.** Observe that the singly linked lists G and H of Fig. 3.4 are also isomorphic, but, in this case, they share some cells. We normally interpret assignment of a value to a variable to mean, "Make a copy of that value." For example, F is a copy of E, in this sense, whereas H is not a copy of G.

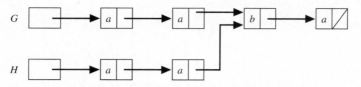

Figure 3.4.   Two equal singly linked lists that share cells.

Having established, for now, the definitions of assignment and equality test-ing, we can implement two Pascal procedures to carry out the corresponding operations for lists. In Program 3.1, *Copy* makes an isomorphic copy, *New,* of the original list, *Old*. It does this copying by traversing *Old* from the first to last ele-ment, adding a new cell to *New* for each element scanned. The list *New* is a copy in the sense we have described.

In Program 3.2, *IsEqual* tests two lists, *One* and *Two,* for equality. It does this testing by traversing them in parallel in the same direction, checking that the cur-rent elements are equal. Observe that *IsEqual* is similar to *Reversal*; see Program 1.2.

```
procedure Copy(Old: LIST; var New: LIST);
{Copy produces a list New from the list Old such that
    New and Old are isomorphic and do not share any
    cells. Copy traverses Old from its first to its last
    element, inserting a new cell into New for each
    element scanned.}

var e: elementtype; Oldpane, Newpane: windowtype;

begin Empty(New);
    if not IsEmpty(Old)
    then begin BeforeFirst(Oldpane,Old);
        Next(Oldpane,Old);
        AfterLast(Newpane,New);
        while not IsAfterLast(Oldpane,Old) do
        begin Examine(e,Oldpane,Old);
            InsertBefore(e,Newpane,New);
            Next(Oldpane,Old)
        end{while}
    end{if}
end{Copy};
```

Program 3.1   A Pascal implementation of a copying algorithm for lists.

```
function IsEqual(One,Two: LIST): boolean;
{IsEqual tests whether two lists One and Two are
    isomorphic by traversing them both in parallel from their
    first to last elements. If every pair of elements is equal
    and the lists have the same number of elements, then the
    lists are isomorphic and IsEqual returns the value true.
    Otherwise, it returns the value false.}

var test: boolean; eOne,eTwo: elementtype;
    Onepane,Twopane: windowtype;

begin BeforeFirst(Onepane,One);
    Next(Onepane,One);
    BeforeFirst(Twopane,Two);
    Next(Twopane,Two);
    test:= true;
    while not IsAfterLast(Onepane,One)
        and not IsAfterLast(Twopane,Two)
        and test do
    begin Examine(eOne,Onepane,One);
        Examine(eTwo,Twopane,Two);
        test:= eOne = eTwo;
        Next(Onepane,One); Next(Twopane,Two);
    end{while};
    IsEqual:= IsAfterLast(Onepane,One)
                and IsAfterLast(Twopane,Two)
                and test;
end{IsEqual};
```

Program 3.2 A Pascal implementation of an equality testing algorithm for lists.

3.3 POLYNOMIAL MANIPULATION

Symbolic computation is the manipulation of objects or symbols, according to some given rules, rather than their evaluation. We consider one such example: single-variable polynomials with integer coefficients. Let the single variable be denoted by x; then,

$$7x^3 - 4x + 2,$$

$$1,$$

$$207x^{32}$$

are examples of such polynomials. Given two polynomials p and q, we want to be able to add p and q, to subtract p from q or vice versa, to multiply p and q, to divide p by q or vice versa, and so on. Observe that these operations must result in polynomials; we are not given a value for x and we do not want the sum of the values of $p(x)$ and $q(x)$, the difference of the values of $p(x)$ and $q(x)$, and so on.

A **polynomial** can be thought of as a list of **terms,** where a term is defined by an integer coefficient and a nonnegative integer exponent. For example, the three polynomials listed previously become

$$(7,3),(- 4,1),(2,0),$$

$$(1,0),$$

$$(207,32)$$

in this framework. We will, however, represent the **zero polynomial** with the empty list. Such a list can be represented with a LIST of *termtype*. The ADT *termtype* has these operations:

1. *Create*: $\rightarrow \mathcal{T}$
2. *ExamineCoeff*: $\mathcal{T} \rightarrow C$
3. *ExamineExp*: $\mathcal{T} \rightarrow X$
4. *ReplaceTerm*: $C \times X \times \mathcal{T} \rightarrow \mathcal{T}$

Here, C is the set of coefficient values, X the set of exponent values, and $\mathcal{T}$ the set of *termtype* values. The operations are self-explanatory except, perhaps, for *Create*, which creates a term with an undefined coefficient and exponent. We can represent *termtype* in Pascal with a record structure:

```
type termtype = record
                   coefficient,exponent: integer;
                end;
```

In the remainder of this section, we let POLY denote a LIST of *termtype*; thus *termtype* replaces *elementtype* in the specification of the LIST operations.

Recall that adding two polynomials requires that we add the coefficients of equal exponent terms. So the addition of

$$7x^3 - 4x + 2$$

and

$$12x^4 - 8x^3 + x^2 + 7$$

gives

$$12x^4 - x^3 + x^2 - 4x + 9.$$

Polynomials are usually represented in exponent-decreasing order; we do not write

$$-4x + 7x^3 + 2$$

or

$$12x^4 + 7x^3 - 8x^3 + x^2 - 4x + 7 + 2;$$

rather, we combine or **collect** terms of the same **order** (the same exponents) and we write

$$7x^3 - 4x + 2$$

or

$$12x^4 - x^3 + x^2 - 4x + 9.$$

The terms of a polynomial are said to be *sorted,* an important concept that we discuss in more detail in Chapter 12. Finally, we do not allow any coefficient to be zero unless it is the only term, in which case the exponent must be zero; we represent zero polynomials with the empty list. Polynomials that satisfy these three conditions are said to be in **canonical form.** We assume that polynomials are in canonical form throughout this section.

To add two polynomials, we scan them simultaneously from highest- to lowest-order terms, adding terms of the same order and copying the higher-order term when the terms do not have the same order. With the previous example, we first copy $12x^4$, since $7x^3$ and $12x^4$ are not of the same order. Then, we add $7x^3$ and $-8x^3$, copy x^2, copy $-4x$, and, finally, add 2 and 7. We give a Pascal version of *Add* in Program 3.3. The simultaneous traversal of P and Q in *Add* is, in the world of sorting, called a **merge;** merging is discussed in more detail in Chapter 12.

In *Add*, we create a new polynomial from P and Q so that P and Q are not destroyed. It is, however, more efficient in space usage, and is sometimes more convenient, to mimic the assignment

$$P := P + Q,$$

rather than

$$R := P + Q.$$

We name the corresponding operation *AddTo*, specified by

```
procedure AddTo (var P: POLY; Q: POLY);
{pre: P and Q are canonical polynomials}.
    post: P after is the canonical polynomial
    that is the sum of P before and Q.}
```

The coding of the operation is left as Exercise 3.4.

```
procedure Add (P,Q: POLY; var R: POLY);
{Add the two canonical polynomials P and Q to give the
    canonical polynomial R. The procedure First returns
    either the window position of the first term or the
    after-last position if the polynomial is zero.
    ExamineExp returns the exponent of a term;
    ExamineCoeff returns the coefficient of a term; and ReplaceTerm
    changes the coefficient and exponent of a term. Finally,
    TailCopy appends a copy of a specified suffix of a polynomial
    to a second polynomial.}
var Ppane,Qpane,Rpane: windowtype;
    Pterm,Qterm,Rterm: termtype;
    Pcoeff,Qcoeff,Rcoeff,Pexp,Qexp: integer;

begin
    if IsEmpty(P) {Q is the result}
    then Copy(Q,R) {See Program 3.1.}
    else if IsEmpty(Q) {P is the result}
    then Copy(P,R) {See Program 3.1.}
    else begin {P and Q are both nonzero }
        First(Ppane,P); First(Qpane,Q);
        Empty(R); AfterLast(Rpane,R);
        while not IsAfterLast(Ppane,P)
                and not IsAfterLast(Qpane,Q) do
        begin
            Examine(Pterm,Ppane,P); Examine(Qterm,Qpane,Q);
            Pexp:= ExamineExp(Pterm); Qexp:= ExamineExp(Qterm);
            if Pexp > Qexp
            then begin InsertBefore(Pterm,Rpane,R); Next(Ppane,P) end
            else if Pexp < Qexp
            then begin InsertBefore(Qterm,Rpane,R); Next(Qpane,Q) end
            else begin ExamineCoeff(Pcoeff,Pterm);
            ExamineCoeff(Qcoeff,Qterm);
                Rcoeff:= Pcoeff + Qcoeff;
                ReplaceTerm(Pexp,Rcoeff,Rterm);
                if Rcoeff <> 0
                then InsertBefore(Rterm,Rpane,R);
                Next(Ppane,P); Next(Qpane,Q)
            end
        end;
        if IsAfterLast(Ppane,P)
        then TailCopy(Qpane,Q,Rpane,R) {Copy the rest of Q to R.}
        else TailCopy(Ppane,P,Rpane,R) {Copy the rest of P to R.}
    end
end;
```

Program 3.3   An addition algorithm for single-variable polynomials.

Subtraction is similar to addition, whereas multiplication is, essentially, repeated addition, and division is repeated subtraction. We leave the coding of these operations to Exercise 3.5.

3.4 LIST REPRESENTATIONS

We now define three representations of LIST: a block representation, a singly linked list representation, and a doubly linked list representation.

3.4.1 A Block Representation

We begin our discussion of representations for LIST with a block representation similar to those for QUEUE and STACK. A list can be represented as a number of contiguous cells of a block from cell 1 onward; see Fig. 3.5. One corresponding Pascal type declaration, for LIST and *windowtype*, is

```
const Lmax = ?; {The predefined maximum size of a list.}
     Lmaxplusone = ?; {Lmaxplusone = Lmax + 1.}
type LIST = record
                cells: array[1..Lmax] of elementtype;
                size: integer;
           end;
     windowtype = 0..Lmaxplusone;
```

We may also use wraparound, as we did for queues; this alternative is explored in Exercise 3.8.

The window operations are easily accommodated in this setting; we use 0 and $size + 1$ to denote the before-first and after-last positions. Insertion and deletion are more difficult here, simply because they may occur within the list, rather than just at the ends. For example, if a window is over cell 4, an insertion before the window forces the items in cells 4, 5, and 6 to shift right by one cell. For the call *InsertBefore(b,w,L)*, we have the before and after situations shown in Fig. 3.6. Observe that, as far as the user is concerned, the window has not moved. It is still over the same element of the list; see the abstract before and after views in Fig. 3.7. Internally, however, the window position has changed.

Similarly, if a window is over cell 4 and we delete the element in the window, we have the before and after situations shown in Fig. 3.8. In this case, the

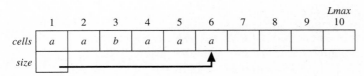

Figure 3.5 A block representation of a list.

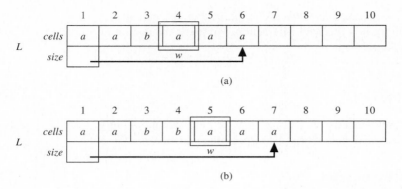

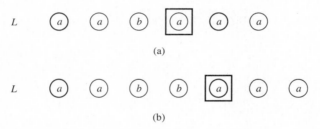

Figure 3.6   The block representation of a list and insertion. (a) Before an insertion before cell 4. (b) After an insertion before cell 4.

Figure 3.7   The user views of the insertion in Fig. 3.4. (a) Before the insertion. (b) After the insertion.

elements in cells 5 and 6 are shifted left by one position, but the window position is the same; we have compacted the representation. Viewed abstractly, *Delete* has moved the window over the next element; see the abstract before and after views in Fig. 3.9. It is not difficult to write the code to accomplish these operations, but we should be wary of boundary situations. We provide the code for some of the operations in Program 3.4; the complete implementation is left to Exercise 3.9.

In the block representation, a deletion can take time proportional to the size of the given list, if we delete an element close to the beginning of the list. Clearly, we wish to avoid this expense if at all possible. One method of avoidance is the topic of Exercise 3.11.

3.4.2   Pointer Representations

As we did with the pointer representations of QUEUE and STACK, we first consider a singly linked list representation. We choose the representation displayed in Fig. 3.10; the corresponding Pascal type definitions are as follows:

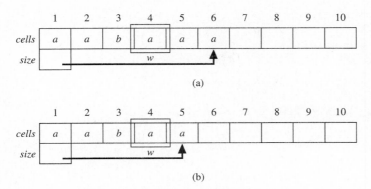

(a)

(b)

Figure 3.8 The block representation of a list and deletion. (a) Before a deletion at cell 4. (b) After a deletion at cell 4.

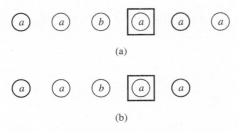

(a)

(b)

Figure 3.9 The user views of the deletion in Fig. 3.4. (a) Before the deletion. (b) After the deletion.

```
type linktype = ↑ celltype;
     celltype = record
                     item: elementtype;
                     successor: linktype
                end;
     LIST = record
                before,after: linktype
            end;
     windowtype = linktype;
```

We have chosen to represent the before-first and after-last positions explicitly, using two sentinel cells. This approach has the advantage that *Previous* is well defined even when the window is over the first element, as is *Next* when the window is over the last element. With this representation, *Empty* produces a linked list, as shown in Fig. 3.11. Also, we have provided two pointers in the header cell, one to the first sentinel and one to the second. The effect of this choice is to give a

```
procedure Empty(var L: LIST);
{pre: vacuous.
    post: L is an empty list.}
begin L.size:= 0 end;

procedure BeforeFirst(var w: windowtype; L: LIST);
{pre: vacuous.
    post: w is the before-first position of L.}
begin w:= 0 end;

procedure Next(var w: windowtype; L: LIST);
{pre: w is not the after-last position of L.
    post: w is the next window position in L.}
begin
    if(w ≥ 0) and (w ≤ L.size)
    then w:= w + 1
    else error ('Outside list in Next')
end;

procedure Replace(e: elementtype; w: windowtype; var L: LIST);
{pre: w is neither the before-first nor the after-last
        position of L.
    post: e is the element in the window w.}
begin
    if (w ≥ 1) and (w ≤ L.size)
    then L.cells[w]:= e
    else error ('Outside list in Replace')
end;

procedure InsertBefore (e: elementtype; var w: windowtype; var L: LIST);
{pre: w is not the before-first position of L.
    post: L after is the same as L before except that e has
          been added before w in L. The window w is over the
          same element in L before and after the insertion.}
var x: windowtype;
begin
    if (w ≥ 1) and (w ≤ L.size + 1) and (w < Lmax)
    then with L do
    begin
        size:= size + 1;
        for x:= size downto w + 1 do
            cells[x]:= cells[x - 1];
        cells[w]:= e; w:= w + 1
    end
    else error('Outside list in InsertBefore')
end;
```

Program 3.4 A block implementation of some of the LIST operations.

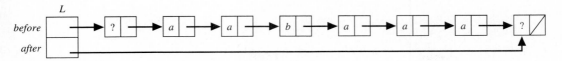

Figure 3.10   A singly linked pointer representation of a list with two sentinel cells.

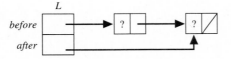

Figure 3.11   An empty list in the singly linked list representation.

constant-time implementation of both *BeforeFirst* and *AfterLast*. We provide the code for *Empty*, *BeforeFirst*, *Next*, and *InsertBefore* in Program 3.5 to show some of the differences between the block and the singly linked list implementations. Because we have a singly linked list, the implementation of *Empty* and *Next* is straightforward. When we implement *InsertBefore*, however, we need to be careful to obtain a constant-time implementation. The problem is that we appear to need the pointer to the previous cell; however, by inserting the new cell *after* the current cell and swapping their items, we sidestep this issue, as shown in Fig. 3.12. This approach, although straightforward, violates the principal motivation for using pointers—we wish to move data only when absolutely necessary. Therefore, in Exercise 3.14, we explore a more appropriate technique; we define the window value to be the link to the cell previous to the cell in the window, rather than the link to the cell in the window. We use this approach when implementing the binary-tree operations in Chapter 5. We can implement *Delete* in a similar manner to the implementation of *InsertBefore*, but *Previous* must return the window position of the previous element.

To find the cell previous to the current cell in a singly linked list, we traverse the list from the first sentinel cell to the current cell. At each step of the traversal, we keep the link of the previous cell, as well as the link of the current cell. This technique ensures that, when the current cell is the cell in the window, we have the link of the previous cell as well; it is called **link coupling.** We give, in Program 3.6, a Pascal version of *Previous*.

Two important issues that we have avoided in the coding of *Next*, *Insert-Before*, and *Previous* are the validity and value of the window variable. Because window values are tied to a specific list, it is possible that a window value is valid for some list, but not for the given one. We explore the problem of window-value validation in more detail in Exercise 3.12.

We can avoid the asymmetry in the implementation of *Next* and *Previous* by using doubly linked lists. In this representation, each cell has both a successor and

```
procedure Empty(var L: LIST);
{pre: vacuous}.
    post: L is an empty list.}
var First, Second: windowtype;
begin
    new(First); new(Second);
    First ↑.successor:= Second;
    Second ↑.successor:= nil;
    L.first:= First; L.second := Second
end;


procedure BeforeFirst(var w: windowtype; L: LIST);
{pre: vacuous.
    post: w is the before-first position of L.}
begin
    w:= L.first
end;


procedure Next(var w: windowtype; L: LIST);
{pre: w is not the after-last position of L.
    post: w is the next window position in L.}
begin
    if w ↑.successor = nil
    then error ('Outside list in Next')
    else w:= w ↑.successor
end;


procedure InsertBefore (e: elementtype; var w: windowtype; var L: LIST);
{pre: w is not the before-first position of L.
    post: L after is the same as L before except that e has
        been added before w in L. The window w is over the
        same element in L before and after the insertion.}
var newptr: windowtype;
begin
    new(newptr);
    newptr ↑.item:= w ↑.item;
    newptr ↑.successor:= w ↑.successor;
    w ↑.item:= e; w ↑.successor:= newptr;
    w:= newptr
end;
```

Program 3.5   A singly linked list implementation of some of the LIST operations.

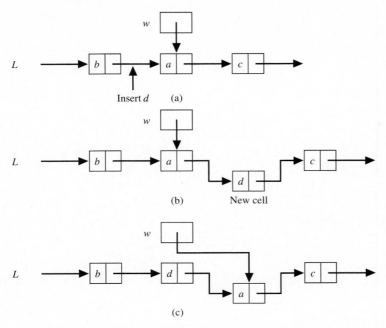

Figure 3.12 Implementation of *InsertBefore* in constant time. (a) Original singly linked list *L*. (b) Insertion of the new cell after the window position. (c) Swapping of the items in the new cell and the current cell, and updating of the window position.

predecessor link, rather than only a successor link. Moreover, we can complete the circle and link the first sentinel cell to the last sentinel cell in both directions, so we can move equally easily forward and backward; see Fig. 3.13. The empty list is then represented as shown in Fig. 3.14.

Circular linked lists have three advantages. First, the header needs to point to only the first sentinel cell, rather than to both. Second, successor and predecessor cells always exist, so testing for the **nil** pointer is avoided. Third, it is an elegant structure. We give the new version of *Previous* in Program 3.7, where we assume the following Pascal type declarations:

```
type linktype = ↑celltype;
       celltype = record
                        item: elementtype;
                        successor, predecessor: linktype
                  end;
     LIST = linktype;
     windowtype = linktype;
```

```
procedure Previous(var w: windowtype; L: LIST);
{pre: w is not the before-first position of L.
    post: w is the previous window position in L.}
var previousptr, currentptr: windowtype;
begin
    if w = L.first {w is over the first sentinel cell.}
    then error ('Outside list in Previous')
    else begin
        previousptr:= L.first;
        currentptr:= previousptr ↑.successor;
        while (currentptr <> w) and (currentptr <> nil) do
        begin
            previousptr:= currentptr;
            currentptr:= currentptr ↑. successor
        end;
        if currentptr = w
        then w:= previousptr
        else error ('Previous undefined')
    end
end;
```

Program 3.6   A singly linked list implementation of *Previous*.

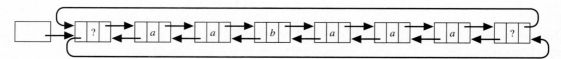

Figure 3.13   The circular doubly linked list representation of a list.

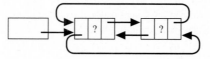

Figure 3.14   The circular doubly linked list representation of an empty list.

Note that a list header now points to only the first sentinel cell, rather than to both sentinel cells. You should implement the other LIST operations for the circular doubly linked list representation; see Exercise 3.15.

```
procedure Previous(var w: windowtype; L: LIST);
{pre: w is not the before-first position of L.
    post: w is the previous window position in L.}
begin
    if w = L
    then error ('Outside list in Previous')
    else w:= w ↑.predecessor
end;
```

Program 3.7 The circular doubly linked list implementation of *Previous*.

3.5 THE SIMPLIST ADT

We introduced, in Section 3.1, the LIST ADT, which provides multiple explicit windows. Sometimes, we do not need such generality; we can program our applications with fewer options. For this reason, we consider an alternative, simpler ADT for lists, the SIMPLIST ADT, which has a single implicit window with explicit window-manipulation operations and only one window-initialization operation, *BeforeFirst*. For the representation of SIMPLIST, we can choose any one of the LIST representations. The underlying purpose of our introduction of SIMPLIST, however, is to demonstrate, with the singly linked list representation, that we can implement all operations of SIMPLIST, apart from *BeforeFirst*, to run in constant time, in the worst case. *BeforeFirst* takes linear time, in the size of the list, in the worst case. We counterbalance the poor worst-case performance of *BeforeFirst* by proving that any sequence of n SIMPLIST operations in this implementation runs in $O(n)$ time. This amortization result establishes that, although some calls of *BeforeFirst* can be time consuming, there cannot be too many of them. In contrast, *Previous* is the time-consuming performer in the singly linked list implementation of LIST, and there is no corresponding amortization result. To achieve this dramatic improvement in performance for SIMPLIST, we use a technique called *pointer reversal*, which provides constant-time performance for *Previous*.

In Section 3.5.1, we specify the SIMPLIST ADT; in Section 3.5.2, we demonstrate how we use pointer reversal to achieve the stated time bounds.

3.5.1 SIMPLIST Specification

Because SIMPLIST, just like QUEUE and STACK, has an implicit window, none of the SIMPLIST operations have window values as arguments or results.

1. *Empty*: $\to L$: The function value *Empty* is an empty list that has two associated window positions, before first and after last.

2. *IsEmpty*: $L \to B$: The function value *IsEmpty(L)* is **true** if L is an empty list; otherwise, it is **false**.

3. *BeforeFirst*: $L \to L$: The function value *BeforeFirst(L)* initializes the window position to be before first in the list L.

4. *IsBeforeFirst*: $L \to B$: The function value *IsBeforeFirst(L)* is **true** if the window is over the before-first position of L; otherwise, it is **false**.

5. *IsAfterLast*: $L \to B$: The function value *IsAfterLast(L)* is **true** if the window is over the after-last position of L; otherwise, it is **false**.

6. *Next*: $L \to L$: The function value *Next(L)* is undefined if the window is over the after-last position of L; otherwise, it is the list L with its window over the next element in L (if there is one; otherwise, it is over the after-last position).

7. *Previous*: $L \to L$: The function value *Previous(L)* is undefined if the window is over the before-first position of L; otherwise, it is the list L with its window over the previous element in L (if there is one; otherwise, it is over the before-first position).

8. *Examine*: $L \to E$: The function value *Examine(L)* is the value of the element in the window if the window is over an element; otherwise, it is undefined.

9. *Replace*: $E \times L \to L$: The function value *Replace(e,L)* is undefined if the window is not over an element in L; otherwise, it is L', where L' is the same as L with the element in the window replaced by e.

10. *InsertAfter*: $E \times L \to L$: The function value *InsertAfter(e,L)* is undefined if the window is over the after-last position in L; otherwise, it is L', where L' is the same as L except that an extra element e occurs after the window position in L.

11. *InsertBefore*: $E \times L \to L$: The function value *InsertBefore(e,L)* is undefined if the window is over the before-first position in L; otherwise, it is L', where L' is the same as L except that an extra element e occurs before the window position in L.

12. *Delete*: $L \to L$: The function value *Delete(L)* is undefined if the window is over the before-first or after-last window position in L; otherwise, it is L', where L' is the same as L except that the element of L in the window has been removed and the window is over the next element or the after-last position in L'.

3.5.2 Pointer Reversal

We discuss only the singly linked list representation and implementation of SIMPLIST; the block and doubly linked list representations are dealt with much

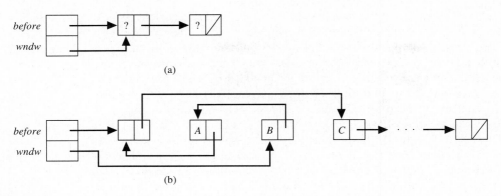

Figure 3.15 The singly linked list representation of SIMPLIST. (a) Representation of an empty list. (b) Representation of a nonempty list with the window over the second element.

like their counterparts for LIST. We have, as we had for LIST, a before-first and an after-last cell. The header has two pointer fields: the first points to the before-first cell and the second gives the window position; see Fig. 3.15. In Pascal, we can represent SIMPLIST with the following declarations:

```
type linktype = ↑ celltype;
     celltype = record
                     item: elementtype;
                     successor: linktype
                 end;
     SIMPLIST = record
                     before,wndw: linktype
                 end;
```

The only window-initialization operation is *BeforeFirst*, so the window begins at the before-first cell, moves down the list by the use of *Next*, moves up the list by the use of *Previous*, and repeats these movements any number of times. At each window position, elements can be inserted, deleted, examined, and replaced. To ensure that *Previous* takes constant time, in the worst case, we reverse the successor link in the next cell whenever we call *Next*. For example, in Fig. 3.15(b), the window is over element *B* as is shown by the value of *wndw*. The successor link of the cell containing *B* points to the previous cell, which contains *A,* and this cell in turn points to the before-first cell; this technique is called *pointer reversal*. Pointer reversal ensures that we can move the window to the previous cell in constant time. But, since we have used the successor link to point to the previous cell, how do we move to the next cell in constant time? The answer to this question is simple: We keep the link to the next cell, of the cell in the window, in the beforefirst cell. We maintain the invariant that the successor link of the before-first cell always points to the cell after the cell in the window.

The advantage of pointer reversal is that the *Delete*, *InsertBefore*, and *Previous* operations can be implemented as constant-time operations, in the worst case, without the extra space needed for doubly linked lists. The disadvantage of pointer reversal is that the coding of these operations is more complex than before, because we need to take into account the reversed links. Although we leave the details of the coding of the operations to Exercise 3.23, we discuss their implementation briefly. The idea behind pointer reversal is to reverse a successor link on each call of *Next*, to undo the reversal of a successor link on each call of *Previous*, and to undo all reversals on each call of *BeforeFirst*. In addition, *Delete* is similar to *Next*, *InsertBefore* and *InsertAfter* modify the reversed-link chain, and *Empty* places the window over the before-first cell. In Fig. 3.16, we show the link changes that *Delete*, *InsertBefore*, and *Previous* must make.

The implementation of the SIMPLIST operations, with pointer reversal, guarantees that cells beyond the current window position are linked as usual, whereas the cells from the before-first cell to the cell in the window are linked in reverse order. A call of *BeforeFirst* must reset all reversed links; otherwise, subsequent calls of *Next* either will give an incorrect cell or will give a correct cell inefficiently. We do not want to swap an inefficient implementation of *Previous* for an inefficient implementation of *Next*; we want an efficient implementation of both. Therefore, we examine how time consuming a sequence of SIMPLIST operations can be. Assume that we apply a sequence of n operations to an empty list. We begin the analysis with the further assumption that no calls of *InsertBefore* occur in the sequence. Then the list can grow only with calls of *InsertAfter*. These insertions, by definition, affect neither the current window nor the cells before that position; they insert cells after the current window position. Now, consider some call of *BeforeFirst* in the sequence, and assume that, just before the call, the window is over the ith cell. (The zeroth cell is the before-first cell.) The call must reset $i-1$ successor links and—and this observation is the important fact—this number of reversed successor links must have been obtained by $i-1$ calls of *Next*. Observe that *Delete*, by definition, does not change the number of cells before the window; therefore, the numbers of reversed links before and after a deletion are the same. So, *BeforeFirst* resets, essentially, only those links that have been reversed by *Next*. This observation implies that the total number of successor links that are reset by all calls of *BeforeFirst* in the sequence cannot be more than the total number of calls of *Next*. In a sequence of n operations, there cannot be more than n calls of *Next*; thus, all calls of *BeforeFirst* cannot reset more than n successor links. As each reset operation takes constant time, we have shown that all calls of *BeforeFirst* take $O(n)$ time.

We now allow a sequence of operations to include calls of *InsertBefore*. Each call of *InsertBefore* increases, by 1, the number of cells before the current window position. So, each call of *BeforeFirst* resets successor links that were either reversed by *Next* or introduced by *InsertBefore*. Thus, once again, there are at most n such links reset by all calls of *BeforeFirst*.

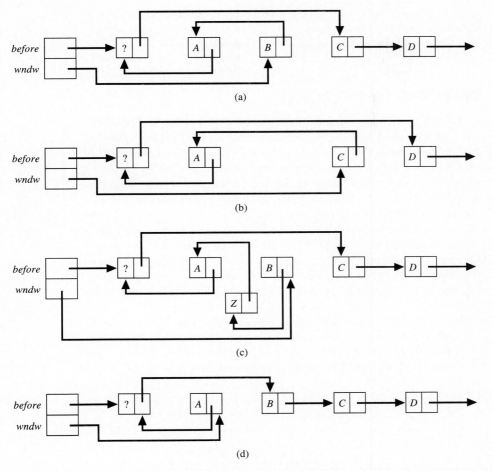

Figure 3.16 Link modification. (a) A singly linked list with pointer reversal. (b) Deletion of *B*. (c) Insertion of *Z* before *B*. (d) A move to the cell before *B*.

We summarize the amortization result as the following fact.

Fact 3.1 *Each sequence of n operations applied to an empty list, in the singly linked list implementation of* SIMPLIST, *takes O(n) time; that is, each* SIMPLIST *operation takes constant time, in the amortized case. In addition, all operations, apart from BeforeFirst, take constant time, in the worst case.*

One final comment. The SIMPLIST implementation that we have analyzed takes a pessimistic view: It assumes that every program that uses SIMPLIST always calls *Previous*. If, however, such a program does not call *Previous*, then the implementation reverses pointers for no reason. An interesting alternative, explored in Exercise 3.24, is to use **lazy pointer reversal;** that is, we reverse pointers on only the first call of *Previous*. It can be shown that, with this technique, a sequence of n SIMPLIST operations also runs in $O(n)$ time.

3.6 PERFORMANCE REPORTS

If we need multiple windows, then we should use the LIST ADT; otherwise, we should use SIMPLIST. In Table 3.1, we provide a checklist for the worst-case (and expected-case) performance of the three implementations of the LIST operations that we have discussed. From the worst-case point of view, the doubly linked list representation is a clear winner; however, we rank the singly linked list representation as our first choice, as shown in Table 3.2. There are two reasons for this choice: Most uses of LIST do not require the operation *Previous*, and the doubly linked list representation requires two pointers for each element. A simple rule of thumb is the following: If we need *Previous*, then we should use the doubly linked list representation; otherwise, we should use the singly linked list representation. The block representation is a clear third; although it has little space overhead, it is not truly dynamic or extendible and, moreover, updates take linear time.

The choice of representation (see Tables 3.3 and 3.4) for the SIMPLIST ADT is clear: It is the singly linked list representation with pointer reversal. This representation is fully dynamic; all operations, apart from *BeforeFirst*, take constant time; and *BeforeFirst* takes constant time, in the amortized case.

Table 3.1 A comparison of the worst-case execution times of the three LIST implementations.

| | LIST implementation | | |
Operation	Block	Singly linked	Doubly linked
Empty	1	1	1
IsEmpty	1	1	1
BeforeFirst	1	1	1
AfterLast	1	1	1
IsBeforeFirst	1	1	1
IsAfterLast	1	1	1
Next	1	1	1
Previous	1	n	1
Examine	1	1	1
Replace	1	1	1
InsertAfter	n	1	1
InsertBefore	n	1	1
Delete	n	1	1

Table 3.2   Performance ratings of the three implementations of LIST.

LIST implementation	Rating	Comments
Singly linked	Excellent	Linear-time *Previous* is only disadvantage
Doubly linked	Very good	Constant time for all operations, but requires two pointers for each element
Block	Satisfactory	Little space overhead; especially good for static or slowly changing lists

Table 3.3   A comparison of the worst-case execution times of the three SIMPLIST implementations.

	SIMPLIST implementation		
Operation	Block	Singly linked	Doubly linked
Empty	1	1	1
IsEmpty	1	1	1
BeforeFirst	1	1[a]	1
IsBeforeFirst	1	1	1
IsAfterLast	1	1	1
Next	1	1	1
Previous	1	1	1
Examine	1	1	1
Replace	1	1	1
InsertAfter	n	1	1
InsertBefore	n	1	1
Delete	n	1	1

[a]This bound is an amortized bound.

Table 3.4   Performance ratings of the three implementations of SIMPLIST.

SIMPLIST implementation	Rating	Comments
Singly linked	Excellent	Amortized constant time for all operations
Doubly linked	Good	Constant time for all operations but requires two pointers for each element
Block	Satisfactory	Little space overhead; good for static or slowly changing lists

3.7   ELEMENT AND WINDOW ASSUMPTIONS

Throughout this text, we examine ADTs that have one ADT parameter: *elementtype*. The advantage of this approach should be clear. We do not need to treat a stack of characters, a stack of real numbers, and a stack of queues in different ways, from the ADT point of view. We do have to be careful, however, about the operations that we assume are available for *elementtype* when implementing its host's operations. We treat *elementtype* as though it is a Pascal scalar type throughout this text. You should be aware that, in many applications, this assumption does not hold; we have sacrificed the validity of Pascal implementations for clarity of exposition. For example, in Pascal we cannot treat a stack of queues the same way as we can a stack of characters. The reason for this disparity is that in Pascal an assignment and an equality test are essentially valid for only scalar values. We cannot use := to assign one queue to another; we cannot use = to test whether two queues are equal.

We have made similar assumptions about the ADT *windowtype*, which we have chosen to abstract the navigation in and manipulation of data structures throughout this text. We also need assignment and equality testing for *windowtype*, and we have opted once more for clarity, rather than for validity, by treating *windowtype* as a scalar type in Pascal. In most cases, we represent *windowtype* as a scalar type (an integer or pointer). There are occasions, however, when we prefer a structured representation—for example, the representation of binary trees in Chapter 5. Typically, we want to be able to extract values from a structured window variable, to assign a window value or position to a window variable, to test two window positions for equality, to look inside a window, and to change what is in a window.

3.8   SUMMARY

We introduced the ADT's LIST and SIMPLIST as abstractions of a list. LIST has explicit windows that provide window initialization and two-way window movement, whereas SIMPLIST has one implicit window with explicit window-manipulation operations. LIST and SIMPLIST are both dynamic in that they allow insertions and deletions. Of the one block and two pointer representations of LIST and SIMPLIST that we studied, *the recommended representation* is the singly linked list, in both cases, because it is efficient and has reasonable space overhead. All LIST operations, apart from *Previous*, take constant time, in the worst case; *Previous* takes linear time. All SIMPLIST operations, apart from *BeforeFirst*, when implemented with pointer reversal, take constant time, in the worst case, and all operations take constant time, in the amortized case. The latter result is the second amortization result that we presented.

We used LIST to highlight what it means for two objects to be equal (to emulate the Pascal equality operator), and what it means to produce a copy of an object (to emulate the Pascal assignment operator).

As an application of LIST, we designed, and partially implemented, a univariate polynomial-manipulation package.

3.9 HISTORY

The LIST ADT is new, but the SIMPLIST ADT is well known; see Horowitz and Sahni (1990) for an early discussion, and Martin (1986) and Welsh and associates (1984) for an in-depth examination.

The manipulation of polynomials is one aspect of symbolic computation which is an increasingly important area of computer science. There are numerous competing systems available. An older, more established one is MACSYMA (Pavel and Wang, 1985; The Mathlab Group, 1988); a more recent successful symbolic computation system is Maple (Char and associates, 1986; 1991).

EXERCISES

3.1: We have argued that QUEUE is not powerful enough to encompass the operations needed by a line-based text editor. Would a "three-windowed queue" that has three implicit windows and *window-positioning* operations be sufficient? Would a "readable queue" that allows reading of elements in the queue without deletion be sufficient? Discuss and explain your answers.

3.2: Specify the LISTII ADT, which has two *implicit windows* and no *explicit windows*. Assume that the two windows can be referred to by the integers 1 and 2, so that we can write *Next*(1,*L*), *Previous*(2,*L*), and so on. Can LISTII be used instead of LIST to implement polynomial manipulation? Explain your answer in detail.

3.3: Generalize the LISTII ADT of Exercise 3.2. The reversal of the pointers X by specifying LISTUN, which has a finite but unbounded number of implicit windows. Again, assume they are referred to by the natural numbers—for example, *Next*(10,*L*), *Previous*(97,*L*), and so on. Compare and contrast LISTUN, LISTII, and LIST.

3.4: Implement and test the new POLY operation *AddTo*, specified in Section 3.3.

3.5: Implement and test the POLY operations of *Subtraction*, *Multiplication*, and *Division*.

3.6: Specify a differentiation operator for POLY. Implement it with the POLY operations.

3.7: Suggest an ADT for multiple-variable polynomials. Describe how you would represent and implement it.

3.8: Implement and test the LIST operations with a wraparound block representation.

3.9: Complete the block implementation of LIST discussed in Section 3.4.

3.10: Given the LISTUN variant of LIST in Exercise 3.3, specify the LISTUN version of the LIST operations. Suggest a representation of LISTUN. Based on your representation, implement the corresponding operations.

3.11: Rather than implementing *Delete* to remove an element immediately in the block representation of LIST, consider a lazy approach in which an element is marked as deleted. You can implement this lazy approach by keeping a present–absent indicator with each element. Implement the LIST operations using this approach, taking advantage of the absent gaps during insertion.

3.12: Consider the block representation of LIST that we have described in Section 3.4.1. The call *Insert(e,w,L)* assumes that the user has ensured that the window *w* belongs to *L* and not to some other list. If we want *Insert* and the other LIST operations to check the appropriateness of the windows they are given, then we must stamp each window variable of a list *L* with "Belongs to *L*."

Suggest a method of incorporating such an association. Provide an implementation of your ideas.

3.13: Complete the singly linked list implementation of LIST given in Section 3.4.2.

3.14: A better representation of window positions in the singly linked list representation than we have used in Section 3.4.2 lets the *windowtype* variable point to the cell previous to the one in the window. Implement and test an implementation of LIST based on this approach.

3.15: Complete the circular doubly linked list implementation of LIST given in Section 3.4.2.

3.16: There are many variations in the specification of LIST in the literature. In this exercise, we consider one that is completely different: It has no explicit windows and no explicit insertion and deletion operations. We call it SLIST, for **simplistic list.** It has the operations *Empty* and *IsEmpty*, as before, and the following six operations. Z is the set of integers, and L is the set of SLIST values.

1. *Size*: $L \rightarrow Z$: The function value *Size(L)* is the number of elements in *L*.
2. *Chop*: $Z \times L \rightarrow L$: The function value *Chop(z,L)* is undefined if |z| is greater than the size of *L*. Otherwise, its value is *L'*, where, if *z* is nonnegative, then *L'* consists of the first z elements of *L*; otherwise, *L'* consists of the last $-z$ elements of *L*.
3. *Catenate*: $L \times L \rightarrow L$: The function value *Catenate(L1,L2)* is a list *L* such that $Chop(Size(L1),L) = L1$, $Chop(-Size(L2),L) = L2$, and $Size(L) = Size(L1) + Size(L2)$.
4. *ExamineFirst*: $L \rightarrow E$: The function value *ExamineFirst(L)* is undefined if *L* is empty; otherwise, it is the first element of *L*.
5. *ExamineLast*: $L \rightarrow E$: The function value *ExamineLast(L)* is undefined if *L* is empty; otherwise, it is the last element of *L*.
6. *Singleton*: $E \rightarrow L$: The function value *Singleton(e)* is a list of size 1 that consists of the single element *e*.

Note that for a list of size 1, *ExamineFirst* and *ExamineLast* return the same value. The constructors are *Singleton* and *Catenate*, the destructor is *Chop*, and the operations *Size*, *ExamineFirst*, and *ExamineLast* are manipulators.

Design, implement, and test an efficient implementation of SLIST. Demonstrate that SLIST can be implemented with the LIST operations, and vice versa.

3.17: We have not included the operator *Size* as a basic operation for LIST. Give at least one advantage and at least one disadvantage of this choice.

3.18: Define the new LIST operation *Find* by *Find*: $\mathcal{E} \times \mathcal{W} \times L \rightarrow \mathcal{W}$ where *find*(*e*,*w*,*L*) is the window position of the earliest appearance of *e* in *L* beyond and including the given window position *w*. If *e* does not appear in these cells, *find*(*e*,*w*,*L*) is the after-last position. Implement this operation for the block and singly linked list representations of LIST.

3.19: Define a new LIST operation *Transpose* by *Transpose* : $\mathcal{W} \times L \rightarrow L$, where *Transpose*(*w*,*L*) is the same as *L*, except that the element in the window *w* has been exchanged with the previous element. If there is no previous element, *L* is not modified. Implement this operation for one of the representations of LIST.

3.20: Using *Transpose* from Exercise 3.19, implement the procedure *Permutation*, which produces a list of all permutations of 1..*n*, beginning with the identity permutation.

3.21: Modify the singly linked list representation of LIST so that an empty list is represented by **nil**; that is, there are no sentinel cells. Implement the LIST operations based on this representation. What difficulties did you encounter? Why did these difficulties occur?

3.22: Define an ADT ILIST, which is the same as LIST except that the positions 1,...,*n*, for a list of size *n*, are made explicit. Thus, we can insert an element before or after position *i*, can delete the element at position *i*, and so on. Discard the window-manipulation operations, references to windows, and any other redundant operations, and add the new operation *Size*. Implement ILIST using a doubly linked representation.

3.23: Complete the pointer-reversal implementation of the singly linked list representation of SIMPLIST that was partially described in Section 3.5.2.

3.24: Design and implement the lazy pointer-reversal technique, for the singly linked list representation, as we discussed in Section 3.5.2. Prove that a sequence of *n* SIMPLIST operations takes $O(n)$ time, and that all operations, apart from *BeforeFirst* and *Previous*, take constant time, in the worst case. Finally, consider an even lazier technique in which not only every call of *BeforeFirst* resets all the reversed links, but also no subsequent pointer reversals take place until there is another call of *Previous*. Prove that this technique can be implemented to run in constant time, in the amortized case, and describe an implementation of the technique.

4

Maps and Arrays

Recall that a **(partial) map**[1] (or function) is a relation between a **domain** D and a **codomain** C such that each element in the domain is related to at most one element in the codomain. Given a map f from D to C and a domain element d, if d is related to some codomain element c with respect to f, then $f(d)$ is defined and we write $f(d) = c$; c is the **image** of d under f. If d is not related to any codomain element under f, then $f(d)$ is said to be **undefined.** The **defined domain** of a map f is the set of all domain elements d such that $f(d)$ is defined. If each codomain element is related to some domain element by the map, then the map is **surjective;** if each codomain element is related to at most one domain element, then the map is **injective;** and if the map is injective, surjective, and total, then it is **bijective.**

Since programming languages such as Pascal, C, and Ada allow user-defined functions or maps, you might well ask why we devote a chapter to this topic. We have two responses to this question. First, there are well-defined functions that cannot be computed in the usual way. For example, during a course on data structures, an instructor may want to know the cumulative average mark of each student. This relationship is clearly a function, but unlike the functions that we usually have in mind, it changes over time; furthermore, we can define it only by providing its domain–codomain pairs. Second, there are functions the images of which are expensive to compute and are computed more than once. Such functions occur, for example, in artificial-intelligence programs. Now, we can avoid recomputation by using the so called **memo functions**—functions that remember results of some or all previous computations. The ADT MAP enables us to define both time-varying functions and memo functions.

---

[1] We prefer to use the term *map,* to distance ourselves from programming-language functions.

Maps whose codomain is the powerset of some set turn out to be important for the representations of GRAPH and DIGRAPH that we examine in Chapter 13. Although such functions fall within the framework of MAP, we nonetheless distinguish them because of efficiency considerations. Also, there are maps, such as arrays in Pascal and in other programming languages, whose domains are Cartesian products of integer ranges. For example, the Pascal declaration

    A: **array**[1..10, -3..3] **of boolean**

is the method that is used in Pascal to introduce a map

    A: {1,2,3,4,5,6,7,8,9,10} × { -3, -2, -1,0,1,2,3} → {**false, true**}.

Indeed, in early programming languages such as FORTRAN, no syntactic distinction was made between a function call (for example, $F(4,2)$) and a reference to an array element (for example, $A(4,2)$). The ADT ARRAY is an abstraction that captures maps of this kind. Although ARRAY is a special case of MAP, we single it out because its domain is a Cartesian product of integer ranges. We can achieve constant-time access to any array value, in the worst case. This property does not hold for MAP, in general, so representations that achieve constant-time access are of particular interest to programming-language designers and implementers, and, at times, to programmers. The design of efficient representations of ARRAY is one instance of a more general problem: *How do we represent efficiently one class of data structures by a second class of data structures?* For example, in Chapter 5, we represent multiway trees with binary trees; in Chapter 6, we represent arrays with binary trees.

In the remainder of this chapter, we first specify MAP and ARRAY, in Section 4.1. In Sections 4.2 and 4.3, we examine the representation and implementation of these ADTs. Finally, in Section 4.4, we consider the representation of sparse arrays, since they occur frequently in real-world applications, such as space-shuttle design.

4.1 MAP AND ARRAY SPECIFICATION

Let D denote a set of domain values, C a set of codomain values, and M the set of functions from D to C. Then, the ADT MAP is specified by the following operations:

1. *Empty*: → $\mathcal{M}$: The function value *Empty* is the map that is undefined everywhere.

2. *IsEmpty*: $\mathcal{M}$→ $\mathcal{B}$: The function value *IsEmpty(M)* is **true** if *M* is undefined everywhere; otherwise, it is **false**.

3. *Codomain*: $\mathcal{D}$× $\mathcal{M}$→ C : The function value *Codomain(d,M)* is *M(d)*. That is, it is undefined if the image of *d* under *M* is undefined; otherwise, it is the image of *d* under *M*.

4. *IsDefined*: $\mathcal{D} \times \mathcal{M} \to \mathcal{B}$: The function value *IsDefined*(*d*,*M*) is **true** if *Codomain* (*d*,*M*) is defined; otherwise, it is **false**.

5. *Assign*: $\mathcal{D} \times C \times \mathcal{M} \to \mathcal{M}$: The function value *Assign*(*d*,*c*,*M*) is the map that we obtain by modifying *M* such that the image of *d* is *c* and the images of all other domain values are unchanged.

6. *Deassign*: $\mathcal{D} \times \mathcal{M} \to \mathcal{M}$: The function value *Deassign*(*d*,*M*) is the map that we obtain by modifying *M* such that the image of *d* is undefined and the images of all other domain values are unchanged.

We specify the ADT ARRAY in a similar way, except that we replace M by A (the set of ARRAY values) everywhere and drop the operations *IsEmpty*, *IsDefined*, and *Deassign*. Note, however, that D is a Cartesian product of integer ranges; hence, in Pascal, *Empty* is equivalent to the declaration of an array, *Codomain*(*d*,*A*) is equivalent to the use of *A*[*d*] in an expression, and *Assign* (*d*,*c*,*A*) is equivalent to *A*[*d*]:= *c*.

4.2 MAP REPRESENTATIONS

Since we can consider a map to be a sequence of domain–codomain pairs, one natural representation of MAP is the LIST, and, therefore, we can use any one of the LIST representations that we introduced in Chapter 3. As we shall see, in Chapters 8, 9, and 10, we can also use TABLE and DICTIONARY to give an efficient representation of MAP. Alternatively, assuming that we are given the ADTs *domaintype* and *codomaintype*, we can declare, in Pascal,

```
type elementtype = record;
                        dom: domaintype;
                        codom: codomaintype
                 end;
```

Conceptually, we then have

```
type MAP = LIST of elementtype;
```

Thus, not only can we use one of the LIST representations to represent MAP, but also we can use LIST itself. When we use one ADT and its operations to represent and implement a second ADT and its operations, we say that we **model** the second ADT with the first ADT. We can model MAP with LIST and implement the six MAP operations in terms of the LIST operations. In Program 4.1, we give the implementations of *Empty* and *Codomain*. The implementation of the remaining four operations is left to Exercise 4.1. Note that *Empty* and *IsEmpty* make trivial calls of the LIST operations *LEmpty* and *LIsEmpty*. The other four operations, however, all require a sequential search within a list. The sequential search implies that the worst-case and expected-case time taken by *Codomain*, *IsDefined*, *Assign*, and *Deassign* is linear in the size of the defined domain of the map.

```
procedure Empty(var M: MAP);
begin LEmpty(M) end;


procedure Codomain(d: domaintype; var c: codomaintype; M: MAP);
var w: windowtype; found: boolean; e: elementtype;
begin
    if LIsEmpty(M)
    then error('{The given map is empty.}')
    else begin
        LBeforeFirst(w,M); LNext(w,M);
        found:= false;
        while not found and not LIsAfterLast(w,M) do
        begin
            LExamine(e,w,M); c:= e.codom;
            found:= e.dom = d; LNext(w,M)
        end;
        if not found
        then error('{The map is undefined for the given domain value.}')
    end
end;
```

Program 4.1   The implementation of the MAP operations *Empty* and
Codomain in terms of the LIST operations.

Because we model MAP with LIST, the efficiency of the implementation of the
MAP operations is dependent on the (perhaps unknown) implementation of the
LIST operations. We may, therefore, prefer to use, directly, one of the LIST representations. From the evaluation, in Section 3.6, of the two basic LIST representations—the block and pointer representations—we know that the pointer representation is the better choice, since it has no predefined maximum list size. On the
other hand, if the domain of MAP is known to be totally ordered, then we can use
the **sorted-block representation,** since this choice decreases the search time. A
sorted block contains the elements in nondecreasing order according to the given
total-order relation; it is **sorted.**

Assume that we are given a block *B* of distinct domain–codomain pairs
sorted according to the total order of the domain. Since the block represents a
map, we can assume that the domain elements that appear in the pairs are distinct.
In many other situations, however, we can have repetitions; We leave you, in
Exercise 4.2, to extend to this case the algorithm that we now give. Given a
domain value *q,* to implement *Codomain*, we want to determine whether a
domain–codomain pair with *q* as its domain value is in *B*. We use divide and conquer to search for *q* efficiently. We give, in Program 4.2, an **integer** function,

```
function BSearch(q: domaintype; B: block; L,U: integer}): integer;
{ The elements of the block B are domain-codomain pairs, and
    the domain is totally ordered. The elements appear
    in the cells L..U of B in domain-sorted order. We assume that
    L ≤ U. If the query domain value q is found in one of these cells,
    then BSearch returns the index of the cell containing q.
    Otherwise, BSearch returns the value 0.
    This searching technique is called binary search.}

var M: integer;

begin M:= (L + U) div 2;
    if L = U {There is only one cell to consider.}
    then
        if B[L].dom = q
        then BSearch:= L
        else BSearch:= 0
    else if q ≤ B[M].dom
        {There are at least two cells to consider; discard one-half
            of the cells, depending on the query q.}
    then BSearch:= BSearch(q,B,L,M)
    else BSearch:= BSearch(q,B,M + 1,U)
end{BSearch};
```

Program 4.2   The Pascal procedure *BSearch*.

BSearch (*q*,*B*,*L*,*U*), that returns the index of the cell containing a pair (*q*,?) if *q* is in *B*[*L*..*U*]; otherwise, it returns 0. First, we observe that if *q* is in *B* and *U* > *L*, then *q* must be in either the first half or the second half, where the first half ends at position $\lfloor (L + U)/2 \rfloor$. This observation follows because the domain elements themselves are distinct and are in sorted order. Second, because the domain elements (and the pairs) are in sorted order, we can determine in which half to look by comparing *q* with the domain element at position $\lfloor (L + U)/2 \rfloor$. We essentially discard half of the array after the midpoint comparison, and we continue with the other half; see Fig. 4.1. We have divided the array, and we now repeat the strategy recursively on the remaining half of it. The method of searching used in *BSearch* is known as **binary search;** at each step, one-half of the remaining elements are discarded. As each step takes constant time, the time taken by *BSearch* depends on only the number of steps (or recursive calls), and this number is independent of the query key. The number of steps corresponds directly to the number of times we can halve the remaining elements; that is, there are $\lceil \log n + 1 \rceil$ steps, yielding $O(\log n)$ search time. This time bound is clearly much better than $O(n)$.

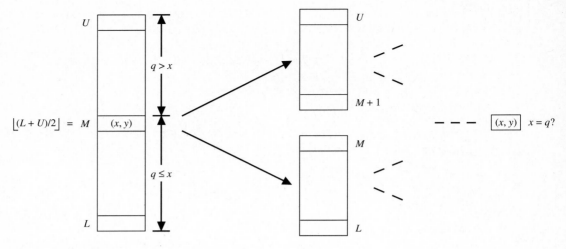

Figure 4.1   Divide-and-conquer search.

4.3   ARRAY REPRESENTATIONS

We present three representations of the ADT ARRAY. The first two—lexicographically ordered and reverse-lexicographically ordered representations—have been in use for decades in programming-language representations of ARRAY. The third method—shell-ordered representation—is presented for its intrinsic interest; it is *extendible,* a term we define in Section 4.3.3. In Section 6.3, we introduce a fourth representation that enables us to incorporate into Pascal programs arrays with execution-time–defined bounds.

4.3.1   Lexicographically Ordered Representation

To make our discussion concrete, we use the example two-dimensional array A of Fig. 4.2; it is an array from $\{1,2,3,4\} \times \{1,2,3,4,5\}$ into some codomain C. We do not need to know the values in C when considering the representation of A; we require only that some prescribed unit of space is needed for each codomain value *in its representation.*

The simplest and oldest representation is based on the lexicographic order of the domain of ARRAY; it is the method used in FORTRAN compilers. An ordered pair (i,j) is **lexicographically earlier** than (i',j') if either $i < i'$ or $i = i'$ and $j < j'$. It is lexicographic because it corresponds to the dictionary ordering of two-letter words. When we write the domain values or **indices** of the example array A in increasing **lexicographic order,** we obtain the ordering

$$(1,1),(1,2),(1,3),(1,4),(1,5),(2,1),...,(4,4),(4,5).$$

A	1	2	3	4	5
1	1	2	3	4	5
2	6	7	8	9	10
3	11	12	13	14	15
4	16	17	18	19	20

(a)

A	1	2	3	4	5
1	1	5	9	13	17
2	2	6	10	14	18
3	3	7	11	15	19
4	4	8	12	16	20

(b)

Figure 4.2 Example array A. (a) The lexicographically ordered and (b) reverse-lexicographically ordered representations of the domain of A.

This order is sometimes called **row-major order,** since we write the first row, followed by the second row, and so on. We indicate the row-major order of the array A in Fig. 4.3 (a) by using the values 1..20 as codomain values. A representation based on this order is now straightforward; we use a block B indexed from 1..20. To guarantee constant-time access we must demonstrate that we can compute the index in B corresponding to each index in A in constant time. To phrase this question more precisely, we define the **addressing function**

$$\alpha : 1..4 \times 1..5 \to \mathcal{N}$$

such that $\alpha(i,j)$ is the index in B corresponding to the index (i,j) in A. Now, for the lexicographic ordering of the domain of A, we have

$$\alpha(i,j) = (i - 1) \times 5 + j.$$

We leave it to you to check, in Exercise 4.4, that this addressing function is correct. Clearly, evaluating it takes constant time. In general, for an $m \times n$ array A, the corresponding lexicographic addressing function α is defined by

$$\alpha(i,j) = (i - 1) \times n + j, 1 \leq i \leq m, 1 \leq j \leq n,$$

or, more generally, by

$$\alpha(\text{row,column}) = (\text{row} - 1) \times \#\text{columns} + \text{column}.$$

Rather than using lexicographic order, we can use **reverse-lexicographic order** as is done in Pascal compilers. We say that $(i,j) <^R (i',j')$ if either $j < j'$ or $j = j'$ and $i < i'$; that is, $(j,i) < (j',i')$. This order is also called **column-major order,** because we write the first column, followed by the second column, and so on. For example, the reverse-lexicographic ordering of the domain of the array A is

$$(1,1),(2,1),(3,1),(4,1),(1,2),...,(3,5),(4,5).$$

We indicate this ordering, in Fig. 4.3(b), by using the indices 1..20 as codomain values. The corresponding addressing function α is defined by

$$\alpha(i,j) = (j-1) \times 4 + i, 1 \leq i \leq m, 1 \leq j \leq n,$$

or, in general, by

$$\alpha(\text{row,column}) = (\text{column} - 1) \times \text{\#rows} + \text{row}.$$

But what if we have a three- or higher-dimensional array? We can generalize the lexicographic and reverse-lexicographic ordering relations as follows. For $d \geq 1$, a d-tuple $(i_1,...,i_d)$ is lexicographically earlier than a d-tuple $(j_1,...,j_d)$ if there is a k, $1 \leq k \leq d$, such that $i_1 = j_1,...,i_{k-1} = j_{k-1}$, and $i_k < j_k$. We say that $(i_1,...,i_d) <^R (j_1,...,j_d)$ when $(i_d,...,i_1) < (j_d,...,j_1)$. So, the domain $1..4 \times 1..5 \times 1..3$ of a three-dimensional array has the lexicographic ordering shown in Fig. 4.3(a), and has the reverse-lexicographic ordering shown in Fig. 4.3(b). The corresponding formulas for $\alpha(i,j,k)$ are

$$(i-1) \times 15 + (j-1) \times 3 + k$$

and

$$(k-1) \times 20 + (j-1) \times 4 + i,$$

respectively. In general, the addressing function for a d-dimensional array indexed by $1..m_k$ in the kth dimension is

$$\alpha(i_1,...,i_d) = (i_1 - 1) \times m_2 \times \cdots \times m_d + \cdots + (i_{d-1} - 1) \times m_d + i_d$$

when it is represented in lexicographic order, and is

$$\alpha(i_1,...,i_d) = (i_d - 1) \times m_1 \times \ldots \times m_{d-1} + \cdots + (i_2 - 1) \times m_1 + i_1$$

when it is represented in reverse-lexicographic order. As we now demonstrate, these addressing functions can be computed with $2d$ arithmetic operations if we precompute the constant terms in the formulas. (Another method of computing the addressing functions with $2d$ arithmetic operations that avoids precomputation is the subject of Exercise 4.5.) We can rewrite the d-dimensional lexicographic addressing function as

$$i_1 \times a_{2,d} + i_2 \times a_{3,d} + \cdots + i_{d-1} \times a_{d-1,d} + i_d + a,$$

which can be further rewritten as

$$(i_1,...,i_d) \cdot (a_{2,d},...,a_{d-1,d},1) + a,$$

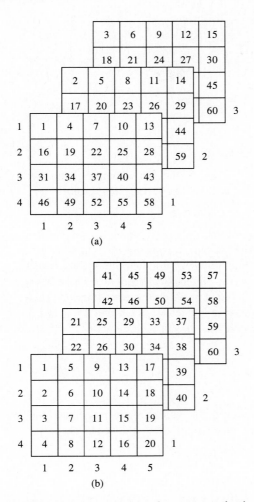

Figure 4.3 An example three-dimensional array. (a) The lexicographic and (b) reverse-lexicographic orderings of the array's domain.

where $a_{k,d} = m_k \times \cdots \times m_d$, $2 \le k \le d - 1$, $a = - a_{2,d} - \cdots - a_{d-1,d}$, and · indicates the inner product of the two vectors. The vector $(a_{2,d},...,a_{d-1,d},1)$ is called the **dope vector.**[2] It has the form shown in Fig. 4.4. Note that the values $a_{k,d}$, $2 \le k \le d - 1$, and a can be precomputed once and for all when the array is created. This precomputation method is extremely useful for compiling array declarations in Pascal and in other programming languages.

---

[2] Strictly speaking, a dope vector also includes the minimum and maximum index, for each dimension of the array.

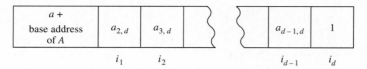

Figure 4.4   The dope vector for a d-dimensional array.

4.3.2 Shell-Ordered Representation

For a d-dimensional array, indexed by $1..m_k$ in the kth dimension, the two addressing functions we introduced in Section 4.3.1 have the general form

$$\alpha : 1..m_1 \times \cdots \times 1..m_d \rightarrow \mathcal{N}.$$

In each case, α is total and, since every two distinct positions in the given array correspond to two distinct positions in the one-dimensional destination array, α is injective. The two addressing functions are, however, not the only injective functions, as we now demonstrate. Given the two-dimensional array A of Fig. 4.2, we can represent it with block B, as shown in Fig. 4.5. We enumerate the indices shell by shell, where the kth shell consists of those indices (i,j) such that $k = \max(i,j)$. To obtain the formula for $\alpha(i,j)$, we observe that the kth shell contains $2k - 1$ elements, so

$$\sum_{l=1}^{k-1} (2l - 1) < \alpha(i,j) \le \sum_{l=1}^{k} (2l - 1),$$

where $k = \max(i,j)$. The two summations in the preceding equation are well known to be the sum of the first k odd numbers; that is, $(k - 1)^2$. In other words,

$$(k - 1)^2 < \alpha(i,j) \le k^2,$$

where $k = \max(i,j)$. If $i < k$, then

$$\alpha(i,j) = (k - 1)^2 + i;$$

otherwise,

$$\alpha(i,j) = k^2 - j + 1$$
$$= (k - 1)^2 + 2k - j.$$

This addressing function is a polynomial in i and j, but it is no longer linear, unlike the lexicographic and reverse-lexicographic addressing functions. Despite this drawback, the address computation takes only constant time; however, the shell addressing function is wasteful of memory. We have to allocate a block that encompasses all the shells needed by the given array, so a tall or long array does not use most of its block. The degenerate and, hence, worst case is the shell representation of a one-dimensional array of size n. It requires n shells and, therefore,

A	1	2	3	4	5
1	1	2	5	10	17
2	4	3	6	11	18
3	9	8	7	12	19
4	16	15	14	13	20

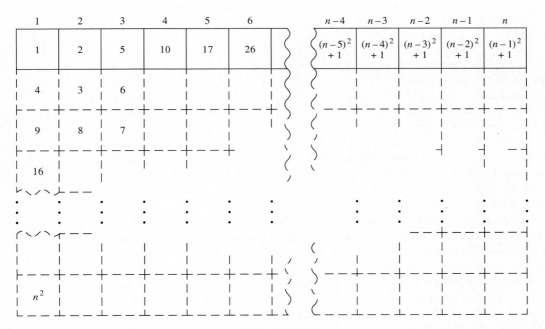

Figure 4.5 The shell ordering of the domain of the example array *A*.

Figure 4.6 A space-inefficient array under the shell ordering.

wastes $n^2 - n$ cells; see Fig. 4.6. On the other hand, shell addressing has something extra to offer, as we discuss in the next subsection.

4.3.3 Extendible Representations

The lexicographic addressing function $\alpha(i,j) = (i-1) \times \#\text{columns} + j$ is a function not only of *i* and *j*, but also of the number of columns. This observation implies that if we have, for example, the 4×5 array *A* of Fig. 4.2, we can add new

	1	2	3	4	5
1	1	2	3	4	5
2	6	7	8	9	10
3	11	12	13	14	15
4	16	17	18	19	20
5	21	22	23	24	25
6	26	27	28	29	30

Figure 4.7 Lexicographically ordered arrays and row extension.

rows by placing them at one end of the array's block and changing only currently undefined values of the addressing function; see Fig. 4.7. The currently defined entries remain unchanged. Thus, if we want to represent arrays such that we can change the number of rows at execution time, then we should use the lexicographically ordered representation. Of course, we can extend the representation of an array only when there is available extra memory contiguous to the array's block. In this case, we can extend the given array by one or more rows without moving the block. This extension takes O(size of row) time, for each additional row. We say that the lexicographic addressing function is **row extendible.** It is not, however, **column extendible;** see Fig. 4.8. We can extend an array, represented lexicographically, by columns only if we are prepared to move the array's entries to new locations and to change the addressing function. Because the lexicographic addressing function is a function of the number of columns of the given array, extending it by one column not only requires additional contiguous memory, but also requires that we change the locations of the currently defined entries. To do column extension, with respect to lexicographic addressing, we need to recompute the representation—an O(size of array) time operation. We do not have to do this recomputation for row extension. Similarly, reverse-lexicographic addressing is column extendible, but is not row extendible; see Exercise 4.6.

Returning to shell-ordered addressing, we see that the associated addressing function is independent of the numbers of rows and columns; it depends on only i and j. This independence means that there is only *one* shell addressing function that is valid for all two-dimensional arrays. It also means that shell-ordered addressing is **extendible,** by both rows and columns; see Fig. 4.9. Such schemes can be useful when we implement programming languages in which arrays are defined by usage rather than by declaration and, therefore, can grow arbitrarily large. A number of other related issues are discussed in Exercises 4.7 and 4.8.

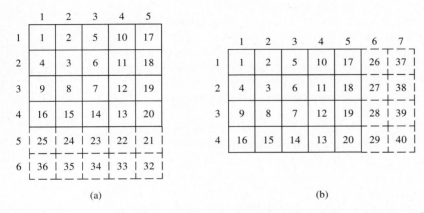

	1	2	3	4	5	6
1	1	2	3	4	5	
2	6	7	8	9	10	
3	11	12	13	14	15	
4	16	17	18	19	20	

(a)

	1	2	3	4	5	6
1	1	2	3	4	5	6
2	7	8	9	10	11	12
3	13	14	15	16	17	18
4	19	20	21	22	23	24

(b)

Figure 4.8 Lexicographically ordered arrays and column extension. (a) The lexicographic ordering of the domain of example array A. (b) The lexicographic ordering of the domain of A when it is extended by one column.

	1	2	3	4	5
1	1	2	5	10	17
2	4	3	6	11	18
3	9	8	7	12	19
4	16	15	14	13	20
5	25	24	23	22	21
6	36	35	34	33	32

(a)

	1	2	3	4	5	6	7
1	1	2	5	10	17	26	37
2	4	3	6	11	18	27	38
3	9	8	7	12	19	28	39
4	16	15	14	13	20	29	40

(b)

Figure 4.9 Shell-ordered addressing and extensions. (a) Row extension. (b) Column extension.

4.3.4 Lazy Initialization

In many applications, we need to assign an initial value to the entries of an array; for example, with bit arrays, the initial value may be 0. Sometimes, we want to initialize the elements to different values; for example, we may want to set the ith position to the value i, in a one-dimensional array. We shall assume, for simplicity, that the initial values of the entries are the same, and that initialization is carried out at declaration time. (The language Ada provides the initialization of an array, at declaration time, with a single value or with different values for the array's entries.) We can modify the specification of *Empty*, in this case, to be *Empty* : $C \rightarrow \mathcal{A}$; the function value *Empty*(*init*) is the array indexed by the domain D that has every entry equal to *init*. The obvious way to implement this operation, for any of the representations we have discussed, is to place the value *init* in each cell of the block allocated for the array. This method takes time linear in the size of the array. Since entries that are never modified are initialized with this scheme, the overhead of initialization may be too high. For this reason, we provide an alternative approach, **lazy initialization,** in which we avoid initializing entries that are never modified. Furthermore, the new scheme maintains constant-time access; its only disadvantage is that it uses much more memory.

The idea underlying the initialization method is simple: Keep a count of the number of entries that have been modified since the call of *Empty*(*init*), and keep their indices in a separate list, the **modified list.** Thus, the call *Empty*(*init*) sets only the count to 0 to give constant-time initialization. For each call *Codomain* (*d*,*A*), we first check whether the index *d* is in the modified list. If *d* is in the modified list, then we know that the corresponding cell in the array's block contains a useful value that we return; otherwise, we return the value *init*. For a call *Assign* (*d*,*c*,*A*), we replace the value in the cell indexed by *d* with value *c,* and we add *d* to the modified list, if it is not already there. This sketch of the initialization method has one serious defect; checking the modified list can take more than constant time. We provide more detail, and demonstrate how we maintain constant-time access.

Apart from the modified list, we maintain a variable *count* of the number of entries modified since initialization, and a **shadow block** of indices into the modified list. The modified list is also represented as a block; see Fig. 4.10. As an example, given a one-dimensional array *A* indexed by 1..13, we have shadow and modified-list blocks also indexed by 1..13. If, immediately after the initialization of *A,* we assign the value *c* to *A*[7], then we also increase *count* to 1, assign the index 7 as the value of the first cell in the modified-list block, and assign the index 1 as the value of the seventh cell in the shadow block. We have created a circular chain for *A*[7] that links the first cell in the modified-list block to the seventh cell in the shadow block; see Fig. 4.11. This circular linking is perhaps confusing, but we can use it to provide constant-time access as follows. A call *Codomain*(*d*,*A*) now involves using the index in the *d*th cell of the shadow block to check directly whether *d* is in the modified-list block. In other words, we determine whether

$$modifiedlist[shadow[d]] = d.$$

If it is, and, moreover, if $1 \leq shadow[d] \leq count$, then the value at position *d* has been modified; otherwise, the value at position *d* is *init*. Note that the second test is crucial to the correctness of this approach. It is possible that, serendipitously, the first condition is satisfied, but the *d*th entry has never been modified. In this

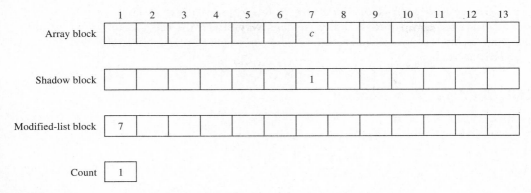

Figure 4.10 Examples of array, shadow, and modified-list blocks.

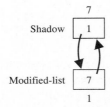

Figure 4.11 A circular chain and a modified entry in the lazy-initialization representation of an array.

case, however, $shadow[d]$ must lie outside the range $1..count$. We leave the details of an implementation of lazy initialization to Exercise 4.9. We can also add to the ARRAY operations an operation that reinitializes an array at any point during its lifetime. This new operation also can be implemented in constant time; see Exercise 4.10.

4.4 SPARSE-ARRAY REPRESENTATIONS

The majority of matrices (that is, two-dimensional arrays of real numbers) that occur when we solve real-world problems—such as space-shuttle design or nuclear-reactor design—have few nonzero entries; they are said to be **sparse.** There is no universal agreement on the number of nonzero entries that is needed to make a matrix sparse; a rule of thumb is that at most 10 percent should be nonzero. In these situations, particularly when we are dealing with very large matrices, we can achieve substantial savings in space (and time) by representing only the nonzero entries. We introduce two representations of arrays that favor sparseness, a **bit-array representation** and an **orthogonally linked list representation**. Other methods are discussed in Exercise 4.11, and in the references given at the end of this chapter.

4.4.1 Bit-Array Representation

Given the square array A

$$\begin{bmatrix} 0 & 4 & 0 & 0 \\ 3 & 0 & 7 & 0 \\ 5 & 0 & 8 & 2 \\ 0 & 9 & 0 & 6 \end{bmatrix},$$

consider its **associated bit array** B_A

$$\begin{bmatrix} 0 & 1 & 0 & 0 \\ 1 & 0 & 1 & 0 \\ 1 & 0 & 1 & 1 \\ 0 & 1 & 0 & 1 \end{bmatrix},$$

where nonzero entries are replaced by 1 and zero entries are unchanged. We have reduced the representation of a sparse array to the representation of a *sparse bit array*. The bit-array representation also requires that the nonzero entries of the given array be in either row-major or column-major order. We choose row-major order, so the example array A is replaced by B_A together with the nonzero vector

$$N_A = [4,3,7,5,8,2,9,6].$$

To access an entry in the sparse array, we traverse the bit array in row-major order and count the number of 1s before the corresponding entry. Thus, accessing an entry takes, in the worst case, time linear in the size of the original array. We can, however, improve the access time by also keeping a vector R_A of cumulative row counts for the array B_A. For our example array A, we have

$$R_A = \begin{bmatrix} 1 \\ 3 \\ 6 \\ 8 \end{bmatrix},$$

and we can now access an element in time linear in the sum of the row and column sizes—a clear improvement. Alternatively, the bit array can be viewed as the **adjacency matrix** of a directed graph (see Chapter 13), and an efficient representation can be obtained directly from efficient graph representations.

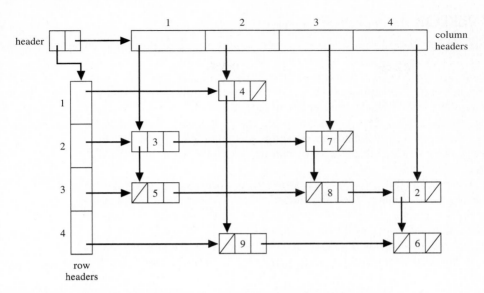

Figure 4.12   The orthogonally linked list representation of a sparse array.

4.4.2 Orthogonally Linked List Representation

We often need to traverse a row or column of an array rapidly—for example, when multiplying two matrices. Unfortunately, the bit-array representation we have chosen favors row traversal over column traversal, so we present an alternative representation that uses **orthogonally linked lists** to provide efficient row and column traversal. The representation is also extendible, whereas the bit-array representation is not. We represent each nonzero entry with a cell that has both a **right link** and a **down link.** The right link gives the cell of the next nonzero entry on the same row; the down link gives the cell of the next nonzero entry in the same column. We can also represent as lists of links the headers for the rows and columns. (We choose blocks of links for efficiency reasons.) The orthogonally linked list representation of the example array A is shown in Fig. 4.12. Note that traversing a sparse array by either rows or columns takes time proportional to the number of nonzero entries in the sparse array.

The major advantage of the orthogonally linked list representation is the latter's flexibility. We can easily change zero elements into nonzero ones and vice versa; we can easily add rows and columns; and we can efficiently traverse a sparse matrix by rows or by columns. The major disadvantages are the overhead involved in accessing an entry and the extra memory needed for the links.

4.5 PERFORMANCE REPORTS

In Table 4.1, we compare the pointer and sorted-block representations of MAP. The sorted-block representation outperforms the pointer representation as far as *Codomain* and *IsDefined* are concerned. This improvement in efficiency, however, implies that *Assign* and *Deassign* have to move elements. For this reason, we choose the sorted-block representation only when the domain is totally ordered and the map is static or nearly static. The pointer representation is the wisest choice in all other circumstances, and is the only choice if the domain is not totally ordered; see Table 4.2. (We shall meet a much better choice, called hashing, in Chapter 9.)

In Table 4.3 we give, for an $n \times n$ array, the performance summary for the four ARRAY representations we have studied. Clearly, the reverse-lexicographically and lexicographically ordered representations are the winners. Not only do they have constant-time performance, but also they are compact; there is no wasted space, as demonstrated by Table 4.4. The shell-ordered representation, on the other hand, achieves constant-time performance and is extendible at the

Table 4.1   A comparison of the worst-case execution times of the two MAP representations.

	MAP implementation	
Operation	Pointer	Sorted block
Empty	1	1
IsEmpty	1	1
Codomain	n	$\log n$
IsDefined	n	$\log n$
Assign	n	n
Deassign	n	n

Table 4.2   The rating of the two MAP representations.

MAP implementation	Rating	Comments
Pointer	Very good	The best general choice.
Sorted-block	Good	Requires a totally ordered domain; extremely good for static or nearly static maps.

Table 4.3 A comparison of the worst-case execution times of the four ARRAY representations.

Operation	ARRAY implementation			
	Lexicographic	Shell	Bit	Orthogonal
Empty	1	1	1	1
Codomain	1	1	n	n
Assign	1	1	n^2	n

Table 4.4 The rating of the four ARRAY representations.

ARRAY implementation	Rating	Comments
Lexicographic	Excellent	Usual representation of arrays
Shell	Very good	An extendible representation
Orthogonal	Very good	An extendible sparse representation that allows efficient row and column traversals
Bit	Very good	A compact sparse representation

expense of wasted space. It is a viable alternative when extendibility is required.

The bit-array and orthogonally linked list representations of sparse arrays have similar performance; both save space by representing only nonzero entries. Changing a zero entry into a nonzero one is time consuming, however, in the bit-array representation, since we have to create space for the new entry in the vector of nonzero values. Hence, *Assign* is an $O(n^2)$ time operation, in the worst case, for the bit-array representation. Moreover, the bit-array representation is compact and nonextendible, whereas the orthogonally linked list representation, although not as compact, is extendible. Another advantage of the orthogonally linked list representation is that traversals by rows and columns take time linear in the number of nonzero entries. For this reason, we rate the orthogonally linked list representation higher than we do the bit-array representation.

4.6 SUMMARY

We introduced the ADT MAP, which allows programmers to define functions that are not easily captured by the standard function-definition facility in programming languages. The ADT ARRAY is a special case of MAP in which the domain is a Cartesian product of integer ranges. It provides an abstraction of the array type in Pascal and in other languages. The special nature of its domain leads to representations that provide constant-time access to codomain values when a domain value is given. We provided three such representations. The first two— the lexicographically ordered and reverse-lexicographically ordered representations—have been used for the representation of arrays in FORTRAN, Pascal, and other programming languages. The third representation—shell-ordered representation—has been used to introduce the notion of extendibility; extendible arrays can grow and shrink without the previously defined values of their addressing function being changed.

Finally, we provided two representations of sparse arrays: the bit-array and orthogonally linked list representations.

4.7 HISTORY

The lexicographically ordered and reverse-lexicographically ordered representations have been used since the early days of computing. Standish (1980) provides a thorough discussion of lexicographic, reverse-lexicographic, and shell-ordered representations. Shell ordering can be viewed as an enumeration of rational numbers, an idea that has been explored by Lew and Rosenberg (1978a; 1978b). The issue of extendibility has been treated exhaustively by Rosenberg (1974), who also has investigated the storage of data structures in a more general framework (Rosenberg, 1978). We have not treated the issue of **proximity-preserving representations,** in which elements "close" to each other in an array are "close" to each other in the array's representation. Refer to the work of Rosenberg (1975) and DeMillo, Eisenstat, and Lipton (1978), for a discussion of this notion.

The representation of sparse matrices is discussed in George and Liu (1981).

EXERCISES

4.1: Complete the implementation of the LIST representation of MAP given in Section 4.2.

4.2: We introduced binary searching in Section 4.2 as a method of improving searching from linear to logarithmic time, when given a sorted block of elements from a totally ordered universe. Design and implement a binary-search procedure for a sorted block of integers that may contain repetitions.

4.3: The binary-search procedure given in Program 4.2 compares the query value with a block value *for equality* only when the repeated halving has left only one block value. We might think that it would be more efficient to test for equality at each midpoint value. Discuss this idea. Specify which of the two approaches is preferable and explain your choice.

4.4: Prove that the lexicographic addressing function $\alpha(i,j) = (i - 1) \times 5 + j$ is correct for an array $A[1..4,1..5]$ whose entries require 1 unit of space. In other words, prove that it maps $1..4 \times 1..5$ to $1..20$ bijectively.

4.5: We have given one method of computing the value of the lexicographic addressing function, for a d-dimensional array, with $2d$ arithmetic operations in Section 4.3.1. Another approach, known as **Horner's rule,** is to use the original formulation of the addressing function as

$$\alpha(i_1,...,i_d) = (i_1 - 1) \times m_2 \times \cdots \times m_d + \cdots + (i_{d-1} - 1) \times m_d + i_d;$$

then, by suitable insertion of parentheses, we can obtain the same result. (This approach provides an efficient method of evaluating any polynomial.) Derive the precise method. Discuss why we do not want to use it for computing the value of an addressing function of an array.

4.6: Demonstrate that the reverse-lexicographic ordering of a two-dimensional array is column extendible but is not row extendible.

4.7: Extend the shell addressing scheme for three-dimensional arrays. How inefficient is the storage utilization in the worst case?

4.8: An addressing function, for a two-dimensional array, that is both row and column extendible must be total, and must map $\mathcal{N} \times \mathcal{N}$ into $\mathbb{N}$ injectively. Prove this assertion.

Design an extendible addressing function that is different from the shell addressing function, but is also easy to compute. [Hint: The function should not be surjective.]

4.9: Implement and test a complete lazy-initialization implementation of ARRAY, based on the lexicographic addressing.

4.10: We can extend the ADT ARRAY to include a new operation that reinitializes an array at any point in the latter's lifetime. Show that the lazy-initialization representation can be extended to this new ADT.

4.11: Perhaps the simplest representation of a sparse array is to represent an array as a list of nonzero entries. To ensure that we can access the entries correctly, we keep the indices of each entry with the entry. Implement the ARRAY operations based on this representation. Analyze the implementation. In addition, analyze the efficiency of lexicographic and reverse-lexicographic traversals under this representation.

4.12: Extend the lexicographic and reverse-lexicographic addressing functions for the case in which each element requires $p \geq 1$ units of space, rather than 1 unit.

4.13: Let $A[1..m,1..n]$ be an array, and let $\alpha_A : 1..m \times 1..n \to 1..mn$ be the corresponding lexicographic addressing function. We conjecture that there is no other bijective addressing function $\beta_A : 1..m \times 1..n \to 1..mn$ such that, whenever $(i,j) < (i',j')$, we have $\beta(i,j) < \beta(i',j')$. Does this conjecture hold? Either prove that it holds or provide a counterexample.

4.14: Upper and lower triangular arrays are common in numerical linear algebra. A two-dimensional array A of order n is **upper triangular** if $A[i,j]$ is well defined only when $1 \leq i \leq j \leq n$. (Alternatively, it is an $n \times n$ matrix in which $A[i,j] = 0$, for $1 \leq j < i \leq n$.) Devise an addressing function, for this kind of array, that maps indices into positions $1..n(n + 1)/2$.

4.15: Generalize Exercise 4.14 to **upper tetrahedral arrays** A of order n and dimension d; that is, $A[i_1,...,i_d]$ is well defined only when $1 \leq i_1 \leq \cdots \leq i_d \leq n$.

4.16: A **band matrix** A of order $n \geq 1$ and **width** $w \geq 1$ satisfies the condition that $A[i,j]$ is well defined only when $|i - j| \leq w - 1$. Devise an addressing function that maps the indices into positions in the range $1..(2w -)n$. Either specify how much space is wasted or prove that no space is wasted.

4.17: Given a two-dimensional array $A[1..m, 1..n]$, we define the distance between $A[i,j]$ and $A[i',j']$ to be $|i - i'| + |j - j'|$. Prove that two positions cannot be farther apart than $m + n - 2$. What is the average distance between two positions?

4.18: Given a two-dimensional array $A[1..m, 1..n]$, we say that $A[i,j]$, $A[i \pm 1, j]$, and $A[i, j \pm 1]$ are **neighbors.** Given an addressing function α, we say that α **preserves proximity** if there is a constant $c > 0$ that is independent of m and n such that

$$|\alpha(i,j) - \alpha(i',j')| \le c,$$

for all neighbors $A[i,j]$ and $A[i',j']$.

    a. Do lexicographic and reverse-lexicographic ordering preserve proximity? Justify your answer.

    b. Does shell ordering preserve proximity? Justify your answer.

    c. Does any addressing function preserve proximity? Justify your answer.

Data Structures and Data Types

Trees and Forests

Trees are ubiquitous. They appear not only as the basis of many data structures, but also in other areas of computer science and in other disciplines. They provide a hierarchical method of structuring data unlike the linear structures—lists, queues, and stacks. There are many uses of trees; we portray several in Fig. 5.1. The genealogical tree is perhaps best known; the organizational tree is a close second. We shall meet the code tree and the trie in the next chapter.

This chapter prepares the way for our use of trees throughout the text. We cover the fundamental notions of binary trees, in Section 5.1, and also the methods to traverse, display, and represent these trees, in Sections 5.3, 5.4, and 5.5, respectively. Binary trees are sufficient for many—but not for all—computer-science applications; we introduce other kinds of trees when they are needed. In addition, we define multiway trees, forests, and orchards.

5.1 TREE DEFINITIONS

We define the trees that we use, with few exceptions, throughout this text: *binary (indexed) trees,* and their more general variant, *multiway (indexed) trees.* We also define the notions of size, height, and level. Finally, we introduce collections of trees—namely, forests and orchards.

5.1.1 Binary Trees

We begin by giving a recursive definition of a **binary (indexed) tree.** A binary (indexed) tree T of n nodes, $n \geq 0$, either is empty, if $n = 0$, or consists of a **root node** u and two binary trees $u(1)$ and $u(2)$ of n_1 and n_2 nodes, respectively, such

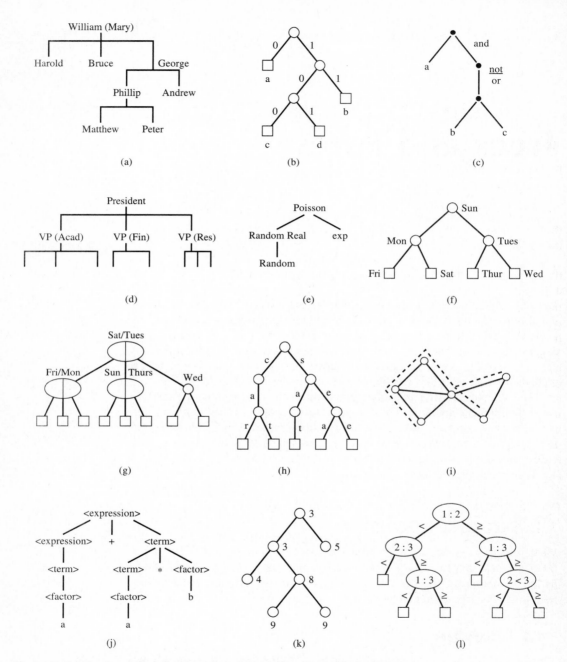

Figure 5.1 Twelve uses of trees. (a) A genealogical tree. (b) A code tree.
(c) An expression tree. (d) An organizational tree. (e) A subprogram
dependency tree. (f) A binary search tree. (g) A 2,3 -tree. (h) A trie.
(i) A spanning tree. (j) A syntax tree. (k) A priority tree. (l) A decision tree.

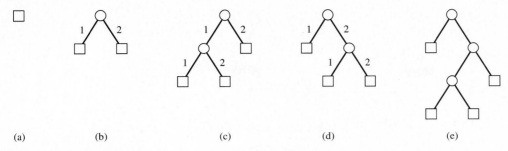

(a)   (b)   (c)   (d)   (e)

Figure 5.2 Five example binary trees. We use □ to denote an empty tree and ○ to denote a node.

that $n = 1 + n_1 + n_2$. We say that $u(1)$ is the **first** or **left subtree** of T, and $u(2)$ is the **second** or **right subtree** of T.

We use the term *indexed* to indicate that a node u has a map associated with it that we also denote by u. Indeed, the map is also an array in the sense of Chapter 4. It is also possible to define a binary tree by associating either a list or a set of trees with each node. These approaches give rise, however, to different classes of trees that do not correspond to the trees used in most computer-science applications.

We display, in Fig. 5.2, binary trees of zero, one, two, and three nodes. We have indicated the domain values of the subtree maps on the **branches** or **edges** of the trees. You should check that these structures are, indeed, binary trees according to the definition. We call ○-nodes **internal nodes** and □-nodes **external nodes**. Note that internal nodes always have two subtrees, whereas external nodes have no subtrees. We always draw trees vertically such that the subtrees of the root are drawn below the root, and left subtrees are drawn to the left of their right siblings.

Sometimes it is convenient to depict only the internal nodes of a binary tree (or of any tree for that matter). When we suppress the external nodes, the trees of Fig. 5.2 appear as shown in Fig. 5.3. Note that we still represent the standalone empty tree by □, but we suppress external nodes elsewhere. The trees in Figures 5.3(c) and (d) are not equal (more strictly, they are not isomorphic), since the left subtree of the root of the tree in Fig. 5.3(c) is nonempty, whereas the left subtree of the root of the tree in Fig. 5.3(d) is empty. Because of the way that we draw binary trees, we can omit the indices without causing any confusion—the way that they are drawn in the plane defines the node maps.

Before examining binary trees in more detail, let us introduce the basic terminology associated with them. Let T be a binary tree with root u, and let v be any node in T. If v is the root of either $u(1)$ or $u(2)$, then we say that u is the **parent** of v, and that v is a **child** of u. If w is also a child of u, and w is distinct from v, we say that v and w are **siblings.** If v is the root of $u(i)$, then v is the **ith child** of u; $u(1)$ is the **left child** and $u(2)$ is the **right child. Grandparent, grandchild,** and other genealogical terminology are used similarly.

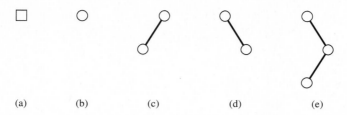

Figure 5.3   The binary trees in Fig. 5.2, with external nodes omitted.

Given a binary tree T of n nodes, $n \geq 1$, we define two useful partial orders on its nodes. Let u and v be two nodes in T. Then v is a **descendant** of u if either v is equal to u or v is a child of some node w and w is a descendant of u. We denote this relation by $desc_T$, and we write $v \, desc_T \, u$. It is not difficult to prove that $desc_T$ is a partial order; see Exercise 5.8. We say that v is a **proper descendant** of u if v is a descendant of u and $v \neq u$. Also note that we can define a relation "ancestor of" as the reverse of the descendant relation.

In a similar manner, we define v to be a **left descendant** of u if v is equal to u, v is a left child of u, or v is a child of some node w and w is a left descendant of u. We denote the relation by $ldesc_T$. The relation $rdesc_T$ can be defined analogously. The relation $ldesc_T$ relates nodes across a binary tree, rather than up and down the tree; it is crucial to the definition of binary search trees (see Section 8.5.1). Given two nodes u and v in a binary tree T, we say that v is **to the left of** u if there is a node w in T such that v is a left descendant of w and u is a right descendant of w. We denote the relation in this case by $left_T$, and we write $v \, left_T \, u$. The relation $left_T$ is a total order; see Exercise 5.10.

The external nodes of a tree define its **frontier.** We normally enumerate the external nodes in left-to-right order in the frontier.

We can count the number of nodes of a binary tree in three ways: by the internal nodes, by the external nodes, or by both. The number of internal nodes of a binary tree is called the tree's **size.** The trees in Figures 5.2(a)–(e) have sizes 0, 1, 2, 2, and 3, and have 1, 2, 3, 3, and 4 external nodes, respectively. The following simple relationship between the size and the number of external nodes is easy to prove either directly or by induction; see Exercise 5.17.

Fact 5.1   *Let T be a binary tree of size $n \geq 0$. Then, the number of external nodes of T is $n + 1$.*

Based on the descendant relation, we define the notions of the height of a tree and the levels of nodes in a tree. Let T be a binary tree. The **height** of T is defined recursively as 0 if T is empty and $1 + max(height(T_1), height(T_2))$ otherwise, where T_1 and T_2 are the subtrees of the root. The height of a tree is the length of a longest chain of descendants. Alternatively, we can number the nodes of T according to the following prescription. Number all external nodes 0, and number each internal node to be one more than the maximum of the numbers of its chil-

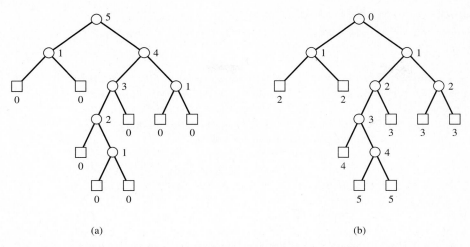

Figure 5.4 Binary trees and numberings. (a) The height numbering. (b) The level numbering.

dren. Then the number of the root is the height of T. In Fig. 5.4(a), we display a tree with its height numbering. The **height of a node** u in T is the height of the subtree rooted at u. We define the **levels** of nodes in a binary tree T by using the following node-numbering scheme. Number the root node 0, and number every other node to be one more than its parent. (If the tree is empty, then the single external node is numbered 0.) Then the number of a node v is that node's level; the level of v is the number of branches on the path from the root to v; see Fig. 5.4(b).

Two kinds of binary trees are of particular interest. First are the **skinny trees,** in which every internal node has at most one internal child; see Fig. 5.5(a). Second are the **complete binary trees** (they are fat trees), in which the external nodes appear on at most two adjacent levels; see Fig. 5.5(b). Within the class of complete trees, we distinguish two subclasses: the **perfect trees** that have all their external nodes on one level, Fig. 5.5(c), and the **left-complete trees** that have the internal nodes on the lowest level in the leftmost possible positions, Fig. 5.5(d). We are interested in skinny and complete trees because, for a given size, skinny trees are the highest possible trees and complete trees are the lowest possible trees.

There is a useful relationship between the height and the size of a binary tree that restricts the allowable heights for a given size and restricts the allowable sizes for a given height. We leave the proof of the following fact to Exercise 5.20.

Fact 5.2

1. *A binary tree of height $h \geq 0$ has size at least h.*
2. *A binary tree of height at most $h \geq 0$ has size at most $2^h - 1$.*

3. *A binary tree of size n ≥ 0 has height at most n.*

4. *A binary tree of size n ≥ 0 has height at least $\lceil \log(n+1) \rceil$; thus, the height is $\Omega(\log n)$.*

Knowing the number of binary trees of a given size is useful in some expected-case analyses of binary trees and in the generation of pseudorandom binary trees. Because binary trees are defined recursively, we obtain, in a natural manner, a recurrence equation for their numbers. Letting $\mathcal{B}_n$ be the number of binary trees of size n, we can obtain the following recurrence equation

$$\mathcal{B}_n = \begin{cases} 1 & n = 0; \\ \sum_{i=0}^{n-1} \mathcal{B}_i\,\mathcal{B}_{n-i-1} & n \geq 1. \end{cases}$$

Its solution, which is beyond the scope of this text, is given as the following well-known fact.

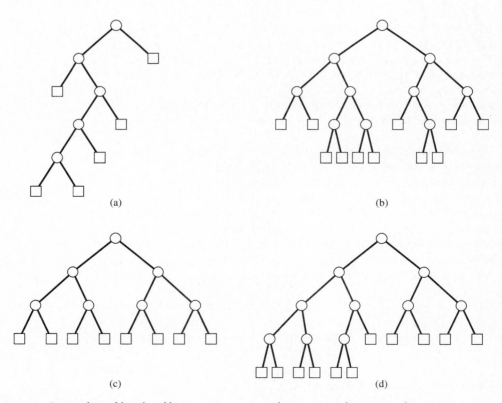

Figure 5.5   Examples of kinds of binary trees. (a) A skinny tree. (b) A complete tree. (c) A perfect tree. (d) A left-complete tree.

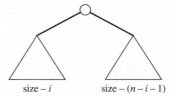

Figure 5.6 Construction of a size-n binary tree.

Fact 5.3 *The number $\mathcal{B}_n$ of binary trees of size n is*

$$\frac{1}{n+1}\binom{2n}{n}.$$

The value of $\mathcal{B}_n$ is known as the **nth Catalan number.** The value of $\mathcal{B}_0$ is 1, because there is only one empty tree. Similarly, the value of $\mathcal{B}_1$ also is 1, because a tree of size 1 must have a root and two empty subtrees. Now, $\mathcal{B}_2$ is 2 because there must be a root node, and this choice leaves two possible choices for the sub-tree of size 1. Observe that $\mathcal{B}_n$ grows rapidly (indeed, exponentially) with respect to n; for example, $\mathcal{B}_{10}$ is already 16,796.

Why does the recurrence equation for $\mathcal{B}_n$ hold? It follows from Fig. 5.6; a size-n binary tree, $n > 0$, consists of a size-i left subtree and a size-$(n - i - 1)$ right subtree, for some i, $0 \leq i < n$. The subtrees are chosen independently, subject to only the size restriction; hence, for fixed i, there are $\mathcal{B}_i \mathcal{B}_{n-i-1}$ choices. As an example, consider $\mathcal{B}_3$, the number of size-3 binary trees. Since $n = 3 \geq 1$, each binary tree of size 3 consists of a root node together with left and right subtrees. The sizes of the two subtrees must sum to 2 by the definition of binary trees; hence, each of the subtrees can have sizes between 0 and 2, as shown in Fig. 5.7. We denote the choices of the subtrees by (0,2), (1,1), and (2,0). Therefore, we see that $\mathcal{B}_3$ is the sum of the number of binary trees of type (0,2), the number of type (1,1), and the number of type (2,0). Substituting with $\mathcal{B}_0$, $\mathcal{B}_1$, and $\mathcal{B}_2$ as appropriate, we find that

$$\mathcal{B}_3 = \mathcal{B}_0\mathcal{B}_2 + \mathcal{B}_1\mathcal{B}_1 + \mathcal{B}_2\mathcal{B}_0$$
$$= 1 \times 2 + 1 \times 1 + 2 \times 1$$
$$= 5,$$

since there are two binary trees of size 2. On the other hand, from the solution to the recurrence equation, we see that

$$\mathcal{B}_3 = \frac{1}{4}\binom{6}{3}$$
$$= \frac{1}{4} \times \frac{6 \times 5 \times 4}{1 \times 2 \times 3}$$
$$= 5.$$

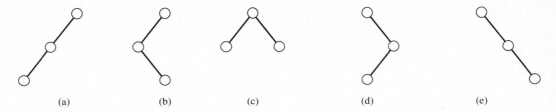

Figure 5.7   All possible combinations of left and right subtrees for a binary tree of size 3.

5.1.2 Multiway Trees

Analogous to our definition of binary trees, we define **multiway (indexed) trees** or simply **trees,** in which the degree of a node is no longer restricted to be 2. A multiway (indexed) tree T of n internal nodes, $n \geq 0$, either is empty, if $n = 0$, or consists of a root node u, an integer $d_u \geq 1$, the **degree** of u, and multiway trees $u(1)$ of n_1 nodes,..., $u(d_u)$ of n_{d_u} nodes such that $n = 1 + n_1 + \cdots + n_{d_u}$; see Fig. 5.8.

A multiway tree T is a **d-ary (indexed) tree,** for some $d > 0$, **if** $d_u = d$, for all internal nodes u in T; see Fig. 5.8(d). A multiway tree T is an **(a,b)-tree,** if $1 \leq a \leq d_u \leq b$, for all u in T; every binary tree is a (2,2) -tree, and vice versa.

Note that an internal node in a multiway tree may have one, two, or more children. The terminology used for binary trees is carried over, with appropriate modifications, to trees. Some aspects of the carryover are explored in Exercise 5.21.

5.1.3 Forests and Orchards

When we remove the root of a tree, we are left with a collection or set of trees called a **forest** of trees. Just as we have different kinds of trees, we also have different kinds of forests. We are particularly interested in **ordered forests,** which we call **orchards. A forest of trees** is a set, possibly empty, of trees. An **orchard of trees** is a list, possibly empty, of trees.

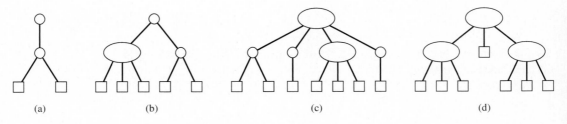

Figure 5.8   Four example multiway trees.

5.2 BINTREE, TREE, AND ORCHARD SPECIFICATION

We have introduced binary trees as structures that have no values associated with their nodes. We assume, however, that the ADT BINTREE has values of type *intelementtype* associated with the internal nodes of a binary tree and of type *extelementtype* with the external nodes, just as we have associated values with the nodes of a list. Taking the analogy further, these values do not have any effect on the BINTREE operations, as long as they satisfy some simple properties that we specify. BINTREE also has explicit windows and window-manipulation operations. Windows can be positioned over any internal or external node, can be moved from a parent to a child, or moved from a child to its parent.

Let $\mathcal{BT}$ denote the set of BINTREEs of *intelementtype* and *extelementtype*, let $\mathcal{I}$ denote the set of values of type *intelementtype*, let $\mathcal{X}$ denote the set of values of type *extelementtype*, and let $\mathcal{W}$ denote the set of values of type *windowtype*. We have the following operations, where $\mathcal{N}$ denotes the set of nonnegative integers:

1. *Empty*: $\rightarrow \mathcal{BT}$: The function value *Empty* is an empty binary tree.

2. *IsEmpty*: $\mathcal{BT} \rightarrow \mathcal{B}$: The function value *IsEmpty(T)* is **true** if *T* is empty; otherwise, it is **false**.

3. *Root*: $\mathcal{BT} \rightarrow \mathcal{W}$. The function value *Root(T)* is the window position of the single external node if *T* is empty; otherwise, it is the window position of the root of *T*.

4. *IsRoot*: $\mathcal{W} \times \mathcal{BT} \rightarrow \mathcal{B}$: *The function value IsRoot(w,T)* is **true** if the window *w* is over the root; otherwise, it is **false**.

5. *IsExternal*: $\mathcal{W} \times \mathcal{BT} \rightarrow \mathcal{B}$: The function value *IsExternal(w,T)* is **true** if the window *w* is over an external node of *T*; otherwise, it is **false**.

6. *Child*: $\mathcal{N} \times \mathcal{W} \times \mathcal{BT} \rightarrow \mathcal{W}$: The function value *Child(i,w,T)* is undefined if the node in the window *w* is external or the node in *w* is internal and *i* is neither 1 nor 2; otherwise, it is the *i*th child of the node in *w*.

7. *Parent*: $\mathcal{W} \times \mathcal{BT} \rightarrow \mathcal{W}$: The function value *Parent(w,T)* is undefined if *T* is empty or *w* is over the root of *T*; otherwise, it is the window position of the parent of the node in the window *w*.

8. *IntExamine*: $\mathcal{W} \times \mathcal{BT} \rightarrow \mathcal{I}$: The function value *IntExamine(w,T)* is undefined if *w* is over an external node; otherwise, it is the element at the internal node in the window *w*.

9. *ExtExamine*: $\mathcal{W} \times \mathcal{BT} \rightarrow \mathcal{X}$: The function value *ExtExamine(w,T)* is undefined if *w* is over an internal node; otherwise, it is the element at the external node in the window *w*.

10. *IntReplace*: $\mathcal{I} \times \mathcal{W} \times \mathcal{BT} \rightarrow \mathcal{BT}$: The function value *IntReplace(e,w,T)* is undefined if *w* is over an external node; otherwise, it is *T*, with the element at the internal node in *w* replaced by *e*.

11. *ExtReplace*: $X \times W \times \mathcal{BT} \to \mathcal{BT}$: The function value *ExtReplace(e,w,T)* is undefined if w is over an internal node; otherwise, it is T, with the element at the external node in w replaced by e.

12. *Insert*: $I \times W \times \mathcal{BT} \to W \times \mathcal{BT}$: The function value *Insert(e,w,T)* is undefined if w is over an internal node; otherwise, it is T, with the external node in w replaced by a new internal node with two external children. Furthermore, the new internal node is given the value e and the window is moved over the new internal node.

13. *Delete*: $X \times W \times \mathcal{BT} \to W \times \mathcal{BT}$: The function value *Delete(w,T)* is undefined if w is over an external node or is over an internal node with no external children; otherwise, it is T, with the internal node in w replaced by w's internal child, if w has one, or by w's left external child otherwise. Furthermore, the window is moved over the replacement node.

This list is not exhaustive; rather, it contains a basic set of operations that we can use to implement algorithms that scan a tree from the root to the frontier. It is important to realize that if we want to add new operations to the ADT BINTREE, to remove operations, or to change operations, then we obtain a new ADT for binary trees. The operation *Child* reflects the indexing in the tree; however, we often replace it with two operations *Left* and *Right*, defined as follows:

1. *Left*: $W \times \mathcal{BT} \to W$: The function value *Left(w,T)* is undefined if the window w is over an external node; otherwise, it is the window position of the left (or first) child of the node in w.

2. *Right*: $W \times \mathcal{BT} \to W$: The function value *Right(w,T)* is undefined if the window w is over an external node; otherwise, it is the window position of the right (or second) child of the node in w.

Insert, as specified, assigns a value to only the new internal node, it does not assign values to the new external nodes. We can, however, use *ExtReplace* to add the needed values.

For TREE, we need both *Degree* and *Child*, specified as follows:

1. *Degree*: $W \times \mathcal{T} \to I$: The function value *Degree(w,T)* is the degree of the node in the window w.

2. *Child*: $\mathcal{N} \times W \times \mathcal{T} \to W$: The function value *Child(i,w,T)* is undefined if the node in the window w is external, or if the node in w is internal and i is outside the range $1..d$, where d is the degree of the node; otherwise, it is the ith child of the node in w.

Since an orchard is a list of binary trees or multiway trees, the ADT ORCHARD, in its most general form, is specified as a composition of LIST and BINTREE (or TREE). Conceptually, we can specify the ADT ORCHARD to be a LIST of BINTREE. To distinguish between the ADT operations of LIST and

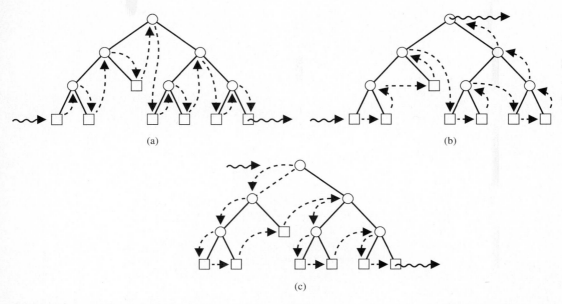

Figure 5.11 Node-visit order in binary-tree traversals. (a) Inorder traversal. (b) Postorder traversal. (c) Preorder traversal.

5.3.2 Level-Order Traversal

We have labeled, alphabetically, the nodes of the binary tree, in Fig. 5.12, so that the alphabetical order of the nodes is the level order. The traversal visits the nodes on each level in left-to-right order; it begins to visit nodes on a new level only when all nodes on all previous levels have been visited. To program a level-order traversal, we need to keep track of the subtrees that must still be traversed. For example, with the tree of Fig. 5.12, after visiting the root node, the traversal has two subtrees to traverse (Fig. 5.13a); after visiting the root of the first subtree, it has two additional subtrees to traverse (Fig. 5.13b); and after visiting the root of the second subtree, it has a further two subtrees to traverse (Fig. 5.13c). The generation order of these subtrees is crucial to the correctness of a level-order traversal. It suggests that we should maintain a list of binary trees when beginning the traversal of a level. After visiting the root of the first subtree in the list, we obtain two subtrees that are to be traversed *only after* all the remaining nodes on the current level are visited. Thus, we should append them to the list. A level-order traversal can be pictured as shown in Fig. 5.14. Initially, we have a list of one binary tree, as shown in Fig. 5.14(a). After visiting the root, we have the list shown in Fig. 5.14(b). We now visit the root B of the first subtree, and this visit spawns two subtrees that are appended to give Fig. 5.14(c). Visiting C causes a further two subtrees to be appended; see Fig. 5.14(d). We provide one further step in Fig. 5.14(e); the remainder of the traversal is left to Exercise 5.28.

```
procedure InorderTraversal(T: BINTREE; Visit: procedure);
{InorderTraversal performs a recursive inorder traversal of the
    binary tree T that visits both internal and external nodes. It uses
    a subsidiary procedure IT that carries the current window position
    as a parameter. When IT visits a node, it invokes the user-defined
    procedure Visit.}
var w: windowtype;

procedure IT(w: windowtype; T: BINTREE);
var v: windowtype;
begin
    if IsExternal(w,T)
    then Visit(w,T)
    else begin
        v:= w;
        {Traverse the left subtree.}
        Left(v,T); IT(v,T);
        Visit(w,T);
        {Traverse the right subtree.}
        Right(w,T); IT(w,T)
    end
end {IT};

begin
    {Initialize the window over the root of T and begin the traversal.}
    Root(w,T);
    IT(w,T)
end;
```

Program 5.1 A Pascal implementation of the inorder traversal of a binary tree.

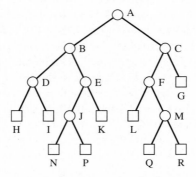

Figure 5.12   Node-visit order in the level-order traversal of a binary tree. The alphabetical ordering of the labeled nodes is the level ordering.

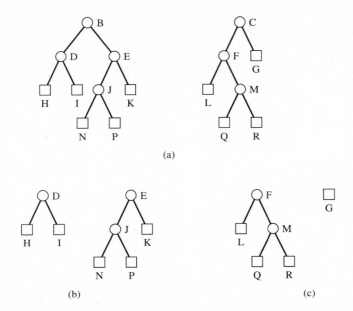

(a)

(b)   (c)

Figure 5.13   States of the level-order traversal of the binary tree in Fig. 5.12.
(a) After visiting the root. (b) After visiting the root's left child.
(c) After visiting the root's right child.

What list operations do we need to support a level-order traversal? We need to create an empty list, to append a value to a list, to examine the first value of a list, and to delete the first value of a list. These are four of the five operations of QUEUE (see Section 1.4.1). Hence, we have an orchard in which the only LIST operations needed are those of QUEUE.

What binary-tree operations do we need? Within a level-order traversal, we need to be able to determine whether the window is over an external node, to examine the node in the window, and to obtain the left and right children of the node in the window. These operations are available to us in BINTREE; therefore, we can implement a level-order traversal as given in Program 5.2. It is iterative, rather than recursive.

The depth-first traversals can also be developed as iterative, rather than recursive, procedures through use of a stack; see Exercise 5.29. Indeed, a generic traversal algorithm can be designed that can be specialized to perform either a depth-first or a level-order traversal, depending on whether a stack or queue is chosen; see Exercise 5.30.

5.3.3 Traversal Analysis

The implementations of the traversals that we have given take $O(n)$ time for a binary tree of size n. Because the traversals visit every node in a binary tree, they

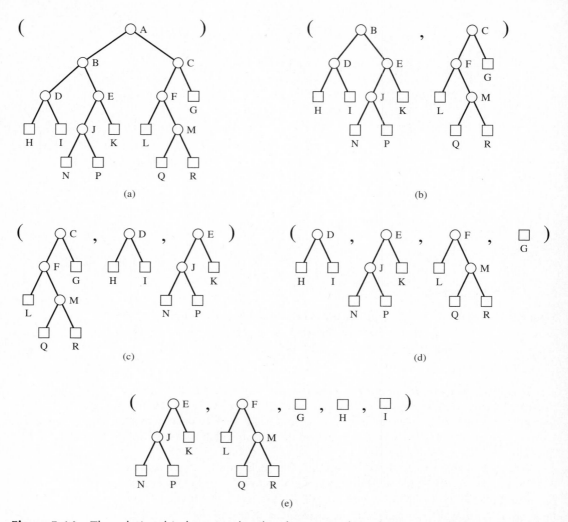

Figure 5.14   The relationship between level-order traversals and queues. (a) The initial queue. (b) After visiting the root node A. (c) After visiting node B. (d) After visiting node C. (e) After visiting node D.

require $\Omega(n)$ time, so we cannot improve the asymptotic running time of the traversals. But how much memory is needed? We have given recursive implementations of the depth-first traversals in Pascal, so they need extra memory for the underlying Pascal stack. (We can, however, rewrite the traversals in iterative form with a user-defined stack, similar to the implementation of the level-order traversal with a user-defined queue.) If each recursive call needs c cells, then a

```
procedure LevelOrderTraversal(T: BINTREE; Visit: procedure);
{LevelOrderTraversal performs a level-order traversal
    of the binary tree T that visits both internal and external nodes.
    It uses a queue of binary-tree windows as a subsiduary
    structure. It initializes the queue to consist of the root window
    of T. The user-defined procedure Visit is invoked whenever
    a node is visited.}
var v,w: window; Q: QUEUE;
begin
    Root(w,T); QEmpty(Q);
    QInsert(w,Q);

    while not QIsEmpty(Q) do
    begin QExamine(w,Q); QDelete(Q);
        Visit(w,T);
        if not IsExternal(w,T)
        then begin
            v:=  w; Left(v,T);
            QInsert(v,Q);
            Right(w,T);
            QInsert(w,Q)
        end
    end
end;
```

Program 5.2 A Pascal implementation of the level-order traversal of a binary tree.

binary tree of height h needs hc cells of stack memory. In the worst case, a tree of size n has height n; if we take a less jaundiced view of reality, however, then we expect the height of a binary tree of size n to be $\approx 2\sqrt{\pi n}$ when all binary trees of the same size are equally likely to occur. Under the probability distribution for binary search trees (see Section 8.5.5), we expect the height of a binary search tree of size n to be $4.31 \ln n + O(n)$. The derivations of these two expected-height values are beyond the scope of this text, even though the implications of the values are easy to see. The expected height of a binary tree is small when compared to that tree's size, and the expected extra memory needed by the depth-first traversals is small compared to the size of the given binary tree.

We can avoid almost all of the requirement for extra memory for a depth-first traversal if we embed the stack in the given tree. We explore two different ways of accomplishing this feat. First, in Section 5.5.3, we introduce threads that enable depth-first traversals to be implemented without a stack. Second, in Section 5.5.4, we introduce a simpler ADT for binary trees that allows us to use pointer reversal when traversing a tree.

When we use the level-order traversal of a binary tree, we cannot avoid the extra memory used by the associated queue. Essentially, the longest queue is obtained from a level that has the most nodes, the width of the traversed tree. We define the **width** of a tree to be the maximum number of nodes on a level. The width and the queue size are closely related; the queue size is never more than twice the width. The expected width of a binary tree, under the assumption that all binary trees of size n are equally likely to occur, is conjectured to be $\sqrt{\pi n/4}$. The expected width of a binary tree under the probability distribution for binary search trees defined in Section 8.5.5 is not known.

5.4 BINARY-TREE DISPLAY

When we test a program, we must ensure that intermediate values are displayed. Since pictorial information is easier to comprehend than lists of values, an intermediate tree is better displayed as a tree than as a list or table. Moreover, whenever a final result is a tree, we prefer to display it as a tree, rather than in some other form such as a list of node values according to some traversal order.

In this section, we describe one method of displaying trees. It assumes that the output medium consists of a fixed grid of cells—for example, a line printer, a matrix printer, or a terminal. Each cell can hold one character, and a character can appear in only a cell. Thus, we ignore high-resolution laser printers, graphics devices, and plotters. There are more appropriate methods for such devices, although the method we describe also can be used.

The method we describe produces tree displays that are compact, but that maintain legibility. We shall concentrate on binary trees; the display of multiway trees is left to Exercise 5.31.

Whatever method we choose to display a tree, the transparency of the tree's structure is enhanced if the display satisfies four basic rules of style.

1. Nodes at the same level should be displayed on the same horizontal line and in the same order.
2. Adjacent levels should be displayed adjacently.
3. The distance between two adjacent displayed levels should be the same throughout the display.
4. Parents should appear above and between their children.

When we draw binary trees, we usually center parents over their children; therefore, we have an additional rule that replaces rule 4:

5. Parents should be centered over their children.

We could satisfy rule 5 by, for each node u, not only centering u over its children, but also forcing u's left subtree to be laid out completely to the left of u and its right subtree to be laid out completely to the right of *u*. Such a display algorithm is the subject of Exercise 5.32. We do not require such a strict separation of left and right subtrees, so the algorithm that we give, *BintreeDisplay*, allows sibling subtrees to overlap when no confusion arises.

BintreeDisplay first assigns tentative horizontal positions to each node in a given tree. Then, based on these tentative positions, it computes their final positions. If a parent has tentative position *i*, then its left child has tentative position *i* − 1 and its right child has tentative position *i* + 1. We traverse the tree in postorder, so the leftmost node in the tree is assigned its final position before any other node is assigned.

Given a node *u* in a binary tree *T*, the **left neighbor** of *u* is the first node to *u*'s left on the same level. If *u* is leftmost on its level, then it has no left neighbor. Because of the traversal order, the left neighbor of a node *u* has already been assigned its final position when we visit *u*. To ensure minimal separation of left and right sibling subtrees, we require that each node be at least two positions to the right of its left neighbor. Thus the tentative position of a node must be at least two positions to the right of the final position of its left neighbor. For example, in Fig. 5.15, the tentative position of node *f* is 0, because its parent's tentative position is + 1. But, its left neighbor *e* has final position 0; so *f*'s tentative position must be + 2. A right shift occurs when we assign a tentative position to node *g*. The initial tentative position of *g* is + 2, but *f*, its left neighbor, has final position + 2, so we move *g* right to position + 4. In this case, the final position of *g* is even farther right, since *g*'s two children have to be moved right as well.

When a node's subtrees have been given their final positions, the node is centered over its children. Observe that the tentative positions of external nodes, perhaps modified by the nodes' left neighbors, are also their final positions. This fact guarantees both convergence and correctness.

To implement *BintreeDisplay*, we need to maintain the final positions of the current left neighbors. There is at most one left neighbor on each level and, ini-

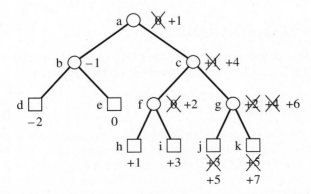

Figure 5.15 Tentative and final positions of nodes produced by *BintreeDisplay*.

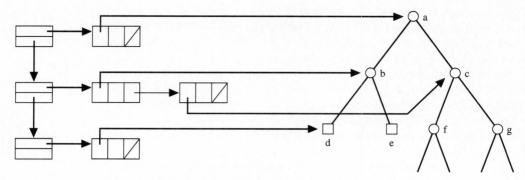

Figure 5.16   The node directory.

tially, there are none. As we wish to display a tree vertically, we need to compute the final positions of every node before we can assign a final position to the root of the tree and display the tree. For this reason, we maintain a directory of nodes, in the given binary tree, arranged in level order and by level. This arrangement is shown schematically in Fig. 5.16. We also keep the final positions of the tree nodes with the latter's directory entries. We have a list for each level, and these lists are also arranged as a list of lists. The list of node-position pairs is abstracted by the ADT *nodelist*, whereas the list of node lists is abstracted by the ADT *levellist*. We rename the *elementtype* ADT associated with *nodelist* as *nodeposition*; it has two entries: *node* and *position*. The final version of *BintreeDisplay* (see Program 5.3) consists of two steps. The initialization step uses *SetUp* to produce the node directory with the final positions of the nodes; see Program 5.4. After the node directory has been computed, the binary-tree layout is produced by *Display*; see Program 5.5. *Display* uses a subsidiary user-provided procedure *PrintNode* which you should supply; see Exercise 5.34.

5.5   BINTREE REPRESENTATIONS

We shall study applications of trees in Chapter 6. Here we consider the block and pointer representations of binary trees; we consider those of trees in Section 5.6.

5.5.1   Block Representations

The first representation of binary trees that we define is based on a representation of the **infinite binary tree.** The infinite binary tree is a binary tree in which every internal node has two internal children. Note that we can obtain every binary tree from the infinite binary tree by pruning the latter's subtrees; we say that every binary tree is a **prefix** of the infinite binary tree. We enumerate the nodes of the infinite binary tree in level order; Fig. 5.17 shows the **level-order enumeration.** We can represent a binary tree with a block using the correspondence between

```
procedure BintreeDisplay(T: BINTREE);
{BintreeDisplay produces a compacted display of the nodes
    of a binary tree; the branches are not shown. It first uses a
    reverse postorder traversal to compute the final positions of
    the nodes as described in Section 5.4, and to create a node
    directory. These actions are the function of SetUp and the sub-
    siduary procedure NLLeftNeighbor. Second, it displays the nodes
    using Display and the user-defined procedure PrintNode.}
var pos: integer; w: windowtype;
    llpane: LLwindowtype; LL: levellist;
    leftmostpos: integer;

    function NLLeftNeighbor(nlpane: NLwindowtype;
        NL: nodelist): integer;
    {NLLeftNeighbor returns the integer position of the binary-tree
        node referenced by the node in the window nlpane of
        the node list.}
    var npos: nodeposition;
    begin NLExamine(npos,nlpane,NL);
        NLLeftNeighbor:= npos.position
    end;
begin
    if IsEmpty(T)
    then writeln(outstream,'Empty tree in the tree display procedure')
    else begin {Initialize the level list.}
        Root(w,T); LLEmpty(LL);
        LLAfterLast(llpane,LL);
        {Compute the positions of the binary tree nodes.}
        leftmostpos:= 0; {This variable keeps track of the
                            leftmost computed position in SetUp.}
        pos:= 0;
        SetUp(w,T,pos,llpane,LL);
        {Display the binary tree using the computed positions.}
        Display(LL,T,leftmostpos)
    end
end;
```

Program 5.3   The binary tree display algorithm.

indices and nodes given by Fig. 5.17; the result is called the **level-order representation.** It provides an **implicit** representation of binary trees, since the
branches of the trees are not represented explicitly, as they are with a pointer representation, as we shall see in Section 5.5.2. For example, the binary tree in Fig.
5.18(a) can be represented with the block shown in Fig. 5.18(b). With this repre-

```
procedure SetUp(w: windowtype; T: BINTREE; var pos: integer;
               llpane: LLwindowtype; var LL: levellist);
{SetUp performs a postorder traversal of the subtree of T
    determined by the window w. On entry, pos is the tentative
    position of the node u in w. SetUp first adjusts this
    position by examining the position of u's left neighbor and ensuring
    that u is at least two units to the right of u's left neighbor.
    After the final positions of the nodes in u's two subtrees are
    computed, the final position of u is computed as the middle position
    between the positions of u's children. SetUp also
    links together the nodes on the same level in a node-position list,
    then links these lists, in turn, with a level list to enable
    Display to traverse the binary tree simply, in level order, to
    obtain the final display.}
var npos: nodeposition; NL: nodelist; nlpane: NLwindowtype;
    rightpos, leftpos: integer;
    rightw, leftw: windowtype; temppane: LLwindowtype;

begin
    if LLIsAfterLast(llpane,LL)
    then begin {Extend the level list by creating an empty node list.}
        NLEmpty(NL);
        LLInsertBefore(NL,llpane,LL); LLPrevious(llpane,LL)
    end;
    LLExamine(NL,llpane,LL);
    NLAfterLast(nlpane,NL); NLPrevious(nlpane,NL);

    if not NLIsBeforeFirst(nlpane,NL)
    then if NLLeftNeighbor(nlpane,NL) + 2 > pos
        then pos:= NLLeftNeighbor(nlpane,NL) + 2;

    if not IsExternal(w,T)
    then begin
        leftw:= w; Left(leftw,T); leftpos:= pos - 1;
        temppane:= llpane; LLNext(temppane,LL);
        SetUp(leftw,T,leftpos,temppane,L);
        rightw:= w; Right(rightw,T); rightpos:= pos + 1;
        temppane:= llpane; LLNext(temppane,LL);
        SetUp(rightw,T,rightpos,temppane,LL);
        {Compute the final position of the node in w.}
        pos:= (leftpos + rightpos) div 2;
    end;
```

Program 5.4   The procedure *SetUp* that is used in the binary tree display algorithm
(continued next page).

```
        {Add the node in w to the appropriate node list.}
        npos.position:= pos; npos.node:= w;
        if pos > leftmostpos
        then leftmostpos:= pos;
        NLInsertAfter(npos,nlpane,NL)
    end;
```

Program 5.4   (concluded)

```
    procedure Display(LL: levellist; T: BINTREE;
                leftmostpos: integer);
    {Display performs a level-order traversal of the binary tree T
        by traversing each node list in the level list LL. During each
        node-list traversal, it displays the nodes on the given level at
        their final positions relative to the leftmost position given
        by leftmostpos.}
    var NL: nodelist; nlpane: NLwindowtype;
        llpane: LLwindowtype; npos: nodeposition;
        currentpos: integer;

    begin LLBeforeFirst(llpane,LL); LLNext(llpane,LL);
        writeln(outstream);
        while not LLIsAfterLast(llpane,LL)
        do begin
            LLExamine(NL,llpane,LL);
            NLBeforeFirst(nlpane,NL); NLNext(nlpane,NL);
            currentpos:= 0;
            while not NLIsAfterLast(nlpane,NL)
            do begin
                NLExamine(npos,nlpane,NL);
                PrintNode(npos.node,npos.position - leftmostpos -
                    currentpos,T)
                currentpos:= npos.position + 1;
                NLNext(nlpane,NL);
            end;
            writeln(outstream);
            LLNext(llpane,LL)
        end
    end;
```

Program 5.5   The procedure *Display* that produces the final display of a binary tree.

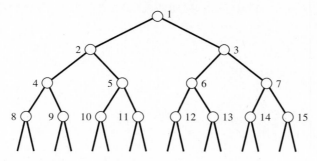

Figure 5.17   The level-order enumeration of the nodes
of the infinite binary tree.

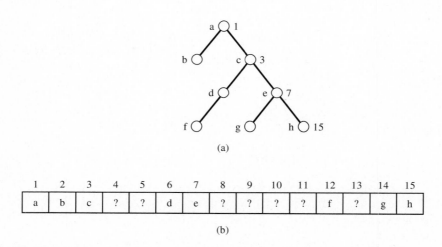

Figure 5.18   Level-order representation of binary trees. (a) A binary tree.
(b) The level-order representation of the tree's internal nodes.

sentation, the highest-numbered node determines the block size; for example, the
highest-numbered node of the binary tree in Fig. 5.18(a) is 15. The level-order
enumeration of the infinite binary tree has a number of important properties, of
which we give only the following, where $\iota(u)$ denotes the index associated with
node u:

1. $\iota(u) = 1$ only when u is the root.
2. The number of the left child of u is $2 \times \iota(u)$.
3. The number of the right child of u is $2 \times \iota(u) + 1$.
4. The number of the parent of u is $\lfloor \iota(u)/2 \rfloor$, unless u is the root, in which
    case it is undefined.

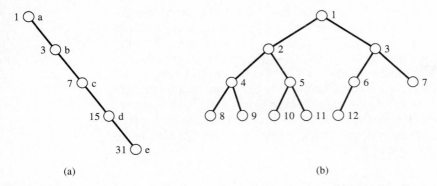

(a)   (b)

Figure 5.19 Level-order representations. (a) Representation of a skinny tree. (b) Representation of a left-complete tree.

These relationships ensure that the BINTREE operations can be implemented in constant time. Much memory can be wasted, however, as shown by the representation of the skinny tree in Fig. 5.19(a); alternatively, no memory may be wasted, as shown by the representation of the left-complete tree in Fig. 5.19(b). The skinny tree requires a block of size 31, but uses only five cells, whereas the left-complete tree requires a block of size 12 and uses all 12 cells. In general, a tree may require a block of $2^h - 1$ cells, for some $h \geq 1$, and use between h and $2^h - 1$ of the cells. In other words, although a binary tree of size n requires only n cells, these n cells may be scattered in a block of size $2^n - 1$. Despite the possibility of wasted memory, the level-order representation can be useful, as we shall see in Chapter 11.

We close this subsection by mentioning one other edgeless representation, the **degree representation.** We enumerate the nodes of a binary tree in postorder, and associate an integer between 0 and 3 with each node. For example, the binary trees of Fig. 5.18(a) and Fig. 5.19(a) are represented as shown in Figures 5.20(a) and (b), respectively. The integer associated with each node indicates whether that node has no internal children (0), a single left internal child (1), a single right

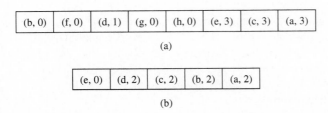

| (b, 0) | (f, 0) | (d, 1) | (g, 0) | (h, 0) | (e, 3) | (c, 3) | (a, 3) |

(a)

| (e, 0) | (d, 2) | (c, 2) | (b, 2) | (a, 2) |

(b)

Figure 5.20 The degree representation of two binary trees. (a) Representation of the tree of Fig. 5.18(a). (b) Representation of the tree of Fig. 5.19(a).

internal child (2), or two internal children (3). These values are easier to comprehend when expressed as the binary numbers 00, 10, 01, and 11, respectively. In
the degree representation, the operation *Right(u)* is easy to implement. Given the
index *i,* in postorder, of a node *u,* the index of *u*'s right internal child, if there is
one, is $i - 1$. On the other hand, the index of *u*'s left child is known only to be earlier than *i,* and the index of *u*'s parent is known only to be later than *i.* Although
the indices can be determined algorithmically (see Exercise 5.35), they are not
immediate. This difficulty is the basis for the study of representations in which
only one edge from each node is represented implicitly, rather than both being
thus represented; see Exercise 5.36.

5.5.2   Pointer Representations

The first pointer representation of binary trees in Pascal follows the recursive definition of binary trees closely:

```
type linktype = ↑celltype;
     celltype = record
                     links: array[1..2] of linktype;
                     item: elementtype;
                 end;
     BINTREE = linktype;
```

The use of a block of two links to point to the two children of a node is close in
spirit to the node map in the definition of binary trees. In the pointer representations of LIST, we have a before-first cell; here, we have a before-root cell. Since
external nodes are similar to the after-last position in a list, we assign cells to
them as we did for the after-last position. To complete the BINTREE representation, we need to define an appropriate *windowtype* representation. The simplest
representation is to let a window be a pointer to the cell representing the node in
the window; see Fig. 5.21.

Rather than taking this simplistic approach, we prefer a more complex representation of a window for two reasons: it illustrates a different approach, and it
avoids parent finding or element swapping during insertion and deletion. (Compare our choice for BINTREE with the choice that we made for the singly linked
list representation of LIST.)

For the new window representation, we require that a window variable point
to the parent of the node in the window; see Fig. 5.21. This change in window
representation is one reason that we introduced a before-root cell. Because an
internal node has two children, the new *windowtype* representation is insufficient
to determine a node uniquely. We resolve this ambiguity by adding to a window
variable a second two-valued field that indicates which child is intended. We use

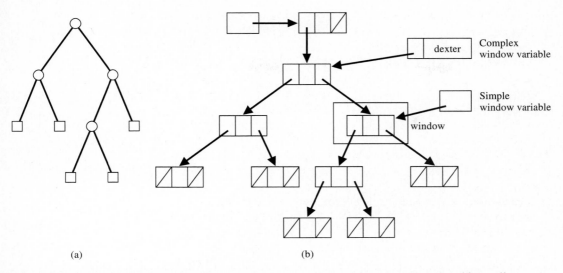

(a)   (b)

Figure 5.21   A BINTREE representation in which external nodes are represented by cells. (a) A binary tree. (b) Representation with the two choices of *windowtype* representation.

the constants *sinister* and *dexter* (the Latin words for left and right) for this purpose. Thus, in Pascal, we have the following additional type declarations:

```
type  directiontype = (sinister,dexter);
      windowtype = record
                       pane: linktype;
                       branch: directiontype
                   end;
```

Pictorially, the two links in a cell that point to the left and right subtrees are split such that the left link appears at the left of the cell and the right link at the right. In Programs 5.6 and 5.7, we provide an implementation of several BINTREE operations based on this representation. It is easy to see that all BINTREE operations, apart from *Parent*, can be implemented to run in constant time. With the singly linked representation of LIST given in Section 3.4.2, we implemented the analogous operation *Previous* by traversing the list from the before-first cell. Similarly, we implement *Parent* by traversing the tree from the root until we reach the parent of the given node. A preorder traversal is the most appropriate traversal. Thus, *Parent* takes $O(n)$ time, in the worst case, with a binary tree of size n. As we shall see in Section 5.5.4, we can obtain a faster implementation of *Parent* when we use a simpler tree ADT. Note that the pointer representations of BINTREE that we suggest are all similar to the singly linked list representation

```
procedure Empty(var T: BINTREE);
begin
    new(T);
    with T ↑do links[1]:= nil
end;


function IsEmpty(T: BINTREE): boolean;
begin
    with T ↑do
        IsEmpty:= links[1] = nil
end;


procedure Root(var w: windowtype; T: BINTREE);
begin
    with w do
    begin branch:= sinister;
        pane:= T
    end
end;
```

Program 5.6   A pointer implementation of *Empty*, *IsEmpty*, and *Root* for binary trees in which external nodes are also represented by cells.

of LIST. We can obtain a constant-time implementation of *Parent* by using the tree analog of doubly linked lists; that is, we add parent links to each cell. This representation is not normally used because of the extra space required for the extra link in each cell. In Exercise 5.37, you are asked to implement this scheme and to suggest when it could be used.

Because an internal node in a binary tree has only two links associated with it, a popular alternative representation is the following:

```
type linktype = ↑celltype;
    celltype = record
                    left: linktype;
                    item: elementtype;
                    right: linktype;
                end;
    BINTREE = linktype;
```

with *windowtype* defined as before. Diagrammatically, there is no change.

If we do not associate values with external nodes, then we can represent these nodes with the pointer constant **nil**. In Fig. 5.22, we show such a pointer representation of a binary tree. On the other hand, if values are associated with external nodes, then, rather than assigning space for links in external nodes, we can use variant records (or discriminated unions), in Pascal and in other program-

```
procedure Left(var w: windowtype; T: BINTREE);
var node: linktype;
begin
    with w do
    case branch of
sinister: begin node:= pane ↑. links[1];
                if node = nil
                then error('No left child ')
                else pane:= node
          end;
dexter: begin node:= pane ↑. links[2];
                if node = nil
                then error('No right child ')
                else begin pane:= node;
                    branch:= sinister
                end
          end
    end
end;

procedure Insert(e: elementtype; w: windowtype; T: BINTREE);
var newnode: linktype;
begin
    with w do
    case branch of
sinister: if pane ↑. links[1] = nil
          then begin new(newnode);
              pane ↑. links[1]:= newnode;
              newnode ↑. links[1]:= nil;
              newnode ↑. links[2]:= nil;
              newnode ↑. item:= e;
          end
          else error('Insertion at an internal node')
dexter: if pane ↑. links[2] = nil
          then begin new(newnode);
              pane ↑. links[2]:= newnode;
              newnode ↑. links[1]:= nil;
              newnode ↑. links[2]:= nil;
              newnode ↑. item:= e;
          end
          else error('Insertion at an internal node')
    end
end;
```

Program 5.7 A pointer implementation of *Left* and *Insert* for binary trees in which external nodes are represented by cells.

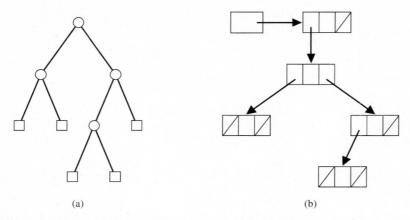

(a)   (b)

Figure 5.22   The BINTREE representation in which external nodes are
represented by the value **nil**. (a) A binary tree.
(b) Its representation.

ming languages, for internal and external nodes. For example, we can declare the
following variant-record type for binary trees in Pascal:

```
type nodetype = (external,internal);
     linktype = ↑celltype;
     celltype = record
                  case node: nodetype of
                      internal: (left: linktype;
                                      item: intelementtype;
                                      right: linktype);
                      external: (item: extelementtype)
              end;
     BINTREE = linktype;
```

As a result, we can represent the binary tree of Fig. 5.22(a), as shown in Fig. 5.23.

5.5.3   Threaded Trees

The depth-first traversals of a binary tree that we have introduced in Section 5.3.1
have two drawbacks. First, they require extra memory for a stack. Second, we
cannot use them to traverse part of a tree. In Section 8.5.7, we implement range
searching for binary search trees by traversing only part of a tree, rather than the
entire tree. (If we need to traverse a subtree completely, then we can use the traversals as we have implemented them in Section 5.3.1.) To avoid the extra mem-
ory used by a stack, we introduce a new operation *InorderSuccessor*: $\mathcal{W} \times \mathcal{BT} \rightarrow$
$\mathcal{W}$. The function value *InorderSuccessor*(w,T) gives the window of the cell that is
the inorder-successor cell of the cell in w. We modify the first pointer representa-

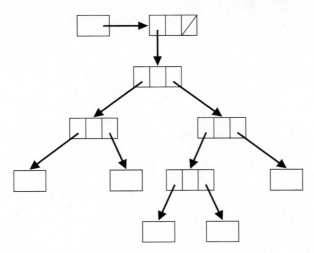

Figure 5.23   The variant-record representation
of the binary tree of Fig. 5.22(a).

tion of a binary tree (see Section 5.5.2) by using the link fields in the cells of the
external nodes. Each left link in an external-node cell points to the inorder-prede-
cessor cell, and each right link points to the inorder-successor cell. If a cell has no
predecessor or no successor, then the corresponding link is **nil**. These extra links
are called **threads.** In Fig. 5.24(a), we give a binary tree and its additional inorder
branches, which are shown with dashed lines; in Fig. 5.24(b), we illustrate the
threaded representation. To distinguish between the original tree links and the
threads, we need 1 extra bit in each link field. All the BINTREE operations, apart
from *Parent*, can still be implemented to run in constant time; see Exercise 5.38.

Given the threaded representation of a binary tree, we can find the inorder
successor of a cell x in the tree as follows. If the right link of x is a thread, then the
cell to which it points is the inorder successor, unless the thread is **nil**, in which
case there is no successor cell. Otherwise, the right link is a tree link. In this case,
the cell given by the right link either has a thread as its left link and is the successor, or it does not and it corresponds to an internal node. If the right child is an
internal cell, then we follow left links until we meet an external cell; this external
cell is the inorder-successor cell. The four different possibilities are shown in Fig.
5.25.

It is clear that any one call to *InorderSuccessor* can take $O(h)$ time for a
binary tree of height h;[1] however, we can use n successive calls to traverse a
binary tree of size n in $O(n)$ time—yet another amortization result. We leave the

[1] Strictly speaking, the time is bounded by the the longest left-descendant path in the tree.

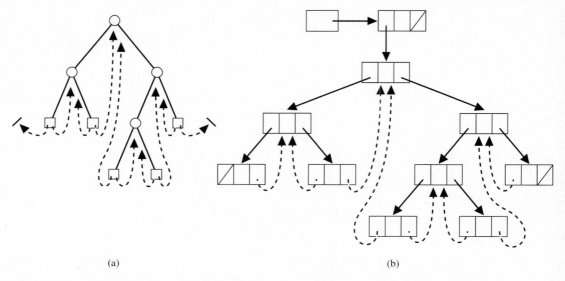

(a)   (b)

Figure 5.24   Threaded representation of BINTREE. (a) A binary tree with additional inorder
branches. (b) Its threaded representation.

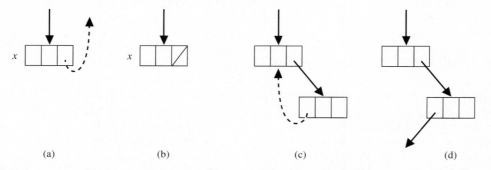

(a)   (b)   (c)   (d)

Figure 5.25   The inorder-successor possibilities of a node in a threaded binary tree. (a) The
right link is a thread and it is not **nil**. (b) The right link is a **nil** thread.(c) The right
link is a tree link, and the cell is gives has a thread as its left link. (d) The right
link is a tree link, and the cell it gives has a tree link as its left link.

proof of this fact to Exercise 5.39. To perform an inorder traversal of a binary
tree, we need to find only the leftmost external node to begin the traversal. The
leftmost external node is always found on the **left spine;** beginning at the root, we
repeatedly branch left until an external node is reached.

It is somewhat surprising that we can use the threads to implement preorder
traversal without a stack in $O(n)$ time, for a binary tree of size n; we leave this
implementation to Exercise 5.40.

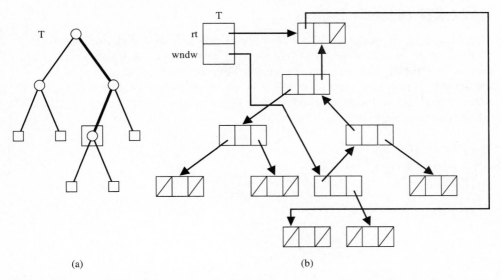

Figure 5.26 The use of pointer reversal in the pointer representation of SBINTREE to avoid using extra memory for a stack. (a) A binary tree and a path drawn with thick branches. (b) The reversed-pointer representation of the tree and path.

5.5.4 Pointer Reversal

We can specify a simpler ADT, SBINTREE, for binary trees, as we did for lists with SIMPLIST. SBINTREE is sufficient for many situations; it has one implicit window and has explicit window-manipulation operations. We leave the details of its specification to Exercise 5.41. Once we have one window, we can use pointer reversal when we navigate in a pointer representation of a binary tree to obtain a constant-time implementation of *Parent*. Also, this technique enables us to avoid using extra memory for a stack during a depth-first traversal, although we still need the extra memory for a queue during a level-order traversal. Finally, we can prove an amortized result for a sequence of SBINTREE operations that corresponds to the amortized result for a sequence of SIMPLIST operations.

Pointer reversal in trees has one problem that pointer reversal in lists does not have; namely, a node has two successors rather than one. Hence, we have no way of knowing which link in a cell has been reversed. For this reason, we use 1 extra bit in each cell. The extra bit is 0 if the left link is reversed and is 1 if the right link is reversed. In Fig. 5.26, we show a binary tree, represented with the first pointer representation, that has three reversed pointers. Note that we define a window variable to be a pointer to the cell in the window. The details of the pointer implementation of the SBINTREE operations are left to Exercise 5.42, as is the proof of the amortization result for a valid sequence of SBINTREE operations on an initially empty tree.

5.6 TREE REPRESENTATIONS

Block representations of multiway trees should be avoided, because they are wasteful of memory; see Exercise 5.45. The pointer representations of binary trees, however, can be adapted for trees. The major difference is that nodes can have any number of children, rather than only two, so we keep the degree of a node with each cell and we represent a node map of pointers with a block, as we did for the first pointer representation of binary trees.

```
const maxdegree = ?;
type linktype = ↑celltype;
     degreetype = 0..maxdegree;
     linkstype = array[1..maxdegree] of linktype;
     celltype = record
                      item: elementtype;
                      degree: degreetype;
                      links: linkstype;
                 end;
     BINTREE = linktype;
```

The implementation of the TREE operations when trees are represented with this **pointer-block representation** is left to Exercise 5.46.

An alternative representation, the **pointer-list representation,** uses a linked-list representation of the node map. The disadvantage of this representation is that the power of indexing is lost; retrieving the ith link takes $\Omega(i)$ time. Despite this drawback, the linked-list representation is useful when the loss of indexing is of little consequence—for example, for high-degree trees that are stored externally (see Chapter 10). The pointer-list representation can be viewed as a map of trees to binary trees in the following sense. (We consider two such maps, one here and one in Exercise 5.49.) For each node in a multiway tree, we add horizontal branches from its first child to its second child, from its second child to its third child, and so on. Then, we remove all parent–child branches except for the parent–first-child branches. This process and its result are illustrated in Fig. 5.27(a). Observe that each node now has at most two branches—one vertical branch and one horizontal branch; thus, the tree is a binary tree (see the redrawn binary tree of Fig. 5.27b). It can be shown that every multiway tree is mapped to a unique binary tree by this process; see Exercise 5.47. We can think of the binary-tree representation of a multiway tree as a formalization of the pointer-list representation. In the pointer-list representation, accessing the first child of a node takes constant time, whereas accessing the ith child requires $\Omega(i)$ time. This fact is confirmed in the binary-tree representation of a multiway tree, because the ith child of a node u in a multiway tree becomes the ith descendant of the node corresponding to u in the binary-tree representation.

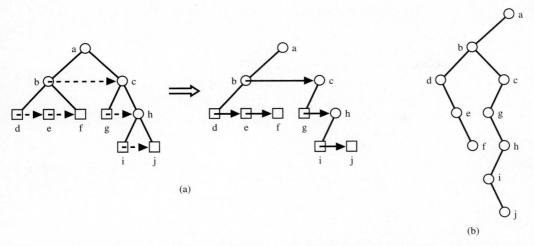

Figure 5.27 Conversion of a multiway tree into a binary tree. (a) The addition of horizontal branches and removal of all parent–child branches apart from the branches to the first children. (b) The resulting tree redrawn.

5.7 PERFORMANCE REPORTS

In Table 5.1, we summarize the asymptotic worst-case and expected-case time bounds for the three binary-tree representations we have introduced. We rate the three schemes in Table 5.2. The pointer representation is a clear winner, since it is

Table 5.1 A comparison of the worst-case execution times of the three BINTREE implementations.

	BINTREE implementation		
Operation	Level-order	Pointer	Degree
Empty	1	1	1
IsEmpty	1	1	1
Root	1	1	1
IsRoot	1	1	1
IsExternal	1	1	1
Child	1	1	n
Parent	1	n	n
IntExamine	1	1	1
ExtExamine	1	1	1
IntReplace	1	1	1
ExtReplace	1	1	1
Insert	1	1	n
Delete	1	1	n

Table 5.2   Performance ratings of the three BINTREE implementations.

BINTREE implementation	Rating	Comments
Pointer	Excellent	Fully dynamic
Level-order	Good	Implicit pointers; constant space overhead
Degree	Satisfactory	Linear time for *Left* and *Parent*

Table 5.3   A comparison of the worst-case execution times of the two TREE implementations.

	TREE Implementation	
Operation	Pointer-block	Pointer-list
Empty	1	1
IsEmpty	1	1
Root	1	1
IsRoot	1	1
IsExternal	1	1
Degree	1	1
Child	1	n
Parent	n	n
IntExamine	1	1
ExtExamine	1	1
IntReplace	1	1
ExtReplace	1	1
Insert	1	1
Delete	1	1

fully dynamic and uses $O(n)$ cells for a binary tree of size n. Its only disadvantage is that *Parent* takes linear time in the worst case. Fortunately, most applications do not need the operation *Parent*, and, in many applications that do need *Parent*, the SBINTREE ADT can be used to give a constant-time implementation of *Parent*. As we have pointed out, the level-order representation can require $2^n - 1$ cells for a binary tree of size n; this storage inefficiency is a serious drawback. Nonetheless, it is an interesting scheme because branches are represented implicitly with no memory overhead, whereas the pointer representation explicitly represents branches as pointers, so it needs additional memory. Since the degree representation is also a block representation that takes linear time, in the worst case, to execute *Left* and *Parent*, it is rarely used.

In Table 5.3, the worst-case time bounds for the two pointer implementations of TREE are summarized. The pointer representation with a block representation of the node map wins easily from this point of view; see Table 5.4. For disk-based

Table 5.4 Performance ratings of the two TREE implementations.

TREE implementation	Rating	Comments
Pointer-block	Excellent	Good for both internally and externally stored trees
Pointer-list	Very good	Good for externally stored trees

multiway trees, however, the pointer representation with a list representation of the node map is also acceptable. For disk-based multiway trees, the time taken to access a child of a node is infinitesimal compared to the time taken for a disk transfer.

5.8 SUMMARY

We introduced the hierarchical data structures known as (indexed) trees in their binary and multiway forms, and described their basic properties. Binary (indexed) trees have nodes with either two children (internal nodes) or no children (external nodes). If a node is internal, we can speak of its first and second child—the children are indexed. Multiway (indexed) trees are defined similarly, except that internal nodes can have one or more children, and they need not have the same number of children. The children are still indexed, however, so that we can speak of the ith child.

We related the height and size of binary trees, and gave a formula for the number of binary trees of the same size. There are $\mathcal{B}_n$ binary trees of size n, for all $n \geq 0$. We specified two ADTs, BINTREE and TREE, that can be used for many tree-based algorithms, as we shall see. In particular, we defined the two basic methods of binary-tree traversal, depth first and level order, and showed how we can implement them using the BINTREE operations. A depth-first traversal explores a tree from the root to the frontier by traversing the first subtree of the root in a depth-first manner and then traversing the second subtree of the root. A level-order traversal, on the other hand, explores a tree level by level. Furthermore, there are three depth-first traversals—preorder, inorder, and postorder—that give rise to prefix, infix, and postfix expressions when an expression tree is traversed.

We have given a tree-display algorithm that creates pleasing displays in time linear in the size of the tree. Moreover, we introduced rules of style for binary-tree displays that can be used to evaluate such displays.

We considered both block and pointer representations of BINTREE and TREE. The implementations of the ADT operations that we have given show the viability of both approaches. For both BINTREE and TREE, we normally choose pointer representations, because they are fully dynamic and also are efficient in both time and space. If we are representing binary trees that have restricted shape, then the level-order representation can be extremely useful, as we shall see in Chapter 11. Block representations of the ADT TREE are not used because they waste space. Normally, the ADT TREE is used for externally stored multiway trees when the nodes are represented with blocks, rather than with lists.

5.9 HISTORY

Trees appeared early in the history of computer science; however, the explicit notion of an indexed tree apparently is new, originating in discussions with Frank Tompa (1990). The binary-tree display algorithm is based on the algorithm of Vaucher (1980). The representations of binary trees and trees discussed here are well known; for example, see Knuth (1968). Threads were first proposed by Perlis and Thornton in 1960. Pointer reversal, in the more general setting of memory management, was presented by Deutsch and Bobrow (1966), Schorr and Waite (1967). Surprisingly, the analysis of the expected height and width of binary trees is recent. Flajolet and Odlyzko (1982) solved the expected-height problem, under the assumption that all trees of the same size are equally likely, and Devroye (1986) solved it for the binary-search-tree model. The expected width of binary trees has been found, under the assumption that all trees of the same size are equally likely, by Aldous (1991); Odlyzko and Wilf (1987) have established both upper and lower bounds on the width of trees (not only binary trees), under the assumption that all trees of the same size are equally likely. The corresponding result for the binary-search-tree model has not been solved.

EXERCISES

5.1: Which of the following drawings represent binary trees?

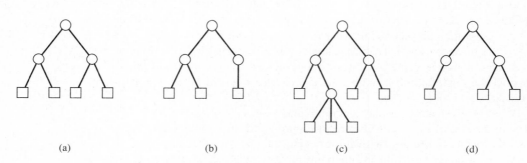

(a)   (b)   (c)   (d)

5.2: Given the following binary trees, is node 1 a descendant of node 2, a sibling of node 2, a parent of node 2, or an ancestor of node 2?

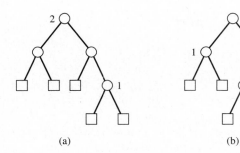

(a)   (b)

5.3: How many binary trees are there of size 4?

5.4: How many multiway trees are there of size 4?

5.5: Draw binary trees of height 4 that have minimum and maximum sizes.

5.6: Which of the following pairs of binary trees are isomorphic?

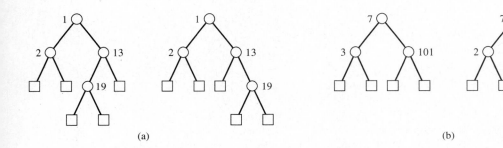

(a)   (b)

5.7: Write a Pascal procedure that, given two nodes in a binary tree, returns their closest common ancestor.

5.8: For a binary tree T, prove that the descendant relations $desc_T$ and $ldesc_T$ are partial orders. Define $rdesc_T$.

5.9: A binary tree defines a descendant relation between nodes in the binary tree. If you are given a relation between nodes in a binary tree, under what conditions is it the descendant relation of a binary tree? Write a Pascal procedure to test whether a relation is the descendant relation of some binary tree.

5.10: Prove that, for a binary tree T, the left-of relation $left_T$ is a total order.

5.11: Generalize to multiway trees the notions of descendant relation and left-of relation.

5.12:   Consider the following operation:

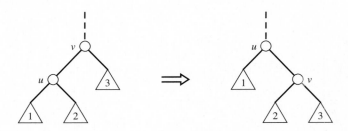

Given two binary trees of the same size, we can transform one of the trees into the other tree using a sequence of these operations. Show that this assertion is true by giving an algorithm that performs this transformation for any two binary trees of the same size.

5.13:   Interpret the nodes of a binary tree to be houses, and interpret the edges to determine paths between the houses. Assume that *Examine*(w,T) returns a house name, and that all house names are distinct. Write a search procedure that returns the shortest path (number of edges) between two given houses in the same binary tree.

5.14:   We say that a binary tree A is a *prefix* of a binary tree B if we can apply the operation

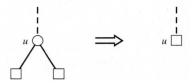

zero or more times to B to obtain a binary tree isomorphic to A. Implement an algorithm to determine whether a binary tree is a prefix of another binary tree. Describe how this algorithm can be used to test for the equality of two trees.

5.15:   We say that a binary tree A is a *suffix* of a binary tree B if we can apply the operation

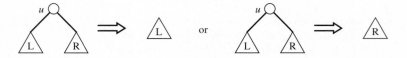

zero or more times to the root of B to obtain a binary tree isomorphic to A. Implement an algorithm to determine whether a binary tree is a suffix of another binary tree.

5.16: We say that a binary tree A is a *subtree* of a binary tree B if we can apply the two operations of Exercises 5.14 and 5.15 zero or more times to B to obtain a binary tree isomorphic to A. Implement an algorithm to determine whether a binary tree is a subtree of another binary tree.

5.17: Prove that the number of external nodes in a binary tree is 1 more than the tree's size.

What relationship is there between the number of external nodes and size of multiway trees of degree $d > 1$?

5.18: Let T be a ternary indexed tree of size n; that is, either T is empty if $n = 0$, or T has a root u and subtrees $u(1)$, $u(2)$, and $u(3)$ such that the sum of their sizes is $n - 1$. For each integer $n > 1$, there are binary trees with n external nodes. Does this fact hold for ternary trees? Either prove that it does or show what numbers of external nodes are possible.

5.19: Generalize Exercise 5.18 to d-ary trees.

5.20: Prove that a binary tree of height at most $h \geq 0$ has size at most $2^h - 1$. Prove that a binary tree of size $n \geq 0$ has height at least $\lceil \log (n + 1) \rceil$.

5.21: Define the terminology for multiway trees that corresponds to the terminology introduced for binary trees in Section 5.1.1.

5.22: We sometimes need to test two data structures for equality. As we pointed out in Section 3.2, equality testing is, in mathematical terminology, isomorphism testing: Two equal structures should have nodes and branches at corresponding places and should have the same values at corresponding nodes.

Design and implement a recursive Pascal Boolean function *IsEqual* that returns **true** if its two binary-tree arguments are equal and returns **false** otherwise. For this purpose, assume the existence of two Boolean functions *InIsEqual* and *ExIsEqual* that determine whether two values of type *intelementtype* and *extelementtype*, respectively, are equal.

5.23: Design and implement a Pascal procedure *Copy* that makes an equal copy of a given binary tree; that is, *Copy(S,T)*, where S and T are both of type BINTREE, assigns a copy of binary tree S to T. The copies should not share any cells.

5.24: Design and implement the following three recursive Pascal procedures that construct binary trees with undefined values at their nodes.
  a. *BuildSkinny(n,T)*, which assigns T a skinny tree of size n.
  b. *BuildMinHt(n,T)*, which assigns T a minimal-height tree of size n.
  c. *BuildLeftComplete(n,T)*, which assigns T a left-complete tree of size n.

5.25: Modify the tree traversals given in Section 5.3 to visit only internal nodes. Modify them to visit only external nodes.

5.26: Design and implement Pascal procedures for the postorder and preorder traversals of binary trees.

5.27: Define depth-first traversals for multiway trees. How do they differ from those for binary trees?

5.28:   Complete the level-order traversal example of Fig. 5.14.

5.29:   Develop an iterative procedure for one of the depth-first traversals of binary trees using a stack.

5.30:   Develop a traversal algorithm for binary trees that performs a depth-first or level-order traversal depending on whether the queue or stack operations are chosen.

5.31:   Suggest two ways of displaying multiway trees. Implement one of your suggestions.

5.32:   It is easier to compute a layout of a binary tree if we require that the left subtree of a node be completely to that node's left, and that the right subtree of a node be completely to that node's right. We can compute the final positions of nodes immediately, when we perform a postorder traversal. Implement and test a new version of *SetUp* that computes the final positions in this manner.

5.33:   *BintreeDisplay* does not print the branches of the displayed trees; modify it to include their printing.

5.34:   *BintreeDisplay* needs the user-defined procedure *PrintNode*; design and implement one version of *PrintNode*.

5.35:   Design algorithms to find the index of a node's left child and a node's parent in the degree representation of a binary tree.

5.36:   We can define a single-branch representation of a binary tree as follows. A binary tree of size n is represented in the first n cells of a block in preorder. The root and the size of the binary tree are assigned to the first cell, and the left and right subtrees are assigned in preorder to the remaining cells in the same way. Each cell holds both a binary-tree node and the size of that node's corresponding subtree. What are the worst-case time bounds for the BINTREE operations using this representation?

Specify the new operation *Sibling* that, given a window w and a binary tree, returns the window over the sibling of the node in w, if there is one. *Sibling* cannot be implemented efficiently with the BINTREE operations; therefore, we specify a new ADT that has *Sibling* and all the BINTREE operations. Implement *Sibling* in the representation described. What is the worst-case performance of your algorithm?

5.37:   Implement and test a pointer representation of BINTREE that includes a parent link in each cell. Under what circumstances would you recommend using this representation?

5.38:   Implement and test the BINTREE operations for the threaded representation of binary trees suggested in Section 5.5.3. Ensure that your implemented operations all run in constant time, apart from *Parent*.

5.39:   Given the operation *InorderSuccessor*, implemented in the threaded representation of binary trees (see Section 5.5.3), prove that an inorder traversal of a binary tree of size n can be implemented without use of extra memory for a stack. Furthermore, prove that this implementation of inorder traversal runs in $O(n)$ time.

5.40:   Given the operation *InorderSuccessor* for binary trees, show how it can be used to implement a preorder traversal without a stack. Prove that, in the threaded representation of Section 5.5.3, your implementation gives an $O(n)$-time traversal for a size-n binary tree.

5.41:   Specify the ADT SBINTREE.

5.42: Using the pointer representation suggested in Section 5.5.4, implement and test the SBINTREE operations. Prove that any valid sequence of n SBINTREE operations on an initially empty tree takes $O(n)$ time.

5.43: Give an example of a binary tree whose structure cannot be uniquely determined from any one of its traversals.

5.44: There are two different traversals of the same binary tree, from which we can reconstruct the unique binary tree. Suggest two such traversals and prove that they allow a correct reconstruction. Give two traversals that do not allow such a reconstruction.

5.45: Explain the observation that block representations are not usually used for multiway trees. Describe how much space these representations waste.

5.46: Implement the ADT operations for TREE using the block-of-links representation.

5.47: Given the map of multiway trees to binary trees described in Section 5.6, show that it is injective. Also extend the map to orchards of binary trees. Prove that your extended map is bijective.

5.48: Implement the map of multiway trees to binary trees given in Section 5.6. What is the performance of your algorithm?

5.49: A second method of representing multiway trees as binary trees is to represent a node of degree 1 with a binary node whose right subtree is never used, and to represent a node of degree $d \geq 2$ with a minimal-height binary tree with d external nodes. We need to distinguish between nodes that correspond to the multiway-tree nodes and those that are additional nodes. One method is to use two colors: black for those nodes that correspond to the original nodes, and red for the additional nodes. We also blacken the external nodes of the binary tree. The two colors can be represented by one bit.

Implement the TREE operations based on this representation. What is the worst-case performance of each of the TREE operations?

5.50: For the transformation of trees to binary trees given in Exercise 5.49, show that the height of the resulting binary tree is bounded by the product of the height of the multiway tree and the logarithm of the maximum degree. Show that the height is not thus bounded for the transformation given in Section 5.6. What bound can you prove in this case?

5.51: Implement an algorithm to transform an expression into an expression tree. Implement an algorithm to transform an expression tree into postfix form.

CHAPTER 6

Applications of Trees

Our purpose in this and later chapters is to demonstrate the breadth of application of trees in computer science. We have used trees to represent arithmetic and Boolean expressions (and indeed other kinds of expressions) in Section 5.3. Expression trees are a valuable representation of expressions, since they provide a simple means to manipulate expressions algebraically. Algebraic manipulation of expressions is useful in symbolic algebra systems and in the compilation of programming languages such as Pascal.

The first applications we consider in this chapter are coding and data compression. In particular, we define optimal variable-length binary codes and code trees and give Huffman's algorithm, which constructs them. Not only does Huffman's algorithm produce optimal variable-length binary codes, but also it does so by using *greediness,* an algorithmic technique that is simple, yet powerful.

Code trees also provide an example of *binary tries*, since they are binary trees in which each internal node has one branch for each symbol 0 and 1. The name *trie* comes from the word re*trie*val. Binary tries are a special case of the more general *multiway tries,* in which each internal node has one branch for each letter in a given alphabet. This notion leads into our second application: a spell checker. We introduce multiway tries as one approach to constructing spell checkers. (We return to tries in Chapter 7, when we use *suffix tries* to provide fast text searching.)

Finally, we introduce a new representation of the ADT ARRAY based on binary tries. The representation can be used to provide arrays with execution-time defined bounds in Pascal—that is, arrays whose bounds can be determined only at execution time, rather than at compile time.

6.1 TEXT, CODES, AND COMPRESSION

Since computer systems represent data as bit strings, whenever we enter data into a computer, they must be transformed into bit strings, such that the identical data can later be derived or output. This transformation is called **encoding;** its inverse is **decoding.** The transformation is defined by a **code.** We define these notions more rigorously before exploring the two basic types of code: fixed-length and variable-length codes. We then define the expected length of a code and demonstrate that we can construct efficiently codes with optimal expected length using Huffman's algorithm.

6.1.1 An Introduction to Codes

Computer systems usually represent or **encode** characters internally with a fixed number of bits. For example, ASCII, the widely used international coding standard, encodes characters with 7 bits; see Table 6.1. Such encodings are called **fixed-length** or **block codes.** Fixed-length codes are attractive because both encoding and decoding are extremely simple; see Exercise 6.1. For coding, we can use a block of integers or **codewords** indexed by characters; for decoding, we can use a block of characters indexed by the codewords. For example, given the sentence

   The cat sat on the mat

and the ASCII code given in Table 6.1, we obtain

   1010100 1101000 1100101 0100000 1100011 1100001 1110100 0100000
   1110011 1100001 1110100 0100000 1101111 1101110 0100000
   1110100 1101000 1100101 0100000 1101101 1100001 1110100

as its ASCII, encoded form. Conversely, given the bit string

   1000100110010111000111101111110010011010011101110110 0111
   0100000110100111100110100000110010111000011110011111001,

we can decode it by chopping it into smaller strings, each of 7 bits, and replacing the bit strings with their corresponding characters—namely,

   1000100(D) 1100101(e) 1100011(c) 1101111(o) 1100100(d) 1101001(i)
   1101110(n) 1100111(g) 0100000( ) 1101001(i) 1110011(s) 0100000( )
   1100101(e) 1100001(a) 1110011(s) 1111001(y).

Block codes are one example of the more general concept of a code, which we now define. Every code can be thought of in terms of a finite alphabet of **source symbols** and a finite alphabet of **code symbols.** Each code maps every finite sequence or **string** of source symbols into a string of code symbols. More formally, letting A be the source alphabet and B be the code alphabet, a code f is an injective map $f: S_A \rightarrow S_B$, where S_A is the set of all strings of symbols from A

Table 6.1   Seven-bit ASCII code.

Octal code	Char	Octal code	Char	Octal code	Char	Octal code	Char
000	NUL	040	SP	100	@	140	`
001	SOH	041	!	101	A	141	a
002	STX	042	"	102	B	142	b
003	ETX	043	#	103	C	143	c
004	EOT	044	$	104	D	144	d
005	ENQ	045	%	105	E	145	e
006	ACK	046		106	F	146	f
007	BEL	047	'	107	G	147	g
010	BS	050	(	110	H	150	h
011	HT	051	)	111	I	151	i
012	LF	052	*	112	J	152	j
013	VT	053	+	113	K	153	k
014	FF	054	,	114	L	154	l
015	CR	055	-	115	M	155	m
016	SO	056	.	116	N	156	n
017	SI	057	/	117	O	157	o
020	DLE	060	0	120	P	160	p
021	DCI	061	1	121	Q	161	q
022	DC2	062	2	122	R	162	r
023	DC3	063	3	123	S	163	s
024	DC4	064	4	124	T	164	t
025	NAK	065	5	125	U	165	u
026	SYN	066	6	126	V	166	v
027	ETB	067	7	127	W	167	w
030	CAN	070	8	130	X	170	x
031	EM	071	9	131	Y	171	y
032	SUB	072	:	132	Z	172	z
033	ESC	073	;	133	[	173	{
034	FS	074	¡	134	\	174	—
035	GS	075	=	135	]	175	}
036	RS	076	¿	136	^	176	~
037	US	077	?	137	–	177	DEL

and S_B is the set of all strings of symbols from B. Injectivity ensures that each encoded string can be decoded uniquely; we do not want two source strings that are encoded as the same string. Throughout this text, we are interested primarily in the code alphabet $\{0,1\}$, since we want to code source-symbol strings as bit strings.

Block codes are also examples of codes that are defined completely in terms of the encoding of their source symbols; that is, for a block code f and for all source strings $a_1 \cdots a_n$, f satisfies $f(a_1 \cdots a_n) = f(a_1) \cdots f(a_n)$. Such codes are called **morphic codes;** the image of each source symbol under f is called a **codeword.** In Chapter 7, we introduce a code that is not a morphic code.

Despite their attractiveness, block codes have one obvious—but unforgiving—trait: n symbols produce nb bits with a block code of length b. For example, if $n = 100,000$, the number of characters to be found in a typical 200-page book, and $b = 7$, then the characters are encoded as 700,000 bits. If we know that our text contains only lower-case letters, digits, and punctuation, then we can design a block code that uses 6, rather than 7, bits. Thus, relative to ASCII encoding, we have compressed the text. In general, for a source alphabet of n symbols, a block code needs at least $\lceil \log_2 n \rceil$ bits to encode each symbol. Thus, the 128 characters in the ASCII table need at least 7 bits. We cannot encode the ASCII characters with fewer than 7 bits; however, we can encode the characters with different numbers of bits depending on their frequency of occurrence. If we use fewer bits for more frequent characters and more bits for less frequent characters, then we expect a source text to be encoded with fewer bits than it would be with a block code. Such a code is called a **variable-length code.**

Variable-length codes, as their name implies, do not necessarily encode each source symbol with the same number of bits. The first major problem with such a code, when we are scanning an encoded message from left to right, is this: How do we know when one codeword is finished and another begins? The example code in Fig. 6.1 demonstrates that, in general, we might not be able to decode an encoded message until we have scanned it completely. Clearly, we would prefer decoding to be instantaneous, with no unbounded delays. To obtain such codes, we require that each codeword not be a prefix of any other codeword. This requirement implies that, for the binary-code alphabet, we should base the codes on **binary-code trees,** which are binary trees whose external nodes are labeled uniquely with the given source symbols, whose left branches are labeled 0, and whose right branches are labeled 1. For example, the binary tree of Fig. 6.2 is a code tree, whereas the tree in Fig. 6.1(c) is not a code tree. The codeword corresponding to a symbol is the bit string given by the path from the root to the external node labeled with the symbol. Hence, in Fig. 6.2, c has codeword 10 corre-

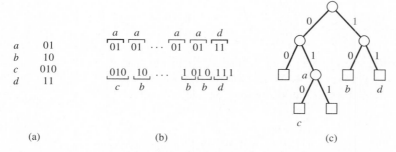

Figure 6.1   An example of unbounded-delay decoding. (a) A code for the symbols *a, b, c,* and *d*. (b) An encoded message that cannot be decoded until we determine whether the last two bits are 01 or 11. (c) The binary tree that corresponds to the code.

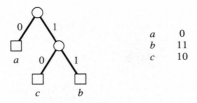

Figure 6.2 A binary-code tree and its prefix code.

sponding to the path: right, left. Every code defined by a code tree satisfies the **prefix property:** *No codeword is a prefix of any other codeword.* This fact follows immediately from the definition of a codeword, since symbols label only external nodes. The prefix property does not hold for the code of Fig. 6.1, since, as we can see, the corresponding tree is not a code tree. Codes that satisfy the prefix property are called **prefix codes.**

The importance of prefix codes stems from the observation that we can uniquely decode an encoded text with a left-to-right scan of the encoded text by considering only the current bit in the encoded text. The decoder can use the code tree for this purpose. The encoded message is read bit by bit. Starting at the root, the decoder moves left when a 0 is read, and moves right when a 1 is read. Whenever an external node is reached, the corresponding source symbol is output and the decoder begins again at the root of the tree. Since no codeword can be extended on the right to give another codeword, decoding is unique. A worked example is given in Fig. 6.3; the implementation of the encoder and decoder for prefix codes is left to Exercise 6.2.

6.1.2 Morse Code

One variable-length code that has been used extensively is Morse code. For example, the Morse encoding of a classic sentence is displayed in Fig. 6.4. The dot–dash encoding reflects the length of the corresponding signal; dot is short and dash is long. As written, Morse code is not a prefix code, because – (T) is a prefix of – · (N). This issue is resolved, in practice, by the addition of a pause at the end

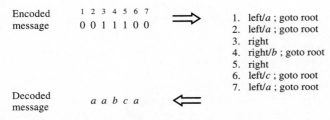

Figure 6.3 An example of decoding for the prefix code of Fig. 6.2.

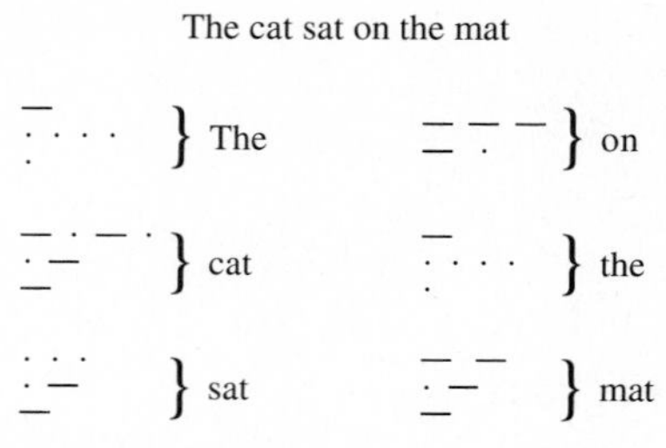

The cat sat on the mat

Figure 6.4   A sentence in Morse code.

of each letter. The pause, denoted by ▷◁, is a long absence of a signal. With the additional signal, we obtain – ▷◁ for T and – · ▷◁ for N. The addition of a new code symbol to the end of every codeword of any code always ensures that the modified code satisfies the prefix property, at the expense of introducing an extra code symbol.

Of course, variable-length codes do not necessarily compress texts; we need to be able to construct good ones. Intuitively, the more frequent a letter is, the shorter its codeword should be; this observation holds for Morse code. In Table 6.2 we give the probabilities of the six most frequent letters and the six least frequent letters from a large corpus of English text, together with their Morse codewords.

6.1.3   Optimal Variable-Length Codes

What makes a good variable-length code? Let $A = a_1,...,a_n$, $n \geq 1$, be the alphabet of source symbols, and let $P = p_1,...,p_n$ be their probabilities of occurrence. In practice, we obtain the probabilities by sampling a corpus of texts that is representative of the text we wish to encode. Now, any binary tree with n external

Table 6.2   The Morse codewords for the six most and six least frequent letters in English. The statistics are taken from Foster (1982).

Letter	Morse code word	Source prob.	Letter	Morse code word	Source prob.
E	·	0.1250	V	· · · –	0.0100
T	–	0.0925	K	– · –	0.0066
A	· –	0.0805	X	– · · –	0.0020
O	– – –	0.0760	J	· – – –	0.0016
I	· ·	0.0729	Q	– – · –	0.0011
N	– ·	0.0710	Z	– – · ·	0.0010

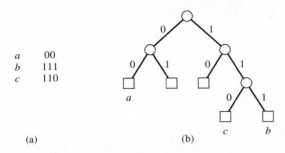

$$
\begin{array}{ll}
a & 00 \\
b & 111 \\
c & 110
\end{array}
$$

(a)   (b)

Figure 6.5   A nonreduced prefix code. (a) The prefix code.
(b) The prefix code's code tree.

nodes labeled with the n symbols defines a prefix code. Conversely, any prefix code for the n symbols defines a binary tree with at least n external nodes. When it gives rise to a binary tree with exactly n external nodes, we say it is a **reduced prefix code.** Fig. 6.5 displays a nonreduced prefix code. Good prefix codes are always reduced, and we can always transform a nonreduced prefix code into a reduced one; the design of an algorithm and a proof of its correctness are left to Exercise 6.3.

To compare different prefix codes for the symbols $A = a_1,...,a_n$ with probabilities $P = p_1,...,p_n$, we consider the number of bits in encoded texts. Let $W = w_1,...,w_n$ be a prefix code for $a_1,...,a_n$, and let $l_1,...,l_n$ be the lengths of $w_1,...,w_n$. Given a source text T with $f_1,...,f_n$ occurrences of $a_1,...,a_n$, respectively, the total number of bits when it is encoded is

$$
\sum_{i=1}^{n} f_i l_i \; .
$$

If we divide the total number of bits by the total number of source symbols in T, then we obtain the **average length of the W-encoding** of the source symbols in the text T. We denote this quantity by ALENGTH(T,W) and define it by

$$
\text{ALENGTH}(T,W) = \frac{\sum_{i=1}^{n} f_i l_i}{\sum_{i=1}^{n} f_i} \; .
$$

Note that this value is not an estimate; it is exact. Now, for long enough texts,

$$
p_i \approx f_i / \sum_{i=1}^{n} f_i;
$$

thus, the **expected length** of the W-encoding of the symbols in a text is

$$\text{ELENGTH}(W,P) = \sum_{i=1}^{n} p_i l_i \, .$$

Observe that the expected length does not depend on the given source text; it depends on only W and P. Now, we can compare two different codes W_1 and W_2 either by comparing, for a given text T, $\text{ALENGTH}(T,W_1)$ and $\text{ALENGTH}(T,W_2)$, or by comparing $\text{ELENGTH}(W_1,P)$ and $\text{ELENGTH}(W_2,P)$. We take the latter course.

Let $A = a_1,...,a_n$ be some source alphabet with associated probabilities $P = p_1,...,p_n$, and let $W = w_1,...,w_n$ and $W' = w'_1,...,w'_n$ be two prefix codes for A. We say W is **no worse than** W' if

$$\text{ELENGTH}(W,P) \leq \text{ELENGTH}(W',P),$$

and we say that W is **optimal** if

$$\text{ELENGTH}(W,P) \leq \text{ELENGTH}(W',P)$$

for all prefix codes W' of A. Having defined optimal prefix codes, we would like to be able to find or construct them efficiently. We begin our hunt for optimal prefix codes by reexamining the relationship between prefix codes and binary trees in somewhat more depth. Given an alphabet A of size $n \geq 1$ and associated probabilities P, any binary tree of size $n - 1$ can be used to give a code tree and, hence, a reduced prefix code for A. All we need to do is to label the n external nodes with the n symbols. In Fig. 6.6, we give two different assignments of the same symbols to the same binary tree, resulting in two different code trees. Clearly there are $n!$ different assignments of symbols to the external nodes of a size $n - 1$ binary tree.

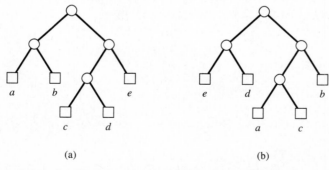

(a)   (b)

Figure 6.6   Two different assignments of the same symbols to a binary tree.

> Given a source alphabet A and associated probabilities P:
>   Step 1: Compute the set S of all reduced prefix codes for A,
>   together with their expected lengths.
>   Step 2: Choose a minimal expected-length prefix code from S
>   as the optimal prefix code.

Figure 6.7   A naive optimal prefix-code construction algorithm.

Since nonreduced prefix codes should have a higher expected length than their reduced counterparts, the following fact should not be too surprising; its proof is left as Exercise 6.4.

Fact 6.1   *For A, P, and W as given in the preceding discussion, where no probability is zero, if W is optimal, then W is reduced.*

Based on Fact 6.1, a naive algorithm for finding an optimal code is shown in Fig. 6.7. To implement it, we need to be able to generate all reduced prefix codes for A. The simplest way of generating them is to turn once more to the binary-tree representation of prefix codes. Because there are $\mathcal{B}_{n-1}$ binary trees of size $n-1$, we see that there are $n!\,\mathcal{B}_{n-1}$ reduced prefix codes to consider in steps 1 and 2 of the algorithm in Fig. 6.7. Observing that $\mathcal{B}_{n-1} \geq 1$, we require $\Omega(n^n)$ comparisons for step 2, since $n! \approx n^n$. The time taken by the algorithm grows exponentially with respect to the number of source symbols. Thus, to be able to find or construct an optimal prefix code in a reasonable time, we need a more efficient construction algorithm. Fortunately, as we shall see in Section 6.1.4, there is a much faster algorithm that uses greediness and takes only $O(n^2)$ time.

6.1.4 Huffman's Algorithm

We wish to solve the following problem: *Given n symbols $A = a_1,...,a_n$, $n \geq 1$, and the probabilities of their occurrence $P = p_1,...,p_n$, respectively, construct an optimal prefix code for A and P.* This problem is an example of a **global optimization problem.** We have shown that a brute-force or exhaustive-search solution is too expensive to contemplate except for small alphabets. Here, we introduce **greediness;** it uses **local optimization** to achieve a globally optimum solution. We build the optimal code incrementally by, essentially, reducing the alphabet by one symbol at each step. We merge the two symbols that have the smallest probabilities into one new symbol. This technique is greediness in action; we choose the *smallest* probabilities. (In general, greediness will force us to choose either the smallest or the largest values. We could assign the next smallest codeword to the next most frequent symbol at each step, but this approach would not guarantee optimality in all circumstances; see Exercise 6.5.)

Before tackling the code-construction problem, we observe that ELENGTH (W,P) is determined solely by the probabilities and the lengths of the codewords. The symbols themselves are irrelevant to this computation. In particular, two

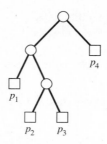

Figure 6.8   A binary tree with external probabilities.

symbols with identical probabilities can exchange codewords without affecting
the expected length. Again, we can best appreciate this effect by viewing a
reduced prefix code as a binary tree; see Fig. 6.8. This view implies that the
lengths of the codewords correspond to the lengths of the root-to-external-node
paths and, hence, the expected length of a given code is also known as the
expected number of node visits, for unsuccessful search, in the corresponding tree
(see Section 10.1.1).

   We are now in a position to introduce and explain **Huffman's greedy algorithm** for solving the problem. It is remarkably simple, and is somewhat more
general than the problem requires in that it needs only positive weights, rather
than probabilities. We demonstrate Huffman's algorithm with the six most frequent letters in English text—$E(0.125)$, $T(0.0925)$, $A(0.0805)$, $O(0.0760)$,
$I(0.0729)$, and $N(0.0710)$. We have given their probabilities of occurrence with
respect to all 26 letters; we have taken the probabilities from the text of Foster
(1982).

   As a first step, we create a forest of code trees, one for each source symbol.
Each code tree consists of a single external node (an empty tree) labeled with its
symbol and weight; see Fig. 6.9. Next we choose two binary trees in the forest
that have the smallest weights associated with their roots—a greedy choice. Intuitively, the final code tree will have a longer path to these symbols than it will to
other symbols. Thus, as we expect, rarer symbols are given longer codewords. In
the example, these symbols are I and N. We replace the two corresponding trees
by a new tree that includes them as subtrees of its root and whose root has weight
equal to the sum of the subtrees' weights. This replacement yields the forest of
Fig. 6.10(a). We repeat the process with the new forest to obtain the forest of Fig.

Figure 6.9   The initial forest of empty binary trees in Huffman's algorithm.

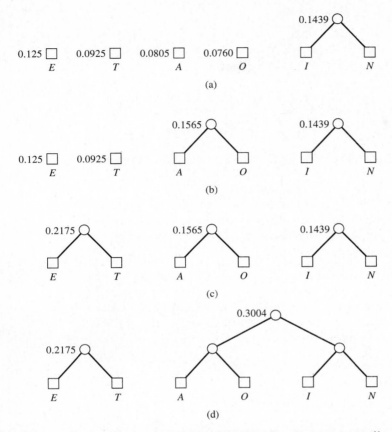

Figure 6.10 The forest of code trees and the first four merges in Huffman's algorithm. (a) After the first merge. (b) After the second merge. (c) After the third merge. (d) After the fourth merge.

6.10(b), then the forest of Fig. 6.10(c), and then the forest of Fig. 6.10(d). Finally, after one more merge, we obtain the singleton forest of Fig. 6.11—the final code tree. The code corresponding to the final code tree is $(A,100)$, $(E,00)$, $(I,110)$, $(N,111)$, $(O,101)$, and $(T,01)$. We compute the ELENGTH of this code by first normalizing the probabilities before we use the previously given formula. We normalize the probabilities by dividing them by the sum of the six probabilities. The ELENGTH of the code is 2.76, an improvement of 0.24 over the shortest block code for the six letters.

Huffman's algorithm can be summarized as shown in Fig. 6.12. Although the approach used by Huffman's algorithm will produce good codes, we need to prove that they are optimal. We leave the proof of the following fact as Exercise 6.6.

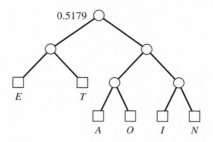

Figure 6.11   The final code tree for the six most frequent English letters.

Fact 6.2   *Given n symbols $A = a_1,...,a_n$ with occurrence probabilities $P = p_1,...,p_n$, respectively, any reduced prefix code for A and P has expected length no less than the expected length of a Huffman code for A and P. Thus, Huffman's algorithm produces optimal codes.*

One aspect of our interest in Huffman's algorithm is the complexity of the latter's data structures—the algorithm uses binary trees and forests. Moreover, to create the initial forest, we need to read a list of symbol–probability pairs. Finally, to encode source text, we require a map that associates symbols to codewords. We break Huffman's algorithm into three basic steps:

1.   Initialize the forest of code trees.

2.   Construct an optimal code tree.

3.   Compute the encoding map (this step is not included in Fig. 6.12).

We tackle only step 2, leaving the other two steps as Exercises 6.7 and 6.8. We use a forest that is a list of (binary) tree–weight pairs; in other words, it is an orchard. The "trees" in the forest are not just trees—they are pairs of binary trees and weights. Hence, we assume the existence of an ADT to reflect this abstraction—namely, *treewtype*. Since *treewtype* variables have two components, we need to be able to examine and replace the components; therefore, we have the

Let F be the forest consisting of n empty trees
   with weights $w_1 , ...,w_n$.

As long as F has more than one tree,
   let T_1 and T_2 be two distinct trees in F with smallest
   weights. Replace T_1 and T_2 in F with a new tree T that
   has weight equal to the sum of the weights of T_1 and T_2,
   T_1 as its left subtree, and T_2 as its right subtree..

Figure 6.12   A high-level version of Huffman's algorithm.

operations *ExamineTree*, *ExamineWeight*, *ReplaceTree*, and *ReplaceWeight*. The procedure *Huffman* is given in Program 6.1. It uses a new BINTREE operation *Construct* that forms a new binary tree by creating a root node and by making two given binary trees as that node's left and right subtrees. Moreover, *Construct* computes the weight of the new root node and returns the corresponding tree–weight pair. *Huffman* also uses two new operations for sequences: *IsSingleton* and *FMin2*. *IsSingleton* tests whether a list consists of exactly one element. It is completely general and can be written in terms of the basic LIST operations; see Exercise 6.9. *FMin2* is, however, a special-purpose function that returns and deletes the two tree–weight pairs with the smallest weights from the given orchard. It is a modification, for our ADTs, of the usual algorithm to find the two minimum values in a list; see Exercises 6.9 and 6.10. If, on the other hand, the initial orchard is in sorted order, with respect to the root weights, then *FMin2* can be implemented extremely simply. To maintain the sorted order of the orchard, an insertion of a newly constructed tree takes linear time. We can avoid this inefficiency with the method discussed in Exercise 6.11.

We are left with the problems of initializing the orchard and constructing the code from the final code tree. The initialization function is given in Program 6.2. Although the encoding-map construction is somewhat more complex, we leave it to Exercise 6.8.

```
procedure Huffman(F: FOREST; var T: BINTREE);
{As long as there are at least two trees in the forest F,
    Huffman replaces the two trees that have the smallest root
    weights with a tree that has those trees as its left and right
    subtrees, and with a weight that is the sum of those trees'
    weights.}
var treewt, treewt1, treewt2: treewtype; wF: Fwindowtype;

begin
    if not FIsEmpty(F)
    then begin
        while not FIsSingleton(F) do
        begin FMin2(treewt1,treewt2,F);
            Construct(treewt1,treewt2,treewt);
            FAfterLast(wF,F); FInsertBefore(treewt,wF,F)
        end;
        FBeforeFirst(wF,F); FNext(wF,F);
        FExamine(treewt,wF,F); ExamineTree(T,treewt)
    end
    else error('An empty forest in Huffman')
end {Huffman};
```

Program 6.1 A Pascal implementation of Huffman's algorithm.

```
procedure Initialize(var F: FOREST);
var wF: Fwindowtype; symbol: char; weight: real;
    T: BINTREE; wT: windowtype;
    treewt: treewtype;

begin
    FEmpty(F); FAfterLast(wF,F);
    while not eof(instream)
    do begin
        read(symbol,weight);
        Empty(T); Root(wT,T);
        ExtReplace(symbol,wT,T); {Create a single external node tree.}
        ReplaceTree(T,treewt); ReplaceWeight(weight,treewt);
        FInsertBefore(treewt,wF,F) {Add weighted tree to forest.}
    end
end {Initialize};
```

Program 6.2   Initialization of the forest or orchard of tree–weight pairs.

6.1.5   An Analysis of Huffman's Algorithm

What is the time required by an implementation of Huffman's algorithm? Step 1, the initialization step, takes linear time; that is, for n symbol–weight pairs, it takes $O(n)$ time. Step 2, as implemented in Program 6.1, is more time consuming. It makes $n - 1$ calls of *Construct* and $n - 1$ calls of *FMin2*. Since we do not maintain the orchard in sorted order, insertion is a constant-time operation, but minima finding uses exhaustive search. Each call of *Construct* takes constant time, because it adds one new node, and a call of *FMin2* with an orchard of n trees makes $O(n)$ comparisons and, therefore, takes $O(n)$ time. Hence, the $n - 1$ calls of *FMin2* take $O(n^2)$ time. Minima finding dominates the time complexity of the code-tree construction; thus *Huffman* takes $O(n^2)$ time.

It is possible to improve the performance of *Huffman* to $O(n \log n)$ time at the expense of a more complex algorithm to find two minima; see Exercise 6.11. Another approach, with the same time bound, uses a more complex structure—namely a priority queue—to represent the forest; see Chapter 11.

Step 3, the coding-function construction, can be implemented to run in $O(n^2)$ time in the worst case; see Exercise 6.8.

6.2   SPELL CHECKING AND TRIES

Text processing has become one of the major applications of computers; hence, it is essential that users can check their spelling on-line easily and quickly. The problem of representing a dictionary for this task is nontrivial; we scratch only the surface of the problem. We use our approach, however, in Chapter 7, when we study strings and string searching in more detail.

6.2.1 Use of Tries

We are given a set of English words, and we want to represent them so that we can check quickly whether a given word is in the set. Rather than treating the words as single units, we treat them as strings of letters. Given a query word X, we test whether it is in the set by first checking whether its first letter agrees with the first letter of any of the given words. We discard, conceptually, all words whose first letter is different from the first letter of X. If any words remain, then we continue by comparing the second letter of X with the second letter of the remaining words, and so on. At each step, we discard some (possibly no) words and continue the matching process with the next letter of X and the next letters of the remaining words. Eventually, when every letter in X has been examined, either some words remain in the set or there are no words left. In the first case, if X is among the remaining words, then we have found it; in the second case, X is not in the set. One refinement of this algorithm is to stop the examination of the letters of X when either one word remains or no words remain. For, when only one word is left, we can check immediately whether it is X. This approach can be formalized with a multiway tree. As an example, we use 10 words taken in sequence from the *Random House Dictionary;* see Fig. 6.13. For simplicity, we assume that the words are formed from only uppercase letters. We use the @ symbol, in addition to the 26 letters of the English alphabet, as an **end-of-word symbol** or **endmarker.** We have chosen @ because it comes immediately before A in the ASCII representation of the letters $A..Z$; thus, $@..Z$ corresponds to the range of integers 64..90 in the ASCII representation. The @ symbol is appended to the end of each word in the set and to the end of each query word to ensure that each string in the set is not a prefix of any other string in the set. For example, MACARONI is a prefix of MACARONIC and MACADAM is a prefix of MACADAMIA, but MACARONI@ is not a prefix of MACARONIC@ and MACADAM@ is not a prefix of MACADAMIA@.

In the multiway-tree representation of the preceding search algorithm for the 10 English words, each internal node has 27 children, one for each symbol in the range $@..Z$; see Fig. 6.14. The @-branch is the first branch of an internal node, the A-branch the second branch,..., and the Z-branch the last branch. Root-to-frontier paths in the tree spell out strings. We require every @-branch to lead to an external node, so that the @ symbol can appear only at the end of strings. There are two kinds of external nodes. First, there are those external nodes that are reached by a path that spells out a prefix of a string in the given set; these are the **active nodes.** The remaining external nodes are not associated with a string in

MACABRE	MACARONI
MACACO	MACARONIC
MACADAM	MACAROON
MACADAMIA	MACAW
MACAQUE	MACCABOY

Figure 6.13   Ten English words.

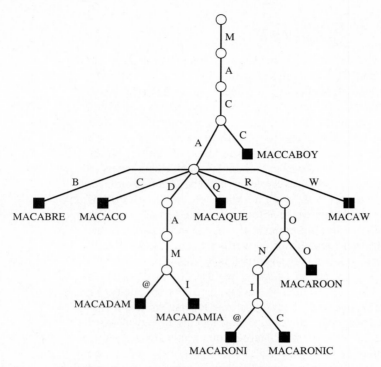

Figure 6.14   The representation of the 10 English words with a multiway trie.

the given set; they are the **inactive nodes.** We indicate the active nodes with ■ and the inactive nodes with □. Each active node u is associated with one string or word, which we denote by *string(u)*. A multiway tree, such as the one in Fig. 6.2, is called a **multiway trie,** because the node map is an array with domain @..Z. *That the children are indexed by the symbols is crucial to this approach.* So, given a symbol a, we can find the ath child of a node by using a constant-time address computation. A multiway trie for n strings, each with an endmarker, has n active external nodes.

Deciding whether a given string $X@ = a_{1..}a_{m+1}$ is in a trie, where $a_{m+1} = @$, takes at most $m + 1$ branchings, one for each symbol; see the high-level algorithm in Fig. 6.15. The search time is independent of the number of words in the trie. The price we pay, however, is the memory overhead, since all internal nodes require $\Omega(d)$ space for d links, where d is the size of the underlying alphabet. We can save space by removing internal nodes that have only one internal or active child and associating strings with branches; for example, MAC appears as a prefix of all 10 words. We explore this idea in Exercise 6.13 and in Section 6.2.2, when we discuss binary tries.

Let $X = a_1 \ldots a_{m+1}$, where a_{m+1} = @ and
$a_1, \ldots, a_m$ are symbols other than @.
Let u be the root of the given trie and $i = 1$.

while (u is not an external node) **and** ($i \le m + 1$) **do**
begin $u := u(a)$; $i := i + 1$ **end**;

if (u is an active external node) **and** ($string(u) = X$)
then X is in the trie
else X is not in the trie;

Figure 6.15 The trie search algorithm.

We have avoided two obvious issues: How do we build a trie for a set of words? How do we perform insertions and deletions? We consider insertion into a trie here; we leave deletion to Exercise 6.14. Based on the insertion algorithm, we can build a trie for a set of words by inserting them one at a time into an initially empty trie.

The idea of insertion is straightforward: We search for the given string (with the appended endmarker) until we fall into either an inactive external node or an active external node for some other string. (If we fall into neither, the string is in the trie.) We illustrate this procedure with the word MACADEMIC and the trie of Fig. 6.14. In Fig. 6.16, we see that the prefix MACAD of MACADEMIC is matched, but the prefix MACADE is not matched; we arrive at an inactive external node. To insert MACADEMIC, we activate the external node and associate with it the string MACADEMIC. The other insertion possibility is that the inserted string falls into an active external node. For example, MACAROONS@ falls into the active node for MACAROON@. In this case, we insert the fewest number of branches to distinguish between the two strings. The time taken for the insertion is linear in the length of the inserted word; that is, the algorithm takes $O(m)$ time, where m is the number of letters in the inserted word. Hence, if we insert a set of words with total length M into an initially empty trie, using repeated insertions, it will take $O(M)$ time.

6.2.2 Binary Tries

Rather than using characters to branch at each node in a trie, we can use the bits in their internal representation. Immediately, since we have only two values, we obtain a binary tree and, since it is used as a trie, we call it a **binary trie.** The code trees of Section 6.1 are binary tries.

Using the 7-bit ASCII representation of characters, @..Z are represented by 100 through 132 in octal. Hence, the 10 English words are represented by the 10

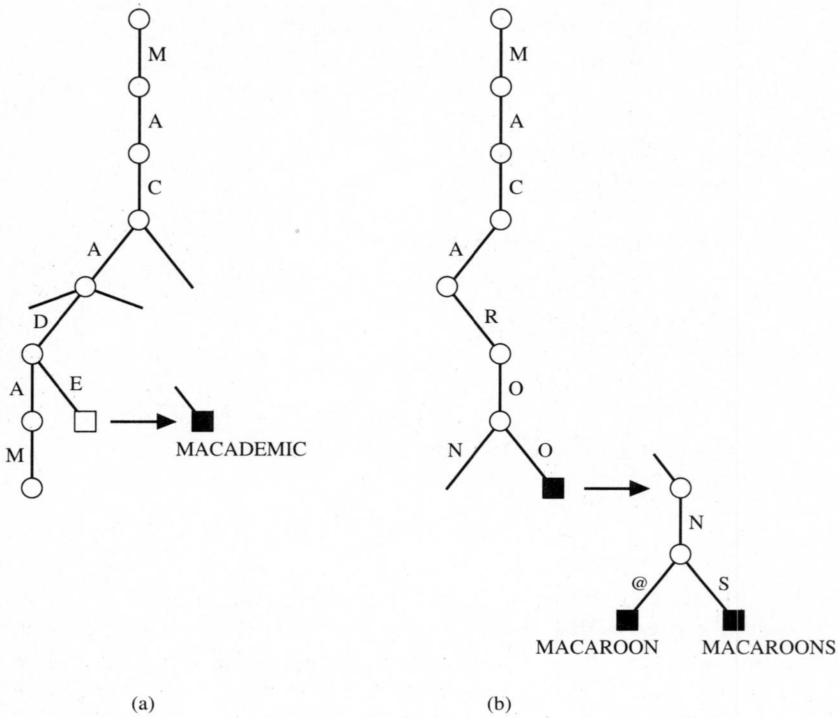

Figure 6.16   Insertion into the trie of Fig. 6.14. (a) Insertion of the word
MACADEMIC. (b) Insertion of the word MACAROONS.

octal strings given in Fig. 6.17. Note that each triple of octal digits denotes 7 bits; hence, MACAW@ is denoted by the bit string 1001101 1000001 1000011 1000001 1010111 1000000. The advantage of binary tries should be clear: Branching at each node is a simple operation. Binary trees are inefficient in their use of space, however, for the same reason as tries are. We can compact them by removing nodes that have one internal or active child, since they do not distinguish any strings in the set. To ensure that searching is implemented correctly, we associate with each node a skip count that indicates how many bits should be skipped. The resulting trie is called a **compact binary trie.** The skip count is added to the current position in the query bit string, *before branching*. We represent the 10 English words of Fig. 6.17 with the compact binary trie of Fig. 6.18. The words in Fig. 6.17 are associated with the corresponding numbered active nodes of the trie. Observe that all external nodes are active in compact binary tries. Because the skipped bits are not checked during a search for a query string, if the search ends at an active node, then we must compare that node's string with the query string. For example, the word TRACK leads to the active node associated with MACCABOY, but the two words are not the same. Indeed, any word having *C* as its fourth letter will end up at the same active node as MACCABOY.

1. MACABRE	115 101 103 101 102 122 105
2. MACACO	115 101 103 101 103 117
3. MACADAM	115 101 103 101 104 101 115
4. MACADAMIA	115 101 103 101 104 101 115 111 101
5. MACAQUE	115 101 103 101 121 125 105
6. MACARONI	115 101 103 101 122 117 116 111
7. MACARONIC	115 101 103 101 122 117 116 111 103
8. MACAROON	115 101 103 101 122 117 117 116
9. MACAW	115 101 103 101 127
10. MACCABOY	115 101 103 103 101 102 117 131

Figure 6.17 The octal strings of the 10 English words in Fig. 6.13.

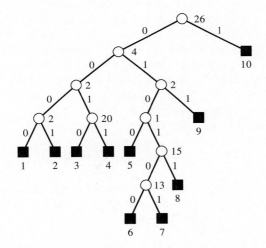

Figure 6.18 A compact binary trie with skip counts.

Compact binary tries are the basis of the PATRICIA trie; see Chapter 7. We leave the design of insertion and deletion algorithms for PATRICIA tries to Exercise 6.15.

6.3 ARRAYS DEFINED AT EXECUTION-TIME

Pascal, in common with most other programming languages, does not support execution-time–defined arrays; the bounds of an array are determined by constants at the time of the array's declaration. We cannot make the declaration, in a procedure or function,

```
var A: array[1..m] of integer;
```

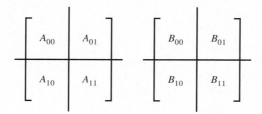

Figure 6.19   Quartering of two matrices A and B in the recursive
definition of their product.

where m is a variable. The value of m must be a constant that is defined at compile time. There are, however, circumstances when such arrays occur naturally. Consider the multiplication of two $2n \times 2n$ matrices A and B. Their product can be defined recursively, rather than in the usual iterative way, as follows. Divide each matrix into four $n \times n$ submatrices, as shown in Fig. 6.19. Then, the product $C = AB$ can be expressed recursively by the four products $C_{ij} = A_{i0}B_{0j} + A_{i1}B_{1j}$, $0 \le i,j \le 1$. If we wish to implement this scheme in Pascal, say, we need to be able to treat A_{ij}, B_{ij}, and C_{ij} as matrices in their own right. In particular, to compute $A_{i1}B_{1j} + A_{i2}B_{2j}$, we need a temporary $n \times n$ matrix to hold the product $A_{i0}B_{0j}$ while $A_{i1}B_{1j}$ is computed. We could use part of a $2n \times 2n$ matrix for this purpose, but this solution wastes considerable space, if we compute each product $A_{ik}B_{kj}$ recursively by the same technique. We need execution-time–defined arrays.

We present one solution to this problem with binary tries; another solution is suggested in Exercise 6.16. For simplicity of presentation, we assume that A, B, and C are $n \times n$ matrices, where $n = 2^p$, for some $p \ge 0$. If $p = 0$, then $n = 1$ and A, B, and C consist of single elements. Rather than indexing the rows and columns of the matrices by $1..n$, we use $0..n - 1$. Each $2^p \times 2^p$ matrix is represented by a perfect binary trie of height $2p$ (see Fig. 6.20), where the matrix entries are associated with the external nodes. Given an index (i,j), $0 \le i,j \le n - 1$, the corresponding external node is found as follows. Express i and j as binary numbers with exactly p bits. Letting $i = i_0...i_{p-1}$ and $j = j_0...j_{p-1}$ be the binary representation of i and j, the external node for (i,j) has the root-to-frontier path labeled by $i_0 j_0 i_1 j_1...i_{p-1} j_{p-1}$. An example for a 4×4 matrix where $p = 2$, is displayed in Fig. 6.21. Element $(0,0)$ is found at the external node determined by 0000, element $(0,3)$ is found at the node determined by 0101, element $(1,1)$ is found at the node determined by (0011), and so on. Observe that the upper-left quadrant A_{00} is the subtrie determined by 00, the bottom-left quadrant A_{10} is that determined by 10, and so on. It is easy to quarter a matrix represented in this way; indeed, it is easy to divide the matrix into $2^q \times 2^q$ submatrices for any q, $0 \le q < p$. The advantage of the binary-trie representation is that we can mimic the declaration of a $2^p \times 2^p$ matrix by constructing, at execution time, a perfect binary trie of height $2p$, *even when p is a variable.* This declaration, however, no longer takes constant time; it takes $O(2^{2p})$ time, linear in the number of matrix entries. Similarly, accessing the

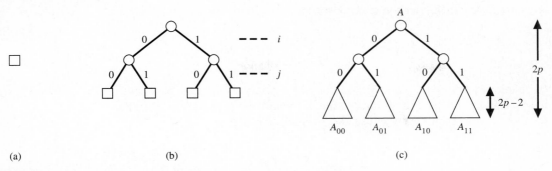

(a)   (b)   (c)

Figure 6.20   The recursive definition of the binary-trie representation of a matrix. (a) The case $p = 0$. (b) The case $p = 1$. (c) The case $p > 1$.

(i,j)th entry no longer takes constant time, it takes $O(p)$ time, logarithmic in the number of entries. In general, for an $m \times n$ matrix, initialization takes $O(mn)$ time and access takes $O(\log m + \log n)$ time. It is possible to use the binary-trie view of a matrix to obtain yet another block representation (see Exercise 6.19) that reduces the initialization time to a constant once more, but that still requires logarithmic access time. Another approach we can take is to use lazy initialization: We add a path in the binary trie when an entry is accessed for the first time; see Exercise 6.21.

The recursive matrix-multiplication scheme lends itself to the implementation of Strassen's faster matrix-multiplication technique. We can multiply two 2×2 matrices, using the preceding recursive method, with eight scalar multiplications and four scalar additions. In general, we can multiply two $2^p \times 2^p$ matrices with eight $(2^{p-1} \times 2^{p-1})$-matrix multiplications and four $(2^{p-1} \times 2^{p-1})$-matrix additions. Letting $M(p)$ denote the number of scalar multiplications used by the

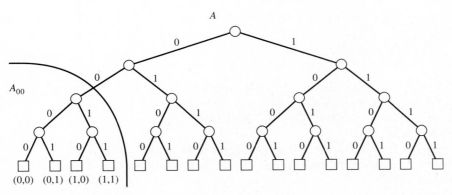

Figure 6.21   The binary-trie representation of a 4×4 matrix.

recursive matrix multiplication method, we obtain the following recurrence equation:

$$M(1) = 8$$
$$M(p) = 8M(p - 1), p \geq 2.$$

Its solution is $M(p) = 8^p$, $p \geq 1$. Strassen observed that, in both cases, only seven multiplications are necessary; thus, a similar recurrence equation for $S(p)$, the number of scalar multiplications used by Strassen's method, is

$$S(1) = 7$$
$$S(p) = 7S(p - 1), p \geq 2.$$

It has the solution $S(p) = 7^p$, $p \geq 1$. We can express these solutions in terms of $n = 2^p$ as $M'(n) = 8^{\log_2 n}$ and $S'(n) = 7^{\log_2 n}$. Using the identity $a^{\log_c b} = b^{\log_c a}$, these solutions are $M'(n) = n^{\log_2 8} = n^3$ and $S'(n) = n^{\log_2 7} < n^3$. The n^3 bound is also the number of scalar multiplications used by the standard matrix-multiplication technique; Strassen was the first person to break the n^3 barrier.

To save one multiplication, we can use the following scheme. We compute the seven intermediate matrices $M_1, ..., M_7$, and then combine them to obtain the C_{ij} matrices:

$$M_1 = (A_{12} - A_{22})(B_{21} + B_{22})$$
$$M_2 = (A_{11} + A_{22})(B_{11} + B_{22})$$
$$M_3 = (A_{11} - A_{21})(B_{11} + B_{12})$$
$$M_4 = (A_{11} + A_{12})B_{22}$$
$$M_5 = A_{11}(B_{12} - B_{22})$$
$$M_6 = A_{22}(B_{21} - B_{11})$$
$$M_7 = (A_{21} + A_{22})B_{11}$$

$$C_{11} = M_1 + M_2 - M_4 + M_6$$
$$C_{12} + M_4 + M_5$$
$$C_{21} = M_6 + M_7$$
$$C_{22} = M_2 - M_3 + M_5 - M_7.$$

The implementation of this matrix-multiplication method is left to Exercise 6.17. Note that, for small matrices, the savings in scalar multiplications is offset by the overhead needed by the method. Only for sufficiently large matrices is this method more efficient.

We make two final comments. We can modify the multiplication algorithm to allow arbitrary square matrices; we leave this modification to Exercise 6.18. Also, the recursive partitioning of a two-dimensional array inherent in the binary-trie representation can be used to provide a block representation. The ordering that is

1	2	5	6	17	18	21	22
3	4	7	8	19	20	23	24
9	10	13	14	25	26	29	30
11	12	15	16	27	28	31	32

Figure 6.22 An ordering corresponding to the binary trie representation of a two-dimensional array.

the basis of this representation is illustrated in Fig. 6.22; we discuss the ordering and representation in Exercise 6.19.

6.4 SUMMARY

We considered three applications of binary indexed trees: coding and compression, spell checking, and array representation. We defined the notions of a prefix code and an optimal prefix code and have introduced Huffman's algorithm that constructs optimal prefix codes. The algorithm also served to introduce the greediness technique, which makes locally optimal decisions and, in this case, produces a globally optimal solution.

The second application, spell checking, introduced tries and binary tries that can be used to check whether a word is in a given set of words in time proportional to its length.

The final application used binary tries, once more, for a novel representation of arrays that enables execution-time–defined arrays to be used in Pascal.

6.5 HISTORY

Huffman's algorithm was developed by Huffman (1952) when he was an undergraduate student at M.I.T.; a presentation in the more general context of coding can be found in the text of Hamming (1986). The observed frequencies of the 26 letters in English are taken from Foster (1982). The notion of a trie was presented by Sussenguth (1963). The trie representation of arrays is discussed in Solntseff and Wood (1977), where these authors' Pascal implementation is given. The representation was discovered independently by Rosenberg (1979) and is studied in more detail in Rosenberg and associates (1979) and in Wood (1978). Cohen and Roth (1975) give another array representation that they use an implementation of Strassen's algorithm. The UNIX utilities `pack` and `unpack` are based on Huffman encoding, and `compact` and `uncompact` are based on adaptive Huffman encoding.

EXERCISES

6.1: Implement, in Pascal, encoding and decoding procedures for ASCII.

6.2: Implement, in Pascal, encoding and decoding procedures for prefix codes. Assume that the encoder is given a map from characters to codewords and that the decoder is given the corresponding code tree.

6.3: Design and implement an algorithm to reduce nonreduced prefix codes such that the resulting prefix code has expected length no greater than the expected length of the given prefix code. What are the time and space requirements of your algorithm?

6.4: Prove that, if no occurrence probability is zero, then every optimal prefix code is reduced. [Hint: Try an argument based on contradiction.]

6.5: Rather than using a greedy algorithm for prefix-code construction that is based on the smallest probabilities, we could use a greedy algorithm that is based on the largest probabilities. Given an alphabet $A = a_1,...,a_n$ of symbols with probabilities $P = p_1,...,p_n$, respectively, at each step we choose that symbol with largest probability and assign it the next smallest codeword. Thus, the most probable symbol is given codeword 0, the next most probable symbol the codeword 10, and so on. When only two symbols remain, we assign them the two remaining codewords of the same length $x0$ and $x1$. Demonstrate that such a scheme does not necessarily produce optimal codes.

6.6: Given n symbols $A = a_1,...,a_n$ with occurrence probabilities $P = p_1,...,p_n$, respectively, prove that any reduced prefix code for A and P has expected length no less than the expected length of a Huffman code for A and P. (This result implies that Huffman codes are optimal.)

6.7: Implement step 1 of Huffman's algorithm—the initialization of the forest of code trees.

6.8: Implement step 3 of Huffman's algorithm by designing a procedure that, given a code tree, outputs the corresponding symbol–code pairs. Modify your approach to produce a list of symbol–code pairs.
      What are the running times of your algorithms?

6.9: Design and implement *IsSingleton* and *FMin2* for *Huffman*.

6.10: Design an efficient algorithm to return the two smallest elements in a list of elements taken from a total order. How many comparisons does your method make, in the worst case, for a list of length n? You can use a fixed (independent of n) amount of extra memory.

6.11: Prove that the weights obtained from the tree-merging step in *Huffman* appear in nondecreasing order. Based on this observation, suggest a different method for obtaining the two minima that uses only two queues and improves *FMin2* to be a constant-time operation, while keeping *InsertBefore* a constant-time operation.

6.12: Take 10 consecutive words from your favorite dictionary and construct a multiway trie for them.

6.13: We have suggested that we can save more space in a multiway trie by removing internal nodes that have only one internal or active child. This removal implies that we conceptually associate strings, rather than symbols, with branches. For example, if we remove such a node that is reached by an α-branch, and a β-branch leads to the internal or active node, then we associate the string $\alpha\beta$ with the original α-branch, and this branch now leads directly to the internal or active child. Observe that when we associate a string with a branch, its first symbol must determine a unique child. So, we cannot have two branches from the same node with strings that begin with the same symbol.

Design insertion and deletion algorithms for this compacted version of a multiway trie. What are the running times of your algorithms? How would you represent a compacted multiway trie?

6.14: Give an algorithm to delete a string from a multiway trie. What is the running time of your algorithm?

6.15: Design insertion and deletion algorithms for the compact binary trie.

6.16: Rather than using a binary trie to represent a two-dimensional array, use a 4-way trie (in which each node has four children), where the children are designated geographically as *NE, SE, SW,* and *NW.* Such a structure corresponds directly to the quartering of the array; it has been called a **pyramid.** Implement matrix multiplication based on this representation.

6.17: Implement and test Strassen's matrix-multiplication algorithm. Design an experiment to compare the recursive multiplication algorithm and Strassen's multiplication algorithm.

6.18: Modify Strassen's multiplication algorithm to allow arbitrary square matrices.

6.19: We can view the quartering of a matrix as a method of obtaining a block representation in the following way. Given a $2n \times 2n$ matrix A, we recursively assign A_{00} to the first n^2 block entries, A_{01} to the second n^2 block entries, and so on. In other words, we assign the quarters in row-major order. Define the corresponding addressing function. How many arithmetic operations does the addressing function take to compute the block position of a matrix entry?

6.20: Design an algorithm to construct a binary-trie representation of a given $2^p \times 2^p$ array. Extend your algorithm to treat arbitrary $m \times n$ arrays. What are the performances of your algorithms?

6.21: Rather than producing a perfect binary trie when initializing an array, we can instead take the lazy approach and produce only an empty trie. Then, when an entry is accessed for the first time, we add the appropriate path to the trie. Implement and test this constant-time initialization technique.

6.22: We can use the binary trie representation of arrays to represent sparse arrays by keeping only the relevant paths. Implement a scheme for dealing with sparse arrays. Compare your scheme with the techniques discussed in Section 4.4.

6.23: Implement algorithms to transform an arithmetic expression into an expression tree and an expression tree into postfix form.

CHAPTER 7

Strings

In Chapter 3, we discussed the uses and the representation of lists or sequences. Why do we now have another chapter on a special kind of sequence, the string?

First, in this chapter, we examine a class of sequences that is restricted not with respect to the operations, but rather with respect to *elementtype*. LIST does not restrict *elementtype* in any way (in Section 6.1, *elementtype* is a binary tree). There are sequences, however, that deserve special treatment—namely, strings. **Strings** are finite sequences of symbols from some specified finite **alphabet** of symbols. In the corresponding ADT, STRING, the values of *elementtype*, the symbols, can be viewed as an integer range $0..m$, for some $m \geq 0$. **Bit strings** and **character strings** are ubiquitous examples of strings.

Second, strings are fundamental. Text files are character strings and binary files are bit strings. Text editors manipulate text files, whereas compilers take text files and produce binary files. Moreover, text files can themselves be viewed as bit strings. This universality of usage has meant that these two specific kinds of strings may appear in programming languages, even though the more general LIST does not; such is the case, for example, in PL/I, Ada, and C. Indeed, there are languages that use the character string as the sole ADT—for example, Snobol. Universality of usage also has meant that compact representations that support the efficient implementation of the string operations are of major interest.

Third, there are some operations that are appropriate for strings but are not as appropriate for sequences in general. For example, the substring operation—which determines whether one string is a substring of a second string—is found in all text editors.

In this chapter, we focus on strings and on their use as text files and in textual databases. Specifically, we consider the basic string operation of pattern matching or substring searching. We examine pattern matching first in a text-editing environment, in Section 7.2, then for a textual database, in Section 7.3. These two environments introduce two different ways in which preprocessing can give efficient solutions. We also show that concentrating on expected-case performance, rather than on worst-case performance, can lead to algorithms that are more practical. We then discuss, in Section 7.4, edit sequences for strings and the problem of determining the minimum edit distance between two strings. This problem introduces dynamic programming, a powerful paradigm that gives efficient solutions to certain optimization problems; we use it again in Chapter 10. The UNIX utility `diff` uses this approach to determine the differences between two text files. With this utility, each line of a text file is a symbol. Next, in Section 7.5, we explore an eminently practical technique for data compression that adapts to the specific source text being encoded. It is the basis of the UNIX utilities `compress` and `uncompress`. The idea of adaptation is also a powerful paradigm; we shall see it in action in Chapters 8 and 10. Finally, in Section 7.6, we examine some representations of strings and report their performance.

We begin by specifying the ADT STRING.

7.1 STRING SPECIFICATION

Let A be an alphabet of symbols, S be the set of STRING values, and N be the non-negative integers. We use the notion of a **position** in a string, rather than the more general notion of a window that we used for lists. For a string of n symbols, the position of the first symbol in the string is 1,..., and the position of the last symbol is n. The **size** of the string is n, the number of symbols in the string. We also refer to position 0, the position before the first symbol in the string, and to the positions $n + 1$,..., the positions after the last symbol of the string. It is natural to access symbols in a string by their position; in many implementations, it is also efficient to do so. Because of this view of strings, we shall use Pascal array notation $S[i]$ to denote $Examine(i,S)$, for a string S, throughout this chapter. (The reader should be aware that this usage does not necessarily imply a block implementation of STRING.) The basic operations of the STRING ADT are thus specified as follows:

1. *Empty*: $\rightarrow S$: The function value *Empty* is the empty string.

2. *IsEmpty*: $S \rightarrow B$: The function value *IsEmpty(S)* is **true** if S is an empty string; otherwise, it is **false**.

3. *Size*: $S \rightarrow N$: The function value *Size(S)* is the number of symbols in S. It is zero if S is the empty string.

4. *Examine*: $N \times S \rightarrow A$: The function value *Examine(i,S)* is undefined if $i < 1$ or $i > Size(S)$; otherwise, it is the symbol at position i.

5. *Replace*: $A \times N \times S \rightarrow S$: The function value *Replace(a,i,S)* is undefined if $i < 1$ or $i > Size(S)$; otherwise, it is S with the symbol in position i replaced by a.

6. *Insert*: $A \times N \times S \rightarrow S$: The function value *Insert(a,i,S)* is undefined if $i < 1$ or $i > Size(S) + 1$; otherwise, it is S with the symbol a at position i and with all symbols at positions $i..Size(S)$ in S now at positions $i + 1..Size(S) + 1$.

7. *Delete*: $N \times S \rightarrow S$: The function value *Delete(i,S)* is undefined if $i < 1$ or $i > Size(S)$; otherwise, it is S without the symbol at position i and with all symbols at positions $i + 1..Size(S)$ in S now at positions $i..Size(S) - 1$.

8. *LeftmostSubstring*: $N \times S \times S \rightarrow N$: The function value *LeftmostSubstring(i,P,S)* is undefined if $i < 1$ or $i > Size(S)$; otherwise, it is the position of the first match of P in S from position i onward. If there is no match, it is zero. A match of P occurs at position j in S if *Examine(j,S)* = *Examine(1,P)*,...,*Examine(j + Size(P) − 1,S)* = *Examine(Size(P), P)*.

7.2 PATTERN MATCHING

Throughout this section, we assume that we are given a **text string** T of length $n \geq 1$ and a **pattern string** P of length $m \geq 1$. We also assume that $m << n$. Furthermore, we assume that $T[n + 1] = T[n + 2] = \cdots = @$, where @ is an **endmarker symbol** that is not in the alphabet of the text and pattern symbols. The endmarker plays a role similar to those of the end-of-line, end-of-record, and end-of-file indicators. Normally, we do not know or wish to compute the size of a string; hence, the endmarker enables us to terminate a search cleanly. We say that P **occurs at position** i in T if $P[j] = T[i + j − 1]$, for all j, $1 \leq j \leq m$; thus, there is a **match** of P in T or P is a substring of T at position i.

There are two related pattern-matching problems. First, for a given P and T, find the *first* or *leftmost occurrence*, if any, of P in T. Second, find *all occurrences* of P in T. For example, these problems correspond to the following commands in the vi text editor under UNIX. (There are similar commands in most text editors.) We have

$$/P/p,$$

which means, "Print the line that contains the first occurrence of P, beginning the search at the current line." We have also

$$/P/gp,$$

which means, "Print all lines containing an occurrence of P in wrap-around order from the current line." These two text-editor commands are probably the most frequently used.

In the Sections 7.2.1, 7.2.2, and 7.2.3, we give a naive algorithm to solve the pattern-matching problems, improve it to give a second solution (the KMP algorithm), and rethink it to give a third solution (the BMH algorithm). The KMP

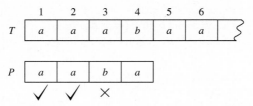

Figure 7.1 The initial pattern position for the naive pattern-matching algorithm.

algorithm demonstrates the power of preprocessing and memory, whereas the BMH algorithm demonstrates that excellent expected-case performance can be obtained by a simpler approach.

7.2.1 A Naive Approach to Pattern Matching

A naive algorithm to solve either of the pattern-matching problems is not difficult to design. Position the pattern below the text so that $P[1]$ is below $T[1]$; see Fig. 7.1 for $P = aaba$ and $T = aaabaa....$ Assume that we are looking for all occurrences of P in T. Compare $P[1]$ with $T[1]$, and compare $P[2]$ with $T[2]$, and so on, until either $P[i] \neq T[i]$ or there is no pattern left; the former corresponds to a failure at position 1 in the text, the latter to a success at position 1. Now slide P one position to the right and compare $P[1]$ with $T[2]$, $P[2]$ with $T[3]$, and so on. With our example, we obtain a match at the second position in T; see Fig. 7.2. The process of comparing and sliding is repeated until $P[m]$ is below $T[n + 1]$. At this point, all matches will have been found; see Fig. 7.3. The corresponding algorithm can be formalized for the specific pattern *aaba* as shown in Program 7.1; unfortunately, although it is simple, it can be extremely inefficient. As an indicator of the matching process, we have included, as a comment with each comparison, the prefix of the pattern currently matched. For example, if we get to the test for equality of $T[i + 3]$ with $'a'$, then we have already matched $'aab'$. We can see why the algorithm is inefficient if we consider the following pathological examples of a pattern and a text. Let $P = a^{m-1}b$ —that is, $m - 1$ as followed by one b— and $T = a^{n-1}b$. At position i of T, we discover a mismatch or match only when comparing $P[m]$ with $T[i + m - 1]$. Moreover, a match occurs at only position

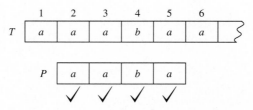

Figure 7.2 A successful match with the naive pattern-matching algorithm.

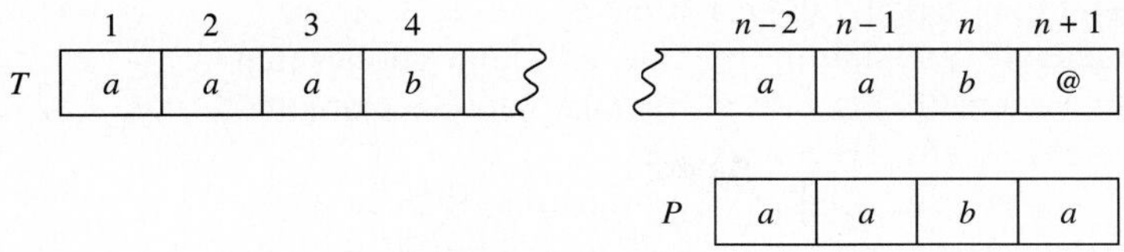

Figure 7.3   The termination position for the naive pattern-matching algorithm.

$n - m + 1$ in T; a mismatch occurs at all other positions i, $1 \le i < n - m + 1$. Now, at each of these positions, we compare exactly m pairs of symbols, whether or not a match occurs. Hence, we make $m(n - m + 1)$ symbol comparisons to find both the first match and all matches. For example, if $n = 10{,}000$ and $m = 10$, we make $100{,}000 - 100 + 10 \approx 100{,}000$ comparisons. We have demonstrated the following fact, expressed formally.

Fact 7.1   *For a pattern of length m and a text of length n, the naive pattern-matching algorithm makes at most mn symbol comparisons in the worst case.*

As with many results of this nature, we are left with a feeling of dissatisfaction. We know that we shall not use such patterns and not have such texts; therefore, how well do we expect the naive algorithm to perform? Assume that we have an alphabet $A = \{a_1, ..., a_c\}$ of $c > 1$ symbols, where p_i is the probability that a_i occurs. Moreover, assume that we have some source that generates symbols independently according to this probability distribution. We can immediately compute the probability p_{eq} that two generated symbols are equal. The probability that two generated symbols are equal to a_i is p_i^2, so the probability p_{eq} is

$$\sum_{i=1}^{c} p_i^2 .$$

Thus, if the probability distribution is uniform (that is, if $p_i = 1/c$) and independent, then p_{eq} is $1/c$.

```
i:= 1; {Initialize the text position.}
while T[i + 4] <> ' @' do
begin
{λ} if T[i] = 'a'
{a}     then if T[i + 1] = 'a'
{aa}         then if T[i + 2] = 'b'
{aab}            then if T[i + 3] = 'a'
{aaba}               then report(i);
     i:= i + 1
end;
```

Program 7.1   A Pascal version of the naive pattern-matching algorithm for the example pattern *aaba*.

Now, define a **random string** of length l to be a string of l symbols, from A, generated by a source independently and uniformly. This definition implies that all symbols from the alphabet are equally likely to occur, and that all pattern and text strings of the same length are equally likely to occur.

Based on these assumptions, we can compute the probability that two random strings P and T of the same length m are equal. For equality of the two strings, we require that $P[1] = T[1],...,P[m] = T[m]$; hence, as each of these equalities is independent of the others, they are all satisfied with probability $1/c^m$. The expected number of symbol comparisons the naive algorithm makes is, however, of more interest. The naive algorithm compares $P[i + 1]$ and $T[i + 1]$ only when $P[1..i] = T[1..i]$. By the previous argument, this latter equality occurs with probability $1/c^i$; thus, a comparison is made at position $i + 1$ with probability $1/c^i$, so the expected number of comparisons made by the naive algorithm on P and T is

$$1 + \sum_{i=2}^{m} 1/c^{i-1} = \frac{c}{c-1}\left(1 - \frac{1}{c^m}\right).$$

Note that, for large m, this number is approximated by $c/(c-1)$.

For a pattern P of length m and a text T of length n, where $n \geq m$, the naive algorithm examines $n - m + 1$ substrings of t of length m. Since, by assumption, each of these substrings is random, the expected number of symbol comparisons made by the naive algorithm is

$$\frac{c}{c-1}\left(1 - \frac{1}{c^m}\right)(n - m + 1).$$

Two typical alphabets are the binary alphabet and ASCII. With the binary alphabet, we expect the naive algorithm to make $\approx 2(n - m + 1)$ comparisons; with ASCII, we expect it to make $\approx n - m + 1$ comparisons. We summarize our findings as the following fact.

Fact 7.2   *For a random pattern of length m, a random text of length n, and an alphabet of size $c > 1$, the naive algorithm makes $\approx cn/(c - 1)$ symbol comparisons, in the expected case, when $m \ll n$.*

Although the naive algorithm has excellent expected-case performance, it has two drawbacks: it has a poor worst-case performance and it repeatedly reexamines text symbols. For these reasons, we consider a more sophisticated algorithm.

7.2.2 The KMP Algorithm

We have proved that the naive algorithm can make $\Omega(mn)$ symbol comparisons in the worst case and $O(n)$ comparisons in the expected case. In this section, we show that we can achieve a worst-case bound of $O(n)$ symbol comparisons by using memory and preprocessing.

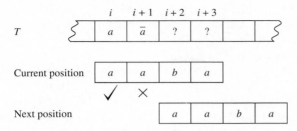

Figure 7.4 An example of when we should slide the pattern beyond the current position in the text.

The naive algorithm (see Program 7.1) always increments i by 1 and repeats the **while** loop when a mismatch occurs. It does not distinguish among the various partial matches; it treats them the same way. As we shall see, it pays to remember the partial match when a mismatch occurs. For example, with $P = aaba$, if $T[i + 1] \neq 'a'$, we can increment i by 2 rather than by 1. If we increment i by 1, then the algorithm recompares $T[i + 1]$ (using the value of i before incrementing) with $P[1] = 'a'$. But we already know that $T[i + 1] \neq P[2] = 'a'$ by the earlier comparison, so this inequality must still hold. Logically, we have that $T[i + 1] \neq P[2]$ and $P[1] = P[2]$ imply $T[i + 1] \neq P[1]$. Hence, we can move the pattern two positions rather than one as is illustrated in Fig. 7.4.

The situation is more complex if $T[i + 2] \neq 'b'$. In this case, $T[i] = 'a'$ and $T[i + 1] = 'a'$. Since $T[i + 2] \neq 'b'$ does not imply, in general, that $T[i + 2] = 'a'$ (normally, we have more than two symbols in the alphabet), we can conclude only that $T[i + 2]$ may be an $'a'$. Thus, the pattern may occur at position $i + 1$; see Fig. 7.5. We should, however, continue by comparing $T[i + 2]$ with $P[2]$, not by comparing $T[i + 1]$ with $P[1]$. The reason for this shift is that $P[1] = P[2]$ and $T[i + 1] = P[2]$ imply that $P[1] = T[i + 1]$ (compare this implication with the previous one).

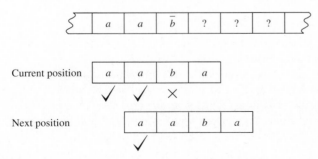

Figure 7.5 An example of when we should slide the pattern, and should continue by comparing the current textual symbol with an earlier pattern symbol.

```
                i:= 1; {Initialize the text position.}
  0: {λ} while T[i + 4] <> ' @' do
            begin
              if T[i] = 'a '
  1: {a}       then if T[i + 1] = 'a'
  2: {aa}         then if T[i + 2] = 'b'
  3: {aab}          then if T[i + 3] = 'a'
     {aaba}            then begin report(i); i:= i + 3; goto 1 end
     {aabā}                    else i:= i + 4 {goto 0}
     {aab̄}                 else begin i:= i + 1; goto 1 end
     {aā}             else i:= i + 2 {goto 0}
     {ā}          else i:= i + 1 {goto 0}
  end;
```

Program 7.2   A Pascal version of the improved naive pattern-matching algorithm.

There are only two possible cases to consider as a result of a mismatch—namely,

1. We continue by comparing $P[1]$ with the next textual symbol; that is, we slide the pattern beyond the current textual position; see Fig. 7.4.

2. We continue by comparing the current textual symbol with some earlier pattern symbol; that is, we do *not* slide the pattern beyond the current textual position; see Fig. 7.5.

Taking these possibilities into account, we obtain the improved pattern-matching algorithm of Program 7.2. We have added comments to display the state of the pattern match at the beginning of each line. So {aab} means that the algorithm is about to test $P[4]$, since $P[1]$, $P[2]$, and $P[3]$ are already matched. Similarly, {$aab̄$} means that a mismatch occurred at position 3 and the pattern must be moved to the right. Note that the integer labels correspond to the highest position matched in the pattern so far.

When a mismatch occurs at pattern position j, the algorithm continues matching at some position k in the pattern, where $k < j$. The value of k is defined uniquely for each mismatch position j; therefore, let $next{:}1..m \rightarrow 0..m - 1$ be the function that specifies this value for each position j in the pattern. With our example pattern, $next(1) = 0$, $next(2) = 0$, $next(3) = 2$, and $next(4) = 0$. Note that, when a mismatch occurs at position j, the algorithm executes **goto** $next(j) - 1$, unless $next(j) = 0$, when the pattern moves past the current text position $T[i]$ and the comparison begins again with $P[1]$ at $T[i + 1]$. In all cases, we are moving the pattern $j - next(j)$ positions.

So far, the new pattern-matching algorithm uses the specific pattern *aaba*, rather than arbitrary patterns. We need to abstract a general pattern-matching algorithm from this new pattern-matching method. To do this abstracting, we col-

```
Compute the function next from P;
i:= 1; j:= 1; {Initialize the pattern and text positions.}
while T[i + m - j] <> ' @' do
begin
    if T[i] = P[j]
    then if j = m
        then begin report(i - m + 1);
            j:= next(m + 1); i:= i + 1
        end
        else begin i:= i + 1; j:= j + 1 end
    else j:= next(j);
    if j = 0 then begin i:= i + 1; j:= 1 end
end;
```

Program 7.3   A Pascal version of the KMP pattern-matching algorithm.

lapse the symbol-matching tests into one general test, as shown in Program 7.3. The general pattern-matching algorithm is called the **KMP algorithm** after Knuth, Morris, and Pratt who designed it. Note that we have extended *next* so that *next*(m + 1) gives the next position in the pattern after a successful pattern match.

We are now in a position to compute the worst-case number of symbol comparisons of the KMP algorithm. Observe that, as a result of each symbol comparison, either i is incremented by 1 or the pattern is moved to the right. Since i can be incremented at most only n times and the pattern can be moved at most only n times, we conclude that the algorithm makes at most $2n$ symbol comparisons in the worst case.

Fact 7.3   *For a pattern of length m and a text of length n, the KMP algorithm makes at most 2n symbol comparisons in the worst case.*

More important, the KMP algorithm never decrements i; that is, it never backs up in the input. Although the KMP algorithm performs at most two symbol comparisons at each textual position *on average,* it may perform many more at some positions. It can be proved that $O(\log m)$ symbol comparisons may occur; see Exercise 7.1. Thus, the KMP algorithm can yield long delays between the reading of two input symbols.

The efficient implementation of the KMP algorithm depends on our ability to compute the *next* function efficiently. We can compute it by using the naive algorithm to match the pattern against prefixes of itself, one prefix for each possible mismatch position. Since there are $m - 1$ such prefixes, the computation of *next* makes $O(m^2)$ symbol comparisons in the worst case. It is possible to compute *next* with $O(m)$ comparisons, in the worst case, by a more complex algorithm that uses the KMP algorithm to match the pattern against itself; see Exercise 7.2. We are more interested, however, in obtaining a pattern-matching algorithm that is faster than both the naive and KMP algorithms.

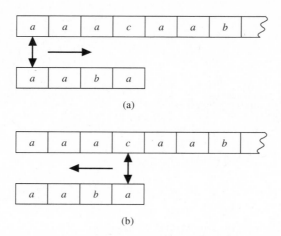

(a)

(b)

Figure 7.6   A comparison of the KMP and BMH pattern-matching methods.
(a) The KMP approach. (b) The BMH approach.

7.2.3   The BMH Algorithm

In the naive and KMP algorithms, we attempt to match the pattern against the text
by moving through both the pattern and the text from left to right; see Fig. 7.6(a).
Boyer and Moore suggested an interesting alternative approach—namely, moving
through the pattern from right to left while moving through the text from left to
right; see Fig. 7.6(b). Horspool suggested a drastic simplification of their original
algorithm. The resulting algorithm, the **BMH algorithm,** makes the same number
of symbol comparisons as the naive algorithm makes, in the worst case, but, in
the expected case, it makes a sublinear number of comparisons. Since the KMP
algorithm makes at least n comparisons, in the expected case, the BMH algorithm
is more efficient.

   One further advantage of the BMH algorithm is that, whenever a textual
symbol is found that does not appear anywhere in the pattern, the pattern is
moved completely past it. In Fig. 7.6(a), the KMP algorithm eventually compares
$T[4] = c$ with $P[3] = b$, where $P = aaba$. It then compares $T[4]$ with $P[2]$ before
moving the pattern past c. On the other hand, the BMH algorithm discovers that
$T[4] = c$ is not in the pattern on the first comparison; hence, it immediately moves
the pattern past that point. This example is, of course, loaded in favor of the BMH
algorithm to illustrate the maximal improvement possible; it can be proved, however, that the BMH algorithm outperforms the KMP algorithm in the expected
case.

   The difference between the BMH and KMP algorithms, apart from the direction of movement through the pattern, is that the BMH algorithm takes into
account the symbols in the text when it encounters a mismatch, whereas the KMP
algorithm ignores them.

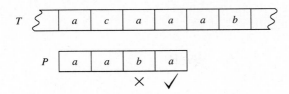

Figure 7.7 Why, for a pattern of length m and each symbol a, $symnext(a) \neq m$ in the BMH algorithm.

Building on the observation in our example, we define a function, called *symnext,* that maps symbols into nonnegative integers. It is defined by

$$symnext(s) = \begin{cases} 0, & \text{if } s \text{ is not in } P[1..m-1]; \\ k, & \text{if } a \text{ is in } P[1..m-1] \text{ and } k \text{ is the rightmost} \\ & \text{position of } s \text{ in } P[1..m-1]. \end{cases}$$

The function *symnext* gives the position in the pattern that should be aligned with the current textual position corresponding to the position m in the pattern. The function *symnext* should be compared with the function *next* of the KMP algorithm; *next* gives the position in the pattern that should be aligned with the current position in the text. We consider only the first $m-1$ symbols in the pattern so that $symnext(P[m]) \neq m$. We thus ensure that the pattern always moves after a mismatch. For example, in Fig. 7.7, if we were to define $symnext('a') = 4$, then a mismatch at position 3 in the pattern and text would imply that the pattern does not move at all.

Assume that some suffix of the pattern has been matched and that the symbol at the next position, say $P[j]$, does not match $T[i-m+j]$. (We maintain the invariant that position i in the text corresponds to position m in the pattern, so i changes only when the pattern slides.) Then, we must slide the pattern such that $P[symnext(T[i])]$ is aligned with $T[i]$. (Notationally, "$P[0]$ is aligned with $T[i]$" means that $P[1]$ is aligned with $T[i+1]$.) We look at only $T[i]$ after a mismatch to determine how we should slide the pattern; we do not look at $T[i-m+j]$, as might be expected. In Fig. 7.8, for $P = aaba$, *symnext* gives a reasonable pattern shift, since $symnext('b') = 3$. Immediately after this shift, we meet c in the text, which does not appear in the pattern, so $symnext('c') = 0$, and we move the pattern completely past this position.

Let us now return to the situation displayed in Fig. 7.7. We have matched the suffix a of the pattern and have found that this match cannot be extended to ba, since the current text symbol is not b. Consider the result of a mismatch at position 3 in the pattern; that is, we have $\bar{b}a$ in the text. Since $symnext('a') = 2$, the pattern slides two places to the right; see Fig. 7.9. A similar argument applied to $\bar{a}ba$ and $\bar{a}aba$ yields the same result.

When we obtain a mismatch between position $i-m+j$ in the text and position j in the pattern, we slide the pattern according to the value of $symnext(T[i])$;

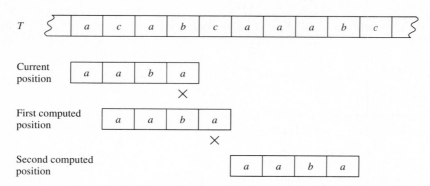

Figure 7.8   Two example pattern shifts in the BMH pattern-matching algorithm.

see Program 7.4. It remains to be proved that an occurrence of the pattern is never missed by the BMH algorithm; we leave the proof to Exercise 7.4. Observe that, unlike in the KMP algorithm, after sliding the pattern, we *always begin matching at the last position of the pattern,* discarding any information about the text we have computed previously. Although we have avoided the problem of computing *symnext,* the computation is not difficult; see Exercise 7.5.

Finally, we wish to know how well the BMH algorithm performs. It requires space proportional to the alphabet size—typically 128 or 256 symbols in practice.

Fact 7.4   *For a random pattern of length m, a random text of length n, and an alphabet of size $c > 1$, where $c \ll n$, the BMH algorithm makes $\approx (n/m) + (n/2c)$ symbol comparisons in the expected case.*

Hence, for a binary alphabet, the BMH algorithm makes $\approx (n/m) + (n/4)$ symbol comparisons, in the expected case; for ASCII, it makes $\approx n/m$ character comparisons in the expected case. For example, if $n = 20,000$, $m = 5$, and $c = 128$, then the BMH algorithm is expected to make ≈ 4000 symbol comparisons. The naive algorithm, however, is expected to make $\approx 20,000$ symbol comparisons.

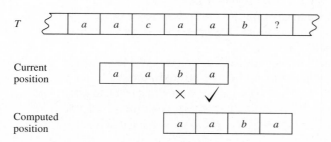

Figure 7.9   What happens after a mismatch at $P[3]$, for the pattern $P = aaba$, with the BMH pattern-matching algorithm.

```
Compute the function symnext from P;
i:= m; j:= m; {Initialize the pattern and text positions.}
while T[i] <> ' @' do
    if T[i - m + j] = P[j]
    then if j = 1
        then begin report(i - m + 1);
                i:= i + m - symnext(T[i]);
                j:= m
        end
        else j:= j - 1
    else begin
        i:= i + m - symnext(T[i]);
        j:= m
    end;
```

Program 7.4   A Pascal implementation of the BMH pattern-matching algorithm.

7.3   SUFFIX AND PATRICIA TRIES

In Section 7.2, we discussed pattern matching in which the pattern was preprocessed but the text was not. This model applies to many text-processing situations in which the text changes over time; therefore, if we preprocessed the text, we would be faced with regular updating of the preprocessed text, which is normally unacceptably expensive. In situations where the text is fairly stable, however, such preprocessing may be a good investment, since it allows for extremely fast pattern matching. For example, it is useful in applications such as electronic dictionaries, encyclopedias, and aircraft manuals.

7.3.1   Suffix Tries

The KMP pattern-matching algorithm together with a *next* function is a **finite-state system** or **automaton.** It reads and "parses" the text. In this section, we preprocess the text, rather than the pattern, to give a finite-state system that reads the pattern but parses the text. The approach we use is based on the following idea. If a pattern P occurs at position i in text T, then P is a prefix of the string $T[i..n]$, which is itself a suffix of T. Conversely, if P is a prefix of some suffix of T, then P occurs in T. These facts suggest the following pattern-matching algorithm.

For a text T (ending with the endmarker @), we list all nonempty suffixes of T apart from @ itself. For a pattern P, we search the list for all suffixes that have P as a prefix. If we sort the list alphabetically before we begin, the search is easier. Indeed, we could do binary search; see Exercise 7.11.

Rather than generate a list of suffixes, we create a compact trie (see Section 6.2.1) of suffixes instead. Then, as we have shown in Section 6.2.1, we can answer a query with a string P in at most $O(|P|)$ time. Recall that, in a trie, each

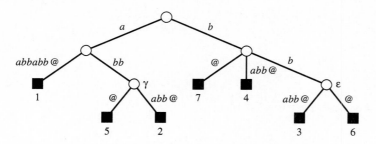

Figure 7.10 The compact trie of suffixes of the text *aabbabb@*.

internal node has as many branches as there are symbols in the underlying alphabet. Furthermore, these branches are indexed by the symbols, so the first branch corresponds to the first symbol of the alphabet, the second branch to the second symbol, and so on. In a compact trie, we associate strings, rather than single symbols, with each branch; however, the first symbol of a string on a branch must be that branch's symbol. We cannot have *ab* and *aab* associated with different branches out of the same node. This property ensures that branching takes place in the same way as in a trie.

We demonstrate the approach with the sample text *aabbabb@*, where @ is the endmarker. We construct a compact trie for all nonempty suffixes of the given text. For the example text, the suffixes are *aabbabb@*, *abbabb@*, *bbabb@*, *babb@*, *abb@*, *bb@*, and *b@*; the suffix @ is irrelevant. The corresponding compact trie is shown in Fig. 7.10, where the external nodes are labeled with the position of the first symbol of the suffix in the text. We call such a trie of suffixes a **suffix trie;** it is defined as a compact trie for the suffixes of a given text such that each active external node is labeled with the position in the text of the first symbol of the corresponding suffix. Now, to determine whether a pattern occurs in the given text, we use that pattern as a query in the suffix trie. At each node on the search path in the trie, the symbol at the current position in the pattern determines a branch. If that branch's string is a prefix of the pattern from the current position onward, then we take the branch and increment the current position by the length of the string. Otherwise, the pattern is not in the trie and hence is not in the text.

For example, with *abb* and the example suffix trie of Fig. 7.10, the search ends at node γ. Hence, *abb* appears in the text at least once and, since the number of active external nodes in γ's subtree is 2, it appears exactly twice. On the other hand, *bbb* causes the search to end at node ε, since there is no active *b* child of ε, and hence *bbb* does not appear in the text. Determination of whether a pattern P of length m appears somewhere in the text takes only at most m node visits; reporting all positions where the pattern appears takes at most $m + 2k - 1$ node visits, where k is the number of occurrences of the pattern in the text. (There are k active external nodes and hence at most $k - 1$ internal nodes in the subtree given by the pattern.)

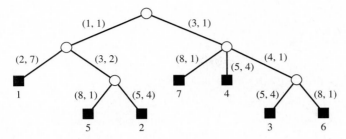

Figure 7.11   A reference version of the suffix trie of Fig. 7.10.

In practice, rather than associating variable-length strings with branches, we replace the strings by references to instances of them in the text. For example, *bb* can be replaced by either (3,2) or (6,2), where an integer pair (i,j) indicates the string $T[i..i + j - 1]$. One version of the example suffix tree of Fig. 7.10, with such replacements, is given in Fig. 7.11. Clearly, the number of node visits in a search is the same as before; however, the space requirements are reduced from $O(n^2)$ cells for the suffix trie, with variable-length strings on its branches, to $O(n)$ cells for the reference version.

7.3.2   Construction of Suffix Tries

Having introduced suffix tries as an efficient data structure for solving pattern-matching queries, we are left with the problem of constructing them. It is possible that all strings in a suffix trie share a nonempty prefix. We associate this prefix with an edge or **hook** to the root node; see Fig. 7.12. From an implementation viewpoint, a suffix trie is given by a pair consisting of a suffix trie (without a hook) and a string. Note that in a suffix trie that contains every suffix of a given text, apart from @, a hook is associated with only either a single symbol or the empty string.

We construct a suffix trie for a text by inserting one suffix at a time into an initially empty suffix trie. We use our example text *aabbabb@* once more. The first suffix is the whole text and, since the suffix trie is empty, we introduce an

Figure 7.12   A hooked suffix trie.

Figure 7.13   Insertion of *aabbabb@* into an empty suffix trie.

external node and a hook; see Fig. 7.13. In this case, the hook contains the whole string. We now insert the suffix *abbabb@*. To do this insertion, we traverse the first edge (the hook). Since it contains a nonempty string, we compare the two strings from left to right until we obtain a mismatch. (Observe that there must be a mismatch.) Such a mismatch occurs at the second position in both strings. We split the branch with a new internal node; see Fig. 7.14. The upper portion of the broken branch is labeled with the common prefix of the two strings, the lower portion is labeled with the remainder of the first string, and the new branch is labeled with the remainder of the inserted string. We repeat this process with *bbabb@*, *babb@*, *abb@*, *bb@*, and *b@*. The first three of these insertions are displayed in Fig. 7.15. If, during the search for the branch to be split, we match a string on a branch completely, we immediately continue the process with the branch's target node and the remainder of the insertion string. We branch from the target node on the basis of the next symbol of the insertion string. This branching is shown in Fig. 7.15(b); *babb@* matches λ on the hook and we branch on *b*, the first symbol of the remainder of *babb@* (in this case, *babb@* itself). This process is seen again in Fig. 7.15(c), since *abb@* arrives at node α with remainder *bb@*; hence, the *b* edge leading to external node 2 is taken. The final result is indeed the suffix trie of Fig. 7.10.

The construction algorithm as described is inefficient. Given the text $a^{n-1}@$, the insertion of $a^{j-1}@$ makes j node visits. Hence, the construction algorithm makes a total of $(n+1)+(n-2)+\cdots+2=n(n-1)/2-1$ node visits; that is, it takes $O(n^2)$ time. The construction algorithm can be improved to run in linear time, but we do not describe that improvement here because it is too complex.

We make one final remark. We normally construct the reference version of the suffix trie, since we discover representatives during the construction algorithm.

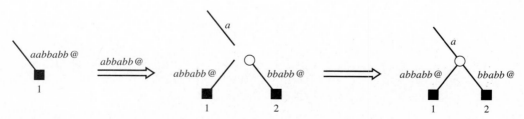

Figure 7.14   Insertion of *abbabb@* into the suffix trie of Fig. 7.13.

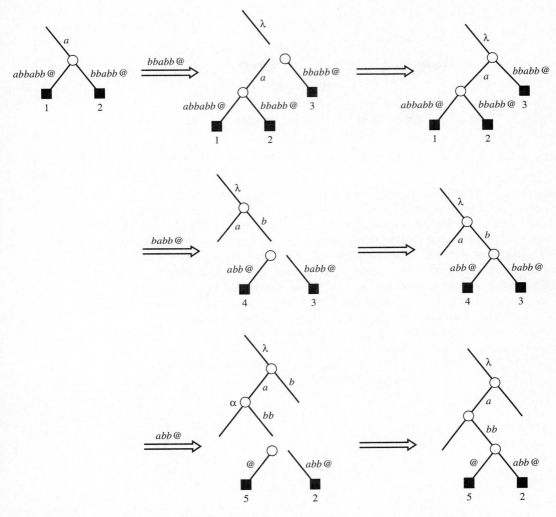

Figure 7.15 Insertion of *bbabb@*, *babb@*, and *abb@* into the suffix trie of Fig. 7.14.

7.3.3 PATRICIA Tries

A **PATRICIA trie** is a compact trie or suffix trie in which strings or their representatives on edges are replaced by single symbols and skip counts; see the discussion of binary tries in Section 6.2.2. PATRICIA is an acronym for "Practical Algorithm To Retrieve Information Coded In Alphanumeric." The suffix trie of Fig. 7.10 can be converted into the PATRICIA trie of Fig. 7.16. Observe that the skip count of each node u in a PATRICIA trie is the length of the string on the branch from u's parent to u in the trie. Furthermore, whenever symbols are

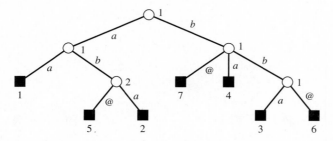

Figure 7.16   The PATRICIA trie corresponding to the suffix trie of Fig. 7.10.

skipped at a node u in a PATRICIA trie, all strings in u's subtree have the same symbols at these skipped positions; we call it the **PATRICIA-trie condition.** This condition enables us to insert a string of length m into a PATRICIA trie in $O(m)$ time; see Exercise 7.14. Searching takes place in much the same way as for suffix tries, but with two differences; see Fig. 7.17. First, on the search string's arrival at a node, the current position in the search string is incremented by the skip count. Thus, the skip count is at least 1. The symbol at the new position is then used to branch from the node. Second, on the search string's arrival at an active external node, the associated string does not necessarily match the search string—it may match at only some of its positions. We need to perform a pattern match at the corresponding position in the text. Observe that, in the PATRICIA trie of Fig. 7.16, *abaa* leads to external node 2, which represents *abbabb@*!

If a text file is small enough to be stored completely in main memory, then the reference version of the suffix trie is the better structure to use. Otherwise, the

```
Given a PATRICIA trie T and a pattern p;
let u be the root node of T and i = 0;

while u is not external and (pᵢ ≠ @) do
begin i:= i + skipcount(u);
    u:= pᵢth child of u;
end;

if u is external
then
    if u is active
    then if string(u) is equal to p, then report success;
            otherwise, report failure;
    else report failure
else report failure;
```

Figure 7.17   A high-level implementation of pattern-matching in a PATRICIA trie.

PATRICIA trie is preferred, because it does not require access to the text file at each internal node, whereas the suffix trie does.

7.4 MINIMUM EDIT DISTANCE

Recall the game in which you are given two words such as PLAY and CARD, and you are asked to transform one into the other by changing one symbol at a time so that each change results in a word. For example, PLAY, PLOY, PLOP, CLOP, COOP, HOOP, HOOD, HOLD, COLD, CORD, and CARD is one such sequence. If we do not require the intermediate strings to be words, we can change PLAY to CARD with four symbol changes.

In this section, we are interested in how we can change one string into another string by means of insertions and deletions of symbols. The replacement scheme we used in the word game could instead use insertions and deletions. For example, PLAY, PAY, PAD, CAD, CARD is one possible transformation sequence.

In a general setting, we have two strings—for example, *aabbaabb* and *bbbaaabbbaaa*—and we want to find a sequence of insertions and deletions that transforms the first string into the second string. For example, we can delete the first two symbols of the first string to give *bbaabb,* and then insert the extra *a*s and *b*s that are needed. Such a sequence is called an **edit sequence,** and its length is called the **edit distance.** In the example, the number of insertions and deletions is eight and, in this case, we cannot complete the task with fewer operations.

The problem we tackle in this section is this: *Given two strings, find the* **minimum edit distance** *between them.* The method we use, with some modification, also can be used to find an edit sequence of minimum length. The problem is another example of an optimization problem: Find a best solution, not just any solution.

We are interested in the problem of finding the minimum edit distance because it provides a way of quantifying the similarity of two strings. Intuitively, *begin* and *bgin* are similar, but *begin* and *end* are not. If we are searching for a particular pattern in a text and it does not occur, we might be interested in finding the closest-matching substring that does occur. If we have two versions of a text file—for example, two drafts of a chapter of a text on data structures—we might want to know how similar they are to each other. If we have two versions of a program that are supposed to give the same results, then we would like to be able to compute the similarity of two outputs obtained from the same input data. The uses of such a tool are boundless. The UNIX utility `diff` is an example of such a program.

How do we compute the minimum edit distance of two strings? In Section 7.4.1, we consider a naive approach to this problem that takes exponential time in the worst case. We then use the experience we have gained to obtain an algorithm that takes time proportional to the product of the lengths of the two given strings.

The improved algorithm uses *dynamic programming,* an important technique that we can use to solve optimization problems that satisfy the optimality principle.

7.4.1 A Naive Algorithm

We begin by stating three facts about the problem. The first fact is that we can always perform all deletions first, and then do all insertions. The second fact is that the minimum edit distance from a string x to a string y is the same as the minimum edit distance from y to x. The reason for this reflexivity is that a deletion in string x corresponds to an insertion in string y, and an insertion in x corresponds to a deletion in y. The third fact is that, in a minimum-length edit sequence, we never insert a deleted symbol and we never delete an inserted symbol.

Based on these facts, a naive algorithm that springs to mind does the following for two strings x and y of equal length. The algorithm first determines whether x and y are equal. If they are not, it deletes one symbol from x and y at all possible positions; this deletion step gives the 1-sets of x and y. If the 1-sets have a string in common, then y can be obtained from x with one deletion and one insertion. Otherwise, we continue by comparing the 2-sets, the 3-sets, and so on. Clearly, the algorithm terminates; on termination, it will have discovered the minimum edit distance of two equal-length strings.

If x and y are of lengths m and n, where $m \leq n$, we can proceed similarly, except that we first delete enough symbols from y that the corresponding deletion set has only words of length m; that is, we construct the $(n - m)$-set of y. For example, with *begin* and *end,* we first delete two symbols from *begin* in all possible ways to give the 2-set

gin ein egn egi bin bgn bgi ben bei beg.

Now, we begin by checking whether *end* is in the 2-set of *begin*; since it is not, we construct the 3-set of *begin* and the 1-set of *end*:

in gn gi en ei eg bn bi bg be

and

nd ed en.

At this stage, we see that *en* appears in the 3-set of *begin* and the 1-set of *end*; hence, the minimum edit distance is $1 + 3$ — that is, 4. The minimum edit distance from *begin* to *end* is realized by the following edit sequence: delete b, delete g, delete i, and insert d after the last symbol.

For two strings of lengths m and n, $m \leq n$, the naive algorithm has a worst-case performance of $O(2^n)$ time, because there are 2^n subsequences of the longer string. We now introduce a more efficient algorithm that makes considerable use of the structure of a minimum-length edit sequence.

7.4.2 A Dynamic-Programming Algorithm

To understand the idea behind the new algorithm, we change our perspective; instead of focusing on the symbols that must be deleted and inserted, we focus on those that are unchanged. These symbols are given as the common string in the naive algorithm. Given a string x of length m, an integer k (where $1 \leq k \leq m$), and positions $i_1,...,i_k$ in x such that $1 \leq i_1 < \cdots < i_k \leq m$; then $x[i_1] \cdots x[i_k]$ is a **subsequence of** x. If $k = 0$, the subsequence is the empty string. Clearly, every subset of $1..m$ determines a subsequence, so there are 2^m subsequences of x. A string u is a **common subsequence** of two strings x and y if u is a subsequence of x and u is a subsequence of y. A string u is a **longest common subsequence (LCS)** of two strings x and y if it is a common subsequence of x and y and there is not a longer string that is a common subsequence of x and y. There can be more than one LCS of x and y; for example, with $x = ac$ and $y = ca$, there are two, a and c. Observe that the minimum edit distance between two strings is the sum of their lengths minus twice the length of their LCS.

We can view an LCS schematically as shown in Fig. 7.18; we connect the unchanging pairs of symbols in the two given strings x and y with straight lines. Note that the lines cannot cross. We now cut each of the two strings into two substrings, $x = x_1 x_2$ and $y = y_1 y_2$, without cutting any connecting line. Once we have done the cutting, we have the following fact: The sum of the minimum edit distances from x_1 to y_1 and from x_2 to y_2 is equal to the minimum edit distance from x to y. This result is an example of the **optimality principle:** *Optimal solutions are composed of optimal subsolutions.* Whenever the optimality principle holds, we can obtain an optimal solution to a given problem by building it up from optimal solutions to smaller subproblems; this technique is called **dynamic programming**.

Rather than cutting two given strings at arbitrary positions, we try to cut them to the right of the rightmost connecting line, by removing at most the last symbol in each string. The optimality principle still holds, but one subproblem is trivialized. The last symbols in x and y may be joined by a connecting line only if they are equal; otherwise, at most one of them can be the endpoint of a connecting line to an earlier symbol in the other string; see Fig. 7.19. For each of the four

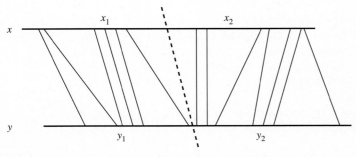

Figure 7.18   A longest common subsequence (LCS) of two strings.

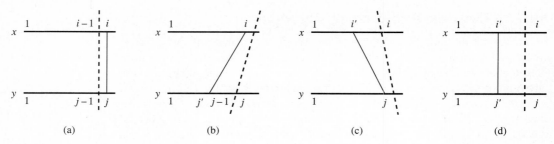

Figure 7.19   The four possible cuts.

possible cuts of the two strings, the edit sequence that produces y_2 from x_2 is trivial. We transform x_2 into y_2 by deleting every symbol in x_2 and inserting every symbol in y_2. Otherwise, we would not be to the right of a connecting line! (It is possible that we cut along a candidate connecting line; that is, the two symbols to the left of the cut may be equal.)

The foregoing discussion suggests the following approach to the problem of minimum edit distance. It is important to remember that we do not know where the connecting lines are to be placed, we are attempting to discover a placement. Given two strings x and y of lengths m and n, respectively, let d_{ij} denote the minimum edit distance between $x[1..i]$ and $y[1..j]$. In this notation, we want to compute d_{mn}. We consider the effect of a cut that cuts off at most the last symbol in each of these substrings; see Fig. 7.19. The rightmost connecting line for the two substrings may connect $x[i]$ and $y[j]$, if $x[i] = y[j]$; may connect $x[i]$ and $y[j']$, for some $j' < j$; may connect $x[i']$ and $y[j]$, for some $i' < i$; or may connect $x[i']$ and $y[j']$, for some $i' < i$ and $j' < j$. When $x[i] = y[j]$, either we ignore their equality, in which case we must delete $x[i]$ and insert $y[j]$, or we consider them to be joined by a connecting line. In the first case, we introduce a cost of 2 units, whereas, in the second case, we introduce a cost of 0 units. The four alternatives lead to the following recurrence equation for d_{ij}:

$$d_{ij} = \min\{d_{i-1,j-1} + 2\delta_{ij}, d_{i,j-1} + 1, d_{i-1,j} + 1\},$$

where $\delta_{ij} = 1$, if $x[i] = y[j]$; otherwise, $\delta_{ij} = 0$.

We give a worked example of the computation of d_{ij}, for the two strings *end* and *begin,* in which we use a matrix representation for the values of d. For convenience, we let i and j take the value 0. By the notation d_{0j}, we mean the minimum edit distance between $x[1..0]$ and $y[1..j]$ —that is, between the empty string λ and $y[1..j]$. Now, the only way to obtain $y[1..j]$ from the empty string is to insert every symbol; hence, $d_{0j} = j$, $0 \le j \le n$. Similarly, $d_{i0} = i$, $0 \le i \le m$. The initial version of the distance matrix is given in Table 7.1.

We now fill in the remainder of the matrix row by row in left-to-right order. The values of d_{1j}, $1 \le j \le n$, are computed from the recurrence equation given previously. For example, d_{11}, the distance from e to b, is the minimum of $d_{10} + 1$, $d_{01} + 1$, and $d_{00} + 2$; that is, it is 2. The next value d_{12} is the minimum of $d_{11} + 1$,

Table 7.1   The initial edit-distance matrix for the two strings *end* and *begin*.

d		λ	b	e	g	i	n
		0	1	2	3	4	5
λ	0	0	1	2	3	4	5
e	1	1					
n	2	2					
d	3	3					

Table 7.2   The final edit-distance matrix for all pairs of prefixes of the two strings *end* and *begin*.

d		λ	b	e	g	i	n
		0	1	2	3	4	5
λ	0	0	1	2	3	4	5
e	1	1	2	1	2	3	4
n	2	2	3	2	3	4	3
d	3	3	4	3	4	5	4

$d_{02} + 1$, and d_{01} (since $x[1] = y[2] = e$); this value is 1. The completed distance matrix is given in Table 7.2. Note that $d_{35} = 4$, as we expected.

Because the algorithm to compute d_{mn} computes all values of d_{ij}, for all i,j, $0 \le i \le m$ and $0 \le j \le n$, it takes $\Omega(mn)$ time. Each entry takes constant time to compute, however, so the algorithm runs in $O(mn)$ time, a distinct improvement over the naive algorithm. We leave to Exercise 7.15 the problem of computing a minimum-length edit sequence for two strings.

7.5 ADAPTIVE DATA COMPRESSION

Data compression is a method of encoding that allows a substantial reduction in the total number of bits required to store a file, compared to conventional methods. For example, a text file of n characters, when encoded using 7-bit ASCII, requires $7n$ bits. However, variable-length encoding methods can use substantially fewer bits in the expected case, typically reducing the number of bits needed by 50 percent. We have already described one such method in Section 6.1—that developed by Huffman. Data-compression methods are compared by their **compression ratio,** which is the ratio of the number of bits in the encoded text to the number of bits in the source text, expressed as a percentage. Huffman encoding gives compression ratios of 55 to 65 percent.

Huffman's data-compression method has two severe disadvantages. First, we must have advance knowledge of the probability distribution of the symbols in the text file if we are to construct a good variable-length code. Either a probability distribution is assumed—for example, the one for English—or it is computed for the given text file by a prescan. Neither of these alternatives is attractive, the first because it may be very different from the unknown distribution of the text, and the second because we may not be able to access the whole text file in advance. We could avoid this difficulty by modifying Huffman's algorithm such that it *adapts* to the probability distribution of the text scanned so far; this adaptation would give a dynamic version of Huffman's algorithm.

The second disadvantage of Huffman's method is that once the code is chosen for the symbols, it is fixed for the whole text; it is globally optimal, but it is not locally optimal. It does not recognize repeated substrings that could be encoded more efficiently; its unit of encoding is fixed in advance. We could obviate this difficulty, to some extent, by encoding pairs (or triples, and so on) of adjacent symbols—that is, **digrams** (or **trigrams**, and so on)—rather than single symbols. This approach, however, increases the size of the code quadratically (or cubically, and so on).

Rather than attempting to overcome these problems by modifying Huffman's algorithm, we prefer to introduce a new method, the **ZLW method,** that deals with these difficulties directly. The acronym ZLW comes from the names of the algorithm's developers: Ziv, Lempel, and Welch. This **adaptive encoding algorithm** recognizes repeated substrings and encodes them more efficiently. The UNIX utilities `compress` and `uncompress` are based on the ZLW method. The ZLW method is the first example of an adaptive algorithm that we use to show that **adaptivity,** in an appropriate setting, can produce more efficient algorithms. ZLW encoding gives compression ratios of 45 to 55 percent, an improvement of 10 percent over Huffman encoding. In Section 7.5.1, we introduce the **ZLW-encoding algorithm;** in Section 7.5.2, we show how **ZLW-decoding** is accomplished. We use the same example to explain both algorithms.

7.5.1 The ZLW-Encoding Algorithm

Huffman's algorithm produces a code tree such as the one shown in Fig. 7.20(a). The corresponding symbol–codeword map can be represented by a height-1 trie, the **source trie,** as shown in Fig. 7.20(b). Just as decoding can be viewed as repeatedly traversing root-to-frontier paths of a code tree, encoding can be viewed as repeatedly traversing root-to-frontier paths of the source trie. But why should we restrict ourselves to height-1 tries? In Fig. 7.20(d), we give a source trie of height 2 with integer codewords, rather than with variable-length binary codewords. The string

adbacbcd

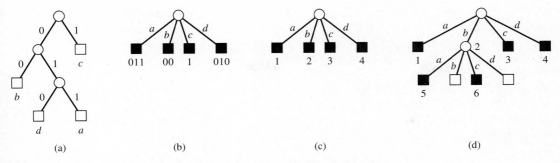

Figure 7.20 Code trees and source tries. (a) A code tree. (b) A standard source trie. (c) A standard source trie with integer codewords. (d) A variable-length source trie with integer codewords.

is partitioned, by the source trie, into the strings or **tokens**

$$a|d|ba|c|bc|b|d,$$

and this partitioning results in the encoded text

$$1453624,$$

whereas the source trie of Fig. 7.5(c) gives

$$142132324.$$

Source tries do not satisfy the prefix property; for example, both b and ba are legal tokens for the source trie of Fig. 7.20(d). Despite this problem, we can partition a source text unambiguously with a source trie, if we do **greedy partitioning;** we continue extending a root-to-frontier path as long as we can. That is why ba is treated as the token ba, rather than as two separate tokens b and a.

With block codes such as ASCII, both the source tokens and codewords are fixed length. With prefix codes, the source tokens are fixed length, but the codewords are variable length. With ZLW coding, both the source tokens and codewords are variable length, so a ZLW encoder has to partition the source into tokens before encoding them. The partitioning of the source text is called **tokenizing,** in analogy with the first pass of a programming-language compiler.

It is this view of encoding that is exploited by the ZLW algorithms. In addition, rather than producing bit strings directly, the ZLW-encoding algorithm produces positive integers. In Fig. 7.20(c), we give an integer code for $a, b, c,$ and d. We can either encode the integers as variable-length bit strings or treat them as short integers in the usual way. We choose the latter approach because of its simplicity.

With prefix codes, we assume, essentially, that both the encoder and decoder know the code before the source text is encoded. With ZLW coding, we assume that the knowledge shared by the encoder and decoder, before a source text is encoded, is the source alphabet and its ordering. Before the encoder begins encoding a new source text, it initializes its source trie to be a height-1 trie for the source alphabet with the initial integer codes of 1,2,..., up to the size of the alphabet, as in Fig. 7.20(c). Normally, we also assume that one of the source symbols occurs at only the end of the source text; it is an *endmarker*. We explain the ZLW-encoding algorithm by way of example using the source text

$$ababcbababaaaa@$$

with the source alphabet $\{a,b,c,@\}$, where @ is the endmarker and the alphabetical order is as given. A high-level implementation of ZLW encoding is given in Fig. 7.21. The initial source trie is shown in Fig. 7.22. As we shall see, the ZLW-encoding algorithm forces the source trie to grow by extending each matched path by one symbol. At each stage, we have a source trie that recognizes one more token. Starting with the source trie in Fig. 7.22, we begin to tokenize the source

```
Given an initial source trie T for m symbols and a text t;
Let last = m be the largest current codeword and i = 1;

while t_i ≠ @ do
begin
    let u be the root node of T;
    while u is not external do
    begin u:= t_ith child of u;
        i:= i + 1
    end;

    last:= last + 1;
    if u is active
    then begin
        emit codeword of u;
        change u into an internal node and add a new
        active external child, with codeword last, as the
        t_ith child of u
    end
    else begin
        emit codeword of u's parent;
        activate u with codeword last
    end
end;
```

Figure 7.21 A high-level implementation of ZLW encoding.

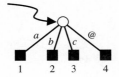

Figure 7.22 The initial encoding trie.

text. Beginning at the root, we discover that *a* is the first token; indeed, the first token is always a single symbol. Hence, we emit its codeword 1 and also add to the trie a new token that consists of the current token followed by the next source symbol. For this example, *b* is the next symbol, so we add the token *ab* to the source trie together with the next integer codeword 5; see Fig. 7.23(a). The next integer, used as a codeword, is always 1 more than the current largest integer used as a codeword. We continue tokenizing the remainder of the source text, *babcbababaaaa@*. Note that the lookahead symbol must not be skipped; otherwise, it will not appear in any token. Now *b* is the next token, so 2 is emitted and the token *ba* is added to the source trie with codeword 6; see Fig. 7.23(b). We continue the tokenization with the suffix *abcbababaaaa@* of the source text and, this time, we see that *ab* is the next token, so its codeword 5 is emitted and the token *abc* is added with codeword 7; see Fig. 7.23(c). This process continues until, eventually, we obtain the token *@*, the termination symbol. At this point, we have the final source trie shown in Fig. 7.24.

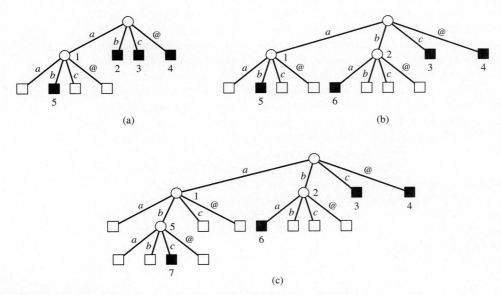

Figure 7.23 The first three steps of the ZLW-encoding algorithm on the example source text.

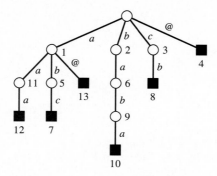

Figure 7.24   The final source trie. For clarity of presentation, the irrelevant branches have been omitted.

The source text has been tokenized as

a	b	ab	c	ba	bab	a	aa	a	$@$
1	2	5	3	6	9	1	11	1	4

The corresponding code sequence is as shown. Can we design a decoding algorithm that decodes such an encoded text correctly? Fortunately, we can.

7.5.2   The ZLW-Decoding Algorithm

The decoder begins with the same source trie as does the encoder; see Fig. 7.20. It reads a sequence of integer codewords and mimics the corresponding actions of the encoder. Therefore, it must reconstruct the same sequence of source tries as the encoder. Assume that the decoder has done this reconstruction for a nonempty prefix of the encoded text that ends with integer i, and that the next integer in the sequence is j. Assume the token of i is x. There are two cases to consider: j is in the source trie, and j is not in the source trie. If j is in the source trie and its corresponding token is ay, for some symbol a and string y, then the encoder will have added the token xa to the source trie with the next integer as its codeword; see Fig. 7.25(a). Therefore, the decoder must add xa to the source trie with the next integer as its codeword and must emit the token ay.

What if j is not in the source trie? This situation can occur, but only in restricted circumstances. It occurs exactly when j corresponds to the token $dx'd$, where $x = dx'$. In other words, the token for j must begin and end with the first symbol of the previously decoded token; see Fig. 7.25(b). In this case, the decoder adds the token $dx'd$ to the source trie with integer codeword j, and it emits $dx'd$ as the token of j.

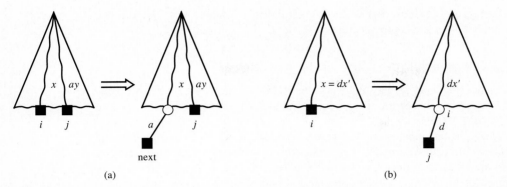

Figure 7.25 The two possible decoding situations. In both cases, the last decoded integer is *i* and the next integer to be decoded is *j*. (a) The interger *j* is in the current source line. (b) The integer *j* is not in the current source line.

We illustrate the decoding algorithm with the same example. We have the encoded text

$$1,2,5,3,6,9,1,11,1.$$

Decoding 1 is straightforward; it causes *a* to be emitted, but nothing else happens. At this stage, we have decoded a nonempty prefix of the encoded text, so we can apply the technique discussed previously. On reading 2, the decoder emits *b* and adds the token *ab* with codeword 5 to the source trie. Similarly, 5 causes *ab* to be emitted and *ba* to be added to the source trie with codeword 6, 3 causes *c* to be emitted and *abc* added to the trie with codeword 7, and 6 causes *ba* to be emitted and *cb* added to the trie with codeword 8. Now the decoder meets 9, and 9 is not in the source trie; see Fig. 7.26. Using the method given previously, we deduce that the decoder must emit *bab,* and we must add *bab* to the trie with codeword 9.

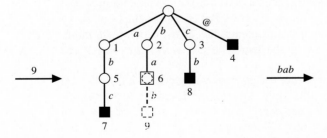

Figure 7.26 The state of play when the decoder reads the integer codeword 9 in the example encoded text.

Comparing the text decoded so far with the original source text, we see that *ababcbabab* is indeed a prefix of the source text.

7.5.3 Implementation and Data Structures

We consider how we might implement the ZLW algorithms. Although we have used a trie as the conceptual structure in both cases, we do not necessarily have to use the ADT TREE.

The ZLW-encoding algorithm needs to be able to navigate down a trie, one branch at a time, to determine whether the current node is external, and, if it is, to determine whether an integer codeword is associated with it. In addition, the algorithm needs to be able to extend the current path with the next source symbol. This operation reduces to either inserting a new internal node and assigning the next integer codeword to one of that node's children, or assigning the next integer codeword to a child of the current node. Given this operation, we can construct the initial source trie from an initially empty trie. All these actions are supported by the ADT TREE operations. Since these operations can be implemented to run in constant time, the ZLW-encoding algorithm can be implemented to run in $O(m + n)$ time, where m is the size of the alphabet and n is the size of the source text; see Exercise 7.16.

The decoding algorithm, on the other hand, needs to be able to navigate up the source trie, one branch at a time. Although its actions can be implemented with the TREE operations, we suggest a different approach: We use a map of integers to strings. Initially, the map is defined for only the source-symbol integers. Thereafter, the ZLW-decoding algorithm needs to determine whether the map is defined for a given integer. If it is, then its codomain is the sought token; otherwise, we use the previous integer in the encoded text to construct a new entry. The astute reader will have already observed that representing the map as a block gives the best performance. If we use integer codewords of 12 bits, then we need a block of size 4096 and the codewords are used as indices. If, further, we represent a token by its last symbol and the integer codeword of the remaining prefix, we need only constant space for each entry. (Note that every nonempty prefix of every token is a token.) With this implementation, the ZLW-decoding algorithm takes $O(m + n)$ time also, where n is the length of the *source text,* not of the encoded text.

If we use 12 bits to represent the integer codewords, then what do we do when we want to add the token 4097 to the source trie? There are two possibilities: either the source trie is unchanged from here on, or the source trie is pruned back so that new tokens can be added. We consider the second possibility; the first possibility is left to Exercise 7.18. The simplest pruning is to cut the source trie back to the initial trie; another possibility is to remove all external nodes, apart from those corresponding to the source alphabet. A comparison of these two approaches is left to Exercise 7.19.

7.6 STRING REPRESENTATIONS

We provide four representations of STRING: the first two are based on the representations of LIST, the third is a combination of a linked-list and block representation, and the fourth is intended to be used for extremely large strings that are stored externally.

7.6.1 LIST Representations

Clearly, any of the LIST representations can also be used to represent STRING. However, each of them has disadvantages.

The block representation is excellent for a substring search, since contiguous symbols are stored contiguously. However, there are two objections to it. First, deleting or inserting a substring is expensive, since it involves moving many symbols to remove a gap or to create a gap. (This objection holds for linked lists, too.) The second, more important, objection is that a maximum length for strings must normally be specified in advance; C uses a block representation. This pre-specification is too restrictive: Either too much space is wasted by a large maximum length being given, or there is the danger of run-time failure because the length was set too short.

The linked-list representations, on the other hand, are inefficient both in space and in time. Although arbitrary length strings are easily accommodated, this accommodation is at the cost of one (or two) pointers for each symbol. If a pointer field is assumed to be 2 bytes and a symbol is assumed to be 1 byte, then a singly linked list requires twice as much space for pointers as it does for symbols. A doubly linked list is even worse—it takes four times as much space for pointers. Asymptotically, these representations use $O(n)$ space for sequences of length n; concretely, however, the multiplicative constant is too high. Similarly, a substring test involves following as many pointers as there are symbols in the substring. Again, asymptotically, such a test takes $O(m)$ time, if m is the length of the substring; concretely, accessing m pointers is normally more time consuming than is moving through the next m positions in a block.

7.6.2 A Chunked-Pointer Representation

Block representations are good for searching because of their contiguity, whereas pointer representations are good for updating because of the linking. Conversely, block representations are bad for updating, whereas pointer representations are bad for searching and storage utilization. These observations suggest that we should try to find a structure that combines the two representations' advantages and minimizes their disadvantages.

We start by dividing strings into fixed-size chunks. Each chunk is represented in a block, and chunks are linked together. In Fig. 7.27, we use chunks of

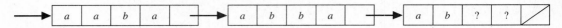

Figure 7.27   A chunked-pointer representation of a string.

size 4 to represent the string *aabaabbaab*. The first problem we meet is this: How do we indicate that the last two positions in the last chunk are not part of the string? Two possible solutions are to reserve one symbol for this purpose (a **void** or **filler** symbol), or to include a count field. The first proposal is fraught with difficulties in that we are usually unable to avoid using any of the symbols in the given alphabet. Therefore, we normally use a count field of, usually, 1 byte. In practice, we need to choose the size of the chunk carefully to ensure good performance.

7.6.3   An External Representation

If we have very large strings, we must almost certainly store them externally. For example, a major dictionary of the English language (such as the unabridged *Oxford English Dictionary*) contains more than 100 million symbols in its machine-readable form. Hence, a two-level structure has emerged—an index block together with an unbounded block for the string. This representation is successful because updates normally are strings, rather than single symbols. Each inserted substring is appended to the current text, and the index is updated to reflect where the new text is stored, whereas each deletion simply causes the index to be updated to avoid the deleted text. For example, given a string in positions $1..n$, the index block contains the pair $(1,n)$. After an insertion of k symbols at position i, the index block contains $(1,i-1),(n+1,n+k),(i,n)$. After a subsequent deletion of text in positions $i-10$ to $i+3$, the index block contains $(1,i-11),(n+5,n+k),(i,n)$. The result of this sequence of operations is illustrated in Fig. 7.28.

The two-level structure can degenerate substantially if many insertions and deletions are carried out. When that happens, the text is reorganized and the index block is reinitialized.

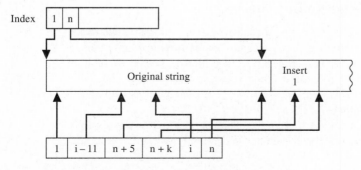

Figure 7.28   A two-level external string representation.

7.6.4 Performance Reports

We content ourselves with examining the worst-case performance of the four string representations. We use the KMP algorithm to implement the *Leftmost-Substring* operation.

The block representation beats every other representation as long as relatively few updates are carried out. Moreover, *LeftmostSubstring* can use the BMH algorithm to obtain sublinear expected-case performance, as indicated in Table 7.3 with the bounds in parentheses. Note that insertion and deletion take linear time in the worst case, even when the update position is already known. This fact is indicated in Table 7.3 by the values in square brackets.

The singly or doubly linked list representations of a string have the disadvantage that finding a position takes linear rather than constant time. Although insertion and deletion take constant time, *if the update position is already known,* we normally do not know the update position, so they take linear time, in the worst case. The positioning problem also affects the performance of the BMH algorithm—the performance is no longer sublinear.

If the size of the chunks is c symbols, then chunking behaves like the pointer representations with a multiplicative constant of $1/c$. Again, the BMH algorithm is no longer sublinear.

Finally, assume that an index block is of size m in the two-level representation. Because the accessing and updating operations need to scan the index block before accessing the string, we see that they must take $O(m)$ time in the worst

Table 7.3 A comparison of the worst-case execution times of the four STRING implementations.

	STRING implementation			
Operation	Block	Pointer	Chunked	Two level
Empty	1	1	1	1
IsEmpty	1	1	1	1
Size	1	1	1	1
Examine	1	n	n/c	$m < 1 >$[a]
Replace	1	n	n/c	$m < 1 >$
Insert	$n[n]$[b]	$n[1]$	$n/c[c]$	$m < U >$
Delete	$n[n]$	$n[1]$	$n/c[c]$	$m < 0 >$
LeftmostSubstring	$n(n/m)$[c]	$n (n)$	$n (n)$	$n (n)$

[a]The values in angle brackets are the number of disk accesses.

[b]The values in square brackets, for insertion and deletion, are the execution times when the update position is given.

[c]The values in parentheses are expected execution times for the BMH algorithm.

Table 7.4   Performance ratings of four implementations of STRING.

STRING implementation	Rating	Comments
Chunked	Very good	Fully dynamic
Block	Good	*LeftmostSubstring* sublinear expected-time; not fully dynamic
Pointer	Satisfactory	Fully dynamic
Two level	Very good	Fully dynamic; fragmentation occurs

case. Once more, the BMH algorithm is inefficient because of the indirectness. For external strings, however, disk accesses are the important measure. Assuming that the index block can be held in main memory (a reasonable assumption), we need only one disk access for *Examine* and *Replace*; U disk accesses for *Insert*, where U is the number of blocks of inserted text; and 0 disk accesses for *Delete*. In Table 7.3, these values are shown, in angle brackets, after the worst-case times.

In summary, as shown in Table 7.4, we prefer the chunked representation over the block and pointer representations, with the two-level representation being the choice for external strings.

7.7 SUMMARY

We have investigated the ADT STRING in some detail. Although it can be subsumed by the ADT LIST, we believe that it is an important concept in its own right, because character and bit strings are so pervasive in the electronic world. The two major differences between the ADTs STRING and LIST are that, in the former, we consider strings to have index positions and we include the operation *LeftmostSubstring*. We have given four representations of strings: block, pointer, chunked, and two-level. The first three are used for internal strings; the chunked representation—a combination of the block and pointer representations—is the representation of choice. The two-level representation is used for external strings. It uses two blocks, an index block and a text block, and it minimizes the number of disk accesses for insertions and deletions.

We have considered two nontrivial approaches to implementing the operation *LeftmostSubstring*: preprocessing the pattern and preprocessing the text. Preprocessing is an important practical technique that can be used in many different situations. We have introduced the KMP pattern-matching algorithm that takes at most $2n$ symbol comparisons, in the worst case, to find all occurrences of a pattern in a text of length n. The BMH algorithm, on the other hand, is an algorithm that is simpler to code and is expected to make $\approx n/m$ symbol comparisons to find all occurrences of a pattern of length m in a text of length n. These two algorithms illustrate a typical tradeoff: an algorithm that is simple to code and has excellent expected-case performance versus an algorithm that is more difficult to code but has very good worst-case performance. In practice, we would choose the BMH algorithm because of its excellent performance and the simplicity of coding its preprocessing step. When we preprocess the text, we obtain even better performance: m node visits to find one occurrence of a pattern of length m. The approach we use introduces the suffix trie, a valuable data structure in its own right.

We have also studied an efficient method of computing the minimum edit distance between two strings and an adaptive method of compressing a string. The problem of finding the minimum edit distance has served to introduce the optimality principle and its algorithmic counterpart, dynamic programming. We shall meet dynamic programming once more in Chapter 10. To compress a string more effectively than Huffman encoding does, we have introduced the ZLW-encoding and decoding algorithms. The ZLW-encoding algorithm has introduced two new ideas: substring encoding and adaptivity. The combination of these two ideas leads to the dramatic improvement of ZLW encoding over Huffman encoding. We shall discuss adaptation further in Chapters 8 and 10.

7.8 HISTORY

The KMP algorithm was discovered independently by Knuth and Pratt, and by Morris; see the history section of their joint paper (Knuth et al., 1977). Knuth derived the algorithm by specializing a construction suggested by Cook (1971) that simulates a deterministic two-way pushdown automaton by a random-access machine, whereas Morris used finite-automata theory directly. The *next* function can be viewed as the transition function of a "conditional" finite automaton: For each state, there are two transitions: one for the current pattern symbol, and one for the next state in case of failure. The BMH algorithm is a simplification of the Boyer–Moore algorithm (1977), developed by Horspool (1980). The empirical evidence for their performance has been confirmed theoretically by Baeza-Yates (1989a; 1989d).

The trie was developed by Sussenguth (1963); the PATRICIA trie was developed by Morrison (1968), although not quite in the form we have presented. The suffix trie was first developed by Weiner (1973), and was improved by McCreight (1976); both authors demonstrated that a suffix trie can be constructed in $O(n)$ time and space from a string of length n. The dynamic-programming algorithm for the problem of finding the minimum edit distance was first designed by Vintsyuk (1968); it has since been rediscovered by many other people (Sankoff, 1972; Wagner and Fischer, 1974; Hirschberg, 1975), as reported in Chapter 1 of the book edited by Sankoff and Kruskal (1983).

Adaptive data compression is important because it allows not only the storage of files in much less space than a block code, such as ASCII, would need, but also transmission of files in much less time than would be required by such a block code. A readable text about text compression is the one written by Bell,

Cleary, and Witten (1990). We discussed Huffman's algorithm in Section 6.1. A dynamic version of Huffman's algorithm was introduced by Gallager (1978); it was extended by Knuth (1985) and Vitter (1987). The UNIX utilities `compact` and `uncompact` are based on adaptive Huffman encoding. Vitter demonstrated that his algorithm takes $2n$ steps. The ZLW-encoding and decoding algorithms are based on those given by Welch (1984), who modified one of the original Ziv–Lempel algorithms (Ziv and Lempel, 1978). The compression ratios of the Huffman and ZLW-encoding methods are taken from Storer's empirical investigations (1988).

The internal representations of strings that we have discussed are standard; see Standish (1980), who also discusses many other variants. The two-level external representation is novel, in this context, and was suggested by Frank Tompa, who used it for the representation of the electronic version of the *Oxford English Dictionary*. It bears some relationship to the notion of difference files—a **difference file** stores the differences between files, rather than the complete files.

EXERCISES

7.1: Prove that a text position may be involved in as many as log m symbol comparisons, in the worst case, in the KMP pattern-matching algorithm.

7.2: The naive approach to computing the *next* function takes $O(m^2)$ time, in the worst case, for a pattern of length m. Implement a more efficient algorithm based on the following ideas. When there is a mismatch at position $i + 1$ of a pattern P, we want to slide P the shortest distance to the right so that we have as large a matching prefix of P as possible. Carry out the following thought experiment. We have two copies P and Q of the pattern. Initially, they are aligned with $P[1]$ opposite $Q[1]$ and $P[m]$ opposite $Q[m]$. Since there is a mismatch with the text at position $i + 1$, we want to determine the largest value of j such that $-1 \le j < i$ and $Q[1..j] = P[i - j + 1..i]$ and $Q[j + 1] \ne P[i + 1]$. This value of $j + 1$ is the value of $next(i + 1)$. To make the computation easier to understand, we introduce an auxiliary function f that is defined in the same way as *next,* except that it requires equality—not inequality—at positions $i + 1$ and $j + 1$.

Now, we can compute $f(i + 1)$ and $next(i + 1)$ recursively as follows. Assume that $f(k)$ and $next(k)$, for all $k \le i$, are known. The first candidate value for $f(i + 1)$ and $next(i + 1)$ is $f(i) + 1$, because at most $Q[f(i) + 1] \ne P[i + 1]$. If these symbols are not equal, then $next(i + 1) = f(i) + 1$; otherwise, $f(i + 1) = f(i) + 1$. In either case, the next candidates for the remaining function value are $f(f(i)) + 1, f(f(f(i))) + 1, \dots$.

Prove that this recursive computation of the two functions takes $O(m)$ time, and that it correctly computes the value of *next*.

7.3: Implement the suggested algorithm to compute the *next* function of the KMP algorithm. Report how well it performs.

7.4: Prove that the BMH algorithm never misses an occurrence of a pattern.

7.5: Design and implement an algorithm to compute *symnext*.

7.6: If we are to simulate the performance of pattern-matching algorithms, we need a pseudorandom text generator. Suggest a method of implementing such a generator, and describe how it might be tested.

7.7: The original Boyer–Moore algorithm is similar to the KMP algorithm in that it examines not only the mismatched text symbol (*symnext*), but also the matched suffix.

Design a pattern-matching algorithm that matches the pattern right to left using only the partially matched suffix, after a mismatch, to slide the pattern. [**Hint:** As in the BMH algorithm, always restart the matching at the last pattern position, and define and use a *next* function.]

7.8: The BMH algorithm moves the pattern, after a mismatch, by examining the text symbol that corresponds to the last symbol in the pattern. It is, perhaps, more natural to move the pattern based on the current mismatched text symbol. Evaluate the performance of such a variant of the BMH algorithm.

7.9: The BMH algorithm shifts a pattern based on the textual symbol opposite the last position of the pattern. The pattern is always moved by at least one position after either a mismatch or a complete pattern match; therefore, why not use the textual symbol that is one position beyond that used in the BMH algorithm? This symbol is not opposite any current pattern position, but it will be, in the BMH algorithm, after the pattern slides to the right. This approach embeds a lookahead into the BMH algorithm; let us call the result the **modified BMH (MBMH) algorithm.**

Compare the MBMH and BMH algorithms on pseudorandom text.

7.10: The idea of using the mismatched text symbol to help the pattern-matching algorithm can be added to the KMP algorithm. Suggest how to incorporate this addition, and compare the resulting algorithm, the **KMP simplified (KMPS) algorithm,** with the KMP pattern-matching algorithm on pseudorandom text.

7.11: Design and implement an algorithm to perform binary search on a sorted block of suffixes of a given text. We normally save space by storing only indexes into the text in the block, creating the **suffix array.** Your algorithm should take $O(m)$ symbol comparisons for a pattern of length m.

A more difficult problem is to construct efficiently such a suffix array from a given text of length n. It is possible to design an algorithm that takes $O(n \log n)$ symbol comparisons to do this construction. Attempt to discover such an algorithm.

7.12: Implement the suffix-trie construction, and design algorithms to solve the following problems:
    a. Given a string, determine a longest repeated substring.
    b. Given two strings, determine a longest common substring.

7.13: Implement the PATRICIA-trie construction and searching algorithms for a large body of text (at least 20,000 symbols).

7.14: Design, implement, and test algorithms for insertion into and deletion from a PATRICIA trie, based on the PATRICIA-trie condition.

7.15: Extend the dynamic-programming algorithm for the minimum edit distance between two strings to find a minimum-length edit sequence.

7.16: Implement the ZLW algorithms using the ADT TREE operations. What are the worst-case running times of your encoding and decoding algorithms?

7.17: Extend the minimum-edit distance problem for two strings in the following two different ways:

    a. Allow the interchange of two adjacent symbols; so, with a string such as *abbabaaaa,* we can obtain *bababaaaa* in one operation. Extend the dynamic-programming algorithm to solve this problem.

    b. Allow different costs for different symbols and operations; so, for example, it may be more expensive to insert an *a* than it is to insert a *p*. Extend the dynamic-programming algorithm to solve this problem.

7.18: Implement the ZLW compression and decompression algorithms. Assume that the source trie is unchanged once the upper bound on integer codewords is reached.

7.19: Implement the two source-trie pruning techniques suggested in the text—namely, prune back to the starting source trie, or prune back the frontier by one level. After you have implemented the two methods, compare their performance.

7.20: Compare the advantages and disadvantages of using fixed-length and variable-length binary encodings of the integer codewords in ZLW compression.

7.21: The suffix trie of a text provides information about that text; for example, it identifies the longest repeated substring. Suggest a compression algorithm based on the suffix trie and longest repeated substrings. Determine how well it performs in comparison to the ZLW method.

8

Sets, Tables, and Dictionaries

We initiate the study of representations for the finite set, which is possibly the most common mathematical and everyday structure. Examples are the sets comprising students in a data-structures course, a project group, a zoo, any committee, and a library.

In computer science, we encounter finite sets of, for example, the identifiers in a program, the words in an on-line dictionary, the programs currently being executed on a system, the courses offered to computer-science students, the records of all undergraduate students, and the faculty and staff in a university.

In this and subsequent chapters, we often refer to an element in a set as a **record.** We do so partly for historical reasons and partly to emphasize that an element normally corresponds to a number of items or **fields**—a record in the data-processing sense. We assume that each record (or element) is identified uniquely by a **(search) key.** A key can be a scalar value, a character string, or a combination of a number of items. In all cases, however, we insist on uniqueness—the key of a record identifies that record uniquely. For simplicity of presentation, we often treat an element as a key, and vice versa. You should, however, bear in mind that a key is usually one field among many.

We first consider sets in general by specifying the SET ADT, before restricting the allowable operations to an important subclass that yields the TABLE and DICTIONARY ADTs. The SET ADT has the set operations *IsMember*, *Union*, *Intersection*, *Difference*, *Size*, and, possibly, *Complement*. In addition, it has the operations *Empty*, *IsEmpty*, *Insert*, *Delete*, and the special set variant of the operation *Examine* that yields a certain element from the given set. The TABLE ADT has only the operations *Empty*, *IsEmpty*, *Insert*, *Delete*, and *IsMember*; the set-theoretic operations are dropped completely. The DICTIONARY ADT has the same operations as TABLE and the additional operations *IsPredecessor*, *IsSuccessor*, *Predecessor*, *Successor*, and *Range*. As we might expect, the reduced number of operations leads to more efficient representations. The names TABLE and DICTIONARY are used interchangeably in many texts, but we distinguish them and treat them separately, since DICTIONARY requires a totally ordered key universe, whereas TABLE does not.

The TABLE ADT abstracts the operations necessary to solve problems of the following form: *Given a set of elements that changes over time by insertion and deletion of elements, determine whether a given element is in the current set.* For example, say the elements are credit-card numbers, and the current set is a set of blacklisted numbers; a query by a salesperson might be, "Is this number on the blacklist?" As another example, if the elements are people's names, then the current set is the set of individuals booked on a particular flight on a particular day; a query is, "Is this particular person booked on this particular flight?" We introduce TABLE representations based on pointers and blocks, in this chapter; one representation based on hashing, a valuable and much-used representation, is discussed in Chapter 9.

The major difference between tables and dictionaries is that we cannot, in general, assume that the key universe of a table is totally ordered. It makes sense, in any dictionary, to ask for the successor or predecessor of a given key, but these operations are not even well defined for all tables. In particular, we can use the *Successor* operation to extract the elements of a dictionary in sorted order with respect to their keys. Two related operations are *Min* and *Max*, which give the minimum and maximum keys in a dictionary, respectively. We often add them explicitly to the DICTIONARY operations. Similarly, it makes sense in a dictionary of employee records to ask, for example, for the records of all employees earning between $58,000 and $60,000 per year, or for all records whose keys lie between two keys K_1 and K_2, where $K_1 \leq K_2$. If $K_1 = K_2$, this operation reduces to an *IsMember* query.

We consider the characteristic function, block, and pointer representations of DICTIONARY and, more important, introduce a new representation based on binary search trees, which are considered in much more depth in Chapter 10. We also establish a logarithmic-time lower bound for searching when the only allowable computation with a key is a key comparison.

8.1 SET, TABLE, AND DICTIONARY SPECIFICATIONS

We begin by specifying the SET ADT; then we specialize it to give the TABLE and DICTIONARY ADTs. Let B and E denote the sets of Boolean values and *element-type* values as before. Then, letting S denote the finite sets of *elementtype* values, we specify the SET operations as follows:

1. *Empty*: $\rightarrow S$: The function value *Empty* is the empty set.
2. *IsEmpty*: $S \rightarrow \mathcal{B}$: The function value *IsEmpty(S)* is **true** if S is the empty set; otherwise, it is **false**.

3. *Insert*: $E \times S \to S$: The function value *Insert(e,S)* is the union of S and the singleton set consisting of e.

4. *Delete*: $E \times S \to S$: The function value *Delete(e,S)* is the difference of S and the singleton set consisting of e; that is, it is all elements in S that are not e.

5. *IsMember*: $E \times S \to B$: The function value *IsMember(e,S)* is **true** if e is a member of S; otherwise, it is **false**.

6. *Union*: $S \times S \to S$: The function value *Union(S_1,S_2)* is the union of S_1 and S_2; that is, it is the set consisting of all elements in S_1 and S_2.

7. *DisjointUnion*: $S \times S \to S$: The function value *DisjointUnion(S_1,S_2)* is the union of S_1 and S_2 if $S_1 \cap S_2 = \varnothing$; otherwise, it is undefined.

8. *Intersection*: $S \times S \to S$: The function value *Intersection(S_1,S_2)* is the intersection of S_1 and S_2; that is, it is the set consisting of all elements that are in both S_1 and S_2.

9. *Difference*: $S \times S \to S$: The function value *Difference(S_1,S_2)* is the difference of S_1 and S_2; that is, it is the set consisting of all elements that are in S_1 and not in S_2.

10. *Size*: $S \to N$: The function value *Size(S)* is the number of elements in S.

11. *Complement*: $S \to S$: The function value *Complement(S)* is the complement of S (it is defined for only finite universes); that is, it is the set consisting of all elements in E that are not in S.

12. *Examine*: $S \to E$: The function value *Examine(S)* is an element of the set S.

The *Examine* operation requires some explanation. Since sets, unlike sequences, do not provide an implicit ordering among their elements, and the elements do not necessarily belong to a totally ordered universe, there are no notions of the first or next elements. It is intended that, for a set S of size n, n successive invocations of *Examine(S)* return its n elements. The *Examine* operation enables us to traverse the elements of any set.

We next specify the TABLE operations as follows, where K denotes a key universe (each element in E is associated with a unique key from K) and T denotes the finite tables of *elementtype* values:

1. *Empty*: $\to T$: The function value *Empty* is the empty set.

2. *IsEmpty*: $T \to B$: The function value *IsEmpty(T)* is **true** if T is the empty set; otherwise, it is **false**.

3. *Insert*: $E \times T \to T$: The function value *Insert(e,T)* is $T \cup \{e\}$.

4. *Delete*: $K \times T \to T$: The function value *Delete(K,T)* is $T - \{e\}$ if there is an element e in T with key K; otherwise, it is T.

5. *IsMember*: $K \times T \to B$: The function value *IsMember(K,T)* is **true** if there is an element e in T with key K; otherwise, it is **false**.

As we can see, the TABLE operations are a proper subset of the SET operations; however, this relationship does not hold for the DICTIONARY operations. We now assume that the key universe K is totally ordered. Thus, letting D denote the finite dictionaries of *elementtype* values, we specify the DICTIONARY operations as follows:

1. *Empty*: $\rightarrow \mathcal{D}$: The function value *Empty* is the empty dictionary.

2. *IsEmpty*: $\mathcal{D} \rightarrow \mathcal{B}$: The function value *IsEmpty(D)* is **true** if D is empty; otherwise, it is **false**.

3. *Insert*: $\mathcal{E} \times \mathcal{D} \rightarrow \mathcal{D}$: The function value *Insert(e,D)* is $D \cup \{e\}$.

4. *Delete*: $\mathcal{K} \times \mathcal{D} \rightarrow \mathcal{D}$: The function value *Delete(K,D)* is $D-\{e\}$ if there is an element e in D with key K; otherwise, it is D.

5. *IsMember*: $\mathcal{K} \times \mathcal{D} \rightarrow \mathcal{B}$: The function value *IsMember(K,D)* is **true** if there is an element e in D with key K; otherwise, it is **false**.

6. *IsPredecessor*: $\mathcal{K} \times \mathcal{D} \rightarrow \mathcal{B}$: The function value *IsPredecessor(K,D)* is **true** if there is an element e in D with a key that is smaller than K; otherwise, it is **false**. Note that there may be no element in D with key K.

7. *IsSuccessor*: $\mathcal{K} \times \mathcal{D} \rightarrow \mathcal{B}$: The function value *IsSuccessor(K,D)* is **true** if there is an element e in D with a key that is larger than K; otherwise, it is **false**. Note that there may be no element in D with key K.

8. *Predecessor*: $\mathcal{K} \times \mathcal{D} \rightarrow \mathcal{D}$: The function value *Predecessor(K,D)* is the element in D that has the largest key that is smaller than K, if there is one; otherwise, it is undefined.

9. *Successor*: $\mathcal{K} \times \mathcal{D} \rightarrow \mathcal{D}$: The function value *Successor(K,D)* is the element in D that has the smallest key that is larger than K, if there is one; otherwise, it is undefined.

10. *Range*: $\mathcal{K} \times \mathcal{K} \times \mathcal{D} \rightarrow 2^{\mathcal{E}}$: The function value *Range(K_1,K_2,D)* is the set of all elements e in D whose keys lie between K_1 and K_2. Note that there may be elements in D with keys K_1 and K_2.

8.2 SET REPRESENTATIONS

We consider two representations for SET. The first representation, which is based on the characteristic function of a set, cannot always be used. The second representation is completely general, it is based on the LIST ADT.

8.2.1 The Characteristic-Function Representation

In this section, we assume that an element and its key are identical; an element contains no other information, apart from its key. Let A be a set of elements from some universe E. Then, the **characteristic function** of A is denoted by $\chi_A : \mathcal{E} \rightarrow \mathcal{B}$ and is defined by

$$\chi_A(e) = \begin{cases} \textbf{\textit{true}} & \text{if } e \text{ is in } A ; \\ \textbf{\textit{false}} & \textit{otherwise.} \end{cases}$$

Thus, a set can be viewed as a total Boolean function and, conversely, a total Boolean function can be viewed as a set.

If E is totally ordered and finite, the elements of E can be enumerated as $e_1 \leq e_2 \leq \cdots \leq e_m$, where m is the cardinality of E and $\leq$ is the total ordering. Immediately, a set A can be represented by a block or vector V, where

$$V[i] = \chi_A(e_i).$$

The representation is illustrated in Fig. 8.1, where we represent **true** by 1 and **false** by 0; V is a **bit vector.** The bit-vector representation of sets is used in the implementation of Pascal's set type—indeed, the Pascal reference language assumes that a bit vector *is* the representation of Pascal's set type. The advantage of this representation is that set operations are translated into efficient bit operations. So, *Insert* changes the appropriate bit to 1, *Delete* changes it to 0, and *IsMember* tests whether it is 1. These operations are constant-time operations, when we can obtain the index of an element e in constant time.

In addition, *Union* is implemented as the disjunction or logical **or** of two bit vectors, *Intersection* is implemented as their conjunction or logical **and**, and *Difference* is reduced to *Complement* and *Intersection*. Hence, each of these operations takes time linear in the size of the universe; that is, it takes $O(m)$ time. In this representation, *Examine* can cycle through the m positions reporting the element given by the next 1 bit. Hence, it takes $O(m)$ time to report all n elements; that is, it takes $O(m/n)$ time amortized over n calls of *Examine*. This simple representation is useful for small universes; for large universes, however, it takes too much space and too much time. Despite these drawbacks, one example of when even relatively large bit vectors are useful is discussed in Exercise 8.2.

We prefer representations that use space linear in the sizes of the sets, take constant worst-case time for *IsMember*, *Insert*, and *Delete*, and take linear worst-

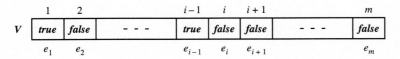

Figure 8.1   The bit-vector representation of a set of elements from a totally ordered universe.

case time for the set-theoretic operations. We can achieve the linear-space bound at the expense of linear-time bounds for *IsMember*, *Insert*, and *Delete* when we use a representation based on LIST.

8.2.2 LIST Representations of Sets

Building on previous ADTs, we can represent a set as a list and, therefore, use any one of the LIST representations given in Chapter 3. Let *A* and *B* be two sets. We examine the three set operations: *Union*, *Intersection*, and *Difference*. We examine other operations in Exercise 8.3. We assume—not unreasonably—that, in each representation, each element appears at most once.

Consider *Union* (*A*,*B*), where the size of *A* is *m* and the size of *B* is *n*. Since *A* and *B* may have elements in common, it is not enough simply to push together the two representations to give the result—duplicates must be weeded out. This fact implies that, for each *a* in *A* (or *b* in *B*), we must check whether *a* is also in *B* (or *b* is also in *A*). A high-level implementation based on this approach is provided in Fig. 8.2; it implies that *Union* takes time proportional to the product of *n* and the time taken by *IsMember* and *Insert*. If the key universe is not totally ordered, then *IsMember* (*b*,*A*) takes $O(m)$ time, and this bound is the best one possible; see Exercise 8.4. Now *Insert* can be implemented to run in constant time, if we assume that the inserted element is not in the given set. Hence, in this case, *Union* takes $O(mn)$ time. It is easy to show that *Intersection* and *Difference* have the same performance.

If, on the other hand, the key universe is totally ordered, we can obtain a more efficient representation by keeping the elements of each set in sorted order with respect to the keys. Then we can implement *Union*, *Intersection*, and *Difference* by **merging.** Usually merging is associated with sorting; merging two sorted lists to give a sorted list is one of the basic operations in merge sort and external sorting; see Chapter 12.

```
{Compute  C = A ∪ B,  for two sets  A  and  B.}

Empty(C);
for  i:= 1 to  Size(A)  do
begin  Examine(a,A);  Insert(a,C)  end;

for  i:= 1 to  Size(B)
do begin  Examine(b,B);
    if not  IsMember(b,A)
    then  Insert(b,C)
end;
```

Figure 8.2   A high-level implementation of *Union* (*A*,*B*).

```
A   =   1    4    9    16   25   36   49

B   =   1    2    4    8    16   32

C   =   ↑
⟹       4    9    16   25   36   49

        1    2    4    8    16   32

        1
⟹       4    9    16   25   36   49

        2    4    8    16   32

        1    1

        ⋮
⟹       25   36   49

        32

        1    1    2    4    4    8    9    16   16
⟹       36   49

        32

        1    1    2    4    4    8    9    16   16   25
⟹       36   49

        1    1    2    4    4    8    9    16   16   25   32
⟹       1    1    2    4    4    8    9    16   16   25   32   36   49
```

Figure 8.3 The merge of two sorted lists.

We implement two-way merging as a synchronous traversal of two sorted lists; in Fig. 8.3, we merge two sorted lists:

$$1, 4, 9, 16, 25, 36, 49$$
$$1, 2, 4, 8, 16, 32.$$

The traversal begins at the first element of each list; denoted by the index pair $(1,1)$. At each step, the smaller of the two indexed elements is output, and the corresponding index is incremented. If the indexed elements are equal, we arbitrarily choose the element from the first list. The merge is completed when the index pair $(m + 1, n + 1)$ is obtained; in this case, it is $(8,7)$.

We can easily modify the merging process to implement *Union*. Whenever the indexed elements are equal, we take one of them and discard the other, incrementing both indexes. For *Intersection*, we always discard the smaller indexed element; when the elements are equal, we take either one and discard the other. For *Difference*, we take the indexed element of the first sequence if it is strictly smaller than the other indexed element; all other elements are discarded.

The time bounds for *Union* , *Intersection* , and *Difference* are now $O(m + n)$, rather than $O(mn)$. These bounds reflect a substantial improvement in performance for such little effort in recoding the basic operations. The advantages of having a totally ordered key universe and making use of it should now be clear.

8.3 TABLE REPRESENTATIONS

We briefly reconsider one of the set representations discussed in the previous section before examining a new method in detail.

8.3.1 SET Representations

As with SET, the block and pointer representations for LIST can be used to represent TABLE. Since we cannot assume that the key universe is totally ordered, *Insert* , *Delete* , and *IsMember* take $O(n)$ time, where n is the size of the table, for each of the representations. Note that we cannot use the bit-vector representation, because the key universe is not necessarily totally ordered, and because, in general, each record contains more than a key.

The advantage of the list representations is that they are simple to program. We now examine an additional representation: lists with adaptive sequential searching. Adaptive sequential searching alleviates the main problem with list representations—namely, bad worst-case behavior—without using extra space.

8.3.2 Lists and Optimal Sequential Search

We have assumed, implicitly, that the records in a table are equally likely to be accessed. But what do we do if they are not? For example, book requests in a university library are not equally likely; typically, the access frequency depends on the reading lists for the currently offered courses. Similarly, in a public library, book requests depend, in general, on the publication dates, book reviews, and best-seller lists. In these situations, as well as in many others, the access-probability distribution of the set is not uniform. Moreover, the distribution changes over time. We first construct a general model for the cost of a table that reflects the expected time taken by a single *IsMember* operation; we then consider the case of a fixed table with a fixed access-probability distribution.

We assume that each table is represented as a list and, for simplicity, we treat elements as keys. Let $e_1,...,e_n$ be the elements or keys in positions 1, ..., n in an n-

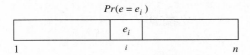

$Pr(e = e_i)$

e_i

1   i n

Figure 8.4   Sequential search with probabilities.

element table, and let $Pr(e = e_i)$ be the probability that a given element e is equal to e_i; see Fig. 8.4. $Pr(e = e_i)$ is the **access probability** of element e_i. Hence,

$$1 - \sum_{i=1}^{n} Pr(e = e_i)$$

is the probability that e is not in the given table. Observe that, if $e = e_i$, then a sequential search with e takes i key comparisons and i probes (a probe is one examination of a cell). If e is not in the table, then a sequential search takes $n + 1$ comparisons and $n + 1$ probes ($n + 1$ rather than n is an arguable number of comparisons, but a reasonable one, if we place e immediately after the last position before searching). The contribution of e_i to the expected number of comparisons or probes is, therefore,

$$i \times Pr(e = e_i)$$

and the contribution of the keys not in the table is

$$(n + 1)(1 - \sum_{i=1}^{n} Pr(e = e_i)).$$

The total contribution of all elements is called the the **expected cost;** it is given by

$$\sum_{i=1}^{n} iPr(e = e_i) + (n + 1)(1 - \sum_{i=1}^{n} Pr(e = e_i)),$$

and we denote its value by $COST(e_1,...,e_n)$. Intuitively, it is the expected number of key comparisons or probes in a table for keys $e_1,...,e_n$ with access probabilities $Pr(e = e_i)$, $1 \leq i \leq n$, when they are represented as a list in the given order. In particular, for the **uniform probability model,** $Pr(e = e_i) = \frac{1}{n}$, $1 \leq i \leq n$, we obtain

$$COST(e_1,...,e_n) = \frac{1}{n} \sum_{i=1}^{n} i = \frac{n + 1}{2}.$$

In other words, we expect to search halfway down the table. If, however,

$$Pr(e = e_i) = \frac{1}{2^i}, 1 \le i < n,$$

and

$$Pr(e = e_n) = \frac{1}{2^{n-1}},$$

then

$$COST(e_1,...,e_n) = \sum_{i=1}^{n-1} \frac{i}{2^i} + \frac{n}{2^{n-1}} < 2,$$

since $2^{n-1} \le n$, for $n \ge 1$. Finally, if we reverse the order of the elements, keeping the same probability distribution, then

$$n - 1 < COST(e_n,...,e_1)$$
$$< n - 2.$$

These results illustrate the wide range that the expected cost may have for a fixed probability distribution. The extremes demonstrated by this example are no accident, as we now prove.

Fact 8.1   *Let $e_1,...,e_n$ be n elements or keys with access probabilities $Pr(e = e_i)$, where $Pr(e = e_i) \ge Pr(e = e_{i+1})$, $1 \le i < n$. Then, over all permutations of the n keys, the* **minimum expected cost** *is $COST(e_1,...,e_n)$, and the* **maximum expected cost** *is $COST(e_n,...,e_1)$.*

Proof: We prove only the first claim; the second is left to Exercise 8.5. Assume that there is some permutation $i(1),...,i(n)$ of the keys that has an expected cost smaller than $COST(e_1,...,e_n)$. Then, there must be some j, $1 \le j < n$, such that $e_j \ne e_{i(j)}$. Choose the smallest such j; see Fig. 8.5. Now $e_j = e_{i(k)}$, for some $k > j$, because of our assumption about j. Exchange $e_{i(j)}$ and $e_{i(k)}$. The expected cost of the sequence after the exchange is

$$COST(e_{i(1)},...,e_{i(n)}) - jPr(e = e_{i(j)}) + jPr(e = e_j)$$
$$- kPr(e = e_j) + kPr(e = e_{i(j)}).$$

Since $Pr(e = e_j) \ge Pr(e = e_{i(j)})$, by assumption, we obtain an expected cost that is no greater than $COST(e_{i(1)},...,e_{i(n)})$. We repeat this transformation until, eventually, we obtain the sequence $(e_1,...,e_n)$. Since each transformation does not increase the expected cost, we have shown that

$$COST(e_1,...,e_n) \le COST(e_{i(1)},...,e_{i(n)}) < COST(e_1,...,e_n);$$

a contradiction.

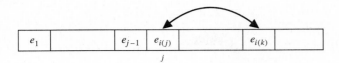

Figure 8.5 The central point in the proof that decreasing probability order is optimal.

Therefore, $COST(e_1,\ldots,e_n)$ is the minimum expected cost, and $e_1,\ldots,e_n$ is one permutation of the elements that achieves it. □

A permutation of $e_1,\ldots,e_n$ that has minimum expected cost is said to be **optimal;** one that has maximum expected cost is said to be **pessimal.**

The probability that an element is not in the table does not affect Fact 8.1, because an unsuccessful search must always probe $n + 1$ cells or do $n + 1$ comparisons in our model. In Exercise 8.6, we consider searching in a sorted table when the elements have nonuniform access probabilities.

The basis of the following discussion is that we are unlikely to know the access probabilities of the elements. (One counterexample to this claim is the problem of determining whether an identifier in a computer program is one of the reserved words in the programming language. In this case, we normally know the access or occurrence probabilities of the reserved words.)

8.3.3 Adaptation and Move-to-Front

Continuing the study of sequential search with not necessarily uniform access probabilities, we consider a more typical situation: The probabilities are unknown and are, perhaps, changing over time. We use **adaptation** to approximate the optimal ordering by applying a fixed permutation after each access. The method is applicable not only to an unknown fixed probability distribution, but also to a time-varying probability distribution. The idea behind the technique is to keep more frequently accessed elements closer to the front of the list. In Exercise 8.7, we explore an alternative approach that approximates the probabilities with frequency counts.

We discuss the **move-to-front adaptive heuristic** that we have already seen in Section 2.3.2. After each successful search, the accessed element is moved to the front of the list. In Fig. 8.6, we display the effect on a list T of the operations *IsMember* (*and,T*), *IsMember* (*and,T*), and *IsMember* (*of,T*). An element is moved into the first position unless it is already there, and the elements in between are pushed one place down in the list.

The move-to-front heuristic can be used with any representation of a list; however, it performs particularly well if a singly linked list is used. In this case, moving an element to the front takes constant time, whereas, in a block representation, it takes time proportional to the element's position. The move-to-front heuristic performs well, in the amortized sense, as we show in Section 8.3.4. We

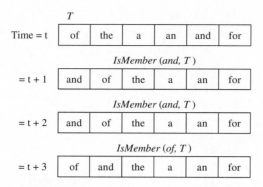

Figure 8.6   An example of the move-to-front heuristic.

first define, for a given query sequence, the notion of the corresponding static optimal list. The **static optimal list** for the keys in a query sequence contains the keys in nonincreasing-frequency order, where the **frequency** of a key is the number of times that the key occurs in the query sequence. The time taken by the move-to-front heuristic with a query sequence is always within a factor of 2 of the time taken by the same query sequence on the static optimal list; that is, we have the following result.

Fact 8.2   *Given a long enough query sequence $e_1,...,e_m$ of keys that is applied to a list containing the keys, the total number of probes with the move-to-front heuristic is never more than twice the total number of probes in the static optimal list for the same keys.*

Although we have discussed how *IsMember* should be modified to include an adaptive strategy, we have ignored *Insert* and *Delete*. Both, however, are easily accommodated. When inserting a new element, we add it to the front of the list. (Assuming that we have already performed an unsuccessful search.) Hence, to treat *Insert*, we: add the new element to the end of the list and then search for it. Deletion is even simpler—we remove the element.

8.3.4   An Analysis of the Move-to-Front Heuristic

We shall carry out an amortized analysis of one of the simpler versions of sequential search. We have a list of n keys and a **query sequence** $e_1,...,e_m$ of keys. We do not allow insertions and deletions. Furthermore, we assume that each key e in the query sequence is in the list; that is, we consider only successful searches. As before, we search the current list of size n sequentially for each element in the query sequence in the order in which it is given, using comparisons.

We compare the performance of the move-to-front heuristic with the performance of the static optimal list for the same query sequence. Hence, conceptually, we apply each query to the optimal list and the current move-to-front list at the same time. To analyze their amortized performance, we introduce an analytic method known as the **banker's paradigm.** The banker's paradigm associates **credits** or a bank account with each key that appears in the lists and maintains a **credit invariant,** for each account, after each query is completed. The units of currency are units of time; each unit corresponds to the time needed by one probe. During the execution of a query sequence on the two lists, some keys accumulate time units that they can use later, and some keys spend time units that they have accumulated. Each key's account is enough to pay for that key to be moved to the front and enough to give to other keys to maintain their credit invariants. Note that the static optimal list for the query sequence does not change during query processing. We initialize the optimal list by counting the number of times that each key appears in the query sequence and ensuring that the list is arranged in nonincreasing-frequency order.

To begin the analysis, we observe that the cost of accessing a key e at position i in a list is i units, because the task takes i probes. We write $opt\text{-}cost(e) = i$ when e is in position i of the static optimal list, and $mtf\text{-}cost(e) = j$ when e is in position j of the move-to-front list. We now show that we can bound the total number of probes used by the query sequence on the move-to-front list by twice the total number of probes used by the query sequence on the static optimal list. The credit invariant we want to maintain is as follows: *For each key e in the lists, the account balance of e is the number of keys before e in the move-to-front list that are after e in the optimal list.* The credit invariant counts the keys that are not in their optimal position with respect to e. Observe that the first key has an account with zero balance. We must initialize the accounts of each key to establish the credit invariant before we process the first query. The account of each key e is maximized when every key before e in the initial move-to-front list is after e in the optimal list. This arrangement gives a maximum total credit of $n(n - 1)/2$ units before the query sequence is executed. After processing a query e, we need to reestablish the credit invariant. We denote the cost of reestablishing the credit invariant by $ci\text{-}cost(e)$, and we prove the following fact.

Fact 8.3 *If the credit invariant holds before IsMember(e,T), then*

1. $ci\text{-}cost(e) < mtf\text{-}cost(e) - 2 \times account(e)$.
2. $mtf\text{-}cost(e) + ci\text{-}cost(e) < 2 \times opt\text{-}cost(e)$.

Fact 8.3.1 motivates the definition of the **credit cost** $cr\text{-}cost(e)$ of a query e as the number of probes used in the move-to-front list plus the units needed to maintain the credit invariant after moving e to the front; that is, $cr\text{-}cost(e) = mtf\text{-}cost(e) + ci\text{-}cost(e)$. Given Fact 8.3.2, we can compare the total costs of a query sequence on the move-to-front and optimal lists as follows. Let $cr\text{-}cost(e_1,...,e_m)$ denote the sum of the total number of probes used in the move-to-front list and the total number of units needed to maintain the invariant after each query, for the query sequence $e_1,...,e_m$. Similarly, let $opt\text{-}cost(e_1,...,e_m)$ denote the total number of probes used in the optimal list for the query sequence $e_1,...,e_m$. Similarly, let cr-

cost(initial) and *cr-cost(final)* denote the total units in the accounts before and after the query sequence is processed. Thus,

$$cr\text{-}cost(e_1,...,e_m) + cr\text{-}cost(initial) - cr\text{-}cost(final)$$

$$\leq \sum_{i=1}^{m} cr\text{-}cost(e_i) + n(n-1)/2 - cr\text{-}cost(final)$$

$$< \sum_{i=1}^{m} [2 \times opt\text{-}cost(e_i)] + n(n-1)/2$$

$$= 2 \times opt\text{-}cost(e_1,...,e_m) + n(n-1)/2.$$

In other words, for query sequences that have length at least n^2, the move-to-front heuristic makes at most twice the number of probes used in the optimal list.

We now establish Fact 8.2. Consider a query e. Let L be the move-to-front list before the query is processed, and let L' be the move-to-front list after the query is processed. Let e appear at position i in L. Then, $mtf\text{-}cost(e) = i$. The $ci\text{-}cost(e)$ of reestablishing the credit invariant is computed as follows. Since e is in the first position in L', its account should be 0. Currently, with respect to L, its account is x, say. Because e is moved to the front of L, the keys that appeared before e in L now have e before them, and some of these keys may have e after them in the optimal list. Whenever that happens, their accounts need to be increased by 1 unit. We show that there are enough units in e's account to pay for these increases.

The number of keys that appear before e in both the optimal list and L is exactly $i - 1 - x$. Therefore, we have to add one unit to the accounts of each of these keys and to remove x units from e's account; that is, $ci\text{-}cost(e) = i - 1 - x - x = i - 1 - 2x$. Thus, $ci\text{-}cost(e) = i - 1 - 2x < i - 2x$, which gives Fact 8.3.1 and also $cr\text{-}cost(e) < 2 \times mtf\text{-}cost(e) - 2 \times account(e)$.

Finally, we compute *opt-cost* (e). The credit invariant implies that exactly x keys that are before e in L are after e in the optimal list. Because there are $i - 1 - x$ keys that appear before e in *both* L and the optimal list, there are *at least* $i - 1 - x$ keys that appear before e in the optimal list. Note that the optimal list can have more than $i - 1 - x$ keys before e, but these extra keys appear after e in L. Now, these observations imply that $opt\text{-}cost(e) \geq i - 1 - x + 1 = i - x$ units. We have already shown that $cr\text{-}cost(e) < 2i - 2x$; therefore,

$$cr\text{-}cost(e) < 2 \times opt\text{-}cost(e),$$

as claimed.

In the preceding analysis, we are allowed to inspect the query sequence in advance for the optimal list, but not for the move-to-front list. We also are not allowed to move keys in the optimal list; once keys are assigned positions, they have to stay there. For this reason, we say that the move-to-front heuristic is **statically optimal,** because it performs within a constant factor of the static optimal list.

Also, we have not allowed insertions and deletions in our analysis. It is, however, a simple exercise to extend the analysis to include them; see Exercise 8.8. Finally, we can also strengthen the result considerably by allowing moves in the optimal list. In this case, the stated bounds still hold, and we say that the move-to-front heuristic is **dynamically optimal.**

8.4 DICTIONARY REPRESENTATIONS

We can view a dictionary as a set; hence, we can represent DICTIONARY with any of the SET representations. These approaches are pursued in Exercises 8.11 and 8.12. Moreover, the characteristic-function representation is extremely good when the elements are the keys and the key universe can be treated as a finite range of consecutive integers.

We first prove that there is a logarithmic-time worst-case lower bound for the *IsMember* operation when we are allowed to compare only keys. Note that the characteristic-function representation beats the lower bound by avoiding key comparisons and using keys as addresses instead. Then, we examine a variant of binary searching, **interpolation searching**, that adapts to the individual search key and, furthermore, has an expected-case performance of $O(\log \log n)$ for an n-element dictionary. This bound is especially interesting because there is a logarithmic expected-case lower bound for the *IsMember* operation when we are allowed only key comparisons.

8.4.1 A Lower Bound for Searching

As we have mentioned in Section 2.4, there are performance barriers that we cannot break through. We prove that such a barrier exists for searching for a query key in a dictionary (the *IsMember* operation). Because it is a dictionary, the keys are taken from a totally ordered universe, and we can use binary search to achieve at most $\lceil \log n \rceil$ comparisons for an *IsMember* operation in a dictionary of size n; see Programs 4.2 and 8.1. We want to show that we can do no better than binary search.

To prove such a lower bound, we need to define a model of computation that captures the kinds of operations that can be used. Since we are dealing with a totally ordered universe and binary search uses key comparisons, we allow comparisons between keys. We can ask whether one key is less than or equal to another key. To avoid irrelevant detail, we specialize the *IsMember* implementation for a fixed-sized, but arbitrarily-sized, dictionary. Let the size be n. The advantage of this specialization is that we can assume that the implementation has no recursion and no loops. (Given a value of n, we can unroll the recursion in *BSearch* of Program 8.1 to give such a program. Therefore, the program can be

```
function BSearch(q: elementtype; D: ourarray;
                    L,U: integer): boolean;
{The keys in the array D are from a totally ordered universe, and
they appear in positions L..U of D in sorted order. We assume
that L ≤ U. If the query q is found in these positions in D, then
BSearch returns true. Otherwise, BSearch returns false.}

var M: integer;

begin M:= (L + U) div 2;
    if L = U
        {There is only one position to consider.}
    then BSearch:= D[L] = q
    else if q ≤ D[M]
        {There are at least two positions to consider, discard one half
            of the positions depending on the query q.}
    then BSearch:= BSearch(q,D,L,M)
    else BSearch:= BSearch(q,D,M + 1,U)
end{BSearch};
```

Program 8.1   A Pascal implementation of binary search.

assumed to consist solely of **if-then-else** statements with key comparisons. In Program 8.2, we specialize *BSearch* for a dictionary of size 3 to give *BSearch*3. Observe that we have included redundant code as comments; in *BSearch*3 the values of *L, M,* and *U* are known in advance.

The lower bound we prove makes no assumptions about the key universe other than that it is infinite and totally ordered. If the key universe is not totally ordered, then we cannot use it for a dictionary.

Having specialized *BSearch* to give *BSearch*3, we now go one step further and abstract *BSearch*3 as a **decision tree** or flowchart in which each node represents a single comparison and the two branches from a node represent the two possible outcomes. For simplicity we also restrict key comparisons to be of only two forms: $q \leq ?D[i]$ and $q \geq ?D[i]$. The tests for equality and inequality are not allowed; they are replaced by two of the given tests. The decision tree corresponding to *BSearch*3 is given in Fig. 8.7. Note that the query key is now implicit in this representation of *BSearch*3, and that a path from the root to an external node corresponds to a sequence of comparisons with some query key in *B-Search*3.

Because the external nodes in a decision tree correspond to the various termination points in *BSearch*3, we know that an external node must correspond to either **true** or **false**. An external node cannot correspond to both **true** and **false**, although it may correspond to neither. For example, a decision tree for a search (not a binary search) with $n = 2$ is given in Fig. 8.8. Note that external node 5 can never be reached, so it is associated with neither **true** nor **false**.

```
function BSearch3(q: elementtype; D: ourarray;
                  {L = 1, U:= 3}): boolean;
{The keys in the array D are from a totally ordered universe, and
they appear in positions L..U of D in sorted order. We assume
that L ≤ U. If the query q is found in these positions in D, then
BSearch3 returns true. Otherwise, BSearch3 returns false.}

{var M: integer;}

begin {M:= (L + U) div 2 = 2;}
    {if L = U}
        {There is only one position to consider.}
    {then BSearch3:= D[L] = q
    else} if q ≤ D[2]
    then {BSearch:= BSearch(q,D,1,2)}
        if q ≤ D[1]
        then BSearch3:= D[1] = q
        else BSearch3:= D[2] = q
    else {BSearch:= BSearch(q,D,3,3)}
        BSearch3:= D[3] = q
end{BSearch3};
```

Program 8.2   *BSearch* specialized for a dictionary of size 3.

Consider the following thought experiment for a decision tree for searching.
For each key e in the universe, "execute" the decision tree with e. Each e will
arrive at some external node. If the decision tree models searching correctly, then
the set of keys that arrive at each external node must be either all in the dictionary
or all outside the dictionary. For example, external node 3 in the decision tree of

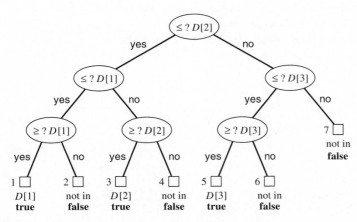

Figure 8.7   A decision tree that corresponds to *BSearch3*.

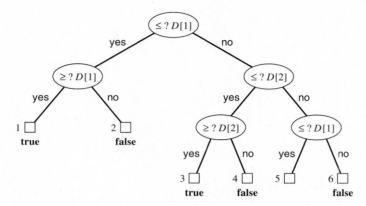

Figure 8.8 A decision tree with unreachable external nodes.

Fig. 8.9 has associated with it all keys in the open–closed interval $(D[1], D[2]]$. Of these keys, only $D[2]$ is in the dictionary; all others are outside the dictionary. If we associate **false** with node 3, we exclude $D[2]$ from the dictionary; if we associate **true** with node 3, we include keys in the dictionary that should be excluded. The algorithm corresponding to the decision tree is *incorrect*. For this reason, we consider only *correct decision trees* for searching.

   Let us summarize what we have discovered so far. Decision trees for searching are an abstraction of comparison-based programs for searching that use only key comparisons and **if-then-else** statements. Conversely, any decision tree, viewed as a high-level flowchart, can be converted into such a program.

   The beauty of the decision-tree abstraction for the searching problem is not only that decision trees can be converted into a program, but also that the length of a path from the root to an external node is the number of key comparisons made on the path by some search key. For example, a search that ends at external node 4 in the tree of Fig. 8.7 has made three comparisons, whereas a search that ends at external node 7 has made two. Since the decision tree can also be viewed as a program, its height gives us the worst-case number of comparisons of any search key. The height of the example decision tree of Fig. 8.7 is 3; hence, no

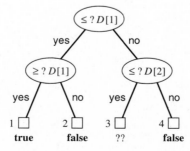

Figure 8.9 An incorrect decision tree for searching.

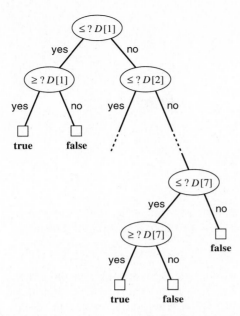

Figure 8.10 A tall decision tree for a dictionary with 7 keys.

search can take more than three comparisons. We might have a tall decision tree, such as the one in Fig. 8.10 for a dictionary of size 7. It has height 8; hence, the corresponding program that implements *IsMember* makes eight comparisons, in the worst case. We leave to Exercise 8.13 the proof that *BSearch*7 makes fewer comparisons, in the worst case.

Let us now return, after this preparatory work, to the discussion of lower bounds for searching using only comparisons and **if-then-else** statements. Recall that to establish a worst-case lower bound B we must show that every algorithm for the searching problem using only the given operations must have a worst-case performance that is at least B. For searching a dictionary of size $n \geq 1$ with keys from a totally ordered universe, we want to prove that $\lceil \log n \rceil$ comparisons is a worst-case lower bound. This problem translates, in the decision tree setting, into establishing a lower bound on the heights of correct decision trees that solve the searching problem. Since decision trees are binary trees, we know from Chapter 5 that if we can establish a lower bound on the numbers of internal or external nodes of decision trees that solve the searching problem, we immediately obtain a lower bound on the trees' heights. Fortunately, we can obtain such a bound, as we now prove.

Fact 8.4 *Given a dictionary of size $n \geq 1$ with keys from a totally ordered universe, the number of external nodes of a correct decision tree that solves the searching problem is at least $2n + 1$.*

Hence, the height of such a decision tree is at least $1 + \lceil \log n \rceil$.

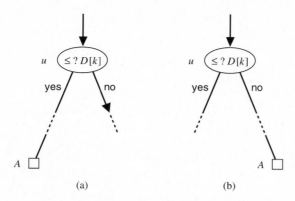

Figure 8.11   If two keys end up at the same external node in a decision tree, then all keys that lie between them end up at the same external node.

Proof: We will prove that there are at least n **true** external nodes; the proof that there are at least $n + 1$ **false** external nodes is left to Exercise 8.14. The idea behind both proofs is the same. If there are fewer **true** external nodes, the decision tree must make some wrong decisions and is, therefore, incorrect. These implications contradict the assumption of correctness.

If there are fewer than n **true** external nodes, either there are no **true** nodes, in which case, because $n \geq 1$, the tree is incorrect, or there is at least one and at most $n - 1$ **true** nodes. The pigeonhole principle implies that there are at least two keys, $D[i]$ and $D[j]$, $1 \leq i < j \leq n$, that are associated with the same **true** external node—A, say. Consider each internal node u on the path from the root to node A. The node u is either a $\leq ?$ or a $\geq ?$ node. In both cases, the path to A will follow either the yes branch or the no branch out of u; see Fig. 8.11. There are four possible cases; we argue about one of them and leave the others to Exercise 8.15. If the node u has a $\leq ?D[k]$ comparison and the A path follows the yes branch, then both $D[i]$ and $D[j]$ are no larger than $D[k]$. Thus, every key in the open interval $(D[i],D[j])$ must follow the same branch. Moreover, this fact holds for every comparison on the A path; hence, every key in $(D[i],D[j])$ must also reach A. Observe that, because the key universe is infinite, there are choices of keys $D[i]$ and $D[j]$ such that the open interval $(D[i],D[j])$ is not empty. Finally, since A is a **true** node, all such keys are reported to be in the dictionary, when they are not. This reporting contradicts the correctness of the decision tree. Therefore, we cannot have two dictionary keys associated with the same external node; there must be at least n **true** external nodes.

Combining this bound with a similar bound for **false** nodes implies that there are at least $2n + 1$ external nodes in every decision tree for n-key dictionaries. Finally, applying the result about the height of binary trees from Section 5.1.1, we know that a correct decision tree must have a height of at least $\lceil \log(2n + 1) \rceil \geq$ $\lceil 1 + \log n \rceil$. □

The lower bound that we have proved is one more than the upper bound attained by *BSearch*. This difference, however, is explained by the observation that *BSearch* also uses $=$? comparisons. If we replace $=$? comparisons by $\leq$? and $\geq$? comparisons, the height of *BSearch*'s decision tree increases by 1.

The lower bound holds for the expected case, too. The proof of this fact also is based on properties of binary trees.

The lower bound for searching in a dictionary of size n should be compared with the lower bound for searching in a table of size n using only $=$? comparisons. Because a table universe does not need to be totally ordered, we can use only $=$? and $\neq$? comparisons. We leave to Exercise 8.4 the proof of the following fact.

Fact 8.5 *Given a table of size n, any searching algorithm that uses only $=$? and $\neq$? comparisons requires at least n comparisons and probes in the worst case.*

8.4.2 Ordered Blocks and Interpolation Search

A binary search of n elements stored in sorted order (with respect to their keys) in a block has an excellent retrieval time of $\lceil \log n \rceil$ probes in the worst and expected cases, while supporting linear-time updates. Indeed, in Section 8.4.1, we proved that we could not do any better in the worst case, and stated that we could not do any better in the expected case. We now give an algorithm that reduces the expected number of probes to $O(\log \log n)$. The obvious question is: Does this upper bound conflict with the expected-case lower bound of $\Omega(\log n)$? At first sight we might think that it does, but a more careful examination of the assumptions for the lower bound reveals that each decision tree depends on only the number and order of the keys. The algorithm we give next, however, uses interpolation in addition. So, there is no contradiction; we have merely demonstrated a truism about lower bounds: *If you want to design an algorithm that is faster than a lower bound, you have to use operations outside the lower-bound model.*

The new search algorithm is based on a simple observation. When looking up a word in a dictionary (for example, *enzyme*), we do not open the dictionary halfway, see whether *enzyme* is there and, if it is not, reopen the dictionary at the appropriate quarter position, and so on. Rather, based on the initial letter "e," which is the fifth letter of the alphabet, we open the dictionary about one-fifth of the way in, since $5/26 \cong 1/5$. We have **interpolated** the position of the words beginning with "e" to be one-fifth from the beginning.

The algorithm just sketched is called **interpolation search.** Given the keys at the current lower and upper positions— e_L and e_U, say—in a dictionary D, we consider the interval $[e_L, e_U]_D$ of all keys in D that lie between e_L and e_U. Similarly, let $[e_L, e_U]$ be the interval of all keys e in the key universe with $e_L \leq e \leq e_U$.

Now, assume that the keys in $[e_L, e_U]_D$ are distributed uniformly, and that $[e_L, e_U]$ is finite. These assumptions imply that the proportion of keys from e_L to q and e_L to e_U in the universe, for some query key q, is the same as the proportion of the keys from e_L to q and e_L to e_U in the dictionary. Using our notation,

$$\frac{\#[e_L,q]}{\#[e_L,e_U]} = \frac{\#[e_L,q]_D}{\#[e_L,e_U]_D} = \frac{\#[e_L,q]_D}{U-L+1}.$$

We can solve this equation to obtain

$$\#[e_L,q]_D = \left\lceil \frac{\#[e_L,q]}{\#[e_L,e_U]} (U-L+1) \right\rceil;$$

hence, we first examine position

$$(L-1) + \left\lceil \frac{\#[e_L,q]}{\#[e_L,e_U]} (U-L+1) \right\rceil.$$

When $\#[e_L,q]/\#[e_L,e_U] = 1/2$, this method reduces to binary search.

Let us look at an example to clarify the approach. Given a block, indexed by 1..100, that contains integer keys from 2001 to 10,000, where do we begin to search for query key 4000? The situation is depicted in Fig. 8.12. By the preceding formula, we probe position

$$\left\lceil \frac{2000}{8000} 100 \right\rceil = 25.$$

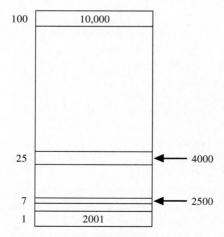

Figure 8.12   An example of interpolation search.

For query key 2500, on the other hand, we probe position

$$\left\lceil \frac{500}{8000} \, 100 \right\rceil = 7.$$

Interpolation search *adapts* to the given query key, whereas binary search is oblivious to the given key.

In interpolation search, as in binary search, if the query key is not found on the first probe, the interpolation is repeated in the appropriate segment of the dictionary. It is possible that at each division of the remaining keys we discard only one key. For this reason, interpolation searching has a worst-case performance of $O(n^2)$ time. We leave to Exercise 8.16 the implementation and simulational evaluation of interpolation searching. In Exercise 8.17, a modification of interpolation searching that guarantees worst-case logarithmic performance is discussed.

8.5 SEARCH TREES AND DICTIONARIES

The lower bound that we have proved in Section 8.4.1 indicates that if we stay within a comparison-based framework, then we should look for dictionary implementations that support updates and queries in $O(\log n)$ time, in the worst case. Search trees are the basis for achieving these bounds, as we shall see in Chapter 10. Here, we are content to define binary search trees, to give several of their properties, to show how updating can be done, to analyze their expected-case performance, and to explain how the different kinds of queries can be implemented.

8.5.1 Binary Search Trees

Recall that a binary tree either is empty or consists of a root node together with a left and right subtree. Fig. 8.13 displays a binary tree with seven internal nodes and eight external nodes—we say it has *size* 7.

Given n distinct keys $K_1 < K_2 < \cdots < K_n$ from some totally ordered key universe, a **binary search tree** for the n keys is a binary indexed tree T of size n whose internal nodes are labeled with the keys so as to satisfy the **binary-search-tree condition:** *For all internal nodes u in T, each key in the left subtree of u is less than the key of u, and the key of u is less than each key in the right subtree of u.* For example, given the 7 days of the week *Sun, Mon, Tues, Wed, Thurs, Fri,* and *Sat,* and their lexicographic ordering

$$Fri < Mon < Sat < Sun < Thurs < Tues < Wed,$$

the tree in Fig. 8.14 is a binary search tree for them. The tree in Fig. 8.15 is not a binary search tree because *Sat* comes after *Fri* in lexicographic order.

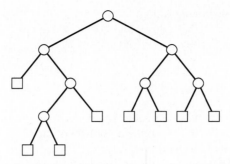

Figure 8.13   An example binary tree.

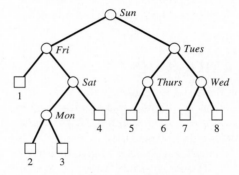

Figure 8.14   A binary search tree for the days of the week with respect to their lexicographic order.

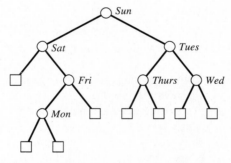

Figure 8.15   A binary tree that is not a search tree.

The binary-search-tree condition guarantees that a simple divide-and-conquer algorithm can be used to solve *IsMember*. Given a key *K* and a binary search tree *T*, we search *T* for *K* using the high-level algorithm given in Fig. 8.16. Each search in a binary search tree terminates either at an internal node, in which case it is successful, or at an external node, in which case it is unsuccessful. For exam-

T is a binary search tree for a set of keys from some totally ordered key universe and *K* is a query key from the same universe. If *K* is in *T*, then the algorithm terminates successfully; otherwise, the algorithm terminates unsuccessfully.

Case 1: *T* is empty—*K* is not in *T*; terminate unsuccessfully.

Case 2: *T* is nonempty.

> **Case 2.1:** $K < key(root(T))$ —repeat the search with the left subtree of *T* replacing *T*.

> **Case 2.2:** $K = key(root(T))$ —*K* is in *T*; terminate successfully.

> **Case 2.3:** $K > key(root(T))$ —repeat the search with the right subtree of *T* replacing *T*.

Figure 8.16   Search in a binary search tree.

ple, searching the day tree of Fig. 8.14 for *Mon* explores the path shown as a thick line in Fig. 8.17(a), whereas searching it for *Keski* (the Finnish word for Monday) gives the path shown in Fig. 8.17(b).

Not only are unsuccessful searches associated with external nodes, but also each external node has an associated **gap** of keys from the universe. In Fig. 8.18, we have redrawn the binary search tree of Fig. 8.14 to highlight this relationship. Immediately, we see that node 2 is associated not only with *Keski,* but also with any string that falls, lexicographically, between *Fri* and *Mon*; that is, node 2 corresponds to the open interval (*Fri,Mon*). This view of search trees is important when we are designing search trees for intervals of keys, rather than for single keys; see Section 15.5.

Rather than associating keys with internal nodes, called **internal search trees,** it is often convenient to associate them with external nodes, called **external search trees.** In this case, we associate **routing** or **separating** values with the internal nodes so that searching can still be carried out efficiently. We can think of an external search tree as an **index** into a file—an additional structure on top of the file structure—as we do in Chapter 10, when discussing external dictionaries. We will assume, for now, that separators and keys are taken from a common universe; in general, however, we do not need this assumption.

Given *n* keys $K_1,...,K_n$ and $n-1$ separators $S_1,...,S_{n-1}$ from some totally ordered key universe such that $K_1 < S_1 \le K_2 < S_2 \le \cdots < S_{n-1} \le K_n$, an **external binary search tree** for the keys and separators is a binary indexed tree *T* with *n* external nodes that are labeled in left-to-right order with the keys, and whose internal nodes are labeled with the separators so as to satisfy both of the following two conditions. First is the **separating condition:** *For all internal nodes u in T, each separator in the left subtree of u is less than the separator of u, and the*

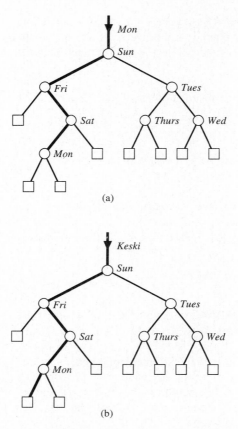

Figure 8.17   Search in the binary search tree of Fig. 8.14. (a) Search for *Mon*.
(b) Search for *Keski*.

separator of u is less than each separator in the right subtree of u. Second is the
key condition: *For all internal nodes u in T, each key in the left subtree of u is
less than the separator of u, and the separator of u is no greater than each key in
the right subtree of u.* The tree of Fig. 8.19 is an external binary search tree for the
days of the week with separators *Mon, Sat, Sun, Thurs, Tues,* and *Wed.* On
the other hand, the tree of Fig. 8.20 is not an external binary search tree because
the key *Fri* is not less than the separator *Fri* and, similarly, the key *Mon* is not less
than the separator *Mon.* The *IsMember* operation, for external binary search trees,
is not difficult to implement. Note that *root*(*T*) is well defined even when *T* consists of a single external node, and an empty tree no longer corresponds to a single
external node. A high-level algorithm for *IsMember* is given in Fig. 8.21.

A search for *Sat* in the external binary search tree of Fig. 8.19 is illustrated in
Fig. 8.22. Since an internal node with the "key" *Sat* is on the path to the external

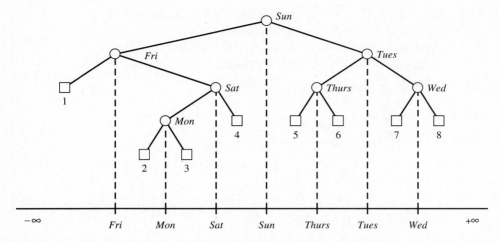

Figure 8.18 The gaps or intervals associated with external nodes in a binary search tree.

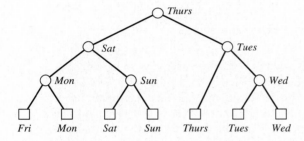

Figure 8.19 An external binary search tree for the days of the week with respect to their lexicographic order.

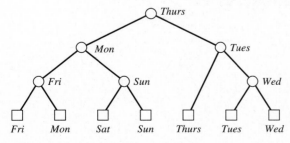

Figure 8.20 A binary tree that is not an external search tree.

T is an external binary search tree for sets of keys and separators from the same totally ordered universe, and *K* is a query key from the same universe. If *K* appears in *T* at some external node, then the algorithm terminates successfully; otherwise, the algorithm terminates unsuccessfully.

Case 1: *T* is empty—*K* is not in *T*; terminate unsuccessfully.

Case 2: *T* is nonempty.

>   **Case 2.1:** *root*(*T*) is internal.

>>   **Case 2.1.1:** *K* < *separator*(*root*(*T*)) —repeat the search with the left subtree of *T* replacing *T*.

>>   **Case 2.1.2:** *K* ≥ *separator*(*root*(*T*)) —repeat the search with the right subtree of *T* replacing *T*.

>   **Case 2.2:** *root*(*T*) is external.

>>   **Case 2.2.1:** *K* = *key*(*root*(*T*)) —*K* is in *T*; terminate successfully.

>>   **Case 2.2.2**: *K* ≠ *key*(*root*(*T*)) —*K* is not in *T*; terminate unsuccessfully.

Figre 8.21   Search in an external binary search tree.

node containing *Sat,* you may well ask, "Why do we not terminate the search earlier?" First, we have assumed throughout that a key is only **part** of a record—it is not the whole of the record. The separator is the key and nothing more; hence, returning the internal node containing *Sat* does not help us to access the information in that key's record. It is only when we reach the corresponding external node that we are able to access the record with key *Sat*. Second, separators do not need to correspond to keys. For example, the external search tree of Fig. 8.23 has separators for which there are no corresponding keys. Hence, a key is guaranteed to be

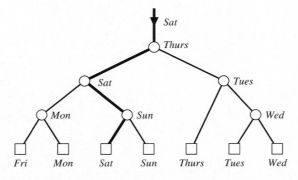

Figure 8.22   The search for *Sat* in the days-of-the-week external binary search tree of Fig. 8.19.

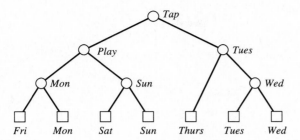

Figure 8.23 Separators in external binary search trees need not be keys.

present only if it is associated with an external node. Separators that do not correspond to keys occur as a result of deletions. This issue is discussed in Exercise 8.19.

8.5.2 Insertion

Search trees are more flexible, with respect to insertion and deletion, than are the LIST implementations of DICTIONARY. Insertion is the simpler of the two operations and, therefore, we study it first. In both cases, we develop algorithms for internal binary search trees; we leave to Exercise 8.20 the development of insertion and deletion algorithms for external binary search trees.

In Fig. 8.17(b), we show the effect of searching for the key *Keski* in the binary search tree of Fig. 8.14. The search ends at the second external node, which corresponds to the gap (*Fri,Mon*), as shown in Fig. 8.18. This unsuccessful search implies that if we add *Keski* to the tree, then it should be added at external node 2 as shown in Fig. 8.24. *Keski* splits the gap (*Fri,Mon*) into two gaps (*Fri,Keski*) and (*Keski,Mon*) associated with the new external nodes 2 and 2.5, respectively. This method—the usual method of insertion—always replaces an external node with an internal node with two external children; see Fig. 8.25. One implementation of *Insert* in Pascal is given in Program 8.3. We now turn to deletion.

8.5.3 Deletion

Deletion and insertion are different in that insertion always takes place at an external node, whereas deletion always takes place at an internal node. In general, we cannot just remove an internal node, since it has two subtrees and, apparently, only one place to reattach them; see Fig. 8.26. When one or both of the subtrees of the to-be-deleted node are empty, however, we can remove the node and reconnect its parent to its nonempty subtree, if there is one. To see that this method is correct, we consider, once more, the binary search tree *T* for the days of the week; see Fig. 8.14. If we perform *Delete (Fri,T)*, the node *u* associated with *Fri* has an empty left subtree, so we can reconnect the tree as shown in Fig. 8.27. Observe

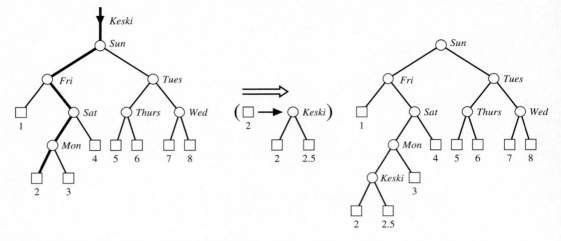

Figure 8.24   The addition of *Keski* to the binary search tree of Fig. 8.14.

that the resulting tree T' *is* a search tree. This fact follows from the observations that: *All keys in the subtree rooted at u in T are less than Sun; and Fri is less than all keys in the left subtree of u in T*. These two observations imply that in T' we have: All keys in the left subtree of the root of T' are less than *Sun*. Hence, T' is a search tree. The general rule is this: *If one subtree of the to-be-deleted node is empty, then replace the node by the other subtree. If both subtrees are empty, then replace the node with the empty subtree.* What do we do when both subtrees of a to-be-deleted node are nonempty—for example, with *Delete (Sun,T)*? Removing the root of *T* leaves two nonempty subtrees, and we want only one tree. Therefore, rather than removing the root, we reduce the problem to removing a node that has at least one empty subtree—the simple case. This idea implies that we should replace *Sun* by some other key in the tree. There are two candidates, the predecessor and successor of *Sun*; that is, *Sat* and *Thurs*. All other keys do not separate the keys in the left and right subtrees. The predecessor of *Sun* is the maximum key in the left subtree of the root—in general, the maximum key in the left subtree of the to-be-deleted node. Replacing *Sun* by *Sat* is all right except that *Sat* now appears twice; we must delete the original appearance of *Sat*; see Fig. 8.28.

Figure 8.25   The insertion of a new key *K* into a binary search tree.

```
procedure Insert(K: key; var D: DICTIONARY);
{D is a dictionary of keys and K is a key from the same
    universe. If K is already in D, then D is unchanged.
    Otherwise, K is added to D. Since D is represented as
    a binary search tree, Insert uses a subsidiary procedure
    Add that determines whether K is in D by mimicking the IsMember
    operation for binary search trees. Only if K is not found is D
    modified. In this case, Add uses the BINTREE operations
    BTInsert and BTReplace to replace an external node with a new
    internal node with key K. The BINTREE operations are identified
    with the prefix BT.}
var w: windowtype;

procedure Add(K: key; var w: windowtype;
                var D: DICTIONARY);
var e: elementtype;
begin
    if BTIsExternal(w,D)
    then begin {K is not in D; add it}
        BTInsert(w,D); {Replace the external node with an internal
            node.}
        BTReplace(K,w,D)
    end
    else begin {w is over an internal node.}
        BTExamine(e,w,D);
        if e < K
        then begin {Continue the search in the node's left subtree.}
            BTLeft(w,D); Add(K,w,D)
        end else
        if e > K
        then begin {Continue the search in the node's right subtree.}
            BTRight(w,D); Add(K,w,D)
        end else {K is in D; do nothing.}
    end
end;

begin
    {Initiate the search and add procedure.}
    BTRoot(w,D); Add(K,w,D)
end;
```

Program 8.3 A Pascal implementation of *Insert* for a dictionary represented as a binary search tree.

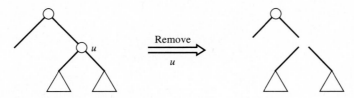

Figure 8.26 The difficulty of removing an internal node
from a binary search tree.

Note that the node *v* associated with the original appearance of *Sat* has an empty
right subtree. The existence of this empty subtree is no accident!

In general, given a nonempty binary search tree *T,* the node containing the
maximum key in *T* always has an empty right subtree. The proof of this fact is
straightforward. Let *u* be the node associated with the maximum key in *T*; see Fig.
8.29. From the binary-search-tree condition, we have that *key(u)* is less than all
keys in *u*'s right subtree. Now, if *u*'s right subtree is nonempty, it contains at least
one key greater than *key(u)*. Hence, because *key(u)* is the maximum key in *T, u*'s
right subtree must be empty. But, how do we find the maximum key in *T*? This
problem is also easy to solve; we just take the right child of the root and each subsequent node until we meet a node with an empty right subtree. The argument
needed to justify this algorithm is similar to the preceding argument; see Exercise
8.23. In summary,

> Find the node *u* with the to-be-deleted key *K*. If *u* has an empty subtree, remove
> *u*; if *u* does not have an empty subtree, find the maximum key *M* in *u*'s left sub-
> tree, replace *K* by *M,* and delete the original *M* from *u*'s left subtree.

The result of deleting *Sun* from the tree in Fig. 8.14, using this strategy, is given in
Fig. 8.28. A partial Pascal implementation of *Delete* is given in Program 8.4; you
are asked to complete it in Exercise 8.24.

You will have observed perhaps that deletion, as we have described it, is
asymmetric. When we delete a key whose node has two nonempty subtrees, we

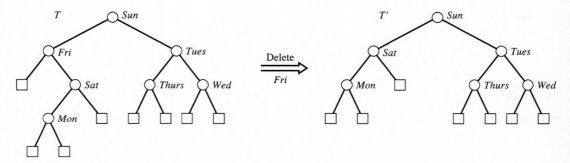

Figure 8.27 The deletion of *Fri* from the binary search tree of Fig. 8.14.

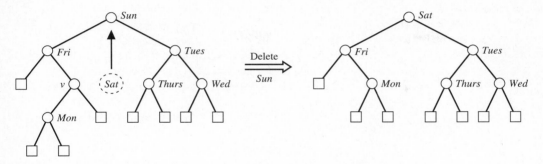

Figure 8.28   The deletion of *Sun* from the binary search tree of Fig. 8.14.

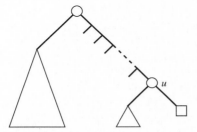

Figure 8.29   The maximum key in a binary search tree. The node
with the maximum key has an empty right subtree.

always choose to remove a node from the left subtree of the key's node. Substantial simulations and analyses have shown that this asymmetry leads eventually to inefficient search trees. Over time, asymmetric deletions skew a binary search tree, whereas, as we show in Section 8.5.5, insertions behave well. **Symmetric-deletion algorithms** behave better than asymmetric ones. We say that deletion is symmetric if it alternates its choices between the predecessor and successor keys, rather than always choosing the predecessor; see Exercise 8.25. An easier method is to flip a coin or hash the to-be-deleted key into 0 or 1, for predecessor and successor; see Exercise 8.25. Whichever method we choose to achieve symmetry, the result is the same: Symmetric deletions produce more efficient search trees than do asymmetric deletions.

8.5.4 A Cost Measure for Binary Search Trees

Given a binary search tree (for example, the one in Fig. 8.30), how do we assess its performance? We must decide what is an appropriate measure of performance. The simplest measure is the number of nodes visited when searching for a key—it corresponds to the number of recursive calls of *IsMember*. A second possible measure is the number of key comparisons that are made. We usually assume that

```
    procedure Delete(K: key; var D: DICTIONARY);
    {D is a dictionary of keys and K is a key from the same
        universe. If K is in D, then K is removed from D.
        Otherwise, D is unchanged. Since D is represented as
        a binary search tree, Delete uses a subsidiary procedure
        Remove that determines whether K is in D by mimicking the IsMember
        operation for binary search trees. Only if K is found is D
        modified. In this case, Remove uses the BINTREE operation
        BTDelete if K's node has at least one external child.
        Otherwise, it finds the predecessor Kpred of K, replaces K
        with Kpred, and removes the original Kpred from K's left
        subtree. The BINTREE operations are identified
        with the prefix BT.}
    var w: windowtype;

    procedure Remove(K: key; var w: windowtype;
                        var D: DICTIONARY);
    var e, Kpred: key;

    begin
        if BTIsExternal(w,D)
        then {K is not in D; do nothing.}
        else begin
            BTExamine(e,w,D);
            if e < K
            then begin
                BTLeft(w,D); Remove(K,w,D)
            end else
            if e > K
            then begin
                BTRight(w,D); Remove(K,w,D)
            end else {K is in D; remove it}
            if the left or right child of the node in w is external
            then BTDelete(w,T)
            else begin
                Find K's predecessor Kpred;
                BTReplace(Kpred,w,D);
                BTLeft(w,D); Remove(Kpred,w,D)
            end
        end
    end;

    begin
        BTRoot(w,D); Remove(K,w,D)
    end;
```

Program 8.4   A Pascal-like implementation of *Delete* for a dictionary implemented
                  as a binary search tree.

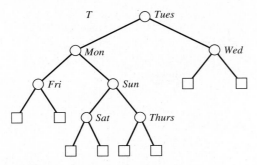

Figure 8.30 An example binary search tree.

a ternary comparison operator is available in this case, rather than the binary comparator we have in Pascal. For binary search trees, the node visit and comparison measures are the same for successful search, and they differ by 1 for unsuccessful search. We choose the number of **node visits** or **probes,** since it is the more appropriate measure for multiway trees; see Chapter 10. For example, in the tree T of Fig. 8.30, a search for *Sun* takes three node visits, whereas a search for *Keski* takes four node visits. Note that the number of node visits for a key or gap is one more than the corresponding node's level. The same keys require three ternary comparisons in each case. In T, the key *Tues* makes the fewest node visits (that is, one node visit), whereas *Sat* and *Thurs* make the most node visits of a successful search (that is, four node visits).

What is the average number of node visits in a successful search in T of Fig. 8.30? There are seven keys that require 1, 2, 2, 3, 3, 4, and 4 node visits; that is 19 node visits in total, or an average of $2\frac{5}{7}$ node visits. Similarly, for the average number of node visits in an unsuccessful search in T, there are eight gaps that require 4, 4, 5, 5, 5, 5, 3, and 3 node visits; that is 34 node visits in total, or an average of $4\frac{1}{4}$ node visits. To compute these averages, we have assumed that each key is equally likely in a successful search, and that each gap is equally likely in an unsuccessful search. The total number of node visits over all successful searches in a tree T is called the **internal path length** of T and is denoted by $IPL(T)$. Similarly, the total number of node visits over all unsuccessful searches in a tree T is called the **external path length** of T and is denoted by $EPL(T)$. More formally, for a binary search tree T, we define $IPL(T)$ and $EPL(T)$ as follows:

$$IPL(T) = \sum_{u \text{ is internal}} (1 + level(u))$$

and

$$EPL(T) = \sum_{u \text{ is external}} (1 + level(u)).$$

If T is of size n, then the average number of node visits in a successful search is $IPL(T)/n$, and in an unsuccessful search is $EPL(T)/(n + 1)$. Just as there is a close relationship between the numbers of internal and external nodes of a binary tree, there is a close relationship between $IPL(T)$ and $EPL(T)$. We leave to Exercise 8.26 the proof of the following fact.

Fact 8.6 *For all binary trees T,*

$$EPL(T) = IPL(T) + 2 \times size(T) + 1.$$

We can also express the path length of a binary tree recursively in terms of the path lengths of that tree's left and right subtrees; the proof is left to Exercise 8.27.

Fact 8.7 *Let T be a binary tree and L and R be the left and right subtrees, respectively, of its root. Then,*

$$IPL(T) = IPL(L) + IPL(R) + size(T),$$

and

$$EPL(T) = EPL(L) + EPL(R) + size(T) + 1.$$

We now analyze the expected internal and expected external path lengths of binary trees.

8.5.5 Analysis of Binary Search Trees

Having chosen the total number of node visits as the cost measure for internal binary search trees, we now examine their performance with respect to this measure. The performance of external search trees is left to Exercise 8.29.

Given a binary search tree we can (1) compute its worst-case and average-case performance, (2) ask for the range of these performances over all trees of the same size, and, finally, (3) ask for the expected-case performance over all trees of the same size. These analyses are progressive refinements of our knowledge about binary search trees; none of them are redundant.

Given a nonempty tree, a worst-case successful search is the key of any node that is as far from the root as possible—the height of the tree. For the tree of Fig. 8.30, the worst case is achieved by both *Sat* and *Thurs*—each requires four node visits. The average number of node visits is given by $IPL(T)/n$ and, for this example tree, as we have already seen, it is $2\frac{5}{7}$ node visits.

But how widely do these performances vary with trees of the same size? For a binary search tree for the days of the week, the worst case can be as low as three node visits for a bushy tree and as high as seven node visits for a skinny tree; see Figures 8.31(a) and (b), respectively. The two examples can be generalized for arbitrary values of n, yielding $\lceil \log_2 n \rceil$ and n node visits, respectively; see Fig.

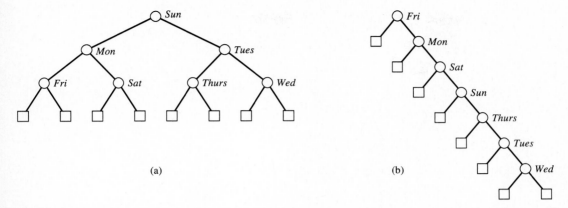

Figure 8.31 Extremal-cost binary search trees for the days of the week. (a) The minimum-cost tree. (b) A maximum-cost tree.

8.32. Serendipitously, the example trees in Fig. 8.32 provide not only the worst-case extremes, but also the extremes in the path length. Thus, we have

$$\sum_{i=1}^{\lceil \log n \rceil} i \cdot 2^{i-1} \approx 0.9 \lceil n \log n \rceil$$

and

$$\sum_{i=1}^{n} i = \frac{n(n+1)}{2}$$

as the minimum and maximum internal path lengths among binary search trees of size n.

A tree cannot be more inefficient than the skinny tree of Fig. 8.32(b) that requires $\Omega(n)$ node visits in both the worst and average cases, and it cannot be more efficient than the bushy tree of Fig. 8.32(a) that makes $O(\log n)$ node visits in both the worst and average cases. *An inefficient search tree behaves like a list, whereas an efficient search tree behaves like an ordered block.*

This analysis leads us to ask at least two further questions: What kinds of trees do we expect to obtain? Can we guarantee efficient, rather than inefficient, trees? We answer the first question immediately; we delay the positive answer to the second question to Chapter 10.

To compute the expected internal path length of binary search trees, we require a probability distribution over trees of the same size. The obvious distribution is the uniform distribution—all trees of size n are equally likely to occur;

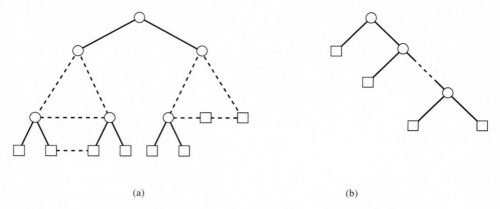

(a)   (b)

Figure 8.32   Extremal-cost binary search trees. (a) A minimum-cost tree.
(b) A maximum-cost tree.

hence, each occurs with probability $1/\mathcal{B}_n$. This assumption leads, however, to results far removed from reality, as simulation shows. Instead, we observe that search trees are usually grown by insertions into an initially empty tree. Therefore, rather than assuming uniformity for the trees, we assume uniformity for the insertion sequences. Of course, in practice, deletions also occur, but we ignore them for two reasons. First, the insertions-only model leads to results that are close to reality; second, analyzing the effect of deletions is an incredibly difficult unsolved problem (Jonassen and Knuth (1978) analyze what happens for binary search trees with *three keys* under deletions and insertions).

Consider n keys $K_1 < \cdots < K_n$ that are inserted, in some order $K_{i_1},...,K_{i_n}$, into an initially empty binary search tree. Observe that if we use the insertion sequence $i_1,...,i_n$, we get exactly the same binary tree, except that it contains the keys $1,...,n$, rather than the keys $K_1,...,K_n$. In other words, the tree we obtain depends on only the relative order of the keys, not on their particular values. For this reason, we consider the insertion of only the keys $1,...,n$ into an initially empty tree using some permutation $(i_1,...,i_n)$ as the insertion sequence. Moreover, we assume that each permutation of $(1,...,n)$ is equally likely to occur as an insertion sequence; that is, each permutation has probability $1/n!$ of occurring.

We want to compute the expected worst-case (or expected height) and expected average-case (or expected internal path length) number of node visits under this model. The expected height was analyzed recently after being open for many years. We merely state the result because its derivation is beyond the scope of this text.

Fact 8.8   *The expected height of a binary search tree of size n is*

$$4.31 \ln n + O(\ln \ln n),$$

under the assumption that all permutations of 1..n are equally likely to occur as insertion sequences.

We now prove the following fact for the expected internal path length.

Fact 8.9 *The expected internal path length of a binary search tree of size n is*

$$1.38n \log n + O(n),$$

under the assumption that all permutations of 1..n are equally likely to occur as insertion sequences.

For convenience, let $I(n)$ denote the **expected internal path length** over all $n!$ permutations of 1..n. Similarly, let $E(n)$ denote the corresponding **expected external path length.** Just as $EPL(T) = IPL(T) + 2n + 1$, so $E(n) = I(n) + 2n + 1$; see Exercise 8.31. Rather than computing $I(n)$ directly, we compute $E(n)$, since it is easier to handle. We derive a recurrence equation for $E(n)$, and then solve it.

The crucial observation is that *the number of node visits made by a search for a key is the same as the number of node visits made when inserting the key.* This observation holds only in the insertions-only model, because nodes and their keys are never moved after they are inserted. Now, when we insert the ith key, we expect to make $E(i - 1)/i$ node visits, since we have already inserted $i - 1$ keys. But, this formula implies that we expect to make $E(0)/1$ node visits for the first key,..., $E(n - 1)/n$ node visits for the nth key; that is,

$$I(n) = \frac{E(0)}{1} + \cdots + \frac{E(n-1)}{n}.$$

Similarly,

$$I(n - 1) = \frac{E(0)}{1} + \cdots + \frac{E(n-2)}{n-1}.$$

Thus, combining these two equations we obtain

$$I(n) = I(n - 1) + \frac{E(n-1)}{n}.$$

But, $E(n) = I(n) + 2n + 1$; therefore, substitution for $I(n)$ and $I(n - 1)$ gives

$$E(n) = \frac{n+1}{n} E(n - 1) + 2.$$

Noting that

$$E(1) = 2,$$

we can unroll $E(n)$ to obtain

$$E(n) = 2 + \frac{n+1}{n} [2 + \frac{n}{n-1} [2 + \cdots \frac{4}{3} [2 + \frac{3}{2} E(1)]...]]$$

$$= 2 + 2 \cdot \frac{n+1}{n} + 2 \cdot \frac{n+1}{n-1} + \cdots + 2 \cdot \frac{n+1}{3} + 2 \cdot n + 12$$

$$= 2(n+1)(\frac{1}{2} + \cdots + \frac{1}{n}) + 2.$$

Since $1 + \frac{1}{2} + \cdots + \frac{1}{n}$ is the nth harmonic number H_n with a value of $\ln n + O(1)$, we obtain

$$E(n) = 2(n+1)(H_n - 1) + 2$$

$$= 1.38n \log n + O(n)$$

and, hence,

$$I(n) = 1.38n \log n + O(n).$$

In other words, we can expect binary search trees to behave like bushy trees, rather than like skinny trees.

8.5.6 Predecessor and Successor Queries

Having demonstrated that binary search trees can be used to answer membership queries efficiently, we next consider the *Predecessor* and *Successor* operations. The *IsPredecessor* and *IsSuccessor* operations are implemented in a similar manner. Recall that, given a dictionary D of keys from a totally ordered universe and a query key K, the result of a successor query with K either is K' in D, where $K < K'$ and K' is the smallest such key in D, or is undefined, in which case $K' < K$, for all K' in D.

For dictionaries, we modify the *IsMember* algorithm for binary search trees to obtain a successor-finding algorithm. The difference between the two algorithms is minor. Letting K be the query key, when K is no less than the key at a node u on the search path, we take the right child of u; see Fig. 8.33. We have merged two tests in the *IsMember* algorithm, because we are not interested in equality. When K is less than the key at a node u on the search path, u's key is a candidate for the successor of K, and we know that there is a successor. If u's key is not the successor, then, by the properties of binary search trees, the successor is to be found in u's left subtree. So, we keep u's key as the latest approximation to the successor and continue the search in u's left subtree; see Fig. 8.33. We leave the implementation of this idea to Exercise 8.32. It is not difficult to show that

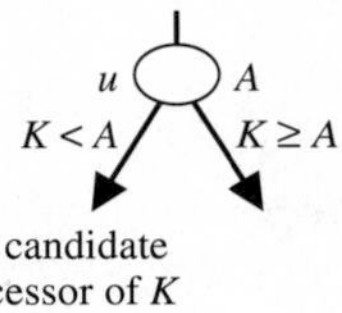

Figure 8.33 Search for a successor in a binary search tree.

these operations can be implemented to run in $O(n)$ time, in the worst case, and $O(\log n)$ time, in the expected case.

8.5.7 Range Queries

We have shown how to perform membership, predecessor, and successor queries in a binary search tree; we now show how to search with a range or interval. We provide two range-querying algorithms and their analyses.

The first implementation of *Range* is based on *IsMember* and *Successor*. Given a dictionary D of keys and two keys K_1 and K_2 such that $K_1 \le K_2$, we want to determine all keys K in D that satisfy $K_1 \le K \le K_2$. For this purpose, we first check whether K_1 is in D. If K is in D, then we report it; otherwise, we do not report it. Whatever the outcome of this membership test, we repeatedly find the successor of the current key in the range, beginning with K_1, until either there are no more keys in the dictionary or a key beyond K_2 is found. This approach guarantees correctness. We leave the implementation of this **marching algorithm** to Exercise 8.33.

The marching algorithm takes $O(rn)$ time, in the worst case, if there are r answers and D has size n. In the expected case, the algorithm takes $O(r\log n)$ time. We can improve these times to $O(r + n)$ and $O(r + \log n)$, respectively, if we add threads to the search tree. We leave the exploration of this variant to Exercise 8.33.

You will have observed perhaps that we have sneaked in a new concept—we have expressed the time bounds of an algorithm not only in terms of its input size, *but also in terms of its output size*. If we do not express the bounds in this way, we are faced with $O(n^2)$ and $O(n \log n)$ time bounds in the worst and expected cases, respectively, because there are $O(n)$ answers in the worst case. Such an analysis is coarse, since we can achieve such bounds with the simplest and most inefficient implementations. (For example, compare each key in the dictionary with the given range—an $O(n)$ time searching strategy.) On the other hand, the expected-case time bound of $O(r + \log n)$ demonstrates that, when r is smaller than $\log n$, the marching algorithm is as fast as *IsMember*, whereas the exhaustive search method examines all n elements, independently of the number of answers.

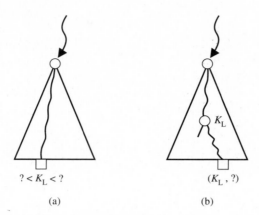

$$? < K_L < ? \qquad\qquad (K_L, ?)$$

(a)   (b)

Figure 8.34   The search path for K_L for the range query $[K_L, +\infty)$ in a
binary search tree. (a) K_L is not in the tree. (b) K_L is in the tree.

Rather than adding threads to a binary search tree, we examine the relationship between the answer nodes and the given range query for a given search tree.
To this end, we first consider the semi-infinite range query $[K_L, +\infty)$, which
denotes the query: Report all keys $K \geq K_L$ that are in D. The symbols $-\infty$ and $+\infty$
play a similar role for key universes that they perform for the set of integers. All
keys are greater than $-\infty$ and less than $+\infty$.

We begin by searching with K_L as before; it traces a root-to-frontier path in
the tree. If K_L is not in the tree, the path stops at an external node with the gap
containing K_L. Otherwise, it has two portions—the first is the path from the root
to the node with key K_L, the second is the path from this node to the external node
whose gap's left end is K_L. These two possibilities are illustrated in Figures
8.34(a) and (b), respectively. In both cases, the worst-case search time is linearly
proportional to the height of the tree. What does this root-to-frontier path tell us
about the range query $[K_L, +\infty)$? Each internal node u, on the path, falls into one
of the three classes displayed in Fig. 8.35. Let the key of node u be A. In Fig.
8.35(a), $K_L < A$, so A is in the range $[K_L, +\infty)$, as are all keys in its right subtree. In
Fig. 8.35(b), $K_L > A$, so A is not in the range and all keys in its left subtree are also
not in the range. In Fig. 8.35(c), $K_L = A$, so A is in the range, all keys in u's right
subtree are in the range, and all keys in u's left subtree are not in the range.

This analysis of the contribution of the nodes on the search path shows that
the keys in the range $[K_L, +\infty)$ are to be found in one of two places in the tree:
Either they are at nodes on the search path, or they are in right subtrees of nodes
on the search path. It is straightforward to discover and report the keys on the
search path, and those in right subtrees can be obtained by traversals of the subtrees, since every key is to be reported. Now, because the traversal of a subtree

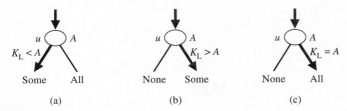

(a)   (b)   (c)

Figure 8.35 The three classes of nodes on the search path of K_L for a range query $[K_L, +\infty)$ in a binary search tree. (a) K_L is less than the node's key. (b) K_L is greater than the node's key. (c) K_L is equal to the node's key.

takes time linear in the size of the subtree, we have designed an algorithm that takes $O(r + \log n)$ time, in the expected case. Moreover, if we are content with knowing where the answers can be found, then we need to report only those nodes on the path whose keys are in the given range. This implication follows because we traverse only the right subtrees of these nodes. Clearly, we expect there to be $O(\log n)$ such nodes, so this approach yields an $O(\log n)$ expected-time algorithm. We can improve it to $O(\log n)$ time in the worst case, by using red–black trees; see Chapter 10.

Finally, let us return to our original problem of a range query $[K_L, K_R]$. We can solve it in a similar manner. The difference is in the number of cases; see Fig. 8.36. Initially, the search follows a single path, depending on whether the range falls wholly to the left or right of a node; see Figures 8.36(a) and (b). This single path can continue until an external node is reached, implying that there are no keys in the range. Usually, however, one of the cases in Figures 8.36(c), (d), and (e) occurs. Either of the first two of these cases transforms the query into a single semi-infinite range query, whereas the third transforms the query into two semi-

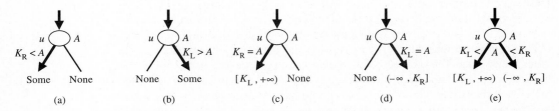

(a)   (b)   (c)   (d)   (e)

Figure 8.36 The five classes of nodes on the search path of a range query $[K_L, K_R]$ in a binary search tree. (a) The range falls to the left of the node. (b) The range falls to the right of the node. (c) K_R is equal to the node's key. (d) K_L is equal to the node's key. (e) The range straddles the node.

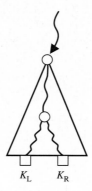

Figure 8.37   The forked search path for a range query in a binary search tree.

infinite range queries. In all cases, the length of the search path is bounded by twice the height of the search tree, so range querying can be implemented to run in $O(r + \log n)$ time in the expected case. The bifurcation of Fig. 8.36(e) can occur at most once, so the search can be viewed as shown in Fig. 8.37. The implementation details are left to Exercise 8.34.

8.6   PERFORMANCE REPORTS

We discuss the representations of SET, TABLE, and DICTIONARY in their presentation order.

The performance of the five SET representations we have covered, in Section 8.2, are summarized in Table 8.1, and their ratings are given in Table 8.2. The best general-purpose SET representation is the unordered-pointer representation, since it makes no assumptions about the universe and it is fully dynamic. There is little merit, by comparison, in using the unordered-block representation.

When the universe is totally ordered, however, we can obtain more efficient representations. Of these representations, the characteristic-function and ordered-pointer representations are the clear winners, and the latter representation is the more general one. The ordered-block representation is a trailing third choice. For the characteristic-function representation to be used, the elements should be the keys, the universe should not be too large, and the universe should be equivalent to a range of consecutive integers. If the universe is too large, then the approach is infeasible, and if the universe cannot be treated as a range of consecutive integers, then the elements cannot be used as indices. For example, the set of primes in some integer range is an example of a universe that should not be used with the characteristic-function representation. Our experience has shown that "too large" means thousands, rather than hundreds, of keys. Although the set-theoretic operations take time proportional to the size of the universe in the characteristic-func-

Table 8.1 A comparison of the worst-case execution times of the five SET implementations.

Operation	SET implementation		
	Characteristic function	Ordered pointer/block	Unordered pointer/block
Empty	m	1	1
IsEmpty	1	1	1
Insert	1	n	n
Delete	1	n	n
IsMember	1	n	n
Union	m	n	n^2
DisjointUnion	m	n	1
Intersection	m	n	n^2
Difference	m	n	n^2
Complement	m	m	mn
Size	1	1	1
Examine	m/n^{a}	1	1

[a]The time for *Examine* is the amortized time over n calls of *Examine*.

tion representation, their bitwise implementation is normally so fast that it beats the ordered-pointer representation.

Three guidelines have emerged from our discussion of the SET representations: (1) avoid using the block representations, (2) avoid using the unordered-pointer representation if at all possible, and (3) choose the characteristic-function representation whenever feasible.

Table 8.2 Performance ratings of the five implementations of SET.

SET implementation	Rating	Comments
Ordered pointer	Excellent	Fully dynamic; efficient set-theoretic operations; for totally ordered universe
Characteristic function	Excellent	Only when elements are the keys and the universe is totally ordered and small
Unordered pointer	Good	Best choice when nothing known about the universe
Ordered block	Good	Predefined size restriction
Unordered block	Satisfactory	

Table 8.3   A comparison of the worst-case execution times of the three
TABLE implementations.

	TABLE implementation	
Operation	Unordered pointer/block	Move to front
Empty	1	1
IsEmpty	1	1
Insert	n	n
Delete	n	$n[2 \times \mathrm{opt}]^a$
IsMember	n	$n[2 \times \mathrm{opt}]$

[a]The values in square brackets are amortized times.

Table 8.4   Performance ratings of the three implementations of TABLE.

TABLE implementation	Rating	Comments
Move to front	Excellent	Easy to code; fully dynamic
Unordered pointer	Good	Little used without the move-to-front modification
Unordered block	Good	Little used

We now turn to TABLE representations. The move-to-front heuristic improves the performance of the unordered-pointer representation substantially. Moreover, it requires only minor changes to the implementation of the search and update operations. Hence, it is the first choice among the representations that we have considered; see Tables 8.3 and 8.4. Again we can dismiss unordered-pointer and unordered-block representations, since they are inefficient.

Finally, we consider the representations of dictionaries. The ordered-pointer representation is not included in the performance measures in Table 8.5, because its performance is the worst of the four representations, so we can dismiss it from realistic consideration immediately. However, it is in the ratings in Table 8.6. Of the remaining three representations, the characteristic-function representation is the first choice, when it can be used. It has the advantage that the operations are easy to code and are extremely efficient. The second choice—a close second—is the binary search tree. Its performance matches the logarithmic lower bound in the expected case, it is fully dynamic whatever the universe size, and its operations are not too difficult to code. As we shall see in Chapter 10 balanced versions of binary search trees perform well in the worst case, too. Finally, we have the ordered block, which provides logarithmic-time searching in the worst case, but takes linear time for updates. Clearly, it is a distant third.

Table 8.5 A comparison of the worst-case execution times of three DICTIONARY implementations.

	DICTIONARY implementation		
Operation	Ordered block	Binary search tree	Characteristic function
Empty	1	1	1
IsEmpty	1	1	1
Insert	n	n	1
Delete	n	n	1
IsMember	$\log n[\log \log n]^a$	$n[\log n]$	1
IsPredecessor	$\log n[\log \log n]$	$n[\log n]$	$(m/n)^b$
IsSuccessor	$\log n[\log \log n]$	$n[\log n]$	(m/n)
Predecessor	$\log n[\log \log n]$	$n[\log n]$	(m/n)
Successor	$\log n[\log \log n]$	$n[\log n]$	(m/n)
Range	$r + \log n[r + \log \log n]$	$n[r + \log n]$	(mr/n)

[a]The values in square brackets are expected-case times.

[b]The values in parentheses are amortized times.

Table 8.6 Performance ratings of four implementations of DICTIONARY.

DICTIONARY implementation	Rating	Comments
Characteristic function	Excellent	Cannot always be used
Binary search tree	Very good	Fully dynamic; not difficult to code; effect of deletions not understood
Ordered block	Good	Overhead of interpolation search outweighs expected-case gains
Ordered pointer	Satisfactory	

8.7 SUMMARY

We have introduced the SET ADT, which provides a basis for incorporating into programs sets and set-theoretic operations such as *IsMember*, *Union*, and *Difference*. Three representations have been examined: characteristic function, block, and pointer. The block and pointer representations can be used for any universe of elements, whereas the characteristic-function representation can be used only when the elements are the keys, the key universe is small and totally ordered, and the key universe can be treated as a range of consecutive integers.

Two important ADTs, TABLE and DICTIONARY, which support only a limited number of set operations, have been introduced. Both restrict the set operations to *Insert*, *Delete*, and *IsMember*, but DICTIONARY has the five additional operations *IsPredecessor*, *IsSuccessor*, *Predecessor*, *Successor*, and *Range*. Although we have considered set representations of TABLE, we have focused our attention on adaptive sequential search with lists. The idea behind adaptive sequential search is to modify the given list of elements on each access so that the ordering of the elements is closer to the optimal ordering. We have carried out an amortized analysis of the move-to-front heuristic to show that this heuristic performs within a factor of 2 of the static optimal list.

For dictionaries, the key universe is required to be totally ordered; thus, the characteristic-function representation gives the most efficient representation. Unfortunately, this representation can be used only when the elements are the keys, the universe is not too large, and the universe can be treated as a range of consecutive integers. We have proved a logarithmic lower bound for the number of key comparisons needed, in the worst case, by any implementation of the *IsMember* DICTIONARY operation that uses only comparisons between keys. We have given an improved searching strategy for ordered blocks—interpolation search—that is more efficient in the expected case. Our main concern, however, has been the introduction of binary search trees, since they provide the basis for efficient implementations of the dictionary operations, as we shall see in Chapter 10. A binary search tree for a set of keys is a binary tree whose nodes are labeled with the keys so that the key of each node is greater than all keys in the node's left subtree and less than all keys in the node's right subtree. An inorder traversal of a binary search tree visits the keys in sorted order. We have also introduced external binary search trees in which keys are associated with the external nodes, rather than with the internal nodes. This notion prepares the way for the study of B$^+$-trees in Chapter 10. We introduced the internal path length as a reasonable cost measure for binary search trees; it is the sum of the lengths of the paths from the root to each internal node. We have proved that the expected path length of a binary search tree is logarithmic in the size of the tree and is within a constant factor of the smallest possible path length. In other words, binary search trees are expected to be efficient. We have also shown how the *Predecessor*, *Successor*, and *Range* operations can be implemented for binary search trees.

8.8 HISTORY

The amortized analysis of the move-to-front heuristic is based on the approach of Sleator and Tarjan (1985a). An asymptotic analysis of sequential search was first carried out by McCabe (1965) and independently by many other researchers (Hendricks, 1976; Rivest, 1976).

The notion of interpolation search was introduced by Peterson (1957); an accessible analysis is given in Perl and Reingold (1977).

The tight bound on the expected height of binary search trees was proved by Devroye (1986), although the upper bound was derived by Robson (1979; 1982) much earlier. Binary search trees were described and their expected-case analysis was derived independently by Booth and Colin (1960), Hibbard (1962), and Windley (1960). The analysis of deletion on binary search trees of size 3 is the subject of an appropriately titled paper, "A trivial algorithm whose analysis isn't," by Jonassen and Knuth (1978). This analysis was extended to size-4 trees by Baeza-Yates (1989c), and a model for the general case was introduced by Culberson and Munro (1989; 1990). A large-scale simulation of deletion algorithms was carried out by Eppinger (1983) and, subsequently, by Culberson (1986).

EXERCISES

8.1: Show how the SET operations can be implemented with the LIST operations.

8.2: You are asked to design a sorting program for records that consist of a single positive integer key in the range 0..10,000. Moreover, you are also told that no two records have the same key. Suggest a method of sorting these records even when internal memory for data is restricted to at most 2 kilobytes.

8.3: Complete the discussion of the implementation of the SET operations using the LIST representation.

8.4: Prove that *IsMember*(a,A), for an element a and a set A of size m, makes at least m = ? and ≠ ? comparisons, in the worst case. This result implies that any implementation of *IsMember* must take at least $\Omega(m)$ time, in the worst case.

8.5: Prove that arranging the elements of a table in order of nondecreasing probability maximizes the expected cost of sequential searching.

8.6: Assume that the key universe is totally ordered. Given a sorted block of keys that have nonuniform access probabilities, suggest a modification of binary search that takes into account their probabilities. Carry out a simulation, and compare your method's performance with the performance of binary search and optimal sequential search for the same set of keys with the same probabilities. How would you modify your method to take into account nonzero unsuccessful search probabilities?

8.7: Implement a sequential search method in which frequency counts are kept as an approximation to the access probabilities. Use the frequency counts to reorganize the elements into optimal order either after each access or after some fixed number of accesses. Compare, by simulation, these two methods with the move-to-front heuristic.

8.8: Extend the amortized analysis of the move-to-front heuristic to include insertions and deletions.

8.9: Construct an example of a list that proves that we cannot remove the factor of 2 in the amortized-time relationship between optimal search and move-to-front search.

8.10: Carry out an amortized analysis of the **counting search heuristic** (keep frequency counts and transpose elements when necessary to maintain nonincreasing frequency order).

8.11: Design and implement a representation for DICTIONARY that is based on LIST. What are the worst-case performances of your implementations of the DICTIONARY operations?

8.12: Design and implement a representation for DICTIONARY based on characteristic functions. What are the worst-case performances of your implementations of the DICTIONARY operations?

8.13: Prove that *BSearch*7 takes fewer comparisons, in the worst case, than does the tall decision tree of Fig. 8.16.

8.14: Prove that, in a decision tree for searching an n-key dictionary using comparisons, there are at least $n + 1$ **false** external nodes.

8.15: Complete the case analysis begun in the proof, given in Section 8.4.1, that a decision tree for the searching problem has at least $2n + 1$ nodes, when the dictionary contains n keys.

8.16: Implement interpolation searching for a block representation of a DICTIONARY. Using your implementation, carry out a simulational experiment to confirm the expected-case performance of interpolation search.

8.17: If we have a multiprocessor machine, we can do binary search with one processor and interpolation search with a second processor, assuming that we use the ordered-block representation of a DICTIONARY. Such parallelism allows us to get the best of both worlds: Guaranteed logarithmic worst-case performance (stop both processes if binary search terminates first), and log-log expected-case performance (stop both processes if interpolation search terminates first). Describe and implement a searching method for a single processor machine, which, based on the two searching strategies, has the same performance as the parallel method we have suggested.

8.18: Extend interpolation searching to strings of symbols.

8.19: Show that deletions in an external binary search tree can produce separators that are not keys, even when all separators in an initial tree are keys.

8.20: Design and implement algorithms for insertion into and deletion from external binary search trees.

8.21: Explain the difference between the average node-visit cost and the expected node-visit cost.

8.22: Rather than using node visits or ternary comparisons, we can use binary comparisons of keys as the basis of a cost measure for binary search trees. Based on this measure, what do extremal-cost binary trees look like? How costly are they?

8.23: Prove the correctness of the algorithm suggested in Section 8.5.3, for finding the maximum key in a binary search tree.

8.24: Complete the partial implementation of *Delete*, for binary search trees, given in Program 8.4.

8.25:   Implement the two alternative deletion algorithms, for binary search trees, that are discussed in Section 8.5.3, and compare the resulting trees with those trees obtained by the standard deletion method of Program 8.4. The two new methods attempt to remove the bias in the standard deletion method. The first method alternately chooses the predecessor and successor keys, rather than always choosing the predecessor key. The second method flips a coin, based on the key, to choose between the predecessor and successor keys.

8.26:   Prove that $EPL(T) = IPL(T) + 2 \times size(T) + 1$.

8.27:   Prove the correctness of the equation given in Section 8.5.5 that relates the path length of a binary tree to the path lengths of that tree's left and right subtrees.

8.28:   We say that a tree is **ternary** if every internal node has three children. Suggest and prove relationships between the size and number of external nodes of a ternary tree, and between the *EPL* and *IPL* of a ternary tree.

8.29:   Derive the expected node-visit cost of external binary search trees.

8.30:   Given the four keys 1..4; which permutations, used as insertion sequences, produce a tallest binary search tree?

8.31:   Prove that $E(n) = I(n) + 2n + 1$.

8.32:   Implement a Pascal version of *Predecessor* or *Successor*, for binary search trees.

8.33:   Implement, for binary search trees, the marching solution to *Range* and compare its performance with the threaded approach.

8.34:   Implement the forked approach to range searching in a binary search tree.

8.35:   Discuss how you would implement the *Predecessor*, *Range*, and *Successor* operations for external binary search trees. Are your implementations simpler or more efficient than those for binary search trees?

C H A P T E R

9

Tables and Hashing

Although we introduced TABLE in Chapter 8, we did not provide an efficient representation of it. We now correct this omission by introducing hashing, a technique that maps the key universe to the indices of a block. Hashing yields excellent performance while retaining simplicity of coding; for these reasons, it has become a standard method for implementing tables. It is important to realize, however, that hashing is limited; we cannot use it to obtain a representation of DICTIONARY that is as efficient as the hash representation of TABLE. In contrast, each representation of DICTIONARY is no less efficient when used as a representation of TABLE.

Normally, with hashing, many keys are hashed to the same cell of a block. They collide. Since a cell normally holds a fixed number of records, we need to provide a strategy to resolve such collisions. We define and compare a number of collision-resolution techniques; we also analyze their expected-case performance. We examine bucketing and separate chaining in Section 9.2 before turning to the most popular method of hashing—open addressing—in Section 9.3. We explain the idea behind open addressing by using linear probing, before introducing double hashing. Open addressing does not support an unlimited number of insertions, just as the block representation of a table does not do so. Therefore, in Section 9.4, we describe an extension of separate chaining and open addressing that is fully dynamic and also is efficient. Called *linear hashing,* it was originally introduced as a method of indexing external tables; however, it also performs well for internal tables. Finally, in Section 9.5, we introduce a variant of linear hashing that uses signatures and a signature index to give one-disk-access retrieval for external tables.

9.1 HASHED REPRESENTATIONS OF TABLE

If we can use the characteristic-function representation of a set as the representation of a table, then insertions, deletions, and member queries can be implemented in constant time. In contrast, the list representations of a table are efficient in their use of space, but insertion and deletion take linear time. A natural question is this: *Can we obtain a representation that is both space and time efficient?* In this section, we introduce a method that has performance close to the characteristic-function approach, *in the expected case.* Moreover, it is closer to the list representation in its use of space.

We introduce hashing in Section 9.1.1; then, in Section 9.1.2, we describe some well-behaved classes of hash functions.

9.1.1 Introduction to Hashing

Let us begin by assuming that the key universe is the set of nonnegative integers, $\mathbb{N}$. (We return to the more general situation in Section 9.1.2.) Further, assume that we have a function $h : \mathcal{N} \to 0..m - 1$, for some $m \geq 1$ (see Fig. 9.1), that uses only arithmetic operations and computes its value in constant time. In other words, we can code h as a one-statement Pascal function. Also, let T be a block, indexed from 0 to $m - 1$, whose entries can be either a record or the special value **void,** which means that the entry does not contain a record. (For simplicity of presentation, we often identify records and their keys.) Then, we can represent a set A of records by setting

$$T[h(a)] = r,$$

where $a = key(r)$, for all r in A, and by setting all other entries to **void.** For example, let $m = 13$, $A = \{22,39,46,54,79,198\}$, and $h(i) = i \bmod 13$, for all i in $\mathbb{N}$. (Note that we have identified the keys and their records in this example.) Now,

$$h(22) = 22 \bmod 13 = 9,$$
$$h(39) = 39 \bmod 13 = 0,$$
$$h(46) = 46 \bmod 13 = 7,$$
$$h(54) = 54 \bmod 13 = 2,$$
$$h(79) = 79 \bmod 13 = 1,$$

and

$$h(198) = 198 \bmod 13 = 3.$$

We obtain the block T of Table 9.1, where **void** $\equiv -1$. We call the function h a **hash function,** since it hashes, or chops up, its argument; we call T a **hash table;** and we call $h(i)$ the **home address** of key i.

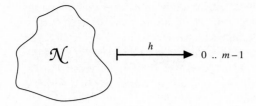

Figure 9.1 An example hash function.

If we are given $B = \{14\} \cup A$, then

$$h(14) = 14 \textbf{ mod } 13 = 1$$

and both 79 and 14 should occupy cell $T[1]$. We say that keys 14 and 79 **collide** under h. We have two possible courses of action. First, we can try to avoid collisions by constructing a different hash function and, perhaps, using a larger hash table. A hash function that maps each record of a set of records to a unique position is said to be **perfect.** Second, we can accept collisions as inevitable and provide methods for dealing with them directly.

It is worthwhile to calculate how many functions there are that map n given keys into n distinct cells of a block of size $m,$ where $1 \leq n \leq m$. Turning this definition around, one key can be assigned any one of m values, the next key any one of $m - 1$ values, and so on. Thus, there are at most $m!/(m - n)!$ perfect hash functions. With the example of $m = 13$ and $B = \{14\} \cup A$, we have $n = 7$; thus, there are at most $\frac{13!}{6!} = 8,648,640$ perfect hash functions that map the elements of B to

Table 9.1 An example hash table.

Index	Keys
0	39
1	79
2	54
3	198
4	−1
5	−1
6	−1
7	46
8	−1
9	22
10	−1
11	−1
12	− 1

seven distinct locations. On the other hand, there are m^n functions that map a set of n elements into a set of m elements, since there are m possible elements to associate with each element in the n-element set. With $m = 13$ and $n = 7$, there are 13^7 functions, or $\approx 63,000,000$ functions. Thus, more than 12 percent of the functions may be perfect hash functions, in this case. However, if we increase n to 10, say, then there are at most $1,038,000,000$ perfect hash functions out of a possible ≈ 140 billion functions; that is, fewer than 1 percent.

It is easy to define a function that maps B to distinct locations, but it is not as easy to find a perfect hash function. You are invited to construct a perfect hash function for B into $0..12$; see Exercise 9.1.

Perfect hash functions ensure that a key can be tested for membership in a given set with *one probe* into the corresponding hash table; that is, in constant time, in the worst case. As we have seen for the set A, however, one insertion can destroy the perfection of a hash function. For this reason, we usually prefer to accept the inevitability of collisions and to deal with them directly *without changing the hash function*. We consider a variety of practical **collision-resolution techniques** in Sections 9.2 and 9.3.

9.1.2 Hash Functions

We have assumed that keys are integers and we have used the modulus function as the hash function. We made these choices for simplicity and convenience of presentation—not for practical reasons. So, what kinds of functions should we use, and how should we hash nonintegral keys? We want to use hash functions that do not show bias over the key space. For example, every constant function is biased, since it maps every key to the same cell. We want keys to be evenly distributed over the range $0..m - 1$, so that retrieval times will not be biased over the key space. Given a block of size m and an integer key x, the hash function

$$h(x) = x \bmod m$$

is one member of a class of hash functions known as **2-universal.** Each member of this class has the form

$$h(x) = ((c_1 x + c_2) \bmod p) \bmod m,$$

where $p > m$ is a large prime, $p > 2^{20}$, c_1 is a positive integer constant less than p, and c_2 is a nonnegative integer constant less than p. The subfunction

$$(c_1 x + c_2) \bmod p$$

is responsible for scrambling or hashing the key x, and the final modulo-m operation serves to map the scrambled key into the block locations. Once we have chosen p and m, we can fine tune the hash function by changing only c_1. The surprising result of changing c_1 is that we obtain a *completely different hash function*. In practice, choosing $c_2 = 0$ has little effect, although theoretically it does have some effect. Choosing $c_2 = 0$ and assigning two different values for c_1 gives two different hash functions that can be used for what is called double hashing; see Section 9.3.2.

If we are programming in C or in a similar lower-level language, then there is another class of hash functions that is also 2-universal, and with which it is easier to work. We assume that the keys are b-bit strings, for some $b > 0$, and $m = 2^l$, for some $l > 0$. Then, we define the **multiplicative-hash function** h as follows:

$$h(x) = (ax \bmod 2^b) \operatorname{\mathbf{div}} 2^{b-l},$$

where $0 < a \leq 2^b - 1$ and a is odd. The advantage of multiplicative hashing is that the modulus and division operators can be evaluated by shifting, rather than by integer division.

What about nonintegral keys—for example, character strings? Essentially, in all such cases, we first produce an integral key and then use one of the 2-universal hash functions. Given a character string $s_1 \ldots s_k$, where the s_i are individual characters, we treat the characters as the digits of an integer to some base b. For example, $b = 37$ works well. Or, more precisely, the internal integer values of the characters are treated as such digits, even though they may be larger than the base b. More precisely, we compute

$$(i_1 \times b^{k-1} + \cdots + i_k \times b^0) \bmod 2^B,$$

for some b and B, where i_j is the internal integer value of s_j, for $1 \leq j \leq k$. Applying modulo 2^B gives the least significant B bits of the result. B is usually 16 or 32 and b is some small odd number, not necessarily prime. We have to be careful to avoid overflow during the computation of the integral key; hence, we normally use modulo arithmetic throughout the computation. For example, for the string $s_1 s_2 s_3 s_4$, we compute

$$(i_1 \times 37^3 + i_2 \times 37^2 + i_3 \times 37 + i_4) \bmod 2^{32}$$

by using Horner's rule and the properties of modular arithmetic to obtain the equivalent form

$$(((((i_1 \times 37 + i_2) \bmod 2^{32}) \times 37 + i_3) \bmod 2^{32}) \times 37 + i_4) \bmod 2^{32}.$$

Because hash functions are used heavily, we want to minimize the number of arithmetic operations they use. For example, **mod** 2^{32} can be accomplished in C with a bit mask and a logical **and**.

Rather than taking one character at a time, we might choose to take two, three, or four at a time. With four at a time, for a string $s_1 \ldots s_{4k}$, we obtain

$$i_{1,4} \times 37^{k-1} + \cdots + i_{4k-3,4k} \times 37^0) \bmod 2^{32},$$

where $i_{j,j+3}$ is the internal integer value of the four characters $s_j \, s_{j+1} \, s_{j+2} \, s_{j+3}$.

Table 9.2   The logical **or** of two 2-bit integers.

or	00	01	10	11
00	00	01	10	11
01	01	01	11	11
10	10	11	10	11
11	11	11	11	11

One final word of warning. It is tempting, particularly when programming in a language such as C, to extract some fixed number of bits from the bit representation of a character string and then, interpreting these bits as an integer, to hash them. For example, we might take the logical **or** of blocks of characters or even single characters. Unfortunately, this technique does not provide a uniform distribution over the integers. For example, consider the logical **or** of two 2-bit integers. All possible combinations are displayed in Table 9.2. Observe that 00 appears once, 11 appears 12 times, and 01 and 10 appear three times each—hardly a uniform distribution. You should avoid using this and similar techniques.

9.2   BUCKETING AND SEPARATE CHAINING

The first method for dealing with collisions is simplistic in the extreme—we allow more than one record to be associated with each cell in a hash table. We assume that each cell in a hash table contains a list of records; see Fig. 9.2. If we represent the list with a block, then we have what is called (fixed-sized) **bucketing,** since each entry has a predefined maximum size. If we use a pointer representation, then we have what is called **separate chaining** or variable-sized bucketing. Thus, the only characteristic distinguishing bucketing from separate chaining is that bucketing uses fixed-sized buckets and separate chaining uses variable-sized buckets. The advantage of both bucketing and separate chaining is that the table operations are easy to implement. We first hash the given key to obtain the bucket in which it should appear; then we perform a sequential search within the bucket. Clearly we can choose to sort the keys in each bucket or to use an adaptive technique (see Section 8.3). We leave these explorations to Exercise 9.2. Here we consider separate chaining in somewhat more detail.

Bucketing suffers from the obvious drawback that buckets can **overflow;** that is, too many records may be hashed to a bucket. In practice, we provide an additional overflow area for those records that cannot fit into their buckets. Although this modification is easily accommodated, it leads to inefficiency. An alternative approach is to recognize that overflows are as inevitable as are collisions. Indeed, when the bucket size is 1, *overflows are collisions*. For this reason, we consider separate chaining.

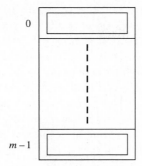

Figure 9.2 A hash table with buckets or chains.

In separate chaining, a hash table is a block of linked-list headers, and each linked list of records is called a **chain.** We treat only the unordered linked list here. Letting the hash function be h and TABLE be represented by **array** $[0..m-1]$ **of** LIST, *IsMember* can be coded as shown in Program 9.1. Observe that, because we use the LIST ADT, the implementation of *IsMember* does not distinguish between fixed-sized and variable-sized buckets.

```
function IsMember(K: keytype; T: TABLE): boolean;
{h is a hash function from the key universe to the indices of the
    hash table T, and K is a key from the key universe. IsMember
    returns true if K is in T; otherwise, it returns false.}
var i: integer; L: LIST; w: windowtype;
    found: boolean; e: keytype;

begin i:= h(K); L:= T[i];
    if LIsEmpty(L)
    then IsMember:= false
    else begin
        LBeforeFirst(w,L); LNext(w,L);
        found:= false;
        while not LIsAfterLast(w,L)
                    and not found do
        begin LExamine(e,w,L);
            found:= e = K;
            LNext(w,L)
        end;
        IsMember:= found
    end
end;
```

Program 9.1 A Pascal implementation of *IsMember* for both bucketing and separate chaining.

When comparing the performance of hashing methods, we normally distinguish between successful and unsuccessful queries or searches. Unsuccessful search in separate chaining always exhausts the chain of the query key, whereas successful search for a query key never exhausts the chain. So, once the home address of a query key is known, hash-table searching is the same as sequential searching; see Section 8.3. It is possible, but highly unlikely, that all keys are hashed to the same address. Therefore, for an n-key table, by the results on sequential search in lists in Section 8.3.2, unsuccessful search makes $n + 2$ probes, in the worst case (we include the probes into both the list header and the after-last cell), whereas successful search makes $n + 1$ probes, in the worst case (we include the probe into the list header). The worst-case performance of separate chaining is as bad as that of sequential search. So, what have we gained?

Separate chaining is a more complex data structure than a singly linked list, but its worst-case performance is the same. As we now show, we have gained with respect to the expected-case performance. As is true in any analysis of hashing methods, the number of elements in the table is less important than is the table's density or load factor. The **load factor** λ of a hash table is the number of records in the hash table divided by the number of cells in the table. For bucketing, the load factor lies between 0 and b, where b is the bucket size; for separate chaining, the load factor can be any nonnegative value. In general, hashing methods have poor worst-case performance, but have extremely good expected-case performance. We prove the following fact in Section 9.2.1.

Fact 9.1   *Assume that each entry in a hash table is equally likely to be accessed, and that each sequence of n insertions is equally likely to occur. Then, a hash table that uses separate chaining and has load factor λ has the following expected-case performance:*

- $s(\lambda) = 2 + \lambda/2$ probes, for successful search
- $u(\lambda) = 2 + \lambda$ probes, for unsuccessful search

9.2.1   Analysis of Separate Chaining[*]

We analyze the performance of three hashing methods in this chapter: separate chaining, uniform hashing, and linear hashing. We can analyze an instance of TABLE in a number of ways—each contributing to our understanding of the representation. In all cases, we consider the performance of *IsMember* to be indicative of the performance of the other operations. This simplification is appropriate because both *Insert* and *Delete* must mimic *IsMember* before they perform an update.

The simplest analysis is for a specific table. Given a hash table of size m, with separate chaining, that holds n keys $K_1,...,K_n$, with c_i keys in chain i, $0 \leq i \leq m$, we can ask:

1. What is the worst-case performance? How slowly can we solve *IsMember*?

2. What is the average-case performance? How fast can we expect to solve *IsMember*?

The worst case is of only slight interest, since it corresponds to the longest chain. The more interesting measure is the average case. Given that p_i is the access probability of K_i, $1 \le i \le n$, the average number of probes in a successful search is

$$\sum_{i=1}^{n} p_i \cdot probes(K_i),$$

where $probes(K)$ is the number of probes needed to find K. This formula should be compared with the expected number of probes in sequential search; see Section 8.3.2. Usually, we assume that all keys are equally likely to be accessed , so the average number of probes becomes

$$\frac{1}{n} \sum_{i=1}^{n} probes(K_i).$$

For unsuccessful search, letting q_i be the probability that a search in chain i of length c_i is unsuccessful, we obtain

$$\sum_{i=0}^{m-1} q_i(c_i + 2)$$

as the average number of probes in an unsuccessful search. Again assuming that the q_i are equal, the average number of probes becomes

$$\frac{1}{m} \sum_{i=0}^{m-1} c_i .$$

Given a static table, the average number of probes is a valid measure of its performance; however, in practice, tables are not static. Hence, we are more interested in the expected values of these measures. In this setting, we are told that a hash table has size m and contains n records, and we assume that it has been obtained by a sequence of n insertions into an initially empty hash table. What do we expect the performance of the resulting hash table to be? The expected worst case (the expected length of the longest chain), is difficult to analyze and is not our primary concern. We consider only the **expected average case,** which we call, simply, the **expected case.**

Assume that each insertion is independent of the previous insertions, and that each cell in the hash table is accessed with equal probability. Then, after n insertions, the expected chain length is n/m; that is, it is the load factor λ. This value implies that an unsuccessful search is expected to take $2 + \lambda$ probes. Now, by the results we have obtained for sequential search in Section 8.3, we expect successful search to end halfway down a chain; that is, it ends after

$$1 + \frac{\lambda(\lambda + 1)}{2\lambda} = \frac{\lambda + 3}{2}$$

probes. Unfortunately, this result is incorrect; there is a fallacy in the argument. The probability of accessing each cell is not necessarily equal for successful search. The longer a chain, the higher the probability that the chain is accessed when we perform a successful search.

First, observe that when we are inserting a new record, the number of probes taken to insert that record is exactly the same as the number of probes to search for that record. Moreover, the number of probes to insert the record corresponds to the number of probes needed for an unsuccessful search. Given a load factor x, $0 \leq x \leq \lambda$, an insertion changes x slightly—by dx, say, to $x + dx$. The expected number of probes to search for this newly inserted record is $u(x) = x + 2$, as we have argued. In a discrete model, we consider the insertion of n records into an initially empty hash table, sum their contributions u_i to the total expected number of probes, and average over the number n of records. In the continuous model that we have adopted, we replace the number of records by the final load factor, replace the contributions by $u(x)$, and replace the sum of the contributions by their integral. Hence, the expected number of probes for successful search in a table with load factor λ is

$$s(\lambda) = \frac{1}{\lambda} \int_0^\lambda (x + 2)dx.$$

Note that the term $(x + 2)dx$ is the expected number of probes in each chain, for unsuccessful search, and λ is the expected number of records in each chain; thus, the expression for $s(\lambda)$, in units, *is* the expected number of probes per record, for successful search. Integrating, we obtain

$$s(\lambda) = \frac{1}{\lambda} \left[\frac{x^2}{2} + 2x \right]_0^\lambda,$$

which evaluates to

$$s(\lambda) = 2 + \frac{\lambda}{2}.$$

These results do not necessarily correspond to reality, because of our assumptions. Table 9.3 shows the results of a simulation of separate chaining that

Table 9.3 The analytic and simulated expected numbers of probes for hashing with separate chaining.

λ	Simulation		Analysis	
	$s(\lambda)$	$u(\lambda)$	$s(\lambda)$ $+ \lambda/2$	$u(\lambda)$ λ
0.1	2.0500	0.9650	2.05	0.1
0.2	2.0750	0.1754	2.10	0.2
0.5	2.2750	0.5351	2.25	0.5
0.9	2.5450	0.9627	2.45	0.9
1.0	2.4650	1.0241	2.50	1.0
2.0	2.9725	2.0022	3.00	2.0
5.0	4.5000	5.0263	4.50	5.0
8.0	6.1075	7.7939	6.00	8.0
9.0	6.4825	9.2566	6.50	9.0
10.0	7.0850	10.0702	7.00	10.0

compares the computed expected numbers of probes with the numbers given by the preceding analysis.

9.3 OPEN ADDRESSING

Although separate chaining is simple to code and is efficient for small load factors, it requires additional space to that already provided by the hash table. We could use **coalesced chaining,** where the chains are in the hash table itself; see Exercise 9.4 for more details. Instead, we consider another alternative, a class of methods called **open addressing.** We store all records in the hash table and deal with collisions uniformly by incrementing the hash-table index and using wraparound (adding an increment to a hash-table index always produces an index into the hash table). It is crucial that, whatever the value of the home address, all locations in the hash table are, in principle, reachable from the home address. We begin by considering the simplest open-addressing technique in which the hash-table index is incremented by 1. Clearly, all cells are reachable from each index with this increment. The method is called *linear-probe hashing* or *linear probing;* it is defined in Section 9.3.1. Because linear probing suffers from clustering, we usually choose an open-addressing method in which the increment depends on the search key. Such a method is called *double hashing;* it is defined in Section 9.3.2. Unfortunately, double hashing is difficult to analyze, so we introduce a third method, *uniform hashing,* that is easier to analyze and that also serves as an approximate model of double hashing; this model is discussed in Section 9.3.3. Finally, in Section 9.3.4, we confront the problem of deletion for open-addressing methods, since it is not as easy to solve as is deletion for bucketing and separate chaining.

9.3.1 Linear Probing

For a hash table of size m, a hash function h, and a key K, let $h_0 = h(K)$ be the home address of K. Then, the **hash sequence** defined by the key K is the sequence

$$h_0, h_1, h_2, ..., h_{m-1},$$

where

$$h_{i+1} = (h_i + 1) \bmod m,$$

for $i \geq 0$. After these preliminaries, we define **linear-probe hashing.** *IsMember* (K, T) first computes $h_0 = h(K)$ with $i = 0$. If $T[h_i]$ is **void,** then K is not in the table. Otherwise, if $T[h_i] = K$, then K is in the table. Finally, if $T[h_i] \neq K$, then we repeat these tests with i replaced by $(i + 1) \bmod m$. Formally, we have the *IsMember* implementation shown in Program 9.2. We can improve the termination test by using the sentinel technique; that is, we replace the key at location h_0 by K—the details are left to Exercise 9.5. Linear probing is hard to beat as far as simplicity is concerned. However, it has one major problem: clustering. To see what clustering is and why it is a problem, we first define *Insert. Insert(K,T)* mimics *IsMember* (K,T) until a void location is found, when K is inserted at the void location.

Assume that each location is equally likely to be the home address of some key. Since the table has m cells, each cell has probability $1/m$ of being the home cell. Each void cell does not have, however, equal probability of being probed; it has only equal probability of being the home cell. Why do we make this distinction? *Because a key is always inserted at the first void cell in the key's hash sequence.* If we have a sequence of s nonvoid cells, then the void cell im-

```
function IsMember(K: keytype; T: TABLE): boolean;
var hi,i: integer; found: boolean;

begin hi:= h(K); found:= false; i:= 0;
    while(T[hi] <> void) and (i < m) and not found do
        begin
            if T[hi] = K
            then found:= true;
            else hi:= (hi + 1) mod m;
            i:= i + 1
        end;
    IsMember:= found
end;
```

Program 9.2 A Pascal implementation of *IsMember* for linear-probe hashing.

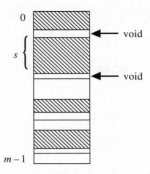

Figure 9.3   Void cells not equally likely to be probed in a linear-probe hash table.

mediately after the sequence has probability $(s + 1)/m$ of being hit by an insertion; see Fig. 9.3. Such an insertion causes the sequence to grow by at least one cell, and by much more if it joins two sequences. This growth is the **cookie-monster effect**—every additional cookie makes the monster grow and, therefore, also makes the monster's appetite grow.

In linear-probe hashing, not only are void cells not equally likely to be the targets of an insertion, but also the sequences of nonvoid cells cause search time to deteriorate. The reason for this deterioration is that whenever a key A probes a nonvoid cell h_i in the hash sequence $h_0,...,h_{m-1}$ of any other key K, it will continue by probing cells $h_{i+1},...,h_{m-1},h_0,....$ In other words, the hash sequences of all keys are identical, when viewed as circular sequences. This similarity ensures that sequences of nonvoid cells continue to grow.

This phenomenon is called **clustering.** We can avoid clustering, to a large extent, by ensuring that different keys that probe, at some point, the same cell, do not subsequently probe the same cells in the same order. In Exercises 9.8 and 9.9, we consider two variants of open addressing that avoid some clustering, and we introduce double hashing, in Section 9.3.2, to eliminate clustering. In Table 9.4, we display two full hash tables, for the same set of keys, formed from two different insertion sequences with linear probing. The first hash table in Table 9.4 is obtained with the insertion sequence

$$11 \; 3 \; 27 \; 99 \; 8 \; 50 \; 77 \; 22 \; 12 \; 31 \; 33 \; 40 \; 53.$$

In total, 28 probes—with an average of 2.1 probes per insertion—are made when the keys are inserted.

The second hash table in Table 9.4 is obtained with the insertion sequence

$$53 \; 40 \; 33 \; 31 \; 12 \; 22 \; 77 \; 50 \; 8 \; 99 \; 27 \; 3 \; 11,$$

which makes 30 probes; that is, an average of 2.3 probes per insertion are made.

Table 9.4 Two full hash tables, for the same keys, obtained with linear probing and using two different insertion sequences.

Index	Key	Number of probes	Home address	Index	Key	Number of probes	Home address
0	77	2	12	0	77	2	12
1	27	1	1	1	53	1	1
2	12	4	12	2	40	2	1
3	3	1	3	3	27	3	1
4	40	4	1	4	3	4	3
5	31	1	5	5	31	1	5
6	53	6	1	6	11	9	11
7	33	1	7	7	33	1	7
8	99	1	8	8	8	1	8
9	8	2	8	9	22	1	9
10	22	2	9	10	99	3	8
11	11	1	11	11	50	1	11
12	50	2	11	12	12	1	12

It is easy to define worst-case insertion sequences. Consider the sequence

$$1\ 14\ 27\ 40\ 53\ 66\ 79\ 92\ 105\ 118\ 131\ 144\ 157.$$

All keys in this sequence hash to the same value; hence, linear-probe hashing reduces to sequential search. The first key makes one probe, the second key two probes, and so on; for a total of $13 \times 14/2 = 91$ probes. The average number of probes, in this case, is 7; that is, it is $(m + 1)/2$.

Similarly, a best-case sequence is

$$0\ 1\ 2\ 3\ 4\ 5\ 6\ 7\ 8\ 9\ 10\ 11\ 12.$$

This sequence makes 13 probes—an average of 1 probe for each insertion.

Finally, we give the expected-case performance results for successful and unsuccessful search with linear-probe hashing. The derivation of these results is beyond the scope of this text. Clearly, the load factor λ satisfies the inequalities $0 \le \lambda \le 1$, for open addressing.

Fact 9.2 *Assume that each entry in a hash table is equally likely to be accessed, and that each sequence of n insertions is equally likely to occur. Then, a hash table that uses linear probing and has load factor λ has the following expected-case performance:*

- $s(\lambda) = \frac{1}{2}(1 + \frac{1}{1-\lambda})$ *probes, for successful search with $\lambda < 1$*

- $u(\lambda) = \frac{1}{2}(1 + \frac{1}{(1-\lambda)^2})$ *probes, for unsuccessful search with $\lambda < 1$*

9.3.2 Double Hashing

We have used linear probing to explain the idea of open-addressing hashing; however, its performance deteriorates rapidly as the load factor increases. Therefore, we turn to double hashing, the most efficient version of open addressing. As we shall see, in double hashing, all unprobed cells are candidates for the next probe. This spread is in sharp contrast to linear probing, in which the adjacent cell is the only candidate cell for the next probe. Double hashing uses two hash functions—one, as before, to compute the home address, and one to compute the increment. We use two 2-universal hash functions of the forms

$$h(K) = (c_1 K \bmod p) \bmod m$$

and

$$g(K) = ((c_2 K \bmod p) \bmod (m - 1)) + 1,$$

where g is the increment hash function. Note that K is hashed, under g, into the range $1..m - 1$ using modulus $m - 1$, rather than m, to ensure that $g(K)$ is never zero. It is possible that some cells are unreachable from the home cell $h(K)$ with increments of $g(K)$ if m is not a prime number; see Exercise 9.10. An alternative approach, called **linear-quotient hashing,** is discussed in Exercise 9.11.

Double hashing eliminates clustering. So, even when $h(K_1) = h(K_2)$, for two distinct keys K_1 and K_2, it is highly unlikely that $g(K_1)$ also is equal to $g(K_2)$. Hence, with high probability, we do not expect the hash sequences of K_1 and K_2 to be cyclic permutations of each other. Since double hashing avoids clustering, clusters do not build up as rapidly as they do with linear probing. We provide two examples of double hashing with $m = 13$, $h(K) = K \bmod \neq 13$, and $g(K) = (7K \bmod 12) + 1$. In Table 9.5, we display the result of inserting the sequence

$$11 \ 3 \ 27 \ 99 \ 8 \ 50 \ 77 \ 22 \ 12 \ 31 \ 33 \ 40 \ 53$$

of 13 keys into a hash table of size 13. The number of probes for each key is given in the second column, and the values of $h(K)$ and $g(K)$ are given in the third and fourth columns. To see the drastic effect of double hashing on the number of probes, we consider the worst-case insertion sequence for linear probing:

$$1 \ 14 \ 27 \ 40 \ 53 \ 66 \ 79 \ 92 \ 105 \ 118 \ 131 \ 144 \ 157.$$

In double hashing, all keys, apart from the first one, use two probes; see the second hash table in Table 9.5.

But what do we expect the number of probes to be in a hash table of size m with load factor λ? It is beyond the scope of this text to analyze double hashing, so we merely state the results. In Section 9.3.3, we analyze a model of double hashing; the results agree with the values we now state.

Table 9.5 Two full hash tables, for two sets of 13 keys, obtained with double hashing.

Index	Key	Number of probes	Home address	Increment	Index	Key	Number of probes	Home address	Increment
0	12	2	12	1	0	53	2	1	12
1	27	1	1	10	1	1	1	1	3
2	33	3	7	4	2	144	2	1	1
3	3	1	8	10	3	79	2	1	2
4	8	2	8	9	4	14	2	1	3
5	31	1	5	2	5	105	2	1	4
6	40	2	1	5	6	40	2	1	5
7	50	4	11	3	7	131	2	1	6
8	99	1	8	7	8	66	2	1	7
9	22	1	9	11	9	157	2	1	8
10	53	5	1	12	10	92	2	1	9
11	11	1	11	6	11	27	2	1	10
12	77	1	12	10	12	118	2	1	11

Fact 9.3 *Assume that each entry in a hash table is equally likely to be accessed, and that each sequence of n insertions is equally likely to occur. Then, a hash table that uses double hashing and has load factor λ has the following expected-case performance:*

- $s(\lambda) = \frac{1}{\lambda} \ln \frac{1}{(1-\lambda)}$ *probes, for successful search with $\lambda < 0.319$*

- $u(\lambda) = \frac{1}{(1-\lambda)}$ *probes, for unsuccessful search with $\lambda < 0.319$*

9.3.3 Uniform Hashing and Its Analysis[*]

Analyzing double hashing—or, indeed, any open addressing method—is a difficult exercise. So we introduce an idealized model of double hashing that is simpler to analyze. For any hash sequence

$$h_0, h_1, ..., h_{m-1},$$

for a hash table of size m, we assume that h_i is chosen uniformly and independently of $h_0,...,h_{i-1}$. This method is called **uniform hashing,** for obvious reasons. We begin by analyzing the expected number $u(\lambda)$ of probes for an unsuccessful search in a uniform-hash table with load factor λ.

Letting the current load factor be λ, the probability that we probe a nonvoid cell is λ, and the probability that we probe a void cell is $1 - \lambda$. Now, as in the analysis of separate chaining, the contribution of an unsuccessful search of exactly c probes to $u(\lambda)$ is

$$cPr(\text{ exactly c probes}).$$

The expected number of probes in an unsuccessful search is the sum of such contributions; that is,

$$u(\lambda) = \sum_{c > 0} cPr \text{ (exactly } c \text{ probes)}.$$

We can rewrite this equation as

$$u(\lambda) = \sum_{c > 0} Pr \text{ ($\geq c$ probes)}$$

by observing that

$$
\begin{array}{rl}
& Pr(\text{ exactly 1 probe}) \\
+ & Pr(\text{ exactly 2 probes}) \ + \ Pr(\text{ exactly 2 probes}) \\
& \quad \vdots \quad \vdots \qquad\qquad\qquad \vdots \quad \vdots \\
u(\lambda) = + & Pr(\text{ exactly } c \text{ probes}) \ + \ Pr(\text{ exactly } c \text{ probes}) + \cdots. \\
& \quad \vdots \quad \vdots \qquad\qquad\qquad \vdots \quad \vdots
\end{array}
$$

Now, summing by columns, rather than by rows, we obtain

$$
\begin{aligned}
u(\lambda) &= Pr(\geq 1 \text{ probe}) + Pr(\geq 2 \text{ probes}) + \cdots \\
&= \sum_{c > 0} Pr(\geq c \text{ probes}).
\end{aligned}
$$

This summation is easier to compute when we substitute for the value of $Pr(\geq c \text{ probes})$. Clearly, by independence,

$$
\begin{aligned}
Pr(\geq c \text{ probes}) &= Pr(\text{ the first } c - 1 \text{ cells are nonvoid}) \\
&= \lambda^{c-1}.
\end{aligned}
$$

Now,

$$
\begin{aligned}
u(\lambda) &= \sum_{c > 0} \lambda^{c-1} \\
&= \sum_{c \geq 0} \lambda^{c} \\
&= \frac{1}{1 - \lambda}.
\end{aligned}
$$

For successful search, we use the observation that the number of probes to retrieve a record is equal to the number required to insert it. Hence, for a uniform

Table 9.6   Comparison of uniform and double hashing.

λ	Hash table size	Simulation of double hashing		Analysis of uniform hashing	
				$s(\lambda)$	$u(\lambda)$
		$s(\lambda)$	$u(\lambda)$	$\ln(1/(1-\lambda)\lambda)$	$1/1-\lambda$
0.1001	1999	1.0400	1.1009	1.0536	1.1112
0.2001	1999	1.1025	1.2368	1.1158	1.2502
0.5006	797	1.4687	2.2500	1.3871	2.0025
0.9007	443	2.5315	10.4496	2.5640	10.0682
0.9112	439	2.9198	11.0395	2.6570	11.2564
0.9211	431	2.9900	12.4781	2.7573	12.6765
0.9511	409	3.2185	18.7522	3.1731	20.4500
0.9900	401	4.0705	81.9430	4.6541	100.2500

hash table with load factor x, the insertion of a new record is expected to take $u(x)$ probes; it increases the load factor by dx, for some small value dx. Hence,

$$s(\lambda) = \frac{1}{\lambda} \int_0^\lambda u(x)dx$$

$$= \frac{1}{\lambda} \int_0^\lambda \frac{dx}{1-x}$$

$$= \frac{1}{\lambda} \ln(\frac{1}{1-\lambda}).$$

In Table 9.6, we give computed values of $u(\lambda)$ and $s(\lambda)$; for comparison, we give the results of a simulation of double hashing.

9.3.4   Dealing with Deletions

Although a TABLE has the operations of *IsMember*, *Insert*, and *Delete*, we have deliberately avoided discussing *Delete*. How can we implement *Delete* for the hashed representations that we have considered?

For separate chaining, implementation of *Delete* is straightforward; we simply delete the record and its cell. For the open-addressing methods, however, it is not as simple. Consider the first hash table of Table 9.7, which is obtained with linear probing. Assume we want to delete the key 27. The obvious deletion method is to search for the key to be deleted and then to empty the key's cell, if the search is successful. This approach yields the second hash table of Table 9.7. If we now perform an *IsMember* query for 53, however, it is unsuccessful,

Table 9.7 An incorrect deletion strategy for linear-probe hashing.

Index	Key		Index	Key
0	77		0	77
1	27[a]		1	−1
2	12		2	12
3	3		3	3
4	40		4	40
5	31		5	31
6	53		6	53
7	33		7	33
8	99		8	99
9	8		9	8
10	22		10	22
11	11		11	11
12	50		12	50

[a]Key 27 is removed.

although 53 is in the hash table. By removing an entry in a hash table constructed with open addressing, we may cause other entries to become unreachable. Therefore, we consider two alternative solutions to the deletion problem.

The first, and simplest, approach is to maintain a **deleted flag** for each entry; it is **true** if the corresponding key has been deleted, and it is **false** otherwise. During an *IsMember* or *Delete* operation, whenever a cell that is marked as deleted is met, a key comparison is not carried out; instead, the next cell in the hash sequence is probed. During an *Insert* operation, once a void location has been found, the first cell that was marked as deleted is replaced by the new key, and its deleted flag is reset.

The second approach is to reorder the keys so that the newly deleted key's cell either is empty or is filled with some other key. Such a reorganization can involve examining all the keys in the table—a time-consuming process. We leave to Exercise 9.13 an efficient implementation of this approach for linear probing.

9.4 DYNAMIC TABLES

The open-addressing techniques discussed in Section 9.3 have two grave disadvantages. First, they provide for insertions, but only up to the size of the hash table. Second, they do not deal elegantly with deletions. We usually handle deletions by marking items as deleted, rather than by removing them. In other words, the TABLE operations are not fully supported. Traditionally, hash tables have been considered to be static entities; recently, however, methods have been developed that implement the TABLE operations in their full generality. We consider one such method here, known as linear hashing. It was introduced for external hashed representations, but it is an excellent candidate for internal hashed representations as well. Furthermore, the analysis of linear hashing is an extension of the analysis of separate chaining.

9.4.1 Linear Hashing

The astute reader has almost certainly observed that separate chaining admits the TABLE operations in their full generality. So why do we look beyond this method? The reason is simple—the performance of separate chaining deteriorates as the number of records grows, because the chains get longer. Linear hashing, as we shall see, can be viewed as a generalization of separate chaining in which the expected chain length is kept within a predefined bound, and, therefore, the performance of linear hashing does not deteriorate.

Initially, we have an empty hash table of size m, where each entry is treated as a variable-sized bucket. During insertion, linear hashing expands the hash table one bucket at a time. We accomplish this expansion by splitting buckets in a predetermined order. We first split bucket 0 into buckets 0 and m, then bucket 1 into buckets 1 and $m + 1$, and so on, until we split bucket $m - 1$ into buckets $m - 1$ and $2m - 1$. We split a bucket whenever the load factor (the average bucket size) is greater than a prespecified upper threshold. During expansion, we need to extend the hash function to cover the new buckets.

Similarly, deletion can cause the hash table to contract. If bucket i is the last bucket that was split and the load factor goes below a prespecified lower threshold, then buckets i and $i + m$ are merged into bucket i.

Once expansion causes the original hash table to double in size, expansion continues with the new hash table. Hence, buckets 0 to $2m - 1$ will be split during the next expansion phase. Expansion can continue indefinitely, but contraction always stops once the original hash-table size is obtained.

We now consider a small example to illustrate these ideas. At each moment, we need to know the following: B, the next bucket to be split; m, the original hash-table size; d, the number of times the table has doubled in size; and h_d, the current or base hash function. Observe that the total number of buckets is $m2^d + B$. Also, we need lower and upper threshold values for the load factor, as well as the total number n of records currently in the hash table. We consider the insertion of the sequence

$$18 \ 5 \ 20 \ 21 \ 14 \ 9 \ 7 \ 15 \ 8 \ 1 \ 12$$

of keys into a hash table of size 3 using the hash function $h_0(K) = K \bmod 3$. Let the lower and upper bounds on the load factor be 1 and 2, respectively. Initially, $B = d = n = 0$; see Fig. 9.4(a). After inserting 18, 5, 20, 21, 14, and 9, we have the situation depicted in Fig. 9.4(b). At this stage, $\lambda = 6/3 = 2$, the upper threshold value. Inserting 7 increases the load factor to 7/3, which is greater than 2, so bucket 0 is split. How do we split a bucket? We extend the base hash function h_0

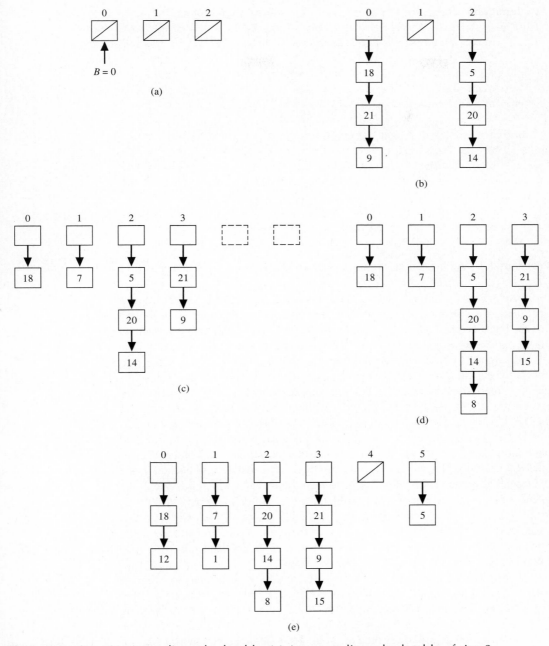

Figure 9.4 Insertion into a linear hash table. (a) An empty linear hash table of size 3. (b) Table after six keys are inserted. (c) Splitting of bucket 0 after 7 is inserted. (d) Table after keys 15 and 8 are inserted. (e) Table after keys 1 and 12 are inserted and two splits have occurred.

```
function IsMember(K: keytype; T: TABLE): boolean;
{The table T is represented by a record that includes the base
    hash modulus, the split hash modulus, and the next bucket B
    to be split.
    IsMember returns the value true if K is in the table;
    otherwise, it returns false.}
var bucket: buckettype;

begin bucket:= K mod T.basehash;
    if bucket < T.B
    then bucket:= K mod T.splithash;

    if K is in bucket T.t[bucket]
    then IsMember:= true
    else IsMember:= false
end;
```

Program 9.3   A Pascal-like implementation of *IsMember* for linear hashing.

to the split hash function $h_1(K) = K$ **mod** 6, since the hash table will eventually double in size. We apply h_1, however, to only the bucket that is about to be split and the buckets that have already been split. We still use h_0 with the unsplit buckets. In our example, $h_1(18) = 0$, so 18 stays in bucket 0, but $h_1(21) = h_1(9) = 3$, so 21 and 9 move to bucket 3, as shown in Fig. 9.4(c). Since bucket 1 is the next bucket to be split, B becomes 1. Note that the load factor is now 7/4, which is less than 2. Continuing, we insert 15 by first computing $h_0(15) = 0$ and, since $0 < B$, we use h_1 giving $h_1(15) = 3$; that is, 15 goes into bucket 3. Next comes 8; $h_0(8) = 2$ gives the correct bucket, since $2 \geq B$, so we obtain the hash table of Fig. 9.4(d). But, the load factor is now 9/4, which is greater than the upper threshold once more, so we split bucket 1. Since bucket 1 contains only 7 and $h_1(7) = 1$, bucket 4 is empty. But, B is now 2. We finally insert 1 and 12 into buckets 1 and 0, respectively, causing the load factor to increase to 11/5 which is, once more, greater than 2; therefore, we now split bucket 2. Since $h_1(5) = 5$; $h_1(20) = 2$; $h_1(14) = 2$; and $h_1(8) = 2$, we obtain the hash table shown in Fig. 9.4(e). At this stage, the table has doubled, so we treat it as though it is the original hash table. Thus, we reset B to 0 and set d to 1, and h_1 becomes the base hash function. The split hash function h_2 is defined as $h_2(K) = K$ **mod** 12.

In Program 9.3, we give a high-level description of *IsMember*; in Program 9.4, we give a high-level description of *Insert*. In both cases, we assume that TABLE is represented as a Pascal record that contains the base hash function, the split hash function, the next bucket B to be split, the number n of records in the hash table, the upper and lower bounds on the load factor, and the hash table t of buckets. Before analyzing the expected-case performance of linear hashing, in Section 9.4.2, we confront one hidden assumption that we have made. We have assumed that a linear hash table can always be extended into a block of main memory that is adjacent to the block containing the current hash table. Clearly, this a dangerous and unwarranted assumption; we cannot guarantee that an adjacent block will always be available, *without moving the hash table*. One simple solution to this difficulty is to use one level of indirection. Rather than assuming that the hash table is in one block of main memory, we assume that it consists of several equal-sized blocks or pages, which we access via a page directory. For example, with a page size of 1024 words, a page directory of size 1024 words can index up to 1 million words—which is more than enough space for a main-memory hash table. Each entry in the page directory is the address of a page of main memory. We access the home cell of a key K in a hash table by extracting from $h(K)$ the number of the page containing the cell. For example, if one record takes 10 words, we can store 102 records in each page. Hence, $h(K)$ **mod** 102 gives the number of the page containing the home cell of K. We leave the details of this paging mechanism to Exercise 9.17.

In Section 9.4.2, we analyze linear hashing, making heavy use of the analysis of separate chaining. Specifically, we prove the following fact.

Fact 9.4 *Assume that each entry in a hash table is equally likely to be accessed, and that each sequence of n insertions is equally likely to occur. Then, a linear-hash table that has load factor λ has the following expected-case performance, in terms of numbers of probes:*

- $s(\lambda) \in [\lambda/2, 2 + 9\lambda/16]$, *for successful search*
- $u(\lambda) \in [2 + \lambda, 2 + 9\lambda/8]$, *for unsuccessful search*

The result is unusual in that it provides ranges of values for the expected numbers of probes, rather than one value in each case.

9.4.2 Analysis of Linear Hashing[*]

At first sight, the analysis of linear hashing appears to be much more difficult than are the analyses of separate chaining and uniform hashing, since the hash table is growing and shrinking with insertions and deletions, respectively. To avoid this difficulty, we simplify the situation by considering only insertions (this simplification is typical). Thus, we need only an upper-threshold value for the load factor; we define this value be λ. For a large hash table, the load factor will be almost constant and will be equal to λ.

At each moment, a linear-hash table can be viewed as two distinct hash tables. One hash table consists of the buckets that have not yet been split; the other hash table consists of the buckets that have been split and the newly created buckets.

Since we use chains to implement the buckets, these two "hash tables" are both hash tables with separate chaining. Moreover, within each hash table, the expected size of each bucket is the same; this fact, clearly, does not hold for the linear-hash table as a whole. Also, the relative sizes of the two parts change during a split.

```
procedure Insert(K: keytype; var T: TABLE);
{The table T is represented by a record that includes the base
    hash modulus, the split hash modulus, the next bucket B to be split,
    the number d of times the table has doubled in size, the
    upper threshold upper, and the number n of records in the table.
    The key K is added to the table T if it is not already present.}
var bucket: buckettype;

begin bucket:= K mod T.basehash;
    if bucket < T.B
    then bucket:= K mod T.splithash;

    if K is in bucket T.t[bucket]
    then {Do nothing—K is already present}
    else begin
        Add K to bucket T.t[bucket];
        T.n:= T.n + 1;

        {Check whether current load factor exceeds upper threshold.}
        if T.n > T.upper * (T.B + T.basehash)
        then begin
            {Split bucket T.t[T.B]}
            if T.B = T.basehash
            then begin {Reset base and split hash moduli.}
                T.B:= 0; T.d:= T.d + 1;
                T.basehash:= T.splithash;
                T.splithash:= 2 * T.splithash
            end
            else T.B:= T.B + 1
        end
    end
end;
```

Program 9.4   A Pascal-like implementation of *Insert* for a linear hashing.

From Section 9.2.1, we know that for separate chaining with a load factor of α we have

$$s_c(\alpha) = 2 + \alpha/2$$

$$u_c(\alpha) = 2 + \alpha$$

as the expected numbers of probes for successful and unsuccessful search, respectively. Let sb, $0 \le sb \le 1$, denote the fraction of the buckets that have been split during the current expansion phase, and let b denote the expected size of an unsplit bucket. Hence, $b/2$ is the expected size of a split or new bucket. Since the load factor of the linear-hash table is to be λ, then the current number of records in the table is equal to the product of λ and the total number $B_u + 2B_s$ of buckets, where B_u is the number of unsplit buckets and B_s is the number of split buckets; that is, the current number of records is $\lambda(B_u + 2B_s)$. But, the current number of records in the table can also be expressed in terms of b, since it is equal to the product of the expected size of an unsplit bucket and the number of split and unsplit buckets; that is, the current number of records is $b(B_u + B_s)$. Hence,

$$b(B_u + B_s) = \lambda(B_u + 2B_s),$$

and, therefore,

$$b = \lambda \frac{B_u + 2B_s}{B_u + B_s}$$

$$= \lambda(1 + \frac{B_s}{B_u + B_s})$$

$$= \lambda(1 + sb).$$

This simple relationship tells us that the expected size of an unsplit bucket grows linearly from λ to 2λ.

We now consider the expected number of probes for a successful search with load factor λ when a fraction sb of the buckets has been split. We denote this value by $s(\lambda,sb)$. Similarly, $u(\lambda,sb)$ is the expected number of probes for an unsuccessful search.

If we probe an unsplit bucket, then the expected number of probes in a successful search is

$$s_c(b),$$

and this number of probes occurs with probability $1 - sb$. Similarly, if we probe a split bucket, the expected number of probes in a successful search is

$$s_c(b/2),$$

and this number of probes occurs with probability sb. Combining these facts with the relationship among b, sb, and λ, we find that

$$s(\lambda,sb) = sb \times s_c(b/2) + (1 - sb)s_c(b)$$

$$= sb(2 + b/4) + (1 - sb)(2 + b/2)$$

$$= sb(2 + \lambda(1 + sb)/4) + (1 - sb)(2 + \lambda(1 + sb)/2)$$

$$= 2 + \frac{\lambda}{4}(2 + sb - sb^2).$$

Similarly, we find that

$$u(\lambda,sb) = 2 + \frac{\lambda}{2}(2 + sb - sb^2).$$

Observe that $s(\lambda,0) = s(\lambda,1) = s_c(\lambda) = 2 + \lambda/2$ and $u(\lambda,0) = u(\lambda,1) = u_c(\lambda) = 2 + \lambda$ as desired; the values of $s(\lambda,sb)$ and $u(\lambda,sb)$ cycle between these values. They are the minimum values for the expected numbers of probes because, whenever $sb \leq sb^2$, either $sb = 0$ or $sb \geq 1$. Clearly, $sb \geq 1$ implies $sb = 1$. The maximum value for $s(\lambda,sb)$ occurs when $ds(\lambda,sb)/dsb = 0$ —that is, when

$$\frac{\lambda}{2}(1 - 2sb) = 0.$$

Since $\lambda > 0$, we have $sb = 1/2$. This value also maximizes $u(\lambda,sb)$. Substitution yields

$$s(\lambda,1/2) = 2 + \frac{9\lambda}{16}$$

and

$$u(\lambda,1/2) = 2 + \frac{9\lambda}{8}$$

to give the upper bounds for the expected numbers of probes.

The maximum values of $s(\lambda,sb)$ and $u(\lambda,sb)$ differ by $\lambda/16$ and $\lambda/8$, respectively, from the minimum values. But how do they vary over a cycle? We close this discussion by giving, without proof, the average expected numbers of probes over a cycle.

Fact 9.5 *Let λ be the load factor of a linear-hash table. Then, the average asymptotic expected numbers of probes over an expansion cycle are*

- $2 + 48\lambda/24$, *for successful search*
- $2 + 13\lambda/24$, *for unsuccessful search*

9.5 EXTERNAL TABLES

When a table is too large to be held permanently in main memory, the TABLE representations that we have presented leave much to be desired. The reason is simple: Disk-access time is orders of magnitude greater than is main-memory–access time. For example, accessing a single character in main memory takes approximately 0.1 microseconds, whereas accessing a single character on disk takes approximately 0.025 seconds. The disk-access time is thus 250,000 times main-memory–access time. Disk-access time and transfer rate dominate all other operations for externally stored structures.

Our purpose, in this section, is to introduce one of the most efficient representations known for external tables from the viewpoint of access time. We do not pretend to cover all the issues in file design here; we advise you to consult the books mentioned in Section 9.8.

We begin by discussing the indexed sequential-access method (ISAM)—the external TABLE or DICTIONARY representation that was in widespread use 20 years ago. We then introduce one efficient external TABLE representation that is based on linear hashing. It supports a one-disk-access *IsMember* operation, although updates are less efficient. To achieve such fast access, it uses an auxiliary index, based on key signatures, which is small enough to be held in main memory.

9.5.1 ISAM

Recall, from Section 2.4.4, that a set of records can be represented on a disk as a set of blocks, each block holding some of the records. The blocks can be assigned randomly or sequentially on the disk, and they are linked together to allow the records to be traversed easily. If we know that the key universe is totally ordered, then representing a set of records in sorted order is inefficient, since the sorted order either degenerates quickly or requires extensive rearrangement after each update. One solution to this problem is to keep a sorted index to the records in main memory. Because files may be very large (1 million records are not uncommon; for example, tax files contain that many records), we cannot keep all keys in main memory. Therefore, the index usually contains a subset of the keys. Also, updates in the file may lead to updates in the index; the index needs to be dynamic as well. ISAM was, historically, the most widely used method for file access, since it solves these problems. Today, however, it has been superseded by hashing methods and by B$^+$-trees.

We now introduce and examine **ISAM** to demonstrate the difficulties inherent in good file-structure design. Initially, we represent a table as a sequential file on a disk sorted by the required key (by block, track, and cylinder). For each cylinder, we construct a **cylinder index** of the highest key in each block of the cylinder. The cylinder index is also stored in the cylinder it indexes. This index is, by construction, also sorted by key. In main memory, we keep a **file index** of the largest keys in each cylinder. The file index is small enough to be kept in main memory during table processing, since a modern disk unit has at most 1000 cylinders. Given a key, we first determine in which cylinder its record must be by searching the file index; see Fig. 9.5. We then make a disk access to retrieve the cylinder index for the given cylinder (the cylinder indexes are stored at a standard position in each cylinder). Finally, we make a block access and a sequential search within the retrieved block to find the record corresponding to the given key. The search for the record has taken two block accesses. This disk-access time is reduced by only one hashing method, which we introduce in Section 9.5.2.

Unfortunately, ISAM deteriorates quickly when insertions occur, because of the method used to insert new records. Initially, each cylinder has some empty tracks for block-overflow records. When a new record is added to a block, old records are shifted to make room for it. If the block is full, then the record with the highest key is pushed out. This record is then moved to an overflow track, and

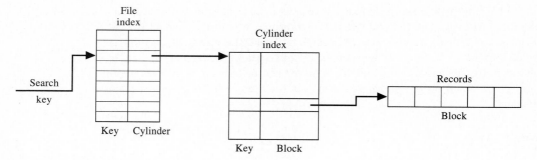

Figure 9.5   Retrieval with ISAM.

its new address is added to the block. Indeed, the address is usually added to the record with the next highest key; see Figures 9.6(a) and (b).

When a second insertion takes place in the same block, the record with the highest key is again pushed into an overflow track and is linked to its predecessor; see Fig. 9.6(c). After many insertions, there are many chains of individual records in the overflow area. To access a record on a chain takes one random block access; therefore, access and update performance degrade significantly. Furthermore, the organization can become worse. When the overflow tracks in a cylinder are filled, further overflow records from that cylinder are stored in an overflow cylinder. Thus, chasing records down a chain may involve disk-head movement; that is, it may take seek time as well as rotational latency and block-transfer time.

One solution to this degradation in performance is to reorganize the file as a sequential file; which is a costly and time-consuming process. Therefore, we prefer to use a table structure that allows insertions and deletions to be carried out without affecting the performance so drastically. External hashing methods accomplish this goal for external tables, and B^+-trees accomplish it for external dictionaires; thus, they have become the only methods used in practice. We consider hashing in Section 9.5.2, and discuss B^+-trees in Chapter 10.

9.5.2 Hashing with One-Disk-Access Retrieval

Linear hashing, which we introduced in Section 9.4, was designed originally for external tables—only recently has the technique been demonstrated to be viable for internal tables. Thus, we can use linear hashing, modified for fixed-sized buckets, as the representation for external tables; see Exercise 9.18. Note that this representation does not require the key universe to be totally ordered. The development of linear hashing for external tables is not difficult. We present a further modification of linear hashing that, although not as useful in general, illustrates the power of hashing methods. The variant of linear hashing that we present provides one disk access for each *IsMember* operation, the fewest disk accesses we can expect. To ensure that only one disk access is used, we use a small internal directory to guide the search for the correct bucket; each bucket has one entry—

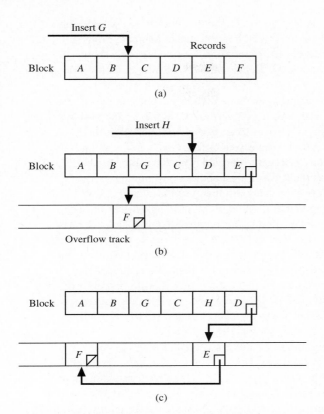

Figure 9.6 Insertion and overflow in ISAM. (a) Record *G* is inserted into a full block. (b) Record *F* is moved to the overflow track and record *H* is inserted. (c) Record *E* is moved to the overflow track and linked to *F*.

its signature—in the directory. The directory expands and shrinks over time, so it needs to be dynamic; however, we ignore the issue of directory representation completely, since the directory is internal and can even be implemented as a list.

We begin by observing that, in an external environment, we use fixed-sized buckets, rather than variable-sized ones. The major effect of this constraint is that it causes overflows, with which we must deal; we avoided this problem with internal linear hashing. We choose the open-addressing technique of linear probing to resolve overflows, because it is simple to use and the bucket increment is the same for all records in the same bucket. (Note that this uniformity is the reason for the inefficiency of linear probing for internal hashing.) Having made this choice, we must also modify linear probing slightly. When we insert a new record, if its **home bucket** is full, then we move records to the next adjacent bucket. If this new bucket is full, then more records are forced out. Overflow has a cascading effect, and the records that are forced out of a bucket do not necessarily belong there. If overflowing records reach the last bucket and cause overflow yet again, then these records are assigned to the following bucket, which will be the last bucket when the next split occurs. Hence, buckets may contain only overflow records.

Modifying insertion for linear hashing with fixed-sized buckets and linear probing is a moderately simple task. We have overlooked, however, the problem of retrieving the overflow records in answer to an *IsMember* query. For this purpose, we introduce signatures and signature sequences. Given a key K and an integer $k > 0$, a **signature** for K is a k-bit value derived from K by some method. A standard technique is to use K as the seed of a pseudorandom-number generator. The higher order k bits of the resulting value are then used as a signature for K. Using a pseudorandom-number generator, we can obtain a **signature sequence** for K by generating a sequence of pseudorandom numbers from K and, for each number, taking the k most significant bits. We denote a signature sequence for key K by $s_1(K), s_2(K), \ldots$. We also need the notion of a **bucket signature**; it is a k-bit value greater than the signatures of all keys in its bucket. To ensure that it is always possible to have bucket signatures that satisfy this condition, we do not allow key signatures to have the maximum value $2^k - 1$. Initially, all bucket signatures are $2^k - 1$; they change only when overflow occurs. Hence, we can use them to test for overflow.

We now modify the insertion of a key K once again. On the initial probe into the home bucket i of K, we insert K into bucket i if there is sufficient space. Otherwise, we compare $s_1(K)$ with the bucket signature $s(i)$. If $s_1(K)$ is greater than or equal to $s(i)$, then K is forced into bucket $i + 1$. Otherwise, records in bucket i with maximal signature values are forced into bucket $i + 1$. (Since we have only k bits for signatures, many records may have the same signature.) At least one record is forced out of the home bucket, and the bucket signature is updated to reflect the signatures of the new records. The insertion procedure continues with the next bucket, and so on. If a key K is being considered for insertion into bucket j and its home bucket is bucket i, then not only is $j \geq i$, but also we use signature $s_{j-i+1}(K)$ to determine what should be done with K.

Insertions increase the load factor and, therefore, we need to be able to expand the linear-hash table. Splitting a bucket, however, is more involved than it is for unmodified linear hashing. When we split a bucket i, we must retrieve all records whose home bucket is at most i and that are stored in bucket i onward. This retrieval implies that all buckets from bucket i onward need to be read. (We need to read buckets, however, only until we meet a bucket that has not overflowed.) Indeed, we have to read the buckets twice. In the first pass, we collect all records with home address at most i, and we reset the bucket signatures to $2^k - 1$. We then separate those records whose home bucket is i and whose home address is still i from those records that must move to bucket $i + m$. In the second pass, we insert all records whose home address is still at most i in the usual way, and then we insert those records whose home address is $i + m$. We must take care to ensure that buckets are read and written only once during each pass; otherwise, updating

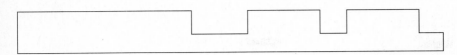

Figure 9.7   The islands resulting from insertions.

is even more inefficient. It is crucial that all records be retrievable after expansion; otherwise, chaos will result. These requirements are the reason that we retrieve all overflowing records from bucket i onward.

Finally, to achieve retrieval with one disk access, we maintain in main memory a list of bucket signatures in bucket order. An *IsMember*(K,T) operation first computes the home address $H(K)$ and the initial signature $s_1(K)$. If the signature of bucket $H(K)$ is greater than $s_1(K)$, then we read the bucket $H(K)$, and K is in the hash table if and only if it is in this bucket. If the signature of bucket $H(K)$ is less than or equal to $s_1(K)$, then we consider buckets $H(K) + 1, H(K) + 2,...$, with signatures $s_2(K), s_3(K),...$, until we find a bucket $H(K) + j$ whose signature is greater than $s_{j+1}(K)$. At this point, the hash table contains K if and only if bucket $H(K) + j$ contains K. A single disk access is sufficient to determine whether this conditions holds.

The computation of the home bucket $H(K)$ of K is the same as the computation for linear hashing in Section 9.4. We keep the number of the bucket that was last split. When $h_i(K)$ is greater than this value, the home address is $h_i(K)$; otherwise, it is $h_{i+1}(K)$.

We leave the details of an implementation to Exercise 9.19; however, we note that the method we have sketched does not perform well on insertions. Because linear probing causes clustering, we obtain large islands of overflowing buckets, which grow as a result of more insertions; see Fig. 9.7. These islands make insertion time consuming. To mitigate the island effect, we can modify the splitting order. Rather than splitting bucket 0, bucket 1, and so on, in this order, we split them, for example, in the following bucket order: 0, 3, ..., 1, 4, ..., 2, 5, ... The effect of such a splitting sequence is to split islands before they get too large and, thus, to reduce insertion time. In practice, we expand more than one bucket at once, the so-called **partial expansion scheme.** With this scheme, we might begin by splitting all buckets 0, 3, and so on, then all buckets 1, 4, and so on, and, finally, all buckets 2, 5, and so on. We use modulo counting to determine which buckets to split; see Exercise 9.20.

We close this section by working through an example of insertions into a one-disk-access linear-hash table. We use the insertion sequence

$$18\ 5\ 20\ 21\ 14\ 9\ 7\ 15\ 8\ 1\ 12,$$

which we used as an example for linear hashing in Section 9.4. We assume a bucket size of 3, an upper bound of 5/2 on the average load factor, and $m = 3$, initially. We begin by inserting the first seven keys; they cause no difficulty, because the load factor is 7/3 and overflow does not occur. The situation at this stage is as shown in Fig. 9.8(a). We now insert 15. Since its home address is bucket 0 and

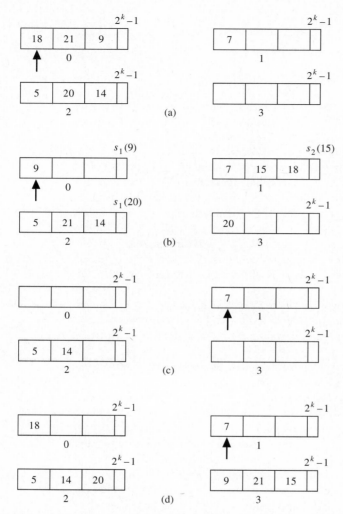

Figure 9.8 Insertion into a linear-hash table with one disk access.
(a) The hash table after the insertion of the first seven keys.
(b) Insertion of 15 causes overflow. (c) The reset linear-hash table
after the first pass during the split of bucket 0. (d) The hash table
after the split of bucket 0.

bucket 0 contains three keys, we have overflow for the first time. Assume that $s_1(15) = s_1(18) = s_1(21) > s_1(9)$; then, bucket 1 overflows, since it contains one key and is given three overflowing keys. Assume that $s_1(7) = s_2(18) < s_2(15) < s_2(21)$. Then, key 21 is forced into bucket 2, and we have overflow again; see Fig. 9.8(b). Finally, assume that $s_1(20)$ is greater than $s_1(5)$, $s_1(14)$, and $s_3(21)$; then, key 20 is forced into bucket 3, the next bucket to be allocated. The insertion of 15 is now complete. However, the load factor of the hash table is now $8/3$; that is, it is greater than $5/2$, the upper bound on the load factor. We must split bucket 0, which contains only key 9. The new home bucket of key 9 is 3, because 9 **mod** 6 = 3. We retrieve the keys that were forced out of bucket 0; that is, we retrieve keys 15, 18, and 21. These keys belong to buckets 3, 0, and 3, respectively. In addition, we must retrieve the other keys that were forced out—namely key 20, which belongs to bucket 2. At this stage, the hash table has been reset, as shown in Fig. 9.8(c). We now insert the retrieved keys again, beginning at the split bucket. Key 18 is inserted into bucket 0; key 20 is inserted into bucket 2; and keys 9, 15, and 21 are inserted into bucket 3. The resulting hash table is shown in Fig. 9.8(d). We leave to Exercise 9.21 the insertion of the remaining three keys.

9.6 PERFORMANCE REPORTS

In the comparison of the performance of the hashing methods that we have examined (see Table 9.8), we do not consider uniform hashing, since it has been included only as an analytical model of double hashing. For internal tables, we have only three competitors: separate chaining, double hashing, and linear hashing. We have rated double hashing as the best method (see Table 9.9), even though it is not fully dynamic. The major reasons for this rating are that double hashing is easy to code and has excellent performance. We rate separate chaining and linear hashing as the next two methods of choice, since they both are fully

Table 9.8 A performance comparison of the six hashing implementations of *IsMember* for TABLE.

		IsMember operation	
TABLE implementation		Successful search	Unsuccessful search
Internal Representations[a]	Separate chaining	$2 + \lambda/2$	$2 + \lambda$
	Linear probing	$1/2(1 + 1/(1 - \lambda))$	$1/2(1 + 1/(1 - \lambda)^{2})$
	Double hashing	$\ln(1/(1 - \lambda))/\lambda$	$1/(1 - \lambda)$
	Linear hashing	$2 + 13\lambda/48$	$2 + 13\lambda/24$
External Representations	Linear hashing[b]	1	1
	One-disk access hashing[c]	1	1

[a]We evaluate the internal methods by the expected numbers of probes.

[b]We evaluate the linear-hashing method by the asymptotic expected number of disk accesses.

[c]We evaluate the one-disk-access hashing method by the exact number of disk accesses.

Table 9.9   Performance ratings of the six implementations of TABLE.

TABLE implementation	Rating	Comments
Double hashing	Excellent	Easy to code; not fully dynamic
Separate chaining	Very good	Easy to code; fully dynamic; deteriorates with increased load factor
Linear hashing	Very good	Not difficult to code; fully dynamic
Linear probing	Satisfactory	Easy to code; not fully dynamic; clustering is a major problem
External linear hashing	Excellent	Choice for external tables; difficult to code
External one-disk access hashing	Very good	Use when searching is dominant operation

dynamic, perform well, and are not difficult to code. Although separate chaining deteriorates rapidly with a high load factor, we prefer it over linear hashing because it is easy to code. Linear probing is not recommended, even though it is easy to code.

For external tables, we recommend linear hashing because it performs so well and expands and shrinks gracefully. The one-disk-access variation of linear hashing should be used only when searching dominates updating. It is a difficult method to implement, and updates are so expensive, in terms of disk accesses, that it is not an obvious method to use. We have included it to demonstrate that the best possible performance is achievable if only for searching. It has been used successfully by a major international airline.

9.7   SUMMARY

Perfect hashing has constant-time performance; however, as a result of insertions, perfect-hash functions are difficult to maintain—or, to put it another way, collisions are inevitable. In this chapter, we studied a variety of collision-resolution techniques: separate chaining, open addressing, and linear hashing. Separate chaining maintains a list of records in each cell of the hash table, where a pointer representation of each list is used. (If the lists are represented as blocks, then we have bucketing.)

In open addressing, we force colliding keys to other available locations in the hash table—the locations are open to any key. We introduced three ways of resolving collisions: linear probing, double hashing, and uniform hashing. Uniform hashing is of only theoretical interest as a model of double hashing. In linear probing, we increment the home address by 1 until we find the given key, we reach an empty cell, or we come full circle. Linear probing suffers from clustering, which causes the access time to deteriorate as the load factor increases; therefore, double hashing is the method of choice. In double hashing, we apply a second hash function to each key to obtain an increment that we add repeatedly to the home address. Double hashing avoids the clustering phenomenon of linear probing, at the expense of a slightly more complex implementation of the table operations. We usually accomplish deletion for open-addressing methods by marking a key as deleted, rather than by removing it and making the entry void. The reason for this approach is that the search path for other keys can be broken if we void an entry.

Apart from separate chaining, all these hashing methods have one major drawback—they have a predefined table size, so they are not fully dynamic. Linear hashing can be considered to be a variant of separate chaining that provides for hash-table expansion to improve performance. Conceptually, we double the hash-table size whenever the chains become too long; practically, we expand the hash table one position at a time whenever the chains become too long. In this way, the work involved in moving keys is spread out, or amortized, over the operations that cause the table to double in size, rather than occurring all at once when the table has already doubled in size. We considered external tables and their classic implementation using ISAM, and showed how linear hashing, which was first introduced for this purpose, can be modified to provide a one-disk-access implementation of *IsMember*, albeit at the expense of more costly *Insert* and *Delete* implementations. For most external tables, unmodified linear hashing is more than adequate. Of the methods we discussed, separate chaining is the only other fully dynamic hashing method; unfortunately, it suffers from a rapid degradation in performance when the load factor is very large with respect to the size of the hash table.

We also analyzed the expected-case performance of three hashing methods: separate chaining, uniform hashing, and linear hashing. The analysis of linear hashing builds on the analysis of separate chaining in a natural way.

9.8 HISTORY

The notion of hashing was apparently suggested by Luhn in 1953; see Section 6.4 of Knuth (1973) for details of the early history of hashing. Perfect hashing was first studied by Sprugnoli (1977), and, subsequently, it has been investigated by many others (Cichelli, 1980; Jaeschke, 1981; Sagar, 1985). Gonnet and Baeza-Yates (1991), Knuth (1973), and Standish (1980) are excellent sources of information about hashing methods. The most influential paper on hashing is the survey by Morris (1968). Carter and Wegman (1979) introduced the notion of universal classes of hash functions. Separate chaining was developed by Williams (1959), and was analyzed by van der Pool (1973). Linear probing was developed by Peterson (1957) and was analyzed by Knuth (1973) in 1962; it was Knuth's first nontrivial analysis of an algorithm. Greene and Knuth (1982) introduce the term *Cookie-Monster effect,* to describe the piling up, or clustering, of records along one hash sequence. Double hashing was introduced by de Balbine (1968), and was analyzed by Guibas and Szemeredi (Guibas, 1976; Guibas and Szemeredi, 1978). The analysis of uniform hashing as an approximation to the analysis of linear probing was reported by Peterson (1957); we have followed the approach of Larson (1983). Linear-quotient hashing was introduced by Bell and Kaman (1970).

The idea of linear hashing was developed by Litwin (1980), but the presentation and analysis are based on the work of Larson (1988a), who demonstrated that this dynamic scheme is suitable for main-memory hash tables. Griswold (1989) suggested that linear hashing could be used for managing strings in a new implementation of the programming language ICON.

The importance of linear hashing for external files was soon recognized, and improvements to the basic scheme were introduced. Larson (1980; 1982) proposed partial expansions to smooth the expected behavior during table expansion, and Larson (1985) suggested linear probing for overflow handling. Gonnet and Larson (1988) introduced the twin notions of signatures and small internal indexes. These ideas culminated in the one-disk-access hashing method of Larson (1988b), on which the scheme described in Section 9.5 is based.

Another successful dynamic-hashing method was developed by Fagin and his coworkers (Fagin et al., 1979); it is called **extendible hashing.** Three surveys of dynamic hashing are those of Enbody and Du (1988), Lewis and Cook (1988), and Scholl (1981).

EXERCISES

9.1:   Find the the smallest prime number m such that the keys

$$\{14,22,39,46,54,79,198\}$$

are hashed to unique addresses under a hash function of the form $h(K) = K \bmod m$.

9.2:   Implement two versions of a hash table with fixed-sized buckets in which the elements within a bucket are either sorted or arranged by adaptive sequential search. Compare the two approaches by simulation. To avoid the overflow problem, do not perform the insertion whenever a bucket is full.

9.3:   Implement two versions of separate chaining in which the chains either are sorted or are arranged by adaptive sequential search. Compare the two approaches for nonuniform access probabilities using simulation.

9.4:   Suggest a method of using chaining within a hash table, implement it, and compare it with separate chaining by using simulation.

9.5:   Implement the TABLE operations using linear-probe hashing, and using the sentinel technique to simplify searching. Since a hash table is of fixed size, ensure that your operations return appropriate error messages when the hash table is full.

9.6: For linear-probe hashing, prove that the total number of probes required to find all records in a hash table is independent of the order in which the records were inserted. Demonstrate, by example, that this fact does not hold for double hashing.

9.7: A simple modification of linear probing increments the hash address by some integer k greater than 1. Does this modification allow all positions to be probed in m increments, whatever the starting address? A positive answer to this question implies that there are no hidden entries in the hash table. If your answer is negative, specify under what conditions this property holds. Does this modification remove or reduce clustering?

9.8: A modification of linear probing is to increment the initial hash address by 1, plus the hash address itself. Under what conditions on the size m of the table can we guarantee that all positions are explored in exactly m probes, from each possible hash-table address? Does this method avoid clustering?

9.9: Another modification of linear probing increments the home address with the square of the number of probes. Under what conditions does this modification allow all positions to be probed? Does it remove clustering?

9.10: Demonstrate that whenever m is not a prime number, there is an increment value that will miss some locations in the hash table in double hashing. Characterize the increment values that ensure that the hash sequence will include every location.

9.11: A variation of double hashing uses the remainder and the quotient given by a modulus m; it is called **linear-quotient hashing.** Thus, $h(K) = K \bmod m$ is the hash function, and $g(K) = ((K \operatorname{\mathbf{div}} m) \operatorname{\mathbf{mod}} (m - 1)) + 1$ is the increment. Implement linear-quotient hashing. Use simulation to compare its performance with double hashing.

9.12: Compare linear probing, double hashing, and uniform hashing, using simulation.

9.13: Suggest an efficient method of removing a deleted record from a hash table, when using linear probing, that either moves some other record into the deleted record's cell or makes that cell void. After the deletion, all records in the hash table, apart from the deleted record, should be accessible by *IsMember*.

9.14: Explain why the approach for deletion you suggested in your answer to Exercise 9.13 cannot be used for double hashing.

9.15: All open addressing methods have excellent expected-case performance, but their worst-case performance is abysmal. One approach to improving the worst-case performance is to reorganize the hash table when inserting a new record. We modify *Insert* for linear-probe hashing by inserting a new record in that record's home cell, even if the home cell is occupied. The record that is forced out (if there is one) is moved to the next cell, and may in turn force out another record, and so on. This modification is called **last-come, first-served hashing,** in contrast to linear probing, which can be called first-come, first-served hashing. Both methods have the same expected-case performance; the difference is that the modified hashing method has a better worst-case performance, as its performance is logarithmic instead of linear. Carry out a comparison of linear-probe hashing and modified linear-probe hashing, by means of simulation, to confirm this assertion.

9.16: Implement the TABLE operations using a linear-hashing representation. Using simulation confirm the performance results for linear hashing.

9.17: Implement linear hashing with a paging mechanism, as suggested in Section 9.4.

9.18: Modify linear hashing to use fixed-size buckets. To accommodate overflowing records, provide an overflow area. Compare the original and modified linear-hashing methods using simulation.

9.19: Implement the TABLE operations using one-disk-access linear hashing. Suggest experiments to determine the performance of one-disk-access hashing. Carry out simulations to verify the performance characteristics of one-disk-access hashing.

9.20: Modify linear hashing so that splits are replaced by groups of splits, using modulo counting to determine which buckets to split at each splitting step. Implement this variation, and compare its performance with that of linear hashing.

9.21: Complete the example of one-disk linear hashing begun in Section 9.5.

10

Dictionaries and Search Trees

Just as in Chapter 9 we studied hashed representations of TABLE in more depth, we now study search-tree representations of DICTIONARY in more depth. In Sections 10.1, 10.2, and 10.3, we consider three approaches to providing efficient, or balanced, search trees for internal dictionaries; then, in Section 10.4, we introduce the standard search-tree representation for external dictionaries. The simplest version of the representation for external dictionaries, given in Section 10.4, provides another class of efficient search trees for *internal* dictionaries. We begin, in Section 10.1, by defining trees that are optimal with respect to a given probability distribution on the key universe. We then demonstrate how we can construct static optimal trees efficiently using dynamic programming, and examine how good they are by comparing them with the entropy of the probability distribution.

In most applications of dictionaries, we expect updates to occur; when we update a static optimal tree, however, the update does not normally preserve optimality. Although we can allow the performance of a static optimal tree to degrade as a result of updates, in the worst case, the tree can be transformed into a listlike structure that has performance far from optimal. For this reason, we examine two schemes for maintaining efficient trees in the presence of updates. In both cases, we maintain the efficiency of the trees by restructuring them after an update. The important property of the restructuring process is that in both cases it is limited to the vicinity of the search path. In Section 10.2, we introduce red–black trees and show that each red–black tree has logarithmic height, in terms of its size. Moreover, we demonstrate that we can update a red–black tree in logarithmic time, in terms of its size, with a constant number of linkage changes. The disadvantage of red–black trees is that they are efficient only with respect to a uniform probability distribution on the keys. If we have a nonuniform probability distribution, then red–black trees can be far from optimal. Therefore, in Section 10.3, we next consider splay trees. Splay trees provide logarithmic search and update time in the amortized case, rather than in the worst case. Furthermore, they adapt their performance to the probability distribution, even when it is not known in advance. We prove that splay trees perform within a constant factor of the static optimal trees studied in Section 10.1.

It is important for external dictionaries to minimize the number of disk accesses, which are excessively time consuming; the time taken by a key comparison can be ignored. To achieve a small number of disk accesses for each operation on the dictionary, we need to use search trees that have degrees much higher than 2 (recall that ISAM takes two disk accesses, in the best case). For, given a fixed number of records, we can produce search trees of smaller height by increasing the tree's degrees. Binary search trees will be substantially higher than a high-degree search tree for the same records; hence, they will require a larger number of disk accesses for each dictionary operation. B^+-trees are efficient multiway search trees that can have high degree. Thus, we can keep the first few levels of a B^+-tree in main memory, in most cases, so two disk accesses suffice to retrieve a record, in the worst case—the same number of disk accesses as is used in ISAM before updates. Moreover, B^+-trees are balanced in that they have logarithmic height, and updates take logarithmic time. They have become the standard representation of external dictionaries because of their efficiency and graceful growth and shrinkage.

The lowest-degree B^+-trees are called $2,3^+$-trees; we use $2,3^+$-trees to illustrate the implementation of the dictionary operations for B^+-trees. $2,3^+$-trees are, however, important in their own right as an alternative, efficient representation of internal dictionaries.

10.1 OPTIMAL BINARY SEARCH TREES

Normally, we expect different records to be accessed with different probabilities, which implies that both successful and unsuccessful searches occur with different probabilities. We have assumed that a dictionary varies over time due to updates. There are, however, situations in which we have no updates at all; in such cases, the set of keys is fixed. One example is the set of reserved words for Pascal. They do not change unless we change the language itself. Moreover, by monitoring a Pascal compiler over time, we can obtain reliable estimates of the key and gap probabilities. In this section, we discuss binary search trees that are *optimal* with respect to a given probability distribution on the key universe. First, we argue that it is worth using optimal binary search trees instead of optimal lists. Second, we provide an algorithm that constructs these trees in $O(n^3)$ time. The construction algorithm uses dynamic programming. Finally, we compare the cost of optimal binary search trees with the entropy of their key and gap probabilities, since the entropy corresponds to the cost of the best possible "tree."

10.1.1 Preliminaries

Let T be a binary search tree for n keys $K_1 < \cdots < K_n$, where p_i is the probability that key K_i is accessed, $1 \le i \le n$, and q_i is the probability that gap (K_i, K_{i+1}) is accessed, $0 \le i \le n$, where $K_0 = -\infty$ and $K_{n+1} = +\infty$. We call the p_i **key probabilities,** and call the q_i **gap probabilities.** We require that

$$\sum_{i=1}^{n} p_i + \sum_{i=0}^{n} q_i \le 1.$$

Now, with this notation,

$$\sum_{i=1}^{n} p_i$$

is the probability that a successful search occurs, and

$$\sum_{i=0}^{n} q_i$$

is the probability that an unsuccessful search occurs. Let $node(i)$ be the node in T with K_i as its key, and let $gapnode(i)$ be the node in T with (K_i, K_{i+1}) as its gap. We can define the **expected number of node visits** in T, $NVCOST\ (T)$, for an *IsMember* operation, as

$$NVCOST\ (T) = \sum_{i=1}^{n} p_i \cdot nodevisits(node(i))$$

$$+ \sum_{i=0}^{n} q_i \cdot nodevisits(gapnode(i)),$$

where $nodevisits(u) = level(u) + 1$. Recall, from Chapter 5, that

$$IPL(T) = \sum_{i=1}^{n} nodevisits(node(i))$$

and

$$EPL(T) = \sum_{i=0}^{n} nodevisits(gapnode(i)).$$

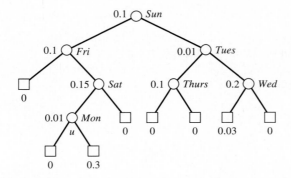

Figure 10.1   A days-of-the-week search tree with probabilities.

If $p_i = \frac{1}{n}$ and $q_i = 0$, then

$$NVCOST\ (T) = \frac{IPL(T)}{n},$$

whereas, if $p_i = 0$ and $q_i = \frac{1}{n+1}$, then

$$NVCOST\ (T) = \frac{EPL(T)}{n+1}.$$

Consider the tree T of Fig. 10.1 with the probabilities: $p_1 = p_{\text{Fri}} = 0.1$; $p_2 = p_{\text{Mon}} = 0.01$; $p_3 = p_{\text{Sat}} = 0.15$; $p_4 = p_{\text{Sun}} = 0.1$; $p_5 = p_{\text{Thurs}} = 0.1$; $p_6 = p_{\text{Tues}} = 0.01$; $p_7 = p_{\text{Wed}} = 0.2$; $q_2 = 0.3$; $q_6 = 0.03$; and all other q_i are 0. Clearly, $NVCOST (T) = 3.33$.

It is often convenient to express the node-visit cost of a tree recursively in terms of the node-visit costs of the subtrees of its root. To this end, the sum of the probabilities associated with the keys and gaps in a subtree is called that subtree's **weight.** If u is a node in a tree T, then we denote its weight by $weight(T(u))$. For example, in the tree T of Fig. 10.1, $weight(T(u)) = 0.31$, where u is the node associated with Mon.

Letting u_{L} and u_{R} denote the left and right children of u, respectively, we prove the following fact.

Fact 10.1   *Let T be a binary search tree of n keys $K_1 < \cdots < K_n$ with key probabilities p_i, $1 \leq i \leq n$, and gap probabilities q_i, $0 \leq i \leq n$. Let u be a node in T; then,*

$$NVCOST\ (T(u)) = NVCOST(T(u_{\text{L}}))$$
$$+ NVCOST(T(u_{\text{R}}))$$
$$+ weight(T(u)).$$

Proof: This equation follows directly from the definition of node-visit cost; namely,

$$NVCOST\,(T(u)) = \sum_{K_i \text{ is in } T(u)} p_i \cdot nodevisits(u, node(i))$$

$$+ \sum_{(K_i, K_{i+1}) \text{ is in } T(u)} q_i \cdot nodevisits(u, gapnode(i)),$$

where $nodevisits(u,v)$ is the number of nodes visited on the path from u to v in T. Partitioning the two sums with respect to the left and right subtrees of u yields

$$NVCOST\,(T(u)) = \sum_{K_i \text{ is in } T(u_L)} p_i \cdot nodevisits(u, node(i))$$

$$+ \sum_{(K_i, K_{i+1}) \text{ is in } T(u_L)} q_i \cdot nodevisits(u, gapnode(i))$$

$$+ \sum_{K_i \text{ is in } T(u_R)} p_i \cdot nodevisits(u, node(i))$$

$$+ \sum_{(K_i, K_{i+1}) \text{ is in } T(u_R)} q_i \cdot nodevisits(u, gapnode(i))$$

$$+ p_l,$$

where K_l is the key of node u. Now observe that each of these sums counts the node visits from u to the node in question, rather than from u_L or u_R, as appropriate. Since this difference is 1, we obtain

$$\sum_{K_i \text{ is in } T(u_L)} p_i \cdot nodevisits(u, node(i))$$

$$= \sum_{K_i \text{ is in } T(u_L)} p_i \cdot nodevisits(u_L, node(i))$$

$$+ \sum_{K_i \text{ is in } T(u_L)} p_i,$$

and similarly for the other three sums. Finally, substituting for each of the four sums, we obtain

$$NVCOST\,(T(u)) = NVCOST(T(u_L))$$

$$+ NVCOST(T(u_R))$$

$$+ weight(T(u))$$

as required. $\square$

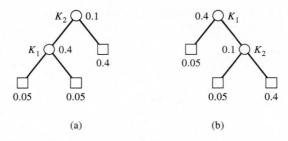

(a)   (b)

Figure 10.2   The candidate trees for the two given keys, K_1 and K_2.
(a) The key K_2 is at the root. (b) The key K_1 is at the root.

Our goal is to construct a binary search tree for given keys, key probabilities, and gap probabilities that has minimum node-visit cost. A natural question is this: Why bother? Why not use optimal sequential search (see Section 8.3.2)? We demonstrate later that optimal binary search trees outperform optimal sequential search methods most of the time. First, we state the construction problem more rigorously: *Given n keys $K_1 < \cdots < K_n$, with key probabilities $p_1,...,p_n$, and gap probabilities $q_0,...,q_n$, construct a binary search tree T, for $K_1,...,K_n$, that has* **minimum node-visit cost** *among all other binary search trees for $K_1,...,K_n$. T is said* to be an **optimal (weighted) binary search tree.**

For example, let $p_1 = 0.4$ and $p_2 = 0.1$, and $q_0 = 0.05$, $q_1 = 0.05$, and $q_2 = 0.4$. Note that we do not give specific keys; we need to know only the keys' ordering. The two possible search trees are shown in Fig. 10.2. Their *NVCOSTs* are

$$3 \times 0.05 + 2 \times 0.4 + 3 \times 0.05 + 1 \times 0.1 + 2 \times 0.4 = 2.0$$

and

$$2 \times 0.05 + 1 \times 0.4 + 3 \times 0.05 + 2 \times 0.1 + 3 \times 0.4 = 2.05.$$

Clearly, the tree in Fig. 10.2(a) has the smaller *NVCOST*—it is optimal. This simple example is not without interest; the optimal tree has the *least probable key* at the root. If we represent this two-key dictionary as an optimal list, then K_1 is in the first position, K_2 is in the second, and all the gaps are after the second position; see Fig. 10.3. The associated cost $COST(K_1,K_2)$, as defined in Section 8.3, is

$$0.4 + 0.2 + 1.5 = 2.1,$$

which is 5 percent more than 2.0, the cost of the optimal tree. We can compare *NVCOST* and *COST*, because both measure the expected number of node visits or

0.4	0.1	0.5
K_1	K_2	
1	2	3

Figure 10.3   The optimal list for the two given keys, K_1 and K_2.

probes. This comparison, however, is for only one example; it is not a general result. We next prove that the result of the comparison holds in general.

Fact 10.2   *Let $K_1 < \cdots < K_n$ be n keys with key probabilities $p_1,...,p_n$ and gap probabilities $q_0,...,q_n$. Denote the binary search tree obtained with the insertion sequence $K_{i_1},...,K_{i_n}$ by $T(K_{i_1},...,K_{i_n})$, where $K_{i_1},...,K_{i_n}$ is some permutation of the n keys. Then,*

$$NVCOST\,(T(K_{i_1},...,K_{i_n})) \leq COST(K_{i_1},...,K_{i_n}).$$

Proof: Consider key K_{i_j} in position j. Its contribution to $COST\,(K_{i_1},...,K_{i_n})$ is jp_{i_j} and its contribution to $NVCOST\,(T(K_{i_1},...,K_{i_n}))$ is $p_{i_j}nodevisits(node(i_j))$. Because K_{i_j} is the jth inserted key,

$$nodevisits(node(i_j)) \leq j.$$

Moreover, the contribution of unsuccessful search to $COST\,(K_{i_1},...,K_{i_n})$ is $q(n+1)$, where $q = q_0 + \cdots + q_n$, and the contribution of unsuccessful search to $NVCOST$ $(T(K_{i_1},...,K_{i_n}))$ is

$$\sum_{i=0}^{n} q_i \cdot nodevisits(gapnode(i)).$$

Again, for all i, $0 \leq i \leq n$,

$$nodevisits(gapnode(i)) \leq n+1,$$

by a similar argument. Together, these inequalities imply that

$$NVCOST\,(T(K_{i_1},...,K_{i_n})) \leq COST(K_{i_1},...,K_{i_n}). \qquad \square$$

Immediately, the optimal tree for $K_1,...,K_n$ is no worse, and usually is better, than the optimal list. Of course, for most sets of keys, key probabilities, and gap probabilities, *NVCOST* is much smaller than *COST*.

Having described our motivation for investigating optimal binary search trees, we need to be able to construct them. Obviously, we would like to obtain a faster algorithm than the exhaustive enumeration algorithm: Compute the *NVCOST* of each of the $\mathcal{B}_n$ search trees and choose one that has minimal *NVCOST*. This algorithm requires $\Omega(2^n)$ steps, which is much too time consuming. Therefore, in Section 10.1.2, we introduce a faster algorithm based on dynamic programming.

10.1.2 A Dynamic-Programming Algorithm

Enumerative or exhaustive search for an optimal tree requires, as we have pointed out, $\Omega(2^n)$ time. This bound is typical of many enumeration problems. Fortunately, dynamic programming often can be used to advantage, as we saw in

Chapter 7. It can be used whenever optimal solutions of problems are simple combinations of optimal solutions of subproblems as is the case here. *An optimal binary search tree has optimal left and right subtrees,* as we prove after introducing some useful notation. On the basis of this fact, we construct optimal subtrees of sizes 1 to n, using smaller optimal subtrees to form larger ones. This approach yields an $O(n^3)$-time construction algorithm.

The notation is as follows. We are given keys $K_1 < \cdots < K_n$, with key probabilities $p_1,\ldots,p_n$ and gap probabilities $q_0,\ldots,q_n$. Since we build only optimal subtrees from contiguous subsequences of the keys, we let $K_{i,j}$ denote the keys $K_i,\ldots,K_j$, where the key sequence is empty when $j < i$. Given a key sequence $K_{i,j}$, we let $p_{i,j}$ denote the corresponding key probabilities $p_i,\ldots,p_j$; we let $q_{i,j}$ denote the corresponding gap probabilities $q_{i-1},\ldots,q_j$; we let $T_{i,j}$ denote the optimal binary search tree for $K_{i,j}$, $p_{i,j}$, and $q_{i,j}$; we let $r_{i,j}$ denote the index of the key of the root of $T_{i,j}$; we let $N_{i,j}$ denote the *NVCOST* of $T_{i,j}$; and we let $W_{i,j}$ denote the weight of $T_{i,j}$.

Rephrasing the construction problem in terms of this notation, we want to find $T_{1,n}$ for $K_{1,n}$, $p_{1,n}$, and $q_{1,n}$. We begin by proving that optimal trees have optimal subtrees.

Fact 10.3 [Optimality Theorem] *Let $K_{1,n}$, $p_{1,n}$, and $q_{1,n}$ be as defined previously. Then, for all i,j, $1 \le i \le j \le n$, if $T_{i,j}$ has K_l as its root key, for some l, $i \le l \le j$, then the left subtree of $T_{i,j}$ is $T_{i,l-1}$ and the right subtree of $T_{i,j}$ is $T_{l+1,j}$. In other words, an optimal binary search tree has optimal subtrees.*

Proof: We argue by contradiction: Assume that the claimed fact does not hold. Then there is a $T_{i,j}$, as shown in Fig. 10.4, for which the left subtree L of the root does not have cost $N_{i,l-1}$ or the right subtree R of the root does not have cost $N_{l+1,j}$. Assume *NVCOST* $(L) \ne N_{i,l-1}$; the other case is symmetric. Now, by assumption, L cannot have minimal *NVCOST*, so *NVCOST* $(L) >$ *NVCOST* $(T_{i,l-1})$. Therefore, we replace L in $T_{i,j}$ with $T_{i,l-1}$ to give a new search tree T for the same keys. Clearly,

$$NVCOST\ (T) < NVCOST(T_{i,j}),$$

because

$$NVCOST\ (T_{i,j}) = NVCOST(L) + NVCOST(R) + weight(T_{i,j}).$$

This inequality contradicts the minimality of the node-visit cost of $T_{i,j}$; therefore, the result holds.   □

Note that the converse of Fact 10.3 does not hold. In Fig. 10.1(b), the subtrees are both optimal, but the tree itself is not.

Because we are dealing with binary search trees, the choice of a root key immediately splits the remaining keys into two contiguous sequences, one for the root's left subtree and one for its right subtree. Therefore, we have to consider not

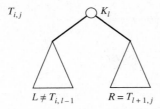

Figure 10.4 The main idea in the proof of the optimality theorem for binary search trees.

all subsets of $K_1,\ldots,K_n$, but rather all contiguous subsequences. This observation reduces the number of trees we have to consider from 2^n to $n + n - 1 + \ldots + 1 = n(n+1)/2$, which is $O(n^2)$. This reduction is the secret of the faster algorithm—the rest of our task is organizing the computation well.

We introduce the algorithm by example, before defining it formally. Let $n = 5$, and let $p_{1,n}$ and $q_{1,n}$ be as given in Table 10.1. We can easily compute the weights of all possible optimal subtrees with the recursive formula

$$W_{i,i-1} = q_{i-1}.$$
$$W_{i,j} = W_{i,j-1} + p_j + q_j.$$

For example,

$$W_{1,1} = W_{1,0} + p_1 + q_1 = 0.06 + 0.21 + 0.11 = 0.38$$

and

$$W_{3,2} = q_2 = 0.02.$$

We obtain Table 10.2 when we display W in matrix form.

The starting point of the algorithm is to provide the $n + 1$ different optimal zero-key trees, $T_{i+1,i},\ 0 \le i \le n$; see Fig. 10.5(a). These trees have associated

Table 10.1 Example key and gap probabilities.

Key or gap				i		
	0	1	2	3	4	5
p_i		0.21	0.15	0.19	0.13	0.02
q_i	0.06	0.11	0.02	0.01	0.06	0.04

Table 10.2   The weights of all optimal trees.

				$W_{i,j}$			
				j			
i	0	1	2	3	4	5
1	0.06	0.38	0.55	0.75	0.94	1.00
2		0.11	0.28	0.48	0.67	0.73
3			0.02	0.22	0.41	0.47
4				0.01	0.20	0.26
5					0.06	0.12
6						0.04

node-visit costs $N_{i+1,i} = q_i$, $0 \le i \le n$. It is convenient to express these costs also in matrix form; see Table 10.3. Next, we compute the optimal one-key trees $T_{i,i}$, $1 \le i \le n$. Since each tree contains exactly one key, it is completely determined by the single key; see Fig. 10.5(b). Because $T_{i,i}$ has subtrees $T_{i,i-1}$ and $T_{i+1,i}$, we can use the recursive formula to compute $N_{i,i}$; namely,

$$N_{i,i} = W_{i,i} + N_{i,i-1} + N_{i+1,i}.$$

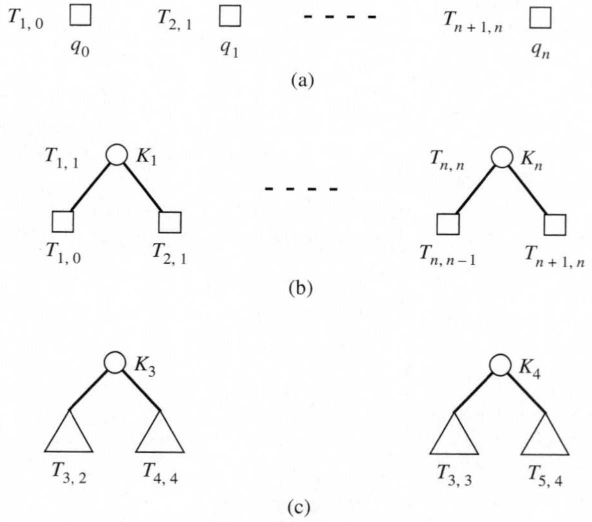

Figure 10.5   Three steps in the construction of an optimal binary search tree, for the example keys and probabilities given in Table 10.1. (a) The optimal zero-key trees. (b) The optimal one-key trees. (c) The two candidates for $T_{3,4}$.

Table 10.3 The node-visit costs of the optimal zero-key trees.

	$N_{i,j}$					
			j			
i	0	1	2	3	4	5
1	0.06					
2		0.11				
3			0.02			
4				0.01		
5					0.06,	
6						0.04

For example,

$$N_{2,2} = 0.28 + 0.11 + 0.02 = 0.41.$$

The two matrices W and N are useful for this purpose. Adding the diagonal entries to the matrix N, we obtain the matrix in Table 10.4. We also provide the first entries for the root matrix r in the same table.

We next compute the costs of the optimal two-key trees. Since there are two keys, we have two choices for the root key. We examine both possibilities in each case. For example, $T_{3,4}$ contains K_3 and K_4. The two candidates for $T_{3,4}$ are shown in Fig. 10.5(c). Since $N_{3,2} + N_{4,4} = 0.02 + 0.27 = 0.29$ and $N_{3,3} + N_{5,4} = 0.25 + 0.06 = 0.31$, the tree in Fig. 10.5(c) with K_3 at the root is chosen as $T_{3,4}$; its node-visit cost is $0.29 + 0.41 = 0.70$. Carrying out a similar computation for each $N_{i,i+1}$, $1 \le i \le n - 1$, we obtain Table 10.5. For optimal three-key trees, we must

Table 10.4 The node-visit costs and root keys of the optimal one-key trees.

$N_{i,j}$								$r_{i,j}$						
			j								j			
i	0	1	2	3	4	5		i	0	1	2	3	4	5
$i=1$	0.06	0.55						1		1				
2		0.11	0.41					2			2			
3			0.02	0.25				3				3		
4				0.01	0.27			4					4	
5					0.06	0.22		5						5
6						0.04		6						

Table 10.5 The node-visit costs and root keys of the optimal two-key trees.

| | $N_{i,j}$ | | | | | | | $r_{i,j}$ | | | | | |
| | | | j | | | | | | | j | | | |
i	0	1	2	3	4	5	i	0	1	2	3	4	5
1	0.06	0.55	1.02				1		1	1			
2		0.11	0.41	0.84			2			2	2		
3			0.02	0.25	0.70		3				3	3	
4				0.01	0.27	0.49	4					4	4
5					0.06	0.22	5						5
6						0.04	6						

Table 10.6 The final node-visit costs and root keys of the optimal trees.

| | $N_{i,j}$ | | | | | | | $r_{i,j}$ | | | | | |
| | | | j | | | | | | | j | | | |
i	0	1	2	3	4	5	i	0	1	2	3	4	5
1	0.06	0.55	1.02	1.55	2.19	2.49	1		1	1	2	2	2
2		0.11	0.41	0.84	1.35	1.63	2			2	2	3	3
3			0.02	0.25	0.70	0.94	3				3	3	4
4				0.01	0.27	0.49	4					4	4
5					0.06	0.22	5						5
6						0.04	6						

examine three candidates for the root of each $T_{i,i+2}$; for optimal four-key trees, we must examine four candidates for the root of each $T_{i,i+3}$; and, finally, for $T_{1,5}$, the only optimal five-key tree, we must examine five candidates for the root. This examination yields the final node-visit cost matrix in Table 10.6, and the final tree of Fig. 10.6. The algorithm we have used is given in Fig. 10.7.

10.1.3 Analysis of the Construction Algorithm

The construction algorithm has to compute $O(n^2)$ entries for the matrices $N_{i,j}$ and $r_{i,j}$. To compute each entry, we compute a minimal-cost tree from the set of candidate trees (one for each choice of root key). At worst, there are are $n-1$ of these candidates. Finding the minimum by exhaustive search takes linear time; therefore, computing each entry takes $O(n)$ time. Combining these two observations,

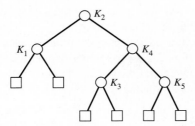

Figure 10.6 The optimal search tree constructed from the probabilities given in Table 10.1 by the algorithm given in Fig. 10.7.

we see that the algorithm takes $O(n^3)$ time, in the worst case. Clearly, it uses $O(n^2)$ space.

This analysis is somewhat crude—we have not specified precisely what we are counting as basic operations. A more detailed analysis shows, however, that the $O(n^3)$ time bound is correct. Using the dynamic-programming approach, we have to compute $\Omega(n^2)$ entries, so we cannot expect to reduce the time bound below this value, unless we can avoid computing the $\Omega(n^2)$ entries. Can we mod-

```
Given keys K₁ < · · · < Kₙ, key probabilities p₁,...,pₙ, and
gap probabilities q₀,...,qₙ, construct an optimal binary search
tree for K₁,...,Kₙ using dynamic programming.

Compute the weights Wᵢ,ⱼ of the optimal trees Tᵢ,ⱼ and
initialize the node-visit costs Nᵢ,ᵢ - ₁, 1 ≤ i ≤ n + 1.
for i:= 1 to n + 1 do
begin Wᵢ,ᵢ - ₁:= qᵢ - ₁;
    Nᵢ,ᵢ - ₁:= qᵢ - ₁;
    for j:= i to n do
        Wᵢ,ⱼ:= Wᵢ,ⱼ - ₁ + pⱼ + qⱼ
end;

for k:= 0 to n - 1 do
    for i:= 1 to n - k do
    begin
        N:= min({Nᵢ,ⱼ - ₁ + N ⱼ + ₁,ᵢ + ₖ : i ≤ j ≤ i + k});
        Let J be the value of j that gives the value of N;
        Nᵢ,ᵢ + ₖ:= Wᵢ,ᵢ + ₖ + N;
        rᵢ,ᵢ + ₖ:= J
    end;
```

Figure 10.7 The optimal-tree construction algorithm.

ify the algorithm, however, to achieve $O(n^2)$ time and space in the worst case? We have a positive answer to this question, which we explain briefly.

We can speed up the construction algorithm by reducing the number of candidate trees that we examine. When computing $T_{i,j}$ we have considered all keys $K_i,...,K_j$ as candidates for the root. The following fact, however, which we do not prove, implies that we can reduce this number substantially.

Fact 10.4 **(Monotonicity)** *For all i, $1 \leq i \leq n$, and for all j, $1 < j \leq n$, the indices of the root keys for $T_{i,j-1}$, $T_{i,j}$, and $T_{i+1,j}$ satisfy*

$$r_{i,j-1} \leq r_{i,j} \leq r_{i+1,j},$$

where $r_{1,0}$ is defined to be $-\infty$ and $r_{n+1,n}$ $+\infty$.

To see how this fact can be used to speed up the algorithm, we observe that instead of finding the minimum among $k + 1$ candidates for *each* value of i, we need to examine at most $r_{i+1,i+k} - r_{i,i+k-1} + 1$ candidates. Hence, for fixed k, we examine

$$(r_{2,k+1} - r_{1,k} + 1) + (r_{3,k+2} - r_{2,k+1} + 1) + \cdots + (r_{n-k+1,n} - r_{n-k,n-1} + 1)$$

candidates, in total, where i ranges from 1 to $n - k$. But this telescoping sum is equal to

$$r_{n-k+1,n} - r_{1,k} + n - k + 1.$$

Since $r_{n-k+1,n} \leq n$ and $r_{1,k} \geq 1$, this sum is less than $2n$; therefore, a suitably revised version of the construction algorithm takes $O(n^2)$ time, rather than $O(n^3)$ time; see Exercise 10.3. Whether there is an algorithm that takes less time remains a tantalizing open problem.

10.1.4 Entropy and Optimality[*]

We can evaluate the efficiency of an optimal tree by comparing its node-visit cost with an independent measure, the entropy of the probability distribution. Let $t_1,...,t_n$, for some $n \geq 1$, satisfy $0 \leq t_i \leq 1$, $1 \leq i \leq n$, and

$$\sum_{i=1}^{n} t_i = 1.$$

Then, $t_1,...,t_n$ is said to be a **discrete probability distribution,** and

$$H(t_1,...,t_n) = -\sum_{i=1}^{n} t_i \log t_i$$

is said to be its **entropy,** where we define $0 \log 0$ to be 0. For example, if $t_1 = \cdots = t_n = 1/n$, then $H(t_1,...,t_n) = \log n$, and if $t_1 = 1$ and $t_2 = \cdots = t_n = 0$, then $H(t_1,...,t_n) = 0$.

Now, given keys $K_{1,n}$ with key probabilities $p_{1,n}$ and gap probabilities $q_{1,n}$, we define $H_{1,n}$ to be the entropy $H(p_1,...,p_n,q_0,...,q_n)$. We can interpret the entropy $H_{1,n}$ to be an idealized node-visit cost, where the term $-\log p_i$ is the ideal "level" of K_i and $-\log q_i$ is the idealized "level" of the gap (K_{i-1},K_i). They are idealized levels because they are real valued rather than integer valued. The following fact, which we do not prove, summarizes the known bounds for the node-visit cost of an optimal tree $T_{1,n}$ in terms of the entropy of its probability distribution.

Fact 10.5

$$H_{1,n} - \log H_{1,n} \le NVCOST(T_{1,n}) \le H_{1,n} + 1 + \sum q_i.$$

So, in an optimal tree, we expect a search to take at most two node visits more than the ideal number. Based on the proof of this fact, we can design tree-construction algorithms that approximate the optimal tree within a constant additive factor, and, also, that are much faster than the optimal construction algorithm. We discuss two example approximation algorithms in Exercises 10.5 and 10.6.

10.2 RED–BLACK TREES

As we have seen in Section 8.5.5, binary search trees perform well in the expected case, but they perform badly in the worst case. In Section 10.1, we posed and solved the problem of obtaining the best possible tree for given keys, key probabilities, and gap probabilities. Unfortunately, this approach assumes that the set of keys is fixed—subsequent insertions and deletions destroy the optimality of the tree. We usually have insertions and deletions; however, at the same time, we want to guarantee performance that is close to the best possible. This situation occurs in environments where we cannot wait too long for the response— for example, in the control of real-time processes as found in a chemical plant or a hospital. We provide two solutions to this problem: red–black trees and splay search trees. Red–black trees guarantee logarithmic worst-case performance for each update and query, whereas splay search trees guarantee only amortized logarithmic performance.

In the remainder of this section, we define red–black search trees, establish a logarithmic upper bound on their heights, and define logarithmic-time insertion and deletion algorithms. In Section 10.3, we treat splay search trees.

10.2.1 Definition and Properties of Red–Black Trees

We begin by defining red–black trees; then we establish that they have logarithmic height. A **red–black tree** is a binary tree whose nodes can be colored either red or black to satisfy the following conditions:

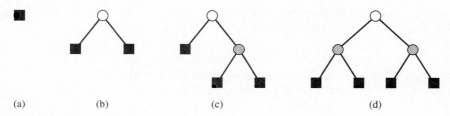

(a)   (b)   (c)   (d)

Figure 10.8   Four red–black trees.

1. **The black condition:** Each root-to-frontier path contains exactly the same number of black nodes.
2. **The red condition:** Each red node that is not the root has a black parent.
3. Each external node is black.

A **red–black search tree** is a red–black tree that is also a binary search tree.

When we display red–black trees, we represent black nodes as solid nodes, red nodes as hatched nodes, and nodes of undetermined color as clear nodes. In Figure 10.8, we give four examples of red–black trees. The tree in Fig. 10.8(a) can be colored only as shown, because of condition (3) in the definition. Similarly, the tree in Fig. 10.8(c) can be colored only as shown. For if the root is colored red, then the remaining internal nodes must be colored black, because of the red condition. However, this implication violates the black condition. Thus, the root must be colored black and, to satisfy the black condition, the other internal node must be colored red, as shown. For most trees, however, there is a choice of coloring.

Not all binary trees can be colored so as to satisfy the three conditions; for example, the size-3 tree in Figure 10.9 is not a red–black tree. To see why it is not, we assume that it is. Then, to satisfy the black condition, either node a is black and nodes b and c are both red, or nodes a, b, and c are all red. In both cases, the red condition is violated.

We now prove that red–black trees have logarithmic height; more precisely, we prove the following fact.

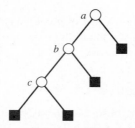

Figure 10.9   A binary tree that is not red–black.

Fact 10.6 *For all $n \geq 1$, every red–black tree of size n has height $O(\log n)$. Thus, red–black trees provide a guaranteed worst-case search time of $O(\log n)$.*

Rather than obtaining an expression for the worst possible height in terms of the size of a red–black tree, we proceed indirectly by considering a tree of smallest possible size for each height. Let $S(h)$ denote the minimum size of a red–black tree of height h; we call trees that attain this size **skinny red–black trees.** What does such a tree look like? If $h = 0$, then $S(h) = 0$; if $h = 1$, then $S(h) = 1$; but what about larger values of h? Consider a tree T of height h, for $h > 1$, that has size $S(h)$. Now T has a root node, a left subtree L, and a right subtree R. Can we say more? Indeed, we can.

Observation 10.1 *Given a skinny red–black tree of height $h > 1$, only one subtree of the root is of height $h - 1$; the other subtree is of smaller height.*

This fact follows because T has minimum size for its height. If L and R have the same height $h - 1$, then, because $h - 1 > 0$, we could replace L by a smaller red–black tree L'—smaller in both height and size. This replacement would give a new red–black tree T', having size less than $S(h)$—a contradiction.

Observation 10.2 *Given a skinny red–black tree of height $h > 1$ such that the right subtree R of the root has height $h - 1$, then R has size $S(h - 1)$.*

If R does not have minimum size $S(h - 1)$, then it can be replaced by a skinnier red–black tree of size $S(h - 1)$, and this replacement, again, contradicts the assumption that T has minimum size $S(h)$. But what about L? Clearly, it must have as many black nodes on each root-to-frontier path as does R. But we can say even more.

Observation 10.3 *Given a skinny red–black tree of height $h > 1$, then L has only black nodes. Therefore, L is a perfect binary tree.*

If L contains a red node, then we remove one of the red node's subtrees and replace the red node with its remaining nonempty subtree. The resulting tree is still red–black, since it still has as many black nodes on each root-to-frontier path as R, and it has smaller size—again, a contradiction. Now, if L is not perfect, then it does not satisfy the black condition. Hence, when $h > 1$, we have deduced that the skinny red–black tree T must look like the tree in Fig. 10.10.

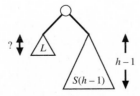

Figure 10.10 A skinny red–black tree—a red–black tree of minimum size for its height.

Finally, we have the following coloring observation, whose proof is left as Exercise 10.9.

Observation 10.4   *For all $h \geq 1$, every red–black tree of height h can be colored such that it has exactly $\lfloor h/2 \rfloor$ black nodes on each root-to-frontier path, and the root is colored black if and only if h is even.*

Therefore, the height of the left subtree of T's root is $\lfloor (h-1)/2 \rfloor$, so we can express $S(h)$ recursively as

$$
\begin{aligned}
S(h) &= 1 + S(h-1) + 2^{\lfloor (h-1)/2 \rfloor} - 1 \\
     &= S(h-1) + 2^{\lfloor (h-1)/2 \rfloor}.
\end{aligned}
$$

It is convenient to eliminate the floor function by unfolding the recursion once to give

$$
S(h) = S(h-2) + 2^{\lfloor (h-2)/2 \rfloor} + 2^{\lfloor (h-1)/2 \rfloor}.
$$

If h is even, then this recurrence equation reduces to

$$
S(h) = S(h-2) + 2^{h/2};
$$

if h is odd, then

$$
S(h) = S(h-2) + 3 \cdot 2^{(h-3)/2}.
$$

Checking these formulas for small values of h, we see that $S(2) = S(0) + 2 = 2$ and $S(3) = S(1) + 3 = 4$, as we expect. We now solve the recurrence equation for even h, the case of odd h is left to Exercise 10.10. Given that

$$
S(h) = S(h-2) + 2^{h/2},
$$

we can unroll the recursion to obtain

$$
\begin{aligned}
S(h) &= \sum_{i=0}^{h/2} 2^i - 1 \\
     &= 2^{1+h/2} - 2.
\end{aligned}
$$

Now, consider a red–black tree of size $n \geq 1$ and even height h. Since $S(h)$ is the size of a smallest red–black tree of height h, we must have $n \geq S(h)$. This fact, however, implies that $n + 2 \geq S(h) + 2 \geq 2^{1+h/2}$. Taking logarithms, we see that

$$
\log(n+2) \geq 1 + h/2,
$$

which gives

$$h \le 2 \log(n + 2) - 2.$$

Rephrasing this result, we have shown that the height of a red–black tree is at most twice the height of the minimal-height tree of the same size, and that it is logarithmic in the size; that is, h is $O(\log n)$.

10.2.2 Promotions and Rotations

Because insertions and deletions in a red–black tree can cause the black and red conditions to be violated, we need to modify the resulting tree to obtain a red–black tree once more. We face similar problems with splay trees. In each case, we use a simple tree transformation—a promotion or rotation—to modify the trees.

Given the subtree rooted at node v in some binary tree T in Fig. 10.11(a), a **single promotion** of v yields the subtree rooted at u in Fig. 10.11(b). An alternative name for this operation is a **left rotation** of u. Similarly, given the subtree rooted at node u in some tree T' in Fig. 10.11(b), a **single promotion** of u yields the subtree rooted at v. Again, an alternative name for this operation is a **right rotation** of v. These two operations are inverses of each other.

The important property of a single promotion is that *a single promotion preserves the binary-search condition*. Thus, every record in a binary search tree T is reachable by an *IsMember* operation both before and after a single promotion in T; there are no unreachable records after a single promotion. (It is easy to define transformations that do not preserve the binary-search condition; see Exercise 10.12.) To see that this property holds, consider the binary tree T in Fig. 10.11(a). The transformation affects only the subtree rooted at u; all nodes outside this subtree are unchanged. Now, by the binary-search condition for tree T,

1. $keys(1) < key(v) < key(u)$.
2. $key(v) < keys(2) < key(u)$.
3. $key(u) < keys(3)$.

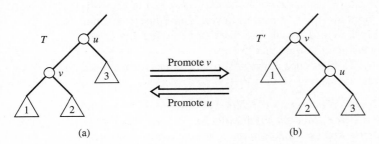

(a) (b)

Figure 10.11 Single promotions or rotations. (a) The initial binary search tree. (b) The binary search that results from the promotion of node v.

Now, for T' to be a binary search tree, we must have

4. $keys(1) < key(v)$.

5. $key(v) < keys(2) < key(u)$.

6. $key(v) < key(u) < keys(3)$.

Inequality (4) follows from (1), (5) is the same as (2), and (6) follows from (1) and (3). This implication also holds in the reverse direction, so we have the following fact.

Fact 10.7 *For T and T' as given in Fig. 10.11, T is a binary search tree if and only if T' is a binary search tree.*

In the literature, the single promotion of node v is often called a **single (left) rotation** at u, and the single promotion of node u a **single (right) rotation** at v.

We need two further transformations, which promote a node two levels rather than one; they are called **2-promotions.** We form the 2-promotions by composing two single promotions. Since a 2-promotion is a composition of two single promotions, it preserves the binary-search condition. First, we have the zig-zag promotion—it comes in two varieties that are mirror images of each other. Given the subtree of Fig. 10.12(a), a **zig-zag promotion of** w yields the tree of Fig. 10.12(c). The mirror image zig-zag promotion of w is shown in Fig. 10.13. We obtain a zig-zag promotion of a node w by promoting w twice.

Second, we have the **zig-zig promotion,** which we need for splay trees but not for red–black trees. In Fig. 10.14, from left to right we have the **left zig-zig promotion** of w, and from right to left the **right zig-zig promotion** of u. We obtain a zig-zig promotion of a node w by first promoting that node's parent and then promoting w. Note that a zig-zig promotion preserves the binary-search condition.

10.2.3 Insertion

As we have proved, red–black trees support the *IsMember* operation in logarithmic worst-case time. The price we have to pay, however, is that insertions into and deletions from a red–black tree can result in a tree that is not red–black; see Fig. 10.15. Therefore, we must demonstrate that the resulting trees can be transformed efficiently into red–black trees once more. We prove that logarithmic time is sufficient time for this transformation.

Fact 10.8 *For all $n \geq 1$, an insertion into or a deletion from a red–black tree of n keys can be performed in $O(\log n)$ time such that the resulting tree is also red–black. Moreover, each insertion and deletion operation takes at most three single promotions; they are said to be of* **constant linkage cost.**

We now prove this fact for insertions; we prove it for deletions in Section 10.2.4. As we shall see, after an insertion into a red–black tree, the transformation

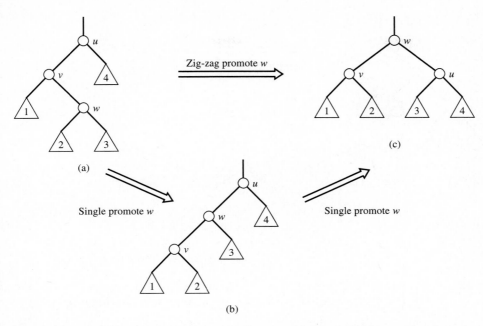

Figure 10.12   The first zig-zag promotion. (a) The initial binary search tree. (b) The tree after the single promotion of *w*. (c) The tree after the second single promotion of *w*.

of the resulting tree into a red–black tree involves color changes and promotions. Initially, we insert a new record into a red–black tree in exactly the same way as we insert a new record into a binary search tree: *The external node corresponding to the search key is replaced by a new internal node that contains the search key and has two external nodes as children.* We must also, however, color the new internal node; we color it red, as we show in the generic example of Fig. 10.16. The effect of this coloring is to preserve the black condition, but the red condition may be violated. The red condition can be violated only if the parent of the new internal node is also red. We must transform this almost red–black tree into a red–

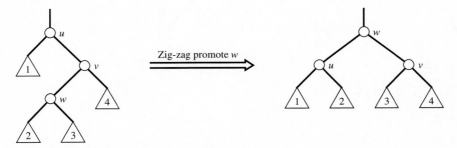

Figure 10.13   The second zig-zag promotion.

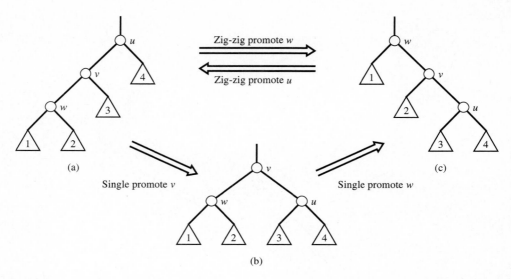

(a)

Single promote v   Single promote w

(b)

(c)

Figure 10.14   The two zig-zig promotions. (a) The initial binary search tree. (b) The tree after the single promotion of v. (c) The tree after the single promotion of w.

black tree. A high-level algorithm to accomplish this transformation is given in Fig. 10.17. There are two straightforward cases to consider (see Fig. 10.18) in which the parent is the root; see case 2 in the high-level algorithm of Fig. 10.17. We assume, in each case, that the black condition holds and that the red condition is violated only as indicated. The solution is simple: Recolor the root black to give a valid red–black tree.

Apart from these two root cases, we have eight other cases; see cases 3 and 4 in Fig. 10.17. We consider only four of them; the other four are symmetric. The four that we consider are displayed in Fig. 10.19. The node u, in each case, has caused the red violation; therefore, its grandparent w must be black (it must have a grandparent; otherwise, it is one of the root cases). Moreover, the parent v of u must have a sibling x because of the black condition, but it may be red or black.

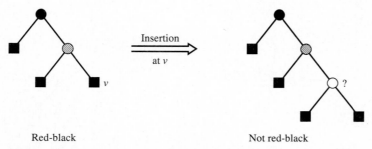

Red-black   Not red-black

Figure 10.15   The red–black property not preserved under insertion.

Figure 10.16   Generic addition of a new internal node.

When x is red (that is, parts (a) and (c) in Fig. 10.19), we recolor v and x black and w red. The recoloring preserves the black condition, but possibly introduces a red violation at w. The violation, if it occurs, is two levels higher in the tree than the original violation; hence, we repeat the transformation recursively. Thus we are left with parts (b) and (d), in Fig. 10.19, in which x is black; they fall to the single and zig-zag promotions, respectively.

In Fig. 10.19(b), we promote the parent v of u and recolor v black and w red. We have essentially redistributed the two red nodes by inserting one red node between the two black nodes w and x. Observe that the black condition holds;

> The node u is a red node in a binary search tree T, and u is the only candidate violating node. Apart from u, the tree T is red–black.
>
> **Case 1:** u is the root. T is red–black.
>
> **Case 2:** u is not the root and its parent is the root. Color its parent black to ensure that T is red–black.
>
> **Case 3:** u is not the root, its parent v is not the root, and v is the left child of its parent w. Let x denote the right child of w.
>
> > **Case 3.1:** x is red. Recolor v and x black and w red; repeat the restructuring with $u := w$.
> >
> > **Case 3.2:** x is black and u is the left child of v. Promote v and recolor v black and w red to ensure that T is red–black.
> >
> > **Case 3.3:** x is black and u is the right child of v. Zig-zag promote u and recolor u black and w red to ensure that T is red–black.
>
> **Case 4:** u is not the root, its parent v is not the root, and v is the right child of its parent w. This case is symmetric to case 3.

Figure 10.17   A high-level description of the recoloring and restructuring algorithm for red–black trees after an insertion.

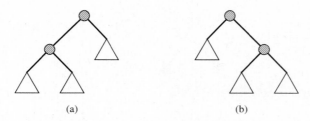

Figure 10.18 The two easily resolved violations of the red condition.
(a) The red node is the left child of a red root.
(b) The red node is the right child of a red root.

moreover, since the new root of the subtree is still colored black, the red condition also holds, and the tree is a red–black tree once more.

Finally, in Fig. 10.19(d), we perform a zig-zag promotion of u and recolor u black and w red. Again, the tree is now a red–black tree.

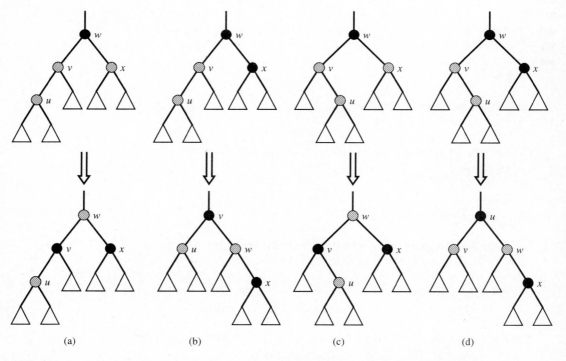

Figure 10.19 The four basic red violations caused by a red node u and their resolution.
(a) u is the left child of its parent and its parent's sibling is red. (b) u is the left child of its parent and its parent's sibling is black. (c) u is the right child of its parent and its parent's sibling is red. (b) u is the right child of its parent and its parent's sibling is black.

The overall picture should be clear; only cases 3.1 and 4.1 in the restructuring algorithm of Fig. 10.17 do not lead to immediate termination. The algorithm must terminate, however, in at most $l/2$ steps, where l is the length of the original path to the modified external node, because the red violation is moved two levels up the tree in the restructuring algorithm. Each case takes a constant number of steps; hence, the transformation, after an insertion, takes $O(\log n)$ steps, because l is $O(\log n)$. Since searching takes $O(\log n)$ steps, insertion takes $O(\log n)$ time in total, in the worst case. Furthermore, an insertion requires at most two single promotions because of cases 3.2, 3.3, 4.2, and 4.3. We say that red–black trees have a constant-linkage-cost insertion algorithm.

10.2.4 Deletion

We delete a record from a red–black tree, initially, in the same way as we delete a record from a binary search tree. If the node u associated with the record has an empty subtree, then we remove u and replace u with u's nonempty subtree, or with an empty subtree if both subtrees of u are empty. Otherwise, u has two nonempty subtrees, so we replace the record at u by its successor record, with respect to their keys, and we delete the node v that contains the record's successor. By definition, the node v has an empty left subtree, so we can delete it straightforwardly. In both cases, we remove a node and replace it with one of its subtrees; see Fig. 10.20 for one of the two symmetric cases. If the node that we remove is

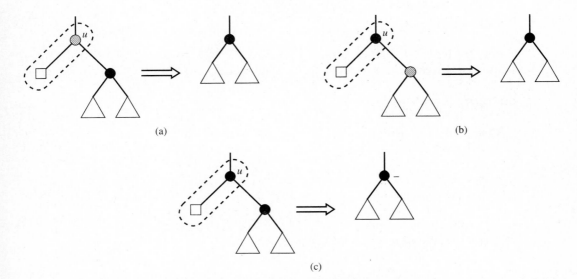

(a) (b)

(c)

Figure 10.20 The removal of a node u from a red–black tree. (a) The node u is red. (b) The node u is black and its internal child is red. (c) The node u is black and its internal child is black; the symbol "−" indicates the root of the violating subtree.

red, then the resulting tree is again red–black; see Fig. 10.20(a). Otherwise, the node we remove is black, and the resulting tree is not red–black, because the replacement subtree has one less black node on its root-to-frontier paths. If the replacement subtree has a red root, however, then we can recolor the root black, and the black condition is satisfied once again; see Fig. 10.20(b). Thus, we are left with the more complex case when the root of the replacement subtree is black; see Fig. 10.20(c). In Fig. 10.21, we give a high-level algorithm to transform an almost red–black tree into a red–black tree. There is one straightforward case to consider (see case 2 in Fig. 10.21) in which u's sibling x is red. We promote x, swap the colors of u and x, and continue with case 3 for u; see Fig. 10.22. This transformation appears to be counterproductive, since it moves u lower in the

The node u is a black node in a binary search tree T, and u is the only candidate violating node. Apart from u, the tree T is red–black.

Case 1: u is the root. T is red–black.

Case 2: u is not the root and its sibling x is red. Let v be their parent. Promote x, swap the colors of v and x, and repeat the algorithm with u.

Case 3: u is not the root, its sibling x is black, and u is the left child of its parent v. Let w denote the left child of x and y the right child of x.

> **Case 3.1:** y is red. Promote x, recolor y black, and swap the colors of v and x to ensure that T is red–black.

> **Case 3.2:** y is black and w is red. Zig-zag promote w, color w the same as v, and recolor v black to ensure that T is red–black.

> **Case 3.3:** y is black and w is black.

>> **Case 3.3.1:** v is red. Recolor v black and x red to ensure that T is red–black.

>> **Case 3.3.2:** v is black (the recoloring transformation). Recolor x red and repeat the restructuring with $u := v$.

Case 4: u is not the root, its sibling x is black, and u is the right child of its parent v. This case is symmetric to case 3.

Figure 10.21 A high-level description of the recoloring and restructuring algorithm for red–black trees after a deletion.

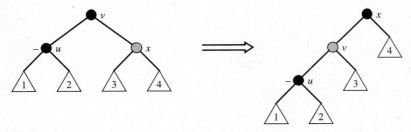

Figure 10.22   Violating black nodes. To ensure that a violating black node u has a black sibling.

tree. It ensures, however, that u's new sibling is black, so case 3 applies immediately.

In case 3 of the restructuring algorithm, v is u's parent, u is the left child of v, x is u's sibling, and w and y are the left and right children of x. If all these nodes are black (case 3.3.2), then we bubble the shortness of u up the tree by recoloring x red and repeating the step with u replaced by v. This recoloring is shown in Fig. 10.23(a); we use the symbol " – " to indicate the root of the violating subtree. The recoloring transformation is repeated as many times as possible. If the violating subtree after this transformation is the whole tree, then it is, once more, red–black. Otherwise, we can no longer apply the recoloring transformation, and the violating subtree is not the whole tree. Thus, one or more of v, w, x, and y is red. The simplest situation is when v is red. In this case, we swap the colors of x and v to give a valid red–black tree; see case 3.3.1 in Fig. 10.21 and the illustration in Fig. 10.23(b).

Finally, we have the two remaining situations: At least one of x's children is red. In case 3.1, y is red, so we singly promote x; see Fig. 10.23(c). Since subtrees 3, 4, and 5 have the same black height as u, recoloring v and y black after the promotion ensures that the black violation is resolved. The half-solid nodes v and x are either both red or both black.

In case 3.2, w is red and y is black, so we zig-zag promote w. Again, the roots before and after the transformation are colored the same and v is recolored black; see Fig. 10.23(d).

We have completed the enumeration of all possible situations, apart from symmetric cases, which are dealt with symmetrically in case 4. Observe that we can apply the promotion of Fig. 10.22 at most once, and similarly for the promotions of Fig. 10.23(c) and (d). Moreover, after we apply the promotion of Fig. 10.22, u has a black sibling and one of the transformations in Fig. 10.23 must apply. Now, we may apply the coloring transformation of Fig. 10.23(a) more than once, but only on the path from the deleted node to the root. Since each transformation takes constant time, deletion takes $O(\log n)$ time and, because it requires at most three single promotions, deletion is of constant linkage cost.

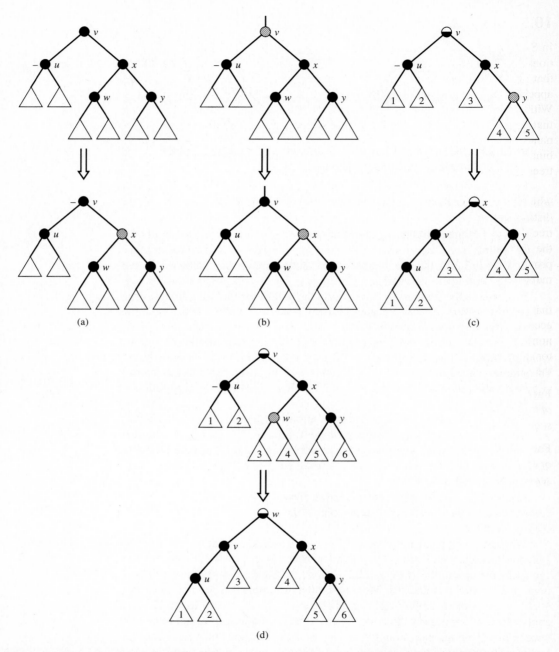

Figure 10.23   The four basic black violations and their resolution. The half-solid nodes in each part are either both red or both black. (a) *u*'s parent and the children of *u*'s sibling are black. (b) *u*'s parent is red and the children of *u*'s sibling are black. (c) The right child of *u*'s sibling is red. (d) The left child of *u*'s sibling is red and its right child is black.

10.3 SPLAY SEARCH TREES

In Section 8.5.5, we saw that, for binary search trees formed by random insertions, an access is expected to take logarithmic time; in Section 10.2, we proved that red–black trees achieve logarithmic access time, in the worst case. Thus it appears that the representation problem for dictionaries is solved completely. With red–black trees, however, we need to maintain 1 bit at each node to indicate that node's color. Not only do these bits take additional space, but their maintenance takes additional time. In addition, we have shown how to construct optimal binary search trees, for given key and gap probabilities; we cannot update optimal trees efficiently, however, while retaining their optimality.

Recalling the success of adaptation for sequential search (see Section 8.3.3), which requires no additional space and no advance knowledge of the probability distribution of the key universe, we explore a similar technique for binary search trees called *splaying*. Whenever we access a record, we move it to the root, just as the move-to-front heuristic moves a record to the front of a list. As we shall prove, in Section 10.3.2, splay search trees are a natural counterpart to the optimal binary trees presented in Section 10.1.

Although any individual access in a splay tree can take linear time, we prove that there cannot be too many such accesses. More specifically, we prove that m accesses take $O(m \log n)$ time, in the worst case, and, moreover, we prove that the number of node visits made by m accesses in a splay tree is within a constant factor of the number of node visits in the optimal binary search tree constructed from the access sequence. That is, we establish the following facts.

Fact 10.9 *Given a binary search tree for n keys and a query sequence $e_1, \ldots, e_m$ of these keys, where $m \geq n$, then the total number of node visits made by the query sequence on the search tree when splaying is used is $O(m \log n)$.*

Fact 10.10 *Given a binary search tree for n keys and a query sequence $e_1, \ldots, e_m$ of these keys, where $m \geq n$, then the total number of node visits made by the query sequence on the search tree when splaying is used is*

$$O\left(n^2 + \sum_{i=1}^{m} N(e_i)\right),$$

where $N(e_i)$ is the number of nodes visited when we are searching the optimal binary search tree constructed for the n keys with the access frequencies given by the query sequence.

Both facts are false for unrestricted binary search trees—we can always construct m accesses that require $\Omega(mn)$ time; see Exercise 10.18. On the other hand, because an individual access can take strictly more than logarithmic time, we should use red–black trees when we need to guarantee logarithmic access time, in the worst case. Fortunately, most applications do not require such a logarithmic guarantee.

We introduce splaying in Section 10.3.1, where we illustrate its effect with an example; then, we analyze splaying in Section 10.3.2.

10.3.1   Splaying

Splaying a node or, equivalently, a record causes the node and its record to be moved to the root. This move-to-root heuristic is similar to the move-to-front heuristic for sequential searching. Given a node u in a binary search tree, a **splay** of u consists of the following two steps: (1) *2-promote u until u can no longer be 2-promoted; (2) if u is not the root, then singly promote u.*

We implement the three DICTIONARY operations in terms of splaying as follows.

1. *IsMember(K,T).* We search T for K in the usual way. If the search is successful, then we splay the node whose key is K; otherwise, we splay the parent of the external node whose gap contains K.

2. *Insert(K,T).* If the search for K is successful, then we splay the node whose key is K. Otherwise, we add a new internal node with key K and splay it.

3. *Delete(K,T).* If the search for K is unsuccessful, then we splay the parent of the external node whose gap contains K. Otherwise, let u be the node whose key is K, v be u's parent, L be u's left subtree, and R be u's right subtree. If L is empty, then we replace u with R and splay v. Otherwise, we splay, within L, the node with the largest key in L. As a result, u has a new left child x with the largest key in L; hence, x has an empty right subtree. Finally, we attach R as the right subtree of x, remove u, replace it with the subtree rooted at x, and splay v; see Fig. 10.24.

You should compare the splay version of *Delete* with the binary-search-tree version of *Delete* in Section 8.5.3.

Before analyzing splay trees, in Section 10.3.2, we work through a detailed example. We begin with an inefficient tree T_0 with keys $1,...,6$ as shown in Fig. 10.25(a)—a left zig-zig tree. *IsMember($1,T_0$)* gives the tree T_1 of Fig. 10.25(b) using two 2-promotions and one single promotion. *Delete($4,T_1$)* causes 3 and 6 to be splayed and results in T_2; see Fig. 10.25(c). *Insert($4,T_2$)* causes two 2-promotions (see Fig. 10.25d) and *IsMember($2,T_3$)* causes one 2-promotion, as does *IsMember($5,T_4$)* (see Figures 10.25e and f). We leave to Exercise 10.19 the implementation details, and to Exercise 10.20 the examination of other splay-related techniques.

10.3.2   Analysis of Splay Trees[*]

We analyze the node-visit cost of a sequence $e_1,...,e_m$ of *IsMember* or query operations applied to a splay tree, and compare it with the node-visit cost of the same sequence applied to the static optimal binary search tree constructed from the

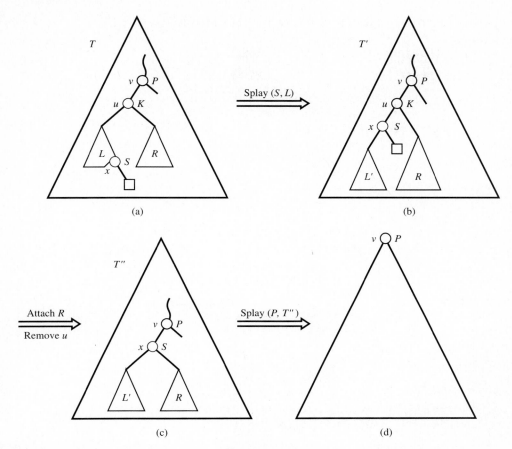

Figure 10.24 Splay deletion of key *K*. (a) The key *K* is at node *u* and *u* has two nonempty subtrees *L* and *R*. (b) Splay, within *L*, the node *x* with maximum key *S* in *L*. (c) Attach *R* as the right subtree of *x*, remove *u*, and reattach *x* to *u*'s parent. (d) Splay *x*'s parent.

same sequence; that is, we prove facts 10.9 and 10.10. We assume that each query e_i is successful; that is, every e_i is in both the splay and optimal trees. The approach we take is similar to, yet different from, the method we used to analyze the move-to-front heuristic. We can use the algorithm in Section 10.1 to construct the static optimal binary search tree for the *n* distinct keys that appear in the query sequence: The gap probabilities are zero, and the key probabilities are given by the number of times that each key appears in the query sequence divided by *m*.

We assume that each key (or its node in the current splay tree) is given a bank account and some initial balance. The initial balance establishes a credit invariant, which we reestablish after we process each query. We use the accounts

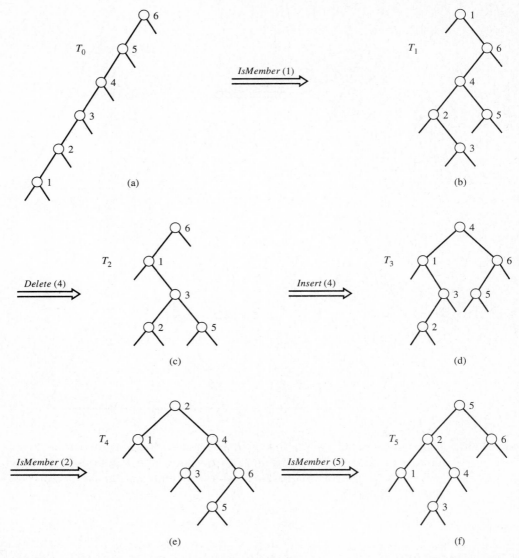

Figure 10.25   Query and update in a splay search tree. (a) An initial search tree for the keys
                   1..6. (b) Query for key 1. (c) Deletion of key 4. (d) Insertion of key 4. (e) Query
                   for key 2. (f) Query for key 5.

to pay for the node visits that are made by a query key, the splay operation, and
the reestablishment of the credit invariant.

   We begin by defining the credit invariant for the keys (and nodes). We assign
a **mass** $m(e) > 1$ to each key e; we shall assign specific masses later to give us the
two facts. Given such a mass assignment, we define the **total mass,** $tm(u)$, of a

node u in the current splay tree, as the sum of the masses of the keys in its subtree. Thus, $tm(u) = m(key(u)) + tm(u_L) + tm(u_R)$, for an internal node u, where each external node has mass 0. Based on the total mass, we now define the **rank**, $r(e)$, of a key e as $2\lfloor \log tm(u) \rfloor$, where u is a node in the current splay tree with $key(u) = e$. Finally, we specify the credit invariant as follows: *The account balance of each key e, with respect to the current splay tree, is $r(e)$ units*. We can reword the credit invariant in terms of nodes in the current splay tree as follows: *The account balance of each node u is $r(e)$ units, where $key(u) = e$*. We shall use the ranks of keys and the ranks of their corresponding nodes in the current splay tree, interchangeably.

Two useful properties of the rank are, first, that $r(u) \geq r(v)$, whenever u is an ancestor of v, and, second (the **equal rank property**), that $r(u) > r(v) + 1$, whenever u has two children v and w with $r(v) = r(w)$. The proofs of these two properties are left to Exercise 10.21.

To establish Facts 10.9 and 10.10, we first compute an upper bound on the cost of a single splay operation. Once we have obtained this upper bound, we can use it to provide an upper bound on the total number of node visits made by the query sequence. Let $cr\text{-}cost(e)$ denote the **credit cost** of splaying e, and define this value as the sum of the number of node visits made when processing the query e, in the current splay tree, and the number of units needed to reestablish the credit invariant after the query e has been processed. We shall prove the following intermediate fact that will enable us to prove Facts 10.9 and 10.10.

Fact 10.11

$$cr\text{-}cost(e) \leq 1 + 3(r(root) - r(e)).$$

A splay operation consists of a number of 2-promotions followed by at most one single promotion. We compute an upper bound on the credit cost of a splay operation by computing upper bounds on the credit costs of single and 2-promotions. We consider the three cases of a single promotion, a zig-zag promotion, and a zig-zig promotion, separately. In each case, we express the credit cost of the operation in terms of the rank of the promoted node, before and after promotion.

The *credit cost of a single promotion* is one node visit plus the units needed to reestablish the credit invariant. In Fig. 10.26(a), the accounts of subtrees 1, 2, and 3 are unchanged; hence, we need to consider only the change in the accounts of nodes a and b as a result of the single promotion of b. This simplification yields a credit cost of

$$1 + r'(a) + r'(b) - r(a) - r(b),$$

where r denotes the rank before promotion, and r' denotes the rank after the promotion. Because $r(a)$ and $r'(b)$ must be equal, by definition, this expression reduces to

$$1 + r'(a) - r(b),$$

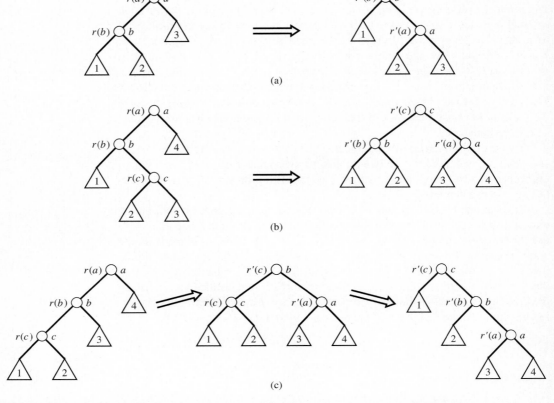

Figure 10.26   The change in the accounts under promotions. (a) A single promotion. (b) A zig-zag promotion. (c) A zig-zig promotion.

and, because $r'(a) \leq r'(b)$, the credit cost is no greater than

$$1 + r'(b) - r(b).$$

The *credit cost of a zig-zag promotion* is two node visits plus the units needed to reestablish the credit invariant. Consider the zig-zag promotion of node c in Fig. 10.26(b). We can ignore the accounts in the subtrees 1, 2, 3, and 4, since they are unchanged, and observe that $r(u) = r'(c)$. The credit cost is, therefore,

$$2 + r'(b) + r'(a) - r(b) - r(c);$$

and, because $r(b) \geq r(c)$, it is no greater than

$$2 + r'(b) + r'(a) - 2r(c).$$

If $r'(a) = r'(b)$, then, by the equal-rank property, $r'(c) > r'(a)$ or $r'(c) - r'(a) \geq 2$, and the credit cost is no greater than

$$r'(c) + r'(b) - 2r(c),$$

which is, since $r'(c) \geq r'(b)$, no greater than

$$2r'(c) - 2r(c).$$

Otherwise, either $r'(c) \geq r'(a) > r'(b)$ or $r'(c) \geq r'(b) > r'(a)$. In both cases, we have $2r'(c) - r'(a) - r'(b) \geq 2$ and, therefore, the credit cost is no greater than

$$2r'(c) - r'(a) - r'(b) + r'(b) + r'(a) - 2r(c);$$

that is, it is no greater than

$$2r'(c) - 2r(c).$$

The *credit cost of a zig-zig promotion* is two node visits plus the units needed to reestablish the credit invariant. Consider the zig-zig promotion of node c in Fig. 10.26(c). Again, we can ignore the contributions of subtrees 1, 2, 3, and 4, and observe also that $r(a) = r'(c)$. The credit cost is, therefore,

$$2 + r'(b) + r'(a) - r(b) - r(c),$$

and it is no greater than

$$2 + r'(c) + r'(a) - 2r(c),$$

because $r'(c) \geq r'(b)$ and $r(b) \geq r(c)$. Clearly, $r'(c) \geq r(c)$. If $r'(c) > r(c)$, then $r'(c) - r(c) \geq 2$, and because $r'(c) \geq r'(a)$, the credit cost is no greater than

$$3r'(c) - 3r(c).$$

On the other hand, if $r'(c) = r(c)$, then we argue that $r(c) > r'(a)$. To see that this property holds, we consider the intermediate tree obtained after the single promotion of b; see Fig. 10.26(c). In this tree: the rank of c is $r(c)$, since c's subtree is unchanged; the rank of a is $r'(a)$, since a's subtree is the same as in the final configuration; and the rank of b is equal to the rank of the root in each of the configurations (that is, $r'(c)$). Now, if $r(c) = r'(a)$, then, by the equal-rank property, the rank of the root of the intermediate tree is greater than $r(c)$. But this fact implies that $r(c) > r(c)$ —a contradiction; so $r(c) > r'(a)$. Thus we obtain immediately that $r'(c) - r'(a) \geq 2$, and substituting for 2 in the credit cost yields a credit cost that is no greater than

$$2r'(c) - 2r(c).$$

In summary, we have proved that a single promotion of a node b has a credit cost no greater than

$$1 + 3r'(b) - 3r(b),$$

and a 2-promotion of a node c has a credit cost no greater than

$$3r'(c) - 3r(c).$$

Computing an upper bound for the credit cost of a splay operation is now straightforward. Each splay operation is a sequence of 2-promotions followed, possibly, by a single promotion. So, splaying a node u has credit cost no greater than

$$3(\sum_{i=1}^{t} r_{i+1}(u) - r_i(u)) + 1 + 3r_{t+2}(u) - 3r_{t+1}(u),$$

where the splay involves t 2-promotions and one single promotion of the node u, r_1 denotes the rank before splaying, and r_i, $2 \le i \le t + 2$, denotes the rank after the $(i-1)$th promotion. This telescoping sum yields

$$1 + 3r'(u) - 3r(u),$$

where $r'(u)$ is the rank of the node u after splaying and $r(u)$ is the rank of u before splaying. Since the node u after splaying is the root node, we can immediately express the credit cost in terms of the rank of the root and the rank of the key of u before splaying as $1 + 3r(root) - 3r(key(u))$.

To complete the analysis of splay trees, we let $cr\text{-}cost(initial)$ be the sum of the account balances of the keys before any splaying takes place, and $cr\text{-}cost(final)$ be the corresponding sum after the query sequence has been processed. Then, the total number $splay\text{-}cost(e_1,...,e_m)$ of node visits needed to process the query sequence $e_1,...,e_m$ is no greater than

$$cr\text{-}cost(initial) - cr\text{-}cost(final) + \sum_{i=1}^{m} cr\text{-}cost(e_i).$$

Since $cr\text{-}cost(final)$ is nonnegative, the total cost is no greater than

$$cr\text{-}cost(initial) + \sum_{i=1}^{m} cr\text{-}cost(e_i).$$

You should compare this relationship with the one we obtained for sequential search in Section 8.3.4. If we let $m(e) = 1$, then $1 \le tm(u) \le n$, for all internal nodes u in the current splay tree. Thus, $0 \le r(e) \le 2\lfloor \log n \rfloor$, for all keys e, and

$$splay\text{-}cost(e_1,...,e_m) \le 2n\lfloor \log n \rfloor 6m\lfloor \log n \rfloor.$$

Now, because $m \geq n$, the total number of node visits made by the query sequence is $O(m \log n)$; we have proved Fact 10.9.

Having bounded the worst-case time taken by a query sequence in a splay tree, we now compare the performances of splay trees and static optimal binary trees. We redefine the mass of a key with respect to the static optimal tree for the given query sequence $e_1,...,e_m$. Let h be the height of the static optimal tree and $N(e)$ be the number of nodes on the path from the root to the node with key e in the static optimal tree. We redefine the mass $m(e)$ to be $3^{h-N(e)}$ and define a new total mass $otm(v)$, for a node v in the static optimal tree, to be sum of the masses of the keys in its subtree. The definition of the total mass $tm(u)$ in terms of $m(key(u))$, for a node u in the current splay tree, is unchanged.

It can be proved by induction (see Exercise 10.22) that $3m(e) \geq otm(v)$, where $key(v) = e$ in the optimal tree. Note that $m(key(root)) = 3^{h-1}$, so $3 (m(key(root)) = 3^h \geq otm(root)$. This inequality, however, implies that

$$m(e) = 3^h 3^{-N(e)}$$
$$\geq otm(root)3^{-N(e)};$$

taking logarithms and rearranging, we obtain

$$\log otm(root) - \log m(e) \leq (\log 3)N(e).$$

But $otm(root) = tm(root)$, because the same keys are in both trees and $m(e) \leq tm(u)$, where $key(u) = e$ in the current splay tree. Therefore,

$$\log tm(root) - \log tm(u) \leq (\log 3)N(e),$$

where $key(u) = e$ in the current splay tree. To complete the analysis, we recall the bound on the credit cost of each query e that we proved—namely,

$$cr\text{-}cost(e) \leq 1 + 3r(root) - r(e).$$

We rewrite this bound as

$$cr\text{-}cost(e) \leq 1 + 6\lfloor \log tm(root) \rfloor - 6\lfloor \log tm(u) \rfloor$$
$$\leq 7 + 6 \log tm(root) - 6 \log tm(u)$$
$$\leq (7 \log 3)N(e),$$

since $\log 3 > 1$ and $N(e) \geq 1$. This inequality bounds the credit cost of a query e in the current splay tree by the number of node visits made by e in the static optimal tree. So to prove Fact 10.10, we need to bound only the sum of the ranks in the initial splay tree. Note that $tm(u) \leq tm(root) = otm(root) \leq 3^h \leq 3^n$, because the height of the optimal tree is at most n. But, $r(e) = 2\lfloor \log tm(u) \rfloor$, where $key(u) = e$ in the current splay tree, yields $r(e) \leq 2n \log 3$, and the sum of all ranks is, therefore, at most $2n^2 \log 3$. So Fact 10.10 follows immediately.

10.4 B$^+$-TREES

Before introducing B$^+$-trees, in Section 10.4.2, we first generalize binary search trees, both internal and external, to multiway search trees, in Section 10.4.1. 2,3$^+$-trees, which can be used for internal dictionaries, are the simplest form of B$^+$-trees; we use 2,3$^+$-trees to illustrate the implementation of the dictionary operations for B$^+$-trees.

10.4.1 Multiway Search Trees

The multiway tree T of Fig. 10.27(a) has degree 4; it has one node w of degree 1; two nodes v and y of degree 2; two nodes u and z of degree 3; and one node x of degree 4. In a binary search tree, we associate one record and key with each binary node, which separates that node's left and right sets of keys. By analogy, because a node of degree d has d sets of keys to separate, we associate $d - 1$ separating keys with the node. A unary node needs $1 - 1 = 0$ keys; a binary node $2 - 1 = 1$ key; a ternary node $3 - 1 = 2$ keys; and a quaternary (or degree 4) node $4 - 1 = 3$ keys. So, the tree T of Fig. 10.27(a) has size 6, 10 external nodes, and needs nine keys to make it into a multiway search tree. Note that the number of external nodes of a tree is a better guide than is the size to the number of keys the tree holds. We now define multiway search trees more formally.

Given n distinct keys $K_1 < \cdots < K_n$ from some totally ordered key universe, a **multiway search tree** for the keys is a multiway tree T with $n + 1$ external nodes whose internal nodes are labeled with key sequences so as to satisfy both the **degree condition:** *A node of degree d is associated with a key sequence of length $d - 1$*; and the **multiway-search condition:** *For all internal nodes u in T,*

$$keys(u_1) < key_1(u) < \cdots < key_{d-1}(u) < keys(u_d),$$

where d is the degree of u, $u_1,...,u_d$ are the d children of u in left-to-right order, $key_i(u)$ is the ith key of u's key sequence, and $keys(u_i)$ is the set of keys in the ith subtree of u.

In Fig. 10.27(b), we display a multiway search tree for the first 9 months of the year, which is obtained from the tree of Fig. 10.27(a). The months are ordered lexicographically. In Fig. 10.28, we give a high-level description of *IsMember* for multiway search trees.

External search trees, in analogy with external binary search trees, have keys associated with external nodes and separators associated with internal nodes. Given n distinct keys $K_1,...,K_n$, and $n - 1$ distinct separators $S_1,...,S_{n-1}$, from some totally ordered key universe such that $K_1 < S_1 \leq K_2 < \cdots < S_{n-1} \leq K_n$, an **external multiway search tree** for the keys and separators is a multiway tree T with n external nodes that are associated with the keys in left-to-right order, and whose internal nodes are associated with separator sequences so as to satisfy the following three conditions: the **degree condition:** *A node of degree d is labeled with a separator sequence of length $d - 1$*; the **separating condition:** *For all internal nodes u in T, $seps(u_1) < sep_1(u) < \cdots < sep_{d-1}(u) < seps(u_d)$, where d is the*

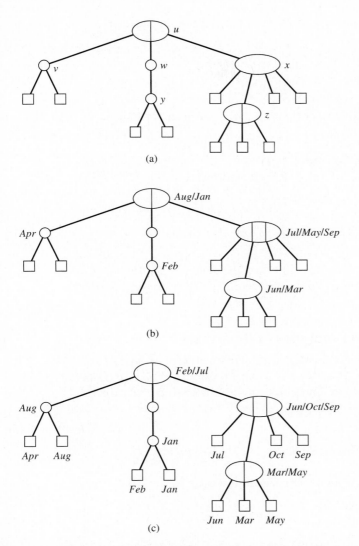

Figure 10.27 Search trees obtained from a multiway tree. (a) A tree of degree 4. (b) A multiway search tree for the first 9 months of the year, ordered lexicographically. (c) An external multiway search tree for the first 10 months of the year, ordered lexicographically.

degree of u, $u_1,...,u_d$ are the d children of u in left-to-right order, $sep_i(u)$ is the ith separator of u's separator sequence, and $seps(u_i)$ is the set of separators in the ith subtree of u; and the **key condition:** *For all internal nodes u in T,*

$$keys(u_1) < sep_1(u) \leq \cdots < sep_{d-1}(u) \leq keys(u_d),$$

T is a multiway search tree, K is a query key, and u is the root of T.

Case 1: u is external. K is not in T; terminate unsuccessfully.

Case 2: u is internal.

> **Case 2.1:** $K = key_i(u)$, for some i, $1 \leq i \leq d_u - 1$. K is in T; terminate successfully.

> **Case 2.2:** $key_{i-1}(u) < K < key_i(u)$, for some i, $1 \leq i \leq d - 1$. [Convention: $key_0(u) = -\infty$.] Repeat the search with $u := u_i$.

Figure 10.28   Search in a multiway search tree.

where d is the degree of u.

In Fig. 10.27(c), we display an external search tree for the first 10 months of the year, obtained from the tree of Fig. 10.27(a). The months are ordered lexico-graphically. In Fig. 10.29, we give a high-level description of *IsMember* for external search trees.

10.4.2   Definition and Properties of B$^+$-Trees

We are now in a position to introduce the only implementation of an external DIC-TIONARY in use today—the B$^+$-tree. When a block is full in ISAM, records that are inserted subsequently into the full block cause overflows of single records. This approach gives rise, over time, to long linked lists of individual records.

T is an external multiway search tree and K is a query key.

Case 1: T is empty. K is not in T; terminate unsuccessfully.

Case 2: T is nonempty.

> **Case 2.1:** $u = root(T)$ is internal. Then, $sep_{i-1}(u) < K \leq sep_i(u)$, for some i, $1 \leq i \leq d - 1$. [Convention: $sep_0(u) = -\infty$.] Repeat case 2 with $u := u_i$.

> **Case 2.2:** $u = root(T)$ is external.

>> **Case 2.2.1:** $key(u) = K$. K is in T; terminate successfully.

>> **Case 2.2.2:** $key(u) \neq K$. K is not in T; terminate unsuccessfully.

Figure 10.29   Search in an external multiway search tree.

Rather than pushing records out one at a time when overflow occurs, we can split the records between the current block and an overflow block. This splitting process will also result in linked lists, but of blocks of records rather than individual records. This approach, together with balancing, is the basis of the B⁺-tree approach. Let us first define B⁺-trees formally, before examining insertion and deletion in detail.

Given an integer $m \geq 1$, a **B⁺-tree T of order** m is an external multiway search tree, over some totally ordered key universe, that satisfies the following three conditions:

1. If the root of T is internal, then the root contains between 1 and $2m$ separators (or has degree between 2 and $2m + 1$).

2. All internal nodes other than the root contain between m and $2m$ separators (or have degrees between $m + 1$ and $2m + 1$).

3. All external nodes are the same distance from the root.

B⁺-trees are used as indexes into a file in two different ways: as a primary index and as a secondary index. When they are used as a **primary index,** the records indexed by them appear at the external nodes; when they are used as a **secondary index,** the keys and record addresses appear at the external nodes—the records appear elsewhere. Often, we need to index a file by more than one key—for example, by name, by salary, and by years of service. In this case, we will have one primary index and several secondary indexes. An external node in a primary-index B⁺-tree will hold, in general, a small number of records (10 to 20, say). This number is called the **bucketing factor** of the B⁺-tree. A secondary-index B⁺-tree may hold 10 times this number of key–address pairs (100 to 200, say).

For simplicity of presentation, we shall treat only B⁺-trees of order 1—also called **2,3⁺-trees**. Also for simplicity, we shall assume that the 2,3⁺-trees are primary indexes with a bucketing factor of 1; that is, one record appears at each external node. In Fig. 10.30, we give a 2,3⁺-tree for the first 8 months of the year. Using the number of node visits or probes to measure access time, we note that, because of condition 3 in the definition of B⁺-trees, it takes the same number of node visits to find all records. Furthermore, the absence of a specific key—unsuccessful search—is demonstrated by the same number of node visits as occurs in a successful search.

Given a B⁺-tree of order $m,$ we obtain the **skinniest tree** when the degrees of the internal nodes are $m + 1,$ and the root is binary; see Fig. 10.31(a). This condition occurs when the B⁺-tree has

$$2(m + 1)^{h - 1}$$

external nodes, where $h \geq 1$ is its height. So, for n keys, the highest possible B⁺-tree of order $m,$ height $h,$ and $n + 1$ external nodes must satisfy

$$2(m + 1)^{h - 1} \leq n + 1 < 2(m + 1)^{h}.$$

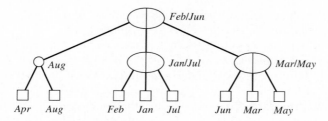

Figure 10.30   An example 2,3$^+$-tree for the first 8 months of the year ordered lexicographically.

Cross-multiplying and taking logarithms, this inequality gives

$$h - 1 \leq \log_{m+1}(n+1)/2 < h;$$

that is, $h = 1 + \lfloor\log_{m+1}(n+1)/2\rfloor$.

Similarly, the **bushiest B$^+$-tree** of order m is obtained when all internal nodes have degree $2m + 1$; see Fig. 10.31(b). It is easy to see that this bushiness occurs when a B$^+$-tree has

$$(2m + 1)^h$$

external nodes, where $h \geq 0$ is its height. For n keys, the lowest possible B$^+$-tree of order m, height h, and $n + 1$ external nodes must satisfy

$$(2m + 1)^h \leq n + 1 < (2m + 1)^{h+1}.$$

Taking logarithms, this inequality gives

$$h \leq \log_{2m+1}(n+1) < h + 1;$$

that is,

$$h = \lfloor\log_{2m+1}(n+1)\rfloor.$$

We have established the following fact.

Fact 10.12   *Given a B$^+$-tree of order m for n keys, its height h lies in the range*

$$\lfloor\log_{m+1}(n+1)/2\rfloor \leq h \leq \lfloor\log_{2m+1}(n+1)\rfloor.$$

Comparing the extreme heights of B$^+$-trees of order m with $n + 1$ external nodes, we can easily derive that, asymptotically, the highest tree is approximately $1 + \log_{m+1}2$ times as high as the lowest tree. Hence, skinny 2,3$^+$-trees are twice the height of bushy 2,3$^+$-trees that have the same number of external nodes. For $m = 99$, this ratio shrinks to ≈ 1.00.

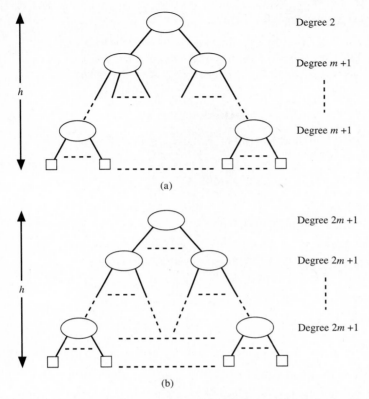

(a)

(b)

Figure 10.31 Extremal B$^+$-trees. (a) A skinny B$^+$-tree of height h. (b) A bushy B$^+$-tree of height h.

Looking at these computations in another way, for $m = 99$, we see that a B$^+$-tree of height 3 has at least $2 \times 100^2 = 20,000$ external nodes. If it has height 4, then the number of external nodes is at least 2 million. We expect that the majority of applications will have at most this number of records. In general, the root will not be binary, so these estimates are pessimistic.

Under reasonable assumptions, internal nodes are expected to be 70-percent full. So a B$^+$-tree of order 100 and height 3 is expected to have 2,744,000 external nodes. This number is much more than the worst-case scenario predicts and is closer to experience. We would expect that a B$^+$-tree of order 100, used as a primary index, would have a bucketing factor of at least 10. Since external nodes are also expected to be 70-percent full, a height-3 B$^+$-tree of order 100 is expected to index $2,744,000 \times 7 = 19,208,000$ records. This number of records is more than sufficient for most purposes. The first two levels of such a B$^+$-tree contain at most 202 nodes, and, if a key can be stored in 8 bytes and an address in 4 bytes, then a full node requires $1600 + 804$ bytes $= 2404$ bytes. Because the first two levels require at most $2404 \times 202 = 485,608$ bytes, they fit easily into main memory.

Analytical results have established the following fact.

Fact 10.13 *Assume that all permutations of 1..n are equally likely to occur as insertion sequences into an initially empty B^+-tree of order m and bucket size b. Under this model, we can expect a B^+-tree of order m and bucket size b, for n keys, to have height*

$$\log_{m+1}(n+1) - \log_{m+1}(2(b+1)\ln 2).$$

So, in particular, when $m = 100$, $b = 10$, and $n = 100$ million, we expect a B^+-tree to have height at most

$$\log_{101}(100{,}000{,}001) - \log_{101}(22 \times 0.6931);$$

that is, it has height at most 4!.

We can summarize the preceding discussion as follows.

Fact 10.14 *In practice, the IsMember operation on a primary-index B^+-tree makes at most two disk accesses and, in a secondary-index B^+-tree, at most three disk accesses.*

Having studied some of the properties of B^+-trees we show, in Sections 10.4.3 and 10.4.4, how we update a $2,3^+$-tree efficiently.

10.4.3 Insertion

Given the $2,3^+$-tree of Fig. 10.30, an unsuccessful search always reaches an external node and nearly always falls to that node's right. For example, a search for *Four,* in the tree of Fig. 10.30, ends at the external node with the key *Feb.* The one exception to this rule is a search for a key smaller than the minimum key in the tree—for example, a search for *Algorithm,* in the tree of Fig. 10.30. In general, because separators do not need to appear as keys, an unsuccessful search can also fall to the left of an external node. When there are many records associated with each external node, the unsuccessful search can end in any one of the associated gaps. We consider a key falling only to the right in the following discussion of insertion, for which we prove the following fact.

Fact 10.15 *Given a B^+-tree T of order m containing n records, we can insert a new record into T in $O(\log n)$ time.*

An insertion always introduces a new external node, a hook into that node (an incomplete edge), and a new separator. For example, the insertion of *Dec* into the tree of Fig. 10.30 first causes a search, then causes the introduction of a new external node to the right of the external node containing *Aug;* see Fig. 10.32(a). Not only is *Dec* associated with the new external node and not only does the external node have a hook, but also the external node has a separator, to separate *Dec* from *Aug.* We choose *Dec* as the separator so that the separating condition is satisfied; see Fig. 10.32(b). We want to add the new external node as a child of

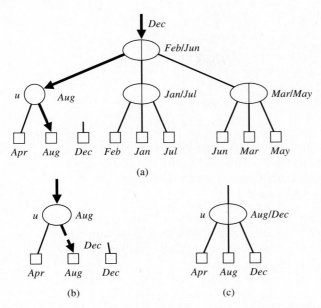

(a)

(b)   (c)

Figure 10.32   Simple insertion into a 2,3⁺-tree. (a) The search for *Dec* in
the 2,3⁺-tree of Fig. 10.30. (b) The addition of *Dec* and its
separator to the example 2,3⁺-tree. (c) Two nodes made
into the children of their "parent," and the addition of the
separator to their parent.

Aug's parent *u*. Conceptually, we break the edge from *u* to *Aug* as shown in Fig.
10.32(b); hence, we obtain, in general, the symmetric situation displayed in Fig.
10.33. Note that when an inserted key falls to the left of an external node, the
result is similar. We now add, to the parent node *u,* two edges to *Aug* and *Dec* and
the separator *Dec*. This final addition yields the tree of Fig. 10.32(c); *u* is now a
node of degree 3.

The insertion of *Sep* into the original tree gives, by similar arguments, the situation depicted in Fig. 10.34(a), which then gives the situation in Fig. 10.34(b).

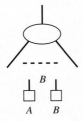

Figure 10.33   The symmetric view of insertion.

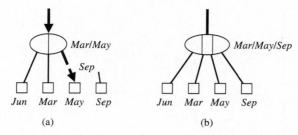

Figure 10.34   Nonsimple insertion into a 2,3$^+$-tree. (a) The addition of *Sep* and its separator to the 2,3$^+$-tree of Fig. 10.30. (b) Two nodes made into the children of their "parent," and the addition of the separator to their parent.

In this case, we change a ternary node into a degree-4 node, a node with three keys. This effect is called **overflow;** the tree is no longer a 2,3$^+$-tree, but we show how it can be transformed efficiently into a 2,3$^+$-tree.

The pattern is now clear: An insertion into a 2,3$^+$-tree adds a new external node, and this addition increases, by 1, the degree of the external node's parent. Clearly, when the degree of the parent is 3, we obtain a parent of degree 4. (In a B$^+$-tree of order m, a parent of degree $2m + 1$ becomes a parent of degree $2m + 2$; the tree is no longer a B$^+$-tree of order m and, indeed, it may no longer be a B$^+$-tree of any order.) We must transform the nearly 2,3$^+$-tree into a 2,3$^+$-tree, and, in general, a nearly B$^+$-tree of order m into a B$^+$-tree of order m. This difficulty is analogous to the difficulty we meet after an insertion into a red–black tree.

Consider the insertion of *Sep* into the tree of Fig. 10.30 once more. After adding a new external node, we obtain a degree-4 parent; see Fig. 10.34(b). Although the tree is no longer a B$^+$-tree of any order, it is an external multiway search tree. To resolve the local overflow, we **split** the degree-4 node into two binary nodes and a separator; see Fig. 10.35(a). In general, we split a node of degree $2m + 2$ into two nodes of degrees $m + 1$ and a separator. The total degree of the two nodes is the same as the degree of the overflowing node, but we have two subtrees where we had only one. The resulting configuration is similar to the starting configuration, but at one level higher in the tree. So we repeat the method given in Fig. 10.34(a); it yields the 2,3$^+$-tree of Fig. 10.35(b). Now the root has three separators, so we have overflow yet again. We split the node as before (see Fig. 10.35c) and pass the problem up to the next higher level. In this case, however, the next higher level does not exist—yet. So we create a new level by introducing a new binary root. The final 2,3$^+$-tree is displayed in Fig. 10.36. Note that the final split increases the height of the tree by 1.

One side effect of the splitting operation is a decided advantage: A node, formerly of degree $2m + 1$, is replaced by two nodes, both of degrees $m + 1$. Further overflow of either of these nodes can occur only after many insertions into their subtrees. This phenomenon is very different from the ISAM situation—once

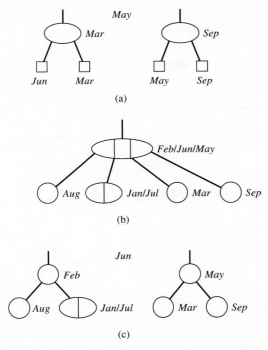

Figure 10.35 Resolution of overflow in 2,3⁺-trees. (a) Splitting of the degree-4 node of the tree of Fig. 10.34(b). (b) Insertion at upper levels in a 2,3⁺-tree. (c) Splitting at upper levels in a 2,3⁺-tree.

overflow begins in a block in ISAM, overflow continues in that block for each subsequent insertion into it.

With the preceding example, we have covered all possible kinds of restructuring. Whenever splitting of a node takes place, it may cause splitting of that

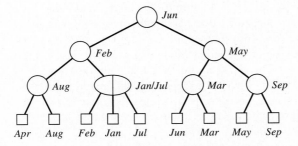

Figure 10.36 The final 2,3⁺-tree after the insertion of *Sep* into the 2,3⁺-tree of Fig. 10.30.

L, R, and T are B$^+$-trees of order m, either L or R is a subtree of T, S is a separator of L and R, and L and R are the same height.

Case 1: Neither L nor R has a parent in T. Introduce a new binary node with separator S, left child L, and right child R. Terminate.

Case 2: Either L or R has a parent u in T, and one of them is the ith child of u. Insert L as the ith child of u, R as the $(i+1)$th child of u, and S as the ith separator. The original children in positions $i + 1$ onward are moved into positions $i + 2$ onward, and the original separators in positions i onward are moved into positions $i + 1$ onward.

Case 2.1: u has at most $2m$ separators. Terminate the restructuring.

Case 2.2: u has $2m + 1$ separators. Split u into two nodes, v with the first m separators and w with the last m separators. Repeat the restructuring with L as $T(v)$, R as $T(w)$, and S as the remaining $(m + 1)$th separator of u.

Figure 10.37   Restructuring of a B$^+$-tree of order m after insertion.

node's ancestors, but *only* of that node's ancestors. So, the insertion algorithm takes $O(\log n)$ time. A high-level description of the restructuring method is given in Fig. 10.37.

10.4.4 Deletion

Having demonstrated that insertion can be carried out as efficiently as can searching (up to a multiplicative constant), we now show that deletion also can be carried out as efficiently as searching. That is, we prove the following fact.

Fact 10.16   *Give a B$^+$-tree T of order m containing n records, we can delete a record from T in $O(\log n)$ time.*

We work through a number of examples of deletion for 2,3$^+$-trees, and indicate how we can generalize the techniques to B$^+$-trees. We begin once more with the 2,3$^+$-tree of Fig. 10.30. To delete *Jan*, we search for *Jan* and remove the corresponding external node, edge, and separator. The corresponding separator is the largest separator in the parent that is no greater than the deleted key. In this case, it is the separator *Jan*; see Fig. 10.38(a). The only exception to this rule occurs when the deleted key is associated with a first or leftmost child. In this case, the smallest separator is removed from the parent. For example, if we delete the key *Feb*, then we also remove the separator *Jan* in its parent.

The effect of a deletion is to reduce the degree of the associated parent by 1; deleting *Jan* changes a ternary node into a binary node—see Fig. 10.38(a). Thus when we delete a key with a binary parent, we obtain a unary parent. For exam-

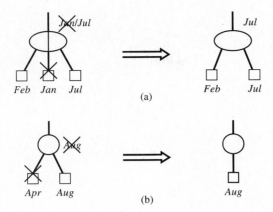

Figure 10.38   Deletion from the 2,3$^+$-tree of Fig. 10.30. (a) Deletion of
Jan. (b) Deletion of Apr.

ple, when we delete Apr, we obtain a unary parent; see Fig. 10.38(b). Such a deletion leaves a multiway search tree that is not a B$^+$-tree of any order. The modified
parent node has **underflowed.** In general, underflow occurs in a B$^+$-tree of order
m when a node with an $(m + 1)$-degree parent is removed; see Fig. 10.39. We
need, as we did when overflow occurs after insertion, to transform the tree into a
2,3$^+$-tree once more (in general, into a B$^+$-tree of order m). We begin to define the
transformation process with our chosen example, the deletion of Apr from the
tree of Fig. 10.30. The unary node, which is produced by the deletion, has an
immediate ternary sibling, so we perform a merge, which is the reverse of a split.
A split produces two nodes and a separator from one overflowing node; a **merge**
takes two sibling nodes and a separator, and combines them into a single node.
The unary node and its immediate sibling have Feb as their separator; see Fig.
10.40(a). The merge is now straightforward; see Fig. 10.40(a). Because the sibling of the unary node is ternary (in general, of degree at least $m + 2$), the resulting node overflows, so we split it into two binary nodes (in general, into two
$(m + 1)$ -degree nodes) and a separator; see Fig. 10.40(b). Normally, a merge followed immediately by a split is called a **rotation** (see Fig. 10.40c), but we prefer
to consider it, at least conceptually, as a composition of a merge and split, a

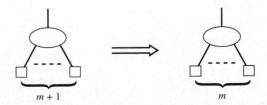

Figure 10.39   Deletion as a cause of underflow in a B$^+$-tree.

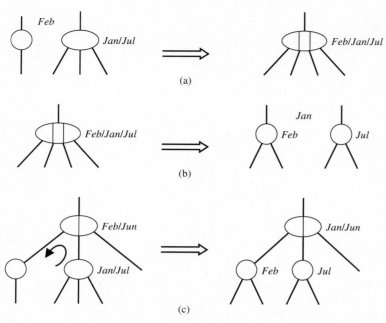

Figure 10.40   Dealing with underflow in a 2,3⁺-tree. (a) Merging of two
nodes and a separator. (b) Splitting of a merged node.
(c) A merge–split rotation.

merge–split, since this view is more general. Since a merge–split preserves the
degree of the parent, the tree is now a $2,3^+$-tree (a B^+-tree) once more.

We now consider the deletion of *Sep* from the tree in Fig. 10.36; it gives a
unary node with a binary sibling as shown in Fig. 10.41(a). When we merge the
unary node with its immediate sibling and their separator *May,* we obtain the tree
of Fig. 10.41(b). We have removed the unary node from the current level, but we
have created a unary node on the next higher level. We deal with this new unary

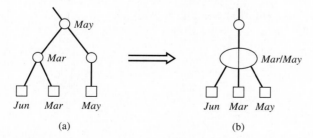

Figure 10.41   The deletion of *Sep* from the 2,3⁺-tree of Fig. 10.36. (a) The resulting unary
node has a binary sibling. (b) The merge of the unary and binary nodes
introduces a unary node at the next higher level.

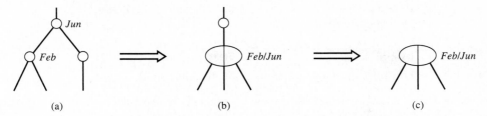

Figure 10.42 Removal of the higher level unary node in the 2,3⁺-tree of Fig. 10.41(c). (a) The node with key *Feb* has one sibling, which is unary. (b) The merge of the unary and binary nodes introduces a unary node at the next higher level. (c) Since the next higher level is the root level, the unary root is removed.

node in a similar way; see Fig. 10.42(a). Again, we have removed a unary node at the expense of introducing another unary node at the next higher level, the root level; see Fig. 10.42(b). This unary node, however, is simple to remove—we chop it off, as in Fig. 10.42(c). The final tree is, in this case, the tree of Fig. 10.30 once more; serendipitously, it is identical to the 2,3⁺-tree we had before we inserted *Sep*.

The general approach to restructuring a B⁺-tree after a deletion is given in Fig. 10.43. We use a merge, in general, when a parent node underflows (it has $m - 1$ separators) as a result of a deletion in a B⁺-tree of order m. Two cases arise. The first case occurs when the underflowing node's immediate siblings have exactly m separators. Either merge gives a node with exactly $2m$ separators and a parent with one less child; see Fig. 10.44(a). This reduction in the degree of the parent may require a merge to be used at the next higher level. The other more usual case occurs when the underflowing node's immediate siblings have more than m separators; see Fig. 10.44(b). The merge is followed immediately by a split (a generalized version of the split used for insertion). If the sibling has k children, then the node of smaller degree after the merge–split has $\lfloor (m + k)/2 \rfloor$ children. Since $k \geq m + 2$,

$$\lfloor (m + k)/2 \rfloor \geq \left\lfloor \frac{(2m + 2)}{2} \right\rfloor$$

$$= m + 1.$$

Similarly, the node of larger degree after the merge–split has $\lceil (m + k)/2 \rceil$ children. Again, since $k \leq 2m + 1$,

$$\lceil (m + k)/2 \rceil \leq \lceil (3m + 1)/2 \rceil$$

$$\leq 2m + 1.$$

So, a merge–split always produces two nodes of degrees between $m + 1$ and $2m + 1$; that is, the tree is a B⁺-tree of order m.

Apart from a node u, which has $m - 1$ separators, the tree T is a B$^+$-tree of order m. u is an underflowing node.

Case 1: u is the root. Remove u and terminate.

Case 2: u is not the root, v is its parent, and u is the ith child of v.

> **Case 2.1:** u has an immediate sibling x with m separators. We assume that x is the immediate left sibling of u; x is the immediate right sibling of u is treated in a similar manner. Let S be the separator of x and u in v. Merge x with u to give a node w with $2m$ separators, which are the m separators of x followed by S and followed, in turn, by the $m - 1$ separators of u. Replace x, S, and u in v with w. The parent v has one less separator; if it underflows, then repeat the restructuring at the next higher level with $u := v$.

> **Case 2.2:** Each immediate sibling of u has at least $m + 1$ separators. We assume that x is the immediate left sibling of u and that it has k separators. Let S be the separator of x and u in v. Merge x with u to give an overflowing node w with $m + k \geq 2m + 1$ separators, which are the k separators of x followed by S followed, in turn, by the $m - 1$ separators of u. Split the node w into two nodes y and z such that y has the first $\lfloor (m + k - 1)/2 \rfloor$ separators of w and z the last $\lceil (m + k - 1)/2 \rceil$ separators of w. The remaining separator S' replaces S in v, and y and z replace x and u as the children of v. The parent v has the same number of separators, so the restructuring terminates; the tree is a B$^+$-tree.

Figure 10.43   Restructuring of a B$^+$-tree of order m after deletion.

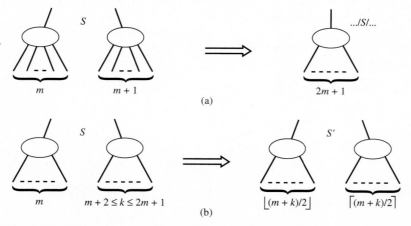

Figure 10.44   A merge in a B$^+$-tree of order m. (a) Situation in which the immediate siblings of an underflowing node have exactly m separators. (b) Situation in which an immediate sibling of an underflowing node has at least $m + 1$ separators.

Finally, since we modify the B^+-tree only on the search path of the deleted key, deletion takes $O(\log n)$ time.

10.5 PERFORMANCE REPORTS

Optimal binary search trees provide a benchmark for splay search trees; they are rarely used in practice (see Table 10.7). When search trees are required—for example, in main-memory databases—we must cater for updates; therefore, we choose binary search trees, red–black trees, splay trees, $2,3^+$-trees, or some other class of balanced trees. (Note that we have included the $2,3^+$-tree as a candidate structure for internal dictionaries.) Which of these four candidates we choose depends on the requirements. Binary search trees are the easiest to implement, but they have linear-time performance in the worst case. Despite this drawback, they are often the first choice. We rate then below red–black trees, $2,3^+$-trees, and splay trees, because of their poor worst-case performance; see Table 10.8.

Splay trees also have a linear-time worst-case performance; however, they guarantee near-optimal performance in the amortized case. In particular, splay trees adapt to the probability distribution, usually unknown, of the key universe. They are not difficult to code, although they are not as easy to code as binary search trees.

When we want to guarantee logarithmic-time performance in the worst case, we should choose red–black trees or $2,3^+$-trees. The updating algorithms for red–black trees are more complex than the updating algorithms for $2,3^+$-trees, but, in most programming languages, the memory required for a node in a $2,3^+$-tree (even a binary node) is more than the memory required for a node in a red–black tree. We rate both choices as excellent.

Table 10.7 A comparison of the execution times of the six search-tree implementations of DICTIONARY.

	IsMember operation	
DICTIONARY implementation	Worst-case time	Expected-case time
Binary trees	n	$\log n$
Optimal binary trees	n	$H_{1,n}$
Red–black trees	$\log n$	$\log n$
Splay trees	n	$\log n$[a]
$2,3^+$-trees	$\log n$	$\log n$
B^+-trees	$\log n$	$\log n$

[a]Note that this bound is an amortized bound for a uniform-probability distribution.

Table 10.8 Performance ratings of six search-tree implementations of
DICTIONARY.

DICTIONARY implementation	Rating	Comments
Red–black trees	Excellent	Dynamic; guarantee logarithmic search time
2,3$^+$-trees	Excellent	Dynamic; guarantee logarithmic search time
Splay trees	Excellent	Dynamic; adapt to unknown time-varying probability distribution
Binary trees	Very good	Dynamic; easy to code; poor worst-case performance
Optimal binary trees	Good	Not dynamic; choice when no updates and probability distribution is known
B$^+$-trees	Excellent	Dynamic; choice for external dictionaries

Finally, for external dictionaries, the B$^+$-tree is the only choice. It is dynamic;
it requires at most two disk accesses for any dictionary operation on most external
dictionaries.

10.6 SUMMARY

We have explored five approaches to obtaining efficient binary search trees—four
for internal dictionaries and one for external dictionaries. The four approaches for
internal dictionaries are optimal trees, red–black trees, splay trees, and 2,3$^+$-trees,
and the approach for external dictionaries is B$^+$-trees. A binary search tree is optimal, for a given set of keys, key probabilities, and gap probabilities, if it has minimal node-visit cost. We have shown how to construct such trees efficiently using
dynamic programming and have compared the trees' performance with the entropy of the probabilities. The entropy can be considered to be an idealized node-
visit cost.

A second approach uses a balance criterion: Nodes are colored red or black,
every red node has a black parent, and all root-to-frontier paths must have the
same numbers of black nodes. We have proved that such trees, called red–black
trees, have logarithmic height, and updates can be carried out in logarithmic time.

The third internal approach, splay trees, uses adaptivity: Whenever a node is
accessed, it (or its parent, if it is external) is moved or splayed to the root. In analogy to sequential search and move-to-front, we have shown that splay trees have
logarithmic amortized performance and perform within a constant factor of static
optimal trees for a given query sequence.

The final internal approach, $2,3^+$-trees, are the lowest-ordered B^+-trees: B^+-trees of order 1. They have logarithmic height, and updates can be carried out in logarithmic time.

External dictionaries should guarantee few disk accesses for each DICTIONARY operation, because disk operations are extremely time consuming in comparison to main-memory accesses. We have introduced B^+-trees, balanced multiway tree structures that satisfy this requirement. A B^+-tree of order m has nodes with between m and $2m$ separators (apart from the root, which has between 1 and $2m$ separators), and every external node is on the same level. Thus B^+-trees have logarithmic height, and updates require only logarithmic time.

10.7   HISTORY

The algorithm to compute optimal weighted binary search trees was developed by Gilbert and Moore (1959), and the improvement using the monotonicity principle was discovered by Knuth (1971). Dynamic programming is an important paradigm that was first identified by Bellman (1957).

The definition of red–black trees and their updating algorithms is based on the presentation in Sarnak and Tarjan (1986). Red–black trees were first introduced by Guibas and Sedgewick (1978), although, under the name **symmetric binary B-trees,** they were developed by Bayer (1972); under the name **half-balanced trees,** they were defined by Olivié (1980; 1982). Olivié proved that half-balanced trees have constant-linkage-cost update algorithms, and he generalized them to α-balanced trees.

Splay trees, introduced by Sleator and Tarjan (1985b), are a modification of the move-to-root trees of Allen and Munro (1978).

B^+-trees, ISAM's first real competitor, were introduced by Comer (1979) as a modification of B-trees, which were devised by Bayer and McCreight (1972) in 1972. Batory (1981) compared B^+-trees to ISAM. A variant of them was implemented and distributed in IBM's VSAM; see the discussion in Comer (1979) and Wagner (1973). Today, they are considered to be the only data structure to use for large external files when the total ordering is important. Their ubiquitousness is discussed in the readable survey article of Comer (1979), and their practical concerns for real systems are covered in Salzberg (1988) and Folk and Zoellick (1987). The analytical result that bounds the heights of B^+-trees was derived by Baeza-Yates (1989c); other analytical results for $2,3^+$-trees and B^+-trees were investigated by Eisenbarth and coworkers (Eisenbarth et al., 1982).

EXERCISES

10.1:   You are given the keys $K_1 = cat$, $K_2 = dog$, $K_3 = kitten$, and $K_4 = puppy$, key probabilities $p_1 = 0.03$, $p_2 = 0.35$, $p_3 = 0.12$, and $p_4 = 0.05$, and gap probabilities $q_0 = 0.05$, $q_1 = 0.00$, $q_2 = 0.10$, $q_3 = 0.30$, and $q_4 = 0.00$.

  a. Construct an optimal binary search tree.
  b. Compute the *NVCOST* of the optimal tree.
  c. Compute the entropy of the probabilities.
  d. Compute the *COST* of the optimal list for the keys.

10.2: The technique for constructing an optimal binary search tree can be adapted to produce a pessimal binary search tree (a maximal *NVCOST* tree). Using the data given in Exercise 10.1, construct a pessimal tree.

10.3: Implement, in Pascal, the suggested speedup of the optimal tree-construction algorithm that is based on the monotonicity principle.

10.4: Given an optimal binary search tree $T_{i,j}$ for keys $K_{i,j}$, probabilities $p_{i,j}$, and zero gap probabilities, insert key K_{j+1} with zero key probability and zero gap probability into $T_{i,j}$ in the usual way to give T. Prove that T is optimal.

10.5: One suggested approximation for a nearly optimal tree is to construct a monotone tree. In a **monotone tree,** the key probabilities associated with internal nodes are arranged in nonincreasing order on all root-to-frontier paths. Because the tree has to be a search tree, when the probabilities are distinct, there is only one possible tree. Give an example monotone tree that shows that monotone trees can be exceedingly costly, compared to their optimal counterparts.

10.6: We can approximate optimal binary search trees in the following way. Given the interleaved sequence of gap and key probabilities (interleaved in the inorder traversal order of any binary search tree for the corresponding keys), we can view the probabilities as points on the line [0,1]. We can produce a balanced tree by taking the key whose key probability interval is closest to 0.5 as the key of the root (if 0.5 lies within a key probability interval, we take that key). We repeat this halving operation for the interleaved sequences and their associated intervals that fall to the left and right of the chosen key. Implement this method. Compare the node-visit costs of the constructed trees, for at least 10 sets of data, with the node-visit costs of the corresponding optimal trees.

10.7: Let T be a binary tree with **frequencies;** that is, each node u in T (external and internal) has an associated nonnegative integer *frequency*(u). We define the **weight of a node** u, denoted by *weight*(u), to be the sum of the frequencies in u's subtree. Finally, we define the **weighted path length of a node** u, denoted by *WPL*(u), to be

$$\sum_{u \in T(u)} frequency(u) nodevisits(u).$$

  a. Prove that, for all internal nodes u in T,
  $$weight(u) = frequency(u) + weight(u_L) + weight(u_R).$$

  b. Prove that, for all internal nodes u in T,
  $$WPL(u) = weight(u) + WPL(u_L) + WPL(u_R).$$

  c. Prove that, for all internal nodes u in T,
  $$WPL(u) = \sum_{v \in T(u)} weight(v).$$

d. Assume that we singly promote a node u in T, where u is the left child of its parent v, to give a new tree T'. Prove that

$$WPL(root(T')) - WPL(root(T)$$
$$= weight(v_R) + frequency(v) - weight(u_L) - frequency(u).$$

10.8: Based on the notions introduced in Exercise 10.7, we propose an adaptive scheme for binary search trees that uses access frequencies. We assume that there are no deletions or insertions; there are only searches. Given n records, we construct a complete binary search tree T of size n such that the frequencies of all internal nodes are 1 and the frequencies of all external nodes are 0. For each query key K, we increment the frequency of K's node u by 1, where u is internal if the search is successful, and is external otherwise. We then singly promote u if it is an internal node and the promotion reduces the $WPL(T)$. We keep weights at only internal nodes, and recompute the frequencies as needed using the relationship

$$frequency(u) = weight(u) - weight(u_L) - weight(u_R),$$

given in Exercise 10.7.

Implement this adaptive heuristic. Compare it with splay trees using the same query sequences.

10.9: Prove, by induction on the height, that every red–black tree of height h can be colored such that there are exactly $\lfloor h/2 \rfloor$ black nodes on each root-to-frontier path and the root node is colored black if and only if h is even.

10.10: Complete the proof from Section 10.2.1 that skinny red–black trees of odd height h have size $3 \cdot 2^{(h-1)/2} - 2$.

10.11: We can generalize red–black trees in the following way. We say that a binary tree is **red-b-black** if it can be colored such that every external node is black and every red node either has at least b black immediate ancestors or is the root. Prove that such trees can be updated in $O(\log n)$ time. Obtain a recurrence equation for the size of skinny red-b-black trees in terms of their heights, and solve it to obtain a bound on the height of red-b-black trees of size n.

10.12: Give a transformation for binary trees that does not, in general, preserve the binary-search condition.

10.13: Solve the following problems for single promotions. The proofs can be found in Culik and Wood (1982).

a. Prove that, for every pair T_1 and T_2 of binary trees of size $n \geq 2$, we can transform T_1 into T_2 with a sequence of single promotions.

b. For all $n \geq 1$ and for every pair T_1 and T_2 of binary trees of size n, define $d_n(T_1,T_2)$ to be the minimum number of single promotions needed to transform T_1 into T_2. Prove that $d_n(T_1,T_2) = 0$ if and only if $T_1 = T_2$, $d_n(T_1,T_2) = d_n(T_2,T_1)$, and $d_n(T_1,T_2) \leq d_n(T_1,T) + d_n(T,T_2)$, for all binary trees T of size n.

c. Prove that, for every pair T_1 and T_2 of binary trees of size $n \geq 2$, $d_n(T_1,T_2) \leq 2n - 2$.

10.14: Given a binary tree T, the **minheight** of a node u in T is the number of internal nodes on a shortest path from u to an external node, and the **maxheight** of u is the number of internal nodes on a longest path from u to an external node. A binary tree is said to be

half-balanced if, for every node u in the tree, $1/2 \leq minheight(T(u))/maxheight(T(u)) \leq 1$. Prove that a binary tree is half-balanced if and only if it is red–black.

10.15: An **AVL** or **height-balanced tree** is a binary tree in which the heights of every pair of sibling subtrees differ by at most 1. Prove, using an approach similar to that for red–black trees (see Section 10.2.1), that AVL trees have logarithmic height. The skinny AVL trees are often called **Fibonacci trees.** Why do you think they are thus named? Design insertion and deletion algorithms for AVL trees that run in logarithmic time.

10.16: Prove that every AVL tree is red–black.

10.17: A **right-sided AVL tree** is a binary tree in which, for every pair of sibling sub-trees, the right sibling is at most 1 higher than the left sibling. Design a logarithmic deletion algorithm for this class of trees. Also design an $O((\log n) \times (\log n))$ -time insertion algorithm.

10.18: Given an empty binary search tree, devise a sequence of m accesses (insertions, deletions, and searches), for any $m > 0$, that requires $\Omega(mn)$ node visits.

10.19: Implement splay search trees and red–black trees. Compare their performance for uniform probability distributions.

10.20: Compare the performance of splay trees with that of search trees in which we only half-splay (splay halfway to the root) on each access.

10.21: Assume that we associate a mass, $m(u) \geq 1$, with each internal node u in a binary tree, and that the total mass $tm(u)$ is the sum of the masses of the nodes in $T(u)$. Let u be a node, in such a binary tree, with two children v and w. Given that $r(w)$ is defined to be $2 \lfloor \log tm(u) \rfloor$, prove that $r(u) \geq r(v)$ and that, if $r(v) = r(w)$, then $r(u) > r(v)$.

10.22: Assume that we associate a mass, $m(u) = 3^{h - N(u)}$, with each internal node u in a binary tree of height h, where $N(u)$ is the number of nodes on the path from the root to u. We also define the total mass $tm(u)$ to be the sum of the masses of the nodes in $T(u)$. Prove that, for all nodes u in the binary tree,

$$3m(u) \geq tm(u).$$

10.23: We have proved, in Section 10.1.1, that the *COST* of the optimal list of n given records, and their key and gap probabilities, is never less than the *NVCOST* of the corresponding optimal binary search tree. The relationship between lists and trees is even closer, however. Let $K_{1,n} = K_1 < \cdots < K_n$ be n keys, where p_i are the key probabilities and q_j are the gap probabilities. Then, for any permutation $I = i(1),...,i(n)$ of $1,...,n$, we can consider $K(I) = K_{i(1)},...,K_{i(n)}$ to be either the arrangement of the keys in a list or the insertion sequence for an empty binary search tree that yields the tree $T(K(I))$. Define a transpose at position j in $K(I)$ as a modification of I that yields I', where $I' = i(1),...,i(j),i(j-1),...,i(n)$. We denote such a transpose by *transpose(I,j)*. Similarly, we define *promote(T(K(I)),j)* to be the tree obtained by promoting the node with key $K_{i(j)}$. In both cases, we assume that $j \neq 1$, since we can neither transpose nor promote when $j = 1$..

  a. Prove that, for $I' = transpose(I,j)$, $T(K(I'))$ is either *promote(T(K(I)),j)* if $K_{i(j-1)}$ is the parent of $K_{i(j)}$ in $T(K(I))$, or is $T(K(I))$, otherwise.

  b. A move-to-front operation on a record at position j in a list can be viewed as $j - 1$ transpositions of the record, and a move-to-root operation of a node at level l in a binary search tree can be viewed as l promotions of the node. Prove, based on the result in part a, that applying move-to-front to a key $K_{i(j)}$ in a list $K(I)$ and then using the resulting sequence as an insertion sequence into an empty binary search tree gives exactly the same tree as we obtain by beginning with $T(K(I))$ and moving $K_{i(j)}$ to the root with single promotions.

10.24: Suggest a representation of multiway search trees for external files. Implement, in Pascal, your representation and the DICTIONARY operations.

10.25: Implement $2,3^+$-trees and the DICTIONARY operations on them. Compare their performance with red–black trees by simulation.

10.26: Suggest a representation for a node in a B^+-tree of order m and, based on this representation, implement B^+-trees and the DICTIONARY operations.

10.27: Set up an experiment to determine, by simulation, the expected height and node visit cost of $2,3^+$-trees. Extend your experiment to determine also the expected number of splits from an insertion. What do your experiments indicate? Do the results correspond to your intuition? If they do not, explain why.

C H A P T E R **11**

Priority Searching

In most discrete-event simulations, current events not only perform some action, but also produce events that are to be invoked later. For example, when we simulate a bank robbery, the event corresponding to the start of the robbery (a note passed to a teller, perhaps) causes many subsequent events: the teller's response; the other robbers' responses; the guard's response; and so on. The simulation must execute the next event—the earliest event that is later than the current one—at each step. If we keep the schedule of events ordered by time—in sorted order—it is easy to pick up the next event. This approach is, however, overkill. We do not need the schedule to be sorted; we need only the next event, at each step of the simulation, which we remove from the schedule, we execute it, and, as a result, we insert new events into the schedule.

Adaptive quadrature is a method for performing numerical integration by subdividing the interval of integration as needed. At each step of the computation, we partition the original interval into subintervals that are not necessarily of equal size. With each interval, we keep its error estimate—an estimate of the difference between the true value of the integral over the interval and the value given by the quadrature method. If all error estimates are less than a given acceptable error, the process terminates. Otherwise, an interval with largest error estimate is replaced by subintervals. Thus, at each step, we need to obtain an interval with maximal error from the list of intervals, delete the interval from the list, and insert new intervals into the list.

In a computer system, processes are usually assigned priorities, which the operating system can use to keep track of the processes. The priorities are usually small positive integers (the smaller the integer, the higher the priority). Clearly, new processes enter the system, currently active processes terminate or become inactive, and the operating system must retrieve, at each invocation, the next process it has to reactivate.

These three examples demonstrate the main subject of this chapter—the PRIORITY QUEUE ADT. We assume that each element or record has an associated priority taken from some totally ordered priority universe. Unlike keys, priorities do not normally identify unique records. Therefore, when we ignore the data associated with the record in a priority queue, we are left with a multiset of priorities, rather than with a set of priorities.

In addition to discussing PRIORITY QUEUE, we consider two-dimensional data for the first time. We introduce the PS QUEUE ADT (PS stands for priority search) that supports the DICTIONARY operations, with respect to the keys of the records, and the PRIORITY QUEUE operations, with respect to their priorities. It has also a new operation, *PriorityRange*, that determines all records that lie within a given key range and are also greater than a given priority. We describe a new data structure, the priority search tree, that we can use to implement PS QUEUE efficiently.

We begin with a formal specification of the PRIORITY QUEUE ADT, in Section 11.1; we then examine some of the representations of PRIORITY QUEUE, in Section 11.2. More specifically, we introduce priority trees, heaps (a space- and time-efficient representation of priority trees), and Fibonacci queues. We return to the topic of Huffman codes as an application of priority queues that are represented as heaps. In Section 11.3, we specify the PS QUEUE ADT and describe a representation based on priority search trees.

11.1 PRIORITY QUEUE SPECIFICATION

Let B denote the *Boolean* values, E denote the set of elements of type *element-type*, P denote the totally ordered priority universe, and $\mathcal{PQ}$ denote the set of all priority queues of elements. We assume that each element in E is associated with a priority from P . A priority queue maintains a set of elements under insertions and deletions, where a deletion removes only an element with the smallest priority.

1. *Empty*: $\rightarrow \mathcal{PQ}$: The function value *Empty* is an empty priority queue.

2. *IsEmpty*: $\mathcal{PQ} \rightarrow \mathcal{B}$: The function value *IsEmpty(P)* is **true** if *P* is an empty priority queue; otherwise, it is **false**.

3. *Min*: $\mathcal{PQ} \rightarrow \mathcal{E}$: The function value *Min(P)* is undefined if *P* is an empty priority queue; otherwise, it is an element in *P* with the smallest priority in *P*.

4. *Insert*: $\mathcal{E} \times \mathcal{PQ} \rightarrow \mathcal{PQ}$: The function value *Insert(e,P)* is a priority queue that consists of all elements in *P* together with *e* (it is $P \cup \{e\}$).

5. *Delete*: $\mathcal{PQ} \rightarrow \mathcal{PQ}$: The function value *Delete(P)* is undefined if *P* is an empty priority queue; otherwise, it is a priority queue that consists of all elements in *P* except for *Min(P)* (it is $P - \{Min(P)\}$).

We often call such a priority queue a **min-priority queue;** a **max-priority queue** is obtained by replacing *Min* with *Max* and "smallest" with "largest." Rather than having the two operations *Min* and *Delete*, we often replace them with a single combined operation:

6. *DeleteMin*: $\mathcal{PQ} \rightarrow \mathcal{E} \times \mathcal{PQ}$: The function value *DeleteMin*(P) is undefined if *P* is an empty priority queue; otherwise, it is an element *e* in *P*, with the smallest priority in *P*, and a priority queue that consists of all elements in *P* except for *e*.

Moreover, we sometimes want to find all records in a min-priority queue that have priorities that are no larger than a given value. This operation is known as a **bounded priority query,** and the name of the corresponding operation is *AtMost*. The corresponding operation for max-priority queues is *AtLeast*.

7. *AtMost*: $\mathcal{P} \times \mathcal{PQ} \rightarrow 2^{\mathcal{E}}$: The function value *AtMost*(p,P) is the set of elements in *P* that have priorities less than or equal to *p*. (It is the empty set if either the priorities of all elements in *P* are greater than *p* or *P* is empty.)

11.2 PRIORITY QUEUE REPRESENTATIONS

The similarity between dictionaries and priority queues is the basis of the first representations that we examine, in Section 11.2.1. We then introduce, in Section 11.2.2, binary priority trees that are similar to binary search trees, except that the ordering is between parents and children, rather than between children. Next, in Section 11.2.3, we provide an efficient implicit representation of priority trees that leads to a much-used structure, the heap; finally, in Section 11.2.4, we introduce the Fibonacci queue, which also allows the priorities of elements in the queue to be reduced efficiently.

11.2.1 DICTIONARY-based Representations

Any one of the representations of DICTIONARY can be adapted for PRIORITY QUEUE. We must modify the representations, however, because of the definition of *Insert* for DICTIONARY—*Insert* adds a new record only if the new record's key is different from the keys in the dictionary. In a priority queue, however, insertion always adds a new record. Fortunately, the modification of the dictionary representations is straightforward. We continue searching during insertion even when we find a record with the same key. We illustrate this approach with two DICTIONARY representations—the sorted linked list and the binary search tree.

Assume that we have priorities 10, 15, 20, 25, 30, 40, and 50. We can represent them in a sorted singly linked list as shown in Figure 11.1(a). If we insert a

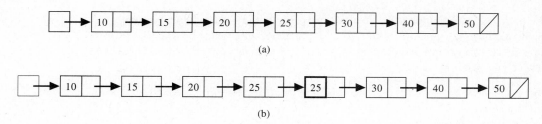

(a)

(b)

Figure 11.1   A sorted singly linked list representation of a priority queue. (a) The initial sorted singly linked list. (b) Insertion of a new record.

new priority—25, say—then we traverse the list until we meet either a priority greater than 25 or the end of the list. Thus, the new priority is inserted before 30 and after 25. (We could traverse the list until we met a priority no less than 25, in which case the new priority would be inserted after 20 and before 25. We have chosen the particular search criterion to ensure fairness—a new record with priority 25 is not removed until all the old records with priority 25 have been removed.) We obtain the list of Figure 11.1(b), where the new priority 25 is outlined with thick lines. We leave to Exercise 11.1 the details of an implementation of priority queues based on this representation.

Given the binary search tree of Fig. 11.2(a), for the example priorities, we again insert 25. In this case, the search criterion is as follows: *Go left if the new record's priority is less than the priority at a node; otherwise, go right.* On reaching an external node, we replace it with an internal node in the usual way. We obtain, therefore, the "binary search tree" of Fig. 11.2(b), where the search path is shown as a dashed line. Observe that the left child of the new internal node corresponds to the gap (25,25); that is, it is empty. Furthermore, the two appearances of the priority 25 are not adjacent in the tree, but they are adjacent in the inorder tra-

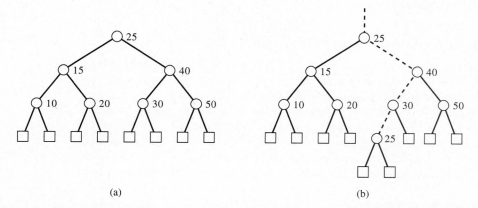

(a)   (b)

Figure 11.2   A binary search tree representation of a priority queue. (a) The initial binary search tree. (b) Insertion of a new record.

versal of the tree and the new record with priority 25 appears after the old record with priority 25.

In a singly linked list, *Min* takes the first record in the list; in a binary search tree, *Min* takes the leftmost record ("Go left *Min*!"). In both cases, because of the insertion strategy, older records are removed before more recent records with the same priority. We have defined a first-in, first-out strategy for records with the same priorities. We leave the details of an implementation to Exercise 11.1. Clearly, red–black trees and splay trees also can be used to represent priority queues.

What are the performances of these representations? For sorted singly linked lists, *Empty*, *IsEmpty*, *Min*, and *Delete* take constant time, but *Insert* takes $O(n)$ time in a priority queue of n records, in the worst and expected cases. For binary search trees, *Empty* and *IsEmpty* take constant time, but *Min*, *Insert*, and *Delete* take $O(n)$ time in a priority queue of n records, in the worst case, and take $O(\log n)$ time, in the expected case. By using red–black search trees, we can obtain logarithmic time, in both the worst and expected cases.

In Sections 11.2.2 and 11.2.3, we develop a representation in which *Min* takes constant time and *Insert* and *Delete* take logarithmic time, in the worst and expected cases.

11.2.2   Priority Trees

Binary search trees carry more information than we require for priority queues— they yield a sorted list with an inorder traversal. Despite this overkill, the underlying structure of a binary tree is a good one—we need only to modify the binary-search condition. As in a sorted singly linked list, we keep a record with smallest priority at the root. Given a binary tree T of $n \geq 0$ internal nodes and n records with priorities, we say that T is a **priority tree** for the records if both of the following conditions hold:

1. Each internal node u of T is associated with a unique record and its priority, which is denoted by **priority(u).**

2. Each internal node u satisfies the **priority condition,**

$$priority(u) \leq priorities(u_L) \cup priorities(u_R),$$

where **priorities(v)** = {$priority(w)$: w is a descendant of v}.

The priority condition implies that the priorities along each root-to-frontier path are in nondecreasing order. In Fig. 11.2(a), we display a priority tree for the priorities 10, 15, 20, 25, 25, 30, 40, and 50; in Fig. 11.2(b), we represent the same priorities with a tree that is not a priority tree. The binary search tree of Fig. 11.2(a) is also not a priority tree.

Given a priority tree, *Min* gives the record associated with the root in constant time; however, the implementation of *Delete* is somewhat more complex than it is for singly linked lists. We do not want to remove the root node, since

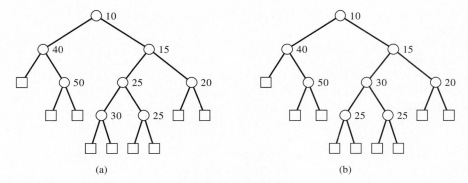

Figure 11.3   Two tree representations of the same priorities. (a) A priority tree.
(b) Not a priority tree.

that gives two priority trees, rather than one. Therefore, we replace the root record
with the record of the root's child that has smaller priority; for the priority tree of
Figure 11.3(a), this priority is 15. Then, we apply the replacement process recursively to the corresponding subtree; in this case, we replace 15 by 20. Finally,
since the node with priority 20 has only external children, we remove it. This
removal yields the tree of Fig. 11.4, which is, once more, a priority tree. We have
bubbled up the replacement values along only one root-to-frontier path. We can
implement *Insert* by inserting the new record at the root and letting it **trickle
down** to reach an appropriate node, where trickling down is similar to bubbling
up, but in the opposite direction. We leave the details of an implementation to
Exercise 11.2. Also, we explore, in Exercise 11.4, the use of red–black trees and
splay trees to obtain efficient implementations of priority trees. We now introduce
an extremely efficient implementation of priority queues based on priority trees.

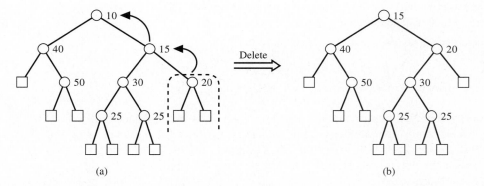

Figure 11.4   The deletion of the record at the root of a priority tree. (a) Removal of
the root record, followed by the bubbling up of the other records.
(b) The final priority tree.

11.2.3 Heaps

Rather than representing priority queues with explicit pointers, as is natural with priority trees, we consider a subclass of priority trees that can be represented implicitly without pointers. Recall from Section 5.1.1 that a *left-complete binary tree* is a binary tree with external nodes on at most two adjacent levels such that the external nodes on the lowest level are leftmost. For each nonnegative integer *n,* there is only one binary tree of size *n* that is left complete; see Section 5.1.1. In Fig. 11.5(a), we display a left-complete priority tree for the example priorities 10, 15, 20, 25, 25, 30, 40, and 50. Observe that the node with priority 50 must be removed when we perform a deletion; otherwise, the resulting tree will not be left complete. Furthermore, the sibling of the node with priority 50, must be replaced by an internal node when we perform an insertion; otherwise, the resulting tree will not be left complete.

We describe how we can ensure that the trees we obtain after an insertion and a deletion are left complete. Consider the insertion of 18 into the priority tree of Fig. 11.5(a). We assume that we maintain a window over the next available exter-

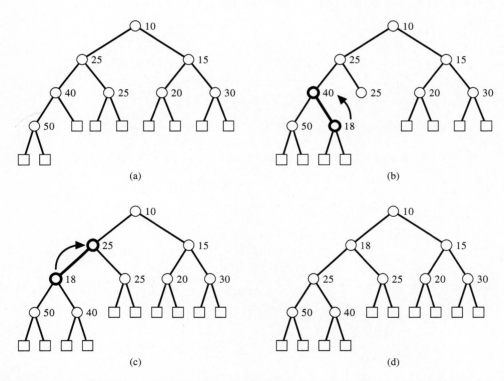

(a)

(b)

(c)

(d)

Figure 11.5   Insertion into a left-complete priority tree. (a) The initial tree. (b) The addition of priority 18 and the first bubble-up step. (c) The second bubble-up step. (d) The final tree.

nal node. We replace the external node in the window by an internal node with associated priority 18; see Fig. 11.5(b). Clearly, the resulting left-complete tree may violate the priority condition. Therefore, we bubble the new record up the tree, exchanging it with its parent's record until the new record reaches the correct position. The bubbling up of 18 needs two exchanges; see Figures 11.5(c) and (d).

Deletion is slightly more complex. Assume that we maintain a window over the rightmost internal node on the lowest level of the tree. We perform a deletion by removing the internal node in the window and replacing the root's priority with its priority. With the priority tree of Figure 11.6(a), we remove the internal node with priority 50 and replace the root priority with 50. This replacement yields the tree of Fig. 11.6(a). Again, in general, the resulting tree may violate the priority condition, although it is guaranteed to be left complete. Observe that, in the example, the resulting tree is not a priority tree. We resolve the priority-condition violation by trickling the new record down the tree, exchanging it with the record of its child with smaller priority, and repeating the exchanges as necessary. The example needs two exchanges; see Figures 11.6(b) and (c).

Although, in principle, we can implement the left-complete priority tree as an explicit tree structure with parent and children pointers, we can implement it

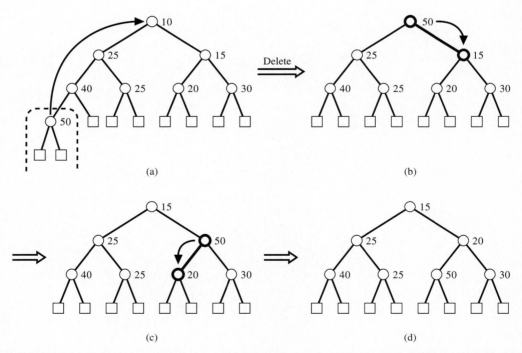

Figure 11.6   Deletion of the root record in a left-complete priority tree. (a) The initial tree. (b) The removal of the record and its replacement. (c) After the first trickle-down step. (d) The final tree after the second trickle-down step.

1	2	3	4	5	6	7	8	9
10	25	15	40	25	20	30	50	

Figure 11.7 The heap representation of the left-complete priority tree of Fig. 11.5(a).

more efficiently without these pointers. We use the level-order representation of a binary tree; see Section 5.5.1. This representation of a left-complete priority tree is called a **heap.** Using this representation, the tree of Fig. 11.5(a) is represented in a block as shown in Fig. 11.7. Because we allow only left-complete trees, there are no gaps in the representation. When there are n records in the tree, the root is always at position 1, the rightmost internal node on the lowest level is always at position n, and the next available external node is at position $n + 1$. Moreover, for a node at position i, its parent is at position $\lfloor i/2 \rfloor$, if $i \neq 1$; its left child is at position $2i$; and its right child is at position $2i + 1$. The pointers are represented implicitly; hence, they do not require any space. Because we have based the heap on a min-priority queue, it is called a **min-heap,** to distinguish it from its companion, the **max-heap.**

Because a heap is based on left-complete binary trees, a heap of size n represents a binary tree of height $\lceil \log(n + 1) \rceil$. Therefore, *Min* takes constant time, *Insert* makes at most $\lceil \log(n + 1) \rceil$ priority comparisons and $\lceil \log(n + 1) \rceil$ exchanges (that is, it takes $O(\log n)$ time), and *Delete* makes at most $2\lceil \log(n + 1) \rceil$ priority comparisons and $\lceil \log(n + 1) \rceil$ exchanges (it takes $O(\log n)$ time). Finally, observe that *AtMost* takes $O(r)$ time, where r is the number of records in the heap that have priorities no greater than the given bound.

A heap is also an attractive data structure, because we can construct a heap for n given records in $O(n)$ time. This attribute of heaps is useful in a number of applications; for example, we use it in *HeapSort* in Chapter 12, and we can use it to obtain an efficient implementation of Huffman's algorithm, as in Exercise 11.5. This time bound is not achievable for red–black *search* trees or, indeed, for any class of search trees, because of the lower bound for the number of comparisons needed to search in a dictionary; see Section 8.4.1. To initialize a heap for n given records, we perform the following two steps. First, we place the n records into positions 1 to n of a block; conceptually, we construct a left-complete tree for the records. Second, we convert the block into a heap—we **heapify** it—by traversing it in reverse level order from frontier to root. We ensure that at each stage of the traversal every node that we have visited is the root of a heap, and, therefore, the subtrees of the node we are visiting currently are both heaps; see Fig. 11.8. Thus, we need to trickle down only the record at the current root node to transform the current subtree into a heap. If the visited node is on level l and the height of the left-complete tree is $h = \lceil \log(n + 1) \rceil$, then the trickle down makes at most $2(h - l - 1)$ comparisons and takes $O(h - l)$ time. On level l, there are 2^l nodes, so level l contributes at most $2^{l+1}(h - l - 1)$ comparisons, or $O(2^l(h - l))$ time, to the overall time of the traversal. Therefore, the sum of these contributions

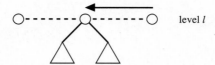

Figure 11.8   A frontier-to-root traversal of a left-complete tree to produce a heap.

gives us the total number of comparisons and the total time taken by heapifying; that is, it gives

$$\sum_{l=0}^{h-2} 2^{l+1}(h-l-1)$$

comparisons. Separating the terms in this summation, we obtain

$$(h-1) \sum_{l=0}^{h-2} 2^{l+1} - 2 \sum_{l=0}^{h-2} l2^{l}$$

comparisons, which gives

$$(h-1)(2^h-1) - (h-2)2^h + 2^h - 4$$

comparisons, using the relationship $S_k = 2S_k - S_k = k \cdot 2^{k+1} - 2^{k+1} + 2$, where

$$S_k = \sum_{l=0}^{k} l2^{l}$$

We simplify the formula, using this relationship, to obtain

$$2^{h+1} - h - 3 = 2n - 1 - \lfloor \log(n+1) \rfloor$$

comparisons when $n = 2^h - 1$. Thus, we need $O(n)$ time to construct a heap for n records. This time bound should be compared with the time needed to construct a binary search tree of minimal height for n keys; see Exercise 11.6.

11.2.4   Fibonacci Queues

Our final representation of priority queues, Fibonacci queues, is based on multi-way priority trees in which nodes do not have a fixed number of children and there can be as few as zero children. The representation is not only interesting, but also useful, because it enables us to implement *Min* and *Insert* in constant time and *Delete* in logarithmic time. Furthermore, it supports a new operation, *Decrease*, that, given a record, decreases that record's priority by a given amount.

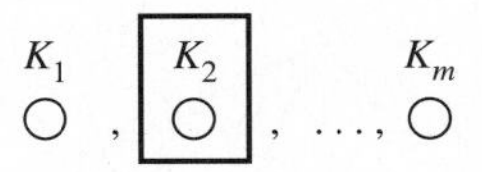

$$K_1 \qquad \boxed{K_2} \qquad K_m$$
$$\bigcirc \quad , \quad \boxed{\bigcirc} \quad , \ \ldots , \ \bigcirc$$

Figure 11.9 The result of a sequence of insertions into an empty Fibonacci queue.

We use this operation for shortest-path algorithms on graphs; see Chapter 13. Although *Decrease* can be implemented with any of the PRIORITY QUEUE representations, it runs in logarithmic time, in the worst case, with, for example, a heap. We can show, however, that *Decrease* runs in constant time, in the amortized case, with Fibonacci queues.

The new data structure is simple and effective. We first ignore the *Decrease* operation and show how the PRIORITY QUEUE operations are implemented.

A **Fibonacci queue** is a forest of trees such that every node in the forest is associated with a unique record; thus, n records are represented by a forest with n nodes. We blur the distinction between internal and external nodes, because an external node (a node with no children) can be given a child, as we shall see. In this setting, we specify that *Empty* produces an empty forest, and that each *Insert* (e,P) adds a priority tree with a single external node to the forest, where the priority of the single node is the priority of e. Thus, after a sequence of insertions, we obtain a forest of single-node priority trees, as shown in Fig. 11.9. To ensure that *Min* is a constant-time operation, we maintain a window over a node with smallest priority. This arrangement implies that, on insertion of a record, that record's priority can be the smallest priority—in which case we move the window. Clearly, *Insert* is still a constant-time operation and, more important, so is *Min*.

We now explain how to implement *Delete* efficiently. We can remove the node in the window in constant time, but we are unable to determine the new placement of the window as efficiently without modifying the structure. We can achieve logarithmic search time, in the amortized case, to place the window, if we merge trees in the forest. Because each tree in the forest is a priority tree, the window is over the root node u of some tree T in the forest. When we remove node u from T, we produce some priority subtrees, which we then add to the forest. After a deletion, we link pairs of trees whose roots have equal degrees until no such pairs exist. (Recall that the degree of a node is the number of its children.) We **link** two trees of equal root degree with root nodes u and v by adding either v as a child of u if $priority(u) \le priority(v)$, see Fig. 11.10(a), or u as a child of v. Note that the degree of the new root is 1 more than the degree of the original root, and observe that a tree with root degree p is perfect and has size 2^p; see Exercise 11.8. Thus, when the priority queue contains n records, each priority tree in the forest has height at most $\lceil \log n \rceil$; after a deletion there can be at most $\lceil \log n \rceil$ trees. These observations imply that *Delete* takes logarithmic time, in the worst case, if we can give an efficient implementation of linking. The key step in the linking process is to find two trees of equal root degree. For this purpose, we can add a **degree index** to the representation that, for each possible root degree, is a list of the trees

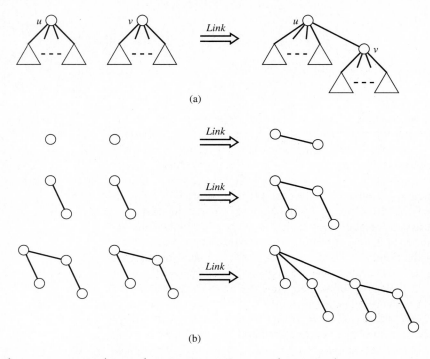

Figure 11.10   Linkage of two priority trees. (a) The general situation.
(b) Linkage of pairs of trees with root degrees 0, 1, and 2.

of that root degree; see Exercise 11.9. In Fig. 11.10(b), we display the result of linking trees with root degrees 0, 1, and 2.

   We are now ready to consider the *Decrease* operation. Assume that we are given a node u, in some tree T in the forest, whose priority is to be decreased. Then we implement *Decrease* in two steps. First, we remove the subtree $T(u)$ rooted at u in T, add it to the forest, and decrease the priority of u. This operation leaves a valid priority tree because u is the root; see Fig. 11.11(a). Also note that the degree of the parent of u in T is decreased by 1. Second, we say that a node x in a tree T is **critical** if after it became the child of its parent as a result of linking it has lost two children as a result of two calls of *Decrease*. Similarly, we say that a node x in a tree T is **subcritical** if after it became the child of its parent as a result of linking it has lost one child as a result of one call of *Decrease*. As soon as a node x in a tree T becomes critical, we remove $T(x)$ from T and add $T(x)$ to the forest. So, after a *Decrease* operation, if the parent of the decreased node becomes critical, then we add its subtree to the forest. This removal can ripple or cascade, since the grandparent of the decreased node can become critical, and so on; see Fig. 11.11(b). Observe that each *Decrease* operation makes at most one node subcritical and removes some critical nodes. Now, k *Decrease* operations can intro-

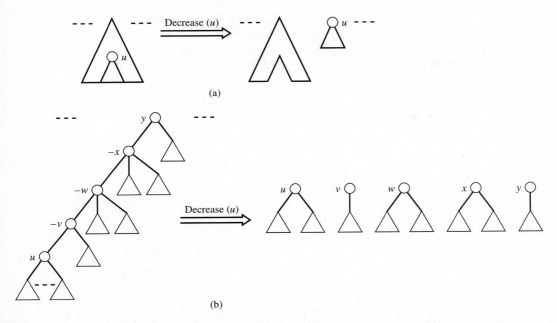

Figure 11.11   The *Decrease* operation. (a) Cutting and reducing. (b) Cutting critical nodes. A minus sign indicates subcritical nodes.

duce at most k subcritical nodes; hence, there can be at most k critical nodes. In other words, *Decrease* takes constant time, in the amortized case.

Although *Decrease* destroys the perfection of the trees in the forest, it does not fragment them too much. Indeed, we show that a node of degree k in a Fibonacci queue has at least F_{k+2} descendants, where F_i is the ith Fibonacci number ($F_0 = 0$, $F_1 = 1$, and $F_{i+2} = F_i + F_{i+1}$).

To establish this result, we consider any node u in a Fibonacci queue. We enumerate u's children in the order they were linked to u, from earliest to latest. Then we show that the ith child v of u has degree at least $i - 2$. Consider when v was linked to u. Just before the linking, u had at least $i - 1$ children (any extra children have been lost after the linking). Thus, because u and v have the same degree, v has at least $i - 1$ children. After the linking, v can lose at most one child without going critical; therefore, v has at least $i - 2$ children.

Now, letting S_k be the smallest possible number of descendants of a node of degree k in a Fibonacci queue, we see that $S_0 = 1$, $S_1 = 2$, and, by definition, $S_{-1} = 1$. Finally, since its child has at least $i - 2$ children,

$$S_k \geq 1 + S_{1-2} + S_{2-2} + \cdots + S_{k-2}.$$

We compare this inequality with the following equality for Fibonacci numbers

$$F_{k+2} = 1 + 1 + F_2 + F_3 + \cdots + F_k,$$

and infer that $S_k \geq F_{k+2}$. We can establish the validity of this inference, which is the source of the name Fibonacci queue, by induction on k.

The implication of this result is that trees in a Fibonacci queue have logarithmic height.

Fact 11.1 *Given an empty Fibonacci queue, a sequence of m PRIORITY QUEUE operations that includes d Delete operations and, possibly some Decrease operations, takes*

$$O(m + d \log n)$$

time, where n is the maximum number of records in the Fibonacci queue at any time during the execution of the sequence.

11.2.5   Performance Reports

We compare only the red–black search tree, heap, and Fibonacci queue representations of PRIORITY QUEUE (see Table 11.1); we do not consider priority trees, since we introduced them only for conceptual purposes. Of the three data structures, heaps and Fibonacci queues are clearly the most efficient representations; see Table 11.2. Heaps are the first choice, because they guarantee logarithmic-time performance, in the worst case, and they have a compact representation without explicit pointers. Fibonacci queues are a close second, because they provide a constant-time implementation of *Insert*, in the worst case, a logarithmic-

Table 11.1   A comparison of the worst-case execution times of the three PRIORITY QUEUE implementations.

	PRIORITY QUEUE implementation		
Operation	Red–black trees	Heaps	Fibonacci queues
Empty	1	1	1
IsEmpty	1	1	1
Min	1	1	1
Insert	$\log n$	$\log n$	1
Delete	$\log n$	$\log n$	$\log n$ [a]
Decrease	$\log n$	$\log n$	1 [b]
AtMost	$r + \log n$	r	?

[1] This time is amortized rather than worst-case time.

[2] This time is amortized rather than worst-case time.

Table 11.2 Performance ratings of the three implementations of PRIORITY QUEUE.

PRIORITY QUEUE implementation	Rating	Comments
Heaps	Excellent	Implicit structure; guaranteed logarithmic worst-case; *AtMost* is linear time in output size.
Fibonacci queues	Very good	Constant time for *Insert*; logarithmic amortized time for *Delete*; uses pointers.
Red–black trees	Satisfactory	

time implementation of *Delete*, in the amortized case, and a constant-time implementation of *Decrease*, in the amortized case. Red–black trees and splay trees, while attaining the same performance as heaps, do so at the expense of using pointers. For this reason, we do not rate them highly.

11.3 PRIORITY SEARCH QUEUES

We introduce a two-dimensional ADT, PS QUEUE, that has both the PRIORITY QUEUE and DICTIONARY operations, and also a new operation, *PriorityRange*. We introduce the need for the new ADT by way of the following problem. We define a **vase** as an axes-parallel rectangle with only three sides—the fourth side is missing and the two parallel sides are semi-infinite in the positive *y* direction; see Fig. 11.3. In addition, we define a **flower** to be a vertical half-line; see Fig. 11.12. The problem that we consider is the **vase query problem:** *Given n flowers in the plane, determine for any query vase V all flowers that lie completely in V.*

We can easily solve this problem in linear time and space by comparing the vase *V* with each flower in turn. If the vase is specified by the coordinates of its corner points and a flower by the coordinates of its endpoint, then we can perform a containment test in constant time. Observe that a flower is contained wholly in a vase if the following two conditions hold simultaneously:

- The *x* coordinate of the flower lies between the *x* coordinates of the vase.
- The *y* coordinate of the flower's endpoint is no smaller than the *y* coordinate of the bottom of the vase.

Clearly, the two conditions can be tested in constant time.

Let a flower *F* be specified by a pair (x^F, y^F) and a vase *V* by a triple (x_L^V, x_R^V, y^V), where *L* denotes leftmost and *R* rightmost. Now, for *F* to be in *V*, we must have

$$x_L^V \leq x^F \leq x_R^V$$

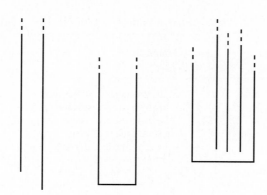

Figure 11.12   Examples of flowers and vases.

and

$$y^V \le y^F.$$

Therefore, to solve the vase query problem, we need to find all flowers that satisfy the *x* inequalities and also the *y* inequality. The *x* inequalities define a range query over the *x* coordinates of the flowers, and the *y* inequality defines a bounded priority query over the *y* coordinates of the flowers. It is possible to solve the range query with a binary search tree and to solve the bounded priority query with a max-priority queue. This method, however, can be extremely inefficient (see Exercise 11.12); we want to report only the flowers that satisfy both queries simultaneously. Therefore, we introduce a new ADT, the PS QUEUE, and a new data structure, the **priority search tree,** to represent the new ADT efficiently.

As we shall see in Section 11.3.2, the priority search tree enables us to solve the vase query problem in $O(r + \log n)$ time, where *r* is the number of reported flowers. The preprocessing time needed to build a priority search tree is $O(n \log n)$.

11.3.1   PS QUEUE Specification

Let B denote the *Boolean* values, E denote the set of elements of type *element-type*, K denote the totally ordered key universe, P denote the totally ordered priority universe, and $\mathcal{PS}$ denote the set of all priority search queues of elements. We assume that each element in E is associated with both a key from K and a priority from P , that each key determines a unique element, but that each priority may be associated with more than one element. A priority search queue maintains a set of elements under insertions and deletions, where a deletion removes either an element with the largest priority or an element with a given key. We omit some of the PRIORITY QUEUE and DICTIONARY operations, to simplify the exposition; you are asked to implement the missing operations in Exercise 11.13.

1. *Empty*: $\rightarrow \mathcal{PS}$: The function value *Empty* is an empty priority search queue.

2. *IsEmpty*: $\mathcal{PS} \rightarrow \mathcal{B}$: The function value *IsEmpty(P)* is **true** if *P* is an empty priority search queue; otherwise, it is **false**.

3. *MaxP*: $\mathcal{PS} \rightarrow \mathcal{E}$: The function value *MaxP(P)* is undefined if *P* is an empty priority search queue; otherwise, it is an element in *P* with the largest priority in *P*.

4. *IsMemberK*: $\mathcal{K} \times \mathcal{PS} \rightarrow \mathcal{B}$: The function value *IsMemberK(K,P)* is **true** if there is an element *e* in *P* with key *K*; otherwise, it is **false**.

5. *Insert*: $\mathcal{E} \times \mathcal{PS} \rightarrow \mathcal{PS}$: The function value *Insert(e,P)* is a priority search queue that consists of all elements in *P* together with *e* (it is $P \cup \{e\}$).

6. *DeleteK*: $\mathcal{K} \times \mathcal{PS} \rightarrow \mathcal{PS}$: The function value *DeleteK(K,P)* is a priority search queue that consists of all elements in *P* except for *e*, where *e* has key *K*. If there is no element in *P* with key *K*, then *P* is unchanged.

7. *DeleteP*: $\mathcal{PS} \rightarrow \mathcal{PS}$: The function value *DeleteP(P)* is undefined if *P* is an empty priority search queue; otherwise, it is a priority search queue that consists of all elements in *P* except for *MaxP(P)* (it is $P - \{MaxP(P)\}$).

8. *PriorityRange*: $\mathcal{K} \times \mathcal{K} \times \mathcal{P} \times \mathcal{PS} \rightarrow 2^{\mathcal{E}}$: The function value *PriorityRange* (K_1, K_2, p, P) is the set of all elements *e* in *P* whose keys lie between K_1 and K_2 and whose priorities are at least *p*.

11.3.2 Priority Search Trees

Priority search trees combine the features of external binary search trees and priority trees; we shall base their definition on max-priority trees. To define them, we use the following ordered pairs of keys and priorities as a running example:

$$(Mon,10),(Tues,5),(Wed,2),(Thur,5), (Fri,6),(Sat,1),(Sun,3),(Work,8).$$

Given a key–priority pair *p,* we use *key(p)* and *priority(p)* to denote its two components; we also write $p = (key(p), priority(p))$. First, we reconsider external binary search trees; see Section 8.5.1. Recall that we associate the keys (and the records containing them) with the external nodes of a binary tree, and we associate separating keys with the internal nodes; we display an external binary search tree for the example key–priority pairs in Fig. 11.13(a). It is important to realize that we associate records with *only external nodes* in this model of external search trees, because we now relax this requirement.

We now think of the key values at external nodes as **validation keys** (the keys at external nodes are exactly those keys that appear in the records in the tree); we no longer require that their associated records be held there. Instead, we allow a record to be associated with any node, but only one, on the search path for

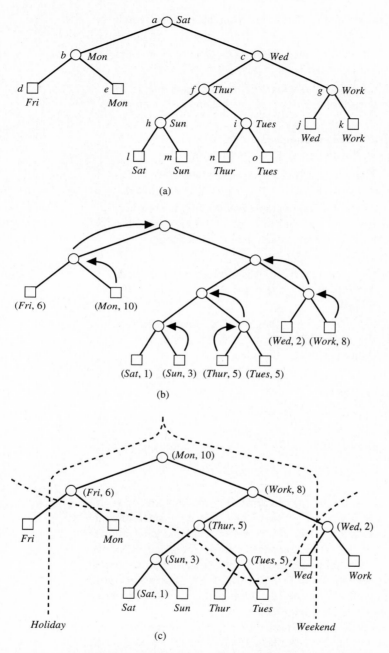

Figure 11.13 Priority search trees. (a) An external binary search tree for the days of the week, ordered lexicographically. (b) Playing of the tournament. (c) The derived priority search tree; we have suppressed the separating keys.

its validation key. For example, the pair (*Thur*,5) can be placed at any one of the nodes *a, c, f, i,* and *n* in the tree of Fig. 11.13(a), since these nodes are on the search path for *Thur*. This separation of the placement of a record from the placement of its key—the validation key—is crucial for the next step. First note, however, that we cannot associate all the records with internal nodes, since there are too few internal nodes.

Because a record can be at any unoccupied node on its search path, it is now straightforward to place the records in max-priority order. We can think of the records starting at the external nodes (see Fig. 11.3b) and playing a tournament, but only the records of sibling nodes play. The winning record in each match is either the one with higher priority or the leftmost one. The winners move up one level, the winners of the new matches are moved up one level, and so on. With the initial tree in Fig. 11.13(b), (*Mon*,10) beats (*Fri*,6), (*Sun*,3) beats (*Sat*,1), (*Thur*,5) beats (*Tues*,5), and, finally, (*Work*,8) beats (*Wed*,2). Thus (*Mon*,10), (*Sun*,3), (*Thur*,5), and (*Work*,8) are promoted. The results of these matches are indicated in Fig. 11.3(b), as are the next three rounds. The tree that results from these promotions has one unfortunate feature: Records may not appear at consecutive nodes on some search paths. For example, the search path to *Wed* has (*Mon*,10), (*Work*,8), and (*Wed*,2) at the first (or root), second, and fourth nodes, respectively. These gaps cause searching problems, so we add a further requirement: *Records must occur at consecutive nodes on their search paths—there must be no gaps—and they must be in nonincreasing priority order.* Thus, we modify the tree obtained from Fig. 11.13(b) by bubbling up records to fill the gaps, while preserving the max-priority order; see Fig. 11.13(c). Observe that the tree is both a search tree, for the keys, and a max-priority tree, for the priorities.

Membership testing is straightforward—we use the query key to determine the search path and to check the record at each node on the path. We terminate the search unsuccessfully when we reach either a node without an associated record or an external node that has a record with a different key. For example, we search for *Work* in the priority search tree of Fig. 11.13(c) by checking the pairs on the right spine. At the second node, we find (*Work*,8). Observe that a range query can be implemented in the same way that it is implemented for binary search trees; see Section 8.5.7.

We can also treat the priority search tree as a max-priority tree—a record with highest priority is found at the root and the records on each root-to-frontier path appear in nonincreasing order. Moreover, we can implement the *AtLeast* operation easily. We carry out a preorder traversal of the priority search tree in which the children of a node are visited only if the parent's priority is at least the given bound.

Finally, the power of the priority search tree is revealed when we combine range searching with bounded priority searching to implement the *PriorityRange* operation. For example, suppose we want to find all records in the tree of Fig. 11.13(c) with keys in the range *Holiday* to *Weekend* and with priorities at least 5. The range search gives the two paths shown with dashed lines in Fig. 11.13(c). We must check the records on the path explicitly for membership, but all records in the subtrees within the two paths have their keys in the range, so we do not have to check them. Also, we must check explicitly the priorities of the records on the two paths, but we need to perform only a bounded priority search in the subtrees within the two paths. Thus, we report (*Fri*,6), (*Mon*,10), (*Thur*,5), (*Tue*,5), and (*Work*,8); see Fig. 11.13(c). We ask you to show how the priority search tree can be used to solve the vase query problem; see Exercise 11.14.

In summary, we have introduced the priority search tree as an efficient implementation of PS QUEUE. In Section 11.3.3, we show that priority search trees can be constructed incrementally by insertions made in a similar manner to those in binary search trees. We also show that the two kinds of deletions can be implemented efficiently as well. We leave you to implement the other DICTION-ARY operations that we have not discussed here (see Exercise 11.13); they can also be implemented efficiently. Finally, we demonstrate that single promotions *almost* preserve the priority-search property, which leads to logarithmic-time updating algorithms for priority search trees based on red–black trees. Because red–black trees have logarithmic height, we can implement the PS QUEUE operations so that *PriorityRange* takes $O(r + \log n)$ time, where r is the number of reported answers and n is size of the tree.

11.3.3   Update of a Priority Search Tree

We touch on three topics: insertion, deletion, and promotion. First, we show that we can insert records into and delete records from a priority search tree as efficiently as we can for binary search trees. Second, we show that single promotions take $O(h)$ time, where h is the height of the given tree. (Compare this bound with the constant-time bound for promotions in binary search trees.) The latter result implies that priority search trees, based on red–black trees, can be updated in logarithmic time. Therefore, the vase problem can be solved with $O(n \log n)$ time and $O(n)$ space for preprocessing with n records, and each vase query takes $O(r + \log n)$ time, where r is the number of reported flowers.

We begin with insertion. Given the priority search tree of Fig. 11.13(c), we insert the record (*Semester*,10). By definition, we must insert a new external node with validation key *Semester* and a new internal node with some separating key. We insert the new record in two phases. First, we search for *Semester* in the tree. Since *Semester* < *Sun*, the search ends at the external node associated with *Sat*. We replace the external node with a height-1 subtree as shown in Fig. 11.14(a) for the general case, and as shown in Fig. 11.14(b) for (*Semester*,10). The new internal node is associated with the separating key *Semester,* and the new external node is associated with the validation key *Semester*. When the external node that we replace is associated with a record, we now associate that record with the new internal node; see Fig. 11.14(a). We have completed the first phase of insertion— the external binary-search-tree phase.

Second, we retrace the search path until we meet either a record with priority higher than that of the inserted record or the root. These two cases for the pair

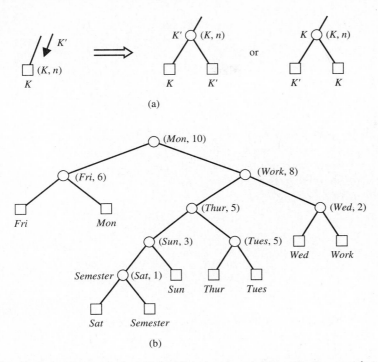

Figure 11.14   Insertion of a new validating key into a priority search tree. (a) The general case. (b) The case of *Semester* in the tree of Fig. 11.13(c).

(K',p') are shown in Fig. 11.15. In both cases, we replace (K,p) with (K',p') and trickle (K,p) down the tree. The difference between trickling a record down a priority search tree and trickling a record down a priority tree is that we must stay on the search path of the trickled record. So the displaced record (K,p) goes to the left or right child, depending on the key K and the separating key at the given node; see Fig. 11.16. In our example, $(K,p) = (Work,8)$, so we obtain the final tree of Fig. 11.17. Clearly, insertion takes $O(h)$ time, in the worst case, in a tree of height h.

There are two deletion operations: *DeleteP*, to delete a record with largest priority, and *DeleteK*, to delete a record with a given key. We develop an efficient implementation of *DeleteK*, since *DeleteP* can be implemented in a similar manner to the implementation of *Delete* for heaps and priority trees. Like insertion, deletion has two phases: A search-tree phase and a priority-tree phase. Because deletion of a record implies that we must remove an external node and an internal node, we must take care that we do not accidentally remove a record other than the one to be deleted. To avoid this difficulty, we carry out the priority-tree phase first. We search for the given key K'; when we find its record, we remove that

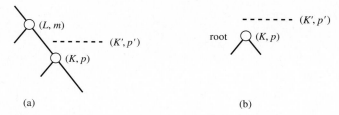

(a)   (b)

Figure 11.15   Finding the correct position for a new record on that record's search path. (a) The search meets a record with lower priority whose parent record has a priority no less than the search priority. (b) The search meets the root and the root's priority is less than the search priority.

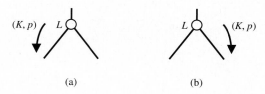

(a)   (b)

Figure 11.16   Trickle down in a priority search tree: the two cases. (a) $K < L$. (b) $K \geq L$

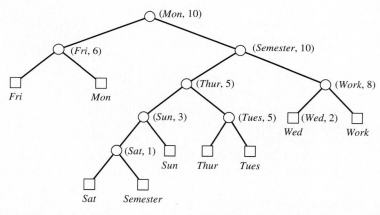

Figure 11.17   The final priority search tree after the insertion of (*Semester*,10) into the tree of Fig. 11.13(c).

record and bubble up another record to fill the gap. Because bubbling up moves records up the tree, it is the standard bubble-up procedure for priority trees (records remain on their search paths). Note that, if the deleted record is associated with an external node or if there are no other records in the subtree of its node, there is no need to bubble up.

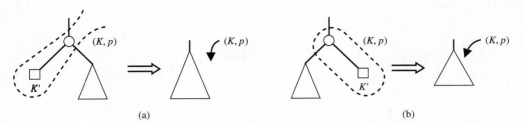

(a)   (b)

Figure 11.18   The removal of an external node in a priority search tree: the two cases.

Second, we delete the validation key K' of the deleted record. When we find the external node associated with K', we remove both it and its parent, and we connect its grandparent to its sibling; see Fig. 11.18. In addition, if the parent is associated with a record with key–priority pair (K,p), we trickle (K,p) down the sibling subtree. There is space for (K,p) in the sibling subtree, since the external node associated with K is in it. Thus, deletion takes $O(h)$ time also.

Finally, we examine promotions. Recall that the two single promotions are defined as shown in Fig. 11.19. Consider the promotion of a node v in a priority search tree; see Fig. 11.19. The promotion preserves the underlying external search-tree condition, because the keys and separators in subtree 1 are no greater than the separator at v, the keys and separators in subtree 2 are greater than the separator at v and no greater than the separator at u, and the keys and separators in subtree 3 are greater than the separator at u (and at v). The priority-search condition is, however, not necessarily preserved. All records in subtrees 1, 2, and 3 have priorities no greater than q, and all records in subtrees 1 and 2 have priorities no greater than p. Therefore, we move (L,q) to node v after promotion, and (K,p) to node u after promotion; see Fig. 11.19. Because $p \leq q$, nodes u and v and subtrees 1 and 2 satisfy the priority condition after the promotion. Subtree 3 may not satisfy the priority condition, but we can easily resolve this difficulty: We trickle (K,p) down subtree 3. The trickle down takes time proportional to the height of subtree 3; that is, it takes $O(h)$ time, where h is the height of the priority search tree.

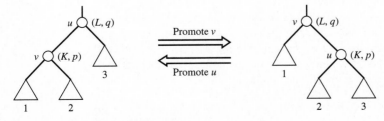

Figure 11.19   The two single promotions in a binary tree.

Table 11.3   The worst-case execution times of the priority-search-tree implementation of PS QUEUE based on red–black trees.

	PS QUEUE implementation
Operation	Priority search trees
Empty	1
IsEmpty	1
MaxP	1
IsMemberK	$\log n$
Insert	$\log n$
DeleteK	$\log n$
DeleteP	$\log n$
PriorityRange	$r + \log n$

Although promotion is no longer a constant-time operation, it still enables us to maintain priority search trees, based on red–black trees, in logarithmic time for each insertion and deletion. We leave the details to Exercise 11.15.

11.3.4   Performance Reports

We have given one representation of PS QUEUE, the priority search tree, that performs extremely well when it is based on red–black trees; see Table 11.3. Observe that it supports *IsMemberK* in logarithmic time.

11.4   SUMMARY

We introduced the PRIORITY QUEUE ADT, which provides the operations of *Empty*, *IsEmpty*, *Insert*, *Delete*, and *Min* for sets of records with respect to their priorities. The three representations that we discussed are the min-priority tree, a tree with the priorities arranged in nondecreasing order along each root-to-frontier path; the heap, an implicit representation of a priority tree that uses only constant space beyond that needed for the priorities (it supports the updating operations in logarithmic time); and the Fibonacci queue, which takes constant time, in the worst case, for all operations apart from *Delete*, which takes amortized logarithmic time, and *Decrease*, which takes amortized constant time. The PRIORITY QUEUE is an appropriate ADT whenever we do not require the records to be sorted in advance, but we need to insert and delete records and to access them in sorted order.

We also introduced the PS QUEUE ADT, which has both the DICTIONARY and PRIORITY QUEUE operations, and the additional operation *PriorityRange*.

We described one efficient representation of PS QUEUE, the priority search tree, which combines priority trees and external binary search trees.

11.5 HISTORY

The heap was introduced by Williams (Williams and associates, 1964) within a sorting algorithm he called *HeapSort*. The efficient construction of a heap from n given records was developed by Floyd (1964). The Fibonacci queue was introduced by Fredman and Tarjan (1987) as a modification of the binomial queue of Vuillemin (1980). Jones (1986) performed a simulational analysis of various PRIORITY QUEUE implementations.

The priority search tree was developed by McCreight (1985) as a byproduct of an attempt to obtain a data structure that would be as efficient as the red–black tree, but for axes-parallel rectangles rather than for one-dimensional points.

EXERCISES

11.1: Implement the singly linked-list and binary-search-tree representations of PRIORITY QUEUE. Compare them using simulation.

11.2: Complete the design of insertion into and deletion from a priority tree. Implement your design. Compare it, using simulation, with the two methods that you implemented in Exercise 11.1.

11.3: Design an implementation of PRIORITY QUEUE based on an external priority tree.

11.4: Implement the heap, the red–black priority tree, and the splay priority tree. Compare them, as representations of priority queues, using simulation.

11.5: Design a new implementation of Huffman's algorithm (see Section 6.1.5) that uses heaps to represent the forest of code trees. What is the worst-case performance of your new algorithm?

11.6: Given n keys from a totally ordered key universe, design a fast algorithm that constructs a minimal-height binary search tree for them. If the n keys are in sorted order, how much time is needed by your algorithm, in the worst case? If the n keys are not in sorted order, how much time is needed in the worst case?

11.7: The algorithm to convert a left-complete tree with records at its nodes into a heap (see Section 11.2.3) can be modified to convert any binary tree of records into a priority tree. Design and implement such an algorithm. Analyze your algorithm's worst-case performance. Given n records with priorities, under what restrictions on the height of a tree does your algorithm run in $O(n)$ time?

11.8: Prove that a priority tree with root degree p in a Fibonacci queue, without the *Decrease* operation, has size 2^p.

11.9: When you link two trees of equal root degree in a Fibonacci queue, the resulting tree has root degree 1 greater than before. Hence, it can be linked with another tree of the same root degree, if one exists. Suggest a method to provide fast access to trees of the same root degree that does not effect the efficiency of the Fibonacci queue.

11.10:   Define a new ADT, MMP QUEUE, that includes the PRIORITY QUEUE operations *Empty*, *IsEmpty*, and *Insert*, both operations *Min* and *Max*, and two deletion operations *MinDelete* and *MaxDelete* that delete only records with smallest and largest priorities. We can represent MMP QUEUE with priority trees in which the priority ordering alternates level by level; thus, levels 0,2,4,..., are min levels and 1,3,5,..., are max levels. The priority of a node in a min level (max level) is the smallest (largest) in its subtree. We call such a tree, an **mm-priority tree.**

> **a.**   Implement the MMP QUEUE operations with an **mm-heap** (a heap in which the priority ordering alternates level by level), such that they run in $O(\log n)$ time, when the heap has size n.
>
> **b.**   Implement an mm-heapify algorithm that, given n records, produces an mm-heap in $O(n)$ time.

11.11:   Another approach to representing MMP QUEUE (see Exercise 11.10) is to associate a pair of records with each node in a priority tree. The pair of records at each node are the records with smallest and largest priorities in the node's subtree. An **interval priority tree,** as it is called, has size $\lceil n/2 \rceil$ for n records. Thus at most one node is associated with one record; for consistency, we assume its priority is repeated to give an interval with one priority.

> **a.**   Prove that the intervals along each root-to-frontier path are nested.
>
> **b.**   Implement the MMP QUEUE operations with an interval heap (the heap equivalent of the interval priority tree), so that they run in $O(\log n)$ time, when the heap has size n.
>
> **c.**   Implement an interval-heapify algorithm that, given n records, produces an interval heap in $O(n)$ time.

11.12:   We have suggested, in Section 11.3.2, that we can solve a priority range query by finding all values that satisfy the underlying *Range* query, finding all values that satisfy the underlying *AtLeast* query, and reporting those values that are in both sets.

Explain, with examples, why this approach provides an inefficient implementation of *PriorityRange.*

11.13:   Implement, with the priority search tree, the PRIORITY QUEUE and DICTIONARY operations that are not given in the specification of PS QUEUE (Section 11.3.1).

11.14:   Demonstrate how the vase query problem (Section 11.3.1) can be solved with the priority search tree. What is the worst-case time bound, in terms of both the input and output sizes?

11.15:   Implement priority search trees using red–black trees.

11.16:   Assume that you are given n vases in the plane, and you need to answer queries of the following form: Given a query vase V, find all vases that it intersects. Sketch an efficient solution to this problem, and derive a worst-case time bound in terms of the input and output sizes.

C H A P T E R **12**

Sorting

We often preprocess data by sorting them, because we can process the sorted data more easily and, usually, more efficiently. Searching for a specific German word in an English–German dictionary with only English-to-German translations is an almost impossible task, whereas searching for an English word in the same dictionary is easy. Similarly, trying to find the name and address corresponding to a given telephone number in a standard telephone directory is, once again, almost impossible, whereas trying to find a number for someone whose name and address we know is easy. In both examples, sorting not only makes a difference—it makes a *substantial* difference. Let us examine a few less obvious examples.

Under UNIX, there is a spelling checker called `spell`; it can operate in both batch mode and individual mode. In individual mode, we give it one word and within 4 seconds it returns an answer. The response time is fast enough. If we want to check the spelling in a 5000-word document (about 10 typeset pages), however, then this method requires

$$5000 \times 4 \text{ seconds} \cong 3 \text{ hours},$$

which is much too slow. Therefore, we choose batch mode, in which the text file is first transformed into a file containing one word on each line. This file is then sorted, duplicates are removed, and the resulting file is then processed by `spell`. This approach takes $\cong 30$ seconds, rather than 3 hours. Sorting plays an important role in obtaining this improvement in performance, although there are other aspects, too.

A second example concerns the initial loading of a B^+-tree (see Section 10.4) when we are given an initial file of n records. We can load a B^+-tree in two different ways. The first method is to begin with an empty B^+-tree and to perform an insertion repeatedly. Each *Insert* operation makes at least one disk access to find

425

the block where the insertion should be made. The disk accesses are independent of one another, however, so they each take

$$\text{average seek time } + \text{ average rotational latency time}$$
$$+ \text{ block transfer time,}$$

in the expected case. (We are ignoring the rewriting of the block after insertion has taken place.) So the total time for the insertion of n records is at least

$$n \times (\text{ast} + \text{arlt} + \text{btt}) \text{ units.}$$

If we first sort the file, however, by the index key, then we can simultaneously build an empty B^+-tree with $\lceil n/b \rceil$ external nodes, where b is the bucket size (the number of records an external node can hold), and fill it using an inorder traversal. With this method, each node is written once; in particular, all records that belong to each external node are available at the same time, so the total time to load the B^+-tree is

$$\text{ast} + \text{arlt} + \lceil n/b \rceil \times \text{btt units.}$$

Because we build the B^+-tree on the fly and the records arrive in sorted order, blocks can be allocated sequentially on the disk; thus, seek time and rotational latency time play a role only when we begin the loading process. Since $ast \gg \text{btt}$, the sequential load time is substantially shorter than the insertion load time. For example, letting $n = 1,000,000$, ast $= 20$ milliseconds, arlt $= 10$ milliseconds, btt $= 1$ millisecond, and $b = 10$, we obtain

$$31,000,000/1000 = 31,000 \text{ seconds}$$
$$\cong 8.6 \text{ hours}$$

for insertion loading, and

$$(30 + 1,000,000/10)/1000 \cong 100 \text{ seconds}$$
$$\cong 2 \text{ minutes}$$

for sequential loading.

We trust that you are convinced that sorting is an important operation that can save considerable time in practical situations. In this chapter, we consider how to sort internally, how well we can expect our chosen methods to perform, and how we can sort externally. Sorting has been the subject of intense study since the advent of computers (even though it predates computers); we touch only the surface of the sorting problem here. We also introduce the notions of presortedness and of nearly sorted files, and discuss how we can take advantage of nearly sorted files to sort them much faster than the normal sorting methods predict.

But let us begin by defining the sorting problem more precisely. We assume that we are given a totally ordered universe K of keys, and that we are dealing with files or sequences of records in which each record has a key from K. Usually we do not require records to be uniquely identified by their keys. When we are given a sequence $R = R_1,...,R_n$ of n records such that the corresponding sequence $K = K_1,...,K_n$ of their keys satisfies the relation

$$K_1 \leq K_2 \leq \cdots \leq K_n,$$

we say that R is **sorted** or in **ascending sorted order.** Note that when two records have the same key, we have more than one sorted order; however, when the keys of the given records are distinct, the sorted order is unique. In general, a sequence R is not in sorted order and we want to rearrange the records into sorted order. The **sorting problem** is this: *Construct an algorithm that for every sequence R of records computes their sorted order with respect to their keys K.* We call such an algorithm a **sorting algorithm.** Mathematically we want to discover a permutation $i : 1..n \rightarrow 1..n$ such that

$$K_{i(1)} \leq K_{i(2)} \leq \cdots \leq K_{i(n)}.$$

In this framework, we say that a permutation i is **stable** with respect to the sequence R of records if

$$K_{i(1)} \leq K_{i(2)} \leq \cdots \leq K_{i(n)},$$

and whenever $K_j = K_l$, $1 \leq j < l \leq n$, we have $i(j) < i(l)$. A stable permutation for R preserves the original ordering of the records with the same key. We say that a sorting algorithm is **stable** when it preserves the original order of multiple appearances of keys, for every given sequence of records.

Given that we have specified, in previous chapters, that keys identify records uniquely, why do we relax this condition now? Consider the use of automatic banking machines (ABMs). Each time you use such a machine to get cash, to deposit a check, or to transfer money from one account to another, you carry out a transaction that consists of the sequence of actions you initiate from the insertion to the removal of your bank card. You and your accounts are uniquely identified by some key; however, you may perform many transactions on the same day. Some bank accounts are updated only once each day; at the end of the day the day's transactions for each account are applied to that account. Clearly, the transactions should be applied to each account in chronological order. Thus if the file of all transactions is sorted by the account keys, to simplify account processing, then the transactions for each account will be adjacent. Furthermore, they should appear in chronological order; that is, the sorting method should be stable.

12.1 COMPARISON-BASED SORTING

In comparison-based sorting methods, we determine the relative order of two records, according to the specified key universe, by comparing only their keys. A **key comparison** is considered to be an atomic operation, and the keys are also considered to be atomic. In Section 12.3, we consider sorting methods that are not comparison-based; instead, they use address computations.

The simplest and best known comparison-based sorting methods are *Bubble-Sort* (because it is one of the first methods taught) as well as *SelectionSort* and *InsertionSort* (because they are the two methods used to sort a hand of playing cards). We consider variations of these basic approaches from the overarching perspective of splitting and joining.

12.1.1 Bubble Sorting

We begin by presenting **bubble sorting** from a new perspective. For simplicity, we assume that the keys are the natural numbers together with their natural ordering $\leq$. Also, we assume that records consist only of keys and that the records are stored in contiguous locations of a block. We use the example block A (shown in Fig. 12.1) throughout. The central idea of *BubbleSort* is to bubble a record with the maximum key to the top of the block. We have used bubbling in Section 11.2.3 to restructure a heap after an insertion; it is exactly the same operation here. We do the bubbling by comparing adjacent records in an overlapping manner, and, whenever two adjacent records are in the wrong order, we transpose them. With the example sequence, we execute the following:

```
{Bubbling the maximum key.}
    for i:= 1 to 7 do
    begin if A[i] > A[i + 1]
        then begin {Transpose the records.}
            temp:= A[i];
            A[i]:= A[i + 1];
            A[i + 1]:= temp
        end{then};
        {Take snapshot of A.}
    end;
```

The bubbling process produces the intermediate snapshots of A shown in Fig. 12.2; we indicate the overlapping pairs of comparisons. The snapshots are taken

	1	2	3	4	5	6	7	8
A	17	8	23	1	12	7	5	1

Figure 12.1 The example block A of eight records.

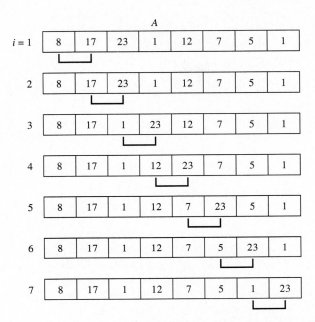

Figure 12.2 Consecutive snapshots of the bubbling process on the block A.

immediately after we execute the loop body, as indicated in the program segment. In general, we bubble records in subblock $A[lower]$, ..., $A[upper]$. The generalization of the program segment to obtain a procedure $Bubble(A,lower,upper)$ is straightforward, so we leave it to Exercise 12.1. $Bubble$ is not, however, without interest; it can be modified to return also an indication that at least one transposition has taken place. For when $Bubble$ does not perform any transpositions, the block is already sorted; see Exercise 12.2.

Given $Bubble$, we can define the procedure $BubbleSort$ given in Program 12.1. The idea is again straightforward; we repeatedly call $Bubble$ on shorter and shorter subblocks. Since each call of $Bubble$ places a record with a largest key in the current top position, this property ensures that we do indeed sort the file. Usually, $BubbleSort$ is written iteratively; we have written it recursively to make explicit the recursive structure of bubble sorting shown in Fig. 12.3. We **split** the original sequence A into two contiguous parts $A[lower..upper-1]$ and $A[upper]$. We sort both parts—trivial for $A[upper]$ —and then **join** the sorted parts again. Joining is trivial in bubble sorting, but splitting is more difficult. We shall see that most comparison-based sorting algorithms have a split–join structure. The specific methods of splitting and joining that we choose provide us with different comparison-based sorting algorithms. In general, we have **hard-split, easy-join** and **easy-split, hard-join** sorting algorithms.

We have spent time on bubble sorting, because the method serves to introduce most aspects of sorting methods and, in particular, of comparison-based

```
procedure BubbleSort(var A: ourarray; lower,upper: integer);
{Bubble sort the records A[lower],...,A[upper].}

begin
    if lower = upper
    then {The records are sorted—do nothing.}
    else begin
        Bubble(A,lower,upper);
        BubbleSort(A,lower,upper - 1)
    end
end;
```

Program 12.1   A Pascal implementation of *BubbleSort*.

sorting methods. We have seen the use of key comparisons, the general structure of sorting methods, and the use of transpositions (the exchanging of adjacent records). Bubble sorting is also, however, a stable sorting algorithm. In the worked example of bubble sorting, key 1 appears twice, but the first appearance of 1 never moves beyond the second appearance of 1; their original order is preserved. We leave you to prove that *BubbleSort* is stable; see Exercise 12.3.

Finally, how badly and how well does *BubbleSort* perform? As described, it is oblivious to the properties of the given sequence, so it always makes

$$upper - lower$$

calls of *Bubble*. Similarly, *Bubble* (A,l,u) performs $(u - l)$ key comparisons and at most $(u - l)$ transpositions. Therefore, when A contains n records, *BubbleSort* takes

$$\sum_{i=1}^{n-1} i$$

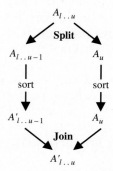

Figure 12.3   The recursive structure of *BubbleSort* in terms of split and join.

key comparisons and at most this number of transpositions; that is, it takes $n(n - 1)/2$ key comparisons and transpositions. Because *BubbleSort* is oblivious to the data, $n(n - 1)/2$ comparisons is also the expected case. Usually we expect *Bubble* to tell us whether the given block is sorted, in which case, *BubbleSort* can terminate immediately. This extension is left to Exercise 12.2; it has no effect on the worst-case performance of *BubbleSort*, but it improves the expected-case performance somewhat. For example, when the records in a sequence are close to their sorted positions, we say that the sequence is **nearly sorted** (a topic to which we return in Section 12.4). If a sequence is nearly sorted, in this sense, then *BubbleSort* performs surprisingly well.

Fact 12.1 *Given a sequence of n records, BubbleSort takes $O(n^2)$ time in both the worst and expected cases. Moreover, it is a stable sorting method.*

12.1.2 Selection Sorting—Hard Split

Bubble sorting uses a maximal key to split a given sequence into two subsequences; it is an example of a **hard-split, easy-join sorting algorithm** in which we *select* the next record, in sorted order, at each step. Here, we explore some other examples of this approach. Normally, splitting by halving (divide and conquer) is standard. If we want to obtain an easy join, however, then the two halves should satisfy the following condition: *All keys in the left half should be no larger than the keys in the right half.* One way to ensure that this property holds is to use the median record to split the keys. Unfortunately, computing the median is a nontrivial task that is best avoided, even though it can be done in linear time, in the worst case. Instead we approximate the median by using the first record of the sequence. This estimation gives us a naive version of *QuickSort*; see Fig. 12.4 for the overall scheme. Given an estimation of the median, *QuickSort* partitions the records into a left part (the records with keys less than the key of the estimated median), a right part (the records with keys greater than the key of the estimated median), and the middle part (the records with keys equal to the key of the esti-

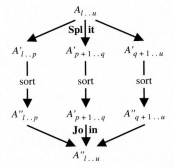

Figure 12.4 The recursive structure of *QuickSort* in terms of split and join.

mated median). Clearly, the records with keys equal to the key of the median record are already in their final sorted positions; there is no need to reconsider them. The left and right parts are then sorted recursively by the same method.

Let us execute *QuickSort* with the example block of eight records. To execute *QuickSort*, we need to decide on a partitioning algorithm. We prefer a partitioning algorithm that operates **in place;** that is it uses only constant additional space. Without this restriction, partitioning is easy; we simply copy the records into a new block. In-place partitioning is, however, more complex. We estimate the median by designating the first record the "median," which we denote by M. We now scan the remaining records from the left and the right simultaneously. The left scan stops when it meets a record with key N that is greater than M, and the right scan stops when it meets a record with a key L that is not greater than M. We exchange the records with keys L and M, and we continue the scans with the next records; see Fig. 12.5(a). We do not have to move records at the right as long as their keys are greater than M's key. Similarly, we do not have to move records at the left as long as their keys are less than M's key. When the scans cross, partitioning is complete. Note that we test for completion *after* the records are exchanged; so we have to exchange the records with keys L and N once again, after completion. When the partitioning is completed, we exchange the record in the first position (with key M) with the record at the completion position of the right scan (with key L); see Fig. 12.5(b). If the left scan does not meet a record

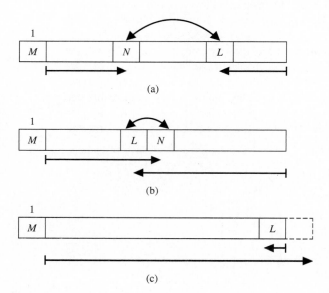

Figure 12.5   Partitioning in *QuickSort*. (a) Two records with keys L and N, with $L \le M < N$ and L beyond N. (b) Normal termination; L and N are adjacent, with L before N. (c) Abnormal termination, with the left scan beyond the block.

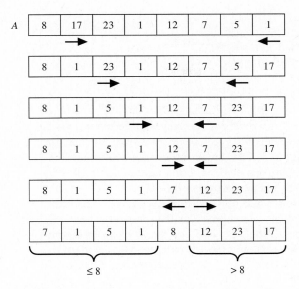

Figure 12.6 Consecutive snapshots of the partioning process with the example block *A*.

with a key greater than *M,* then it will scan beyond the end of the block; see Fig. 12.5(c). We can avoid this difficulty by using a sentinel (see Exercise 12.4), or by using a different median-estimation method (see Exercise 12.5). In Fig. 12.6, we show how the partitioning algorithm works with $M = 8$, the first record. The results of subsequent partitionings, caused by recursive calls of *QuickSort*, are displayed in Fig. 12.7.

QuickSort can perform badly; for example, when it is given a sorted sequence of size *n,* it requires $\Omega(n^2)$ comparisons. Assuming, however, that each permutation of *n* records with distinct keys is as equally likely to occur as is any other permutation of the *n* records, *QuickSort* makes $O(n \log n)$ comparisons, in the expected case. This performance can be seen quite easily when we observe that the partitioning process mimics insertion into an initially empty binary

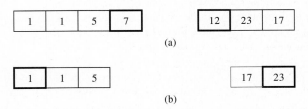

Figure 12.7 The partitions of *QuickSort* for the block *A*. (a) After the first recursive calls. (b) After the second recursive calls.

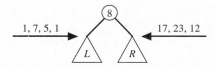

Figure 12.8   *QuickSort* and binary-search-tree insertion.

search tree. With our example, $M = 8$ becomes the root key, and the other records are sent into the left or right subtree, depending on whether they are less than (or equal to) or greater than M; see Fig. 12.8. The comparisons made by the partitioning algorithm are exactly the comparisons made with the root key. Similarly, in the left subtree *L,* 1 becomes its root and the partition is trivial.

Thus, the number of comparisons made by *QuickSort* for a given sequence is the number needed to construct a binary search tree with the same sequence. If all sequences of size n are considered equally likely to occur, then the expected number of comparisons made by *QuickSort* is the expected external path length of the corresponding binary search tree. This value is shown, in Section 8.5.4, to be $O(n \log n)$.

In practice, more than one record is used to estimate the median; for example, we can use the median of the first, middle, and last records—a technique called the **median-of-three** estimation. Also, when the number of records falls below a prespecified threshold, some other sorting method, such as *BubbleSort*, is usually used. If, however, we always select a record with largest key (or a record with smallest key), rather than estimating the median, then *QuickSort* reduces to *SelectionSort*—another basic $O(n^2)$-time sorting algorithm. More important, when we first preprocess the records, so that selecting a record with largest key is less time consuming than is scanning all the records, we arrive at *HeapSort*, which we consider in somewhat more detail.

In *HeapSort*, we first convert a given block of records into a max heap; see Section 11.2.3. Once this conversion is done, we sort by recursively selecting a record with largest key, deleting it from the heap, and placing it in the next available position (the previous last position) of the block. When we remove a record from a heap of size m, we free cell m, so we can place the deleted record in cell m. Because we delete the record with largest key at each step, we guarantee that the records are placed in the freed cells in nonincreasing key order. Since a largest record can be found and deleted by *DeleteMax* with $O(\log n)$ comparisons, this aspect of *HeapSort* takes $O(n \log n)$ comparisons, *in the worst case,* for n records; see Section 11.2.3. Thus we obtain a sorting algorithm that takes $O(n \log n)$ time, in the worst case. Given the example block *A, HeapSort* produces the max heap shown in Fig. 12.9. In this example, only 8 and 23 are exchanged to produce a max heap. *DeleteMax* removes 23 and bubbles down the 1 taken from the last position. Bubbling frees the last position, in which we place 23. The process is repeated six more times, after which the block is guaranteed to be sorted; see Fig. 12.10. *HeapSort* can be viewed as an optimized version of *SelectionSort*.

We summarize the results we have obtained as follows.

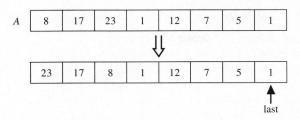

Figure 12.9 The max heap for *HeapSort* with the example block *A*.

Fact 12.2 *Given a sequence of n records,*

1. *QuickSort takes $O(n^2)$ time, in the worst case, and $O(n \log n)$ time, in the expected case. It is not stable.*
2. *HeapSort takes $O(n \log n)$ time, in both the worst and expected cases. It is not stable.*

We leave you to demonstrate that *QuickSort* and *HeapSort*, as described, are not stable; see Exercise 12.6.

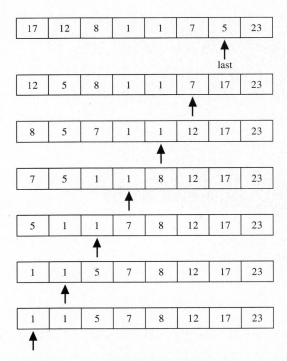

Figure 12.10 Consecutive snapshots of the repeated *DeleteMax* operation in *HeapSort*.

12.1.3 Insertion Sorting—Hard Join

A pack of 52 playing cards has four **suits** of 13 cards each—namely, clubs (♣),
diamonds (♦), hearts (♥), and spades (♠)—and each suit has **ranks** 2, 3,..., 10,
jack, queen, king, and ace. We define a total order for a pack of cards as follows:
*One card is less than a second card if either the suit of the first is earlier (alpha-
betically) than the suit of the second, or they are of the same suit and the rank of
the first card is earlier (in the preceding list) than the rank of the second.* So
5♣ < 3♥ < 4♥, and 10♦ < Q♦ < A♦. This ordering is used in bridge, hearts, and
whist, for example.

Insertion sorting is one method that card players use to sort their hands of
cards. As its name implies, we insert records one at a time into their correct positions. This process is illustrated in Fig. 12.11; we consider, during a left-to-right
scan, each card in turn, inserting each card into its correct position among the
sorted cards to its left. The only problem is, How do we find the correct position?
We describe **linear insertion,** which gives rise to *LinearInsertionSort*. On reaching the record at position *i,* we scan back to, at most, position 1 to find the
record's position *j*. We then create a gap for the record at position *j* by moving
records from positions *j* to *i* − 1 one place to the right. For simplicity, we combine
the gap creation with the backward scan, bubbling the record in position *i* into its
correct position using transpositions; see Program 12.2.

Since the records to the left of the current record are sorted during *Linear-
InsertionSort*, we can also use binary search; this modification yields *Bi-
naryInsertionSort*, described in Exercise 12.8. A major application of insertion

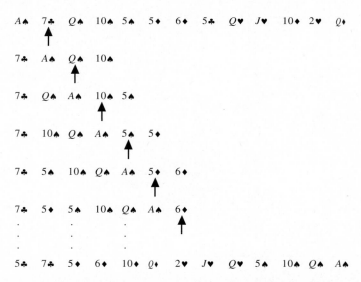

Figure 12.11   Consecutive snapshots of *LinearInsertionSort* for a hand of cards.

```
{We assume that A has a position 0 that is used to hold a
    sentinel value. The current record is at position i in A.}

j:= i;
A[0]:= A[i]; {Set the sentinel value.}
while A[j] < A[j - 1] do
begin {Transpose A[j] and A[j - 1].}
    t:= A[j - 1]; A[j - 1]:= A[j];
    A[j]:= t; j:= j - 1
end;
```

Program 12.2   Combination of gap creation and position finding in linear insertion.

sorting is in each pass of *ShellSort*; see Exercise 12.9. In each pass, each record is close to its final position, so linear insertion is efficient.

The structure of *LinearInsertionSort* is shown in Fig. 12.12; insertion sorting consists of easy splitting followed by hard joining. Rather than splitting off one record at a time, however, we can choose to split the sequence into two halves. This approach leaves us with two sorted halves which have to be joined, so we merge them. This sorting method is called *MergeSort*. Merging is an important concept in its own right; we introduced it in Section 3.3, and we use it in Section 12.5 as the basis of external sorting. We illustrate merge sorting with the running example; see Fig. 12.13.

We merge two sorted sequences by scanning them from left to right simultaneously. At each step, we append the record with the smaller key, chosen from the two current records of the two sequences, to the end of the output sequence. If the two current records have equal keys, then we append the earlier record, where by "earlier" we mean the record whose position is earlier in the block. (This choice

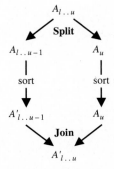

Figure 12.12   The recursive structure of *LinearInsertionSort* in terms of split and join.

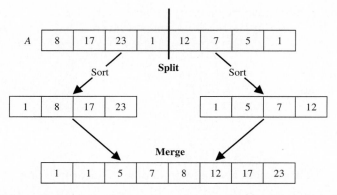

Figure 12.13 Illustration of the strategy of *MergeSort* with the block *A*.

is crucial, since it ensures that *MergeSort* is stable.) The first three steps with the two sorted sequences of size 4 from Fig. 12.13 are shown in Fig. 12.14. Eventually, one sequence is exhausted. With this example, the second sequence is exhausted before the first sequence; see Fig. 12.15. At this stage, the remaining

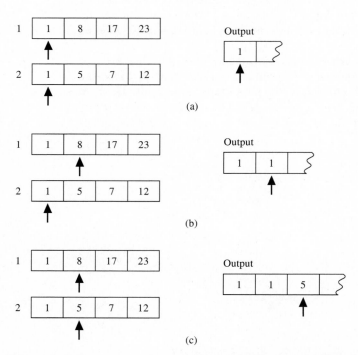

Figure 12.14 Initial snapshots of the merging of two sorted subblocks.

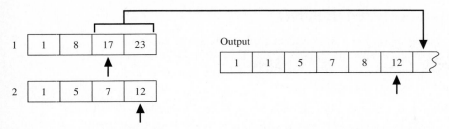

Figure 12.15 The situation when one subblock is exhausted during merging.

records in the other sequence are appended, in sorted order, to the end of the output sequence. You can verify the correctness of this algorithm by observing that we maintain three sorted sequences: two input sequences and one output sequence. Initially, the output sequence is empty; finally, the input sequences are both empty. At each step, all records in the output sequence have keys that are no greater than the keys of all the remaining records in the input sequences, and a new record from the input sequences is appended to the output sequence. The new record has a key that is no smaller than the key of any record in the output sequence and no larger than the key of any record in the input sequences; hence, the invariant is maintained.

As described, merge sorting uses an intermediate block for merging. For this reason, it is usually used only when the records are in a linked list, since in this situation the use of extra space can be avoided. (We can also avoid extra space when we use a block, by merging in place, but the method is nontrivial to implement; see Exercise 12.10.) Merge sorting makes $O(n \log n)$ comparisons and data movements, in the worst and expected cases; that is, it takes $O(n \log n)$ time, in the worst and expected cases. To see why these bounds hold, we let $C(n)$ be the maximal number of comparisons used by *MergeSort* with sequences of size n. Then we obtain the following recurrence equation:

$$C(n) = \begin{cases} 0, & \text{if } n = 1; \\ C(\lceil n/2 \rceil) + C(\lfloor n/2 \rfloor) + n, & \text{otherwise.} \end{cases}$$

When $n > 1$, *MergeSort* makes two recursive calls—one that takes at most $C(\lceil n/2 \rceil)$ comparisons and one that takes at most $C(\lfloor n/2 \rfloor)$ comparisons—and performs a merge that takes $n - 1$ comparisons. This recurrence equation is standard. Its solution is given by the results in Section 2.5; that is, $C(n)$ is $O(n \log n)$. In other words, we have established the following fact. We leave to Exercise 12.11 the proof that *MergeSort* is a stable sorting algorithm.

Fact 12.3 *Given a sequence of n records, MergeSort takes $O(n \log n)$ time, in the worst and expected cases. Moreover, MergeSort is stable.*

12.2 SORTING: A LOWER BOUND

We have described sorting algorithms that perform well in the worst case; we have shown that, of these algorithms, the fastest take at least $cn \log n$ comparisons, in the worst and expected cases, for some constant $c \geq 1$. We now prove that this lower bound holds for a general model of sorting.

Fact 12.4 *Every sorting method that uses only key comparisons to determine each record's final position in sorted order requires $\Omega(n \log n)$ key comparisons to sort n records, in the worst case.*

The value $n \log n$ is an impermeable barrier; we can do no better without changing the rules. In Section 12.3, we demonstrate that we can obtain a linear-time sorting algorithm when we relax the key-comparison requirement.

We begin by considering how we might sort a sequence $x = x_1, x_2, x_3$ of three numbers. If we use *BubbleSort*, then we proceed as follows: Compare x_1 and x_2, transposing the values if necessary. Compare x_2 and x_3, transposing the values if necessary. Finally, compare x_1 and x_2 again, transposing their values if necessary. When we write a program for this process without loops, we obtain Program 12.3. It is a nonrecursive and specialized version of *BubbleSort*; see Program 12.1. Not surprisingly, since they both use comparisons, *BubbleSort3* is similar to *BSearch3* of Section 8.4.1. The crucial observation about *BubbleSort3* is that each execution path corresponds to a unique initial relationship among x_1, x_2, and x_3. For example, if $x_1 < x_3 < x_2$, then execution terminates at the comment {Sorted 2}. Similarly, if $x_3 < x_2 < x_1$, then execution terminates at {Sorted 6}. Now, the relative order of the three numbers corresponds to a permutation of the numbers, with respect to their sorted order; for example, $x_1 < x_3 < x_2$ corresponds to the permutation (1,3,2). The termination positions depend on only the relative order of the records, not on their specific keys, so we need to consider only the input values 1, 2, and 3. Thus, the input $x_1 = 1$, $x_2 = 3$, and $x_3 = 2$ and permutation (1,3,2) terminate at {Sorted 2}.

We abstract the execution paths of a comparison-based sorting algorithm with paths in a decision tree in which the nodes correspond to pairwise comparisons. *BubbleSort3* gives the decision tree of Fig. 12.16. We suppress the transpositions so that all comparisons are relative to the original sequence and the external nodes are associated with their corresponding permutations. We suppress all references to the specific block x by referring to only the indices into x, and by making the comparison <? implicit. Since three records have six possible orderings, it should be no surprise to find that the decision tree has six external nodes—one for each permutation. The worst-case performance of *BubbleSort3* is the height of the tree, because each node corresponds to a comparison and the longest path determines the maximum number of comparisons. Similarly, the best-case and expected-case performances correspond to the length of the shortest root-to-frontier path and to the average external path length (we assume that all input permutations are equally likely to occur).

```
procedure BubbleSort3(var x: ourarray);
var t: elementtype;
begin
    if x[1] < x[2]
    then if x[2] < x[3]
        then {Sorted 1}
        else begin
            t:= x[2]; x[2]:= x[3]; x[3]:= t;
            if x[1] < x[2]
            then {Sorted 2}
            else begin
                t:= x[1]; x[1]:= x[2]; x[2]:= t
                {Sorted 3}
            end
        end
    else begin
        t:= x[1]; x[1]:= x[2]; x[2]:= t;
        if x[2] < x[3]
        then {Sorted 4}
        else begin
            t:= x[2]; x[2]:= x[3]; x[3]:= t;
            if x[1] < x[2]
            then {Sorted 5}
            else begin
                t:= x[1]; x[1]:= x[2]; x[2]:= t
                {Sorted 6}
            end
        end
    end
end;
```

Program 12.3   *BubbleSort3*: Sorting three records without loops.

Each comparison-based sorting algorithm for n input values gives a decision tree with at least $n!$ external nodes, one for each permutation. Because decision trees are easier to handle than are algorithms, we would like decision trees and sorting algorithms to be interchangeable. We have to be careful, however, since it is easy to provide examples of decision trees that do not correspond to any sorting algorithm; see Fig. 12.17. The tree for three records in Fig. 12.17(a) has only five external nodes—one too few. External node 2 corresponds to two permutations, and external node 4 does not correspond to any permutation. The decision tree in Fig. 12.17(b), for two records, has three external nodes—one too many—and external node 2 does not correspond to any permutation. This decision tree does, however, have a corresponding sorting algorithm, albeit an inefficient one.

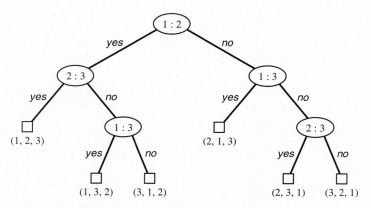

Figure 12.16   The decision tree for *BubbleSort3*.

Informally, a decision tree for n records corresponds to some sorting algorithm when each external node corresponds to at most one permutation. Such a decision tree has at least $n!$ external nodes.

In Section 5.1.1, we proved that a binary tree with m external nodes has height at least $\lceil \log m \rceil$. Hence, a decision tree with at least $n!$ external nodes has height at least $\lceil \log n! \rceil$. Now, $n! = \Omega(n^n)$, according to Stirling's approximation to $n!$, thus the height of the decision tree is at least $\Omega(n \log n)$. In other words, any comparison-based sorting algorithm requires $\Omega(n \log n)$ comparisons, in the worst case. This lower bound also holds in the expected case, but we do not prove this fact here.

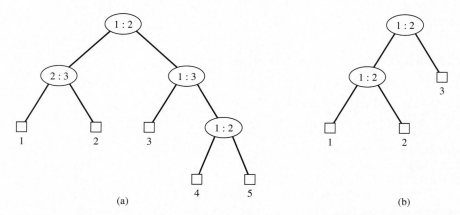

Figure 12.17   Two nonstandard decision trees. (a) External node 2 corresponds to two permutations. (b) External node 2 does not correspond to any permutation.

12.3 DIGITAL SORTING

We now introduce a sorting method that takes $O(n)$ time, in the worst case. This sorting method is faster than the sorting methods introduced in Section 12.1, and it is also faster than the lower bound of $\Omega(n \log n)$ time that we proved in Section 12.2. It achieves this improved performance by changing the rules; it places records by address computation and thus avoids key comparisons. Clearly, we can treat keys from a totally ordered universe as the indices of a block. We can then sort a file by emptying the cells of the block, reading the file, and assigning the records to the cells that their keys index. Finally, we can scan the block and collect the records in the nonempty cells in sorted order. We should not use this approach, however, when the key space is very large, since the time taken to initialize the block, and subsequently to read it, is much too long. (We cannot, of course, use this approach if the key universe is infinite.) There are two possible modifications to this method that can be used when the key space is large but finite. The first modification is to use buckets of consecutive keys, rather than individual cells for keys. It gives rise to a sorting method called *BucketSort*, which provides some essential ideas. The second modification is to decompose keys into "digits," and to use the digits as bucket addresses. For this reason, we call it digital sorting.

12.3.1 Bucket Sorting

Given a sequence of records, *BucketSort* distributes the records into b buckets by interpolation. It estimates or computes the minimum and maximum keys in the input, called *minkey* and *maxkey,* respectively. We associate $\lceil (maxkey - minkey + 1)/b \rceil$ contiguous key values with each bucket; let this number be denoted by *bsize*. Now, given a record with key K, where $minkey \le K \le maxkey$, it is added to the bucket indexed by

$$\left\lceil \frac{K - minkey + 1}{bsize} \right\rceil;$$

see Fig. 12.18. We consider the buckets to be queues, so that the arrival order of records is preserved to ensure stability. The records in each bucket are sorted by either the same technique applied recursively or some other method. Finally, the sorted buckets are joined in their natural order—namely, the records in bucket 1, followed by the records in bucket 2, and so on.

Although we expect n/b records to be placed in each bucket, we cannot guarantee this number. Indeed, in the worst case, $n - 1$ records may be placed in *minkey*'s bucket. Thus *BucketSort* takes $O(n^2)$ time, in the worst case. It can be shown, under the assumption that all permutations of n given records are equally likely to occur, that *BucketSort* takes $O(n)$ time, in the expected case, when $n \approx b$. The astute reader might observe that we can compute easily the number of

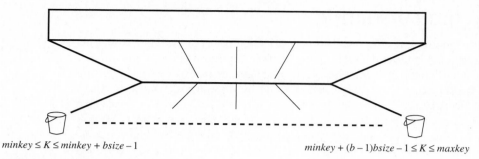

$minkey \leq K \leq minkey + bsize - 1$ $minkey + (b-1)bsize - 1 \leq K \leq maxkey$

Figure 12.18   The first pass of *BucketSort*.

records and use it as the number of buckets. Thus we obtain an $O(n)$-time sorting algorithm, in the expected case. The reason that we do not use this approach in practice is that, as we have explained, it is time consuming in the worst case.

There are situations when we know the range of key values, and, furthermore, the range is of reasonable size. These situations are a golden opportunity for *BucketSort*. In many other situations, we can use the first pass of *BucketSort* to produce a good approximation to a sorted sequence, which is then easy to sort by some other method.

12.3.2 Digital Sorting

Let us return to the example hand of cards in Fig. 12.11. Rather than using *InsertionSort*, we can do a two-pass sort. In the first pass, we have four buckets: one each for clubs, diamonds, hearts, spades. In the second pass, each of these buckets is divided into 13 buckets: one each for 2, 3, ..., J, Q, K, A. We are doing a two-pass bucket sort with a variable number of buckets. With our sample hand, we obtain the buckets of cards separated by suits, after the first phase, as shown in Fig. 12.19. After the second phase, each of the suit buckets is distributed into rank buckets. Since there is at most one card in each rank bucket, we need to catenate only the rank buckets to obtain each suit sorted by rank. The second pass is completed in a third phase as indicated in Fig. 12.19. Finally, the first pass is resolved in a fourth phase, when the suit buckets (now sorted by rank) are catenated to give the sorted hand.

This example demonstrates the idea behind digital sorting—the keys are known to be a sequence of digits *from some small range of values,* and we sort the records with respect to the digits of their keys, one digit at a time. If we use digit comparisons, however, instead of key comparisons, the sorting algorithms would be no faster than the algorithms that we have discussed. The crucial idea is to avoid key and digit comparisons as much as possible. We avoid them completely in digital sorting, by using digits as addresses of buckets. There is one major difference, however, between bucket sorting and digital sorting. During one pass of

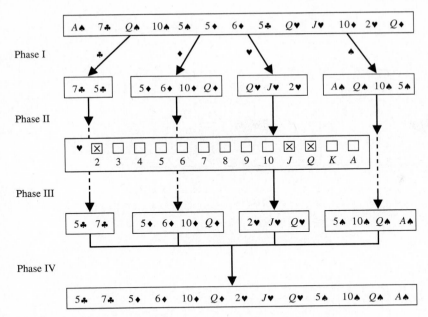

Figure 12.19 The two-pass *BucketSort* of a hand of cards.

digital sorting, we distribute the records according to one of the digits of their keys and then we collect them again, whereas in bucket sorting, we collect the records only once, after the repeated distributions. More precisely, in the *i*th pass, we sort the *i*th least significant digit; in particular, we sort the least significant digit on the first pass and the most significant digit on the last pass. Thus for card hands, we first sort by rank and then by suit, as shown in Fig. 12.20. (Note that, for playing cards, the most significant digit is rightmost—not leftmost, as it is for the normal way we write integers.) Since two distinct keys can have identical digits at some positions, digital sorting must deal with multiple appearances of digits. Indeed, for correctness, we require that each pass of digital sorting be stable. Therefore, we treat the buckets as queues, so that their contents are maintained in arrival order.

Digital sorting was once a much-used electromechanical sorting method. When programs were typed or punched onto 80-column cards, it was easy to scramble a deck of cards, so the last eight columns were used to hold a sequence number. A deck of punched cards could then be sorted using digital sorting with a punched-card sorting machine. In some programming languages, there are restrictions on the length of identifiers, and in some computer systems, there are restrictions on the length of user ids. Digital sorting is an ideal method to use, in these settings, if we want to sort a set of identifiers.

We summarize the performance of digital sorting as follows:

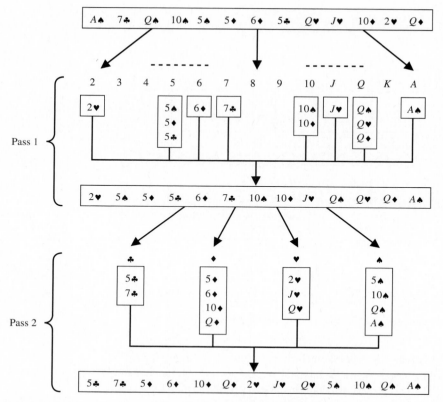

Figure 12.20   The two-pass *DigitalSort* of a hand of cards.

Fact 12.5   *The digital sorting of n records with d-digit keys takes O(dn) time, in the worst and expected cases. For fixed d, digital sorting is a linear-time sorting algorithm.*

12.4 ADAPTIVE SORTING

It is often the case, in reality, that a given file is already nearly sorted. For example, a bibliography file for use with BibTEX and LATEX may be nearly sorted, so BibTEX should not need to spend the same amount of time sorting the file as it would spend on a random permutation of the file. Another example comes from one solution to a clustering problem, for a set of points in the plane. The points are sorted with respect to their distance from some designated point, using any of the sorting algorithms that we have discussed. The designated point is then moved slightly, and we want to sort the points again, with respect to the new position of the designated point. Clearly, the distances have changed little; therefore, the rel-

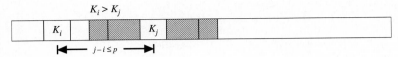

Figure 12.21 The condition for a sequence to be *p*-sorted.

ative order of the points hardly will have changed. There is **coherence,** as the graphics community calls it. Thus if we already have the points sorted according to the original position of the designated point, then the points are nearly sorted with respect to the new position of the designated point. A third example comes from the first pass of *BucketSort*. As a result of bucketing, we have split the file into groups, and the groups, not the records, are sorted. Therefore, the file we form by joining the groups is nearly sorted. There are many different notions of nearly sortedness; we explore one such notion in this section.

With each of the three examples, the question is this: Can we sort faster in a comparison-based model than the lower bound would have us believe? To see that we can, we consider a slight generalization of the bucket-sorting example. Assume that we are given a sequence $K = K_1,...,K_n$ of n keys. An **inversion** is a pair (i,j) such that $1 \leq i < j \leq n$ and $K_i > K_j$. Clearly, a sequence is sorted when it has no inversions. We say that K is p-**sorted**, for some $p \geq 0$, when, for all inversions (i,j), we have $j - i \leq p$; see Fig. 12.21. Note that p is 0 if and only if K is sorted, since in an unsorted file there must be an inversion and the distance between the keys in the inversion is at least 1. Also, if K is sorted, then it is p-sorted, for all $p \geq 0$; but if K is p-sorted, for some $p > 0$, it does not need to be sorted; see Exercise 12.13.

Each of the comparison-based sorting algorithms we have discussed requires, in the worst case, $\Omega(n \log n)$ time to sort a p-sorted sequence. But we now describe a sorting algorithm that takes $O(n \log p)$ time in the worst case, for a sequence of n records, where p is the smallest value for which the sequence is p-sorted. Since $0 \leq p < n$, $\log p$ is $O(\log n)$ and the algorithm takes $O(n \log n)$ time, in the worst case, when we ignore the p-sortedness of the sequence. Surprisingly, the algorithm does not need to know p in advance; it **adapts** its behavior to the unknown value of p. When p is small, we obtain a linear-time sorting algorithm.

The **adaptive sorting algorithm,** *TryToMergeSort*, proceeds as follows. It is a variant of *MergeSort* with a different splitting policy. We use **modulo-two splitting of K;** that is, one half consists of all odd positions in the original sequence, and the other half consists of all even positions. We denote the two halves by K_{odd} and K_{even}. After splitting the sequence into two halves, we try to merge them. If the two halves are sorted, then the merge succeeds and *TryToMergeSort* terminates. Otherwise, at least one of the two halves is unsorted, so *TryToMergeSort* is called recursively on both halves. Observe that the attempt to merge takes time linear in the size of the given sequence; hence, a coarse upper bound on the total number of comparisons taken by *TryToMergeSort* is $O(n \log n)$, the same as for

MergeSort. We can obtain a tighter bound, however, by using the following observation.

Observation 12.1   *If K is p-sorted, for some p > 0, then K_{odd} and K_{even} are $\lfloor p/2 \rfloor$-sorted.*

Hence, the depth of recursion in *TryToMergeSort* is bounded by $\lceil \log p \rceil$. At this depth, *TryToMergeSort* has a sorted sequence as input, which implies the following fact.

Fact 12.6   *Given a sequence of n records, TryToMergeSort takes $O(n \log p)$ time, in the worst case, and, for fixed p, it takes linear time. Moreover TryToMergeSort is stable.*

The stability of *TryToMergeSort* can be established by the same method you use to establish the stability of *MergeSort* in Exercise 12.14. There is a lower bound, which we do not prove, for sorting *p*-sorted sequences of *n* records; it tells us that $\Omega(n \log p)$ comparisons are required, in the worst case. Thus, based on this fact, *TryToMergeSort* is optimal.

12.5   EXTERNAL SORTING

The sorting methods discussed in Sections 12.1 and 12.3 are internal sorting methods; they assume that we can hold the files to be sorted completely in main memory. Although we can adapt these methods to sort extremely large files that we cannot hold in main memory, we do not normally sort externally in this way. The underlying reason is that comparisons and exchanges are no longer a realistic measure of a sorting algorithm's performance. *Rather, we count disk accesses.* As an example, we examine in somewhat more detail how we can implement *MergeSort* for external files. We then investigate, in Section 12.5.1, how we can modify *MergeSort* to give an external sorting method—multiway merge sort—that is the most popular sorting method for external sorting.

Generally, external sorting methods **scan** or **make passes** over a file many times, rearranging some parts of the file during each pass. For example, *MergeSort* can be viewed as a multiple-pass sorting method in which the first pass merges adjacent pairs of sorted subfiles of size 1, the second pass merges adjacent pairs of sorted subfiles of size 2, and so on; see Fig. 12.22. The sorted subfiles are normally called **runs.** When we use this approach without any modification, each record access is random. Assume that we are given a file of *n* records of equal size stored in *M* blocks, with *b* records in each block ($n = M \times b$). Then *MergeSort* takes $\lceil \log n \rceil$ passes, and each pass makes *n* sequential record accesses. Thus it takes

$$\approx \lceil \log n \rceil \times n/b \times \text{btt} = \lceil \log n \rceil \times M \times \text{btt units of time}$$

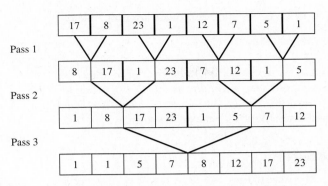

Figure 12.22 *MergeSort* as a multiple-pass sorting method.

to sort the file. (We have ignored all details of how this method can be implemented, and we have ignored the time taken by the internal operations, since the overall time is dominated by the disk-transfer time.) For $n = 1,000,000$, ast = 20 milliseconds, arlt = 10 milliseconds, b = 10, and btt = 1 millisecond, sorting takes

$$\approx 2,000,000/60,000 \approx 33 \text{ minutes.}$$

We can improve this naive implementation by recognizing that it is better to sort each block internally on the first pass, and on the second pass to merge adjacent pairs of blocks. Immediately we have fewer passes; *MergeSort* takes $\lceil \log M \rceil$ passes rather than $\lceil \log n \rceil$, and, hence, modified *MergeSort* takes

$$\approx \lceil \log M \rceil \times M \times \text{btt units of time}$$

to sort the file. For the example file and times, it takes

$$\approx 1,700,000/60,000 \approx 28 \text{ minutes;}$$

we have saved 5 minutes. We can improve *MergeSort* even further by sorting a number of adjacent blocks on the first pass, rather than sorting only one block. Assume that k blocks can be held in main memory at the same time. Then on the first pass we sort the first k blocks, then the second k blocks, and so on. Subsequent passes are the same as before, except that in the second pass we can merge the first k blocks with the second k blocks, the third k blocks with the fourth k blocks, and so on. This improvement reduces the number of passes to

$$\lceil \log(M/k) \rceil,$$

and, hence, reduces the sorting time to

$$\approx \lceil \log(M/k) \rceil \times M \times \text{btt units of time.}$$

For the example file and times, with $k = 8$, this approach yields a sorting time of

$$\approx 1,400,000/60,000 \approx 23 \text{ minutes};$$

we have saved a further 5 minutes. The message should be clear: *The longer we can make the sorted runs on the first pass, the fewer passes and disk accesses we need, and, hence, the faster we can sort the file.* This maxim leads us to discuss multiway merge sort, the standard external sorting method in use today.

12.5.1 Multiway Merge Sort

When adapting *MergeSort* to sort external files, we used two-way merging of adjacent runs. We can improve *MergeSort* substantially, however, by using a **multiway merge** that merges more than two runs at each merge step. For example, in Fig. 12.23 we have four runs; in Fig. 12.23(a) these runs are merged in pairs, as in *MergeSort*, to give two runs and then, on the next pass, one run. We compare the two-way merge with the four-way merge of Fig. 12.23(b). In one pass of the four-way merge, the four runs are merged into one run. Thus we need only one pass of the file to sort that file!

In general, when we perform m-way merging on each pass, we need only

$$\lceil \log_m M \rceil \text{ passes},$$

rather than $\lceil \log_2 M \rceil$ passes; we save

$$\approx \log_2 M - \log_m M \text{ passes}$$

$$= \log_2 M (1 - \frac{1}{\log_2 m}) \text{ passes}.$$

The larger the value of m, the larger the saving *in the number of passes*. There is, however, a down side to this saving: we are no longer reading sequentially. Indeed, even for two-way merging our analysis leaves much to be desired. Assume that we have space in main memory for C blocks, excluding buffer areas. When we have two runs of exactly C blocks, we cannot hold them in main memory at the same time. We read the first halves of each run into main memory and merge them. When one half is exhausted, we read its corresponding second half; we then continue merging until the remaining first half is exhausted, when we read its second half, and continue merging. During the merge and reads, we are also writing. Indeed, writing is interleaved with reading. If we assume that we read and write pieces of the same size, then we have four reads and four writes. In the one-disk model, each read and each write involves a seek. So we can approximate the time for the two-way merge of two runs, each consisting of C blocks, by

$$8 \times (\text{ast} + \text{arlt}) + 4 \times C \times \text{btt units of time}.$$

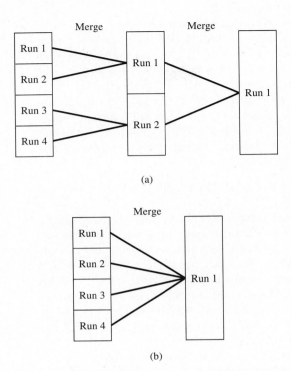

(a)

(b)

Figure 12.23 Merge of four runs. (a) Two-way merging. (b) Four-way merging.

Actually, there are only three write seeks for the four read seeks, so we should use a multiplicative factor of 7 in the first term; however, using a factor of 8 gives sorting-time estimates that are close to reality. Furthermore, we use m-way merging, in practice, when the estimate is even closer to reality. When we have two disk units available, we can read from one disk and write to the second; thus we avoid write seeks, but not read seeks. The corresponding estimation for the two-disk model is left to Exercise 12.15. Returning to the one-disk case, the second term in the equation for the two-way merge is the time needed to read and write $2C$ blocks. Thus a single two-way merge pass of a file takes

$$M/2C \times (8 \times (\text{ast} + \text{arlt}) + 4 \times C \times \text{btt}) \text{ units of time,}$$

since there are M/C runs. It is convenient to consider the number P of pieces (or halves) that are read and written, rather than the number of runs. Each piece contains $C/2$ blocks; hence, $P = 2M/C$ and the time taken for a single pass can be expressed as

$$2P \times (\text{ast} + \text{arlt}) + 2M \times \text{btt} \text{ units of time.}$$

This formula depends on only the number of pieces and the number of blocks in the file; the second term is the time taken to read the file twice when we ignore seeks. Observe that the second pass has runs of size $2C$, but the number P of pieces remains the same! So the time taken by each pass is the same.

What sorting times do we expect in practice? We use our assumed values for disk access: ast = 20 milliseconds, arlt = 10 milliseconds, and btt = 1 millisecond. We consider a file of 1 million records, each of 2400 bytes. We assume that each block holds exactly one record, so $b = 1$ and $M = 1,000,000$. Further, assume that $C = 4000$ blocks; that is, $P = 2M/C = 500$ pieces. Under these assumptions, one pass of a two-way merge, for runs of C blocks, takes

$$2 \times 500 \times (20 + 10) + 2 \times 1,000,000 \times 1 \text{ milliseconds,}$$

or approximately 34 minutes. Initially, there are $M/C = P/2 = 250$ runs of size C. After one pass, there are 125 runs of size $2C$; after two passes, there are 63 runs of size $4C$; and so on. Sorting takes $\lceil \log_2 250 \rceil = 8$ two-way merge passes and, hence, 8×34 minutes; that is, it takes ≈ 4.5 hours. We compare the sorting time with the coarse estimate derived at the beginning of the section with $b = 10$. We repeat the derivation with $b = 1$, to obtain an estimate of 333 minutes or, approximately, 5.5 hours to sort the file of 1 million records. We have reduced the time by 1 hour, because we begin with runs of size C. We consider, in Section 12.5.3, the time it takes to obtain these initial runs.

Rather than using two-way merge, why not use four-way merge, or even a higher-order merge? We know that when we increase the degree of the merge, we reduce the number of passes, but does this increase in degree also reduce the merging time?

Since we have a fixed main-memory capacity C, we must hold smaller portions of the runs in main memory at the same time. For four-way merge, the number P of pieces is no longer $2M/C$, but rather is $4M/C$, since each piece has $C/4$ blocks. Apart from this modification, we obtain the same formula; namely, each pass takes

$$2 \times P \times (\text{ast} + \text{arlt}) + 2 \times M \times \text{btt units of time.}$$

Under our assumptions, $P = 4,000,000/4000 = 1000$ pieces. So, one pass takes

$$2 \times 1000 \times (20 + 10) + 2 \times 1,000,000 \text{ milliseconds,}$$

and this value is approximately 34 minutes again. But, we need only $\lceil \log_4 250 \rceil = 4$ passes; that is, four-way merge needs only

$$\approx 2.25 \text{ hours,}$$

or half the time taken by two-way merge.

In general, for m-way merge, $m \geq 2$, we have $m \times M/C$ pieces and $\log_m(M/C)$ runs. We leave to Exercise 12.16 the computation for $m = 5, 6, 7,$ and

8. There is, however, a bottleneck. We can find a threshold value of m beyond which no gain in performance is obtained. Each time we double m, we double the number of pieces, and the number of passes shrinks a little. Thus, when the total seek time for one pass begins to dominate the sequential reading of the file, doubling m no longer reduces the overall sorting time; rather, it increases the overall sorting time. In Section 12.5.2, we discuss a simple technique for implementing multiway merge.

12.5.2 Replacement–Selection

We use replacement–selection to implement multiway merging. Assume that we are performing an eight-way merge; then, we need to merge eight runs at the same time. We need to find a record with a smallest key in the eight runs, to move it to the output, and to repeat the process until all eight runs are exhausted. Since a smallest key must appear in one of the initial records of each of the eight runs, we need to examine only these eight records. Once we find a smallest key, its record is output, and the process is repeated with the second record in the same run and the remaining seven records. We have **selected** a record with a smallest key, and have **replaced** it by the next record in its run; this strategy is called **replacement–selection.** We implement replacement–selection using a replaceable heap. Since we know that we always have eight runs to merge in each pass, we want to delete a record from a heap without shrinking it. **Replaceable heaps** have exactly this feature; they support a new PRIORITY QUEUE operation, *Replace*: $\mathcal{E} \times \mathcal{PQ} \to \mathcal{PQ}$. *Replace(e,P)* replaces an element that has minimum priority in P with e. We implement it by replacing the current root record with the new record and letting the new record trickle down.

For example, in Fig. 12.24, we give a replaceable heap for eight runs. The internal nodes are associated with the keys of the first records in the eight runs, and the root key is a minimal key. We should output first the record with key 39, since 39 is the smallest key. We can find its record by keeping, with the key, a pointer to the corresponding record. Although we have separated the nodes from their runs in Fig. 12.24, in practice they are identified. Since run 5 has the smallest key, 39, its first record is output and is replaced by the second record, in run 5, with key 43. Key 43 trickles down the heap, and key 40 is now the smallest key. The replaceable heap implements replacement–selection in a natural manner. Eventually, one of the runs is exhausted; at that time, we perform a *Delete*, rather than a *Replace*, so that the heap shrinks.

The number of comparisons made by an m-way merge, using a replaceable heap, is at most $n\lceil \log_2 m \rceil$, for an n-record file, whereas the naive method takes nm comparisons.

12.5.3 Creation of Initial Runs

Until now, we have ignored the creation of the initial runs. When we have space for C blocks, we can read C blocks at a time, sort them by some standard method

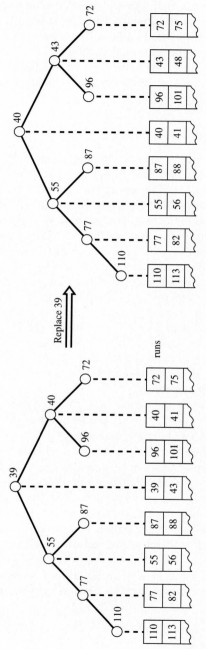

Figure 12.24 The removal of the root key in a replaceable heap and its replacement from the same run.

(for example, *HeapSort*), and output a run of *C* blocks. This method interleaves the reads from and writes to the file, so, when there is only one disk unit available, we need to perform a seek before each read and write of *C* blocks. The time taken is, therefore,

$$2M/C \times (\text{ast} + \text{arlt}) + 2M \times \text{btt units of time}$$

to create initial runs of size *C*. The example file and timings takes

$$500 \times (20 + 10) + 2 \times 1,000,000 \text{ milliseconds,}$$

or about 34 minutes. When we have only one disk unit available, we can do no better; see Exercise 12.17. With two disk units, however, we can improve the performance by reading the file from one disk unit and writing it to a second unit; thus the input and output of the file are both sequential. To improve the performance even further, we create runs that are expected to be $2C$ blocks or $2m$ records long by using replacement selection with an m-way merge, where m is the number *of records* that can be held in *C* blocks, see Fig. 12.25. In our example, each record is one block long, so we use *C*-way merge. How does replacement–selection work in this case? We first read in *C* records and create a replaceable heap for them using keys and run numbers. We always have two run numbers, the **current run number** and the **next run number.** Initially, the current run number is 1 and the next run number is 2. We extend the $\leq$ relation for keys to pairs consisting of keys and run numbers as follows: *Given two records with keys K_1 and K_2 and run numbers r_1 and r_2, respectively, $(r_1, K_1) \leq (r_2, K_2)$ whenever either $r_1 < r_2$, or $r_1 = r_2$ and $K_1 \leq K_2$.* The first *C* records have run number 1.

The idea behind our strategy stems from a simple observation. Rather than reading *C* records, sorting them, and outputting them, we output records with smallest keys first, and replace their records with new records; as long as the new keys are no less than the last key we output, we can add them to the current run. If any new keys are smaller than the last key we output, then we place their records in the next run. More precisely, the record of the current minimum pair (r, K) is output, and a new record with some key K' is read in. If K' is greater than or equal to K, then we replace the pair (r, K) with (r, K') in the heap; otherwise, we replace (r, K) with $(r + 1, K')$.

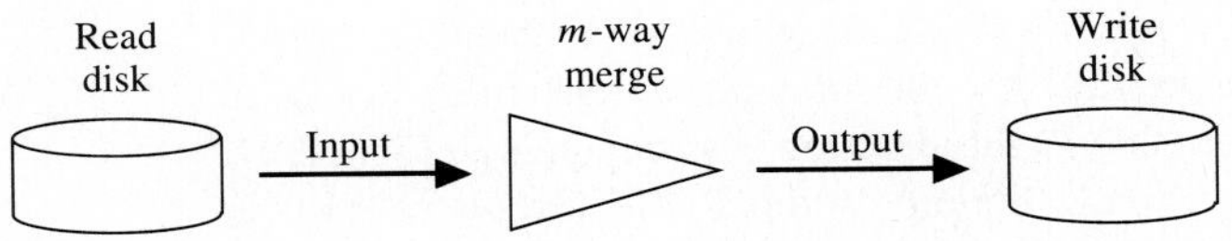

Figure 12.25 The use of two disks in an m-way merge.

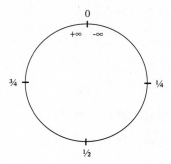

Figure 12.26   The circular track for the interval [0,1) corresponding
                   to the key space.

In this way, we obtain runs that are at least m records long, but they may be much longer. We might expect that they are longer by $m/2$ records, but it turns out that this expectation is overly pessimistic, as we now demonstrate.

Fact 12.7   *If we have space for m records in main memory, then replacement–selection using m-way merge produces runs that have expected length 2m.*

Assume that the key of each newly input record is equally likely to be at each position in the key space ($+\infty, -\infty$). We can abstract this situation using a graphic argument based on falling snow and a snowplow.

Let the key space be modeled by a circular track with positions (or keys) from the closed–open interval [0,1) corresponding to the key space ($+\infty, -\infty$); see Fig. 12.26. Snowflakes, corresponding to newly input records, fall uniformly on the track. A snowplow, corresponding to the most recently output key, is moving around the track in a clockwise direction. It is plowing the snow, corresponding to the output of the most recently output keys, as it moves around the track; that is, records are output in nondecreasing key order. The amount of snow on the track, at any time, corresponds to the number m of records in main memory.

The snowplow begins its first run at position 0, and plows clockwise until it reaches position 0 again. It then begins its second run, and so on. The speed of the snowplow is inversely proportional to the height of the snow it meets: The deeper the snow, the slower the snowplow is. After some time (this implication can be derived formally), the snowplow reaches its steady state and travels at some constant speed. This steady state implies that the snowplow must meet the same depth d of snow at each position; that is, the situation is as depicted in Fig. 12.27. When the snowplow passes position 0, there must already be d units of snow at position 0, but at position $1/2$ there must be only $d/2$ units of snow, because snow is still falling. The depth must decrease linearly with the distance from 0, so $1 \times d/2$ snowflakes must have already fallen when the snowplow passes position 0, and the snowplow clears $1 \times d$ snowflakes in one circuit because it meets snow

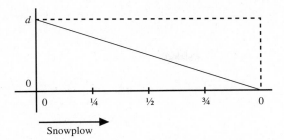

Figure 12.27   The steady-state situation for the snowplow.

of depth d everywhere. Since the number of fallen snowflakes corresponds to the number of records m that can be stored in main memory, we obtain

$$1 \times d/2 = m.$$

Hence,

$$d = 2m$$

is the number of snowflakes cleared in one circuit; that is, a run is expected to consist of $2m$ records.

12.6   PERFORMANCE REPORTS

We can divide the sorting algorithms that we have discussed into four classes: internal comparison-based sorting, internal digital sorting, internal adaptive comparison-based sorting, and external sorting. *HeapSort* and *MergeSort* have guaranteed worst-case optimal performance, and *MergeSort* is stable and is easier to code than *HeapSort*; see Tables 12.1 and 12.2. *QuickSort* is important and popular; although it takes quadratic time in the worst-case, it is optimal in the expected case. In practice, *QuickSort* is extremely fast, as the film "*Sorting Out Sorting*" (Baecker, 1982) demonstrates. It sorts files faster than either *HeapSort* or *MergeSort*. The main disadvantages of *QuickSort* are that it is difficult to code well and it is not stable. The remaining two methods, *BubbleSort* and *LinearInsertionSort*, are included for their historic interest, and because *LinearInsertionSort* is used in each pass of *ShellSort* and also is adaptive. They are both easy to code and are often used to sort small files. *TryToMergeSort* is effective when a file is nearly sorted; it is easy to code and adapts optimally to the disorder in a file. *DigitalSort* is also effective when it is appropriate—that is, when we need to sort fixed-length character strings or integers.

When we need to sort external files held on disks, *MultiWay Merge* is *the* method of choice. Although this method is nontrivial to code, many sort utilities that use it are available.

Table 12.1 A comparison of the worst-case execution times of eight sorting methods.

Sorting method	Worst case	Expected case	Stability
BubbleSort	n^2	n^2	yes
HeapSort	$n \log n$	$n \log n$	no
LinearInsertionSort	n^2	n^2	yes
MergeSort	$n \log n$	$n \log n$	yes
QuickSort	n^2	$n \log n$	no
TryToMergeSort	$n \log p$	$n \log p$	yes
DigitalSort	nd	nd	yes
MultiWay Merge	$n \log n$	$n \log n$	yes

Table 12.2 Performance ratings of the eight sorting methods.

Sorting method	Rating	Comments
MergeSort	Excellent	Worst-case optimal; stable
QuickSort	Very good	Expected-case optimal; fastest comparison-based sorting method; not stable
HeapSort	Very good	Worst-case optimal; in place; not stable
LinearInsertionSort	Satisfactory	Quadratic performance; in place adaptive to nearly sorted files
BubbleSort	Satisfactory	Quadratic performance; in place
TryToMergeSort	Very good	Optimally adaptive; stable; easy to code
DigitalSort	Very good	Easy to code; linear time; restricted application
MultiWay Merge	Excellent	Best external sorting method; stable; but nontrivial to code

One final comment: Most of the sorting methods that we have studied are stable. The obvious exceptions are *HeapSort* and *QuickSort*. It is possible to modify these two methods to obtain stable sorting algorithms, but this modification results in more complex code and degraded performance.

12.7 SUMMARY

We have discussed the sorting problem for both internal and external files, and we have distinguished between comparison-based and address-based sorting algorithms for internal sorting. Comparison-based sorting is based on the primitive operation *"compare two given keys,"* whereas address-based sorting is based on the operation *"compute the address of a given key."* We have also exploited the split–join view of sorting algorithms to provide insight into their differences. The split–join view is based on the observation that comparison-based sorting methods have the following generic structure: *Split a file into a number of parts, sort each part recursively by the same method, and join the sorted parts together.*

We have shown that $\Omega(n \log n)$ comparisons are required to sort a file of n records, in the worst case, with any comparison-based sorting algorithm, and have given sorting algorithms that achieve a matching upper bound, in the worst case. Digital sorting beats the comparison-based lower bound by avoiding key comparisons and using address computation; it takes linear time, in the worst and expected cases.

Of the sorting algorithms we have presented, *MergeSort*, *HeapSort*, and *QuickSort* are the best methods for internal sorting. Moreover, *MergeSort* is the easiest to code correctly, so it is the method we recommend when you have to code a sorting algorithm. *QuickSort* is, however, usually available as a sort utility; for example, as `sort` under UNIX. Digital sorting is an appropriate choice when the keys are strings, of characters or digits, and they have a predefined length.

We have touched on the topic of nearly sorted files and adaptive sorting algorithms. We have given a comparison-based sorting algorithm, *TryToMergeSort*, that sorts faster than the comparison-based lower bound, when it is given a file that is nearly sorted according to the maximal distance between the keys in an inversion.

Finally, for external sorting, we have argued that there is only one choice— multiway merging with replacement selection.

12.8 HISTORY

Knuth's text (1973) is a veritable compendium of sorting; it is complemented by the handbook of Gonnet and Baeza-Yates (1991) that summarizes known facts concerning various sorting algorithms. In addition, the text of Lorin (1975) is a useful and readable source of sorting methods. The split–join view of sorting was proposed by Merritt (1985). Stable sorting is addressed by Horvarth (1978). *TryToMergeSort*, an algorithm that is optimal, in the worst case, with respect to the p-sortedness of the input, was developed by Estivill-Castro and Wood (1989). Estivill-Castro and Wood (1992) surveys the state-of-the-art of adaptive sorting algorithms. The seminal paper on nearly sortedness is that of Mannila (1985). The snowplow model for the determination of the size of initial runs when using replacement–selection was suggested by E.F. Moore, and the presentation is based on that given by Knuth (1973, 254–255). A pragmatic approach to external sorting, on which we base Section 12.5, is found in Salzberg (1989). Two complementary investigations of external mergesort which discuss nearly sortedness are those of Estivill-Castro and Wood (1991), and Zheng and Larson (1992).

EXERCISES

12.1: Modify *Bubble* to bubble elements only within the indices *lower* to *upper* of the given block.

12.2: Modify *Bubble* as in Exercise 12.1, and also modify it to return an indication that at least one transposition has taken place during its call. Moreover, modify *BubbleSort* to terminate immediately when the given block is sorted.

12.3: Prove that *BubbleSort* (Section 12.1.1) is stable.

12.4: Design a Pascal partitioning algorithm for use in *QuickSort* that uses a sentinel to prevent the left scan from going beyond the right end of the block.

12.5: Design a Pascal partitioning algorithm for use in *QuickSort* that uses the median-of-three estimation of the median to prevent the left scan from going beyond the right end of the block. The median-of-three method uses the records in the first, middle, and last positions. It sorts them and uses their median as an approximation to the median of the given records.

12.6: Prove that *HeapSort* and *QuickSort*, as described in Section 12.1.2, are not stable.

12.7: The partitioning step of *QuickSort* can be modeled using elements of three colors as follows. Given an array $A[L..U]$ of red, white, and blue elements, design an efficient algorithm to partition them into three blocks, the first consisting of red elements, the second of white elements, and the third of blue elements. The algorithm can use only one additional variable to hold a colored element and can perform only exchanges of the elements. (Thus it cannot count the numbers of each color and then fill the array accordingly.) The problem is often called the Dutch-Flag problem.

12.8: Modify *LinearInsertionSort* by using binary search to place each element. Design and carry out a simulation experiment that compares binary insertion with linear insertion. Describe your results.

12.9: Rather than splitting a sequence into two halves, we can split it into m subsequences using **modulo splitting.** Let $A = A_1,\ldots,A_n$ be a sequence, and let m, $1 \leq m \leq n$, be an integer. Then we obtain the m subsequences

$$A_{[1]} = A_1,A_{m+1},A_{2m+1},\ldots,$$
$$A_{[2]} = A_2,A_{m+2},A_{2m+2},\ldots,$$
$$\cdot \quad \cdot$$
$$\cdot \quad \cdot$$
$$\cdot \quad \cdot$$
$$A_{[m]} = A_m,A_{2m},A_{3m},\ldots.$$

This method of splitting is used as the basis of a sorting method known as *ShellSort*. We sort each subsequence using linear insertion sort, perform a trivial join, and then repeat the process with a different value of m. *ShellSort* is given an unsorted sequence and a decreasing modulus sequence $m_k > m_{k-1} > \cdots > m_1$, where k is a function of n and $n > m_k$. It sorts by first sorting the m_k subsequences and then sorting the m_i subsequences for i ranging from $k-1$ down to 1.

    a. Show that $m_1 = 1$ is necessary to ensure that A is sorted at the end of the process described here.

b. Linear insertion can be accomplished in two different ways. We have described a method that inserts the next element e by searching from the end of the current sorted portion to find e's position. We could have searched forward from the beginning of the current sorted portion to find e's position. Which method is preferable in the context of *ShellSort*? Explain your answer.

[You might want to design several experiments to gain insight into these two methods. For this purpose, use the decreasing modulus sequence

$$2^k - 1, 2^{k-1} - 1, ..., 2^2 - 1, 2^1 - 1,$$

where $k = \lceil \log n \rceil$.]

c. Compare, using simulation, the modulus sets $\{2^i - 1 \rightarrow 1 \le i \le \lceil \log n \rceil\}$ and $\{2^i 3^j \rightarrow i,j \ge 0 \text{ and } 2^i 3^j < n\}$ when used as decreasing modulus sequences in *ShellSort*. You should monitor the number of comparisons and the number of data movements on each pass and in total.

12.10: Design and implement an algorithm for merging two sorted subblocks of a block in place; that is, using only constant additional space.

12.11: Prove that *MergeSort* (Section 12.1.3) is a stable sorting algorithm.

12.12: You are given no more than 100,000 records, each consisting of only a unique key from 1..100,000. How can you sort them? How can you sort them if the machine you are using cannot hold all the records in main memory at one time?

12.13: Give a sequence of integers that is 1-sorted, but not 0-sorted. Argue informally why it is not 0-sorted. Generalize the example to show that there are sequences that are $(p + 1)$-sorted but not p-sorted, for all $p \ge 0$.

12.14: Prove that *TryToMergeSort* (Section 12.4) is stable.

12.15: This exercise discusses multiway merge.
a. Consider the two-way merge of two runs of C blocks under the assumption that two disk units are available. Give a formula that approximates the time taken by the merge.
b. Extend the preceding formula to give the approximate time taken to carry out one pass of two-way merge for M blocks.
c. Using the values given in the text for disk performance (Section 12.5), compute the time taken to sort, by two-way merge, 1 million records, each of size 2400 bytes, when one block holds exactly one record and $C = 4000$ blocks.

12.16: In Section 12.5, we have computed the savings in the number of passes, when moving from two-way to four-way merging. Complete the computations for m-way merging, for the values $m = 5, 6, 7$, and 8.

12.17: When discussing the production of initial runs for multiway merge with one disk unit (Section 12.5.3), we stated that it is impossible to reduce the time to produce sorted runs of size C. Explain why this statement holds.

C H A P T E R 13

Graphs and Digraphs

Graphs, directed and undirected, are the preeminent modeling tool for real-world problems, as well as being of interest in their own right. An airline-route map is a familiar example; see Fig. 13.1. Another example is a prerequisite graph of computer science courses; for example, Fig. 13.2 shows one for the University of Waterloo.

These two examples demonstrate the two different kinds of graphs: The route map is undirected, whereas the prerequisite graph is directed. In the prerequisite graph, we wish to show not only that course CSII is related to course CSIII, but also that CSII is a prerequisite for CSIII. So we use a directed edge from course CSII to course CSIII. In contradistinction, we assume that the relation between two cities in the route map is symmetric—if we can fly from one city to a second city by some airline, we can fly also in the reverse direction by the same airline. If this property does not hold, then we use a directed graph to represent a route map.

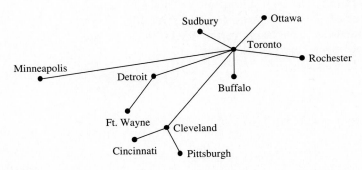

Figure 13.1 An airline route map.

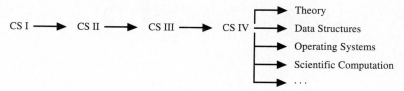

Figure 13.2 A prerequisite graph of computer science courses
at the University of Waterloo.

Graphs and digraphs (the usual name for directed graphs) are, at the same time, simple notions, which explains their universality of usage, and complex objects, which explains the ongoing interest in them and the challenge of them. In this chapter, we focus on the data-structuring aspects of graphs, rather than exploring graphs in their own right. To carry out this exploration, we need to have some understanding of the properties of graphs and, hence, of how graphs are used. For this reason, we examine fundamental graph problems and algorithms.

We introduce, in Section 13.1, the basic notions associated with graphs and digraphs, before we specify the DIGRAPH ADT and, implicitly, the GRAPH ADT. In Section 13.2, we discuss briefly the two standard representations of DIGRAPH and GRAPH. In Sections 13.3 and 13.4, we tackle a number of problems for graphs and digraphs and show how we can solve them using the corresponding ADT operations. Because graph traversals are basic to many graph algorithms, we demonstrate that we can perform them using the GRAPH and DIGRAPH operations. Finally, in Section 13.5, we return to the issue of memory management. We demonstrate not only how memory can be managed, but also how the memory-management problem can be modeled as a digraph problem.

13.1 GRAPH AND DIGRAPH SPECIFICATIONS

We begin by defining formally the notions of a digraph and graph and some of the terminology associated with them before specifying the corresponding ADTs.

A **directed graph** or **digraph** G consists of a finite set N of nodes or **vertices** and a set $E \subseteq N \times N$ of **directed edges;** we write $G = (N,E)$. An edge (s,t) is directed from s, the **source vertex,** to t, the **target vertex.** We say that t is a **successor** of s. Note that we allow edges from a vertex to itself.

Given a digraph $G = (N,E)$, a sequence

$$u_0, u_1, ..., u_m$$

of vertices from N is a **path,** if

$$(u_i, u_{i+1})$$

is in E, for all i, $0 \le i < m$. Intuitively, we can walk from u_0 to u_m along edges of G according to their direction. It is a **simple path** if we can walk from u_0 to u_m without revisiting a vertex—that is, whenever $i \ne j$, $u_i \ne u_j$. When $u_0,...,u_m$ is a path in G and $u_0 = u_m$, we say that it is a **cycle.** It is a **simple cycle** if $u_0,...,u_{m-1}$ is also a simple path.

A **graph** G consists of a finite set N of vertices and a set of E **edges;** we write $G = (N,E)$. An edge is defined by a set of two distinct vertices; thus, $\{a,b\}$ is an edge between a and b, where a and b are distinct. We say that two vertices a and b are **adjacent** if $\{a,b\}$ is in E. We can treat a graph as a digraph in which every edge $\{a,b\}$ is represented by two directed edges (a,b) and (b,a). Hence, we also consider b to be a successor of a and vice versa, in this case. The notions of path and cycle carry over to graphs in a straightforward manner. The **complete graph** for a set N of vertices has edge set

$$\{\{a,b\} : a,b \text{ in } N, a \ne b\};$$

it is the set of all possible edges between distinct pairs of vertices.

Having defined the elementary notions of graphs and digraphs, we now specify the DIGRAPH ADT. We allow the addition and removal of vertices and edges, and the replacement and examination of vertex and edge values. To navigate around a digraph, we can determine the number of vertices in a digraph and the number of successors of a given vertex. We can also obtain some vertex of a given digraph and obtain a successor of a given vertex.

Let G denote the set of digraphs whose vertices and edges have values of type *elementtype* (denoted by E). When these values are numerical, they are usually called **vertex weights** and **edge weights.** For convenience, we have chosen the vertex and edge values to be from the same set of values E; however, it is straightforward to modify the specification to have different sets of values. The vertices in a digraph are identified uniquely with **identifiers** from some totally ordered **identifier space** I that is usually the set of natural numbers.

1. *Empty*: $\rightarrow G$: The function value *Empty* is the empty digraph that has no vertices and no edges.

2. *IsEmpty*: $G \rightarrow B$: The function value *IsEmpty(G)* is **true** if G is an empty digraph; otherwise, it is **false.**

3. *InsertVertex*: $I \times E \times G \rightarrow G$: The function value *InsertVertex(id,e,G)* is the digraph that we obtain by adding a new vertex with identifier *id* and value e to G. If there is already a vertex in G with identifier *id,* then the operation is undefined.

4. *DeleteVertex*: $I \times G \rightarrow G$: The function value *DeleteVertex(id,G)* is the digraph that we obtained by removing the vertex with identifier *id* from G. If there is either no vertex in G with identifier *id* or the vertex *id* is the source or target vertex of an edge, then the operation is undefined.

5. *InsertEdge*: $I \times I \times \mathcal{E} \times G \rightarrow G$: The function value *InsertEdge* (*ids,idt,e,G*) is the digraph that we obtain by adding a new edge (*ids,idt*) with value *e* to *G*. If one or both of the identifiers *ids* or *idt* is undefined, then the operation is undefined, and if there is already an edge (*ids,idt*) in *G*, then the operation is undefined.

6. *DeleteEdge*: $I \times I \times G \rightarrow G$: The function value *DeleteEdge(ids,idt,G)* is the digraph that we obtain by removing the edge (*ids,idt*) from *G*. If there is no edge (*ids,idt*) in *G*, then the operation is undefined.

7. *ExamineVertex*: $I \times G \rightarrow \mathcal{E}$: The function value *ExamineVertex(id,G)* is the value associated with the vertex *id* in *G*. If there is no vertex *id* in *G*, then the operation is undefined.

8. *ReplaceVertex*: $\mathcal{E} \times I \times G \rightarrow G$: The function value *ReplaceVertex* (*e,id,G*) is the same as *G*, except that the value associated with the vertex *id* is *e*. If there is no vertex *id* in *G*, then the operation is undefined.

9. *ExamineEdge*: $I \times I \times G \rightarrow \mathcal{E}$: The function value *ExamineEdge* (*ids,idt,G*) is the value associated with the edge (*ids,idt*) in *G*. If there is no edge (*ids,idt*) in *G*, then the operation is undefined.

10. *ReplaceEdge*: $\mathcal{E} \times I \times I \times G \rightarrow G$: The function value *ReplaceEdge* (*e,ids,idt,G*) is *G*, except that the value associated with the edge (*ids,idt*) is *e*. If there is no edge (*ids,idt*) in *G*, then the operation is undefined.

11. *Size*: $G \rightarrow \mathcal{N}$: The function value *Size(G)* is the number of vertices in *G*. It is zero if and only if *G* is empty.

12. *SuccessorSize*: $I \times G \rightarrow \mathcal{N}$: The function value *SuccessorSize(id,G)* is undefined if *id* is not the identifier of any vertex in *G*; otherwise, it is the number of successors of the vertex *id* in *G*. It is zero if and only if *id* has no successors.

13. *Vertex*: $G \rightarrow I$: The function value *Vertex(G)* is the identifier of some vertex in *G*. If *G* is empty, then the operation is undefined. A sequence of *Size(G)* calls of *Vertex(G)* returns each vertex once and only once.

14. *Successor*: $I \times G \rightarrow I$: The function value *Successor(id,G)* is undefined if *id* is not the identifier of any vertex in *G*; otherwise, it is the identifier of some successor of vertex *id* in *G*. If *id* has no successors, then the operation is undefined. A sequence of *SuccessorSize(id,G)* calls of *Successor(id,G)* returns each successor once and only once.

We note that if we interleave insertions and deletions of vertices or edges with *Vertex* or *Successor*, then the results of these two operations are not always well defined.

We leave the specification of the GRAPH operations to Exercise 13.1, since it is similar.

13.2 GRAPH AND DIGRAPH REPRESENTATIONS

Because we model the GRAPH ADT with DIGRAPH, we discuss representations for only DIGRAPH. Furthermore, we rarely, if ever, represent digraphs (or graphs) in the "natural" way—that is, by nodes and links (or pointers). This approach is different from the representations for LIST and BINTREE, for example, where links are a common implementation method. For this reason, we normally identify the vertices of a digraph (or graph) with the integers $1..n$, when the given graph or digraph has n vertices.

The edge set E of a digraph $G = (N,E)$ can be viewed as a (partial) function $f_E : N \rightarrow 2^N$; hence, we can model DIGRAPH using the ARRAY ADT with domain N and codomain 2^N. Since we assume that I is the set N of natural numbers and the vertices are identified by the integers $1..n$, a block that is indexed by $1..n$ and has values that are subsets of $1..n$ is an obvious representation. The subsets can be represented by the SET ADT. If we use the LIST representation of SET, then we obtain the **adjacency-list** representation of f_E. On the other hand, because the sets in this framework are subsets of $1..n$, we can also represent each set as a Boolean block indexed by $1..n$. We obtain a block of blocks or a two-dimensional array representation of f_E, the **adjacency-matrix** representation. These representations are the only two choices that we consider when we discuss the time and space requirements of a graph or digraph algorithm. At all other times, we consider the representation of f_E to be a block with a set codomain. As a result of this viewpoint, *Successor* can be implemented with the *Examine* operation for SET, and *InsertEdge* can be implemented with the *Insert* operation for SET.

For example, the digraph of Fig. 13.3(a) can be represented by the block of blocks of Fig. 13.3(b) or the block of linked lists of Fig. 13.3(c). We capture these two representations with the following type declarations in Pascal. First, we give the the type definitions for the adjacency-matrix representation:

```
type idtype = 1..Maxvertex;

SET = record
          vertexvalue: elementtype;
          successorindex: idtype;
          S: array[idtype] of boolean
      end;
DIGRAPH = record
              vertexcount: idtype;
              vertexindex: idtype;
              adj: array[idtype] of SET
          end;
```

We have added some extra fields in the type definition for convenience and efficiency. First, *vertexcount* is used to hold the current number of vertices. Second,

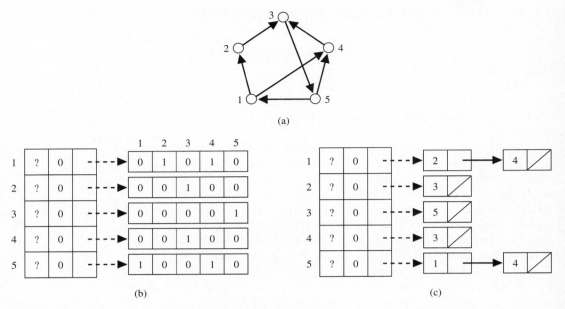

Figure 13.3   Digraph representations. (a) An example digraph. (b) The block of blocks or adjacency-matrix representation of the example digraph. The dashed lines indicate that the target block is included in its source cell. (c) The block of lists or adjacency-list representation of the example digraph. The dashed lines indicate that the target linked list is included in its source cell.

vertexindex is used by *Vertex* to obtain the next vertex, and *successorindex* is used by *Successor* to obtain the next successor. We have associated values only with vertices, and not with edges; however, it is easy to modify the definition to include edge values.

For the adjacency-list representation, we need to replace the definition of *S* in SET by

$$S: \text{LIST } \textbf{of } \textit{idtype},$$

and to change the type of *successorindex* to correspond to this change. We provide a Pascal implementation of *Empty*, *ExamineVertex*, and *Vertex* in Program 13.1, based on the adjacency-matrix representation. We leave you to implement the remaining operations; see Exercise 13.2. Also, we leave you to implement the DIGRAPH operations based on the adjacency-list representation; see Exercise 13.3. Observe that repeated calls of *Successor(id,G)* involve scanning a row vector in the adjacency-matrix representation; hence, it takes $O(n)$ time to return all successors once. On the other hand, the adjacency-list representation takes $O(SuccessorSize(id,G))$ time. This difference between the two representations is crucial to the efficiency of many graph algorithms. As we shall see in Section

```
procedure Empty(var G: DIGRAPH);
begin with G do
    begin vertexindex:= 0;
        vertexcount:= 0
    end
end;


procedure ExamineVertex(var e: elementtype;
                i: idtype; G: DIGRAPH);
begin with G do
    begin if (i <= 0) or (i > vertexcount)
        then error(' Attempting to examine a nonexisting vertex.')
        else e:= adj[i].vertexvalue
    end
end;


procedure Vertex(var i: idtype; var G: DIGRAPH);
begin with G do
    begin vertexindex:= vertexindex + 1;
        if vertexindex = vertexcount + 1
        then vertexindex:= 1;
        if (vertexindex <= 0) or (vertexindex > vertexcount)
        then error ('Attempting to retrieve a nonexisting vertex.}')
        else i:= vertexindex
    end
end;
```

Program 13.1 A Pascal implementation of three DIGRAPH operations based on the
                  adjacency-matrix representation.

13.3.2, we can traverse a digraph in $O(n + e)$ time using the adjacency-list representation, where n is the number of vertices and e is the number of edges. With
the adjacency-matrix representation, a traversal takes $O(n^2)$ time. Furthermore,
the space requirements are different. The adjacency-matrix representation uses
$O(n^2)$ space, whereas the adjacency-list representation uses $O(n + e)$ space.

13.3 DIGRAPH ALGORITHMS

We consider two digraph problems in this section. The first problem is to organize the steps of a recipe into an appropriate order—a topological sorting or
scheduling problem. It leads to two subproblems—namely, determine whether a
given digraph has a cycle, and topologically sort an acyclic digraph. The second
problem is to find a shortest path in an edge-weighted digraph from a given
source vertex to a given target vertex, if such a path exists. We use the two prob-

lems to demonstrate that depth-first and breadth-first traversals are basic tools for solving graph problems.

13.3.1   A Scheduling Problem

Baking recipes consist of the quantities of the ingredients and a set of instructions, or tasks, with an explicit ordering (and often an implicit ordering). We ignore the quantities in the following discussion. For example, the tasks associated with making a rhubarb cake are as follows:

1. Clean and peel rhubarb stalks.
2. Cut rhubarb into 2-centimeter pieces.
3. Scatter rhubarb evenly over cake mix.
4. Put milk and butter in a pan and bring to boil.
5. Pour egg–sugar mix onto hot milk and butter.
6. Beat eggs and sugar until white.
7. Stir cake mix until smooth.
8. Mix flour and baking powder and add to egg–milk mix to give cake mix.
9. Pour cake mix into large greased shallow pan.
10. Bake cake mix for 20–25 minutes at 200°C to give cake.

The tasks have been grouped according to their main ingredient, not according to the order in which they should be carried out. Observe that steps 1, 2, and 3 are in their correct order; we cannot put the rhubarb on the cake mix until it is cleaned, peeled, and cut. The inherent ordering of the steps can be captured by a digraph, a **task digraph**—its vertices are steps and there is a directed edge from a vertex i to a vertex j if step i is to be carried out before step j. In Fig. 13.4(a) we have displayed the basic ordering information. All other ordering information can be obtained from this basic ordering by the following rule: *If i should be done before j and j should be done before k, then i should be done before k.* For example, since 4 is to be done before 6 and 6 before 5, clearly 4 is to be done before 5, so we can add an edge directed from 4 to 5. If we repeat the application of this rule, then we obtain the digraph shown in Fig. 13.4(b). We have computed the **transitive closure** of the task digraph of Fig. 13.4(a)—a fundamental operation on digraphs (and graphs). What we want to do, however, is to order the steps so that later steps should never have to be completed before earlier steps. Such an ordering is called a **topologically sorted ordering.** A topologically sorted ordering is, after all, the way we usually follow a recipe. Note that, in general, there is more than one topologically sorted ordering. With the example recipe and its task digraph of Fig. 13.4(a), we can easily see that the ordering

$$4,6,5,8,7,9,1,2,3,10$$

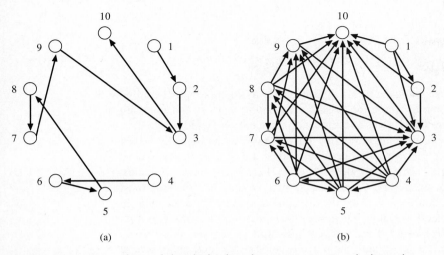

(a)   (b)

Figure 13.4 Digraphs and the rhubarb-cake recipe. (a) A task digraph representation of the inherent ordering of the steps in the recipe. (b) The digraph representation of the complete ordering of the steps inherent in the recipe—the transitive closure of the task digraph in (a).

is topologically sorted, as is

$$1,2,4,6,5,8,7,9,3,10,$$

and even

$$1,4,6,2,5,8,7,9,3,10.$$

But,

$$1,2,3,4,5,6,7,8,9,10$$

is not a topologically sorted ordering, because 6 should be completed before 5, 8 before 7, and 9 before 3. At this stage, you should consider how many different topologically sorted orderings there are for this example; see Exercise 13.4.

How do we obtain a topologically sorted ordering for hundreds and thousands of tasks? For example, consider the tasks involved in the construction of a new office building, the arrangement of an office shuffle, or the completion of a university degree. First, let us define the **scheduling** or topologically sorted ordering problem more precisely as follows: *We are given* $n \geq 1$ *tasks* $T_1,...,T_n$ *subject to* **constraints** *of the following form:* T_i *must be completed before* T_j. *Produce a permutation* $T_{i_1},...,T_{i_n}$ *of* $T_1,...,T_n$, *such that, whenever* $j < k$, *there is no*

Figure 13.5 A two-task digraph with no topologically sorted ordering.

constraint: T_{i_k} must be completed before T_{i_j}. We can always represent a scheduling problem with a digraph in which the tasks correspond to vertices and there are edges (T_i, T_j) whenever there is a constraint that T_i must be completed before T_j.

We can easily construct digraphs that do not have a topologically sorted ordering; for example, the two-task digraph displayed in Fig. 13.5 does not have any topologically sorted ordering for the two tasks. There are only two schedules, 1,2 and 2,1; in both cases, however, there is a conflict, because the final task must be completed before the first one. That the digraph has a cycle is no accident. In general, we observe the following: *Whenever a task graph has a cycle, it has no topologically sorted ordering.* Every **acyclic digraph** (a digraph that has no cycles) has, however, at least one topologically sorted ordering; see Exercise 13.5. Therefore, the first step in obtaining a topologically sorted ordering from a task digraph is to determine that the task digraph has no cycles and, therefore, that a topologically sorted ordering exists.

There is a close relationship between sorting and topological sorting, since, given n distinct numbers, $x_1,...,x_n$, their constraints correspond to the pairwise ordering, x_i is to be "completed" before x_j when $x_i < x_j$. The topologically sorted ordering for the x_is is unique, and it corresponds to sorting the x_is into ascending order. The topological sorting problem is, therefore, a generalization of the sorting problem, which is the reason for its name. In Sections 13.3.2 and 13.3.3, we show how to test a digraph for acyclicity and how to sort topologically an acyclic digraph (often called a **dag,** for directed acyclic graph).

13.3.2 Acyclicity and Traversals

Given a digraph, we can determine whether it has a cycle by traversing it. Recall that a traversal of a data structure visits each vertex exactly once by walking along each edge, so it takes time linear in the size of the structure (if moving from one vertex to another takes constant time). Graphs and digraphs have two basic traversal orders—**depth first** and **breadth first.** The successors of vertices in graphs and digraphs are unordered, so there is no predetermined order for exploring successors of a vertex. You should compare the definitions of digraphs in Section 13.1, and of trees in Section 5.1. We have defined trees such that the successors of a tree node are ordered. (Most representations of graphs and digraphs, however, impose an ordering on successors and, in practice, this ordering is used. It has the advantage that two depth-first (or breadth-first) traversals of a graph or digraph that begin at the same vertex, will visit vertices in the same order.)

To determine whether a digraph has cycles, we explore all simple paths—if none of these paths are cycles, then the digraph has no cycles. A digraph has a cycle if and only if it has a simple cycle; see Exercise 13.6.

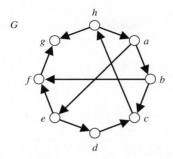

Figure 13.6   The example digraph *G*.

We use the digraph *G* of Fig. 13.6 to illustrate the traversal algorithms. Depth-first traversals of digraphs (and of graphs) are similar to depth-first traversals of trees with the following differences. Because there is no ordering of successors and because we visit a vertex when first meeting it, there is only one depth-first traversal. A further difference is that we can meet a vertex many times, and the only method of avoiding visiting it many times is to mark it as visited when we first meet it. When traversing a tree, we do not need to mark its nodes as visited; see Exercise 13.7.

Since digraphs (and graphs) do not have root vertices or designated entry vertices, a traversal can begin at any vertex. For example, let us begin at vertex *h* in *G*. We visit *h*, mark it, and then continue the traversal by moving to each successor of *h* in some order. We picture the traversal order by building a **traversal orchard**—a conceptual structure that is never implemented. Recall from Section 5.1.3 that an orchard is an ordered forest of trees. Assume that we continue the traversal by moving to vertex *g*. We visit vertex *g* and mark it. Since *g* has no successors, we continue with the "next" successor of *h*—namely, *a*. The traversal orchard grows as shown in Fig. 13.7. Node *a* has two successors; we assume that we explore *b* and then *e*. As we traverse *G* from *b*, we find that *b* also has two successors. We assume that *f* is the first successor; its only successor is the vertex *g*, which we have already visited. We know that the vertex *g* has been visited, because it is already in the traversal orchard and it has been marked. We indicate the edge that we do not take as a dashed edge in the traversal orchard, and we retreat to vertex *b*, which has an unexplored successor. These steps are shown in Figures 13.7(d) through (f). Continuing with vertex *c*, the second successor of *b*—see Figures 13.7(g) and (h)—we find that its only successor, *h*, has been visited. Again, we indicate the edge not taken as a dashed edge. This dashed edge is different from the first one, however; it connects a vertex to one of that vertex's ancestors—*h* is an ancestor of *c*—whereas the dashed edge from *f* to *g* does not have this property. Since *h* is an ancestor of *c*, there is a simple path from *h* to *c* and an edge from *c* to *h*. Et voilà ! A cycle. So, *G* is not acyclic.

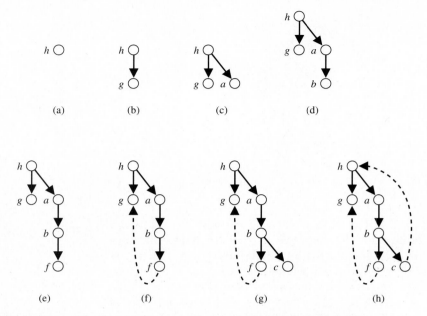

Figure 13.7   The first eight steps of a depth-first traversal of G.

From the viewpoint of acyclicity testing, the traversal can terminate at vertex c; however, we continue the traversal for illustrative purposes. The final traversal orchard is shown in Fig. 13.8(a). If we begin the traversal at vertex f, say, then we obtain a different traversal orchard; see Fig. 13.8(b). After reaching g, we continue the traversal at some arbitrary unvisited vertex; in this case, we continue with vertex e. The depth-first traversal algorithm is described recursively in Fig. 13.9.

We have learned that we can adapt the depth-first traversal algorithm for trees to give a depth-first traversal algorithm for digraphs. A Pascal implementation is given in Program 13.2, based on the DIGRAPH operations. How fast is *DepthFirstTraversal*? We need to visit every vertex and to traverse every edge, so it requires $\Omega(n + e)$ time, where n is the number of vertices and e is the number of edges, in the given digraph. An examination of *DepthFirstTraversal* should convince you that the time depends only on the time taken by the ADT operations: *Size*, *SuccessorSize*, and *Successor*. The operations *Size* and *SuccessorSize* take constant time, and e calls of *Successor* take $O(e)$ time with the adjacency-list representation. (With the adjacency-matrix representation, the e calls take $O(n^2)$ time.) Thus, we are able to implement *DepthFirstTraversal* to run in $O(n + e)$ time using $O(n + e)$ space, and these bounds are optimal.

We now consider the breadth-first traversal of a digraph. A breadth-first traversal begins by visiting some vertex, visiting all that vertex's successors, then visiting all of their successors, and so on. For the digraph of Fig. 13.6, if we begin

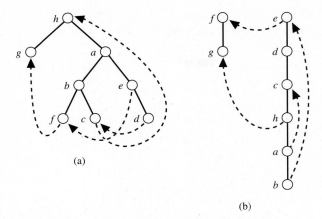

Figure 13.8 Two depth-first traversal orchards for digraph *G*.

For each vertex *u* in a given digraph *G*,
　　if *u* is unvisited, then visit *u* and traverse
　　　　the digraph starting from each of its successors;
　　　　otherwise, terminate the traversal.

Figure 13.9 A high-level recursive description of the depth-first traversal of a digraph.

at vertex *h*, then we obtain the traversal orchard given in Fig. 13.10. Serendipitously, we obtain exactly the same traversal orchard as we did with depth-first traversal when we began at the same vertex *h*. This occurrence is unusual, even when we explore the successors of each vertex in the same order; normally, two traversals give different orchards. For example, in Fig. 13.11(a), we have another depth-first traversal of *G* and, in Fig. 13.11(b), we have the corresponding breadth-first traversal. The successors are explored in the same order as before, except that we assume that the successors of *b* are explored in the order *c* followed by *f*. We leave you to design a Pascal implementation of breadth-first traversal and to analyze its performance; see Exercise 13.8. Breadth-first traversal can be used also as a basis for acyclicity testing; see Exercise 13.9.

13.3.3 Topological Sorting

We now assume that we are given a dag and we want to produce a schedule for its vertices that does not conflict with the constraints given by the dag itself; it should be a topologically sorted ordering. For example, with the dag *H* of Fig. 13.12 (a), the schedule

$$h, a, g, d, b, e, c, f$$

```
procedure DepthFirstTraversal(G: DIGRAPH);
var visited: array[1..Maxvertex] of boolean;
    i,n: integer;

procedure DFT(i: integer; G: DIGRAPH);
var j,s: integer;
begin
    if visited[i]
    then {Exit immediately.}
    else begin
        {Visit vertex i.}
        visited[i]:= true;
        s:= SuccessorSize(i,G);
        for j:= 1 to s do DFT(Successor(i,G),G)
        {Note that, by definition, s calls of Successor(i,G)
            return the s successors of vertex i.}
    end
end;

begin
    n:= Size(G);
    for i:= 1 to n do visited[i]:= false;

    for i:= 1 to n do DFT(i,G)
end;
```

Program 13.2 A Pascal implementation of the depth-first traversal of a digraph.

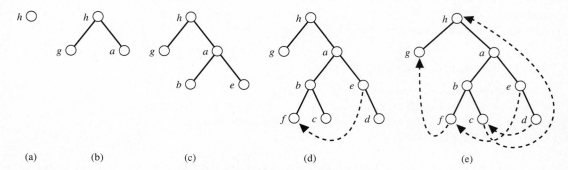

(a)   (b)   (c)   (d)   (e)

Figure 13.10 Snapshots of a breadth-first traversal of digraph *G*.

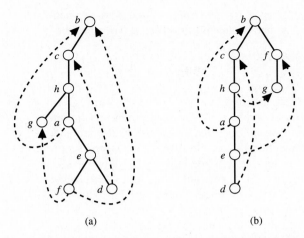

(a)   (b)

Figure 13.11 Corresponding orchards for depth-first and breadth-first traversals of digraph *G*. (a) A depth-first traversal. (b) A breadth-first traversal.

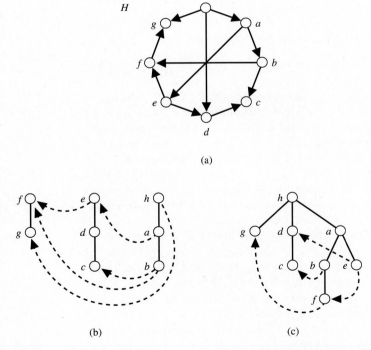

Figure 13.12 Dags and depth-first traversals. (a) The example dag *H*. (b) A depth-first traversal of *H* from vertex *f*. (c) A depth-first traversal of *H* from vertex *h*.

is not a topologically sorted ordering, since g occurs before b and there is a path from b to g, and d occurs before e and there is an edge from e to d. The schedule

$$h,a,e,b,f,d,c,g$$

is, however, a topologically sorted ordering.

We first extend the definition of the postorder traversal of a binary tree, given in Section 5.3.1, to multiway trees and orchards. To traverse a multiway tree in postorder, we traverse the subtrees of each node before visiting that node and, moreover, we traverse the first subtree, then the second subtree, and so on. To traverse an orchard in postorder, we traverse the first tree in postorder, then the second, and so on. Now, to sort topologically the vertices of a dag, we use depth-first traversal and the following observation: *A postorder traversal of a depth-first orchard visits the vertices in reverse topological order.* We first show that this observation holds for a depth-first orchard of the example dag, before arguing that it holds in general. Two possible depth-first orchards for the example dag are shown in Figures 13.12(b) and (c). In a postorder traversal of a tree, we traverse the subtrees of a vertex before visiting the vertex, and we traverse the subtrees in left-to-right order. Also, we traverse the trees in an orchard in left-to-right order. Therefore, given the orchard in Fig. 13.12(b), we obtain the postorder traversal

$$g,f,c,d,e,b,a,h;$$

given the orchard in Fig. 13.12(c), we obtain the postorder traversal

$$g,c,d,f,b,e,a,h.$$

Reversing these two sequences, we obtain two topologically sorted orderings of the vertices. Checking this fact is a laborious task, since we have to ensure that every descendant of each vertex in the dag appears later than the vertex itself. Why does this approach work? We consider the kinds of edges that we add to a vertex u in a depth-first traversal orchard. If a vertex u has no edges from it, then it has no descendants in the given dag. So, in a topological ordering, it must appear after all its ancestors; in a reverse topological ordering, it must appear before all its ancestors. But a postorder traversal, by definition, produces this ordering.

If a vertex u has edges from it, then they can be dashed or solid edges. What do these edges tell us about u's position in a topological ordering? An edge of either kind from u indicates that u has descendants and that it should appear before them in a topological ordering; that is, it should appear after them in a reverse topological ordering. In a postorder traversal, u is visited after its solid-edge descendants, so we have to consider only its dashed-edge descendants. But a dashed edge from u leads to a vertex occurring earlier in the depth-first traversal, and such vertices are of two possible kinds:

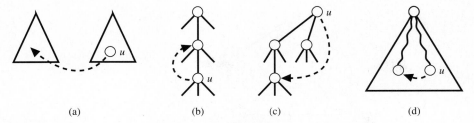

Figure 13.13 The four kinds of dashed edges from a vertex u in a depth-first traversal orchard. (a) From u to a different tree to its left. (b) From u to one of its ancestors. (c) From u to one of its descendants. (d) From u to a vertex that has a common ancestor.

1. A dashed edge from u leads to a vertex in a different tree, and this tree is, by definition, to u's left; see Fig. 13.13(a).

2. A dashed edge from u leads to a vertex in the same tree as u, in which case (1) it is an ancestor of u in the tree, see Fig. 13.13(b); (2) it is a descendant of u in the tree; that is, to u's left, see Fig. 13.13(c); or (3) it is a descendant of the root of the tree—that is, it is to u's left—see Fig. 13.13(d).

Case 2.1 cannot occur, because the digraph is acyclic; the other three cases may occur and, in each of them, u is visited later than the corresponding vertices in a postorder traversal. Thus, u appears after its descendants in a postorder traversal, and this ordering agrees with the reverse topological ordering of the vertices of the given dag.

Using the adjacency-list representation, we can implement topological sorting so that it runs in $O(n + e)$ time using $O(n + e)$ space. An implementation combines the depth-first traversal of a dag and the postorder traversal of the depth-first traversal orchard to produce a single traversal of the graph. The key observation is that the depth-first traversal visits vertices in preorder; in a postorder traversal, we visit vertices on any root-to-frontier path, in a depth-first tree, in frontier-to-root order, the reverse of the visit order in depth-first traversal. We do not need to construct the depth-first orchard explicitly; we leave the details to Exercise 13.10.

13.3.4 Minimum or Shortest Paths

Assume that you are in Toronto, Ontario, and wish to fly to Raleigh, North Carolina,; because you are a nervous flyer, you want to minimize the in-the-air (or flight) time. To solve this and similar problems, we represent the airline-connection network as a digraph in which vertices are airports, edges are nonstop flight connections, and nonnegative integer weights on the edges are the usual in-the-air

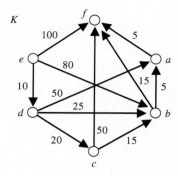

Figure 13.14   The example weighted digraph K.

time of the corresponding flight. We use a digraph, rather than a graph, because the flight time from one city to a second city is not necessarily the same as the flight time from the second city to the first city. (We ignore multiple connections and assume, for simplicity, that all nonstop flights from one airport to a second have the same in-the-air time.) A path from Toronto to Raleigh provides a sequence of nonstop flights, and the sum of the weights on the corresponding edges gives the total in-the-air time for the sequence. Our problem becomes this: *Find a path from Toronto to Raleigh that minimizes the in-the-air time.*

Abstracting this problem further, we have a digraph with nonnegative integer weights on its edges and two vertices s (for source) and t (for target). Letting the **cost** or **length** of a path in the digraph be the sum of the weights on the edges in the path, we wish to find a minimum-cost path from s to t. Such a path is called a **minimum** or **shortest path from s to t**. (In Exercise 13.13, we consider the **all-pairs shortest-path problem:** *Find the shortest paths between all distinct pairs of vertices.*) For example, given the weighted digraph K of Fig. 13.14 with source vertex e and target vertex f, a shortest path from e to f is

$$e,d,b,a,f,$$

which has a cost of $10 + 25 + 5 + 5 = 45$. Compare this path with the paths

$$e,f$$

and

$$e,d,a,f,$$

which have costs 100 and 65, respectively. With our small example, we could examine all simple paths from e to f, compute their costs, and take any path that has minimum cost. In general, however, we are given large digraphs, so we soon falter when we attempt exhaustive examination, because of the exponential number—in terms of the number of vertices—of paths. We avoid the exponential blowup by using greediness again. We attempt to find a global minimum (or maximum) by taking a partial solution and extending it incrementally with local minima (or maxima). The resulting algorithm is called **Dijkstra's algorithm.**

Dijkstra's algorithm traverses a given digraph one vertex at a time, beginning with the source vertex s, to find the shortest paths from s to all the vertices it has visited. We, however, use Dijkstra's algorithm to find only the shortest path from s to t; the minor extension to obtain them all is left as Exercise 13.11. The traversal splits the vertices into two disjoint sets: the **visited vertices** V and the **unvisited vertices** U. Initially, for a digraph, $G = (N,E)$, we have $V = \{s\}$. At each traversal step, the unvisited vertices are the vertices in $N - V$. The traversal discovers larger and larger subgraphs of the given digraph by adding one unvisited vertex to V at each step; it does not "know" the whole graph until it has visited all the vertices. We, therefore, maintain *the length of a shortest path from s to each vertex in N, subject to the restriction that "shortest path" means a minimum-cost path that passes through only vertices in V*. This maintenance criterion is the traversal invariant, and we call such paths V-paths. If there is no V-path from s to an unvisited node u, then we define the cost of the path from s to u to be $+\infty$.

Note that when we have visited all the vertices in a digraph, $V = N$ and an N-path is just a path, so a shortest N-path from s to t is a shortest path from s to t. We have a somewhat stronger result though. If we stop the traversal algorithm as soon as we visit vertex t, then, even if we have not visited all the vertices in the digraph, we can guarantee that we have already found the shortest path from s to t. This stronger result is established later in this section. First, how do we maintain the traversal invariant efficiently? Whenever we add a vertex to V, we may need to change some of the shortest V-paths. Fortunately, as we shall see, this change can be done efficiently.

Without more ado, let us describe Dijkstra's algorithm, work through the algorithm with the example digraph K, and, finally, prove the algorithm's correctness. We give a high-level version of Dijkstra's algorithm in Fig. 13.15. We are given an edge-weighted digraph, $G = (N,E)$, and vertices s and t in N. At each step of the traversal, we have a set of visited vertices V such that $V \subseteq N$, s is in V, and V satisfies the traversal invariant, and we want to add an unvisited vertex from U to V. We use the notation $wt(x,y)$ to denote the weight of the edge (x,y) in E, and $D(x)$ to denote the length of a shortest V-path or shortest **distance** of x from s. Initially, $V = \{s\}$, $D(s) = 0$, and, for all u in $N-\{s\}$, $D(u)$ is $wt(s,u)$ if there is an edge from s to u, and $+\infty$, otherwise.

We visit an unvisited vertex u if it satisfies the **greedy criterion:** *For all z in $N - V$,*

$$D(u) \le D(z).$$

We illustrate Dijkstra's algorithm with the example digraph K. Initially, since the source vertex is e, we have $V = \{e\}$, $D(b) = 80$, $D(d) = 10$, $D(f) = 100$, $D(e) = 0$, and $D(u) = +\infty$, for all other unvisited vertices u. Because the next vertex to be visited must be a successor of at least one vertex in V, the only possible candidates to be added to V are b, d, and f. The greedy criterion specializes, in this case,

Given a digraph $G = (N, E)$ with nonnegative weights on its edges
and two vertices s and t, find a shortest path from s to t.

We begin by initializing the visited set V, the unvisited set U,
and the V-path distance function D.

```
V:= {s}; U:= N - {s};
For all w in N, D(w):= + ∞;
For all u in U such that (s,u) is in E,
    D(u):= w(s,u);

while t ∉ V do
begin
    Let u in U have minimum D(u) value.
    V:= V ∪ {u}; U:= U - {u};
    For all w in U such that (u,w) is in E,
        D(w):= min(D(w),D(u) + w(u,w))
end;
```

Figure 13.15   A high-level version of Dijkstra's algorithm to find a shortest path in a digraph
from a source vertex s to a target vertex t.

to the following: Which u in $\{b,d,f\}$ satisfies $D(u) \leq D(z)$, for all z in $\{b,d,f\}$?
Clearly, we choose d, since $\mathrm{wt}(e,d) < \mathrm{wt}(e,b) < \mathrm{wt}(e,f)$. The traversal and the
shortest V-paths are shown as a sequence of snapshots in Fig. 13.16. We have
reversed the direction of the edges of the shortest paths in Fig. 13.16, so that we
can represent the shortest paths efficiently; we call this technique the **reversed-
edge technique.** We have reversed the direction of the edges so that the shortest
V-paths are easily rediscovered, and we have added the distance of each vertex
from e as a vertex weight. (This extension is not included in the high-level algorithm of Fig. 13.15.) Whenever a shortest path to an unvisited vertex is modified,
we need to change only its predecessor on the current path to be its predecessor
on the new path, which is always the newly visited vertex. We now update D.
$D(a)$, $D(b)$, and $D(c)$ are reduced to $D(a) = 60$, $D(b) = 35$, and $D(c = 30)$. The set
V of visited vertices is now $\{e,d\}$, and unlisted candidates must be successors of d
or e. Hence, a, b, c, and f are candidates, and we visit c, since $D(c) = 30$ and this
cost is the smallest for the vertices in $N - \{e,d\}$. We obtain the shortest V-paths by
adding the new vertex c and its connecting edge (d,c) to the traversal set; see Fig.
13.16(c). Since b and f are successors of c, at most $D(b)$ and $D(f)$ are reduced by
the addition of c. In fact, $D(b)$ is unchanged, but $D(f) = 80$.

Continuing the greedy process, the next set of candidates is $\{a,b,f\}$. Clearly,
we should visit b next, in which case, $D(a) = 40$ and $D(f) = 50$. Only a and f are
unvisited at this point; hence, we should add a to V and set $D(f)$ to 45. We obtain
the snapshot of Fig. 13.16(e). Finally, we add f to V and we have found a shortest
path from e to f. We have found also the shortest V-paths, for all vertices in V from
e.

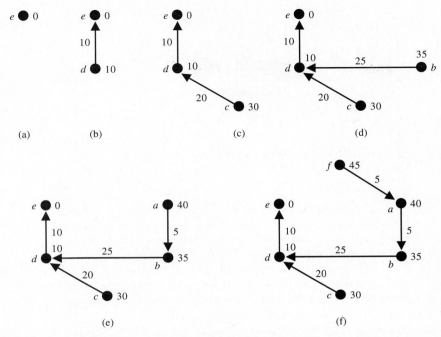

Figure 13.16 The six successive steps in Dijkstra's algorithm for source vertex e in the example digraph K.

What is surprising is that we never have to change the shortest path from s to a vertex once that vertex has been added to V. This effect of greediness is crucial to the algorithm's correctness, efficiency, and simplicity. There are two steps needed to demonstrate this fact. First, we argue that when we add a new vertex u to V, the shortest V-path to u is a shortest path to u. Second, we argue that the distance function D is maintained correctly by Dijkstra's algorithm. In both cases, we argue by contradiction.

First, when we add a new vertex u to V, we assume that the shortest V-path to u is not the shortest path to u. Hence, there is a shorter path that first leaves V to go to some vertex x in U, and then, perhaps, goes in and out of V several times before arriving at u; see Fig. 13.17. This assumption, however, implies that the V-path from s to x is shorter than the V-path from s to u. In other words, $D(x) < D(u)$, and Dijkstra's algorithm would have chosen to add x rather than u to V.

Second, when we add u to V, consider the value of $D(w)$, for each w in $N-(V \cup \{u\})$. If there is an edge from u to w, then Dijkstra's algorithm compares $D(w)$ and $D(u) + wt(u,w)$, and reduces $D(w)$ if the $(V \cup \{u\})$ -path to w is shorter than the V-path to w. The only remaining possibility is that there is a shorter $(V \cup \{u\})$ -path from s to u, from u to some node x in V, and from x to w, as shown in Fig. 13.18. But the shortest path from s to x is a V-path, and it is no

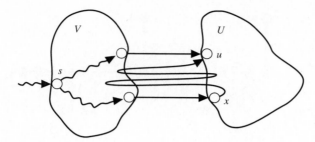

Figure 13.17   Shortest paths and *V*-paths. An implied shortest
path that is not a *V*-path.

longer than the $(V \cup \{u\})$-path from s to x via u, because x was added to V before u. Thus the V-path from s to w via x is no longer than the $(V \cup \{u\})$ -path from s to w via u and x. Hence, D(w) can be reduced when u is added to V only by a new path from s to w via u and the edge (u,w).

The set of shortest distances can be maintained with four operations: *Min*, *Delete*, *Insert*, and *DecreaseDistance*. These operations can be implemented with a Fibonacci queue in which the records are the vertices of the given digraph and the priority of the record is the current shortest distance of its vertex from s.

Using the adjacency-list representation, observe that, for w in $N - V$, D(w) is updated only when (u,w) is in E. Thus, D is updated at most e times and the Fibonacci queue takes $O(e)$ time for the e *DecreaseDistance* operations. Choosing a minimum-valued D(u) and deleting its record takes $O(\log n)$ amortized time in a Fibonacci queue; since there are $n - 1$ greedy steps, they take $O(n \log n)$ time in total. Combining these observations, we see that Dijkstra's algorithm can be implemented, with the adjacency-list representation, to run in $O(e + n \log n)$ time, using $O(n + e)$ space. (If we use the adjacency-matrix representation, then Dijkstra's algorithm takes $O(n^2)$ time and space. We leave the details to Exercise 13.12.)

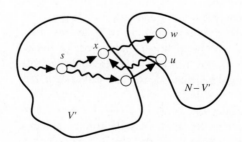

Figure 13.18   Modification of shortest paths after vertex selection in the shortest-path
algorithm. How the shortest path to vertex w can change after selecting
vertex u.

When we want to find the shortest paths from every vertex to every other vertex (the all-pairs shortest-path problem), we can repeat Dijkstra's algorithm n times. This method gives an $O(ne + n^2 \log n)$-time solution, but the Floyd–Warshall algorithm—see Exercise 13.13—takes $O(n^3)$ time and uses $O(n^2)$ space. In the worst case, the two algorithms take the same time, $O(n^3)$, but the simplicity of the Floyd–Warshall algorithm ensures that that algorithm has a smaller multiplicative constant hidden in the big-oh notation. Despite this simplicity, Dijkstra's algorithm is faster than the Floyd–Warshall algorithm when e is smaller than $O(n^2)$.

13.4 GRAPH ALGORITHMS

We consider two problems that can be modeled and solved using graphs. The first problem is whether we can walk from a source plank to a target plank on a building site without getting muddy feet. This problem leads to the path-connectedness and connected-component problems. Second, we consider the problem of drawing scatter plots efficiently. It leads to the minimal-tour problem, which is, unfortunately, an intractable problem. Therefore, we investigate an approximation algorithm that is based on the efficient construction of minimum spanning trees for an edge-weighted graph. Again, depth-first and breadth-first traversals are central to the algorithms we present.

13.4.1 Walking the Planks

A typical building site is covered with knee-deep clay mud and is littered with wooden planks that provide mud-free walkways. We are on plank s and want to walk to plank t without jumping across gaps or wallowing in mud; see Fig. 13.19(a). Can we do it?

We first rephrase this problem in terms of graphs. Given a configuration of planks, we construct a graph that models their connectivity. Let each plank be a vertex in the graph; whenever two planks cross each other, in some way, there is an edge between their corresponding vertices. For example, in Fig. 13.19(a), plank 4 crosses planks 3 and 10, so the associated graph has edges between vertices 4 and 3, and between vertices 4 and 10; see Fig. 13.19(b). Observe that it is natural to use *undirected* edges here, since whenever we can walk from s to t, we can walk from t to s. In this setting, the query, "Can we walk from plank s to plank t?" becomes "Is there a path from vertex s to vertex t?" The graph model captures the essential properties of the planks and discards the inessential ones. But how do we answer the path question?

We say that two vertices s and t are **connected** in a graph, $G = (N,E)$, if there is a path from s to t in G. Connectedness is an equivalence relation: Each vertex is, trivially, connected to itself; if a vertex s is connected to a vertex t, then t is connected to s; and, finally, if a vertex s is connected to a vertex t, and t is connected to a vertex u, then s is connected to u. Because connectedness is an equiv-

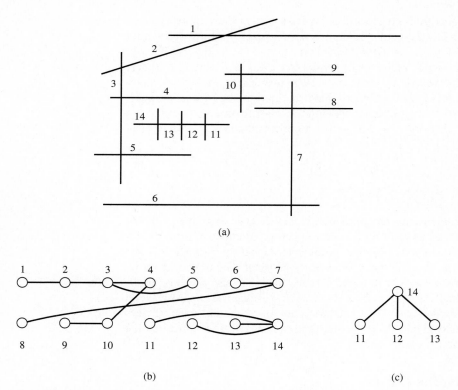

(a)

(b)   (c)

Figure 13.19 Planks and graphs. (a) An example of planks on a muddy
building site. (b) The corresponding graph. (c) A connected
component of the planks graph.

alence relation, its equivalence classes are sets of vertices that are connected to
one another. For example, in Fig. 13.19(b), the set {11,12,13,14} of vertices is an
equivalence class with respect to connectedness. Each equivalence class determines a subgraph of the original graph, called a **connected component.** Moreover, a connected component has no edges to any vertices in the remainder of the
graph—it is a **disconnected subgraph.** A connected component is an equivalence
class of vertices together with all their edges. So the set {11,12,13,14} determines
the connected component given in Fig. 13.19(c).

Our interest in connected components stems from the following relationship
between path existence and connected components: *There is a path from s to t if
and only if s and t are in the same connected component.* This relationship leads
to two different approaches to the path question. In the first approach, we are
given a graph and a pair of vertices; in the second approach, we are given a graph
and, subsequently, pairs of vertices. In both cases, we want to determine, for a
given pair of vertices, whether the vertices are connected in the graph. The two

versions are called the **off-line** and **on-line** versions, respectively, of the connectivity problem. In the off-line problem, we must explore the graph to see whether *s* and *t* are connected; in the on-line problem, we can preprocess the graph to find its connected components before answering any queries. We provide algorithms for path connectedness and connected components in Sections 13.4.2 and 13.4.3, respectively.

13.4.2 Path Connectedness

The problem we consider here is this: *Given a graph G and two vertices s and t in G, is there a path that connects s and t in G?* This problem is similar to the problem of determining whether there is a cycle in a given digraph, and it falls to a similar approach—we traverse the graph starting at either vertex *s* or vertex *t*. We use a depth-first traversal so that the minor differences between the traversal of a graph and the traversal of a digraph are highlighted. Consider the example graph *L* given in Fig. 13.20, and assume that $s = g$ and $t = b$. We treat the edges as pairs of directed edges, from *g*, we reach *h*, say, via an edge, then *c*, and then *a*; see Fig. 13.21. From *a*, we explore the edges to *c* and *h*, before taking the edge to *b*. At this point, we have reached *b* while exploring the depth-first tree rooted at *g*; hence, *g* and *b* are connected. Alternatively, if $t = d$, say, then the previous traversal continues after reaching *b*, giving rise to the depth-first tree of Fig. 13.22(a). Since *d* is not in this tree, it is not connected to *g*.

Using the adjacency-list representation, this algorithm can be implemented to run in $O(n + e)$ time, using $O(n + e)$ space. The adjacency-matrix representation is considered in Exercise 13.14.

13.4.3 Connected Components

We provide one solution to the following problem: *Given a graph, $G = (N,E)$, determine its connected components.* We then use the connected components to answer efficiently queries of the following form: Are two given vertices *s* and *t* in the same connected component of *G*?

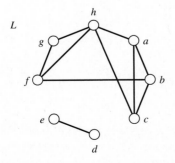

Figure 13.20 The example graph *L*.

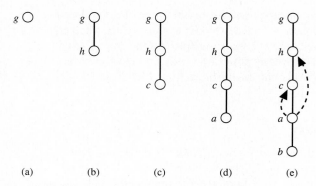

Figure 13.21   The first five steps in a depth-first traversal
                of the example graph *L*.

By now, the basic approach should be clear—we perform a depth-first traversal of *G,* and each tree in the depth-first orchard corresponds to a connected
component. Continuing the depth-first traversal we began in Fig. 13.21, we complete it by starting at either vertex *d* or vertex *e*. We choose to begin at vertex *d,*
and we obtain the second and final tree in the depth-first orchard; see Fig.
13.22(b). Thus, the graph of Fig. 13.20 has two connected components. These
components are $G_1 = (\{a,b,c,f,g,h\}, E_1)$, where

$$E_1 = \{\{a,b\},\{a,c\},\{a,h\},\{b,c\},\{b,f\},\{c,h\},\{f,g\},\{f,h\},\{g,h\}\},$$

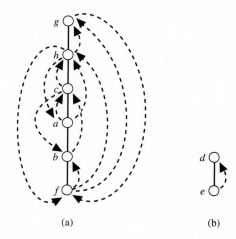

Figure 13.22   Components and depth-first traversal trees. (a) A depth-first
                traversal tree for one component of *L*. (b) A depth-first traversal
                tree for the other component of *L*.

and $G_2 = (\{d,e\},E_2)$, where

$$E_2 = \{\{d,e\}\}.$$

Clearly, we can accumulate the vertices and edges of each component as we traverse the graph, so the algorithm runs in $O(n + e)$ time and uses $O(n + e)$ space.

Finally, to answer queries of the form, "Are s and t in the same component?" we number the components and attach a component number to each vertex during the traversal. Therefore, to answer a query for s and $t,$ we check only whether they have the same component number; the check can be implemented to take constant time.

13.4.4 Minimum Spanning Trees

After moving into a new building, we need to connect some electrical equipment that is scattered throughout the building. The building has built-in ducts to hold such connections, and we want to connect the equipment so as to minimize the total length of the connections, since wire is expensive and longer wire is less reliable. For example, the graph P in Fig. 13.23 abstracts such a problem, where the vertices correspond to equipment or sites, the edges correspond to ducts, and the weight of an edge $e = (x,y)$ corresponds to the distance from x to y through duct $e.$

What exactly does it mean to connect the sites? The connecting strategy we use is that there should be a path from each site to every other site. Thus the sites and their connections must form a single connected component—it is a **connected subgraph** of the given graph that contains the same vertices as the original graph, and we call it a **spanning subgraph.** We want to find a minimum-cost

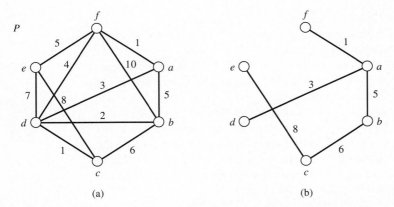

Figure 13.23   Weighted graphs and spanning trees. (a) The example
weighted graph P. (b) A spanning tree of P.

spanning subgraph of a given graph, where we define the **cost** of an edge-weighted graph G to be the sum of the graph's edge weights, and we denote it by $COST(G)$. We claim that we need to consider only those spanning subgraphs that are free trees; they are called **spanning trees.** An example spanning tree of the graph P is given in Fig. 13.23(b). A **free tree** is a graph that is connected and acyclic. It is straightforward to establish that a free tree of n vertices has exactly $n - 1$ edges and that adding a single edge to a free tree produces a cycle; see Exercise 13.15. Assume that we have a graph G with nonnegative edge weights and a minimum-cost spanning subgraph S of G. If S is not a free tree, then it has a cycle, and we can remove at least one edge from this cycle of S to give a spanning subgraph S' of G such that the cost of S' is no greater than the cost of S. If S' is a free tree, then we are done; otherwise, we repeat the edge-removal process on S' instead of S until we obtain a free tree. Since we never increase the cost of a subgraph by removing an edge, the final free tree that we obtain has a cost no greater than the cost of S. Thus we need to consider only minimum-cost spanning trees; they are called **minimum spanning trees.** We can now abstract the wiring problem as the following: *Given a graph with nonnegative edge weights, find a minimum spanning tree of the graph.* One obvious algorithm is to enumerate all spanning trees, to compute their costs, and to select one that minimizes the cost. Unfortunately there can be exponentially many (in terms of e) spanning trees of a connected graph. So we are interested in a more efficient algorithm.

We will use greediness once more, growing a minimum spanning tree one vertex at a time. The algorithm, called **Prim's algorithm,** is based on the following fact, as are all minimum-spanning tree algorithms.

Fact 13.1 *Assume that $G = (N,E)$ is an edge-weighted connected graph, and that V is a proper subset of N. If, among all edges between V and $N - V$, the edge $\{v,w\}$ has smallest weight, then there is a minimum spanning tree of G that includes the edge $\{v,w\}$.*

We argue as follows. Let $T = (N,E_T)$ be a minimum spanning tree of $G = (N,E)$ such that $\{v,w\}$ is not in E_T. Thus there is an edge $\{v',w'\}$ in E_T with v' in V and w' in $N - V$. By assumption, we cannot have both $v' = v$ and $w' = w$. Moreover, the edge $\{v',w'\}$ is the only edge that connects V to $N - V$ in T; otherwise, T is not a free tree. Since T is a spanning tree of G, there is a path, through the vertices of V, from v' to v, and there is a path, through the vertices of $N - V$, from w' to w; see Fig. 13.24. Now add the edge $\{v,w\}$ to T and remove the edge $\{v',w'\}$ from T to give T'. Since T is a spanning tree, there is a path from v to every vertex in V and from w to every vertex in $N - V$, so T' is also a spanning tree. Finally, because the edge $\{v,w\}$ has lowest weight among all edges connecting V to $N - V$, its weight is no greater than the weight of $\{v',w'\}$. In other words, $COST(T') \le COST(T)$ and T' is a minimum spanning tree that includes the edge $\{v,w\}$.

Prim's algorithm chooses any vertex u in $G = (N,E)$ as the initial vertex. It partitions N into two disjoint sets $V = \{u\}$ and $N - V$. Applying the preceding claim, it considers all edges from V to $N - V$, selecting an edge with smallest

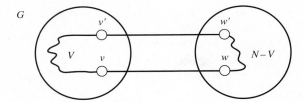

Figure 13.24 A minimum spanning tree with a smallest weight edge between V and $N - V$.

weight. This edge contributes a new vertex that is added to V. The greedy step is then repeated until all vertices have been added to V and, hence, to a minimum spanning tree. For example, with the graph P of Fig. 13.23, if we begin with vertex f, then we obtain the sequence of partial minimum spanning trees shown in Fig. 13.25. We know that the edge added at each step is in *some* minimum spanning tree; hence, we are assured that the final spanning tree *is* a minimum spanning tree. In the example, the cost of the minimum spanning tree is 12. Compare this spanning tree with the spanning tree given in Fig. 13.23(b) that has cost 23.

Prim's algorithm is simple and elegant, but how do we implement it efficiently? At each step we need to find an edge of smallest weight between two sets of vertices, and to add a new edge and vertex to the partial minimum spanning tree. Therefore, we keep, for each vertex in $N - V$, an edge of smallest weight connecting it to a vertex in V, if there is such a vertex. We call this set of edges the **closest set.** We can now find easily an edge of smallest weight between the two sets—we simply examine the, at most, $\#N - \#V$ edges. Having chosen an edge $\{v,w\}$ with smallest weight, we remove it from the closest set and update the closest set, because w may be closer than other vertices in V to some vertices in $(N - V) - \{w\}$. With care, updating of the closest set can be accomplished in $O(n)$ time. Thus Prim's algorithm can be implemented to run in $O(n^2)$ time and space, using the adjacency-matrix representation. We leave you to provide an implementation in Pascal; see Exercises 13.16 and 13.17.

13.4.5 Scatter Plots and Minimal Tours

Assume that we are given a set of points that we want to display as a scatter plot using a graph plotter. Most graph plotters obey simple commands of the following form: Move the pen to position (x,y), raise the pen, lower the pen, and draw a fat dot. Initially, and finally, the graph plotter is at position $(0,0)$, the origin, and we assume that the given points have been scaled to match the graph plotter's coordinate system. An example plot of 12 points is shown in Fig. 13.26. Now, although we are free to choose the ordering or schedule of the points, we assume that the graph plotter plots the points in the order that we give it. But, as we are interested in only the final plot, how much difference does this choice make? "A lot," is the answer, since different schedules give different sequences of graph-

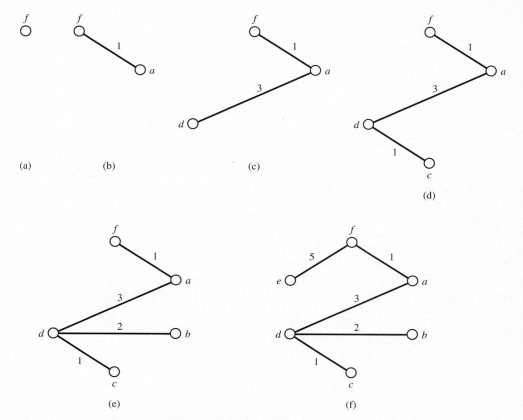

Figure 13.25   Six snapshots of Prim's algorithm on graph *P*.

plotter movements. Because the graph plotter is an electromechanical device, each movement takes time proportional to the sum of the distances moved in the *x* direction and the *y* direction; that is, $d((x,y),(x',y')) = |x' - x| + |y' - y|$. This measure of distance is called L_1 distance. In addition, there are start-up and stop times, but these times are independent of the choice of schedule, so we ignore them.

With the example set of points, consider the two different schedules shown in Fig. 13.27. The hidden plotter movements are indicated with directed edges—they form a tour of the vertices. In Fig. 13.27(a), the plotter moves $2 + 1 + 1 + 1 + 1 + 1 + 5 + 1 + 1 + 1 + 1 + 1 + 7 = 24$ units, whereas, in Fig. 13.27(b), it moves $12 + 10 + 9 + 8 + 7 + 6 + 5 + 6 + 7 + 8 + 9 + 10 + 7 = 104$ units—more than *four* times as far! When we are plotting a very large point set, this disparity in the distances can be much, much greater.

Not surprisingly, we can view the plotter problem as a graph problem. The origin and each point are vertices, and, for every pair of distinct vertices, we have

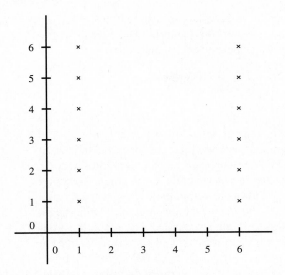

Figure 13.26 An example plot of 12 points.

an edge that is weighted by the L_1 distance between them—it is a complete edge-weighted graph. More generally, we have an edge-weighted connected graph, $G = (N, E)$, where the weights are nonnegative numbers. A **tour** of such a graph G is a simple cycle of all the vertices of G; that is, it is a sequence

$$u_0, u_1, \ldots, u_n$$

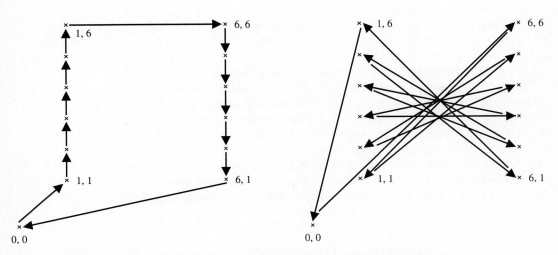

Figure 13.27 Two different plotting schedules for plotting the 12 example points in Fig. 13.26.

of the vertices of G, such that u_i is adjacent to $u_{i+1}, 0 \le i < n, u_0 = u_n$, and $N = \{u_1, ..., u_n\}$. A tour is also called a **Hamiltonian cycle.** The **cost** of a tour $u_0, ..., u_n$ is the sum of the weights on the associated edges; that is,

$$COST(u_0, ..., u_n) = \sum_{i=0}^{n} \text{wt}(u_i, u_{i+1}).$$

We say that a tour is **minimal** when no other tour has smaller cost.

In the general setting, determining whether a graph even has a tour is an intractable (but solvable) problem. In other words, all known algorithms to solve this problem take time that is exponential in the size of the given graph. Computer scientists conjecture that there is no algorithm to determine whether a graph has a tour, which runs in polynomial time in the size of the given graph. Furthermore, not only is this problem in a class of problems called NP (denoting non-deterministic polynomial-time problems), but it is as hard (in terms of time) to solve as is any other problem in this class—it is said to be **NP-complete.** Informally, problems that are in NP can be solved by the guess-and-verify technique: *Guess a solution, and verify that the proposed solution is indeed a solution.* The tour problem fits into this category, since we can guess some schedule

$$u_0, u_1, ..., u_n$$

for the vertices in the graph, such that $u_0 = u_n$ and $N = \{u_1, ..., u_n\}$; then we can verify whether the schedule is a tour in $O(n)$ time with the adjacency-matrix representation, and in $O(n^2)$ time with the adjacency-list representation. (We need to check whether there are edges $\{u_i, u_{i+1}\}$ in G, $0 \le i < n$.) Furthermore, since there are $n!$ different candidate schedules (the schedule $u_0, u_1, ..., u_n$ is the same as $u_2, ..., u_n, u_1, u_2$, for example), we can enumerate the schedules. Based on the enumeration of the schedules, we can derive an $O(n^{2+n})$-time algorithm that determines whether the graph has a tour, and to give a tour if there is one.

From this preliminary discussion, we should not expect the problem of finding a minimal tour to be simpler than that of determining whether there is a tour. It can be shown that finding a minimal tour is also an intractable problem. So we are interested in developing efficient algorithms that produce tours that are nearly minimal and that guarantee how bad such tours are with respect to the minimal tour. We give a simple approximation algorithm based on minimum spanning trees that requires two assumptions. First, we assume that the given graph is complete; second, we assume that the edge weights satisfy the triangle inequality. The triangle inequality states that, for all u, v, w in N,

$$\text{wt}(u, w) \le \text{wt}(u, v) + \text{wt}(v, w).$$

The triangle inequality is satisfied for the scatter-plot problem and for similar problems based on distances in the plane.

We use three observations:

1. A minimum spanning tree can be found efficiently.
2. If G is an edge-weighted, connected graph, S_{min} is a minimum spanning tree of G, and T_{min} is a minimum tour of G, then $COST(S_{min}) \leq COST(T_{min})$.
3. We can construct a tour T from S_{min} such that $COST(T) \leq 2 \times COST(T_{min})$; in other words, the cost of T is never more than twice the cost of the minimum tour.

The first observation has been demonstrated in Section 13.4.4, so we consider only the second and third observations here. Given any tour T of G, removing any edge from T gives a spanning tree S of G. Since edge weights are nonnegative (they may be zero),

$$COST (S) \leq COST(T).$$

But S_{min} satisfies $COST(S_{min}) \leq COST(S)$, for all spanning trees S of G and, in particular, for any spanning tree obtained from T_{min}; hence,

$$COST (S_{min}) \leq COST(T_{min}).$$

Thus the cost of a minimum spanning tree provides a (coarse) lower bound on the cost of a minimum tour.

We next show how to construct a tour from a spanning tree of a complete graph. Given the complete graph of Fig. 13.28(a) and one of its spanning trees in Fig. 13.28(b), we can produce a tour from it in the following way. First, we replace, conceptually, each edge by two directed edges, directed in opposite ways; see Fig. 13.29(a). Then we march around the vertices along the directed edges, never repeating a directed edge; for example,

$$a,e,a,c,d,c,a,b,a$$

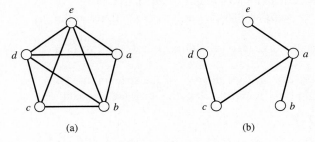

(a)   (b)

Figure 13.28 Complete graphs and spanning trees. (a) A complete graph. (b) One of its spanning trees.

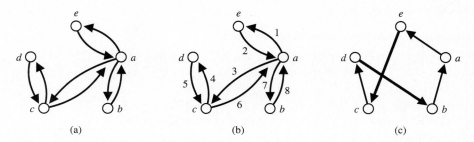

Figure 13.29 Spanning trees, marches, and tours. (a) The directed version of the spanning tree of Fig. 13.28(b). (b) A march derived from the directed spanning tree. (c) The tour derived from the march.

is such a **march.** We indicate the march in Fig. 13.29(b) by numbering the edges from one to eight in the order they are visited. This march is *not* a tour, since vertices are revisited; however, its cost is twice the cost of the spanning tree.

We now show how we can convert a march into a tour. We follow the march, replacing repeated vertex visits by shortcuts; for example, the third vertex in the example march is vertex *a* once more, so we remove the revisit to give

$$a,e,c.$$

Similarly, we next meet *c* for a second time and *a* for a third time, so we remove both revisits to give

$$a,e,c,d,b,a.$$

Because the original graph is complete, we know that the short-cut edges $\{e,c\}$ and $\{d,b\}$ are in the given graph; therefore, this schedule is a tour. The final tour is shown in Fig. 13.29(c), where the short-cut edges are shown in double thickness.

Returning to the minimum-tour problem, we can find an approximate solution by (1) finding a minimum spanning tree, (2) constructing a march of the spanning tree, and (3) converting the march into a tour. It is not difficult to prove that we can implement these three steps so that they run in $O(n^2)$ time, in the worst case.

We now prove how costly such a tour can be with respect to the cost of a minimal tour.

Because any march has a cost that is twice the cost of the spanning tree *S* from which it is derived, a tour *T* derived from a march must satisfy the inequality

$$COST\ (T) \le 2 \times COST(S).$$

The reason is simple: When converting a march into a tour, we replace sequences of edges in the march with a single edge; that is, a path of the form

$$u_k,...,u_l$$

is replaced by the single-edge path

$$u_k, u_l.$$

Now, by the triangle inequality,

$$wt(u_{l-2}, u_l) \leq wt(u_{l-2}, u_{l-1}) + wt(u_{l-1}, u_l);$$

repeating this reduction, we find that

$$wt(u_k, u_l) \leq wt(u_k, u_{k+1}) + \cdots + wt(u_{l-1}, u_l).$$

Since each shortcut satisfies such an inequality, we have shown that the cost of the derived tour is, indeed, at most twice the cost of the given spanning tree. We begin the construction of an approximate tour T_{app} with a minimum spanning tree S_{min}, so T_{app} satisfies

$$COST(T_{min}) \leq COST(T_{app}) \leq 2 \times COST(S_{min}) \leq 2 \times COST(T_{min}).$$

We leave you to implement this approximation technique in Exercise 13.18.

13.5 MEMORY MANAGEMENT

We introduced, in Section 1.5.4, the memory-management problem in the restricted setting of QUEUE. The following discussion delineates two issues of memory management: whether it is system or user initiated, and whether there are links between the blocks. For example, orphaned blocks can occur in Pascal both because we can have links between blocks and because Pascal depends on the user-initiated release of such blocks. A third issue of memory management is whether blocks of fixed or different sizes are available. In the UNIX file system, for example, blocks have a fixed size (usually 512 bytes), whereas in any multiprogramming system, blocks of different sizes are used. Variably sized blocks lead to what are known as the fragmentation and scatter problems; as a result, a request might not be able to be filled, because no free block is large enough, although there are sufficient free cells in total.

After defining a model for memory management in Section 13.5.1, we solve a number of memory-management problems in Sections 13.5.2 to 13.5.6.

13.5.1 A Memory-Management Model

We make a number of assumptions consistent with most memory-management situations. We assume that the available memory is a block of cells indexed from $1..m$, for some integer m that is often a power of 2. A cell is a fixed-sized unit of memory, such as a byte, word, or page. We assume that there are many users, rather than just one, and that each user's request is satisfied by the return of a subblock of the block of cells. When we are discussing the system-initiated release of

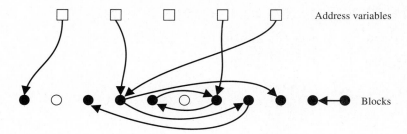

Figure 13.30   A digraph model of the memory-management problem. Solid
circular nodes correspond to rented blocks; clear circular
nodes correspond to free blocks.

subblocks, the system must know where the interblock links are stored in a block.
For, at the bit level, links and values are just bit sequences—there is no intrinsic
difference between them. In addition, we assume that link arithmetic is not used.
Otherwise, in system-initiated memory-management systems, it would not be
possible to know who references whom! Finally, we assume that there are address
variables, which are not stored in the available memory, that point to some of the
allocated or rented blocks.

   We can model the free and rented memory with a digraph in which vertices
correspond to address variables and subblocks, and edges correspond to address-
variable links and interblock links. We illustrate the digraph model in Fig. 13.30,
in which we use square nodes to denote address variables and circular nodes to
denote subblocks.

   Any solution to the memory-management problem is an implementation of
the three memory-management operations: *Initialize*, *Request*, and *Return;* see
Section 1.5.4.

13.5.2   The Simple Case: Fixed-Sized Blocks

Assume that we want only blocks of some predetermined size b and that there are
no interblock links. It is convenient, in this case, to think of the available memory
as a block $1..m$ of cells, where each cell is a block of size b. Each cell is either
rented or free, and the memory manager keeps track of the free cells (or, alternatively, of the rented cells), so that the manager can easily determine whether a
request can be filled. We begin by considering the user-initiated request and
release of cells. Initially, all cells are free; later, some of them are free. The memory manager must maintain a set of free cells under the following operations:
remove a free cell from the set, add a rented cell to the set and make it free, and
test whether the set of free cells is empty. We can use any of the set representations for this purpose. Two specific possibilities are characteristic functions and
linked lists. In both cases, we need to remember that memory is a limited
resource; we are willing to provide a small predetermined amount of extra memory, but no more. The reason for this restriction should be clear: We want to max-

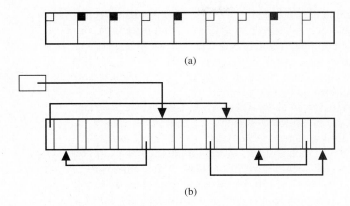

Figure 13.31 Freedom representation. (a) The embedded bit vector or rented–free indicators. (b) The embedded free list.

imize the available memory for the users. Thus we do not want to keep a separate bit vector of free cells, or a separate linked list of free-cell addresses, as we do in Section 1.5.4. (The bit vector has m bits, and the linked list has m free-cell addresses and m links.) To avoid the space overhead, we **embed** a bit vector directly in the block of cells, if each cell has 1 unused bit, which is a reasonable assumption in most settings; see Fig. 13.31(a). We call these bits **rented–free indicators.** Similarly, we embed a linked list in the block of cells by linking together the free cells directly to obtain a free list; thus a cell must contain at least $\lceil \log_2 m \rceil$ bits—again a reasonable assumption in most settings; see Fig. 13.31(b). We leave the implementation of the operations *Initialize*, *Request*, and *Return*, using these two methods, to Exercise 13.21, where we ask you to compare their performance.

With the user-initiated release of blocks, these ideas provide efficient solutions; when we require system-initiated release, however, they fall short. The reason is simple. The memory manager needs to be able to determine when a rented block should be returned. Rather than dealing with this issue here, we consider it in the context of variably sized blocks, in Section 13.5.3.

13.5.3 Variably Sized Blocks

We now consider the management of variably sized blocks. Each request is for a block of at least one cell. The issues we face are how to keep track of the free cells, to fill a request, to handle returned blocks, and to handle scatter and fragmentation.

Because blocks are not of fixed size, we embed a free list in the subblocks of free cells. We leave you to explain why we do not use a bit vector in this context in Exercise 13.22. Thus we need a fixed number of extra cells, over and above the user's requirements, in each rented block to hold a free–rented indicator and the size of the block. Let f denote this number of cells. Similarly, in each free block we need space for a free–rented indicator, the size of the free block, and a free-list link; we assume that each free block is larger than $2f$ cells so that it can hold this information. We assume that the number of bits needed to hold a link is the same as the number of bits needed to hold a size. Furthermore, we assume that the first cells of a block contain the free–rented indicator followed by the block size and, in the case of a free block, followed by the free-list link.

Consider a request for a block of b cells, where $b > 0$. Clearly, such a block has to have size at least $b + f$. The simplest strategy we can use to satisfy the request is to scan the free list until we meet the first block that has size at least $b + f$, **first-fit allocation.** Once we find such a block, we split it into a left part of size $b + f$ and a right part. The right part should have size at least $2f$, since it has to be linked into the free list. In practice, we create blocks of size at least *Bmin,* for some *Bmin* $\geq 2f$. If the right part is smaller than *Bmin,* then we do not split the block; we allocate the whole block. Before allocating the free block, we remove it from the free list and indicate that it is rented. We might prefer to use **best-fit allocation,** in which case we scan the whole free list to determine the smallest free block of size at least $b + f$. The advantages and disadvantages of these two allocation methods are the subject of Exercise 13.23.

It is possible that there is no free block of size at least $b + f$, yet the total number of free cells is more than $b + f$. There can be two reasons for this phenomenon. First, the free space may have been broken up into small free fragments as a result of repeated requests and returns; the free cells are **fragmented** in the available memory; see Fig. 13.32(a). So, although there are sufficient contiguous free cells to satisfy the request, we do not know it. We discuss this phenomenon when we discuss the return of rented blocks later in this section and also in Section 13.5.4. Second, the rented blocks may be so **scattered** throughout the memory that there are insufficient contiguous free cells to satisfy the request; see Fig. 13.32(b). We can solve the **scatter problem,** as it is called, by moving the rented blocks to create sufficient contiguous free cells. This process is called **compaction;** we discuss it in more detail in Section 13.5.5. Of course, it is possible that the total number of free cells is insufficient for the latest request, so compaction and fragmentation removal will not enable the memory manager to grant the request. This situation

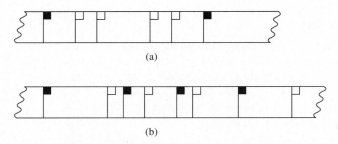

(a)

(b)

Figure 13.32   Fragmentation and scatter in available memory.
(a) Contiguous free fragments. (b) Scattered free fragments.

leaves us with two further possibilities. First, if there are any rented blocks that are not reachable from any address variable, then we can recycle them as free blocks. This process is known as **garbage collection;** we discuss it in more detail in Section 13.5.6. Second, if all these approaches fail, then we can store the contents of some of the rented blocks on disk and reuse the blocks to satisfy the request. This approach is known as **memory swapping;** it is usually used with virtual-memory systems and a discussion of it is beyond the scope of this text.

We now consider the return of rented blocks. When the user returns a rented block, we can reset the free–rented indicator and insert the block at the beginning of the free list. Unfortunately, the effect of this simplistic approach is that the free space is fragmented, over time, into small free fragments, since adjacent free fragments are not discovered and, hence, are not merged. Since fragmentation can cause a request to be unsatisfiable, even when there are sufficient contiguous free cells, we must solve the fragmentation problem. We present one solution that is another application of the laziness principle—*do nothing if possible; otherwise, do nothing until you must do something*. We first met the laziness principle when we introduced the Fibonacci queue in Section 11.2.4; we performed insertions lazily. Here, we use the simplistic method of returning rented blocks until the memory manager has a request that cannot be filled. Then, and only then, we recompute the free list by scanning the memory and merging adjacent free blocks. Observe that this approach is a feasible one, since each free and rented block contains not only a free–rented indicator, but also the block's size. We examine the first block in the cells indexed by 1 onward. Thus if the first block is free, then we merge it with the following block, if that block is also free. This merging process is repeated until we either exhaust the available memory or meet a rented block. In both cases, we add the free block to the new free list. If we have exhausted the available memory, then we have finished the scan; otherwise, we continue the scan until we either meet a free block or exhaust the memory. In Exercise 13.24, other more traditional solutions to the fragmentation problem are explored, and are compared with the lazy method.

We can solve the fragmentation problem by using one of the buddy systems for memory management. We discuss one of these systems, the binary buddy system, in Section 13.5.4.

13.5.4 The Buddy Systems

Rather than allowing blocks to be of any requested size, buddy systems restrict the permissible block sizes. In particular, they allow sizes

$$1 < s_1 < \cdots < s_m,$$

for some $m > 0$, where s_m is the total number of cells in the memory, and an index i of a block size s_i is called a **block-size index.** When a user requests a block of b cells, the memory manager allocates a block of size s_i, where

$$s_{i-1} < b + f \le s_i.$$

If no such block exists, then a block of size s_{i+1} is split into two blocks or **buddies,** a left buddy of size s_i and a right buddy of size $s_{i+1} - s_i$. Because $s_{i+1} - s_i$ must be a permissible block size, we have

$$s_k = s_{i+1} - s_i,$$

for some k, $1 \leq k \leq i$. When $k = i$, we obtain the **binary-buddy system;** when $k = i - 1$, we obtain the **Fibonacci-buddy system** (see Exercise 13.25); and when $k < i - 1$, we obtain the **order-k–buddy systems** (see Exercise 13.26). The advantage of a buddy system is that the blocks, their sizes, and their positions are predetermined. Its obvious disadvantage is that space is wasted when the size b of a requested block is much smaller than the size of the allocated block. We describe the binary-buddy system in somewhat more detail.

With each block, we store the block-size index, rather than the block size. To satisfy a request efficiently, we link together free blocks of the same size in a free list. The free lists are accessible from a block $1..m$ of m free-list headers; that is, the free list for blocks of size s_i is given by the header at position i. If there is a free block of the appropriate size s_i, then it is removed from its free list, the free–rented indicator is changed, and its address is returned. If there is no free block of size s_i, then we split a free block of size s_{i+1} into two free blocks, each of size s_i. Again, if there is no free block of size s_{i+1}, then we first split a free block of size s_{i+2} to obtain two free blocks of sizes s_{i+1}. Then we split one of the blocks of size s_{i+1}. In general, we repeatedly split a free block of size s_{i+l}, for some $l \geq 1$, when we cannot satisfy the request immediately.

When we return a rented block of size s_i, we could just add it to the ith free list. This method causes fragmentation, so we join the returned block with its buddy, if its buddy is also free. The result is a larger free block; if its buddy is free, then we join them, and repeat the free-buddy joining until it can no longer be done. Now the buddy of a block of size s_i is also of size s_i; but we must know the answer to the question, "Who is my buddy?" Since we know the address α of the first cell in the returned block of size s_i, we need to determine only whether $\alpha - 1$ is an even or odd multiple of s_i. If $\alpha - 1$ is an even multiple of s_i, then the returned block's buddy is immediately to s_i 's right; otherwise, the returned block's buddy is immediately to s_i 's left. This observation is not difficult to validate, so we leave its validation to Exercise 13.27.

13.5.5 Compaction

In any memory-management scheme for variably sized blocks, both the fragmentation and scatter problems need to be solved, for there may be a sufficient number of free cells, even though there are insufficient contiguous free cells. One solution to the scatter problem is to relocate the rented blocks to have the lowest possible addresses and, therefore, to amalgamate the free cells into one free block. This process is called **compaction.**

We leave you to explore, in Exercise 13.28, a straightforward compaction algorithm, which requires space for an additional link in each block. Here we

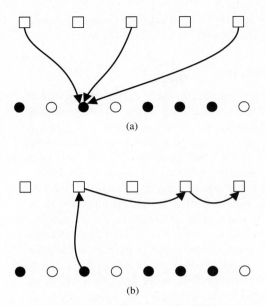

Figure 13.33   Compaction and linking. (a) Multiple address variables
pointing to the same rented block. (b) The corresponding
linked list.

describe a compaction algorithm that requires 1 extra bit, for a data–link indicator, in each address variable and each block. We assume that many address variables may point to each rented block. We scan all address variables and, for each
rented block, we link the address variables that point to it and make the rented
block a list header; see Fig. 13.33. Since we have not assigned space in a rented
block for the extra link, we use at most f cells of the data area for it, and we set the
data–link indicator to *link*. The link field in an address variable is used to hold the
evicted data, and the address variable's data–link indicator is set to *data*. When a
subsequent address variable is found that points to the same rented block, it is
inserted into the rented block's list; see Fig. 13.33(b).

In the second step, we scan the blocks in the available memory from lowest
to highest addresses to compute the number of free cells and to move rented
blocks. If a block is free, then we add its size to the cumulative free-space count;
otherwise, we move the block to the left by exactly the cumulative free-space
count. (If the data–link indicator of a rented block is set to *data,* then it is not ref-
erenced by any address variable, so we can treat it as a free block.) Once the
rented block is moved, we traverse its address-variable list and make the address
variables point to the new block location. When we meet the last address variable
on the list, we transfer the evicted data to their original area in the rented block,
before modifying its link field. Finally, the data–link indicators of the last address
variable and the rented block are changed.

Once all rented blocks have been relocated, the remaining cells are free, so a new free block is created and the free-list header is reinitialized to point to it.

13.5.6   Fixed-Sized Linked Blocks

In LISP and its successors, data are represented with linked lists of blocks, where each block has two fields, a head and tail (or car and cdr, to use the original LISP terminology), each of which can be an atom or a pointer. An **atom** is, depending on the specific implementation, either a value or a pointer to a value; we assume for simplicity that it is the former. Because we have fixed-sized blocks, we find it convenient, once more, to think of the available memory as a block of blocks. For user-initiated release, we can use the techniques discussed in Sections 13.5.2 to 13.5.5. The issues we wish to address here, however, are system-initiated block reclamation (called *garbage collection*) and orphans. We assume that we can distinguish between an atom and a pointer; in practice, 1 bit is used to distinguish them. As before, we assume that we can access the address variables and that we maintain a free list of blocks.

Each block in the available memory can be free, rented and in use, or rented and orphaned. With system-initiated block reclamation, we have to find the blocks that are rented and orphaned, since these blocks can be freed. A block is **rented and in use** if it is reachable by a sequence of links from some address variable, and it is **free** if it is reachable from the free-block list header. Immediately, all remaining blocks are **rented and orphaned.** This observation suggests the following idea: First, we color all blocks red; second, we color all blocks green that are reachable from some address variable; third, we collect the remaining red blocks and add them to the free list. We can model this approach with a group of digraphs that have designated source vertices; see Fig. 13.30. Reachability can then be solved by depth-first search, as we have seen in Section 13.3.2. We need 1 bit in each block for the coloring and, because of space restrictions, we should implement the depth-first traversal nonrecursively with constant extra space. Indeed, if we have 1 further bit available in each block, then we can implement depth-first traversal using pointer reversal; see Sections 3.5.2 and 5.5.4. The extra bit is used to indicate which of the two possible link fields has a reversed pointer. The color and reversal bits, together with previous and current pointer variables are sufficient to perform a nonrecursive depth-first traversal of each digraph in the group. The algorithm is called the Deutsch–Schorr–Waite algorithm; the details of its implementation are left to Exercise 13.29.

13.6   PERFORMANCE REPORTS

We summarize, in Table 13.1, the worst-case time bounds for the adjacency-list and adjacency-matrix representations of graphs and digraphs in terms of n, the number of vertices in a graph or digraph, and m, the maximum possible number

Table 13.1 A comparison of the worst-case execution times of the two GRAPH and DIGRAPH representations.

Operation	GRAPH and DIGRAPH implementation	
	Adjacency list	Adjacency matrix
Empty	1	1
IsEmpty	1	1
InsertVertex	1	1
DeleteVertex	1	1
InsertEdge	$n[1]^a$	1
DeleteEdge	n	1
ExamineVertex	1	1
ReplaceVertex	1	1
ExamineEdge	n	1
ReplaceEdge	n	1
Size	1	1
Vertex	$m - n(m/n)^b$	$m - n(m/n)$
SuccessorSize	1	1
Successor	1	$m - n(m/n)$

[a]The time bound in square brackets for *InsertEdge* is valid when the operation is used only for the initialization of a graph or digraph.

[b]The times in parentheses are amortized over n calls.

of vertices. Note that m is a constant—only n varies. In both representations, we assume that we have direct access to a vertex, its value, and the number of successors and that we maintain a count of the number of vertices. The adjacency-matrix representation provides constant-time access to an edge, whereas the adjacency-list representation forces a sequential search for an edge; it takes linear time. The *Vertex* operation scans the header block, in both representations, to obtain the next vertex in the graph. Because the header block has size m, n calls of *Vertex* take $O(m)$ time. If m is not too much larger than n, then each call of *Vertex* takes constant time, when averaged over n calls of *Vertex*. The adjacency-list representation is more efficient than is the adjacency-matrix representation when we examine successors, because we can find all successors of a vertex in $O(n)$ time, whereas finding all successors takes $O(m)$ time in the adjacency-matrix representation. Therefore, as shown in Table 13.2, we recommend the adjacency list representation.

One final note. In many applications, including the algorithms discussed in this chapter, *InsertEdge* is used only to construct the initial graph; therefore, in these situations, we can implement it to run in constant time with both representations.

Table 13.2   Performance ratings of the two representations of DIGRAPH and GRAPH.

GRAPH and DIAGRAPH implementation	Rating	Comments
Adjacency list	Excellent	Space efficient; slow for random edge accesses.
Adjacency matrix	Very good	Quadratic space; slow successor chasing.

13.7 SUMMARY

We introduced the ADTs DIGRAPH and GRAPH that correspond to the mathematical notions of a digraph and graph, respectively, and we discussed two representations for them. The two representations are the adjacency matrix, a block of Boolean blocks that corresponds to the characteristic function of the edge set, and the adjacency list, a block of lists that corresponds to the lists of successors of each vertex. We also investigated how the choice of representations affects the performance of a variety of graph algorithms. Almost all graph algorithms are based on one of the two possible traversals—namely, depth-first traversal, which is similar to the preorder traversal of a tree, and breadth-first traversal, which is similar to the breadth-first traversal of a tree.

We illustrated how digraphs and graphs are used to solve a number of problems; through these solutions, we uncovered one new algorithmic notion, topological sorting, and made extensive use of greediness. Topological sorting is the rearrangement of the elements of a sequence so that the constraints among them are not violated. Sorting is a special case of topological sorting.

We presented some of the basic algorithms and data representations for a number of variants of the memory-management problem. In particular, many of the variants can be modeled as digraph problems, and then solved using digraph algorithms.

13.8 HISTORY

Hopcroft and Tarjan (1973) were the first people to promote depth-first traversal and the adjacency-list representation of graphs and digraphs. Topological sorting was developed by Kahn (1962).The shortest-path algorithm was developed by Dijkstra (1959); the minimum-spanning-tree algorithm was developed by Prim (1957). The scatter-plot problem is the geometric version of the traveling-salesperson problem, a well-known intractable problem (Garey, Graham, and Johnson, 1976). Garey and Johnson (1979) provide an excellent guide to intractable problems.

The monograph by Tarjan (1983a) provides an excellent introduction to a number of other graph algorithms and supporting data structures. Bondy and Murty (1976) provide a good general introduction to graph theory.

The issue of efficient memory management is crucial to the implementation of operating systems (see Silberschatz, Peterson, and Galvin (1991)), and programming languages (see Aho and colleagues (1988) and Knuth (1968)). The buddy systems were first published by Knowlton (1965); the Fibonacci-buddy systems were investigated by Hinds (1975) and Hirschberg (1973). The compaction scheme that we presented in Section 13.5.5 was developed by Morris (1978). The nonrecursive implementation of the depth-first marking algorithm for memory management was developed by Deutsch and Bobrow (1966) and by Schorr and Waite (1967). Cohen (1981) surveys garbage-collection schemes in detail, and Appel (1990) discusses more recent results.

EXERCISES

13.1: Specify the GRAPH operations in a similar manner to the specification of the DIGRAPH operations in Section 13.1. *Successor* and *SuccessorSize* should be replaced by *Adjacent* and *Degree*, respectively.

13.2: Complete the partial implementation of the DIGRAPH operations given in Program 13.1.

13.3: Implement and test an implementation of the DIGRAPH operations based on the adjacency-list representation.

13.4: How many different topologically sorted orderings are there of the task digraph in Fig. 13.4?

13.5: Prove that a digraph has a topologically sorted ordering if and only if it is acyclic.

13.6: Prove that a digraph has a cycle if and only if it has a simple cycle.

13.7: Why do we not need to mark the nodes in a tree as visited when we perform a depth-first or breadth-first traversal?

13.8: Give a high-level description of the breadth-first traversal of a digraph. Implement and test a Pascal procedure derived from it. What are the time and space requirements of your algorithm?

13.9: Design and test an algorithm that checks whether a digraph is acyclic by using a breadth-first traversal.

13.10: Implement and test the topological-sorting algorithm described in Section 13.3.3. It should combine a depth-first traversal of a digraph with a postorder traversal of the resulting traversal orchard.

13.11: Extend the given version of Dijkstra's algorithm to find a shortest path from s to each vertex that can be reached from s.

13.12:   Prove that Dijkstra's algorithm takes $O(n^2)$ space and time when we use the adjacency-matrix representation.

13.13:   An alternative approach to solving the all-pairs shortest-paths problem is based on the matrix view of a digraph and was developed by Floyd (1962) and Warshall (1962). Given three $n \times n$ integer matrices A, B, and C, we define the sum $C = A + B$ by

$$C_{i,j} = min\{A_{i,j}, B_{i,j}\},$$

and we define the product $C = A \times B$ by

$$C_{i,j} = min\{A_{i,1} + B_{1,j}, ..., A_{i,n} + B_{n,j}\}.$$

Moreover, let A^i, $i \geq 1$, denote the product of A with itself i times and

$$A^{[i]} = A + A^2 + \cdots + A^i.$$

  a. Define $A_{i,i} = 0$ and $A_{i,j}$ to be the weight of the edge between vertices i and j, where $A_{i,j} = +\infty$ if there is no edge between i and j. Prove that $A_{i,j}^{[n]}$ is the shortest distance between i and j.

  b. The Floyd–Warshall algorithm is defined in a way slightly different from that implied in part a. Rather than blindly computing all the powers of A, at the kth step it computes $A^{(k)}$, the shortest distances between pairs of vertices whose paths can go only through vertices $1, ..., k$. This computation involves only $A^{(k-1)}$ and the vertex k, since

$$A_{i,j}^{(k)} = min\{A_{i,j}^{(k-1)}, A_{i,k}^{(k-1)} + A_{k,j}^{(k-1)}\}.$$

Based on this recurrence, give a simple algorithm to compute $A^{(n)}$. What is the worst-case time taken by your algorithm?

  c. Modify the two algorithms given in parts a and b to give the shortest paths as well.

13.14:   We have suggested, in Section 13.4.2, an algorithm, based on depth-first traversal, that determines whether there is a path from a given vertex s to a second vertex t. What are the time bounds of the algorithm if the adjacency-matrix representation is used? Can breadth-first traversal be used to solve this problem? If it can be, sketch an algorithm; otherwise, explain why it cannot be used.

13.15:   Prove that a free tree has $n - 1$ edges if it has n vertices. Prove that adding a single edge to a free tree introduces a cycle.

13.16:   Implement and test Prim's algorithm using the adjacency-matrix representation.

13.17:   Implement Prim's algorithm using the adjacency-list representation to obtain a time bound of $O(n + e \log n)$ and a space bound of $O(n + e)$.

13.18:   Implement the approximation technique for printing scatter plots based on minimal spanning trees.

13.19:   Define a maximum spanning tree of an edge-weighted graph as a spanning tree that has maximum cost, where the cost of a subgraph is the sum of the weights of the subgraph's edges. Suggest an efficient algorithm to find a maximum spanning tree and determine its worst-case time and space bounds.

13.20: Suggest an approximation algorithm, based on maximal spanning trees (see Exercise 13.19), for printing scatter plots that maximizes the distance traveled and the time taken by a graph plotter.

13.21: In Section 13.5.2, we presented two methods to implement the memory-management operations for fixed-sized blocks: an embedded bit vector and an embedded free list. Implement these two methods. Compare their performance analytically and by simulation.

13.22: When we are managing variably sized blocks (see Section 13.5.3), an embedded bit vector is an inappropriate method of keeping track of the free and rented blocks. Why is this assertion true?

13.23: When we are managing variably sized blocks (see Section 13.5.3), the memory manager can allocate free blocks by using the first-fit or best-fit strategies. Discuss the advantages and disadvantages of these two methods.

13.24: In Section 13.5.3, we present a lazy method to solve the fragmentation problem. Two other approaches suggest themselves.

    a. When we are returning a block, the memory manager can examine the adjacent blocks in available memory and, if at least one of them is free, can merge them and update the free list. For the data representation we have given, what is the worst-case time requirement of this algorithm?

    b. Another approach is to keep the free list sorted by block address in which the memory manager inserts the returned block into the free list and then examines the adjacent blocks in the free list. If at least one of them is adjacent, then the manager can merge them and update the free list. What is the worst-case time requirement of this algorithm?

    c. Compare the lazy method with the two methods we have defined.

13.25: The major problem with the Fibonacci-buddy system is answering the question, "Who is my buddy?" The reason is that the blocks to the left or right of a given block could be buddies, and there is no simple address calculation that determines which one it is. One approach to this problem is to add extra information to each block, a **left-buddy count.** If a block of size s_{i+1}, with a left-buddy count of b, is divided into a left buddy of size s_i and a right buddy of size s_{i-1}, then the left-buddy count of the left buddy is $b + 1$, and the left-buddy count of the right buddy is 0. The left-buddy count of a block tells us how many times the block is consecutively the left buddy of a left-buddy block.

When we return a block of size s_i at position p, we use the left-buddy count as follows: If the block has left-buddy count 0, then it is a right buddy and its left buddy has size s_{i+1} at position $p - s_{i+1}$; otherwise, it is a left buddy and its right buddy has size s_{i-1} at position $p + s_{i-1}$. If the block's buddy is free, then we combine the two blocks and reset the left-buddy count of the combined block. If the left-buddy count was b, then it becomes $b - 1$.

Design an efficient implementation of a memory-management scheme based on the Fibonacci-buddy system.

13.26: Adapt, for order-k–buddy systems, the technique suggested in Exercise 13.25 to determine whether a block is a left or right buddy.

13.27: Prove the correctness of the technique given in Section 13.5.4 to determine whether a block has a left or right buddy in a binary-buddy system.

13.28: Design an algorithm for the compaction of variably sized blocks, when there is sufficient space in every block for an additional link.

13.29: Implement the Deutsch–Schorr–Waite algorithm for the garbage collection of fixed-sized blocks with at most two link fields. You should use variant records if you choose Pascal.

C H A P T E R

14

Partitions

We consider how to maintain partitions of a set. A **partition** of a set is a collection of subsets such that each element of the set appears in exactly one subset; hence, the subsets are pairwise disjoint. We call the subsets of a partition **classes,** because a partition can be identified with an equivalence relation over the set, and conversely. Thus the classes are exactly the equivalence classes of the relation. Recall that an equivalence relation is a binary relation that is reflexive, symmetric, and transitive.

For example, we have a muddy building site that has been strewn with wooden planks to make mudfree walkways; see Fig. 14.1. Locally, we know that plank c crosses plank d; therefore, when we can get to plank c, we can also get to plank d, and conversely. We have a set of crossing pairs—in this case,

$$\{\{a,b\},\{b,c\},\{c,d\},\{c,f\},\{d,e\},\{g,h\}\}.$$

Given two planks, a start plank and a finish plank, we want to know if we can walk, mudfree, from the start plank to the finish plank. When we cannot, we will take the four-wheel drive vehicle. We have seen this problem in Section 13.4.1, when we discussed connected components; we use it again to illustrate a different solution strategy that uses partitions.

The set of crossing pairs of planks defines a binary relation R over the set $P = \{a,b,c,d,e,f,g,h\}$ of planks as follows. A crossing pair $\{x,y\}$ tells us that we can walk directly from x to y and vice versa, so we include both (x,y) and (y,x) in R. We say that R is **symmetric.** Because we can always walk from every plank to itself, we include the pair (x,x) in R, for every x in P; thus, R is **reflexive.** Finally, whenever we can walk from a plank x to a plank y and from plank y to a plank z, we can also walk from x to z. R should be **transitive.** We need to add the minimum number of ordered pairs of planks to the reflexive, symmetric relation R so

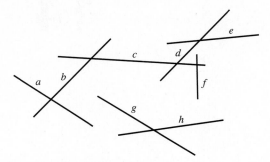

Figure 14.1   Planks on a muddy building site.

that the resulting relation is also transitive. Stated formally, we need to form the relation's transitive closure. The resulting relation is an equivalence relation that partitions P into mudfree walk sets and leaves us with the simpler problem: *Are the start and finish planks in the same mudfree walk set?* If they are not, then we cannot get from one to the other without either jumping or getting mud on our shoes.

As a second example, assume that we have a programming language in which we can state explicitly that two identifiers are synonyms of each other. From a programmer's point of view, this statement means that the two synonyms share a common value and can be used interchangeably; from a compiler writer's point of view, these two apparently distinct variables are to be identified—their storage representation is the same. Ignoring the dangers of this statement, let us consider how a compiler might process a synonym list such as

synonym $(a,b),(c,d),(e,f),(a,g),(g,c).$

Since a is a synonym of both b and $g,$ it follows that b and g are synonyms. Similarly, because c is a synonym of d and g is a synonym of $c,$ we can infer that d and g are synonyms, as are a and $c,$ a and $d,$ b and $c,$ and b and $d.$ The set $\{a,b,c,d,g\}$ is a set of mutual synonyms; that is, every identifier in the set is a synonym of every other identifier. The compiler must discover sets of mutual synonyms. The synonym list defines a binary relation R over the set $\{a,b,c,d,e,f,g\}$ of identifiers, and the mutual-synonym sets are a partition of it. Because $R,$ as defined by the synonym list, is not necessarily an equivalence relation, we need to compute the equivalence relation E that it defines. By the nature of synonymity, when x and y are synonyms, so are y and $x;$ E is symmetric. Also, every identifier x is a synonym of itself; E is reflexive. Finally, if x and y are synonyms and y and z are synonyms, then x and z are synonyms; E is transitive. The relation R does not necessarily satisfy any of these properties, although we have $R \subseteq E.$ To obtain E from $R,$ we extend it by adding the additional pairs given by the above observations; we form the **reflexive, symmetric, transitive closure** of $R.$ E is the smallest relation that contains R and is reflexive, symmetric, and transitive. Once we know what to compute, we need to determine only how we can compute the synonym sets efficiently.

There are many more examples of the use of partitioning in the literature. In all of them, we are essentially given the identity partition, $\{\{e\}: e$ is an element$\}$, of some set of elements. We must maintain the partition under the *Equivalence* operation that makes two elements equivalent and the *IsEquivalent* operation that, for two given elements, is **true** if the elements are equivalent; otherwise, it is **false**. An ADT that has these operations is called the PARTITION ADT. Observe that the two operations *IsEquivalent* and *Equivalence* are sufficient to solve the synonym and mudfree walk problems: For each pair (x,y) in the given list, make x and y equivalent, if they are not already equivalent. In the case of the synonym problem, the final equivalence classes are the synonym sets. In the case of the planks problem, after processing the list, we determine whether the start and finish planks are equivalent. If they are equivalent, then we can walk mudfree from start to finish; otherwise, we must use a vehicle.

We first specify the PARTITION ADT, in Section 14.1; then we consider two representation scenarios. In the first scenario, in Section 14.2, we assume that the given set is a range $1..n$, for some n that is not too large. In the second scenario, in Section 14.3, we relax this assumption and allow the given set to be a finite set from any universe. As we shall see, the range assumption enables us to obtain extremely efficient representations, whereas we cannot obtain such efficient representations when the assumption is relaxed. Finally, in Section 14.4, we specify a new ADT, PPARTITION, that has the same operations as PARTITION together with a new operation *Undo*, which undoes the last *Equivalence* operation that has not been undone; therefore, *Undo* enables a user to return to a previous partition—to go back to the past.

14.1 PARTITION SPECIFICATION

Let E be a set of element values, B be the set of Boolean values, and P be the set of PARTITION values.

1. *Identity*: $\to \mathcal{P}$: The function value *Identity* is the identity partition of the set $\mathcal{E}$; that is, $\{\{e\}: e$ is in $\mathcal{E}\}$.

2. *IsEquivalent*: $\mathcal{E} \times \mathcal{E} \times \mathcal{P} \to \mathcal{B}$: The function value *IsEquivalent*(e,f,P) is **true** if e and f are in the same class of the partition P; otherwise, it is **false**.

3. *Equivalence*: $\mathcal{E} \times \mathcal{E} \times \mathcal{P} \to \mathcal{P}$: The function value *Equivalence*(e,f,P) is the partition P in which the classes in P containing e and f are replaced by their union. Thus, the result is P if and only if e and f are in the same class in P.

14.2 REPRESENTATIONS IN PARTICULAR

In many cases, the set of elements associated to an instance of PARTITION is the range of integers $1..n$, for some n that is not too large. We develop representations under this restriction in this section. When we do not have such a restricted set of *elementtype*, the representations are somewhat more complex, as we shall see in Section 14.3. We prefer to discuss the implementation of *IsEquivalent* and *Equivalence* in terms of two more basic operations called *find* and *link* that use class representatives. The **representative** of a class in a partition is one element in the class. The function value *find*(e,P) is the representative of the class in P that contains e, and the function value *link*(e,f,P) is the union of the classes in P whose representatives are e and f. The link operation is defined only when $e \neq f$, in which case the representative of the new class is either e or f. Thus we can implement *IsEquivalent*(e,f,P) by the Boolean expression *find*(e,P) $=$ *find*(f,P). Moreover, we can implement *Equivalence*(e,f,P) as the call *link* (*find*(e,P),*find*(f,P),P), if *find*(e,p) $\neq$ *find*(f,p), otherwise, we do nothing.

All the representations we encounter are based on multiway unordered trees (and forests) in which we need to follow only parent links. This observation leads to the first representation.

14.2.1 The Parent-Link Forest Representation

We represent each class as an unordered tree that has only parent pointers and has one node for each element in the set. Strictly speaking, we do not have trees, since the parent of the root is defined to be the root. In Fig. 14.2, we display the classes $\{a\}$, $\{a,b\}$, $\{a,b,c,d,e\}$, and $\{a,b,c,d,e\}$. The representation is not unique; also, it has the interesting feature that each node can have arbitrarily many children—the degree of a tree is not fixed in advance. The representative of each class is the element appearing at the root in its representation; the classes given in Fig. 14.2 have representatives a, a, a, and c, respectively.

We can now implement the operation *find*(x,P) straightforwardly. If the x node is its own parent, then x is the representative of the class containing x. Otherwise, we evaluate *find*(y,P), where the y node is the parent of the x node. For

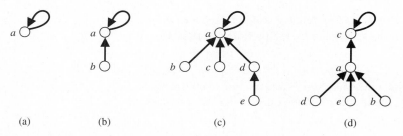

   (a)   (b)   (c)   (d)

Figure 14.2 Four examples of the parent-link tree representation of classes.

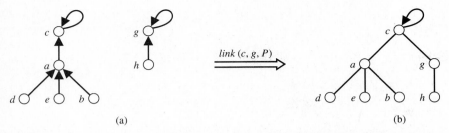

Figure 14.3 The implementation of *link* in the parent-link representation. (a) The representation of two classes. (b) The result of linking the two classes.

example, *find(e,P)* with the tree of Fig. 14.2(d), results in *find(a,P)*, which results in *find(c,P) = c*, giving *c* as the representative of the class containing *e*.

The operation *link(x,y,P)* for two distinct representatives *x* and *y* is particularly simple: Make *y* a child of *x*. In Fig. 14.3, we display one possible result of executing *link(c,g,P)*. In general, *Equivalence(x,y,P)* is *P* if *find(x,P) = find(y,P)*; otherwise, it is *link(find(x,P),find(y,P),P)*.

How do we represent a forest of unordered trees? The representation we use is simple, yet subtle; it is a cursor implementation of a forest. We use a block with both indices and values from 1..*n*. So, if *n* = 8 and *a, b, c, d, e, f, g,* and *h* are the integers 1, 2, 3, 4, 5, 6, 7, and 8, then we have the block of Fig. 14.4 for the three classes {*a,b,c,d,e*}, {*f*}, and {*g,h*}, where the first and last classes are represented as shown in Fig. 14.3(a).

Although *link* is easy to implement, it causes inefficiency, since it can produce trees of linear height. For example, for the range 1..8, the value P_3 of

$$Equivalence\ (4,3,Equivalence(3,2,Equivalence(2,1,Identity)))$$

is the tree of Fig. 14.5(a). The operation *link* has caused inefficiency, because, for example, *find(1,P_3)* has to follow four links to obtain the representative 4. In general, for a range 1..*n*, *find(i,P)* may follow *n* links; thus, because *IsEquivalent* and *Equivalence* both call *find*, they take linear time, in the worst case. As we shall see in Section 14.2.2, we can reduce the time bound for *find* at the expense of making the implementation of *link* slightly more difficult to code.

1	2	3	4	5	6	7	8
3	1	3	1	1	6	7	7
a	*b*	*c*	*d*	*e*	*f*	*g*	*h*

Figure 14.4 A block representation of parent-link trees.

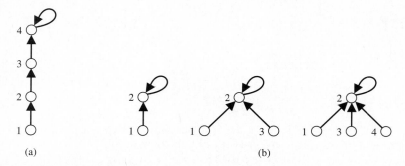

Figure 14.5   The value of *Equivalence (4,3, Equivalence (3,2,*
                   Equivalence (2,1,Identity))). (a) With the *link* implementation.
                   (b) With the *hlink* implementation.

14.2.2 Height Linking

Rather than connecting two trees arbitrarily, when we link them, we insist that the
"smaller" tree be attached to the root of the "larger" tree. This strategy balances
the trees in the forest, as we will show.

We compare trees by their height, where the **height of a node** u in a tree T is
the height of the subtree $T(u)$ of T. The use of size rather than height is explored in
Exercise 14.4. Because each representative e determines a unique node, we can
write *height(e)* without confusion. We modify the implementation of *link* to take
the heights of its given trees into account; we call it *hlink* to denote **height linking**
and to distinguish it from *link* in the following discussion. The function value
hlink(e,f,P) is the forest that we form from the forest that represents P by attaching f to the root of e, if *height(e)* $\geq$ *height(f)*; otherwise, it is the forest that we
form by attaching e to the root of f. Note that, if *height(e)* = *height(f)* before the
linking operation, then, after the linking, *height(e)* is increased by 1. For example,
the value of

$$Equivalence\ (4,3,Equivalence(3,2,Equivalence(2,1,Identity)))$$

is defined by three trees displayed in Fig. 14.5(b). Since we need to keep the
height with each node, each entry in the block representation, consists of a height
and a link field, rather than a link field alone. To see that the use of *hlink* balances
the trees in the forest, we establish the following fact.

Fact 14.1   *If a parent-link tree which is formed by a sequence of hlink opera-*
tions has height $h \geq 1$, then its size is at least 2^{h-1}.

We prove Fact 14.1 by induction on h. The underlying idea of the proof is that a
tree of smallest size of a given height must have been formed by linking two trees
of equal height. Since the basis, $h = 1$, is trivial, we consider only the induction

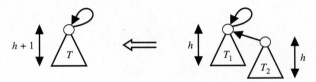

Figure 14.6   The structure of a smallest tree of height $h + 1$.

step. We assume that the fact holds for some height $h \geq 1$. Consider a parent-link tree T of height $h + 1$ of smallest possible size. Since $h + 1 \geq 2$, T must have been formed by linking two trees T_1 and T_2. Clearly, the heights of T_1 and T_2 are either h or $h + 1$. Because T is a tree of height $h + 1$ of smallest size, T_1 and T_2 must both be of height h; see Fig. 14.6. Now, $size(T) = size(T_1) + size(T_2)$, and the induction hypothesis implies that $size(T) \geq 2 \times 2^{h-1} = 2^h$. Finally, any parent-link tree T' of height $h + 1$ satisfies $size(T') \geq size(T)$, so the fact holds in general.

We need the converse of Fact 14.1.

Fact 14.2   *If a parent-link tree which is formed by a sequence of hlink operations has size $m \geq 1$, then its height is at most $\lceil \log(m + 1) \rceil$.*

A direct consequence of these facts is that if we have n elements, then each *hlink* and *find* operation takes $O(\log n)$ time, in the worst case. This time bound is a significant improvement over the time bounds for *link* and *find*. Can we reduce the time even further? Surprisingly we can, as we demonstrate in Section 14.2.3.

14.2.3   Halving

We have improved the implementation of the PARTITION operations by replacing *link* with *hlink*; we now modify *find* to improve the implementation further. The technique is ingenious, yet simple; the proof of its performance is not simple, however, so we omit the proof. We change the implementation so that *find* reattaches every other node on the search path, apart from the last and next-to-last nodes, to their grandparents; see Fig. 14.7. The technique is called **halving;** to distinguish this new version of *find* from the original version, we rename the operation *hfind*. To perform halving, we scan a node-to-root path only once; we leave you to work through the details of an implementation; see Exercise 14.7.

If we use both *hfind* and *hlink*, then the operations *IsEquivalent* and *Equivalence* still take $O(\log n)$ time, in the worst case. If we consider a sequence of m PARTITION operations, however, then the amortized time is now much less; it is $O(m\log^* n)$, where we define $\log^* n$ as follows. For $i \geq 0$, define $\log^{(i)} n$ recursively as

$$\log^{(i)} n = \begin{cases} n, & \text{if } i = 0; \\ \log(\log^{(i-1)} n), & \text{otherwise.} \end{cases}$$

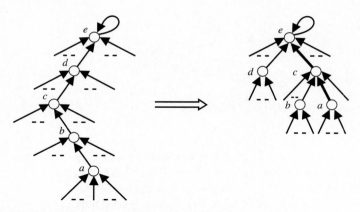

Figure 14.7   The halving technique. The reattached edges are
shown as thick lines.

Now,

$$\log{}^*n = \min(\{i : \log^{(i)} n \le 1\});$$

in other words, $\log{}^*n$ is the smallest number of applications of logarithm (to the
base 2) that produces a value no larger than 1. In Table 14.1, we give the values of
$\log^{(i)}n$ and $\log{}^*n$ for the first six transition values of n. Since $2^{65,536}$ is already
greater than the number of atoms in the universe, for all practical purposes,
$\log{}^*n \le 5$; that is, we can consider $\log{}^*n$ to be a constant.

   In summary, when the element values are from a small range $1..n$, we can
implement m calls of *IsEquivalent* and *Equivalence* to run in $O(m \log n)$ time by
using *hlink* and *find*. Furthermore, if we use *hfind* and *hlink*, then the m operations
take $O(m \log{}^* n)$ time; that is, almost linear time. In both cases, each individual
operation takes $O(\log n)$ time, in the worst case.

Table 14.1   The first six transition values for $\log{}^*n$.

n	$\log n$	$\log \log n$	$\log^{(3)}n$	$\log^{(4)}n$	$\log{}^*n$
1	0	–	–	–	0
2	1	0	–	–	1
4	2	1	0	–	2
16	4	2	1	0	3
65,536	16	4	2	1	4
$2^{65,536}$	65,536	16	4	2	5

14.3 REPRESENTATIONS IN GENERAL

When the elements in the PARTITION ADT are not a small subrange of the integers, we cannot use directly the representations given in Section 14.2. For example, if the elements are integers, if they do not form a subrange, and if the smallest subrange that contains them is much larger than the set of elements, then we cannot afford the space for a block indexed by the smallest enclosing subrange. We must look elsewhere for solutions. Conceptually, we use a TABLE or DICTIONARY ADT to map the elements into a small subrange, so that the representations for the PARTITION ADT of Section 14.2 can be used. In practice, we merge the two ADT representations into one representation, as we shall demonstrate. Although we can still use parent-link trees to represent classes, we can no longer use direct access to arrive at the node containing a given element. We must use some other kind of access. Two methods suggest themselves: binary search trees and hashing. We consider these two alternatives briefly: binary search trees in Section 14.3.1 and hashing in Section 14.3.2.

14.3.1 Binary Search Trees

Recall that search trees may be used only when the underlying keys are from some total order. If they are not from a total order, then we use hashing. The advantage of search trees is that we do not need to know the set of elements in advance; the structure grows gracefully. In both cases, however, the representation consists of two parts: a search structure and a forest of parent-link trees. We represent each element once in the structure; therefore, in the case of search trees, each node contains an element, left and right children links, a height, and a parent link for its parent-link tree. It is important to realize that we represent two kinds of trees simultaneously, so the parent of a node u is *not* u's parent in the search tree, but rather is u's parent in the parent-link forest. In Fig. 14.8(a), we have drawn search-tree links as continuous lines and parent links as broken lines. In Fig. 14.8(b), we have displayed the corresponding parent-link forest separately.

The operation *Identity* now creates an empty structure—the identity partition is represented implicitly. The operation *find*(*a,P*) first determines whether *a* is in the search tree. (This operation is an *IsMember* operation for the dictionary.) If *a* is in the search tree, then the corresponding parent links are followed until a repeated parent link is found. Otherwise, *a* is not in the search tree, so it is inserted and the parent link of the new node is initialized to point to the new node. The operation *hlink*(*a,b,P*) is unchanged. Hence, the search-tree implementation of the dictionary enforces a linear worst-case time for each call of *find* and *hlink*.

Rather than using binary search trees plain and simple, we can improve the performance of the implementation by using red–black trees (Section 10.2) to guarantee logarithmic worst-case time; see Exercise 14.10. We can improve the implementation even more by allowing *find* to return a window, rather than a rep-

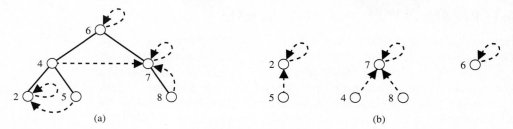

Figure 14.8   Binary search trees and parent-link trees. (a) The combination of a binary search tree and a parent-link tree. (b) The corresponding parent-link tree.

resentative, and *hlink* to take two windows as its arguments. This change in specification enables *hlink* to be a constant-time operation, whereas *find* remains a logarithmic time operation when red–black trees are used; see Exercise 14.11. The crucial observation is that we cannot achieve the $O(m \log^* n)$ time bound of Section 14.2.3, because we need additional search time for the elements.

14.3.2 Hashing

Since we need to perform only the *IsMember* and *Insert* operations for the elements, hashing is a viable approach. A hash table, indexed by $1..m$, has three fields—one for the element, one for its height, and one for its parent link. Although we can use any open addressing method, we recommend double hashing because it gives the best performance. If *find* returns the hash-table index of the representative and *hlink* takes hash-table indices as arguments, then *hlink* and *find* become $O(\log n)$-time operations, in the expected case. If we replace *find* with *hfind*, then we expect m operations to take $O(m \log^* n)$ time; thus, this approach is the method of choice. We leave you to evaluate it further in Exercise 14.12.

14.4 BACK TO THE PAST

Most text editors have a command that allows a user to undo one or more previous commands—to go back to a previous state. For example, in vi, u means "undo the last change"; in particular, u followed by u does not change anything! The idea of undoing a sequence of computation steps occurs in many different settings; we focus our attention on graphics editors. Typically, graphics editors allow users to construct scenes that are composed of separate figures, such as lines, curves, boxes, polygons, and ellipses. They also include editing operations, so that a user can move individual figures, copy figures, and rotate figures, for example. To make editing easier, they also include the group and ungroup operations that enable a user to treat a group (set or class) of figures as one compound figure and to decompose a compound figure into its original components once

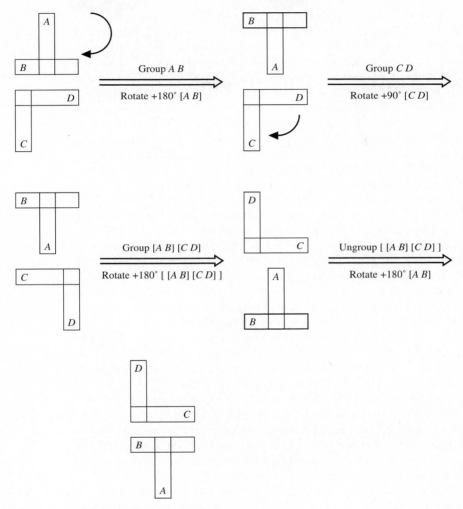

Figure 14.9 Grouping, ungrouping, and rotating.

more. Thus a user can rotate a group of figures with one rotation operation, rather than with a separate rotation operation for each figure in the group; see Fig. 14.9.

Clearly a set of figures is partitioned by a grouping operation, since each figure must appear in only one current group. Initially a set of figures is partitioned into the identity partition; each figure is a class. A grouping operation is the same as *Equivalence* and, in this framework, an ungrouping operation is called *Undo*. Unlike u in vi, *Undo* must undo the latest *Equivalence* operation that has not been undone. We show using rotations, see Fig. 14.9, how we can move four figures into a new configuration with the group and ungroup operations.

After this introduction of a new operation for partitions, we specify the operation $Undo: \mathcal{P} \to \mathcal{P}$ formally as follows. The function value $Undo(P)$ is undefined if P is the identity partition; otherwise, it is the partition before the latest *Equivalence* operation that has not been undone. We call the associated ADT, which has the PARTITION operations and *Undo*, the PPARTITION ADT (for **past partition**).

To implement PPARTITION efficiently, we need to maintain a historical record of the result of the *Equivalence* and *Undo* operations, a **history.** Since each *Undo* undoes one previous *Equivalence*, we maintain only a history of the results of the *Equivalence* operations that have not been undone. The challenge we face is to maintain an *Equivalence* history compactly and to implement *Undo* efficiently. We consider one approach that yields an $O(\log n)$ -time implementation of the PPARTITION operations, in the worst case.

We return to the *find* and *hlink* implementation of the PARTITION operations of Sections 14.2.1 and 14.2.2. Each call of *hlink* links a smaller-height tree to a larger-height tree; *it does not change either tree in any other way* and neither does *find*. Thus the result of each *Equivalence* operation can be represented by a window over the node that is no longer a root node. Since we need to maintain the results of only those *Equivalence* operations that have not been undone and since we access them in a LIFO manner, we use a stack of windows. Each call of *Undo* takes the top window w, if there is one. It resets the parent link of the node in w to point to the node in w; thus, it has undone the corresponding *Equivalence*. It is possible, however, that the heights of the two resulting trees were the same before the *Equivalence* operation; hence, in this case, it is possible that the height r of the node in w is 1 less than the height s of the other root node. Unfortunately the converse implication does not hold. For, if s is greater by 1 than r, then s may have been increased by an earlier *Equivalence* operation. Therefore we need not only to keep the window over the nonroot node, but also to keep a height-increment indicator with each window. The height-increment indicator has one of two possible values: the height of the new root node did increase when the node in the window became a nonroot node, or the height did not increase. Using this additional information, *Undo* determines whether to decrement s by 1.

The STACK operations take constant time, in the worst case; therefore, the implementation of *hlink* that we have sketched takes constant time. Clearly, *Undo* takes constant time, and *find*, which is unchanged, takes $O(\log n)$ time, in the worst case. In summary, we can implement the PPARTITION operations in $O(\log n)$ time, in the worst case. Furthermore, this performance result holds also when the given universe is not a range $1..m$, by the results of Section 14.3.1.

To reduce these time bounds further, we can use *hfind* with *hlink* and *Undo*. Because subtrees are modified by *hfind*, however, we need to keep additional information with each node in the partition forest, which we use to reconstruct a subtree when undoing an *Equivalence*. The details of this approach are beyond the scope of this text; see Section 14.7 for references to the literature. It leads, however, to an $O(\log n/\log\log n)$-time implementation of the PPARTITION operations, in the amortized sense.

14.5 PERFORMANCE REPORTS

The message of this chapter should be clear by now; see Tables 14.2 and 14.3. We use height linking to implement *Equivalence*, since it is easy to modify the *link* representation and code. If we require almost constant time for the PARTITION operations, then we also use *hfind*. Although *hfind* is not as easy to code as is *hlink*, it is not difficult to code. Finally, if we have to use a table or dictionary to represent the set of elements, then we recommend double hashing, because it runs in constant time, in the expected case.

Table 14.2 A comparison of the worst-case execution times of five PARTITION implementations.

| | PARTITION implementation | | | | |
Operation	Parent link	Height linking	Height linking and halving	Red–black	Double hashing
Identity	n	n	n	1	1
IsEquivalent	n	$\log n$	$\log^* n$[a]	$\log n$	$\log^* n$
Equivalence	1	$\log n$	$\log^* n$	$\log n$	$\log^* n$

[a]The $\log^* n$ values are amortized times for a sequence of m operations.

Table 14.3 Performance ratings of five implementations of PARTITION.

PARTITION implementation	Rating	Comments
Height linking and halving	Excellent	Easy to code; almost constant time
Height linking	Very good	Easy to code; logarithmic time
Parent-link	Poor,	
Double hashing	Excellent	Almost constant time in expected case
Red–black	Very good	Logarithmic time

14.6 SUMMARY

We introduced the PARTITION ADT to solve the problem of maintaining partitions (or equivalence classes) of sets under the operations: to form the identity partition, to test whether two elements are equivalent, and to make two elements equivalent. The basis for all the representations that we discussed is a forest of parent-link trees. When the domain is a small subrange, *Equivalence* and *Is-Equivalent* can be implemented extremely efficiently. When the domain is not a small subrange, we can use either binary search trees or hashing in conjunction with the parent-link tree representation. In this setting, we prefer to use double hashing because of its excellent expected-time performance.

We also introduced the PPARTITION ADT that has a new operation *Undo* that undoes the latest *Equivalence* operation that has not been undone. It is the first example of an ADT that has history; we can recover previous partitions by the use of *Undo*.

14.7 HISTORY

The early versions of FORTRAN included an EQUIVALENCE statement that identified synonym pairs; see Arden, Galler, and Graham (1961). Galler and Fischer (1964) gave an implementation of *find* that reattaches all nodes on the search path as children of the root. It is called **path compression** and is useful elsewhere; see the survey paper of Tarjan (1979a). The notion of height linking was introduced by Tarjan and van Leeuwen (1984) under the name of **ranked linking,** and the notion of halving was introduced by van Leeuwen and van der Weide (1977; Tarjan and van Leeuwen, 1984). Tarjan and van Leeuwen (1984) present, in a readable form, a number of new results for PARTITION; they also reprove a number of known results. Tarjan (1979b) and Tarjan and van Leeuwen (1984) established the corresponding $\Omega(\log^* n)$ lower bound in a separable pointer model of computation. The extension of PARTITION to PPARTITION was suggested by Mannila and Ukkonen (1986a; 1986b), who used it to model resolution and backtracking in PROLOG. Subsequently, Westbrook and Tarjan (1987) demonstrated tight lower and upper bounds of $O(\log n/\log \log n)$ amortized time.

A survey paper by Galil and Italiano (1991) is an extremely good source for results on other variations of PARTITION.

EXERCISES

14.1: Given a connected graph, you can compute a spanning tree by using the PARTITION ADT. Implement and test such an algorithm. Analyze its time complexity.

14.2: Design and implement a representation of PARTITION based on LIST using either linked lists or blocks. Analyze the time complexity of your algorithm.

14.3: Give a sequence of m PARTITION operations that achieve $\Omega(mn)$ time, when *link* and *find* are used.

14.4: Rather than using the height of trees to implement *link*, we can use their size instead; see Galler and Fischer (1964). Explore this alternative representation. Prove that it also gives a logarithmic-time implementation of the PARTITION operations.

14.5: An alternative representation of PARTITION uses height-1 trees to represent the classes, where all the elements in a class appear as the children of some root node. In this representation, we implement *link* by attaching the children of one root as the children of the other root. Implement new versions of *find* and *link* based on this representation. Analyze the time complexity of these operations.

14.6: Using the representation of PARTITION defined in Exercise 14.5, modify your *link* implementation to make the children of the root in the smaller tree the children of the root of the larger tree. The implementation of *find* is unchanged. What are the worst-case and amortized-case times for these operations?

14.7: Carry out a simulational evaluation of PARTITION based on *hlink* and *hfind*.

14.8: Give a sequence of m PARTITION operations that achieve $\Omega(m \log n)$ time, when *hlink* and *find* are used.

14.9: Implement *find* by using **path compression;** that is, reattach every node on the search path to the root node. Call this version of *find* *pcfind*. Prove that *link* and *pcfind* give a logarithmic-time implementation of the PARTITION operations.

14.10: Implement and test a general representation of PARTITION based on red–black trees, *find,* and *hlink*.

14.11: Specify the *find* and *link* operations in terms of windows. Implement and test a general representation of PARTITION based on this approach.

14.12: Carry out a simulational evaluation of a general representation for PARTITION based on double hashing, *hfind*, and *hlink*.

PART III

Preview

CHAPTER 15

Further Topics

New efficient data structures continue to be developed. The realm of data structures is fluid, with ever changing borders; data structures are born, some die, some attain fame, and the majority are little known. We have attempted, in this text, to provide data structures that have demonstrated both their worth and their survival of the fluctuations of popularity. We have, however, restricted our attention to data structures for records, records with keys, and records with priorities; that is, for zero- or one-dimensional attributes. The only exception is the introduction of priority-search trees, in Section 11.3. One-dimensional attributes have a longer history and are better understood; efficient data structures are known and are comparatively well established. Furthermore, a working knowledge of data structures for one-dimensional attributes provides a firm foundation for the study of data structures for multidimensional attributes. To offset this deliberate bias, we examine briefly, in this final chapter, some data structures for two-dimensional points and objects. Before this introduction, we first consider, in Section 15.1, skip lists, a new implementation of the DICTIONARY ADT; see Chapters 8 and 10. This structure has attracted much attention, because it uses randomization and is easy to implement. Then, in Sections 15.2, 15.3, and 15.4, we introduce three data structures for multidimensional point sets: quad trees, k-d trees, and grid files. The quad tree is used for two-dimensional point sets, and we restrict our discussion of k-d trees and grid files to two-dimensional point sets also. The first two of these structures are used for point sets in main memory, whereas the grid file is used for external point sets. Rather than specifying new ADTs for multidimensional point sets, we consider a number of different searching operations that such ADTs should have. For example, given the coordinates of all cities in a state or province, we can easily envisage queries of the form: Which cities are

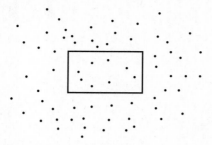

Figure 15.1   A two-dimensional range query.

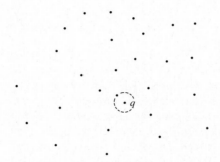

Figure 15.2   A two-dimensional nearest-neighbor query.

inside a given range (or rectangle; see Fig. 15.1)? Which city is closest to a given point (see Fig. 15.2)? Which cities are on a given vertical or horizontal line (a **partial-match query;** see Fig. 15.3)? Alternatively, when we have a state or province divided into its voting districts or ridings, it is natural to ask of a particular location: Which district or riding is it in (a **region query;** see Fig. 15.4)?

Next, we consider data structures for objects other than points in one- and two-dimensional space. In Section 15.5, we define the segment tree, a data structure that can represent line segments in one dimension, and the range tree, a data structure that can represent points in one dimension. We use segment trees and range trees to construct a hierarchical tree structure for rectangles, in Section 15.6. Finally, in Sections 15.7 and 15.8, we consider two general problems for data structures: how to make data structures dynamic and efficient, and how to make them remember the past or be persistent.

The presentations are, by necessity, brief; we touch only the surface of the data structures and the problems that they can be used to solve.

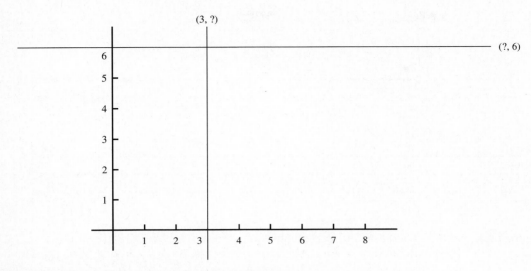

Figure 15.3 Two-dimensional partial-match queries.

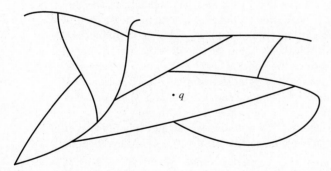

Figure 15.4 A two-dimensional region query.

15.1 SKIP LISTS

In Section 8.2, we used a sorted linked list to represent DICTIONARY. The major advantage of sorted lists is their simplicity; simplicity in concept and simplicity of coding. Their major disadvantage is their inefficiency; *Insert*, *Delete*, and *IsMember* take $O(n)$ time in a sorted list of n records, in both the worst and expected cases. We can, however, improve the search time by adding extra pointers, as we demonstrate in Fig. 15.5. In Fig. 15.5(a), we have a sorted linked list

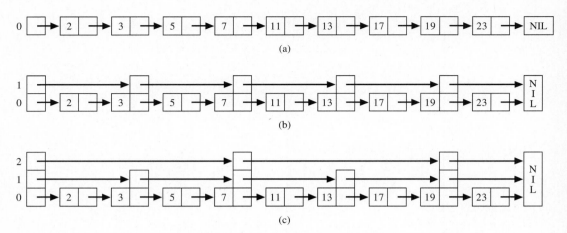

Figure 15.5   Sorted linked lists and skip pointers. (a) A sorted linked list for the primes 2,...,23. (b) The addition of pointers that skip one record. (c) The addition of pointers that skip three records.

for the prime integers 2,...,23; in Fig. 15.5(b), we have added extra pointers that skip one record, rather than none; and in Fig. 15.5(c), we have added pointers that skip three records and one record. We define the **level** of a node in a list to be k if the node has $k + 1$ pointers. We demonstrate how to use these extra pointers by searching for 8 in the list of Fig. 15.5(c). We begin the search at the topmost level, level 2, and discover that 8 is between the nodes 7 and 19. We now drop down to level 1 and continue the search from node 7. We discover that 8 lies between node 7 and 13. Finally, we drop down to level 0 and search from node 7. We discover that 8 lies between 7 and 11; therefore, we know that 8 is not in the list.

In general, given a static sorted list of n records, we can add skip pointers to obtain a **complete skip list** that achieves logarithmic search time. A level k node has $k + 1$ pointers that skip $2^k - 1, 2^{k-1} - 1, \ldots, 2^0 - 1$ nodes. Moreover, we arrange level k nodes at positions $i2^k$, for $i \geq 0$. Immediately, the topmost level is $\lceil \log n \rceil$ and the total number of pointers is only double the number in the original linked list. Thus we can search a complete skip list rapidly; however, the resulting structure is impractical to update. A complete skip list is similar to a complete binary tree, and the difficulty of updating it is similar to the difficulty of updating a complete binary tree. In both cases it is easy to insert or delete a record, but it is inefficient to maintain the balanced structure of the extra skip pointers in the linked list and the completeness of the binary search tree.

Recently, Munro, Papadakis, and Sedgewick (Munro et al., 1992) have introduced a version of this structure that can be updated and searched in logarithmic time. Here, we present Pugh's original version of the structure (Pugh, 1990), called **skip lists**, which use randomization.

Rather than attempting to maintain a uniform arrangement of pointers at the various skip levels, we maintain the proportion of level k nodes. Observe that, in

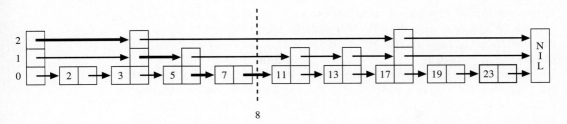

Figure 15.6   A skip list for the primes 2,...,23.

the complete skip list, 50 percent of the pointers are at level 0, 25 percent at level 1, and, in general, $(100/2^{k+1})$ percent at level k. Thus, on insertion, we introduce a level 0 node with probability 1/2, a level 1 node with probability 1/4, and, in general, a level k node with probability $1/2^{k+1}$. Moreover, a level i pointer in a node no longer skips exactly $2^i - 1$ nodes; instead, it points to the next node of level i or higher. The effect of these changes is that insertions and deletions require only local modifications; the level of a node is decided on insertion, and it never changes.

We have already explained how we search for a record in a complete skip list, we search for a record in a skip list in exactly the same way. For example, with the skip list in Fig. 15.6, when we search for a record with key 8, we are left between nodes 7 and 11 on level 0. We have indicated by thick lines the links that we have followed.

If we wish to insert a new record with key 8, then we would follow the same search path and discover that it should be placed between nodes 7 and 11. We must now not only insert the new record at this position, but also randomly generate its level and add the appropriate links. For example, if 8 is inserted as a level 2 node, then we must reset all the links cut by the vertical dashed line in Fig. 15.6; we obtain the new links indicated by thick lines in Fig. 15.7(a). If, however, 8 is

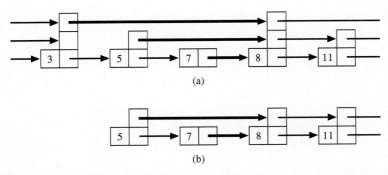

Figure 15.7   Randomized insertion of 8 into the skip list of Fig. 15.6. (a) As a level 2 node. (b) As a level 1 node.

inserted as a level 1 node, we need to reset only two links, as shown in Fig. 15.7(b). To be able to reset the links efficiently during a search, we maintain, for each level, the last node visited. We leave the details of this maintenance as part of Exercise 15.1.

The remaining problem is the random generation of the level of a new node. We have observed that, in a complete skip list, one-half of the nodes with level i pointers have level $(i + 1)$ pointers. Rather than hard wiring the value $1/2$, we assume that a fraction p of the nodes with level i pointers have level $(i + 1)$ pointers, where $0 < p < 1$. Hence, the level count is first initialized to 0. Then, to generate the level of a new node, we repeatedly obtain a pseudorandom number between 0 and 1. If the number is less than p, then we increase the level count by 1; otherwise, we terminate the generation. Thus we obtain a level 0 node with probability $1 - p$, a level 1 node with probability $p(1 - p)$, and a level i node with probability $p^i(1 - p)$. It is possible that we obtain a node with a level that is much higher than the number of records in the skip list. To avoid this pathological situation, we truncate a generated level if it is higher than $\log_{1/p} n$, where n is the current size of the skip list; we denote this value by $L(n)$. (Note that, when $p = 1/2$, $L(n) = \log_2 n$, the maximum level of a complete skip list.) Clearly, $L(n)$ grows and shrinks as the skip list grows and shrinks; therefore, it appears that we need to reevaluate $L(n)$ whenever we insert or delete a record. We normally, however, bound the number of levels in advance by estimating the maximum number of records that we will store in the skip list. We leave you to work out the details; see Exercise 15.1.

15.2 QUAD TREES

We introduce the quad tree, a data structure for two-dimensional point sets that is easily generalized to provide a data structure for d-dimensional point sets. As we shall see, it allows *IsMember* and *Range* queries to be implemented easily, albeit not always efficiently. The quad tree was introduced by Finkel and Bentley (1974); Samet (1989a; 1989b) has written an excellent text on the quad tree, its variants, and its usage. Recalling that binary search gives rise to the notion of binary search trees, we generalize binary searching to **quartering search.** Given a query point q, we begin the search at a **split point,** dividing the plane into four quarters by splitting it horizontally and vertically through the split point. This approach is illustrated in Fig. 15.8 with point a. We have reduced the search of the plane to the examination of one quadrant. For example, if q is the point shown in Fig. 15.8, then we compare points a and q and determine that we should continue the search for q in the lower-right quadrant of a. This quadrant contains three points, b, c, and d. If we select b as the split point, then we quarter *only* the lower-right quadrant as shown in Fig. 15.8. Since q is to the left of and above b, we continue the search in the shaded rectangle in Fig. 15.8. Since it contains only one point—namely c—we compare the two points and discover that q is not in the given set.

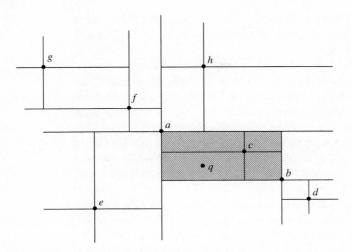

Figure 15.8 Quartering search in the plane.

Before we use binary search, we first sort the points so that a binary search always halves the number of points that need to be examined at each step. We might expect that we could first "sort" a two-dimensional point set so that quatering search quarters the number of points at each step. Unfortunately we cannot sort a two-dimensional point set so that this property always holds. Consider the set of diagonal points in Fig. 15.9. However we quarter them, we cannot reduce the number of points in *all* quadrants to be at most $n/4$. Indeed, this specific point set guarantees that, in every recursive quartering, at least two quadrants will be

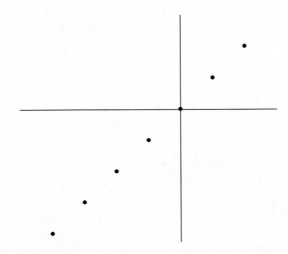

Figure 15.9 Quartering does not necessarily quarter a point set.

empty. You are asked to verify this fact in Exercise 15.2. In general, for a point set of size n, we can guarantee only that each quadrant contains no more than $n/2$ points—the same as for binary search.

We can define the split point by minimizing, over all quarterings, the maximum of the numbers of points in the four quadrants, which is an application of the **minimax principle.** This choice of split point ensures that, given n diagonal points, there are at most $n/2$ points in each quadrant. To implement the minimax principle in this setting, we sort the points primarily by their x values and secondarily by their y values and choose the median point as the split point. This choice guarantees that there are at most $\lceil n/2 \rceil$ points in each quadrant. If we do not have to use one of the given points as a split point, then we can obtain a simpler splitting policy; see Exercise 15.3.

We have ignored the time taken for a query. The algorithm that we have described takes linear time, since we must discard points at each step of the search; unlike in binary search, it appears that we cannot discard points except by examining all points in the current quadrant. So, unlike doing binary search in one dimension, it appears that in two dimensions we cannot search in time faster than linear. The basic reason is that there is no total ordering for two-dimensional point sets that corresponds to quartering search.

We can, however, obtain a more efficient search algorithm if we first build a multiway search tree that reflects the quartering-search pattern. We describe a four-way search tree in which each node has four children—one for each quadrant—and each internal node contains one point; this structure is called a **quad tree.** For example, the point set in Fig. 15.8, quartered as shown, gives rise to the quad tree of Fig. 15.10. The correspondence between the four children of a node and the quadrants is shown in Fig. 15.10; we refer to the children by their compass direction and index interchangeably.

A search—for a point q, say—begins at the root of a given quad tree. We determine in which of the four quadrants the point can be and continue the search

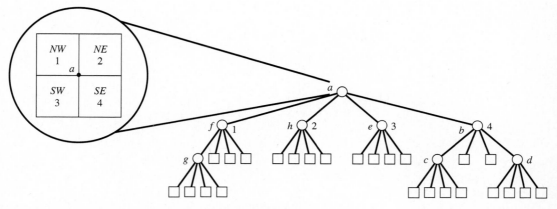

Figure 15.10 A quad tree for the point set in Fig. 15.8.

at the corresponding child. To ensure that searching is done correctly, we must be careful how we associate points with quadrants. We use the following scheme. If $p = (x_p, y_p)$ is the point at some node, then we associate a query point $q = (x_q, y_q)$ with the southern halfplane when $y_q < y_p$. Similarly, we associate q with the western halfplane when $x_q < x_p$. So the NE-quadrant consists of all points $q \neq p$ such that $x_q \geq x_p$ and $y_q \geq y_p$. It is not difficult to confirm that, for a quad tree Q, an *IsMember* query takes $O(height(Q))$ time, in the worst case.

Because of space limitations, we do not discuss the updating of a quad tree; we leave updating to Exercise 15.4. Rather, we discuss how we can construct efficient quad trees, when we know the point set in advance, and how efficient range and co-range searching are. Range searching is a more important operation when we have multidimensional point sets, whereas membership testing is less important. First, in Section 15.2.1, we demonstrate that we can construct quad trees of logarithmic height, for all sets of distinct points, and we show that the construction can be done efficiently. Second, in Section 15.2.2, we analyze the worst-case time for range and co-range searches in a quad tree of minimum height.

15.2.1 The Construction of Quad Trees

Given a set of n distinct points in the plane, we can construct a quad tree of logarithmic height by the method we have already suggested. We sort the points primarily by their x values and secondarily by their y values, and split them into two halves around their median. For example, with the set of 18 points displayed in Fig. 15.11, their median is j as indicated. Having selected j, we partition the remaining points into four subsets, corresponding to the four quadrants, and repeat this process for each subset in turn. By implementing this quartering process carefully, we can maintain the sorted order of the four subsets. The quad tree has logarithmic height, because at each node we divide the remaining points into at least two halves. Hence, the time, $T(n)$, taken to construct a quad tree for n points can be expressed by the following recurrence equation, when the time for

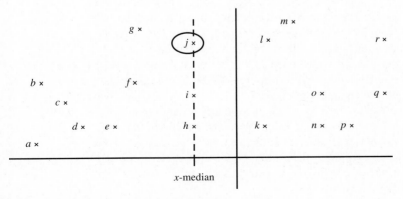

Figure 15.11 A point set and its median.

sorting is excluded. We have

$$T(1) = a,$$

$$T(n) = T(n_1) + T(n_2) + T(n_3) + T(n_4) + an,$$

where a is a positive constant, $n = 1 + n_1 + n_2 + n_3 + n_4$, and $n_1 + n_3 = n_2 + n_4$, because of the partitioning method. The linear term an measures the contribution of median selection and partitioning. The recurrence equation for $T(n)$ has the solution $O(n \log n)$, which you are invited to verify; see Exercise 15.5.

15.2.2 Range and Co-Range Queries

Assume that we are given a quad tree of size n and minimum height $\lceil \log_4 n \rceil$, and we wish to perform a range query on it. How much time does the range query take, in the worst and expected cases? Before examining these questions in more detail, we observe that the answer to a query consists of at most n points, so the worst-case run time is, trivially, $O(n)$. This bound is misleading, however, since it depends on the time to report the, at most, n answers. To isolate reporting time, we prefer to express the time bounds in terms of the size of the input *and* the size of the output, as we have done for range queries in Section 8.5.7. So instead of having a time function $T(n)$, we have a time function $T(n,r)$, where r is the number of reported answers. In this framework it is clear that $T(n,r)$ is $O(n)$ for a range query, but it is possible that this upper bound can be reduced. For example, for a binary search tree of size n and logarithmic height, a one-dimensional range query takes $O(r + \log n)$ time; see Section 8.5.7. Furthermore, as we have shown in Section 8.5.7, this bound can be reduced to $O(\log n)$ time, when we report only where the answers can be found, rather than providing them! Indeed, this bound holds for a co-range query too, where a **co-range query** gives all points that are outside the given range.

We demonstrate that, in a quad tree of minimum height, a range query takes $O(r + \sqrt{n})$ time, in the worst case. The case of co-range queries is left to Exercise 15.6. As with one-dimensional range querying, we analyze what can happen to a query range at each node during the search. Beginning at the root of the given quad tree, a range is preserved as long as it falls completely inside a quadrant; see Fig. 15.12(a). Eventually, either we reach an external node or the query range is split into two semi-ranges, see Fig. 15.12(b), or four quarterplanes, see Fig. 15.12(c). In both cases, the element at the node is in the range. At the next level, a semi-range may be preserved, see Fig. 15.13(a), split into a semi-range and a slab, see Fig. 15.13(b), split into two quarterplanes, see Fig. 15.13(c), or split into two quarterplanes and two halfplanes, see Fig. 15.13(d). Similarly, a quarterplane may be preserved, see Fig. 15.14(a), split into a quarterplane and a halfplane, see Fig. 15.14(b), or split into a quarterplane and two halfplanes, see Fig. 15.14(c). Thus we are left with two cases to consider—slabs and halfplanes. A slab may be split into two slabs or four halfplanes, see Fig. 15.15, whereas a halfplane may be split into two halfplanes, see Fig. 15.16.

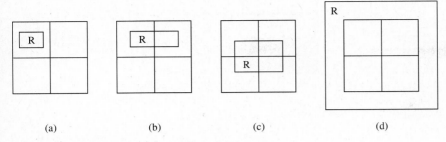

Figure 15.12   The four kinds of range query.

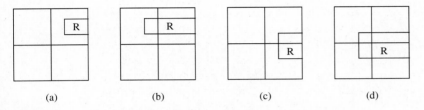

Figure 15.13   The four kinds of semi-range query.

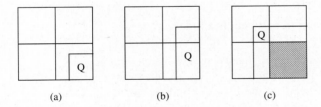

Figure 15.14   The three kinds of quarterplane query.

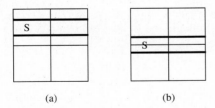

Figure 15.15   The two kinds of slab query.

Observe that quarterplane and halfplane queries may cause the reporting of a whole subtree; see Figures 15.14(c) and 15.16(b). The elements at nodes are reported only in the cases shown in Figures 15.12(c), 15.13(d), 15.14(c), 15.15(b), and 15.16(b). It is not difficult to see that a range that is split at each level into a combination of quarterplanes (the corners) and halfplanes (the edges)

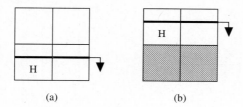

Figure 15.16   The two kinds of halfplane query.

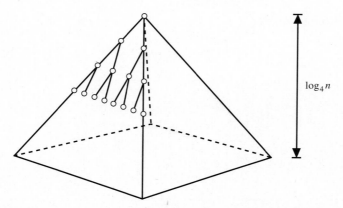

Figure 15.17   The face of a quad tree, which is a binary tree.

maximizes the number of pieces and, hence, the worst-case search time. A worst-case range query consists of Fig. 15.12(c) at the root, Fig. 15.14(c) at its four children, and Figures 15.14(c) and 15.16(b) at the 12 grandchildren, and so on. In the worst case, we traverse the four **faces** of the quad tree; see Fig. 15.17. Because a face corresponds to a binary tree and its height is $\lceil \log_4 n \rceil$, its frontier has at most $2^{\lceil \log_4 n \rceil}$ external nodes; that is, it has $O(\sqrt{n})$ external nodes. Hence, the four faces contain $O(\sqrt{n})$ nodes—the number of nodes visited, in the worst case, by a range query. Thus a range query takes $O(r + \sqrt{n})$ time, in the worst case, in a quad tree of logarithmic height. (This bound holds also in the expected case when a quad tree is built by incremental insertions.)

15.3 *k*-d TREES

Although the quad tree is a remarkably adaptive data structure, it is based on quartering the plane, and this choice prevents a true quartering of a given point set, in general. We introduce another data structure for two-dimensional point sets that avoids this difficulty most of the time; we call it the **2-d tree.** The underlying idea is similar. We recursively subdivide the plane; however, at each step we divide the plane with respect to only one coordinate. We alternate coordinates to

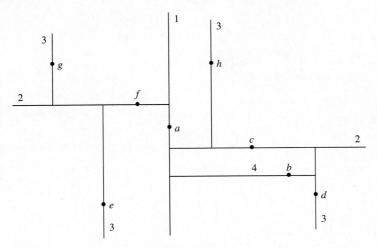

Figure 15.18   Halving of search in the plane.

obtain the final division. The 2-d tree is the two-dimensional version of the **k-d tree,** which was developed by Bentley (1975). The discussion of 2-d trees is based on the work of Bentley and his coworkers (Bentley, 1975; Bentley, 1979b; Friedman et al., 1977).

   In Fig. 15.18, we split the points of Fig. 15.8 by this method. The order of splitting is shown: first, a vertical split through *a*; second, *independent* horizontal splits through *f* and *c*; and so on. The corresponding 2-d tree is shown in Fig. 15.19, together with the corresponding splitting coordinates.

   One advantage of 2-d trees is that the point set of Fig. 15.9 can now be partitioned efficiently; see Fig. 15.20. Nonetheless there are point sets that are bad—for example, the point set in Fig. 15.21(a). In general, whenever we have two or more points that are horizontally or vertically collinear, the partitioning method may not halve the current point set. This problem occurs because the *x*-coordinate (and *y*-coordinate) values need not be distinct. We solve this problem by compar-

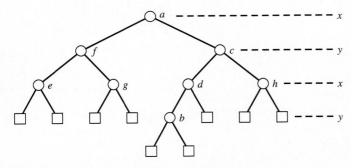

Figure 15.19   A 2-d tree for the points in Fig. 15.8.

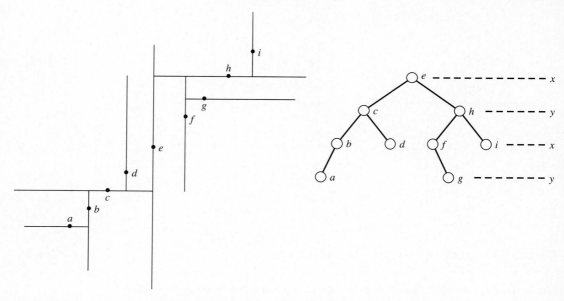

Figure 15.20   A bad point set for quad trees is good for 2-d trees.

ing the ordered pairs (x_i, y_i) when comparing x values. In other words, for two points (x_i, y_i) and (x_j, y_j), whenever $x_i = x_j$, we compare y_i and y_j. Similarly, rather than comparing points by only their y values, we compare the pairs (y_i, x_i) and (y_j, x_j). This approach ensures that the points in Fig. 15.21(a) give rise to the 2-d tree in Fig. 15.21(b).

In Sections 15.3.1, 15.3.2, and 15.3.3 we consider how to construct 2-d trees, how to carry out partial-match search, and, finally, how to carry out nearest-neighbor search.

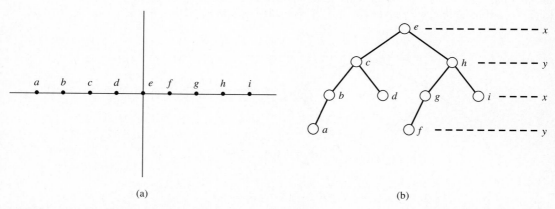

Figure 15.21   Bad point sets and 2-d trees. (a) A bad point set. (b) A suggested 2-d tree.

15.3.1 The Construction of 2-d Trees

To construct 2-d trees, we use an approach that is similar to the construction
method for quad trees. Given a set S of n points in the plane, we determine their x
median, M, and use M to partition S into S_L, S_R, and $\{M\}$. As we have already
mentioned, we compare x values by comparing the ordered pairs of coordinates,
and we compare y values by comparing the reversed ordered pairs of coordinates.
The difference is that we now treat S_L and S_R independently. Each of them is partitioned with respect to their y median, and so on. The partitioning process gives a
2-d tree of logarithmic height. By performing careful implementation and by sorting S separately by x and y before starting the construction, we can construct an
$O(n \log n)$-time construction algorithm; see Exercise 15.7.

Alternatively, we can construct a 2-d tree by repeatedly inserting records into
an initially empty 2-d tree. This approach gives, in the worst case, a 2-d tree of
height $O(n)$ and internal path length $O(n^2)$; see Exercise 15.8. Fortunately, the
expected internal path length of 2-d trees is $O(n \log n)$; hence, the expected-case
performance of 2-d trees is similar to the expected-case performance of binary
search trees.

15.3.2 Partial-Match Search

A two-dimensional partial-match query has the form $(x_q,?)$ or $(?,y_q)$; that is, it
matches those points that have the same x projection x_q or the same y projection
y_q, respectively. We can, in two dimensions, view $(x_q,?)$ as the vertical line with
equation
$x = x_q$. We give an algorithm for two-dimensional partial-match search in a minimum-height 2-d tree; we prove that it takes $O(r + \sqrt{n})$ time, in the worst case,
where r is the number of reported answers. The algorithm is remarkably simple.
Given an $(x_q,?)$ query (a $(?,y_q)$ query is treated similarly), there are four cases to
consider during the search. The first three occur on an x level; the fourth occurs
on a y level. At a y-level node u, see Fig. 15.22(d), the search continues at both
children—it bifurcates. In addition, when the x coordinate of the point at u is
equal to the query value, u's point is reported.

At an x level node u, the x value, x_u, of u's point influences the search. If
$x_q < x_u$, then we take only the left branch, see Fig. 15.22(a); if $x_q > x_u$, then we

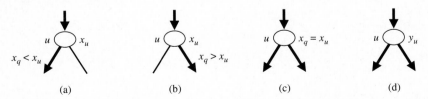

Figure 15.22 The four cases in a partial-match search. (a) The query x value
is less than the node x value. (b) The query x value is greater
than the node x value. (c) The query x value is equal to the
node x value. (d) The query at a y level node.

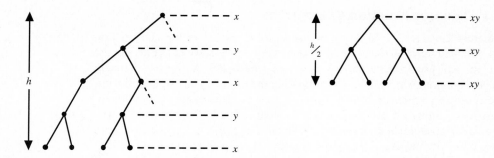

Figure 15.23   Partial-match search in a 2-d tree with $x_u \neq x_q$, for every x-level node u.

take only the right branch, see Fig. 15.22(b); and if $x_q = x_u$, then we report u's point and take both branches, see Fig. 15.22(c). (The latter case occurs because of the searching policy for equal x coordinates.)

Clearly, the worst case is given by case (c) in Fig. 15.22 on x levels; it appears to imply that the whole 2-d tree is traversed and, thus, a partial-match search takes $O(n)$ time, in the worst case. A closer examination shows, however, that it takes $O(r + \sqrt{n})$ time. There are two possible cases. We may never meet a node u on an x level with $x_u = x_q$, in which case we always take one branch on the x levels and both branches on the y levels. If we conceptually keep only the explored nodes, then the resulting unary-binary tree can be compressed into a binary tree of one-half the height and, therefore, of only $\sqrt{n}$ nodes; see Fig. 15.23. In the other case, we meet a node u on an x level with $x_u = x_q$. In this case, although we must explore both children of $u,$ we need to explore only one child of each grandchild of u. This implication follows because a grandchild v is on an x level, and, if $x_v = x_q$, then we must report all points in one subtree of v and explore the other subtree. This situation is shown in Fig. 15.24, where, from the definition of a 2-d tree, subtree 2 must contain only records (x_q,y), for some y. Thus, only subtree 1, in Fig. 15.24, needs to be explored further; thus, in the worst case, only $\sqrt{n}$ nodes are explored.

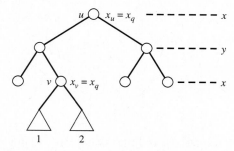

Figure 15.24   Partial-match search in a 2-d tree at the great-grandchildren of a node u for which $x_u = x_q$.

15.3.3 Nearest-Neighbor Search

We are given a set S of n points in the plane, and a query point $q = (x_q, y_q)$; we want to know a closest point in S to q. There may be more than one closest point; in that case, we report one of them. To measure closeness, we use the standard measure of distance in the plane. Nearest-neighbor search can be considered to be a generalization of predecessor and successor search for one-dimensional point sets; see Section 8.5.6.

A nearest-neighbor query can be viewed as a circular-range query, centered on q, where the circle is initially of infinite radius. Each time we obtain some candidate point p in S that is inside the circle, we shrink the circle so that p is on its circumference. The two possible positions of a new point p are shown in Fig. 15.25. If S is represented by a 2-d tree, then first we search for q in the 2-d tree. During the search, we determine whether the current node's point is inside the current circle of q. If it is inside the current circle, then we shrink the circle. In either case, we continue the search. This algorithm appears to run in $O(\log n)$ time, when the 2-d tree has height $O(\log n)$. Unfortunately, we may miss the closest point if we do nothing more, because q's circle may overlap the other half of the region at each node on the search path. For example, in Fig. 15.25(a), p is at an x node and the circle overlaps the left halfplane. Hence, it is possible that a closer point may be found there.

To ensure that we always find a closest point, when the search reaches an external node and an exact match has not been found, we retrace the search path and, whenever q's current circle overlaps the other halfplane, we search in that half. For example, p is at an x node, in Fig. 15.25(a), and, when we return to that

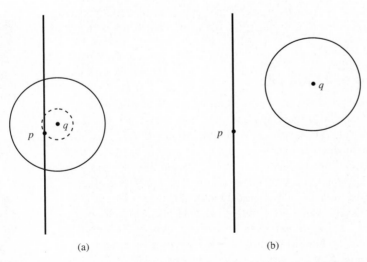

(a)   (b)

Figure 15.25 Circular ranges and new points. (a) When a range shrinks.
(b) When a range does not shrink.

node, q's circle still overlaps the left halfplane; thus, we continue the search in that node's left subtree.

The search algorithm outlined here can be inefficient, in the worst case—namely, it can take linear time. However, in the expected case, when 2-d trees are constructed to be of minimum height or are grown by random incremental insertions, it takes $O(\sqrt{n})$ time—a substantial improvement.

15.4 GRID FILES

Computer-science researchers have recognized that multidimensional data and searches are part and parcel of many real-world applications—for example, in geographical and architectural databases. One implication of this usage is that we need to provide not only efficient updating, but also efficient multidimensional searching *for externally stored data.* We have already faced this issue for one-dimensional data in Chapters 9 and 10, where we recommended linear hashing and B$^+$-trees, because they make few disk accesses, in the worst case. Here, we introduce the grid file, an excellent multidimensional-file organization that does not discriminate between dimensions, expands and contracts gracefully under insertions and deletions, takes few disk accesses for exact-match queries, and handles partial-match and range queries efficiently. The grid file was introduced by Nievergelt and associates (Nievergelt et al., 1984) in a readable paper that presents convincing experimental results.

Anyone who has read about or taken part in search-and-rescue missions will understand the grid-file approach. Rather than organizing the data (impossible in search and rescue), we organize the data space. In search-and-rescue missions, we divide the region to be searched into a grid pattern. The grids are numbered and they are covered one at a time, usually by different searchers. This idea is the basis of the grid file.

15.4.1 The Definition of a Grid File

We consider a two-dimensional grid file throughout the section; the extension to three or more dimensions is straightforward, if somewhat tedious. We use points in the plane as data, where the data space is within the rectangle [x_{min}, x_{max}, y_{min}, y_{max}] —**the grid space.** As they are in any external organization, the data are held in buckets; their maximum size is denoted by b. We divide the grid space into cells or **grid blocks** with separating **grid lines;** see Fig. 15.26. Note that m horizontal and m vertical grid lines define m^2 grid blocks. So, with 10 million points, we use a 1000×1000 grid, when we require each grid block to hold, on average, 10 points. Thus, the 1 million grid blocks are defined by only 2000 grid lines—and these grid lines can be held in main memory. In general, we assume that the grid lines can be held in main memory.

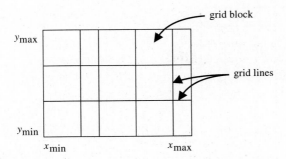

Figure 15.26 A grid space, grid lines, and grid blocks define a grid directory.

The crucial decision in the design of a grid file is that the grid blocks contain the addresses of the buckets that hold the points, rather than the buckets themselves. This decision has a major effect on the storage utilization and on the efficiency of adding and removing grid lines. Thus the grid blocks form a **grid directory.** Since the grid lines are in main memory, we can retrieve the grid block containing a given query point in one disk access, and we can retrieve its associated bucket (if there is only one) in one additional disk access—two disk accesses in total.

This simplistic analysis requires that each grid block be associated with at most one bucket; however, we may have more than one grid block assigned to the same bucket. Indeed, we allow any rectangular set of grid blocks to be assigned to the same bucket; see Fig. 15.27(a). We do not allow nonrectangular sets of grid blocks; see Fig. 15.27(b). There are two basic reasons for rectangular bucket assignment. First, ranges are rectangular, so allowing only rectangular bucket assignments prevents retrieval of too many points that are not in a given query range. Second, and more important, rectangular bucket assignments are easier to split and merge. As we deal with insertions in Section 15.4.2, we now consider exact-match, partial-match, and range queries.

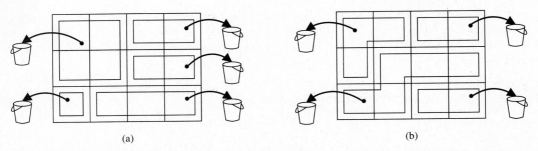

(a)   (b)

Figure 15.27 Grid blocks and buckets. (a) A valid assignment. (b) An invalid assignment.

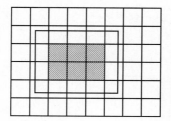

Figure 15.28   A range query on a grid file.

We have left many details unspecified—for example, the organization of the grid lines. Since the horizontal grid lines are defined by only y values, we can use any dictionary organization. Observe that, for a query point $q = (x_q, y_q)$, we want to find the closest horizontal grid lines that enclose y_q. This query is a successor and a predecessor query; hence, a table organization should not be used. Because disk-access time is orders of magnitude greater than the time taken for a successor and predecessor query, we might well choose a linked-list representation of a dictionary.

Having determined the indices of the grid block that contains the query point, we must retrieve it from disk. Because the grid directory has fixed-sized grid blocks (each block is associated with one disk address), the location on the disk of each grid block can be computed from its indices. For example, based on lexicographic ordering for the allocation of grid blocks (see Section 4.3.1), the page containing the given grid block can be computed easily.

Once we have found the correct grid block, we can retrieve its bucket and compare the query point with the points in the bucket. Again note that exhaustive searching within a bucket is acceptable in the context of external files.

A partial-match query—for example $q = (x_q, ?)$ —is implemented in a similar manner. The major difference is that a vertical slab of grid blocks and their associated buckets must be examined.

Finally, any range query intersects a rectangular set of grid blocks; see Fig. 15.28. The bordering grid blocks are the only ones that may contain irrelevant points, and the nonbordering grid blocks contain only relevant points (the shaded grid blocks in Fig. 15.28). Note that the chosen grid–bucket association implies that bordering grid blocks can involve grid blocks completely outside the range, because they are associated with the same bucket.

15.4.2   Updating of a Grid File

Initially, we assume that there is only one grid block—the complete data space— and, for ease of discussion, that the bucket capacity is three records. If we have three records in the grid file, then we have the situation displayed in Fig. 15.29(a). The insertion of one more record causes the bucket to overflow. We split the grid space vertically by adding a new vertical grid line and introducing two new

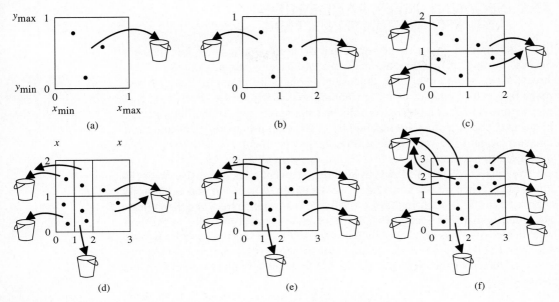

Figure 15.29   Snapshots of insertions into a single-block grid file.

replacement buckets; see Fig. 15.29(b). The records in the old bucket must be distributed between the two new buckets. Assume that the leftmost bucket overflows after two more insertions. This time, we add a new horizontal grid line; see Fig. 15.29(c). We alternate splitting of the grid space by an x line and a y line, although other protocols could be used. The new grid line cuts across the whole grid space, but we split only the bucket associated with the grid block (0,1,0,1) in Fig. 15.29(b); see Fig. 15.29(c). This principle is crucial—each overflow splits exactly one bucket.

Assume that two more records are inserted into block (0,1,0,1). We add a new vertical grid line and split the corresponding bucket to obtain Fig. 15.29(d). Continuing our example, if the next two records enter block (2,3,1,2), then they cause overflow, but we do not introduce a new grid line. The bucket is associated with two grid blocks, so we replace it by two buckets and redistribute the records giving Fig. 15.29(e). If a further record is inserted into block (2,3,1,2), then the new bucket overflows immediately. This time we have to add a new grid line—a horizontal one—and to replace the bucket; see Fig. 15.29(f). This latest insertion has the side effect of associating four grid blocks with one bucket—those grid blocks in the rectangle (0,2,1,3). The introduction of new grid lines maintains the rectangular association of grid blocks to buckets—another reason for choosing the condition in the first place.

Once the number of grid lines is reasonably large, insertions will normally cause only bucket splitting; we will rarely add new grid lines. This observation is the key to the efficiency of the grid file for large point sets.

15.5 SEGMENT TREES, RANGE TREES, AND SEGMENT INTERSECTION

The least complex object, apart from a one-dimensional point, is a line segment, interval, or range in one-dimensional space. We have identified a number of data structures for representing one-dimensional points; we now introduce the **segment tree,** which enables us to do stabbing search efficiently. Given a set A of line segments and a point q in one-dimensional space, we say that the line segments in A that contain q are **stabbed** by q. We shall use the segment-tree structure to help us solve the **segment-intersection problem:** *Given a set of (one-dimensional) line segments, report all pairwise intersections.*

We begin, in Section 15.5.1, by defining segment trees and discussing stabbing search. Then, in Section 15.5.2, we demonstrate insertion and deletion for segment trees. In Section 15.5.3, we briefly introduce range trees and their update algorithms. Finally, in Section 15.5.4, we solve the segment-intersection problem. The segment tree was developed by Bentley (1977), and was first used by Bentley and Wood (1980) to solve the rectangle-intersection problem. Samet (1988) has surveyed the data structures available for this problem, as well as for other rectangle problems.

15.5.1 The Definition of Segment Trees

The basic idea of the new data structure is that we take the gap view of binary search trees, which we introduced in Section 8.5.1, and modify it for external binary search trees. We assume that the endpoints of the segments are known in advance and, for illustration, that they are in the integer range 1..16. Although segments are closed intervals (the endpoints belong to the segments), we treat them as closed–open intervals.

We begin with an external binary search tree for the possible endpoint values; we display an external binary search tree for the 16 example points in Fig. 15.30. Now we associate the closed–open interval $[i, i+1)$ with external node i and the closed–open interval $[i, j+1)$ with each internal node u, where i is the minimum value in $T(u)$ and j is the maximum value in $T(u)$. In the tree of Fig. 15.30, node α represents the interval $[5, 9)$, node β represents the interval $[11, 13)$, and node γ represents the interval $[15, +\infty)$. Let *interval*(u) denote the interval associated with node u.

Given such a tree structure T, we can represent a segment $S = [i, j)$ by marking, with S, all nodes u in T that satisfy the **segment-search condition:**

$$interval(u) \subseteq S \text{ and } interval(parent(u)) \nsubseteq S.$$

For example, with the line segments $A..F$, given in Fig. 15.30, we have marked the nodes that satisfy the segment-search condition. The set of segments that marks a node is called a **node list;** we can represent node lists with doubly linked lists.

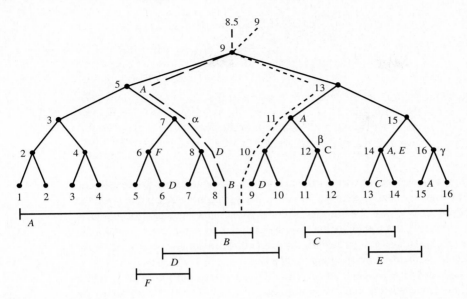

Figure 15.30 A segment tree.

Having defined the segment tree, we now demonstrate stabbing search. For the example segment tree in Fig. 15.30, we consider the query 8.5. We perform a membership search for 8.5 in the segment tree; it traces out the search path that we have indicated with a dashed line. We report all segments in all node lists on the path—in this case, A, D, and B. By definition, these three segments are the only segments that contain 8.5. If the query value is 9, then we expect to report the same three segments. The search path for 9, indicated by a dotted line, yields, however, only A and D; B is not reported because it is not on the search path. This anomaly occurs because we do not represent the right endpoint of segments. The solution is, however, straightforward: We search for both the query value and its predecessor; see Exercise 15.12. Observe that, for a segment tree of size n and height h, a stabbing query takes $O(r + h)$ time, where r is the number of reported answers. If h is $O(\log n)$, then stabbing search takes $O(r + \log n)$ time, and this bound is optimal in a comparison-based model of computation.

15.5.2 Updating of a Segment Tree

We assume that the allowable endpoints of segments are known in advance and do not change over time. We can then construct a segment tree for the endpoints that has empty node lists—a **skeleton segment tree.** Moreover, we can construct it to have minimum height; that is, it has height $O(\log n)$, for n endpoint values. Insertions into and deletions from the skeleton segment tree never change the underlying tree structure; they change only the marking (the node lists). We say that this structure is **semi-dynamic,** since, although it does not allow new end-

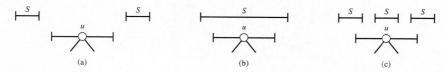

Figure 15.31   Segments and nodes in a segment tree. (a) The segment and
the node's interval are disjoint. (b) The segment contains the
node's interval. (c) The segment intersects, but does not
contain, the node's interval.

point values to be inserted or endpoint values to be deleted, it does not restrict the
number of line-segment insertions. Thus, it allows multiple segments with the
same endpoints values to be inserted; hence, we assume that each segment is
identified uniquely with some name. We use integers to name the segments. (In
Exercise 15.13, we ask you to design, for segment trees, an insertion scheme for
line segments with arbitrary endpoint values.)

We now describe the insertion scheme. Given a segment tree T of height h
and size $n - 1$, we wish to insert a new segment $S = [\text{left}(S),\text{right}(S))$ into T. We
essentially carry out a partial preorder traversal of T, which we describe recursively as follows. We begin at the root node of T, and we compare S with the interval at the root node. Since the root node is not handled any differently from any
other node during the insertion, we outline the general case of S meeting a node u.
There are three cases to consider; they are illustrated in Fig. 15.31. First, in Fig.
15.31(a), S and the node's interval are disjoint; we terminate the traversal. Second, in Fig. 15.31(b), the node's interval is contained in S; we mark the node with
S and terminate the traversal. Third, in Fig. 15.31(c), the node's interval is not
contained in S, but they have points in common; we continue the traversal at both
children of the node. When S contains u's interval, we do not continue the traversal with u's children; therefore, the algorithm marks with S those nodes in T
that satisfy the segment search condition.

We now argue that the insertion algorithm visits at most four nodes on each
level of the segment tree, and that it marks at most two nodes on each level.
Clearly, when a segment S intersects the interval of a node u, but does not contain
that interval (see Fig. 15.32), the algorithm visits both children t and v of u. If S
intersects, but does not contain, the intervals of t and v, then the algorithm visits
the four grandchildren—$w, x, y,$ and z—of u. But now the algorithm visits at most
four great grandchildren of u, because even if, for example, S intersects all four
intervals of $w, x, y,$ and z, it must contain the intervals of x and y; see Fig. 15.32.
Hence, only the children of w and z are explored further, in this case.

We have demonstrated that insertion visits at most four nodes on each level;
you should see clearly that it marks at most two nodes on each level. Therefore, in
a height-h segment tree, n segments mark $O(nh)$ nodes, in the worst case. If h is
$O(\log n)$, then n segments take $O(n\log n)$ space, in the worst case. Moreover,

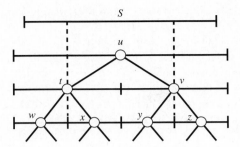

Figure 15.32   Insertion and visited nodes on each level of a segment tree.

Bucher and Edelsbrunner (1983) prove that n segments use $O(n \log n)$ space, in the expected case.

Finally, we discuss deletion. It is trivial to find the nodes marked by a segment S: All we have to do is to remove the marks. If we implement the node list as a doubly linked list, then finding S in a node list takes $O(n)$ time, in the worst case, when there are n segments in the tree. Hence, if the tree is of height h, then deletion takes $O(hn)$ time! We can reduce this worst-case bound by linking the appearances of S into a superimposed circular list; we need to find only one appearance of S to be able to delete all appearances of S. Thus, the use of an **appearance list** reduces the time bound of deletion to $O(h + n)$ —that is, to $O(n)$. We can reduce the time bound to $O(h)$ by using an auxiliary binary search tree for the names of the n segments; that is, if $n = O(\log n)$, then deletion takes $O(\log n)$ time, in the worst case. We leave you to fill out the details of the deletion algorithm in Exercise 15.14.

15.5.3 Range Trees

In Section 8.5.7, we discussed range searching with binary search trees. We noted that a range search in a binary search tree for n points takes $O(\log n)$ time, when the tree has height $O(\log n)$ and we report only where we can find the answers. We now introduce a new semi-dynamic data structure, the **range tree,** which uses this property to attain $O(\log n)$ -time updates and $O(r + \log n)$ -time range search. The secret is that we must know the n point values in advance such that each instance of the structure contains points with some of these values. Clearly, the structure is similar to the segment tree; therefore, the description is brief. We ask you to flesh out the the implementation in Exercise 15.15. As with segments, we distinguish between the name of a point and its value or coordinate.

Given n point values in one dimension, we construct an external binary search tree for them. To ensure efficiency, we construct a minimum-height tree; its height is $\lceil \log n \rceil$. This structure is fixed; we insert and delete point names by marking. For example, given a point name p with value x, we mark with p, all nodes in the tree on the path from the root to the external node for x. The set of point names that marks a node is a node list once more; we can represent node lists with doubly linked lists.

The advantage of range trees is that when we perform a range search, we do not need to traverse any subtrees. If all the point names in a subtree are inside a given range, then we merely report the point names in the node list of the subtree's root. Thus, a range search takes $O(r + \log n)$ time, where r is the number of answers. The use of external search trees, rather than internal search trees, implies that we need report only point names in node lists; see Exercise 15.16.

We implement deletion by the same technique that we described for deletion in segment trees. We link the appearances of each point name and keep the point names in a red–black tree, for example; see Exercise 15.15.

The range tree is more complex than we need for one-dimensional range search; however, for two-dimensional queries it is extremely useful as we shall see in Section 15.6.

15.5.4 Segment-Intersection Search

Segment trees support membership and stabbing queries; however, they do not support, efficiently, the detection of segment intersections. There are four types of segment intersections of a query segment Q with a given segment S; they are illustrated in Fig. 15.33. We can detect the intersections given in Figures 15.33(a) and (c) by using the left endpoint of Q as a stabbing query. Similarly, we can detect the intersection given in Fig. 15.33(d) by using the right endpoint of Q as a stabbing query. (But we will also report the intersection given in Fig. 15.33(c) twice!) Thus, we have missed the intersection given in Fig. 15.33(b), which is a range query for line segments. Although it is possible to modify the segment tree to support range queries efficiently (see Exercise 15.17), we suggest an alternative approach. We use a segment tree for the intersections in Figures 15.33(a) and (c), and a range tree for the intersections in Figures 15.33(b) and (d). We observe that *two line segments Q and S intersect if and only if $left(Q) \in S$ or $left(S) \in Q$.* Thus, we construct a range tree for the left endpoints of the given segments and use Q as a range query.

Assume that we are given the segment and range trees for a set A of n segments, and that they have height h. Then, by the discussion in Sections 8.5.7, 15.5.1, and 15.5.3, we can report all segments that intersect a query segment Q in $O(r + h)$ time, where r is the number of intersecting segments. If we ensure that h is $O(\log n)$, then we obtain a time-optimal structure for segment intersections. As

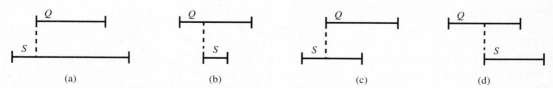

(a)   (b)   (c)   (d)

Figure 15.33 The four kinds of segment intersections.

we proved in Section 15.5.2, it is not a space-optimal structure, since each segment may mark $O(h)$ nodes in the segment tree.

We can use a different characterization of the intersection of two segments; namely, two line segments Q and S intersect if and only if $left(Q) \leq right(S)$ and $left(S) \leq right(Q)$. We can then use a priority search tree, rather than the structure we have described; see Section 11.3 and Exercise 15.18. Another alternative structure, the **interval tree,** is also based on external binary search trees, but the search condition is defined differently. Given such a tree structure T, we can represent a segment $S = [i,j]$ by marking, with S, the node u in T that satisfies the **interval-search condition:**

$$separator(u) \in S \text{ and } separator(parent(u)) \notin S.$$

In addition, the node lists are organized as binary search trees for the endpoints of the segments. The interval tree was developed by Edelsbrunner (1983a; 1983b); its advantage over the segment tree is that, because each segment appears in only one node list, the interval tree for n segments uses $O(n)$ space. We leave you to implement stabbing search and segment-intersection search in the interval tree as Exercise 15.19.

15.6 HIERARCHICAL TREES AND RECTANGLES

We address the following problem in this section. *Given a set of n rectangles, discover all pairs of intersecting rectangles.* We can solve this off-line or batch problem by comparing all pairs of rectangles, which takes $O(n^2)$ time and uses $O(n)$ space. We sketch an alternative solution that takes $O(r + n \log^2 n)$ time and uses $O(n \log^2 n)$ space, in the worst case, where r is the number of intersecting pairs. The solution is based on the algorithm and data structures we gave in Section 15.5 to find all pairs of intersecting segments. Bentley and Wood (1980) solve this problem by using the plane-sweep technique to reduce the rectangle-intersection searching to segment-intersection searching. Thus, they obtain an algorithm that runs in $O(r + n \log n)$ time and uses $O(n \log n)$ space, in the worst case. The structures we describe in this section, however, were used by Six and Wood (1982) to solve the three-dimensional variant of the rectangle-intersection problem.

We have provided, in Section 15.6, a new data structure for segment-intersection search; we now describe how we can extend this structure for rectangles in the plane and rectangle-intersection search. As with segment trees, see Section 15.5, we assume that the allowable endpoints values are integers known in advance. Moreover, we assume that each rectangle is identified uniquely by some name that we assume is also an integer. The technique that we shall introduce is applicable only to **axes-parallel rectangles** as displayed in Fig. 15.34.

The crucial observation is that the set of points that define a rectangle can be represented as the Cartesian product of the x interval and y interval given by its x

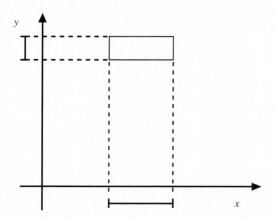

Figure 15.34   An axes-parallel rectangle and its projections.

projection and y projection, respectively; see Fig. 15.34. This decomposition suggests that we can solve stabbing queries for rectangles by composing the results of a stabbing query for the rectangle's x intervals with the results of a stabbing query for the rectangle's y intervals. A simplistic composition is to compute the intersection of the results of the two queries; a more efficient approach is to perform the y-stabbing query on the results of the x-stabbing query. We describe, in Section 15.6.1, a hierarchical tree structure that supports this cascading approach to stabbing queries; then, in Section 15.6.2, we extend the method for rectangle-intersection queries. Finally, in Section 15.6.3, we discuss how we can construct hierarchical trees efficiently.

15.6.1 Stabbing Search

In Section 15.5, we introduced the segment tree, for one-dimensional line segments, that supports stabbing search. Using the interval decomposition of a rectangle, we can represent the x intervals of the given rectangles in a segment tree. Each node u in the segment tree has an associated node list of rectangles whose x intervals contain u's interval. Now, we replace u's node list with a segment tree for the y- intervals of the rectangles in u's node list; see Fig. 15.35. This structure, which we call a **segment–segment tree,** can be used to answer stabbing queries efficiently, if we ensure that the trees at the two levels of the hierarchy have logarithmic height. Given a stabbing query $q = (x_q, y_q)$, we search the x-segment tree with x_q and then for each node on the search path, we search the associated y-segment trees with y_q. We report all rectangles in the node lists on the search paths in the y-segment trees. Since the x-segment tree has logarithmic height, we examine $O(\log n)$ y-segment trees, and, since each y-segment tree has logarithmic height, we examine $O(\log^2 n)$ node lists. Thus, stabbing search takes $O(r + \log^2 n)$ time, where r is the number of rectangles stabbed by the query point.

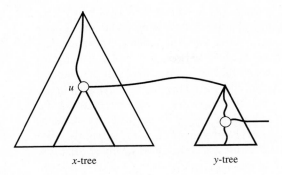

Figure 15.35 A segment–segment tree.

15.6.2 Rectangle-Intersection Search

Given a set of n rectangles in the plane, we first want to discover all the rectangles that intersect a given query rectangle. As we demonstrated, in Section 15.5, we need both a segment tree and a range tree to solve segment-intersection queries. Thus, we use four hierarchical tree structures to solve rectangle-intersection queries: We need segment and range trees at each level to detect all possible intersections. Thus we have a segment–segment tree, a segment–range tree, a range–segment tree, and a range–range tree. In each case, the first-level trees are based on the x intervals of the rectangles and the second-level trees are based on the y intervals of the rectangles. A rectangle query is decomposed into four different queries: an x-stabbing y-stabbing query, an x-stabbing y-range query, an x-range y-stabbing query, and an x-range y-range query. If we ensure that all trees have height $O(\log n)$, then a rectangle-intersection query takes $O(r + \log^2 n)$ time, where r is the number of reported intersections. Now, to find all intersecting pairs of rectangles in the given set, we construct the four two-level trees for the n rectangles, *in skeletal form,* and insert one of the rectangles. Then we repeatedly choose a new rectangle, use it as a rectangle-intersection query, and then insert it. This algorithm reports each intersecting pair only once, takes $O(r + n \log^2 n)$ time, and uses $O(n \log^2 n)$ space, in the worst case.

15.6.3 Construction of Hierarchical Trees

Because we know the x and y coordinates of the corners of the n given rectangles in advance, we can build a skeletal hierarchical tree, of height $O(\log n)$, in $O(n^2)$ time using $O(n^2)$ space. Once they are built, we can insert each rectangle into the four hierarchical trees in $O(\log^2 n)$ time and perform a rectangle-intersection query in $O(\log^2 n)$ time. Such a statement enables us to carry out any number of rectangle-intersection queries efficiently. Clearly, $O(n^2)$ time is too much and the space requirement is too high. But, because we are the given the n rectangles in advance, we can use them to reduce the time and space requirements of the construction. To illustrate the idea, we reexamine the construction of a range–segment tree, for n given rectangles. Assume that we insert the left endpoints of the x intervals of the rectangles into a skeletal x-range tree. Then each endpoint appears in $O(\log n)$ node lists, since the x-range tree has height $O(\log n)$. Thus, n rectangles use $O(n \log n)$ space. We now traverse the x-range tree and, for each node u, we construct a skeletal y-segment tree for the y intervals of the rectangles in u's node list. Clearly, the skeletal range–segment tree that we obtain by removing the node lists uses $O(n \log n)$ space, instead of $O(n^2)$ space—a significant reduction. To arrive at a comparable time bound, we have to avoid locally sorting the endpoints of the y intervals of the rectangles in each node list. (Locally sorting one node list takes $O(n \log n)$ time, in the worst case; hence, sorting n node lists takes $O(n^2 \log n)$ time.) We avoid local sorting by inserting the rectangles twice into the x-range tree, once sorted by their bottommost y coordinates and once sorted by their topmost y coordinates. We keep two separate node lists at each node, which we then merge, in linear time, to obtain the endpoints of the y intervals in sorted order. Globally sorting the rectangles takes $O(n \log n)$ time, and inserting them takes $O(n \log n)$ time; hence, we can construct a skeletal range–segment tree in $O(n \log n)$ time. A similar approach can be used for the other three hierarchical trees.

15.7 DYNAMIZATION

In many applications of multidimensional data structures, we have insertions and deletions of objects; hence, the data structures should be dynamic. Unfortunately, most of these data structures do not support efficient updating; for example, k-d trees do not, as we shall demonstrate. With binary search trees, on the other hand, we are able to maintain logarithmic-height subclasses of them in logarithmic time, in the worst case; for example, we can do so with the red–black trees. For this reason, we are interested in providing general techniques that make an essentially static structure dynamic. Such a technique is called a **dynamization technique.** In Section 15.7.1, we demonstrate that 2-d trees do not support the promotion operation efficiently; then, in Section 15.7.2, we introduce one dynamization technique. The specific technique we discuss was developed by Bentley (1979b), and by Bentley and Saxe (1980). Overmars (1983) has investigated dynamization techniques thoroughly. The term *dynamization* was introduced by van Leeuwen and Wood (1980).

15.7.1 Promotions and *k*-d Trees

The promotion operation underlies every rebalancing algorithm for binary search trees. We first show that there is no similar operation for 2-d trees; we leave you to demonstrate, in Exercise 15.20, a similar result for quad trees.

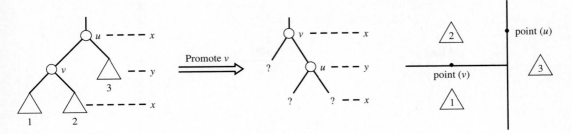

Figure 15.36 Promotions and 2-d trees.

Assume that we have the 2-d tree shown in Fig. 15.36, and we want to promote v. What happens to the node u and the subtrees 1, 2, and 3? This node and these subtrees are associated with regions of the plane as shown in Fig. 15.36. If v is promoted to be the root of this subtree, then node u becomes its right child. The node u is now on the y level, rather than on the x level. But the points in subtree 3 that are all x-greater than the points of u and v, are not y-greater than the point of u. In other words, promotion does not preserve the 2-d search property. Therefore, instead of a local transformation that both preserves 2-d trees and enables us to rebalance them, we use a completely different approach.

15.7.2 Dynamic 2-d Trees

Rather than modifying a given 2-d tree after updating it, as we do for red–black trees, we rebuild it. Since rebuilding is inefficient, we represent a point set with an orchard of 2-d trees. The orchard is determined by the binary expansion of the current size of the set; for example, when it has nine elements, its representation consists of one 2-d tree of size 8, and one of size 1. Each 2-d tree in this representation has size a power of 2, and there is at most one 2-d tree of each size. Since we rebuild individual trees as needed, we ensure that each tree has the form shown in Fig. 15.37—namely, a perfect binary tree with a single dangling node at the leftmost position in the bottom level.

We can think of the orchard of 2-d trees as a clothesline with 2-d trees, rather than clothes, hanging from the line. For example, the point set of size 8 of Fig. 15.8 is represented by four 2-d trees—three of them empty; see Fig. 15.38. Observe that the 2-d tree of size 8 is different from the one in Fig. 15.38. To search and update this structure, we first note that there are $\lceil \log n \rceil$ 2-d trees in the representation of a set of size n. This observation implies that we can access the $\lceil \log n \rceil$ root nodes in $O(\log n)$ time. The general searching strategy is to search in each of the 2-d trees and to combine the answers to give the overall answer. Whenever this strategy works correctly for a class of searching problems, we say that the searching problem is **decomposable.** For example, exact-match, partial-match, range, co-range, and nearest-neighbor queries are decomposable.

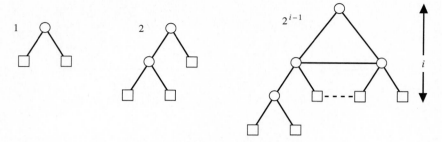

Figure 15.37 Perfect 2-d trees with one dangling node of sizes 1, 2, and 2^{i-1}.

Consider an exact-match or *IsMember* query q. If q is in the given point set, then it must be in one of the 2-d trees hanging on the clothesline. We test each one in turn. Since a search in subtree i, $0 \le i \le \lceil \log n \rceil$, takes i node visits, in the worst case, overall *IsMember* takes

$$\sum_{i=0}^{\lceil \log n \rceil} i,$$

or $O(\log^2 n)$ node visits, in the worst case. Thus searching takes $O(\log^2 n)$ time. We solve a nearest-neighbor query by carrying out a nearest-neighbor query for each 2-d tree and finding the nearest point among the, at most $\lceil \log n \rceil$, answers. It is easy to show that this algorithm is correct. Let S be a set of points that is partitioned into two disjoint subsets A and B ($A \cup B = S$ and $A \cap B = \emptyset$). For a point q, we denote the nearest neighbor of q in S by $S(q)$. Then, for any point q, the nearest neighbor of q in S is the nearer neighbor of $A(q)$ and $B(q)$. In other words, $S(q)$ is in $\{A(q),B(q)\}$. Hence, a nearest-neighbor query is implemented as $O(\log n)$ nearest-neighbor queries, each taking $O(\log n)$ node visits, in the ex-

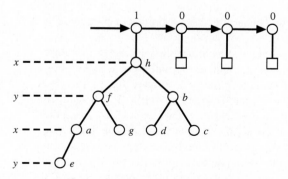

Figure 15.38 A clothesline of 2-d trees.

Figure 15.39 The eight-point set of Fig. 15.8 with eight additional points.

pected case. Thus a nearest-neighbor query takes $O(\log^2 n)$ time overall, in the expected case.

The implementation of the other queries is left to Exercise 15.21. We turn, here, to the problem of updating the representation. We consider only insertions, since deletions are considerably more difficult.

Everyone knows how to add 1 to a binary number. Beginning at the lowest-order bit or the right end, we flip each 1 bit until either the first 0 bit is reached, in which case we flip it, or the bit positions are exhausted, in which case we add a 1 bit at the new position. This addition algorithm is the basis of the insertion algorithm. Consider our initial example of eight points $(8 = (1000)_2)$. Insert the new point i; see Fig. 15.39. Since the 2-d tree in position 0 is empty, we just create a one-node 2-d tree with i as its only point; see Fig. 15.40(a). Again, we add a new point—j, say. The 2-d tree in position 0 is no longer empty—it corresponds to a 1 bit. We replace it by an empty 2-d tree, and now we have two points, i and j, to insert at position 1. But position 1 has an empty 2-d tree, so we replace it with a 2-d tree of size 2; see Fig. 15.40(b). The next interesting event occurs when two more points—k and l, say—are inserted in this order, one at a time. The point k creates a 2-d tree of size 1 at position 0. The point l replaces this tree with an empty 2-d tree and carries k and l to position 1. Because the tree at position 1 is nonempty, it is replaced by an empty 2-d tree, and the four points i, j, k, and l are carried to position 2. Now there is an empty tree at position 2, so we replace it with a 2-d tree of size 4; see Fig. 15.40(c). After four further insertions, of r, s, t, and u, the whole orchard expands by one position, yielding the orchard of Fig. 15.40(d).

Because an insertion can cause all the trees in the orchard to be rebuilt, insertions take $O(n)$ time, in the worst case. Fortunately, the amortized bound is much lower, as we now show. If we insert n points into an initially empty structure, where $n = 2^k$, for some $k \geq 0$, then we construct a 2-d tree of size 2^i at position i

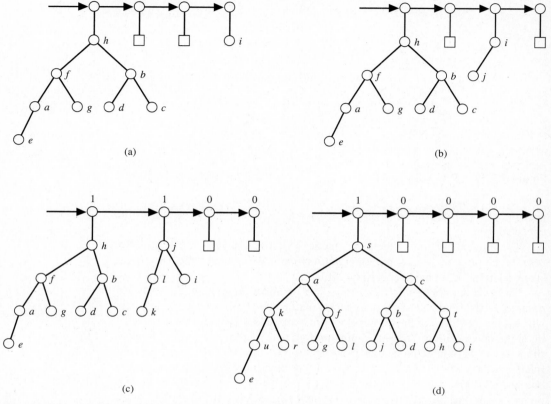

Figure 15.40 The insertion of the additional points into the clothesline of Fig. 15.38.

exactly 2^{k-i} times. Because it takes $O(m \log m)$ time to construct a 2-d tree of size m, the insertion of n points takes

$$\sum_{i=0}^{k} (2^{k-i} \times i2^{i})$$

time. We can take the term 2^k outside the summation and simplify the resulting summation to obtain

$$2^k \sum_{i=0}^{k} i;$$

that is, the insertion of n points takes $O(2^k \times k^2)$ time. Because $k = \lceil \log n \rceil$ and $n = 2^k$, the amortized construction time is $O(\log^2 n)$ for each point.

Deletion can be carried out in the same amortized time bound, but it is more difficult. Moreover, we can transform the amortized time bounds into worst-case time bounds by amortizing the construction work using a technique called **partial rebuilding;** see Overmars (1983).

15.8 PERSISTENCE

In Section 14.4, we described an extension of the PARTITION ADT that provides an undo operation, which can be used to reconstruct a previous instance of the ADT, to return to the past. Here, we describe an extension to the DICTIONARY ADT that modifies the *IsMember* and *Successor* operations (and the other search operations) to search in the past. Although we can implement the operations by reconstructing the dictionary for the given time and applying the standard *IsMember* or *Successor* operations to it, we demonstrate that there are more efficient implementations. For simplicity, we consider only modified versions of *IsMember* and *Successor* that are specified as follows.

1. *IsMember*: $\mathcal{K} \times \mathcal{N} \times \mathcal{D} \rightarrow \mathcal{B}$: The value of *IsMember(K,t,D)* is **true** if there is an element with key K in D at time t; otherwise, it is **false**.

2. *Successor*: $\mathcal{K} \times \mathcal{N} \times \mathcal{D} \rightarrow \mathcal{E}$: The function value *Successor(K,t,D)* is the element e in D at time t, whose key is the successor of K, if there is one; otherwise, it is undefined.

We assume that updates occur at times 1,2,... and that they occur in the present; we do not allow updates in the past (or the future). This version of persistence was called **partial persistence** by Driscoll and associates (Driscoll et al, 1989; Sarnak, 1986) who presented the first space-efficient general implementation of persistence. They reserved the term **persistence** or **full persistence** for structures that allow updates at any time, rather than only in the present. An application of their techniques to the point-location problem has been developed by Sarnak and Tarjan (1986).

We examine a number of techniques for making binary search trees persistent. Although the techniques can be extended to red–black trees, B$^+$-trees, and other structures, we do not do that here. In Section 15.8.1, we introduce simple techniques for the implementation of persistence, one of which we then refine, in Section 15.8.2, to give path copying, and which we further refine, in Section 15.8.3, to give limited-node copying.

15.8.1 A Few Simple Techniques

Each record in a dictionary has an associated lifetime $[t_i, t_d]$ from the time t_i when the record was inserted to the time t_d when it was deleted. Thus, perhaps the simplest solution is to time stamp a record with its insertion time (and deletion time if applicable) and to keep all the records that have been inserted in one binary search tree. If there have been m insertions, then this solution uses $O(m)$ space, and we can even use red–black trees to achieve $O(\log m)$ access time, in the worst

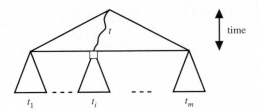

Figure 15.41   Persistence by tree copying.

case. With *IsMember(K,t,D)*, we search the associated binary search tree T_D for a record with key K. If there is no such record, then we return the value **false**. Otherwise, there is a record with key K in T_D, and we return **true** if and only if t is no earlier than the record's insertion time and no later than its deletion time. Since we must keep all m inserted records, which were inserted at m different times, $O(\log m)$ is a reasonable upper bound for *IsMember*. We shall reduce this upper bound by using the sortedness, with respect to time, of the insertion order. With *Successor(K,t,D)*, however, we see immediately that using a single binary search tree is suboptimal. It is straightforward to find the successor of K in a single binary search tree in $O(\log m)$ time; however, it need not be a successor at time t. We must scan the successors of K in inorder to find the first one that was current at time t. Clearly, in the worst case, this search takes $O(m)$ time.

   One solution to the *Successor* problem is to keep separate trees for each update. Whenever we update a tree, we make a new copy of it, update the copy, and time stamp the copy with its creation time. We can maintain a red–black tree of creation times, so that, given a *Successor(K,t,D)* or *IsMember(K,t,D)* operation, we first find the latest search tree with creation time $\bar{t}$ no greater than t; see Fig. 15.41. This search takes $O(\log m)$ time if there have been m updates. We then carry out either a successor or membership search on the resulting tree. Since $\bar{t}$ is the last update time that is not after time t, we guarantee the correctness of the search strategy. The total search time is $O(\log m + \log n_{\bar{t}})$, where $n_{\bar{t}}$ is the number of records available at time $\bar{t}$. Since $n_{\bar{t}}$ is $O(m)$, the total search time is $O(\log m)$. The space requirement is horrendous; it is $O(m^2)$. We can, however, reduce the space bound, using path copying, as we shall demonstrate in Section 15.8.2.

15.8.2   Path Copying

Making a new copy of a search tree each time that we perform an update is a powerful technique. Its major drawbacks are the time to make the copies and the total space requirement; m updates produce m trees that use $O(m^2)$ space, in the worst case. We can reduce the space usage by copying only part of each tree. In this section, we introduce path copying, and, in Section 15.8.3, we introduce limited-node copying. Although we focus on binary search trees, we will make side remarks about red–black trees. When we insert a node into or delete a node from a search tree, we change the tree only on the search path; see Fig. 15.42(a). This

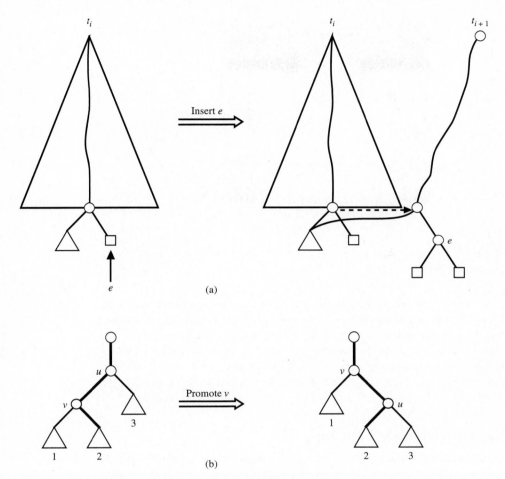

Figure 15.42 Persistence and path copying. (a) Path copying after insertion. (b) Promotions change only the search path.

property holds also for promotions; see Fig. 15.42(b). So, rather than copying the whole tree, we merely copy the search path. Path copying was developed independently by a number of researchers (Krijnen and Meertens, 1983; Myers, 1982; Myers, 1984; Reps et al., 1983; Swart, 1985); a similar technique was used by Kung and Lehman (1980) and by Kwong and Wood (1982) in the development of concurrent-access methods for search trees. More precisely, we copy the nodes on the search path. For insertion, we create a new internal node to replace the current external node (see Fig. 15.43a); for deletion, the copy of the parent of the deleted node is linked to one of the children of the deleted node (see Fig. 15.43b). Since we copy the root node, we can search a tree at time t as before; the major difference is that we will be switching from one copy to another copy during a

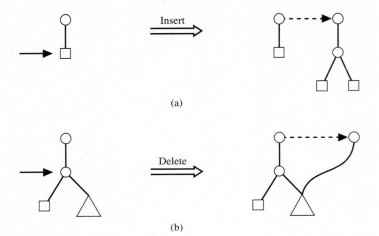

Figure 15.43   Persistence by path copying. (a) Copying after an insertion.
(b) Copying after a deletion.

search. We do not, however, need to know that the switches are occurring. If we
are using path copying with binary search trees, then we expect that m updates
will use $O(m \log m)$ space. By using red–black trees, we can guarantee the
$O(m \log m)$-space bound, in the worst case. Ideally, we would like $O(\log m)$
search time, using $O(m)$ space, in the worst case. In Section 15.8.3, we present a
modification of path copying that reduces the space bound to $O(m)$ space, *in the
amortized case.*

15.8.3 Limited-Node Copying

To reduce the space requirements of persistent search trees even further, we do
not produce a new root node for each update. Rather than distinguishing versions
at the root node, we distinguish them much later on the search path. Thus we no
longer copy a complete search path, but rather copy only part of a search path; the
technique called **limited-node copying** was introduced by Driscoll and associates
(Driscoll et al., 1989; Sarnak, 1986). One implication of this approach is that we
no longer perform one search in time followed by a standard key search; rather,
we interleave time and key searching.

   Each node in a binary search tree now has three links, rather than two. These
links are the usual left and right links, and a new link, **the overflow link,** which is
initially empty. When we want to change one of the children of a node, we use the
overflow link to hold the change, if it is free. With the overflow link, we keep
both the time of the update and which child it represents. If the overflow link is
already in use and is not free, then we copy the node. We give the copy the latest
left and right children; thus its overflow link is free. If the copied node is the root,
then we have produced a new root; otherwise, the copy is an overflow child of the

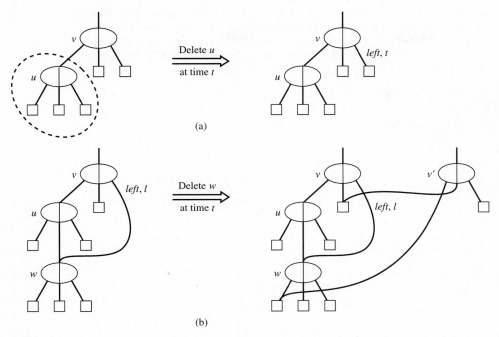

Figure 15.44   Persistence by limited-node copying. (a) The overflow link of the parent of the copied node is free. (b) The overflow link of the parent of the copied node is not free.

copied node's parent. But the parent's overflow link may not be free, in which case we must copy the parent. In Fig. 15.44, we illustrate limited-node copying with deletion; in Fig. 15.44(a), the parent of the copied node has a free overflow link, whereas in Fig. 15.44(b) it does not. Clearly, in the worst case, we can copy a complete search path; however, it can be proved that m updates introduce $O(m)$ new nodes, in total. Thus limited-node copying uses $O(1)$ space, in the amortized case.

The beauty of this technique is that it can be applied to red–black trees, B$^+$-trees, and many other linked data structures.

EXERCISES

15.1:   Complete the implementation of the operations for skip lists. Compare the performance of skip lists with that of binary search trees, using simulation.

15.2:   Prove that, for a diagonal point set, a quartering always produces at least two empty quadrants.

15.3: Since quad trees are a generalization of binary search trees, we can generalize external binary search trees to give external quad trees. In an external quad tree, the internal or separating nodes contain values that may not be from the given point set. Demonstrate that we can obtain a simpler splitting policy, for a given set of points in the plane, compared to the minimax splitting policy introduced in Section 15.2.

15.4: Design insertion and deletion algorithms for quad trees. Analyze their worst-case performance.

15.5: Prove that the recurrence

$$T(1) = a,$$
$$T(n) = T(n_1) + T(n_2) + T(n_3) + T(n_4) + an,$$

where $n = n_1 + n_2 + n_3 + n_4 + 1$ and $n_1 + n_3 = n_2 + n_4$, has the solution $O(n \log n)$.

15.6: Prove that, in a quad tree of minimum height, a co-range query can be answered in $O(r + \sqrt{n})$ time.

15.7: Design and implement an algorithm to construct a minimum-height 2-d tree, from a set of n points, that takes $O(n \log n)$ time.

15.8: Prove that incremental insertion into an initially empty 2-d tree can give rise to a tree with linear height and quadratic internal path length.

15.9: Design algorithms for range, co-range, and partial-match search in a 2-d tree. What are the worst-case performances of your algorithms in terms of the size and the number of reported answers?

15.10: Continue the grid file example in Section 15.4.2 by adding 10 more points.

15.11: Implement an internal version of the grid file for various bucket sizes. Carry out a simulation to evaluate its performance, in terms of number of bucket accesses; the minimum, maximum, and average number of records in the buckets; and the number of buckets and grid blocks.

15.12: Because we represent a line segment as a closed–open interval in a segment tree, a membership search with the right endpoint of a segment will not discover the segment. We have suggested implementing a stabbing query by performing both a membership and predecessor query with the stabbing point. Design an algorithm that implements stabbing search in this way. Analyze the worst-case performance of your algorithm.

15.13: Design insertion and deletion algorithms for segment trees, when you are not given the endpoint values in advance. Assume, however, that the endpoint values are integers. Analyze the worst-case performance of your algorithms.

15.14: Complete the details of the insertion and deletion algorithms for segment trees with a fixed set of endpoint values, as described in Section 15.5.2.

15.15: Complete the implementation of the range tree that we began in Section 15.5.3.

15.16: Implement a range tree that is based on an internal binary search tree. Compare the "internal" range tree algorithms with the "external" range tree algorithms we introduced in Section 15.5.3; in particular, is it sufficient to report only node lists in an internal range tree?

15.17: Suggest a modification of segment trees that will allow them to handle range queries. Analyze the worst-case performance of your algorithms.

15.18: Two segments, Q and S, intersect if and only if $\text{left}(Q) \leq \text{right}(S)$ and $\text{left}(S) \leq \text{right}(Q)$. Suggest an algorithm to solve the segment-intersection problem that is based on this characterization and that uses priority-search trees.

15.19: Design algorithms for the insertion and deletion of line segments from an interval tree (see Section 15.5.3), when the endpoints are known in advance. Then, design algorithms for stabbing search and segment-intersection search. In all cases, analyze the worst-case performance of your algorithms.

15.20: Prove that any operation in a quad tree that is similar to a promotion does not preserve the quad-search property.

15.21: Design algorithms for range, co-range, and partial-match search in an orchard of 2-d trees. For an orchard that contains n points and has $O(\log n)$ trees, analyze the worst-case performances of your algorithms in terms of n and the number of reported answers.

References

A.V. Aho, J.E. Hopcroft, and J.D. Ullman. *The Design and Analysis of Computer Algorithms*. Addison-Wesley, Reading, MA, 1974.

A.V. Aho, R. Sethi, and J.D. Ullman. *Compilers: Principles, Techniques, and Tools*. Addison-Wesley, Reading, MA, third edition, 1988.

D.J. Aldous. The continuum random tree II: An overview. In M.T. Barlow and N.H. Bingham, editors, *Stochastic Analysis*, pages 23–70, Cambridge University Press, Cambridge, England, 1991.

B. Allen and J.I. Munro. Self-organizing binary search trees. *Journal of the ACM*, 25:526–535, 1978.

A.W. Appel. Garbage collection. In P. Lee, editor, Topics in Advanced Language Implementation, MIT Press, Cambridge, MA, 1990.

B.W. Arden, B.A. Galler, and R.M. Graham. An algorithm for equivalence declarations. *Communications of the ACM*, 4:310–314, 1961.

R. Baecker. *Sorting Out Sorting*. Computer Systems Research Group, University of Toronto, Toronto, Ontario, Canada, 1982. Movie.

R.A. Baeza-Yates. Expected behaviour of B$^+$-trees under random insertions. *Acta Informatica*, 26:439–471, 1989.

R.A. Baeza-Yates. Efficient text searching. PhD thesis, Technical Report CS-89-17, Department of Computer Science, University of Waterloo, Waterloo, Ontario, Canada, 1989.

R.A. Baeza-Yates. Improved string searching. *Software—Practice and Experience*, 19:257–271, 1989.

D.S. Batory. B$^+$-trees and indexed sequential files: A performance comparison. In *Proceedings of the Eleventh ACM SIGMOD Conference*, pages 30–39, 1981.

R. Bayer. Symmetric binary B-trees: Data structure and maintenance algorithms. *Acta Informatica*, 1:290–306, 1972.

R. Bayer and E.M. McCreight. Organization and maintenance of large ordered indexes. *Acta Informatica*, 1:173–189, 1972.

J.R. Bell and C.H. Kaman. The linear quotient hash code. *Communications of the ACM*, 13:675–677, 1970.

T.C. Bell, J.G. Cleary, and I.H. Witten. *Text Compression*. Prentice-Hall Advanced Reference Series. Prentice-Hall, Inc., Englewood Cliffs, NJ, 1990.

R.E. Bellman. *Dynamic Programming*. Princeton University Press, Princeton, NJ, 1957.

J.L. Bentley. Multidimensional binary search trees used for associative searching. *Communications of the ACM*, 18:509–517, 1975.

J.L. Bentley. Algorithms for Klee's rectangle problems. Technical report, Department of Computer Science, Carnegie-Mellon University, Pittsburgh, PA, 1977.

J.L. Bentley. Decomposable searching problems. *Information Processing Letters*, 8:244–251, 1979.

J.L. Bentley. Multidimensional binary search trees in database applications. *IEEE Transactions on Software Engineering*, SE-5:333–340, 1979.

J.L. Bentley and J.B. Saxe. Decomposable searching problems: I. Static-to-dynamic transformation. *Journal of Algorithms*, 1:301–358, 1980.

J.L. Bentley and D. Wood. An optimal worst-case algorithm for reporting intersections of rectangles. *IEEE Transactions on Computers*, C-29:571–577, 1980.

J. Bishop. *Data Abstraction in Programming Languages*. International Computer Science Series. Addison-Wesley, Reading, MA, 1986.

J.A. Bondy and U.S.R. Murty. *Graph Theory with Applications*. Macmillan, London, 1976.

A.D. Booth and A.J.T. Colin. On the efficiency of a new method of dictionary construction. *Information and Control*, 3:327–334, 1960.

R. Boyer and S. Moore. A fast string searching algorithm. *Communications of the ACM*, 20:762–772, 1977.

W. Bucher and H. Edelsbrunner. On expected- and worst-case segment trees. In F.P. Preparata, editor, *Computational Geometry*, volume 1 of *Advances in Computing Research*, pages 109–125, JAI Press, Greenwich, CT, 1983.

J.L. Carter and M.N. Wegman. Universal classes of hash functions. *Journal of Computer and System Sciences*, 18:143–154, 1979.

B.W. Char, G.J. Fee, K.O. Geddes, G.H. Gonnet, and M.B. Monagan. A tutorial introduction to Maple. *Journal of Symbolic Computation*, 2:179–200, 1986.

B.W. Char, K.O. Geddes, G.H. Gonnet, B.L. Leong, M.B. Monagan, and S.M. Watt. *Maple V Language Reference Manual*. Springer-Verlag, New York, NY, 1991.

R.J. Cichelli. Minimal perfect hash functions made simple. *Communications of the ACM*, 23:17–19, 1980.

J.C. Cleaveland. *An Introduction to Data Types*. Addison-Wesley, Reading, MA, 1986.

J. Cohen. Garbage collection of linked data structures. *Computing Surveys*, 13: 341–367, 1981.

J. Cohen and M. Roth. On the implementation of Strassen's fast multiplication algorithm. *Acta Informatica*, 6:341–355, 1975.

D. Comer. The ubiquitous B-tree. *Computing Surveys*, 11:121–137, 1979.

S.A. Cook. Linear-time simulation of deterministic two-way pushdown automata. In *Proceedings of the IFIP Congress 1971*, pages 172–179, North-Holland., Amsterdam, The Netherlands, 1971.

J.C. Culberson. *The Effect of Asymmetric Deletions on Binary Search Trees*. PhD thesis, Department of Computer Science, University of Waterloo, Waterloo, Ontario, Canada, 1986.

J.C. Culberson and J.I. Munro. Explaining the behaviour of binary search trees under prolonged updates: A model and simulations. *Computer Journal*, 32:68–75, 1989.

J.C. Culberson and J.I. Munro. Analysis of the standard deletion algorithm in exact fit domain binary search trees. *Algorithmica*, 5:295–312, 1990.

K. Culik and D. Wood. A note on some tree similarity measures. *Information Processing Letters*, 15:39–42, 1982.

G. de Balbine. *Computational Analysis of the Random Components Induced by a Binary Equivalence Relation*. PhD thesis, California Institute of Technology, Pasadena, CA, 1968.

R.A. De Millo, S.C. Eisenstat, and R.J. Lipton. Preserving average proximity in arrays. *Communications of the ACM*, 21:228–231, 1978.

L.P. Deutsch and D.G. Bobrow. An efficient incremental automatic garbage collector. *Communications of the ACM*, 9:522–526, 1966.

L. Devroye. A note on the height of binary search trees. *Journal of the ACM*, 33:489–498, 1986.

E.W. Dijkstra. A note on two problems in connexion with graphs. *Numerische Mathematik*, 1:269–271, 1959.

E.W. Dijkstra. *A Discipline of Programming*. Prentice-Hall, Inc., Englewood Cliffs, NJ, 1976.

J.R. Driscoll, N. Sarnak, D.D. Sleator, and R.E. Tarjan. Making data structures persistent. *Journal of Computer and System Sciences,* 38:86–124, 1989.

H. Edelsbrunner. New approach to rectangle intersections: Part I. *International Journal of Computer Mathematics*, 13:209–219, 1983.

H. Edelsbrunner. New approach to rectangle intersections: Part II. *International Journal of Computer Mathematics*, 13:221–229, 1983.

B. Eisenbarth, N. Ziviani, G.H. Gonnet, K. Mehlhorn, and D. Wood. The theory of fringe analysis and its application to 2-3 trees and B-trees. *Information and Control*, 55:125–174, 1982.

R.J. Enbody and H.C. Du. Dynamic hashing schemes. *Computing Surveys*, 20:85–114, 1988.

J.L. Eppinger. An empirical study of insertion and deletion in binary search trees. *Communications of the ACM*, 26:663–669, 1983.

V. Estivill-Castro and D. Wood. A new measure of presortedness. *Information and Computation*, 83:111–119, 1989.

V. Estivill-Castro and D. Wood. External sorting, initial run creation, and nearly sortedness. Research Report CS-91-36, Department of Computer Science, University of Waterloo, Waterloo, Ontario, Canada, 1991.

V. Estivill-Castro and D. Wood. A survey of adaptive sorting algorithms. *Computing Surveys*, 24, 1992, to appear.

R. Fagin, J. Nievergelt, N. Pippenger, and H.R. Strong. Extendible hashing—A fast access method for dynamic files. *ACM Transactions on Database Systems*, 4:315–344, 1979.

N.J. Fine. The Jeep problem. *American Mathematical Monthly*, 54:24–31, 1947.

R.A. Finkel and J.L. Bentley. Quad trees: A data structure for retrieval on composite keys. *Acta Informatica*, 4:1–9, 1974.

P. Flajolet and A.M. Odlyzko. The average height of binary trees and other simple trees. *Journal of Computer and System Sciences*, 25:171–213, 1982.

R.W. Floyd. Algorithm 97: Shortest path. *Communications of the ACM*, 5:345, 1962.

R.W. Floyd. Algorithm 245: Treesort3. *Communications of the ACM*, 7:701, 1964.

M.J. Folk and B. Zoellick. *File Structures: A Conceptual Toolkit*. Addison-Wesley, Reading, MA, 1987.

C.C. Foster. *Cryptanalysis for Microcomputers*. Hayden Book Company, Rochelle Park, NJ, 1982.

M.L. Fredman and R.E. Tarjan. Fibonacci heaps and their uses in improved network optimization algorithms. *Journal of the ACM*, 34:596–615, 1987.

J.H. Friedman, J.L. Bentley, and R.A. Finkel. An algorithm for finding best match in logarithmic expected time. *ACM Transactions on Mathematical Software*, 3:209–226, 1977.

D. Gale. The Jeep once more or Jeeper by the dozen. *American Mathematical Monthly*, 77:493–501, 1970.

Z. Galil and G.F. Italiano. Data structures and algorithms for disjoint set union problems. *Computing Surveys*, 23:319–344, 1991.

R.G. Gallager. Variations on a theme by Huffman. *IEEE Transactions on Information Theory*, IT-24:668–674, 1978.

B.A. Galler and M.J. Fischer. An improved equivalence algorithm. *Communications of the ACM*, 7:301–303, 1964.

M.R. Garey, R.L. Graham, and D.S. Johnson. Some NP-complete geometric problems. *Proceedings of the Eighth Annual ACM Symposium on Theory of Computing*, pages 10–22, 1976.

M.R. Garey and D.S. Johnson. *Computers and Intractability: A Guide to the Theory of NP-Completeness*. W.H. Freeman and Company, New York, NY, 1979.

A. George and W.H. Liu. *Computer Solution of Large Sparse Positive Definite Systems*. Prentice-Hall Series in Computational Mathematics. Prentice-Hall, Inc., Englewood Cliffs, NJ, 1981.

E.N. Gilbert and E.F. Moore. Variable length encodings. *Bell System Technical Journal*, 38:933–968, 1959.

G.H. Gonnet and R. Baeza-Yates. *Handbook of Algorithms and Data Structures: In Pascal and C*. International Computer Science Series. Addison-Wesley, Reading, MA, second edition, 1991.

G.H. Gonnet and P.A. Larson. External hashing with limited internal storage. *Journal of the ACM*, 35:161–184, 1988.

R.L. Graham, D.E. Knuth, and O. Patashnik. *Concrete Mathematics: A Foundation for Computer Science*. Addison-Wesley, Reading, MA, 1989.

D.H. Greene and D.E. Knuth. *Mathematics for the Analysis of Algorithms*. Birkhäuser, Boston, MA, second edition, 1982.

D. Gries. *The Science of Programming*. Texts and Monographs in Computer Science. Springer-Verlag, New York, NY, 1981.

W. Griswold. Improving the performance of sets and tables in ICON. *The Icon Newsletter*, 31:3–5, 1989.

The Mathlab Group. *MACSYMA Reference Manual, Version 13*. Laboratory for Computer Science, M.I.T., Cambridge, MA, 1988.

L.J. Guibas. *The Analysis of Hashing Algorithms*. PhD thesis, Department of Computer Science, Stanford University, Stanford, CA, 1976.

L.J. Guibas and R. Sedgewick. A dichromatic framework for balanced trees. In *Proceedings of the 19th Annual Symposium on Foundations of Computer Science*, pages 8–21, 1978.

L.J. Guibas and E. Szemeredi. The analysis of double hashing. *Journal of Computer and System Sciences*, 16:226–274, 1978.

R.W. Hamming. *Coding and Information Theory*. Prentice-Hall, Inc., Englewood Cliffs, NJ, second edition, 1986.

W.J. Hendricks. An account of self-organizing systems. *SIAM Journal on Computing*, 5:715–723, 1976.

T.N. Hibbard. Some combinatorial properties of certain trees with applications to searching and sorting. *Journal of the ACM*, 9:13–28, 1962.

J.A. Hinds. An algorithm for locating adjacent storage blocks in the buddy system. *Communications of the ACM*, 18:221–222, 1975.

D.S. Hirschberg. A class of dynamic memory allocation algorithms. *Communications of the ACM*, 16:615–618, 1973.

D.S. Hirschberg. A linear space algorithm for computing maximal common subsequences. *Communications of the ACM*, 18:341–343, 1975.

J.E. Hopcroft and R.E. Tarjan. Efficient algorithms for graph manipulation. *Communications of the ACM*, 16:372–378, 1973.

E.C. Horvarth. Stable sorting in asymptotically optimal time and space. *Journal of the ACM*, 25:177–199, 1978.

E. Horowitz and S. Sahni. *Fundamentals of Data Structures in Pascal*. Computer Software Engineering Series. Computer Science Press, San Francisco, CA, third edition, 1990.

R.N.S. Horspool. Practical fast searching in strings. *Software—Practice and Experience*, 10:501–506, 1980.

D.A. Huffman. A method for the construction of minimum-redundancy codes. *Proceedings of the IRE*, 40:1098–1101, 1952.

G. Jaeschke. Reciprocal hashing: A method for generating minimal perfect hashing functions. *Communications of the ACM*, 24:829–833, 1981.

A.T. Jonassen and D.E. Knuth. A trivial algorithm whose analysis isn't. *Journal of Computer and System Sciences*, 16:301–322, 1978.

D.W. Jones. An empirical comparison of priority-queue and event-set implementations. *Communications of the ACM*, 29:300–311, 1986.

A.B. Kahn. Topological sorting of large networks. *Communications of the ACM*, 5:558–562, 1962.

K.C. Knowlton. A fast storage allocator. *Communications of the ACM*, 8:623–625, 1965.

D.E. Knuth. *Fundamental Algorithms*. Volume 1 of *The Art of Computer Programming*. Addison-Wesley, Reading, MA, 1968.

D.E. Knuth. *Seminumerical Algorithms*. Volume 2 of *The Art of Computer Programming*. Addison-Wesley, Reading, MA, 1969.

D.E. Knuth. Optimum binary search trees. *Acta Informatica*, 1:14–25, 1971.

D.E. Knuth. *Sorting and Searching*. Volume 3 of *The Art of Computer Programming*. Addison-Wesley, Reading, MA, 1973.

D.E. Knuth. Dynamic Huffman coding. *Journal of Algorithms*, 6:163–180, 1985.

D.E. Knuth, J.H. Morris, and V.R. Pratt. Fast pattern matching in strings. *SIAM Journal on Computing*, 6:323–350, 1977.

T. Krijnen and L.G.L.T. Meertens. Making B-trees work for *b*. Technical Report IW 219/83, The Mathematical Centre, Amsterdam, The Netherlands, 1983.

H.T. Kung and P.L. Lehman. A concurrent database manipulation problem: Binary search trees. *ACM Transactions on Database Systems*, 3:339–353, 1980.

Y.-S. Kwong and D. Wood. A new method for concurrency in B-trees. *IEEE Transactions on Software Engineering*, SE-8:211–222, 1982.

P-Å. Larson. Linear hashing with partial expansions. *Proceedings of the Sixth VLDB Conference*, pages 224–232, 1980.

P-Å. Larson. Performance analysis of linear hashing with partial expansions. *ACM Transactions on Database Systems*, 7:566–587, 1982.

P-Å. Larson. Analysis of uniform hashing. *Journal of the ACM*, 30:805–819, 1983.

P-Å. Larson. Linear hashing with overflow-handling by linear probing. *ACM Transactions on Database Systems*, 10:75–89, 1985.

P-Å. Larson. Dynamic hash tables. *Communications of the ACM*, 31:446–457, 1988.

P-Å. Larson. Linear hashing with separators—a dynamic hashing scheme achieving one-access retrieval. *ACM Transactions on Database Systems*, 13:366–388, 1988.

J.S. Lew and A.L. Rosenberg. Polynomial indexing of lattice points. I: General concepts and quadratic polynomials. *Journal of Number Theory*, 10:192–214, 1978.

J.S. Lew and A.L. Rosenberg. Polynomial indexing of lattice points. II: Nonexistence results for higher-degree polynomials. *Journal of Number Theory*, 10:215–243, 1978.

T.G. Lewis and C.R. Cook. Hashing for dynamic and static internal tables. *IEEE Computer*, 21(10):45–56, 1988.

R.C. Linger, H.D. Mills, and B.L. Witt. *Structured Programming: Theory and Practice*. The Systems Programming Series. Addison-Wesley, Reading, MA, 1979.

W. Litwin. Linear hashing: A new tool for file and table addressing. *Proceedings of the Sixth VLDB Conference*, pages 212–223, 1980.

H. Lorin. *Sorting and Sort Systems*. The Systems Programming Series. Addison-Wesley, Reading, MA, 1975.

H. Mannila. Measures of presortedness and optimal sorting algorithms. *IEEE Transactions on Computers*, C-34:318–325, 1985.

H. Mannila and E. Ukkonen. On the complexity of unification sequences. In *Proceedings of the 3rd International Conference on Logic Programming*, pages 122–133, Springer-Verlag, New York, NY, 1986. Lecture Notes in Computer Science 225.

H. Mannila and E. Ukkonen. The set union problem with backtracking. In *Proceedings of the 13th International Colloquium on Automata, Languages, and Programming (ICALP 86)*, pages 236–243, Springer-Verlag, New York, NY, 1986. Lecture Notes in Computer Science 226.

J.J. Martin. *Data Types and Data Structures*. Prentice-Hall International Series in Computer Science. Prentice-Hall, Inc., Englewood Cliffs, NJ, 1986.

D.E. Matthews, 1990. Personal Communication.

J. McCabe. On serial files with relocatable records. *Operations Research*, 13:609–618, 1965.

E.M. McCreight. A space-economical suffix tree construction algorithm. *Journal of the ACM*, 23:262–272, 1976.

E.M. McCreight. Priority search trees. *SIAM Journal on Computing*, 14:257–276, 1985.

S.M. Merritt. An inverted taxonomy of sorting algorithms. *Communications of the ACM*, 28:96–99, 1985.

B. Meyer. *Object-Oriented Software Construction*. Prentice Hall International Series in Computer Science. Prentice-Hall, Inc., Englewood Cliffs, NJ, 1988.

D.S. Moore. *Statistics: Concepts and Controversies*. W.H. Freeman and Company, San Francisco, CA,1979.

F.L. Morris. A time- and space-efficient garbage compaction algorithm. *Communications of the ACM*, 21:662–665, 1978.

J.H. Morris. Types are not sets. In *Conference Record of ACM Symposium on the Principles of Programming Languages*, pages 120–124, 1973.

R. Morris. Scatter storage techniques. *Communications of the ACM*, 11:35–44, 1968.

D.R. Morrison. PATRICIA—practical algorithm to retrieve information coded in alphanumeric. *Journal of the ACM*, 15:514–534, 1968.

J.I. Munro, Th. Papadakis, and R. Sedgewick. Deterministic skip lists. In *Proceedings of the Third Annual ACM-SIAM Symposium on Discrete Algorithms*, pages 367–375, 1992.

E. Myers. AVL dags. Technical Report TR 82-9, Department of Computer Science, University of Arizona, Tucson, AZ, 1982.

E. Myers. Efficient applicative data types. In *Eleventh Annual ACM Symposium on Principles of Programming Languages*, pages 66–75. ACM, 1984.

G.J. Myers. *Reliable Software Through Composite Design*. John Wiley & Sons, Inc., New York, NY, 1975.

J. Nievergelt, H. Hinterberger, and K.C. Sevcik. The grid file: An adaptable, symmetric multikey file structure. *ACM Transactions on Database Systems*, 9:38–71, 1984.

A.M. Odlyzko and H.S. Wilf. Bandwidths and profiles of trees. *Journal of Combinatorial Theory: B*, 42:348–370, 1987.

H.J. Olivié. *A Study of Balanced Binary Trees and Balanced One–Two Trees*. PhD thesis, Departement Wiskunde, Universiteit Antwerpen, Antwerp, Belgium, 1980.

H.J. Olivié. A new class of balanced search trees: Half-balanced search trees. *RAIRO Informatique théoretique*, 16:51–71, 1982.

M.H. Overmars. *The Design of Dynamic Data Structures*. Volume 156 of *Lecture Notes in Computer Science*. Springer-Verlag, New York, NY, 1983.

R. Pavelle and P.S. Wang. MACSYMA from F to G. *Journal of Symbolic Computation*, 1:69–100, 1985.

Y. Perl and E.M. Reingold. Understanding the complexity of interpolation search. *Information Processing Letters*, 6:219–222, 1977.

A.J. Perlis and C. Thornton. Symbol manipulation by threaded lists. *Communications of the ACM*, 3:195–204, 1960.

W.W. Peterson. Addressing for random access storage. *IBM Journal of Research and Development*, 1:130–146, 1957.

C.G. Phipps. The Jeep problem: A more general solution. *American Mathematical Monthly*, 54:458–462, 1947.

R.C. Prim. Shortest connection networks and some generalizations. *Bell System Technical Journal*, 36:1389–1401, 1957.

W. Pugh. Skip lists: A probabilistic alternative to balanced trees. *Communications of the ACM*, 33:668–676, 1990.

T. Reps, T. Teitelbaum, and A. Demers. Incremental context-dependent analysis for language-based editors. *ACM Transactions on Programming Languages and Systems*, 5:449–477, 1983.

R.L. Rivest. On self-organizing sequential search heuristics. *Communications of the ACM*, 19:63–67, 1976.

J.M. Robson. The height of binary search trees. *Australian Computer Journal*, 11:151–153, 1979.

J.M. Robson. The asymptotic behaviour of the height of binary search trees. *Australian Computer Science Communications*, 4:88–98, 1982.

A.L. Rosenberg. Allocating storage for extendible arrays. *Journal of the ACM*, 21:652–670, 1974.

A.L. Rosenberg. Preserving proximity in arrays. *SIAM Journal on Computing*, 4:443–460, 1975.

A.L. Rosenberg. Data encodings and their costs. *Acta Informatica*, 9:273–292, 1978.

A.L. Rosenberg. Encoding data structures in trees. *Journal of the ACM*, 26:668–689, 1979.

A.L. Rosenberg, D. Wood, and Z. Galil. Storage representations for tree-like data structures. *Mathematical Systems Theory*, 13:105–130, 1979.

T.J. Sagar. A polynomial time generator for minimal perfect hash functions. *Communications of the ACM*, 28:523–532, 1985.

B. Salzberg. *File Structures: An Analytic Approach*. Prentice-Hall, Inc., Englewood Cliffs, NJ, 1988.

B. Salzberg. Merging sorted runs using large main memory. *Acta Informatica*, 27:195–215, 1989.

H. Samet. Hierarchical representations of collections of small rectangles. *Computing Surveys*, 20:271–309, 1988.

H. Samet. *Applications of Spatial Data Structures*. Addison-Wesley, Reading, MA, 1989.

H. Samet. *Fundamentals of Spatial Data Structures*. Addison-Wesley, Reading, MA, 1989.

D. Sankoff. Matching sequences under deletion–insertion constraints. *Proceedings of the National Academy of Sciences of the U.S.A.*, 69:4–6, 1972.

D. Sankoff and J.B. Kruskal. *Time Warps, String Edits, and Macromolecules: The Theory and Practice of Sequence Comparison*. Addison-Wesley, Reading, MA, 1983.

N. Sarnak. *Persistent Data Structures*. PhD thesis, Department of Computer Science, Courant Institute of Mathematical Sciences, New York University, New York, NY, 1986.

N. Sarnak and R.E. Tarjan. Planar point location using persistent search trees. *Communications of the ACM*, 29:669–679, 1986.

M. Scholl. New file organizations based on dynamic hashing. *ACM Transactions on Database Systems*, 6:194–211, 1981.

H. Schorr and W.M. Waite. An efficient machine-independent procedure for garbage collection in various structures. *Communications of the ACM*, 10:501–506, 1967.

R. Sedgewick. *Algorithms*. Addison-Wesley, Reading, MA, second edition, 1988.

A. Silberschatz, J.L. Peterson, and P.B. Galvin. *Operating System Concepts*. Addison-Wesley, Reading, MA, third edition, 1991.

H.-W. Six and D. Wood. Counting and reporting intersections of d-ranges. *IEEE Transactions on Computers*, C-31:181–187, 1982.

D.D. Sleator and R.E. Tarjan. Amortized efficiency of list update and paging rules. *Communications of the ACM*, 28:202–208, 1985.

D.D. Sleator and R.E. Tarjan. Self-adjusting binary search trees. *Journal of the ACM*, 32:652–686, 1985.

N. Solntseff and D. Wood. Pyramids: A data type for matrix representation in Pascal. *BIT*, 17:344–350, 1977.

R. Sprugnoli. Perfect hashing functions: A single probe retrieval method for static sets. *Communications of the ACM*, 20:841–850, 1977.

T.A. Standish. *Data Structure Techniques*. Addison-Wesley Series in Computer Science. Addison-Wesley, Reading, MA, 1980.

J.A. Storer. *Data Compression: Methods and Theory*. Computer Science Press, San Francisco, CA, 1988.

E.H. Sussenguth, Jr. Use of tree structures for processing files. *Communications of the ACM*, 6:272–279, 1963.

G. Swart. Efficient algorithms for computing geometric intersections. Technical Report TR 85-01-02, Department of Computer Science, University of Washington, Seattle, Washington, 1985.

R.E. Tarjan. Application of path compression on balanced trees. *Journal of the ACM*, 26:690–715, 1979.

R.E. Tarjan. A class of algorithms which require non-linear time to maintain disjoint sets. *Journal of Computer and System Sciences*, 18:110–127, 1979.

R.E. Tarjan. *Data Structures and Network Algorithms*. Volume 44 of *BMS-NSF Regional Conference Series in Applied Mathematics*. Society for Industrial and Applied Mathematics, Philadelphia, PA, 1983.

R.E. Tarjan and J. van Leeuwen. Worst-case analysis of set union algorithms. *Journal of the ACM*, 31:245–281, 1984.

P. Thomas, H. Robinson, and J. Emms. *Abstract Data Types: Their Specification, Representation, and Use*. Oxford Applied Mathematics and Computing Science Series. Oxford University Press, Oxford, England, 1988.

F.W. Tompa. Data structure design. In A. Klinger, K.S. Fu, and T.L. Kunii, editors, *Data Structures, Computer Graphics, and Pattern Recognition*, pages 3–30, Academic Press, New York, NY, 1977.

F.W. Tompa. A practical example of the specification of abstract data types. *Acta Informatica*, 13:205–224, 1980.

F.W. Tompa, 1990. Personal Communication.

J.A. van der Pool. Optimum storage allocation for a file in steady state. *IBM Journal of Research and Development*, 17:27–38, 1973.

J. van Leeuwen and T. van der Weide. Alternative path compression techniques. Technical Report RUU-CS-77-3, Department of Computer Science, University of Utrecht, Utrecht, The Netherlands, 1977.

J. van Leeuwen and D. Wood. Dynamization of decomposable searching problems. *Information Processing Letters*, 10:51–56, 1980.

J.G. Vaucher. Pretty printing of trees. *Software—Practice and Experience*, 10:533–561, 1980.

T.K. Vintsyuk. Speech discrimination by dynamic programming. *Cybernetics*, 4:52–57, 1968.

J.S. Vitter. Design and analysis of dynamic Huffman codes. *Journal of the ACM*, 34:825–845, 1987.

J. Vuillemin. A unifying look at data structures. *Communications of the ACM*, 23:229–239, 1980.

R.A. Wagner and M.J. Fischer. The string-to-string correction problem. *Journal of the ACM*, 21:168–173, 1974.

R.E. Wagner. Indexing design considerations. *IBM Journal of Research and Development*, 17:351–367, 1973.

S. Warshall. A theorem on Boolean matrices. *Journal of the ACM*, 9:11–12, 1962.

P. Weiner. Linear pattern matching algorithms. In *Conference Record of the IEEE 14th Annual Symposium on Switching and Automata Theory*, pages 1–11, 1973.

T.A. Welch. A technique for high-performance data compression. *IEEE Computer*, 17(6):8–18, 1984.

J. Welsh, J. Elder, and D. Bustard. *Sequential Program Structures*. Prentice-Hall International Series in Computer Science. Prentice-Hall, Inc., Englewood Cliffs, NJ, 1984.

J. Westbrook and R.E. Tarjan. Amortized analysis of algorithms for set union with backtracking. Technical Report TR-103-87, Department of Computer Science, Princeton University, Princeton, NJ, 1987.

F.A. Williams. Handling identifiers as internal symbols in language processors. *Communications of the ACM*, 2:21–24, 1959.

J.W.J. Williams. Algorithm 232. *Communications of the ACM*, 7:347–348, 1964.

P.F. Windley. Trees, forests, and rearranging. *Computer Journal*, 3:84–88, 1960.

N. Wirth. Program development by step-wise refinement. *Communications of the ACM*, 14:221–227, 1971.

N. Wirth. *Systematic Programming: An Introduction*. Prentice-Hall, Inc., Englewood Cliffs, NJ, 1973.

D. Wood. A comparison of two methods of encoding arrays. *BIT*, 18:219–229, 1978.

D. Wood. *Paradigms and Programming with Pascal*. Computer Software Engineering Series. Computer Science Press, San Francisco, CA, 1984.

R.T. Yeh, editor. *Data Structuring*. Volume IV of *Current Trends in Programming Methodology*. Prentice-Hall, Inc., Englewood Cliffs, NJ, 1978.

E. Yourdon. *Techniques of Program Structure and Design*. Prentice-Hall, Inc., Englewood Cliffs, NJ, 1975.

L.-Q. Zheng and P.-Å. Larson. Speeding up external mergesort. Research Report, Department of Computer Science, University of Waterloo, Waterloo, Ontario, Canada, 1992.

J. Ziv and A. Lempel. Compression of individual sequences via variable-rate coding. *IEEE Transactions on Information Theory*, IT-24:530–536, 1978.

INDEX